MARKETING COMMUNICATIONS

⑤SAGE | **50** YEARS

SAGE was founded in 1965 by Sara Miller McCune to support the dissemination of usable knowledge by publishing innovative and high-quality research and teaching content. Today, we publish more than 750 journals, including those of more than 300 learned societies, more than 800 new books per year, and a growing range of library products including archives, data, case studies, reports, conference highlights, and video. SAGE remains majority-owned by our founder, and on her passing will become owned by a charitable trust that secures our continued independence.

Los Angeles | London | Washington DC | New Delhi | Singapore

SECOND EDITION

MARKETING COMMUNICATIONS

John Egan

Los Angeles | London | New Delhi
Singapore | Washington DC

Los Angeles | London | New Delhi
Singapore | Washington DC

SAGE Publications Ltd
1 Oliver's Yard
55 City Road
London EC1Y 1SP

SAGE Publications Inc.
2455 Teller Road
Thousand Oaks, California 91320

SAGE Publications India Pvt Ltd
B 1/I 1 Mohan Cooperative Industrial Area
Mathura Road
New Delhi 110 044

SAGE Publications Asia-Pacific Pte Ltd
3 Church Street
#10-04 Samsung Hub
Singapore 049483

Editor: Matthew Waters
Assistant editor: Nina Smith
Production editor: Sarah Cooke
Copyeditor: Sharon Cawood
Proofreader: Dick Davis
Indexer: Martin Hargreaves
Marketing manager: Alison Borg
Design: Francis Kenney
Typeset by: C&M Digitals (P) Ltd, Chennai, India
Printed and bound in Great Britain by Ashford
Colour Press Ltd

© John Egan 2015
This edition published 2015
First edition published by Thomson Learning 2007

Library of Congress Control Number: 2014936261

British Library Cataloguing in Publication data

A catalogue record for this book is available from the British Library

ISBN 978-1-4462-5902-3
ISBN 978-1-4462-5903-0 (pbk)

A ... r products are printed in the UK using FSC papers and boards.
W ... ers are used as measured by the Egmont grading system.
We undertake an annual audit to monitor our sustainability.

Contents

IMAGE AND BRAND MANAGEMENT

MARKETING COMMUNICATIONS PLANNING

UNDERSTANDING MARKETING RESEARCH

CAMPAIGN TACTICS AND MANAGEMENT

CAMPAIGN MEDIA AND MEDIA PLANNING

ADVERTISING

SALES PROMOTION

PUBLIC RELATIONS

SPONSORSHIP AND PRODUCT PLACEMENT

DIRECT AND DIGITAL MARKETING

PERSONAL SELLING, POINT OF SALE AND SUPPORTIVE COMMUNICATIONS

INTEGRATED MARKETING COMMUNICATIONS

INTERNAL COMMUNICATIONS

MARKETING CHANNELS AND BUSINESS-TO-BUSINESS COMMUNICATIONS

ETHICAL MARKETING AND THE REGULATORY ENVIRONMENT

THE COMMUNICATIONS INDUSTRY

GLOBAL MARKETING COMMUNICATIONS

THE CHANGING FACE OF MARKETING COMMUNICATIONS

ABOUT THE AUTHOR

Professor John Egan is Head of the Department of Marketing at Regent's University, London. He is Chair of the Academy of Marketing, the major UK academic marketing organisation, and Chair of the Learning Advisory Group, formally the Senate, of the Chartered Institute of Marketing. He is a Chartered Marketer, a Fellow of the Higher Education Academy and a Freeman of the Worshipful Company of Marketers.

Professor Egan has a long publishing career and is the Editor of The Marketing Review and on the editorial boards of the European Journal of Marketing, the Journal of Political Marketing and Marketing, Intelligence & Planning. He has authored books on Marketing Communications and Public Relations and his textbook Relationship Marketing is now in its fourth edition and has been translated into Russian, Simple Chinese and Mandarin.

He entered academia in 1997 following a career in luxury retailing initially with American Department Stores and later with Mappin & Webb, Crown Silversmiths, and Garrard, Crown Goldsmiths. Prior to his appointment at Regent's University Professor Egan was at London South Bank University where, in addition to his academic marketing responsibilities, he was Faculty Director of Marketing and External Communications responsible for all aspects of marketing in the Faculty.

PREFACE

When the first edition of this book was published in 2007 the world of Marketing Communications was a different place. IPhone was launched in that year and Facebook was barely two years old. Digital was in its infancy. In the years in between we seem to have become dominated by digital media. We carry around smart phones and iPads, we watch digital TV (often while surfing social media) and the technologies are converging.

So is this a radically different book from its predecessor? Yes in that no Marketing Communications book can fail to recognise the affect that digital media has had on all the Marketing Communications tools and especially advertising. However, much of the theory behind good communications is still valid today as in the past. Indeed it seems that many of the mistakes of the past are being repeated in the mistaken belief that they will somehow work because it's now digital.

So what is different about this edition? It incorporates new thinking in the field of marketing communications building substantially in some areas. The number of chapters remains the same (thus fitting well into modular teaching plans) although the content of several have been rejigged. All the end-chapter case studies have been revised with up-to-date subject matter and more will be made available on the supporting website.

There were many kind words said about the first edition. I believe this one is better and I hope you do too. If you have any comments to make on the book I would be pleased to hear from you.

Professor John Egan
London

GUIDED TOUR

LEARNING OBJECTIVES

Having completed this chapter readers wo

- Understand the reasons behind the gr
  marketing communications

- Be aware of the main developments i
  communications industry

- Have a general understanding of
  their part in an integrated camp

- Recognise the part played b
  process

Learning Objectives provide a bulleted outline of what you will learn from reading the chapter.

Glossary Terms appear in the margins for quick reference where they are discussed in the text for the first time. These terms are also available in the back of the book as part of a full Glossary.

Cost-per-thousand (CPT)
A measure for comparing the cost-effectiveness of media, calculated by dividing the cost of an advertisement in one particular medium by the circulation.

FMCG
Fast-moving consumer goods (such as those sold in supermarkets).

seen
the com
(McKenn
image of a
heavily criti
of study into
(2002) notes,
the promotio
desired respo
tion does co
regardless

It seems
ated and
as a qu
how
f

 insight: Radio Ad

Not everyone was convinced that ne
about the new medium of radio an
*wireless music box has no imaginable c
particular?".* Although he or she evidentl
of potential advertisers were to use t

Although the history of marketing
earlier times was, by the middle
developing best practice. Mar
r this growing industry

Insight boxes provide industry examples to help you make ties between theory and real life practice and events.

summary

This chapter introduced a simple def... history of such communications ove... mix approach to marketing as well as ... markets that are driving these trends... mix and the overlapping nature of co... to target marketing communicatio... total market orientation and the ... nd the media, old and new...

Summaries capture the key concepts covered in the chapter to help ensure you are meeting the learning objectives.

Review Questions allow you to test your knowledge and understanding of the chapter.

? review questions

1. How would you define marketing

2. Explain the principle of integrate

3. What are Borden's '12 elements

4. What is the difference betwee

5. How would you define a 'm

6. What would you consi approach to a co...

discussion quest

The art of marketing communicatio... advertising has been used and con...

What do you believe is the danger 'advertising'?

What are the main perceived sh... their implications be?

Discussion Questions help you develop your analytical and critical thinking skills by reflecting on a set of questions with classmates; or individually.

case study: 1.1 Amb

by Nicola Clark, Marketing 24

Olympic sponsors have been warned to br
marketing ahead of the London 2012 Olyn
    LOCOG [London Organising Commi
restrictions to protect sponsors, su
portunity for brands to hijack t
restrictions on digital

End of chapter Case Studies show you how the main issues of the chapter are applied to real life marketing situations, with reflective questions at the end to test your understanding of the case study.

Further Reading provides suggestions for other reading sources about the chapter topic from both books and academic journals.

further reading

- Petty, R.D.(2013) 'From Puffery to Pena
  Concerns' *Journal of Historical Researc*

- Balmer, M.T. and Greyser, S.A. (2006) '
  branding, corporate communications
  of Marketing, 40 (7): 730.

- Leahigh, A.K. (1993) 'The histor
  Fall, 38 (3): 24–5.

$SAGE

Instructor Resources   Student Reso

Marketing Communications
by John Egan

Student Resources

1. MARKETING
   COMMUNICATIONS: PAST AND
   PRESENT

2. MARKETING
   COMMUNICATIONS THEORY

   BUYING BEHAVIOUR

   AND BRAND
   ENT

Marketing Communications

Welcome to the companion website for the secon
Communications by John Egan.

This website offers additional study materi
ahead of the pack:

For Students:

- Web Links

Visit: study.sagepub.com/egan

MARKETING COMMUNICATIONS: PAST AND PRESENT

1

LEARNING OBJECTIVES

Having completed this chapter, readers would be expected to:

- Understand the reasons behind the growth of marketing communications

- Be aware of the main developments in the marketing communications industry

- Have a general understanding of marketing communication's tools and their part in an integrated campaign

- Recognise the part played by different media in the communications process

INTRODUCTION

When the question 'what is **marketing communications**?' is asked, the likelihood is that there will be as many answers as there are respondents. One of the most common responses is likely to be simply **advertising** because it is the most visible tool in the marketing communications (**marcoms**[1]) mix and there is little doubt that for many years the promotional function was dominated by mass advertising. Indeed, prior to the twentieth century the term advertising was used for what might contemporaneously be called marketing (in its widest sense). Even today, commentators frequently use the terms interchangeably.

Over the past two decades, however, the term marketing communications has steadily eclipsed that of advertising and promotion when describing how an organisation presents itself and its brands to its audience, whoever that audience might be. This text will,

---

[1] Marcoms is a frequently used short form for marketing communications and is used throughout this book to avoid too much repetition of the longer form.

therefore, take, in the first instance, a simple working definition of 'marketing communications' as:

> the means by which a supplier of goods, services, values and/or ideas represents itself to its target audience with the goal of stimulating dialogue, leading to better commercial or other relationships.

This simple definition serves to emphasise the idea of reaching out to an audience, whether the organisation is a commercial, not-for-profit, government or other type of collective and trying to establish a dialogue. It is designed to reflect the underlying communications objective and either specifically or indirectly inform, differentiate, remind, reassure and/or persuade the target audience to act. Alongside this, it should be remembered that marketing communications is constantly evolving and in a state of constant dynamic flux, influenced by both wider environmental factors and, more directly, media development, budgetary demands and (most important of all) consumer attitude. To reinforce this, it is worth considering the considerable changes on all levels since the first edition of this book was published in 2008.

However, despite present and future change, marketing communications today is the outcome of evolution and, as such, it is valuable to look at what went on in the past.

MARKETING COMMUNICATIONS HISTORY

Marketing communications activities were practised long before they were analysed and defined in the twentieth century. Table 1.1 notes some of the marketing communication milestones throughout its long history of development and innovation. Nevett (1982), in his review of advertising history, urges us to 'not indulge in speculation as to whether prehistoric cave paintings, Babylonian inscriptions, the ten commandments or the writings on the wall at Balthazar's feast constitute advertising', and yet, in their own way, they all represent communication of one kind or another. In commercial terms, early examples of publicity included the Babylonian tablets bearing the marks of various craftsmen, such as an ointment maker, a scribe and a shoemaker. Ancient Greece provides clear evidence of what today would be recognised as advertising or sales promotion. Criers, whose main occupation was the proclamation of new laws, were also available for hire by traders to help promote their wares. Someone who availed himself of this service was Aesclyptöe, an Athenian cosmetics vendor whose advertisement (a forerunner of today's jingles) ran (Nevett 1982):

> For eyes that are shining, for cheeks like the dawn,
> for beauty that lasts after girlhood has gone,
> for prices in reason, the woman who knows,
> will buy her cosmetics at Aesclyptöe.

By Roman times, advertising was in widespread use. The best preserved examples of this come from the ruins of Pompeii, destroyed by the eruption of Vesuvius in AD 79, where there are not only numerous examples of signs (e.g. a mill for a baker, a boot for a shoemaker, a ham for a butcher, a goat for a dairy, etc.) but actual advertisements written on walls. For example, one of the earliest known tourism adverts was on the walls of Pompeii (Russell & Lane 2005) and read:

> Traveller
> Going from here to the Twelfth Tower
> There Sarinus keeps a tavern
> This is to request you to enter
> Farewell

TABLE 1.1   Historical development of Marketing Communications

Circa	
3000 BC	Babylonian tablet bearing inscription of an ointment maker, a scribe and a shoemaker
400 BC	Criers in ancient Greece
79 AD	Poster advertisements preserved following Vesuvius eruption
1140	Criers widely employed in France
1441	Moveable type invented (Guttenberg)
1477	First English advertisement (William Caxton)
1525	First advertisement printed in a news sheet (Germany)
1610	Newspapers circulating in Germany and the Netherlands
1614	Earliest known law restricting advertising prohibited shop signs from extending more than eight feet (England)
1622	First English newspaper
1625	First English newspaper advertisement
1655	Use of the term 'advertising' becomes established
1657	First English language publication devoted entirely to advertising (*The Publick Advertiser*)
1740	First printed outdoor posters (hoardings) appeared in London
1786	First known advertising agent (William Taylor)
1841	First advertising sales agency in the USA (*Volney-Palmer*)
1871	First known research into advertising effectiveness (*A Guide to Advertising*)
1891	First account executive (J. Walter-Thompson, USA)
1917	Association of British Advertising Agents (ABBA) formed which later became the *Institute of Incorporated Practitioners in Advertising* and is now the *Institute of Practitioners in Advertising (IPA)*
1926	Commercial radio introduced (USA)
1930	Radio Normandy broadcasts advertising to UK market
1947	Commercial television introduced (USA)
1955	Commercial television introduced (UK) First advertisement – *Gibbs* SR toothpaste
1971	Email first developed (Ray Tomlinson)
1980	CERN launched ENQUIRE programme (Tim Berners-Lee), which allowed scientists to interact from diverse locations
1989	Proposal for World Wide Web (WWW) by Tim Berners-Lee
1991	First web page created First web cam broadcast 2G (second-generation wireless phone technology) launched
1994	Yahoo launched (formerly Jerry's Guide to the World Wide Web)
1995	Commercialisation of the internet (encryption developed by Netscape that made financial transactions more secure); Infoseek (early search engine) launched
1998	Google established 3G telephony launched (in Japan)
2004	Web 2.0 launched
2005	Facebook launched
2006	Twitter launched 4G telephony launched (in South Korea)
2007	First iPhone launched

Sources: Nevett 1982; Wells et al. 1997; Russell & Lane 2005; Chapman 2009

In the centuries that followed the demise of the Roman Empire (commonly known as the 'dark ages'), evidence of marketing communications activity is scarce and it is not until the twelfth century that we can again pick up the thread. In 1140, criers (still known by the Latin title of Praeco) were widely employed in France. By the end of that century, Paris had sufficient criers to warrant the appointment of two master-criers, one for each bank of the Seine (Nevett 1982). Although the earliest written mention of such criers in England was in 1299, they almost certainly existed long before this date.

By the fifteenth century, little had changed since Roman times. The principal media for announcements and promotion were criers and signs, the latter usually painted directly onto an available wall or affixed to shops or other commercial establishments. Inns vied with one another by creating conspicuous illustrated signs to advertise their services to a largely illiterate audience. This accounts for many of the unique public house names that have survived to the present day (e.g. Hole in the Wall, The Green Man, etc.). In England in 1614, the first law in restraint of such advertising prohibited signs from extending more than eight feet (2.44 metres) from a building (Russell & Lane 2005).

One of the forerunners of modern advertising were the 'siquis', handwritten bills common in England in the sixteenth and seventeenth centuries. Originally, these were used to advertise clerical positions and set out the requirements for the post. They were in Latin and usually began *si quis* (if anybody). The name stuck and soon these notices were taking a variety of subject matter such as lost and found, runaway apprentices, etc. (Russell & Lane 2005).

THE AGE OF PRINTING

The first really modern innovation came with the invention of the printing press. This opened up a range of possibilities for advertising to be displayed, taken away or kept for further reference. The earliest example of a printed poster advertisement in English was a 3 by 5 inch (7.6 x 12.7 cm) bill, promoting the 'Pyes of Salisbury', a set of rules for the clergy. It was printed by William Caxton around 1477, about 40 years after Guttenberg's original invention. The poster included the plea, 'Pray do not pull down this advertisement'.

Printing was also a major part of the evolution of newspapers, which themselves were to play such an important part in the development of advertising over the succeeding centuries. Although the Romans posted daily government newsletters known as *acta diurna* as early as 59 BC, the forerunner to the newspaper was probably the manuscript newsletters, copies of which were circulated in the Middle Ages by banking houses. The first example of a printed advertisement was probably in such a German news pamphlet around 1525. By 1610, records show that newspapers were beginning to circulate widely in Germany and the Netherlands. Although a principally news-bearing medium, advertising soon became the principal means by which production and distribution costs could be offset. The first English language newspaper was *The Weekly Newes of London*, published in 1622, and the earliest example of an advert in an English newspaper can be traced to 1625. The first publication in the 'New World' of North America was *Public Occurences Both Forreign and Domestick*, which appeared in 1690 but for only one edition! The first American newspaper to carry advertising (in this case, advertising a reward for the capture of a thief) was the *Boston Newsletter* in 1704 (Wells et al. 1997).

THE INDUSTRIAL REVOLUTION

Although it had an ancient past, the roots of modern marketing communications are firmly associated with the Industrial Revolution. Prior to this, the vast number of producers each made a limited number of products and delivered them for consumption locally. Traders would bring their goods to market and sell them according to local supply and demand. Between 1740 and 1821, a major transformation took place in UK manufacturing that would ultimately spread to many parts of the world. The Industrial Revolution saw a major switch from individual artisans to mass production in huge custom-built factories. Mass-produced goods manufactured in one location required wide distribution to sustain production levels. New distribution channels were developed (railways, canals, etc.) to cope with this expansion of traffic but how was consumer demand to be generated? Mass production was all very well, but it also required mass consumption to be sustainable!

Manufacturers identified the mass media as the vehicle to stimulate demand and began to make use of advertising in two distinct ways[2] (Nevett 1982). The first was to offer retailers advertising space as an inducement to buy more stock. For example, in 1780 William Jones, a London chemist and druggist, offered a free advertisement in selected local newspapers to stockists who bought a dozen bottles of his *Tincture of Peruvian Bark*. The second strategy was to promote direct to the consumer with a view to informing the public about the product and building up confidence in its benefits. It was important, therefore, to ensure that your product (with your mark or brand) was not mistaken for the competition. This was an example of what today would be called 'brand building'.

Such was the growing proliferation of advertising in the eighteenth century that in 1758 Samuel Johnson wrote that they 'are very negligently perused, and it is therefore necessary to gain attention by magnificence of promise and by eloquence, sometimes sublime and sometimes pathetick'.

Yet Johnson appeared to have a sense of advertising's growing appeal when in 1760 he wrote, 'the trade of advertising is now so near to perfection that it is not easy to propose any improvements'.

During this period, the principle mass media were newspapers and magazines. In the UK, the number of newspaper titles rose from 25 in 1700 to 258 in 1800. UK annual paper production, between 1800 and 1860, rose from 11,000 tons to 100,000 tons. In the USA, the number of newspapers more than doubled between 1830 and 1860 (from 1200 to 3000) and the number of magazines increased by over 250% between 1850 and 1880 (from 700 to 2400). Mass advertising in these periodicals was generating the necessary 'hungers' that led to mass consumption (Varey 2002).

Poster advertising too continued to increase during the period, such that it was becoming a problem akin to that of 'fly-posting' today. Daniel Defoe, in *A Journal of the Plague Year*, described the proliferation of poster advertising by the middle of the seventeenth century:

> it is incredible, and scarce to be imagin'd, how the Posts of Houses and Corners of Streets were plastered over with Doctors Bills, and Papers of ignorant fellows; quacking and tampering in Physick, and inviting the People to come to them for Remedies; which was generally set off, with such flourishes as these, (viz) INFALLIBLE preventive Pills against the Plague. NEVER FAILING Preservatives against the infection. SOVERAIGN Cordials against the corruption of the body … I take notice of these by way of Specimen: I could give you two or three dozen of the like, and yet have abundance left behind. (cited in Nevett 1982)

Patent (or quack) medicine suppliers were, during this period, major proponents of advertising on both sides of the Atlantic, with an importance to the industry

---

[2]   In later times, these would be called 'push' and 'pull' strategies (see Chapter 5).

akin to that of cigarette or alcohol advertisers in the mid to latter part of the twentieth century. In an age where the threat of serious, even fatal disease, was ever present, such 'magic remedies' were in great demand. In the USA by the 1870s, patent medication was the largest single category in advertising and continued to dominate this medium until the end of that century. On the downside, the fraudulent claims of the quack remedies were an early example of how one sector can give the whole of advertising a bad name (Russell & Lane 2005).

Patent medicines affected marketing communications in other ways too. Because of the (supposed) qualities of these medicines, it was desirable that each unit should be packaged separately so that it could carry a notice about the patent and a warning against infringements and imitators. According to Nevett (1982):

> [as] sordid though this form of enterprise unquestionably was, the medicine vendors may well be regarded as the pioneers of modern marketing, branding their products, advertising them widely and distributing them over large areas of the country.

The term advertising, which, prior to the mid-nineteenth century, referred to any and all promotional activity, came to be more narrowly defined in this period as 'paid for mass media communication' and was the tool that led the significant development of brands and markets from the late nineteenth century through to the 1950s. Even as early as the nineteenth century, leading advertisers, such as *Schweppes, Crosse & Blackwell* and *Lea & Perrins*, were running campaigns that covered wide areas of the UK. In the USA, large-scale advertising during the second half of the nineteenth century helped lay the foundations for the growth of such present-day companies as *American Express, American Tobacco, Campbell's Soup, Carnation, Coca-Cola, Colgate-Palmolive, Eastman-Kodak, Sears, Roebuck & Co., Quaker Oats, Heinz, Libby, Pillsbury, Procter & Gamble* and *Nabisco*, to name but a few (Sivulka 1998).

Although, as early as 1630, an advertising agency model was said to be operating in France (Varey 2002), little detail is known. The claim to be the first recognisable advertising sales agency is often credited to Volney-Palmer in the USA, established in 1841. However, despite the rather diverse definitions of the term agency, the title probably goes to William Taylor who, in the *Maidstone Journal* of 1786, described himself as an advertising agent. James White was another UK pioneer who founded his agency in 1800, and Charles Barker another who established his business in Birchin Lane, London in 1837. By this time, many leading agents were offering all the services that might be required in the preparation and execution of a campaign (Nevett 1982). By 1880, advertising agencies were common in most of Britain's principal towns and cities.

Fly-posting
Posters randomly affixed to walls rather than licensed hoardings.

THE MODERN ERA

By the turn of the century, the marketing communications industry was entering its more modern phase. Advances in printing technology were creating formats that could be used creatively by advertisers. In addition, catalogues, in their various forms, were to become the means by which small towns and rural communities would become part of the consumption machine. As the twentieth century progressed, the introduction of, first, commercial radio stations and, later, television, was to see broadcasting taking over from printed messages as the dominant advertising media. This period also saw the recognised growth of other marketing communications tools such as public relations and sales promotion. As early as 1900, powerful business interests employed public relations (PR) professionals to 'defend their special interests against muckraking journalism

Quack medicine
Derives from the arcaic Dutch word *quacksalver* (hawker of salve) – a derogatory term used to describe the promotion of unproven or fraudulent medicines.

and government regulation' (Cutlip et al. 2006). The Great War (1914–1918) had seen the value to governments and commerce of propaganda (a word that had a less harsh meaning than today), and PR departments were there to exploit it. Sales promotion (as a means of incentivising sales rather than simply advertising product) grew with the fast-developing retail industry, and in particular with the advent of department stores, variety chain grocery stores and, later in the twentieth century, supermarkets.

---

insight: Radio Advertising

Not everyone was convinced that new technology was the way forward in advertising. When asked about the new medium of radio, an anonymous potential investor was said to have retorted: 'The wireless music box has no imaginable commercial value. Who would pay for a message sent to nobody in particular?' Although he or she evidently got this wrong from an investment perspective, later generations of potential advertisers were to use the same argument against the mass media.

Although the history of marketing communications is ongoing, the informality, and perhaps naiveté, of earlier times was, by the middle of the twentieth century, being replaced by increased creativity and developing best practice. Marketing education was coming to the fore as the provider of professionals for this growing industry. The advertising industry in particular saw huge growth in the second and third quarters of the twentieth century. By the end of it, however, it was the 'newer' marcom tools that were coming to prominence. By 2000, two-thirds of spend on marketing communications was below the line (i.e. marcom tools, excluding advertising; see Figure 1.4), a reversal of the situation seen 50 years before (Varey 2002), although there are indications that the age of digital media (banner ads and pay-per-click) has stopped and perhaps reversed this decline.

THE DIGITAL REVOLUTION

The biggest developments around the end of the twentieth century and into the new millennium have collectively been called 'the digital revolution'. In the very short time that has passed since 1989 when Tim Berners-Lee, working at the CERN laboratories, put forward a proposal for the World Wide Web (originally called MESH), both personal and commercial communications have changed beyond recognition. Existing communications media (television, radio, print, etc.) have not only embraced digital technology but have crossed boundaries into the online world. By 1995, the first commercialisation of the internet was apparent and Netscape developed encryption technology that made financial transactions more secure. In the same year, the first sale was made on 'Echo Bay' (which later became *eBay*). Amazon.com also started in 1995, although it did not make a profit until 2001. Email was first developed in 1971 by Ray Tomlinson, although the first web-based mail service (Hotmail) did not arrive until 1996. Search engines became so much a part of life that their advertising potential soon became apparent. Market leader *Google*, founded in 1998, was by 2011 earning $37.9 billion in advertising and other revenues. So established is the company that a new verb (to google) has entered the lexicon. Social media and social networking sites have grown in popularity since 2004 and, according to Traffikd, there are over 400 different portals from the general networking (e.g. *Facebook*) to the highly specialised (e.g. Vegetarian & Vegan Recipe Exchange). Tribes' website lists over 78,000 member-created groups, adding to the ability to interact with like-minded people. The iPhone (first launched by *Apple* in 2007) started the 'app' (application software) revolution and took mobile phone marketing into a major new dimension. By 2010, *Apple* had authorised over 500,000 apps with social and commercial applications. In addition to locating where you are, mobile phones can now direct you to the nearest shop or restaurant of your choice. QR (quick response) codes, now found widely in press, magazine and poster advertising, can also be read by these smartphones. Consumers scan these codes and get further details on events, reviews, promotions and other information from online links. Such is the importance of online technology that no self-respecting organisation is without a website and a new functional position (the webmaster) has become central to marketing strategy.

Will the digital revolution change marketing communications? The answer is yes and no. Yes, in that convergence of media allows for communications perhaps at a fraction of the cost and at a far greater speed than in the past. No, in that online and off-line will still require creativity and craft in order to get the message across. As with all the innovations that proceeded it (print, radio, television, etc.), digital tools will not replace what went before but rather augment it. As its predecessors, digital media will have its positives and negatives.

FIGURE 1.1   Enterprise

Below the line
All marketing communications tools, excluding advertising (e.g. sales promotion, public relations, etc.).

Few practitioners of this or any other century were quite as blatant as this American maker of headstones:

Here lies
**Jane Smith,
wife of Thomas Smith,
marble cutter,**
This monument was erected by her husband as a tribute to her memory and a specimen of his work. Monument of the same style 350 Dollars.

Source: McPhee1982

MARKETING COMMUNICATIONS EDUCATION

Marketing communications education has followed the growth of general marketing education from its early discussions at the beginning of the twentieth century, particularly with regards to advertising. It was, however, during the period between 1920 and 1950 that it developed (initially out of the study of economics and a concentration on food distribution), spread through schools and colleges around the world and became an important adjunct to business life. By 1950, Business Education was firmly established in the USA and there were signs of activity in other western markets. During this 'golden age of marketing'

(1950–1970), the public appetite for new goods and services was at its height. Marketing, particularly advertising, became an important stimulant to growing economies. UK advertising expenditure (in real terms) rose significantly from £102m in 1950 to £323m in 1960 and £554m in 1970. It would appear that modern marketing could sell anything and that modern marketing communications, and in particular advertising, could deliver the customers that manufacturers and suppliers required. As Kennedy and Ehrenberg (2000) noted, 'good old-fashioned mass-marketing approaches are what made brands'.

The studies of marketing in general and marketing communications in particular developed from their perceived importance to economic growth. Most commonly, marketing communications (or promotion) was seen (and still largely continues to be seen) as the fourth and most visible aspect of the ubiquitous **marketing mix** (de Pelsmacker et al. 2007). In this regard, it is seen to combine with the three other elements (product, place and price) to create a unique marketing profile for a particular product or brand. The basic task of the marketer, it was held, was to combine the four elements into a marketing programme to facilitate an exchange with consumers in the marketplace (Belch & Belch 2011). The **4Ps** (product, place, price and promotion) model, developed by McCarthy (1960), was, however, itself a distillation of Borden's (1964) 'twelve elements of a marketing programme', many of which were recognisable themselves as marketing communications tools, as shown in Figure 1.2.

4Ps or the marketing mix
A model of marketing which incorporates product, place, price and promotion.

FIGURE 1.2 Borden's elements of a marketing programme

Product planning	Personal selling	Display	Pricing
Advertising	Servicing	Branding	Promotions
Physical handling	Channels of distribution	Packaging	Fact finding and analysis

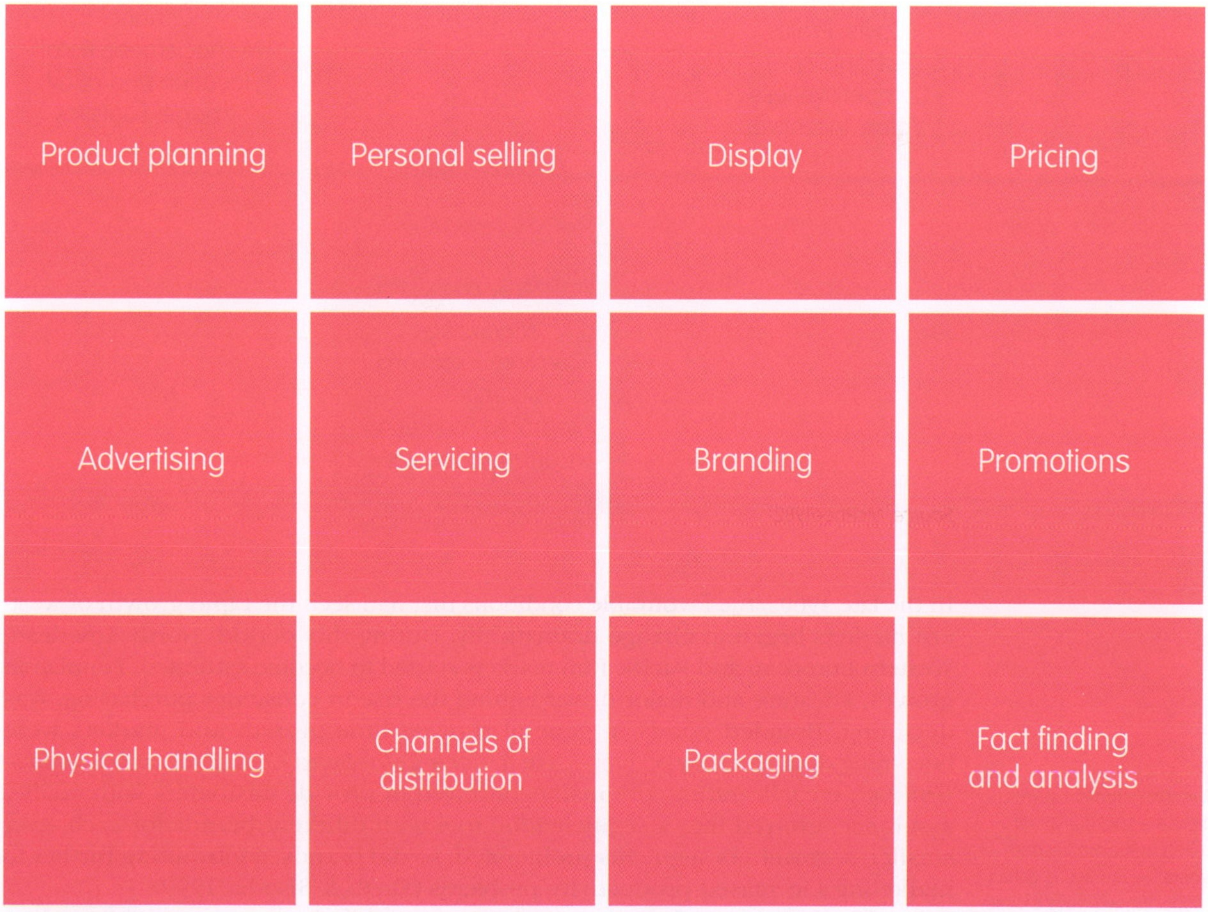

It was the simplified 4P marketing framework, rather than the more comprehensive 12 elements, that were quickly adopted by students, teachers and practitioners alike, as a straightforward, easy to remember and intuitively rational marketing model. The so-called 'golden era of marketing' (1950–1970) was a time of high consumer trust, effective mass advertising, growing prosperity, homogeneous demand, poorly developed distribution channels and, above all, dominant manufacturing power (O'Driscoll & Murray 1998: 396), and the 'brand management model' or 'toolbox approach' (Grönroos 1994) of the marketing mix appeared to be working very effectively indeed.

FIGURE 1.3   4Ps of marketing

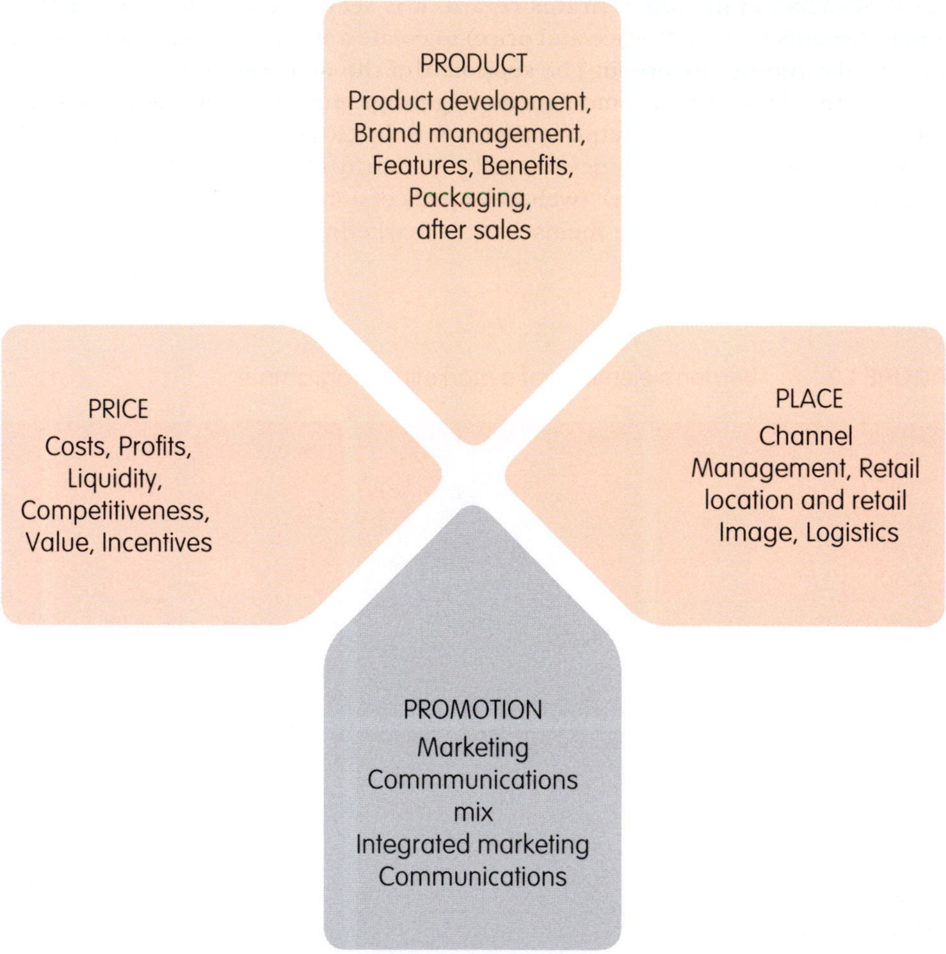

PRODUCT
Product development, Brand management, Features, Benefits, Packaging, after sales

PRICE
Costs, Profits, Liquidity, Competitiveness, Value, Incentives

PLACE
Channel Management, Retail location and retail Image, Logistics

PROMOTION
Marketing Communications mix Integrated marketing Communications

In the late 1960s, the favourable conditions that had seen the rapid growth of western markets began to change dramatically. During this period, North American, Western European and Pacific Rim markets started to become saturated. Population growth, a feature and major driver behind the rise in consumer purchasing, was declining. Branded goods in general showed little growth and markets were becoming dominated by **oligopolies** (e.g. *Coca-Cola–Pepsi Cola, Procter & Gamble–Unilever*, etc.). Branding, originally conceived to provide customers with quality assurance, evolved into a segmentation tool with different brands for each, ever smaller, segment. As segments proliferated, so did brands, contributing further to marketing's increased productivity problems (Sheth & Sisodia 1999).

Mature markets, as these economies were rapidly becoming, exhibited characteristics that differentiated them from growth markets (Christopher 1996). In

Oligopolies
A market situation in which there are few, dominant sellers in the market and where the marketing action of one firm will have a direct effect on the others.

particular, consumers, faced with a surfeit of goods and services, were to become much more demanding. Marketing Communications functions such as advertising, public relations, sales promotion and direct marketing, were becoming more sophisticated, but this only resulted in commercial clutter which made it 'more difficult for brands to be seen or heard' (Duncan 2002: vii). In this buyer's market, customers began to realise the attractiveness of their spending power and began to take advantage of it. Customers were becoming much more sophisticated and were less easily persuaded by marketing messages.

During this period, it was becoming evident that the perceived benefits of marketing communications tools, particularly advertising, were in decline, as the media market (television, radio and magazines in particular) fragmented, causing the **cost-per-thousand**[3] rates of most media to increase substantially. Other major changes included the development of own brands from dominant fast-moving consumer goods **(FMCG)** retailers. Increasingly, these retailers were looking not for brand-building advertising to support their businesses but '**below the line**' (see Figure 1.3) in-store promotions as an incentive to stock branded lines. The main casualty at this time was the advertising industry. During the period 1966 to 1974, the number of people involved in UK advertising (as opposed to other forms of marketing communications) fell by almost a third from 20,000 to 14,000. In recent years (2009 onward), however, advertising has seen a renaissance associated with the digital marketing boom. The differentiation needed to distinguish one communication from another has been inherited by lean, highly creative and smaller agencies competing for more and more business where new technologies are helping reinvent the processes associated with the industry.

FIGURE 1.4   Above and below the line

The various marketing communications tools are frequently referred to as **'above the line'** (advertising) or **'below the line'** (all other marcom tools). This has a historical foundation and is based on the way that agencies (which for most of the twentieth century were principally advertising agencies) invoiced their clients. Advertising was

INVOICE	
6 Insertions Evening Globe	£ 12,000
6 Insertions Daily Globe	£ 12,000
3 Insertions Sunday Globe	£ 4,000
Sub Total	£ 28,000
In-store Promotional Literature	£ 5,000
New product launch event	£ 5,000
Total	£ 38,000

placed with the media at an agreed rate. The agency would invoice this total amount to their clients. When paying the media owner for the space the agency would deduct an agreed percentage of 10% or 15%. Other services of the agency (sales promotion, public relations activities etc.) were additional costs added on after the main charge for advertising space. The invoice might look like this; Thus advertising was referred to as **'above the line'** (i.e. included in the main media costs) and other tools **'below the line'**. In addition, some marketers refer to Direct Marketing (which in theory overlaps both advertising and promotion) as **'through the line'**. This terminology may eventually fade away as many agencies have moved away from commission-based earnings to fee-based earnings.

---

[3]   Cost-per-thousand (CPT) is a frequently used ratio comparing the costs between different media.

Perhaps the biggest changes of all are the consumers who, it would appear, no longer respond as readily to traditional forms of advertising and promotion as they did decades before. Clients too are much more demanding, requiring better results from their communications. Marketing communications is being driven towards greater accountability with companies increasingly favouring a database approach to measure effectiveness. As Evans (2003) notes, 'count them out and count them back in again'.

In the Business Education field, marketing and marketing communications were seen to be changing, yet the concepts and theories that were still promulgated by the communications industry were from the bygone age of the 1950s and 1960s (McKenna 1991; Christopher & Baker 2000). The 4Ps approach promoted the image of a 'toolbox' (Grönroos 1995) of science-orientated marketing that was heavily criticised as 'a neglect of process in favour of structure', leading to a 'lack of study into many of the key variables' (Christopher et al. 1991: 8). As Varey (2002) notes, marketing communications is nearly always presented in texts as the promotion of producer and product to a predetermined audience to elicit a desired response – if only it were that easy! In reality, everything an organisation does communicates something about the firm and its goods and services, regardless of whether the marketer accepts this and acts on it (Grönroos 2000).

It seems clear that marketing communications is moving in a more 'sophisticated and eclectic direction' than was previously the case (Evans 2003). As well as a questioning of the marketing mix orthodoxy, there are evident changes in how marketing communications are perceived and practised. Marketers are being forced, by ever-turbulent market conditions, to find new or outstanding ways to communicate with their customers. None are complete replacements for previous practice, which continues in parallel. Indeed, part of the new communications' thinking is the greater variety of tactical approaches now being used.

Cost-per-thousand (CPT)
A measure for comparing the cost-effectiveness of media, calculated by dividing the cost of an advertisement in one particular medium by the circulation.

FMCG
Fast-moving consumer goods (such as those sold in supermarkets).

DEVELOPMENTS IN MARKETING COMMUNICATIONS

Marketing strategies in general and marketing communications in particular are always adapting and changing to accommodate to changing market circumstances. There are currently four major developments that have permeated all sectors of the industry. These perceived developments are shown in Table 1.2.

TABLE 1.2   Developments in marketing communications

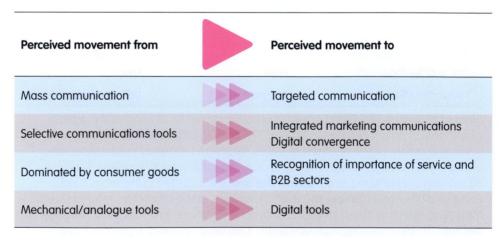

Perceived movement from		Perceived movement to
Mass communication		Targeted communication
Selective communications tools		Integrated marketing communications Digital convergence
Dominated by consumer goods		Recognition of importance of service and B2B sectors
Mechanical/analogue tools		Digital tools

MASS VS. TARGETED COMMUNICATION

Mass communication, as we have noted, was at the heart of marketing communications from the Industrial Revolution through to the last quarter of the twentieth century. The challenge to this dominance has come from two principal directions:

- philosophical   the development of relationship marketing
- technological   the ability to analyse and target individual customers (sometimes called 'one-to-one marketing').

These developments do not sound the death-knell of mass communication (it would be difficult to imagine companies such as *Coca-Cola* or *Kellogg's* wholly giving up on mass advertising) but it is no longer automatically assumed that, for example, television adverting is the most effective tool and medium to reach all customers. A distinction is being made between broad, untargeted, communication and more personal, targeted communication. Both types have, needless to say, their own particular strengths and weaknesses. De Pelsmacker et al. (2007) looked at the advantages and disadvantages of targeted (personal) communication in comparison with mass communication, and the contrasting results are shown in Table 1.3.

The developments in data collection and processing, the increased sophistication of the internet and other electronic media, together with the availability of tools (e.g. *Google* Analytics) to measure their effectiveness, seem to indicate that this movement from mass to targeted communication will continue into the future.

One-to-one marketing
A concept that proposes that customers can be individually targeted.

TABLE 1.3   Personal versus mass communications

	Personal communications	Mass communications
Reach big audience		
• Speed	Slow (PS) Fast (DM)	Fast
• Cost per customer	High	Low
Influence on individual		
• Attention value	High	Low
• Selective perception	Relatively lower	High
• Comprehension	High	Moderate/Low
Feedback		
• Direction	Two-way	One-way (generally)
• Speed of feedback	High	Low
• Measuring effectiveness	Accurate	Difficult/Impossible

PS =Personal selling DM = Direct marketing

Source: de Pelsmacker et al. (2007)

SELECTIVE VS. INTEGRATED MARKETING COMMUNICATIONS (IMC)

A second feature in the development of modern marketing communications is a shift towards an integrated communications approach. Integrated marketing communications (IMC) is, in theory, the process of using promotional tools in a unified way so that a synergy of communications is created (Semenik

2002: 8). According to Paul Simons, Chairman and Chief Executive of *Ogilvy and Mather UK*:

> marketing communications must become more integrated … the various elements of promotion devoted to informing, persuading and inducing action from a range of target audiences must be studied, analysed, planned and implemented in a co-ordinated and effective manner. (cited in Smith & Taylor 2002: viii)

The fundamental principle of IMC is that it takes a holistic approach to communication and drives an organisation to consider the total impact of all their communications activities at any one time. IMC directly impacts marketing planning by acknowledging that all aspects of organisational communication have a potential to influence all stages of the buying process.

An IMC approach should influence all brand messages, not just those regarded as traditional marketing communications (Duncan 2002). This is regarded by many as an important concept as it recognises that non-marketers are also transmitting important messages to customers (directly and indirectly) and that many of these messages are not necessarily under the control of a traditional marketing department (e.g. helplines). As a consequence, it is important that any individuals working in marketing have a broad appreciation of the various marketing communications channels, whether or not they fall within their own specialist field.

Despite its seeming advantages, IMC is not fully accepted in academia nor fully adopted in the communications industry, largely because of its supposed difficulty to implement. Others argue that it is simply the basis under which organisations have always wanted to operate but, for various reasons, they have been unable to operationalise it. As Martin Sorrell, CEO of WPP, has noted, 'A good idea unco-ordinated is still better than a lousy idea that is well-coordinated'.

The concepts and tactics suggested by an IMC approach are covered in more detail in Chapter 15.

CONSUMER GOODS ORIENTATION VS. TOTAL MARKET ORIENTATION

Relationship marketing
To 'identify and establish, maintain and enhance and, when necessary, terminate relationships with customers and other stakeholders, at a profit so that the objectives of all parties involved are met; and this is done by mutual exchange and fulfilment of promises' (Grönroos 1994).

Service-dominant logic
Traditional marketing had an exchange model based on goods. Service-dominant logic suggests a new approach in which service provision rather than goods or services is fundamental in any exchange.

Another major change, closely associated with **relationship marketing** and more recently **service-dominant logic** (Vargo & Lusch 2004), is the movement away from the domination of consumer goods marketing and, in particular, from American consumer goods practice of the 1950s (O'Driscoll & Murray 1998: 409) towards a more holistic model that incorporates business-to-business (B2B) and services – both very substantial sectors in their own right. These latter categories were frequently regarded as 'exceptional' in relation to consumer goods marketing because they did not seem to quite fit the existing marketing models. In many traditional marketing books, services and business-to-business (or industrial marketing) were covered by largely unconnected chapters at the end of the text which simply noted the differences between them and consumer goods.

In the business-to-business area, researchers[4] observed the existence of lasting buyer–seller relationships in business markets and pointed out the severe shortcomings of traditional marketing theory to capture and explain this phenomenon (Håkansson & Snehota 2000). The relative importance of the various marcoms tools was what was most apparent in this field. This was never a sector

---

[4]   These researchers mainly belonged to what became known as the Industrial Marketing & Purchasing Group (IMP).

that invested heavily in mass advertising, while personal selling was prevalent because it was seen to have a greater influence given the characteristics of the market.

In the service sector, an area that was rapidly becoming dominant[5] in many western markets, the traditional marketing models again appeared to be a poor fit. In an attempt to adapt (rather than revolutionise), new models were proposed based on the original marketing mix. To the original 4Ps (Product, Place, Price and Promotion) it was suggested adding People, Physical Evidence, Processes (Booms & Bitner 1981), Political Power, Public Opinion and other Ps to fill the perceived gaps. But even these were not quite enough. A new perspective on marketing was growing based on relationships and, in particular, that point (or points) where the customer interacts with the employee – the customer interface. It is here that the so-called 'moment of truth' arises – when business is lost or won.

The relationship marketing perspective (as it became known) went further as it emphasised the importance of all of an organisation's relationships (employees, suppliers, etc.), not just the customer–supplier dyad. This perspective has a number of implications for marketing communications strategy. As well as the obvious need to communicate at, as well as before, the point of sale, this emphasises the importance of internal marketing and training of staff (see Chapter 16), as well as an organisation's corporate relationships. In addition, external communications take on an important role in the fostering, development and maintenance of long-term relationships both between organisations and between organisations and consumers. The concept, however, is not altruistic but an adoption to modern marketing conditions. As Foxall et al. (1998) note:

> consumer-orientated management [is not] an optional extra. It is an essential corporate outlook in affluent, competitive societies in which consumers enjoy unprecedented levels of discretionary income and the power of choice that makes that happen.

The importance of these themes will be developed further in later chapters.

MECHANICAL/ANALOGUE TOOLS VS. DIGITAL TOOLS

It is undeniable that the digital revolution has changed the way marketing communications are perceived and practised. The relentless movement towards digitalisation has engulfed each of the traditional media (press, radio, television) in turn while, at the same time, making them (and more) available through the World Wide Web, on personal computers and smartphones.

While it has been a boon in so many ways (see Chapter 13), it has brought with it a number of problems. Since the early days, advertising was used to offset the cost of information (e.g. newspapers) and leisure (e.g. television programmes). It is nothing new to suggest as this commentary, attributed to Les Brown suggests

> In day-to-day commerce, television is not so much interested in the business of communications as in the business of delivering audiences to advertisers. People are the merchandise not the shows. The show is merely the bait.

However, digital broadcasting has enabled viewers to 'zip' and 'zap' their way past commercial messages. Media owners are, therefore, searching for how they

---

[5]   By the middle of the 1990s, over 75% of the working populations of the UK and the USA were in service industries.

can make up for loss of advertising revenues as organisations switch to a plethora of new platforms.

The second problem is the so-called 'democratisation' of the internet. Commercial companies have looked on in envy at how home-made videos can 'go viral' and sought to emulate this through their own (frequently highly creative) messages. However, commercial organisations are treated with contempt if they try to pass off their professionally-made videos as those of amateur admirers.

Further convergence of media is inevitable as is the growth in the number of messages we receive each day. Managing this process may prove increasingly difficult.

MARKETING COMMUNICATIONS TOOLS AND MEDIA

A clear distinction should be made between marketing communications tools and the media that may carry their messages:

- marcom tools: the processes by which marketers develop and present an appropriate set of communications stimuli (e.g. advertising, public relations, etc.)
- media: those channels through which the communications are carried (e.g. television, internet, etc.).

It is important not to confuse 'tools' and 'media' as they have different characteristics and serve different roles. It is also important to make the distinction because aspects surrounding electronic media (e.g. the internet) are frequently positioned as processes set apart from other aspects of marketing (e.g. e-marketing, internet marketing, etc.). From the perspective of marketing communicators, the internet and other electronic channels are additional mediums of communication. Like all other media, they have their strengths and weaknesses (see Chapter 8).

MARKETING COMMUNICATIONS TOOLS

Marketing communications mix
The tools used in marketing communications such as advertising, sales promotion, public relations, personal selling, direct marketing, etc. (also referred to as the **promotional mix**).

A simple way of conceptualising marketing communications options is to use the analogy of a toolbox. Thus, the various elements of communications delivery, sometimes called the **marketing communications mix** or **promotional mix,** consists of a set of tools that can be used in different combinations and with different intensities to create a strong message for the target audience. There is far from total agreement as to what constitutes the finite list of marketing communications tools, nor is there full agreement as to the definitions of each. As a general rule, the larger the number of tools proposed, the narrower the defined boundaries. As an indication of the different perspectives, the following are the views of some notable writers on marketing communications, as shown in Table 1.4.

This text tries to chart its way through the forest of definitions by first concentrating on those that most (but certainly not all) agree are central tools of marketing communications (i.e. advertising, sales promotion, public relations, personal selling) and using these as a base on which to explore those tools with specific characteristics (e.g. direct marketing, sponsorship, etc.). An indication of the close association and overlapping nature of the tools can be seen in Figure 1.5.

The major characteristics of the major marcom tools are shown in Table 1.5. The different tools, as one might expect, have different strengths and weaknesses,

TABLE 1.4   Marketing communications tools

AUTHOR (DATE)	MARKETING COMMUNICATIONS TOOLS
Lancaster & Massingham (1993); Lane & Russell (2001)	advertising, sales promotion, public relations, personal selling
Fill (2009)	advertising, sales promotion, public relations, personal selling, direct marketing
Belch & Belch (2011)	advertising, sales promotion, publicity/public relations, personal selling, direct marketing, interactive/internet marketing
Smith & Taylor (2002)	advertising, sales promotion, publicity/public relations, personal selling, direct marketing, sponsorship, exhibitions, packaging, point of sale/merchandising, word-of-mouth, e-marketing, corporate identity
Shimp (2010)	mass media advertising, on-line advertising, sales promotion, store signage (point-of-sale), packaging, direct mail, opt-in email, publicity, event & cause sponsorship, personal selling
Duncan (2000)	mass media advertising, sales promotion, public relations, personal selling, merchandising, point-of-purchase (point-of-sale), packaging, speciality advertising (premiums), licensing, direct (response) marketing, e-commerce, internal marketing, events & sponsorship, trade shows (exhibitions) customer service

FIGURE 1.5   The overlapping nature of marketing communications tools

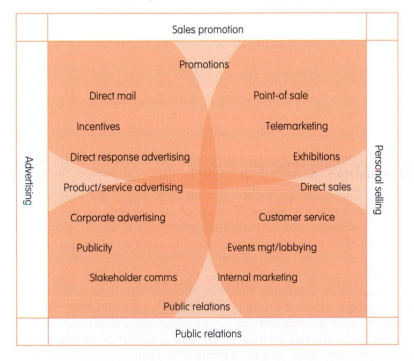

which will be discussed in greater detail in later chapters, but there are a number of other critical considerations that also need to be taken into account when planning campaigns, which include:

1 The amount of time available to develop the communications message and format
2 How much control is required over its delivery
3 The extent of financial resources available for its creation
4 The skills and expertise available for its creation
5 The respective levels of credibility that each tool and its delivery media bestow on the organisation/brand
6 The relative size and geographic scale of the target audience.

TABLE 1.5   Marcom tools characteristics

Advertising	A non-personal form of mass communication with a high degree of control over design and placement but potentially a low degree of persuasion and credibility. It is never either neutral or unbiased.
Sales promotion	The use of incentives to generate a specific (usually short-term) response. Capable of targeting and with a high degree of control over design and placement. Generally regarded as having low credibility although cause-related promotions may have a very positive effect. They are seen to add value for consumers but may bring forward future sales.
Personal selling	A personal communication with potential buyers with the intention of making a sale. This may initially focus on developing a relationship but will always have 'closing the sale' as the ultimate objective.
Public relations	'The art and social science of analysing trends, predicting their consequences, counselling organisations' leadership and implementing planned programmes of action which will serve both the organisation's and the public's interest' (Mexican Statement (1978))
Direct marketing	Seeks to target individual customers with the intention of delivering personalised messages and building a relationship with them based on their responses to direct communication.

Because of their different strengths and weaknesses, some tools are seen to be more effective in certain situations and to achieve more particular objectives than others. In Chapter 2, there is a discussion on the 'hierarchy of effects models' and in Chapter 3 a fuller discussion regarding buyer behaviour. Suffice at this time to note that a rational model of buyer behaviour suggests that consumers pass through various stages before purchase.

In effect, the model suggests that customers must be aware and interested before desire can develop and the purchase is ultimately made. In addition, there is the importance of the experience of the purchase itself on future behaviour to be considered. With the differing objectives in mind, we can predict the importance of the various marketing communications tools at different stages in the process.

As this model and Table 1.6 suggest (as a generalisation), advertising and public relations are tools that develop brand relationships over time, while personal selling and sales promotion are seen as shorter-term stimuli to purchase. Again, as a generalisation, advertising and sales promotion are seen to be under the editorial control of the marketer while public relations and personal selling (because of the fickleness of human beings) are seen as less controllable.

FIGURE 1.6 Effectiveness of marketing communications tools

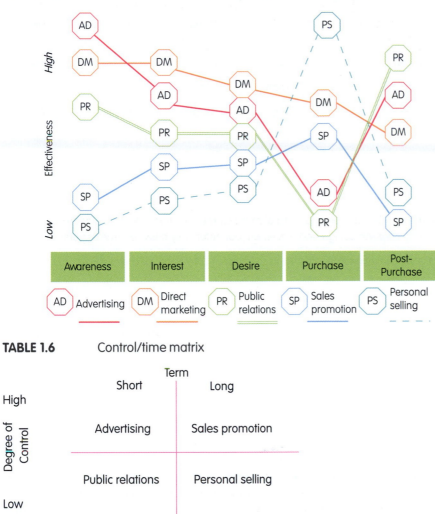

TABLE 1.6 Control/time matrix

	Term	
	Short	Long
High		
	Advertising	Sales promotion
	Public relations	Personal selling
Low		

Degree of Control

The choice of which marketing communications tools to use is determined by the characteristics associated with each tool. There are summaries of these characteristics in Table 1.7, and they will be discussed further in relevant chapters.

TABLE 1.7 Key characteristics of major marketing communications tools

Communications	Advertising	Sales promotion	Public rel'ns	Pers'l sales	Direct marktg
Ability to deliver personal message	*Low*	*Low*	*Low*	*High*	*High*
Ability to reach large audience	*High*	*Med*	*Med*	*Low*	*Med*
Level of interaction	*Low*	*Low*	*Low*	*High*	*High*
Credibility given by target audience	*Low*	*Low*	*High*	*Med*	*Med*
Costs	Advertising	Sales promotion	Public rel'ns	Pers'l sales	Direct marktg
Absolute costs	*High*	*Med*	*Low*	*High*	*Med*

(Continued)

TABLE 1.7   (Continued)

Communications	Advertising	Sales promotion	Public rel'ns	Pers'l sales	Direct marktg
Cost per contact	Low	Med	Low	High	High
Wastage	High	Med	High	Low	Low
Size of investment	High	Med	Low	High	Med
Control	Adver-tising	Sales promotion	Public rel'ns	Pers'l sales	Direct marktg
Ability to target particular audiences	Med	High	Low	Med	High
Ability to redeploy as circumstances change	Med	High	Low	Med	High

Source: Marketing Communications, Fill © Pearson Education 2009 (used with permission)

MEDIA

Some marketing managers and agencies consider 'media' to include communic-ations tools (e.g. sponsorship, point of sale) as well as mainstream media (tele-vision, press, etc.). In this text, media is defined as the medium through which the message is channelled rather than the strategy behind the message delivery. That is to say that marketing communications medium is any medium capable of carrying a message to one or more people. This does not mean that all media are a form of hollow pipe capable of carrying all types of message to all types of audience. Each again has its own particular strengths and weaknesses, a concept that will be expanded on in later chapters.

The list of different media never stands still. Just as the twentieth century saw the introduction of broadcast media, current technological developments are helping to differentiate brands from the crowd. For example, stimulated by the need to counter a growing ambivalence, particularly to advertising, by increasingly sophisticated consumers, marketers are looking beyond traditional media to find new and better ways of communicating with their customers. This has meant a growing number of spectacular campaigns involving light projection onto famous landmarks, huge poster-like messages on building sites, giant representation of products, public service vehicles transformed and all-singing, all-dancing flash dances in public places. Known collectively by the term **alternative** or **ambient media**,[6] it is best described as communications with a 'wow' factor (see Insight for alternative terms). That is advertising that is *not* in a traditional media and is clever, witty or daring and which causes consumers to stop and pay attention. Needless to say, once the medium for these messages becomes too commonplace (and no longer 'wow's us) it ceases, by definition, to be ambient media.

Another medium with the potential for generating a 'wow factor' is video (often uploaded to, and available to view from, sites such as *YouTube*). When such a

Alternative or ambient media
Often associated with outdoor media and best described as anything that introduces a 'wow factor' capable of attracting attention and curiosity.

Guerrilla marketing
A marketing tactic, originally described by Jay Conrad Levinson, which uses surprise and/ or unconventional (and sometimes personal) interaction to promote products, services, ideas, etc. and which intends to get maximum results from minimum outlay.

---

[6]   A term first coined by the Concord Agency.

> ◉ **insight: Alternative marketing vehicles – future of marketing**
>
> **A**.C. Nielsen's (2003) *Consumer Insight Magazine* notes the confusing number of terms for those alternative attempts to reach the consumer, by-passing traditional media vehicles. They include: **buzz marketing**, **street marketing**, **guerrilla marketing**, **renegade marketing**, **virtual marketing**, **ambush marketing** (see case study), **vanguard marketing**, **ambient marketing**, **covert marketing**, **under-the-radar marketing**, **diffusion marketing** and **viral marketing**. All refer to new mediums often aided significantly by '**word of mouth**' and developed to bypass the consumer's growing apathy to traditional forms of communications.

video catches on (as measured by the number of views it achieves), it is said to have gone viral. However, it is more often non-commercial videos that reach this vaulted status.

Changing viewpoints and new opportunities are challenging much of the traditional thinking on media selection. Media selection has traditionally been based on such measurements as '**opportunities to see**' or response rates. Today we are faced with a much greater challenge of establishing an understanding of how people use the various media. This challenge too will be followed up in Chapter 9.

Opportunities to see (OTS)
A measure used by media buyers to estimate how many times the target audience may see a message.

DISPUTED TERRITORIES

With most business and marketing texts there are areas of disagreement; marketing communications is no exception and three such issues are given below. Although these will be discussed in their respective sections, it is doubtful that this will be to everyone's satisfaction. These include:

- *whether personal selling should be part of the marketing communications mix.* Many would argue not. The perspective taken in this text is that it is an important means of communicating with the customer, particularly in the retail and business-to-business (B2B) sectors and as such should be included
- *whether 'public relations' (PR) has become 'debased' and replaced variously by Corporate Affairs, Corporate Communications and/or Public Affairs (Dolphin & Fan 2000: 97).* Although there is evidence in the marketplace that job titles are changing away from PR towards those noted, this text maintains PR as a core area while discussing the implications of Corporate Communications
- *whether the internet and other digital media should be regarded as a new type of marketing or whether it is just another communications medium.* While recognising the importance of e-communications, this text chooses to regard it as an important medium of communication rather than a new marketing approach.

summary

This chapter introduced a simple definition of marketing communications and presented a short history of such communications over the centuries. It reviewed the twentieth-century marketing-mix approach to marketing, as well as more current thinking, and related this to the changing nature of markets that are driving these trends. The chapter noted authors' different views on the promotions mix and the overlapping nature of communications tools. In particular, it looked at the move from mass to target marketing communications, the move away from the narrow consumer goods perspective to a total market orientation and the digital revolution. It also reviewed the different communications tools and the media, old and new, associated with them.

review questions

1. How would you define marketing communications?

2. Explain the principle of integrated marketing communications.

3. What are Borden's '12 elements' of a marketing programme?

4. What is the difference between 'above the line' and 'below the line'?

5. How would you define a 'moment of truth'?

6. What would you consider to be the main challenge of an integrated marketing communications approach to a company?

7. Define 'marketing tools' and 'media'.

8. List the tools you might find in the marketing communications toolbox.

9. What are the main characteristics of sales promotion?

10. Give an example of 'alternative' media.

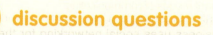

discussion questions

1. The art of marketing communications goes back a long way. How do you think the way in which advertising has been used and constructed will have evolved over that time and why?

2. What do you believe is the danger to a company in simply seeing marketing communications as 'advertising'?

3. What are the main perceived shifts in the development of marketing communications and what might their implications be?

case study 1.1: Ambushing the Olympic Games

by Nicola Clark, *Marketing*, 24 May 2011

Olympic sponsors have been warned to brace themselves for a barrage of online guerrilla marketing ahead of the London 2012 Olympics.

LOCOG [London Organising Committee of the Olympic and Paralympic Games] has grappled with restrictions to protect sponsors, such as limits on outdoor and TV advertising, but experts say the opportunity for brands to hijack the Olympics online remains 'huge'. With LOCOG facing a challenge to impose restrictions on digital marketing, official sponsors are being warned they can expect 'open season' when it comes to making the most of the Olympics online.

'It is a grey area. The restrictions based on TV and outdoor advertising don't matter anymore, especially in the UK with the BBC', said Steve Martin, chief executive of *M&C Saatchi Sports & Entertainment*. 'The smart marketers are one step ahead when it comes to social media. It's not as if official sponsors will be taking out superinjunctions to stop brands advertising online', he added.

While LOCOG argues it will be able to police breaches (see below), Nathan McDonald, managing partner of *We Are Social*, said the guerrilla social marketing activity will be highly evolved. 'The opportunities are huge. For example, you could check-in near Olympics venues and get targeted by local offers', added McDonald.

Meanwhile, brands such as *British Airways* are failing to maximise the potential brand-boost of the Olympics by neglecting search strategies, according to new research. Hannes Ortner, head of linguistics services and analysis at *Locaria*, which has been auditing the search capabilities of Olympic partners, said *BA* is letting itself down. 'These brands need to ensure they personalise their strategies for local markets. *BA*'s Chinese websites jump into English and destroy the user journey', he said.

Source: Reproduced from *Marketing Magazine* with the permission of the copyright owner, Haymarket Media Group Limited

Statement: LOCOG response

There are challenges with international enforcement of legal rights where social networking is involved. However the principle remains – if a business uses social networking for the clear purposes of ambush marketing in the UK, we can take action for infringement of our legal rights.

If the ambush activity is outside of the UK, we will work with the IOC and the relevant National Olympic Committee to address the issue – in many countries there are similar laws to those which apply in the UK which prevent ambush marketing of the Olympic Games and these can be used where relevant.

Case study questions

1. Why should Olympic sponsors be protected from ambush marketing?
2. In what ways might non-sponsor companies seek to take advantage of a sponsored event?

further reading

Balmer, M.T. and Greyser, S.A. (2006) 'Corporate marketing: integrating corporate identity, corporate branding, corporate communications, corporate image and corporate reputation', *European Journal of Marketing*, 40 (7): 730.

Leahigh, A.K. (1993) 'The history of – quote, unquote – public relations', *Public Relations Quarterly*, 38 (3): 24–5.

O'Barr, W.M. (2005) 'A brief history of advertising in America', *Advertising and Society Review*, 6 (3).

Petty, R.D. (2013) 'From puffery to penalties: a historical analysis of US masked marketing policy concerns', *Journal of Historical Research in Marketing*, 5 (1): 10–26.

Shapiro, S.J. (2005) 'Looking backward – and ahead', *Journal of Public Policy & Marketing*, 24 (1): 117–20.

Sivulka, J. (1998) *Soap, Sex and Cigarettes: A Cultural History of American Advertising*. Belmont, CA: Wadsworth Publishing.

Swain, W. (2004) 'Perceptions of IMC after a decade of development: who's at the wheel, and how can we measure success?', *Journal of Advertising Research*, 44 (1): 45–65.

Thomas, C. and Guinn, O. (2006) 'How nothing became something: white space, rhetoric, history, and meaning', *Journal of Consumer Research*, 33 (1): 82.

REFERENCES

Belch, G.E. and Belch, M.A. (2011) *Advertising and Promotion: An Integrated Marketing Communications Perspective*, 9th edn. New York: McGraw-Hill.

Booms, B.H. and Bitner, M.J. (1981) 'Marketing strategies and organisation structures for service firms', in J. Donnelly and W.R. George (eds), *Marketing of Services*. Chicago, IL: American Marketing Association.

Borden, N.H. (1964) 'The concept of the marketing mix', *Journal of Advertising Research*, June: 2–7.

Chapman, C. (2009) The History of the Internet in a Nutshell. Available at: www.sixrevisions.com/ [accessed 18 March 2012].

Christopher, M. (1996) 'From brand values to customer values', *Journal of Marketing Practice*, 2 (1): 55–66.

Christopher, M. and Baker, S. (2000) 'Relationship marketing: tapping the power of marketing', in Cranfield School of Management, *Marketing Management: A Relationship Marketing Perspective*. Basingstoke: Macmillan.

Christopher, M., Payne, A. and Ballantyne, D. (1991) *Relationship Marketing*. Oxford: Butterworth-Heinemann.

Cutlip, S.M., Allen, H.C. and Broom, G.M. (2006) *Effective Public Relations*, 9th edn. Upper Saddle River, NJ: Prentice Hall.

De Pelsmacker, P., Geuens, M. and Van den Bergh, J. (2007) *Marketing Communications: A European Perspective*, 3rd edn. London: Prentice Hall.

Dolphin, R.R. and Fan, Y. (2000) 'Is corporate communications a strategic function?', *Management Decision*, 38 (2): 99–106.

Duncan, T. (2002) *Using Advertising and Promotion to Build Brands*. New York: McGraw-Hill.

Evans, M.J. (2003) 'Marketing communications changes', in S. Hart (ed.), *Marketing Changes*. London: Thomson.

Fill, C. (2009) *Marketing Communications: Interactivity, Communities and Content*, 5th edn. Harlow: Financial Times/Prentice Hall.

Foxall, G.R., Goldsmith, R. and Brown, S. (1998) *Consumer Psychology for Marketing*, 2nd edn. London: Cengage Learning.

Grönroos, C. (1994) 'From marketing mix to relationship marketing. towards a paradigm shift in marketing', *Management Decision*, 32 (2): 4–20.

Grönroos, C. (1995) 'Relationship marketing: the strategy continuum', *Journal of the Academy of Marketing Science*, 23 (4): 252–4.

Grönroos, C. (2000) 'Creating a relationship dialogue: communication, interaction and value', *The Marketing Review*, 1: 5–14.

Håkansson, H. and Snehota, I.J. (2000) 'The IMP perspective: assets and liabilities of business relationships', in J.N. Sheth and A. Parvatiyar (eds), *Handbook of Relationship Marketing*. Thousand Oaks, CA: Sage, pp. 69–93.

Kennedy, R. and Ehrenberg, A. (2000) 'The customer profiles of competing brands', 29th European Marketing Academy Conference, Erasmus University, Rotterdam.

Lancaster, G. and Massingham, L. (1993) *Marketing Management*. New York: McGraw-Hill.

Lane, W.R. and Russell, J.T. (2001) *Advertising: A Framework*. Upper Saddle River, NJ: Prentice Hall.

McCarthy, E.J. (1960) *Basic Marketing: A Managerial Approach*. Homewood, IL: Irwin.

McKenna, R. (1991) 'Marketing is everything', *Harvard Business Review*, Jan.–Feb.: 39–45.

Nevett, T.R. (1982) *Advertising in Britain: A History*. London: Heinemann.

Nielsen, A.C. (2003) 'Alternative marketing vehicles: future of markets', *Consumer Insight Magazine*, June, www.marketingpower.com [accessed 31 October 2005].

O'Driscoll, A. and Murray, J.A. (1998) 'The changing nature of theory and practice in marketing: on the value of synchrony', *Journal of Marketing Management*, 14 (5): 391–416.

Russell, J.T. and Lane, W.R. (2005) *Kleppners' Advertising Procedure*, 16th edn. Upper Saddle River, NJ: Pearson Education.

Semenik, R.J. (2002) *Promotion and Integrated Marketing Communications*. London: Thomson Learning.

Sheth, J.N. and Sisodia, R.S. (1999) 'Revisiting marketing's generalisations', *Journal of Academy of Marketing Science*, 17 (1): 71–87.

Shimp, T.A. (2010) *Advertising, Promotion and Supplemental Aspects of Integrated Marketing Communications*, 8th edn. London: Thomson Learning.

Sivulka, J. (1998) *Soap, Sex and Cigarettes: A Cultural History of American Advertising*. Belmont, CA: Wadsworth.

Smith, P.R. and Taylor, J. (2002) *Marketing Communications: An Integrated Approach*, 3rd edn. London: Kogan Page.

Varey, R.J. (2002) *Marketing Communications, Principles and Practice*. London: Routledge.

Vargo, S.L. and Lusch, R.F. (2004) 'Evolving to a new dominant logic for marketing', *Journal of Marketing*, 68 (Jan.): 1–17.

Wells, W., Burnett, J. and Moriarty, S. (1997) *Advertising Principles and Practice*, 4th edn. Upper Saddle River, NJ: Prentice Hall.

USEFUL WEBSITE

Explore advertising history at the History of Advertising Trust: www.hatads.org.uk/

For additional materials that support this chapter and your learning, please visit:
study.sagepub.com/egan

MARKETING COMMUNICATIONS THEORY

2

LEARNING OBJECTIVES

Having completed this chapter, readers would be expected to:

- understand the theories and concepts behind the practice of marketing communications

- appreciate the importance of message source characteristics

- describe the important elements of a successful message and the effects of message repetition

- recognise the importance of opinion formers and opinion leaders in the wider communications process

- understand the concepts associated with 'hierarchy of effects' models and their application to campaign strategy.

INTRODUCTION

Communication is a word that is not wholly without controversy. Most dictionary definitions suggest that it can mean *either* the giving *or* the exchange of information. Yet the traditional marketing viewpoint was that the marketer produced and communicated messages while consumers received and consumed them – a distinctly one-way process. In a changing consumer environment, the validity of this traditional viewpoint has been challenged and today most marketers would define effective marketing communications as, by necessity, a two-way exchange.

COMMUNICATION MODEL

Early models of the communication process reflected the 'one-way' communication approach. Klapper's (1960) '**hypodermic effect**' or '**magic bullet**' encapsulated the notion that communication was the transfer of ideas, feelings, knowledge and/or motivation from one person's mind to another.

Hypodermic effect
An early model of marketing communications that inferred communication was one way (also known as **magic bullet**).

It was Wilbur Schramm (1955) who developed what was to become accepted as the basic model of mass communication (see Figure 2.1). As a demonstration of the communications process, it is wonderfully simplistic in its imagery. Despite this, the vital element is the quality of the linkages between each element. It is these linkages that have a significant impact on the success of the communication. Schramm's communication model implies two-way correspondence as there are response and feedback mechanisms built in. The sender or the source may also alter or adapt messages and/or the media as required.

FIGURE 2.1   Basic communications model

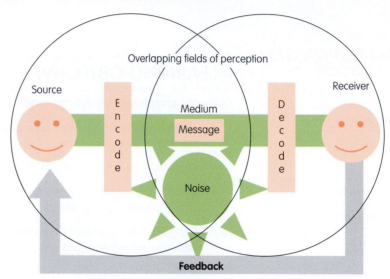

Source
The originator of the message (also refers to the person delivering the message).

Message
The vehicle by which an idea is transmitted via a medium (e.g. television).

Encode, encoded (messages)
Putting the idea into a format (e.g. speech, print, etc.) using a combination of appropriate words, pictures and symbols so that it can be transmitted via a medium.

Figure 2.1 is an adaptation and development of Schramm's original model. Here the **source** identifies the need to transmit a **message**. The message is made up (or **encoded**) into a format (e.g. speech, print, etc.) using a combination of appropriate words, pictures, symbols (see Table 2.1), music, etc. It is important to note the importance of communications other than words to our understanding of messages. It is estimated, for example, that in a message, the verbal part (words) accounts for 7%, the vocal part (tone, dialect, accent) 38% and the non-verbal part (body language) 55% (Abrantes 2006).

TABLE 2.1   Encoded messages

Symbolic communication methods

Method	Implication
Letters/Numbers	Progression and/or status (e.g. XJ6, XJ8), size (1500, 2000)
Space	Freedom, richness, elegance.
Artefacts	Status (e.g. quality watches)
Movement (kinetics)	Emotion, body movements (e.g. shrug of shoulders, folded arms)
Smell	Atmosphere, desire (e.g. coffee, fresh bread)
Touch	Quality (e.g. furniture, fabric)
Colour	Feature (e.g. white = purity, red = danger)

It should be noted that much 'silent communication' changes from culture to culture. Indeed, poor understanding of cultural differences leads to 'ethnocentrism' – the practice of assuming that others think and believe as you do. These cross-cultural differences can lead to misunderstanding or total rejection of the communication. This will be developed further in Chapter 20.

Although words themselves are only a minor part of any communication, they evidently (when associated with vocal elements) play an important part in the message being understood. In the English language, there are about three-quarters of a million words (OED 2014) although native speakers use only around 5,000 regularly. The meaning of words can be:

- **denotative** (having meaning for everybody) or
- **connotative** (having meaning unique to the individual).

As the latter can be understood by different individuals in different ways, marketers need to know and understand their target audience. In terms of the Basic Communications Model, this means their fields of perception must overlap. This perceptual understanding should include the effect of:

- **semiotics**: the study of signs and symbols in a language (see Table 2.2)
- **syntactics**: the grammatical arrangement of words
- **semantics**: the branch of linguistics concerned with meaning.

The word semiotics derives from the Greek *semeion*, meaning 'a mark, sign, trace or omen'. Semioticians see the whole of social culture as comprising of signs. Material objects are important (literally, '**sign**ificant') for the meanings we give to them. The study of semiotics (or semiology) is usually traced back to Swiss linguist Ferdinand de Saussure (1857–1913) and American philosopher Charles Sanders Pierce (1839-1914). As with any academic school of thought, it has its passionate supporters and hostile detractors but it does serve as a useful basis for identifying many of the formal patterns in the creation of meaning in aspects of modern culture and in particular the media. According to de Saussure, a '**sign**' was anything that makes meaning and was composed of a signifier (anything that signifies, e.g. a written word) and the signified (that which the signifier refers to). The letters r-o-s-e placed together in a certain order (rose) may conjure up the image of a flower, which is the literal (denotative) meaning of the word it forms. The image of the rose may also relate to love, passion, tenderness and more. These connotative associations, based on socially derived meanings, form the basis of the narratives and myths behind much iconic advertising (e.g. *Coca-Cola* Santa, *Marlboro* Cowboy, *Guinness* The Surfer and *Nike* Just Do It).

Silent communication
A non-verbal communication such as a shrug of the shoulders.

Denotative
Words having meaning for everybody.

Connotative
Words having meaning unique to the individual.

Semiotics
The study of signs and symbols in a language.

Syntactics
The grammatical arrangement of words.

Semantics
The branch of linguistics concerned with meaning.

TABLE 2.2   Signs and symbols in language

Signs

			Example
1	Icon	a sign that looks like an object or represents it visually in a way that most people could relate to	No Smoking sign; wheelchair access
2	Index	a sign that relates to the object by a causal connection	Yawn *equates to* boredom; sweat *equates to* thirst
3	Symbol	an artificial sign created for a purpose or meaning	Olympic rings; Facebook 'like' symbol

Syntactics refers again to meaning. Some communications can be grammatically correct but incomprehensible, while others might be incorrect (e.g. Beanz meanz Heinz) but are perfectly understandable. This demonstrates that the rules governing syntax are distinct from the meanings words convey.

Semantics has particular cultural and subcultural importance. The definition of a word or phrase, for example, is not always the same for all audiences, even if they notionally speak the same language. The term 'wicked' is one illustration of this. According to most dictionary definitions, it means 'morally bad … mischievous or roguish' (HarperCollins 2011). To most young people, however, it means formidable, remarkable and excellent. The words, therefore, not only need to be in a language that the receiver understands but their ascribed cultural meanings also need to be taken into account.

Clever use of the language can also add to the effectiveness of the message. In particular, communicators use:

- **simile**: a figure of speech involving the comparison of one thing with another (e.g. 'like *Murphys* I'm not bitter')
- **metaphor**: the application of a name or phrase which is imaginatively but not literally applicable (e.g. '*Lenor* is like a breath of fresh air')
- **allegory**: an extended metaphor; the representation of abstract ideas or principles by characters, events, places, etc., or where the meaning or message is represented symbolically (e.g. the *Rimmel* London Look).

Medium/Media
A means of carrying the message (also referred to as **media channel**), such as television, radio, newspapers, etc.

Direct marketing
Seeks to target individual customers with the intention of delivering personalised messages and building a relationship with them based on their responses to direct communication.

Word of mouth (WoM)
Marketing messages that circulate around from person to person (or persons via electronic communications).

Viral marketing, buzz marketing or street marketing
Marketing spread by word of mouth; alternatively, marketing materials created by the brand owner that are passed on and spread 'virus-like' around the internet.

Mass media
Largely untargeted media, including newspapers, television, radio, etc.

Slice-of-life advertising
Advertising that uses simulated 'real-life' situations and where the viewer is encouraged to get involved with the action.

Brand values
Those values associated with a brand (e.g. status, youth, etc.).

The message from the sender to the receiver travels via some sort of **medium** (or **media channel**), which may be personal (e.g. via a salesperson) or non-personal (e.g. via an advertisement). Personal mediums include face-to-face communications and certain media associated with **direct marketing** (telemarketing, electronic mail, etc.). **Word of mouth** (WoM) is a particularly powerful personal medium. Research at Northeastern University suggests that over 15% of all our conversations make reference to a company, brand, product or service (Carl 2006). With the development of the internet has come the growth of online reviews. According to research by Nielsen (2009), 78% of consumers trust these reviews compared to 35% who believe the claims of advertisers. In recent years (and particularly since the advent of digital technology), marketers have begun to concentrate their minds on how to promote WoM through strategies variously known as **viral marketing**, **buzz marketing** or **street marketing**. These strategies encourage the spread of positive messages (virus-like) through the online community. For example, the film *Ted* in 2012 used viral marketing to build up word of mouth for the film. *Volkswagon, T.Mobile* and *Apple* gained 62.7 million, 28.4 million and 27.8 million views, respectively, of their *YouTube* commercials in 2011, largely through word of mouth. *Hotmail* could never have expanded its network without the viral-like effect of messages on every email despatched through their system. However, as with communications in all media the *planned* transmission of accurate or even positive messages, travelling through a chain of individuals, cannot be guaranteed.

Non-personal mediums are characterised by what has become known as **mass media**. This term includes newspapers, television, radio, etc. Information received directly from a non-personal source is, generally, less persuasive than information obtained from a personal medium. The mass media is not, however, above attempting to increase credibility by 'personalising' the messenger(s). This may be done by creating around the message a homely or familiar situation (e.g. a family eating a meal). This so-called '**slice-of-life**' advertising encourages the receiver to imagine themselves in that particular situation (see Chapter 9), thus encouraging them to feel comfortable and at ease with the images and messages presented, identify with them and recognise the associated **brand values** that complement them (see also **source attractiveness** below). As an example of the enduring nature of this form of advertising, in March 2012 *Premier Foods* announced the launch of a brand new campaign featuring the home-loving Oxo family which first aired in 1983.

Decoding (effectively the recognition of the meaning presented by the words, pictures, symbols, music, etc.) is affected by the receiver's **field of perception**[1] which encompasses the perceptions, experiences, attitudes and values of the receiver. The more the source understands about the receiver (and vice versa), the easier it will be to decode the message successfully. To put this another way, the greater the overlap between the source's and the receiver's 'fields of perception', the more likely it is that they will understand each other (see Figure 2.1).

Effective communication, therefore, is where the recipient receives and comprehends the message that the sender transmits. Ineffective communication is where the message is:

- misunderstood and/or
- misinterpreted and/or
- rejected.

Communication is an interpersonal activity which is highly dependent on the social context in which it takes place. Therefore:

- the sender needs to identify in advance the target audience and how they will receive it
- the sender will need to persuade the receiver that the message is worth listening to
- there needs to be a clear, and as far as possible, unobstructed route or channel (**medium**) through which the message can be sent, received and understood
- the sender needs evidence (**feedback**) that the message is not only received but is understood and having the desired effect.

Clarity of understanding (created by overlapping fields of perception) is, therefore, also required if **feedback** is to be interpreted by the source in the right way (see Figure 2.1). Feedback is the reaction(s) a receiver makes, having received the message. It is important to the source as they can verify whether the message has been received correctly (e.g. a favourable reaction) and whether the receiver has acted on it (increased sales, etc.).

As communication and greater understanding develop over time, feedback may become more complex and include **complaints** (also called customer '**voice**') or **suggestions** that may benefit the company and its relationship with its customers in the longer term. Feedback is also, generally, better utilising personal than non-personal mediums. Feedback is, for example, likely to be clearer and more immediate in a personal (face-to-face) selling situation than in some other form of response (letter, email, etc.). At the other extreme, feedback from mass media advertising (brand building rather than direct response) can be unclear and/or only become clear over time.

SOURCE CHARACTERISTICS

The accurate transfer and acceptance of messages is highly influenced by the characteristics of the source (i.e. where/who the message comes from or appears to come from) of the message. Kelman (1961) suggests that **source credibility, source**

Decoding
Translating the message into understandable ideas/concepts.

Field of perception
An individual's range of understanding. Overlapping fields of perception enable understanding (also referred to as realm of perception and realm of understanding).

Feedback
Information regarding the receiver's reaction to a message used as a measure of understanding and, where appropriate, response to any call to action (e.g. a sale).

Complaints
A statement that a particular situation (or series of situations) gives rise to dissatisfaction (also called **customer voice**).

Suggestions
Constructive feedback from staff, customers and others with a stake-holding in the organisation.

Source credibility
How much confidence the receiver has that the source can provide an expert and/or objective opinion.

Source attractiveness
How attractive and persuasive the source is and how much the source identifies with the consumer.

Source power
Where compliance with the request involves a real or perceived reward or actual or apparent avoidance of punishment.

---

[1]   Also called the **realm of perception** or **realm of understanding**.

TABLE 2.3   Source characteristics

Characteristic	Description	Example
Source credibility	How much confidence the receiver has that the source can provide an expert and/or objective opinion	A former police officer endorsing a security system
Source attractiveness	How attractive and persuasive the source is and how much the source identifies with them*	*Either* a celebrity *or* (at the other extreme) an ordinary person like you
Source power	Where compliance with the request involves a real or perceived reward or actual or apparent avoidance of punishment	An aggressive sales person, a threat to well-being, etc.

Source: Kelman (1961)

Note: *Retailers often select sales staff whose profile is similar to that of their customers.

Trust
A confidence in someone or something. There are three forms of trust: institutional trust, character-based trust and process-based trust.

Expertise
Expertise includes aptitude, required training and experience and is domain specific.

Institutional trust
Trust that is based on the rule of law (e.g. minimum standards legislation) or qualification (e.g. doctors, lecturers, etc.).

Character-based trust
Trust in individuals (particularly important in personal selling).

Reputation
Trust and confidence built up over time and based on past performance.

attractiveness and **source power** are the three factors that most define the source characteristics of the messenger (see Table 2.3).

Source credibility is associated with recognised objectivity and includes two additional important constructs: **trust** and **expertise**.

Trust itself can take one of three forms (Pickton & Broderick 2001):

- **institutional trust**: based on the rule of law (trust based on minimum standards legislation) or qualification (e.g. doctors, lecturers, etc.)
- **character-based trust**: trust in individuals (particularly important in personal selling)
- **process-based trust**: trust built up over time (i.e. **reputation**).

Whatever combinations of these forms of trust are present will determine the way the message is received and ultimately believed. Trust may take time to develop but can be lost in a very short time, indeed as many financial institutions discovered following the financial crises. According to a US Gallup poll, confidence in banks, for centuries held in high esteem, fell by 25 points (from 58% to 23%) in the period June 2002 to 2011.

Expertise includes aptitude, required training and experience and is domain specific. For example, you may trust a former police commissioner to tell you about home-security equipment but not necessarily follow their advice on holidays abroad. A famous footballer may successfully endorse sportswear but is less likely to be as influential in the financial services market.

Source attractiveness is associated with identification or relationship-seeking behaviour. This may be aspirational or simply identifiable with an everyday situation. An example of the latter is 'slice-of-life advertising', first introduced by *Procter & Gamble* in the 1950s, where the target audience is easily identifiable in the advertisement attending to some everyday problem (e.g. blocked drains, high credit card bills, etc.).

Aspiration also relates to situations we might dream of seeing ourselves taking part in (e.g. an opening night party, the Ambassador's reception (*Ferrero Roche*)). This association between the aspiration and the product or service may change the receiver's perception of it. Another important example of the importance of attractiveness relates directly to the celebrity endorsement. Ever since Lillie Langtry appeared on a pack of *Pears* soap in 1893, stars have lent their names to the promotion of branded products (Mistry 2006). Communicators have always found that messages from stars of stage, screen and television are generally received well and it is believed that their influence may even have increased in recent years with the growth of the so-called 'cult of celebrity' where famous (or infamous) and/or broadly recognisable characters compete for appearances in magazines and broadcast media. So powerful is the 'pull' of some celebrity names that sportsman David Beckham, whose deal with *Adidas* is the biggest in football, brought his total earnings in 2010/11 to around $40 million.

The credibility of the celebrity is important in creating a believable link between the meaning(s) associated with that celebrity and the product or service they are promoting (Pickton & Broderick 2001). For example, Charlotte Church was chosen to front a *Walker's Sensation* crisp campaign. According to the company, 'the Welsh singer was selected because she is a real women, with a luxury life-style', which they felt 'fitted perfectly with the Sensations brand' (Mistry 2006). Meanwhile, Gary Lineker, who has been associated with *Walker's* since 1994, has recently signed a contract extension to take his relationship with the brand into its third decade. Such is the growth of the 'cult of celebrity' that it is calculated that at least one in four television advertisements now use celebrities, up from one in eight 10 years ago (2006).

When source credibility is called into question, however, companies will frequently attempt to dissociate themselves as quickly as they possibly can from even the most famous celebrities. Michael Jackson's parting with *Pepsi Cola* was one such example, as was that of Kate Moss, the face of several cosmetic and fashion houses, who was publicly dropped by several sponsors following a drugs allegation (only to be re-employed by, for example, *Calvin Klein* once the initial bad publicity had died down). More recently, Tiger Woods was dropped unceremoniously by *Gillette, AT&T, Gatorade, Accenture* and other sponsors following his much publicised marital problems.

Source power is where the source of the message has the power to punish or reward and where influence is largely sought through compliance. This may be associated with sales promotions (buy now offer ends soon), penalty warnings (e.g. reminders to get in tax returns by a certain date) or promotions largely based on developing feelings of guilt (e.g. if you die are your children protected?).

Not only are the clarity and source credibility important but also crucial is what else is happening as the message is 'transmitted', as this can affect its reception. Noise (not the volume per se but anything that disturbs the proper reception of the message) is a complicating factor that may influence the quality of the reception and/or the feedback. This may be because the number/content/attraction of other messages both within and outside of the channel distracts the receiver(s). Noise may be deliberately introduced, for example, in so-called 'spoiler campaigns', where the competition deliberately introduces a competing, conflicting or denigrating message to counter the message from the source (tabloid newspapers frequently run spoiler campaigns against one another's promotions and politicians regularly denigrate opponents' messages).

Brand confusion is one outcome of indistinct communication. Suppliers of products or services with very similar names, characteristics or benefits may find it difficult to distinguish their message from that of others. This is particularly true where the base product or service is the same or similar to other products or services. In these situations, the more unique the message in terms of content and execution, the less likely it is that brand confusion will occur. At the other end of the scale, if the presentation of the message is so unique and memorable that it overshadows the product or service itself, it is equally detrimental. This is known as **vampire creativity** and it occurs primarily when the communication is *too* original, *too* entertaining or *too* involving (Wells et al. 1997), and where the creativity of the agency is remembered ahead of the product or service it is seeking to promote.

Noise
Anything that interferes with the proper delivery of the message (e.g. competing messages).

Spoiler campaigns
Where the competition deliberately introduces competing, conflicting or denigrating messages to counter the message from the source.

Brand confusion
Any misunderstanding concerning brand values and benefits – an outcome of indistinct communication.

Vampire creativity
Occurs when the communication is *too* original, *too* entertaining or *too* involving, such that it distracts the consumer from the brand message. This leads to consumers remembering the advertising but not the brand it was associated with.

insight: Benetton

In the 1990s, *Benetton* built up a reputation with the public for advertising that many would regard as shocking. These included AIDS patient David Kirby in his final moments at Ohio State Hospital, a newborn baby still attached to its umbilical cord and pictures of inmates waiting on death row. Twenty years later, *Benetton* launched its 'Unhate' campaign in order to recreate some of the public attention of earlier days. In an interview with *Marketing Magazine* in 2012, Worldwide Communications Director of the *Benetton Group*, Gianluca Pastore, said ' To be controversial is a style and heritage from the United Colours of *Benetton'*. He claims, however, that they are not being controversial for the sake of being controversial, rather they 'want to be consistent to the history of the brand'. The 'Unhate' campaign included images of Pope Benedict XVI kissing Imam Sheikh Ahmed el-Tayeb and US President Barack Obama kissing (in different images) the Chinese leader Hu Jintao and Venezuelan Communist leader Hugo Chavez. The big change from the pre-millennium campaigns is that what was previously an outdoor poster or print campaign now uses digital media to foster a dialogue with customers in addition to the traditional mediums.

Source: *Marketing Magazine*, 1 August 2012

Repetition
Repeat exposure to the brand message (also referred to as frequency).

Repetition is seen as beneficial to the reception of the message. Research by Mano (1996) suggests that respondents who have been exposed to an advertisement once before (as compared to respondents who are exposed for the first time) appear to evaluate the message as more favourable and less dull. Wells et al. (1997) note that psychologists maintain that you need to hear a message a minimum of three times before it crosses the threshold of perception and enters into memory. Gary Lineker's relationship with *Walkers*, which began in 1995 (and was extended by another three years in January 2012), reveals how repetition can strengthen the association for consumers who are already aware of the endorsement (Mistry 2006). Jingles, catchy tag-lines and memorable music also aid memorability.

Decay
Corruption of a message over time.

Wear-out
Consumer boredom and/or irritation at a repeated communication.

Researchers have also found that information **decays** at a 'negatively decelerating rate' with 60% of the initial yield of information (from, for example, an advertisement) having decayed within six weeks (Fill 2001) On the other hand, showing a message too often can also lead to consumer boredom or **wear-out**. Wear-out is essentially a point at which a level of exposure has been reached, after which continued exposure results in negative rather than positive feelings. Effectively, the communications become irritating. Reasons for this irritation include that they:

Transformational
Image-dominant, brand-building messages.

- are unbelievable, exaggerated and over-dramatised situations
- include unsympathetic characters
- involve continuous brand comparison and brand repetition
- include information-orientated messages (as opposed to **transformational** or image-dominant messages)

- are hard-sell (as opposed to soft-sell)
- include satire, provocation and eroticism (versus music, sentimental situations and warmth).

Wear-out is thought to cause individuals to use **selective attention** and switch off after a certain number of exposures and/or to use counter-argument against both the message and the medium monotony (Petty and Cacioppo 1979).

Selective attention
The process of screening out information that does not interest us and selectively processing the information that does. Messages that successfully bypass 'selective attention' are likely to be perceived positively.

FIGURE 2.2   Wear-out

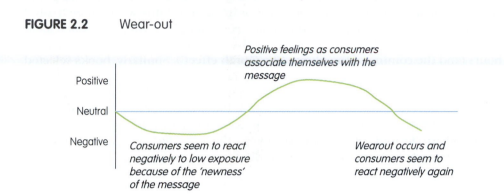

It would appear that wear-out appears more for some types of message than for others. For example, complex messages, minor changes in advertisement execution, short or slow commercials and non-food *do not* seem to experience the negative effects of a high exposure rate, while humorous, long, fast-paced, image-dominant and transformational commercials *do* suffer from high repetition levels (de Pelsmacker et al. 2007).

It is important to note that all of the above are generalisations because every consumer reacts differently due to their individual attitudes and values, as will be discussed in Chapter 3. Some companies recognise the irritation that certain advertising provokes and may seek to take advantage of it (see Insight).

insight: Go Compare

In summer 2012, billboards advertising the UK price comparison site Go Compare suffered what looked like a rash of vandalism. What was surprising, however, is that they were defaced before they reached their destination. The message 'Go compare' was altered to read 'Go and get some singing lessons', 'Go jump off a cliff', 'Go get a new job' and simply 'Go away'. According to Nick Hall, Go Compare's head of marketing: 'We know some people find the character irritating and this is us saying "we get it".' The poster campaign was followed a few weeks later by a television advertisement which showed TV celebrity Sue Barker blowing up the annoying singing tenor.

TWO-STEP MODEL

The simple communications model shown in Figure 2.1 assumes that the message travels direct to the intended recipient. This 'one-step communications' model does not, however, reflect the way many commercial and other messages are received in the real world. When a customer wants to buy something, where the specifications are complex or expenditure is high (or both) and/or where that purchase affects their self-image, the consumer may seek advice on the potential purchase or follow the perceived trend(s) in the market. Alternatively, they may be recommended by others to take some purchasing decisions they had not previously considered.

The two-step model, therefore, introduces the concept of **opinion formers** and **opinion leaders**, as shown in Figure 2.3. Opinion formers are people with influence or authority over our lives. They might be journalists, broadcasters, analysts, politicians, scientists or anyone with some real or imagined status who can be trusted (rightly or wrongly) to impart good advice. For example, a ringing endorsement by Oprah Winfrey of *Amazon*'s Kindle led to the product selling out in a few hours (and the coining of the phrase 'the Oprah effect'). Similarly, books selected by Richard Madeley and Judy Finnegan regularly make it to the top of bestseller lists and have launched the careers of many new authors. So-called **advertorials** (where an advertisement is designed to look like newspaper or magazine copy) also seek to take advantage of journalistic endorsement. Here, 'paid-for' advertising is made to look like editorial copy, in the knowledge that the latter will carry considerably more influence than the former.

FIGURE 2.3   Two-step communications model

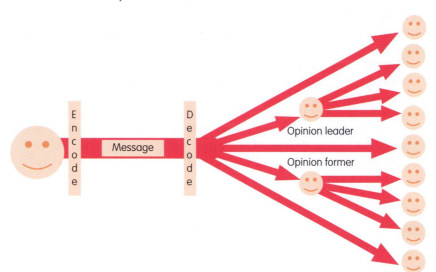

Opinion leaders are also influencers but may not be formal experts. They do not necessarily provide advice but consumers are prone to follow them. They are often, but not always, from a higher social status than their immediate contemporaries and frequently more gregarious. Their opinion is regularly sought on one or more different subjects and they may be asked to endorse many different products. In the world of clothing, they are often called **fashion icons**, examples of which include celebrities such as David Beckham and Lady Gaga.

Opinion leadership can be simulated in advertising by using testimonials or creating backdrops (e.g. a laboratory) that signify professionalism or status. Opinion leaders will frequently take risks and be among the first to adopt new styles, visit exotic places and purchase new products. The rest of society may then follow but not all at once (see **diffusion of innovation**).

Collectively, opinion formers, opinion leaders and any others that help to 'pass on the message' might be called **connectors.** Marketers also know them

Opinion formers
People with potential influence or authority over our lives, such as journalists, broadcasters, analysts, politicians, scientists or anyone with some real or imagined status who can be trusted (rightly or wrongly) to impart good advice.

Advertorials
Advertising in a format that mimics a magazine or press editorial.

Opinion leaders
May not be formal experts. They do not necessarily provide advice but consumers are prone to follow them. They are often, but not always, from a higher social status than their immediate contemporaries and frequently more gregarious.

Fashion icons
Celebrity fashion leaders (e.g. David Beckham and Lady Gaga).

Diffusion of innovation
The way that new product or service developments (e.g. mobile telephones) enter the market. Rogers' (1983) theory of diffusion suggests that various consumers adopt over different time periods. These he called innovators, early adopters, early majority, late majority and laggards.

Connectors
A collective name for opinion formers and opinion leaders and others (e.g. family) who help to carry the message to the consumer (also referred to as **influentials, carriers, trendsetters** and **evangelists**).

variously as **influentials, carriers, trendsetters** and **evangelists** (Nielsen 2003). **Alternative (or ambient) media** (see Chapter 1) often relies on the influence of connectors who have mastered what sociologists call 'weak-tie' or 'social ambience' (Nielsen 2003). The larger their network of social acquaintances, the more 'power' connectors wield in society and the better positioned they are to trigger trends. Indeed, any source of social influence can be considered a potential audience for marketing communications, including social and cultural groupings often called **reference groups** (Pickton & Broderick 2001). These could include family, work colleagues and social and religious groups.

> **Reference groups**
> Groups with whom consumers associate themselves, e.g. faith groups, social groups.

As noted above, opinion leaders frequently take risks and are among the first to adopt new products or services, while the rest of society will only follow in time. This process of staggered adoption (of new products, fashion, etc.) over time, by different sections of society, is called **diffusion** (Rogers 1983).

FIGURE 2.4   Diffusion of innovation

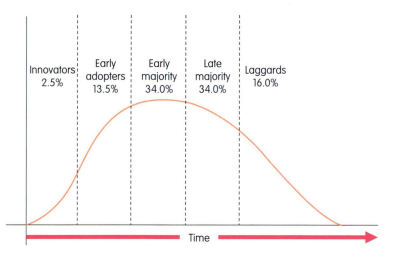

Diffusion of innovation over time is said to follow a pattern approximately as illustrated in Figure 2.4. The first into the market are seen as the **innovators**. These are those customers who are at the forefront of trends, particularly in technical innovation. They are likely to have a high disposable income and are willing to pay a high price for being first in the market. Innovators are estimated to represent 2.5% of the (eventual) total market. Next are the **early adopters**. This group frequently consists of the opinion leaders noted above and their entry into the market is significant. They are generally younger with an above average education and/or income and represent around 13.5% of the market. The **early majority** (34%) represent the first move towards general acceptance and the speed of adoption can be seen to have increased considerably. The **late majority** (34%) are more sceptical of new ideas but, as the saying goes, 'the luxuries of one generation become the necessities of the next' and they eventually come on board. By now the majority of the market will have adopted the innovation. The last 16% are called the **laggards** and these are often the most technology (or innovation) averse. Ultimately, however, as in the case of radios, televisions, refrigerators, and perhaps latterly mobile telephones, they too adopt the innovation.

> **Innovators**
> Those customers who are at the forefront of trends, particularly in technical innovation. They are likely to have a high disposable income and are willing to pay a high price for being first in the market.
>
> **Early adopters**
> Frequently the opinion leaders. Their entry into the market is significant. They are generally younger with an above average education and/or income.
>
> **Early majority**
> Entry of the early majority of customers represents the first move towards general acceptance. The speed of adoption can be seen to have increased considerably by this stage.
>
> **Late majority**
> Sceptical of new ideas, these customers eventually take up the innovation.
>
> **Laggards**
> Sometimes technophobic, this is the last group to take up an innovation.

FIGURE 2.5   Product life cycle

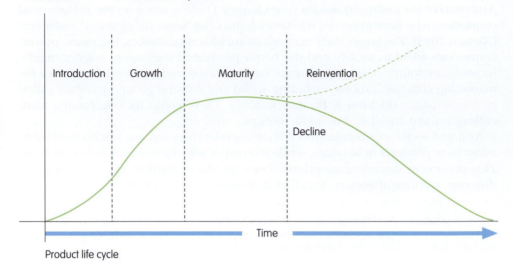

Product life cycle

The **product life cycle** (PLC) is another concept that emerged from research on adoption and diffusion of information. A typical life cycle (see Figure 2.5) could be hypothesised as consisting of an introductory period, a period of growth, a maturity phase and ultimately decline, unless the product brand can be reinvented (as, for example, *Harley Davidson* or *Brylcreem*). The importance of the life-cycle concept has been challenged significantly over the years, particularly because of the difficulty in knowing where in the life cycle a product/brand is supposed to be at any one time. Even if its scientific application is dubious, it is useful in explaining the rationale behind the differences in marketing communications strategy at different stages of a company's and/or brand's evolution. The implication of this is that not only do the tools and strategies change depending on whether the communicator wishes to gain attention, create interest, stimulate desire or generate action (see hierarchy of effects models in Figure 2.6), but that the particular life-cycle characteristics of the product or service need be taken into account. Table 2.4 shows how a brand's perceived position on the PLC may be seen to determine its marketing and marketing communications objectives and the strategies and marcom tools used to achieve them.

FIGURE 2.6

	KNOWLEDGE		FEELING		MOTIVATION →ACTION
AIDA Strong 1925	Attention	Interest	Desire		Action
DAGMAR Colley 1961	Awareness	Comprehension		Conviction	Purchase
Lavidge and Steiner 1961	Awareness	Knowledge	Liking	Preference	Conviction Purchase
Wells et al 1965	Awareness Perception	Understanding			Persuasion
	COGNITIVE		**AFFECTIVE**		**CONATIVE**

TABLE 2.4   Life cycle effects on marcom strategy

	Introduction	Growth	Maturity	Decline
Marketing objectives	Help early adopters adopt	Quickly gain market share	Expand market share and build customer/ distributor loyalty	Maintain dominant market position and consider brand extensions
Marcom objectives	Create awareness and interest/ desire among innovators	Strengthen brand preference (with customers and distributors). Encourage wider trial and use	Increase frequency of use and/or suggest possible new uses	Minimise promotion but retain brand values. Perhaps create specialist niche
Marcom strategy (tools in order of priority)	PR/Publicity Personal selling Advertising Sales promotion	Advertising Personal selling Sales promotion PR/Publicity	Advertising Dealer promotions Sales promotions PR/Publicity	Reduced media expenditure

Source: Smith & Taylor 2004

HIERARCHY OF EFFECTS MODELS

From the earliest days of consumer research, it was noted that it was rare for consumers to make instant unsupported decisions. Instead, it was proposed that consumers went through a number of stages prior to purchase. The many concepts developed to show this have become collectively known as **hierarchy of effects** models. Hierarchy of effects models are some of the oldest of all marketing models, first appearing in 1898, continuing to have prominence into the 1980s and (despite revisions in thinking) arguably still having important resonance today. As with all models, they should be recognised for what they are – attempts to simplify complex processes – and not truths. They may prove useful, however, in explaining the thinking behind marketing communications strategy.

Proponents of the traditional hierarchy framework suggest that audiences respond to messages in a very ordered way that is first **cognitive** (thinking), then **affective** (feeling) and third **conative** (doing) (Barry & Howard 1990). Cognition is typically defined as 'mental activity', as reflected in knowledge, beliefs or thoughts that someone has about some aspect of their world (1990). Advertisers have historically relied on measures of memory (such as **recall**) to operationalise cognition. So, for example, in *Marketing's Adwatch Survey* respondents are asked by the pollster 'which of these TV commercials do you remember seeing?' The affective component is any degree of feeling and emotion, in a general sense, which can be attributed to the brand. This is often associated with what is known as **brand personality** (see Chapter 4). Conation refers to either the intention to perform 'a behaviour' (e.g. purchase) or the behaviour itself.

One of the earliest attempts to model the effect of marketing communications was the **AIDA model**, generally attributed to Strong in 1925 (but which actually originated with St Elmo Lewis in 1898 and which was first published in a trade magazine in 1910). Initially designed to represent the stages through which a salesperson should take a prospect to make a sale, this later became the basic framework against which persuasive communication, particularly advertising, was thought to work. AIDA stood for **attention, interest, desire** and **action** and represented the stages the rational consumer was supposed to pass through before the ultimate purchase. This can be superimposed on the hierarchy model, as shown

Hierarchy of effects models
Models that purport to show how marketing communications can help the buying process. AIDA and DAGMAR (see Glossary) are among the best known.

Cognitive
The process of thinking involving the mental processes of memory, perception, judgement and reasoning.

Affective
Feeling processes relating to moods, feelings, attitudes and emotions.

Conative
Doing/action processes; behaviour directed towards positive action.

Brand personality
The character and essence of a brand; the perceived lifestyle associations and values (e.g. status, fashion, quality, etc.).

AIDA model
Generally attributed to
Strong (1925), the model
was designed to represent
the stages through which
a salesperson should
take a prospect but was
later adopted as a basic
framework to explain how
persuasive communication
(mainly advertising) works.
AIDA stands for attention,
interest, desire and action.

Attention
Notice taken of
something or someone;
in communications
theory, attention must be
gained before a message
can be delivered.

DAGMAR
DAGMAR (defining
advertising goals for
measuring advertising
results) was Colley's
(1961) formula for setting
communications-
orientated objectives.

in Figure 2.6. Later models similar in construction were also developed to explain the communications process. They include DAGMAR (defining advertising goals for measuring advertising results), which was Colley's (1961) suggested formula for setting communications-orientated objectives, Lavidge and Steiner (1961) and Wells et al. (1997) who were also trying to represent the communications process in their hierarchy models.

What is most evidently missing from the above models is the post-purchase effect. This is the effect on future decision making, having experienced consumption. Evidently, a good consumption experience is likely (but not certain) to lead to other purchases. As early as 1911, Sheldon added 'permanent satisfaction' as the final step in the Lewis/Strong model to create **AIDAS**. This was an early recognition of the now recognised importance of post-purchase (Barry & Howard 1990). As part of his theory of adoption, Rogers (1983) suggested that there were various stages, including knowledge, persuasion, decision (adopt/reject), implementation and confirmation (continued adoption, discontinuance, continued rejection). Bovée et al. (1995) took this further by suggesting that this post-purchase period is the point when advertising (and the other marketing communications tools) should be used to bolster the customer's sense of satisfaction about the action or purchase, and that this phase represents the beginning of a new cycle in the communication process.

FIGURE 2.7   Extended hierarchy of effects models

	KNOWLEDGE		FEELING		MOTIVATION →ACTION	POST PURCHASE
AIDA(S)	Attention	Interest	Desire	Action		(Satisfaction)
Rogers	Awareness				Decision	Confirmation
			Persuasion		Implementation	
Bovée et al	Awareness	Acceptance			Ownership	
	Comprehension		Preference			Reinforcement
	COGNITIVE		**AFFECTIVE**		**CONATIVE**	**CONATIVE**

Involvement
The degree of perceived
relevance and personal
importance attached
to the purchase.

In their review of hierarchy of effects models, Barry and Howard (1990) noted that while there is little disagreement among researchers regarding the importance of the three stages of the hierarchy, there has been significant disagreement regarding the order of the three stages. The traditional hierarchy of effects model makes the assumption that consumers always go along the rational path of [learning] →[feeling] →[doing]. Although this might be considered logical and rational, our knowledge of the way people work suggests that rationality is not always a human strongpoint. Table 2.5 shows examples of where alternate paths (B to D) to consumption can be seen to be taking place. Although there are in theory six combinations of the three elements, A–D represent the most persuasive matches. Table 2.5 also introduces the concept of involvement as a measure of how important (in monetary and/or other terms) the consumer regards the purchase to be. These represent:

TABLE 2.5 Alternative effects hierarchy

	Involvement	Description	Examples
A: [learning] ➔[feeling] ➔[doing]	High	*Informative* Classic hierarchy	High ticket items, e.g. jewellery
B: [feeling] ➔[learning] ➔ [doing]	High	*Affective* Self-esteem, ego	e.g. sports cars, perfume
C: [feeling] ➔[doing] ➔[learning]	Low	*Social* Personal taste	e.g. pizza, an inexpensive gift
D: [doing] ➔ [learning] ➔[feeling]	Low	*Habitual* Routine behaviour	e.g. shampoo, newspaper

A: The classical hierarchy discussed previously and frequently referred to as the '**extended problem-solving**' model. Purchase decisions are characterised by their importance (high involvement) and rational decision making. Examples include the purchase of high-ticket items such as jewellery.

B: High involvement again but where less information may be required, perhaps because the brand image is strong. It is associated with status items such as sports cars and quality watch brands.

C: Often characterised as '**limited problem solving**', this might be described as 'life's little pleasures' or impulse purchases. These are affected by personal taste and include, for example, a gift for a friend.

D: Habitual and routine behaviour, for example the purchase of a newspaper.

These alternate means of consumer decision making relate directly to involvement and **experience**.[2] Involvement, as noted previously, is the degree of perceived relevance and personal importance attached to the purchase. Experience is the extent to which the consumer has accumulated prior knowledge of the product or service concerned (see Figure 2.8). Looking at decision making in this way enables a matrix to be created that has direct connections with those factors discussed as A to D above.

Extended problem solving
A model where purchase decisions are characterised by their importance (high involvement) and rational decision making.

Limited problem solving
Known and familiar purchases (modified or straight re-buys) with medium involvement in the purchase.

Experience (in relation to purchasing)
The extent to which the consumer has accumulated prior knowledge of the product or service.

FIGURE 2.8 Problem solving

Experience \ Involvement	*High*	*Low*
High	Extended problem solving A	C Limited problem solving
Low	Status seeking or brand loyalty B	D Habit or variety seeking

2 This also has some relevance in relation to the weak theory of advertising (see Chapter 9).

The key advantage of discussing the hierarchy of effects models, irrespective of any debates about accuracy, is their recognition that brand awareness is important. Another benefit is that they again help distinguish between the likely objectives at each stage of the model. Although hierarchy of effects models were largely used to explain the characteristics of advertising, they are useful as a predictor of the relative importance of all the marketing communications tools at various times during the process (see Figure 2.9). Differing objectives mean different strategic approaches, which in turn mean use of the most effective tool(s) for the situation. Advertising and PR are, for example, the tools most effectively used for learning and developing feelings over time. Sales promotion and personal selling are more immediate 'action' tools. This is illustrated in Figure 2.9.

Notwithstanding the contribution the classical hierarchy models have made, and continue to make, they have a number of shortcomings:

- There is no empirical proof that suggests consumers actually go through each stage.
- Hierarchy models do not take account of the potential for interactions between stages.
- Post-purchase experience is often not included.

Brand attitude
How the consumer feels about the brand.

Front-of-mind awareness
Maintaining awareness of the brand in the consumer's mind.

Hierarchy of effects models and related frameworks consider **brand awareness** as a prerequisite for **brand attitude** formation and subsequently conclude that affective responses cannot be formed or purchases made without having awareness of the brand. Most companies, therefore, strive for what is frequently known as **front-of-mind awareness**, in effect establishing your brand before all others in the mind of the consumer.

Despite their evident shortcomings, the models discussed in this chapter present a framework for concepts and theories that can be examined and challenged in the light of observed consumer behaviour.

FIGURE 2.9   Hierarchy of effects and relevant marcom tools

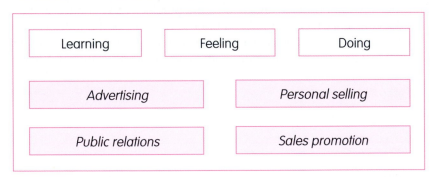

RATIONAL VS. EMOTIONAL APPEALS

Much of what has been discussed in this chapter might be termed rational responses to the messages put in front of us as consumers. Rational messages attempt to prove the usefulness and quality of the product or service, often stating benefits or statistics to justify the facts presented. However, human beings are more emotionally programmed than even we ourselves realise. In messages designed to appeal to our emotions, attractive photography (perhaps representing children/parents/friends, nostalgic scenes or other settings designed to stir our emotions) and music are used to heighten responses. Humans even react in a less than rational way, even when they know they are being manipulated. 'Three for the price of two' and other 'offers' tempt us to over-purchase or make selections on the basis of the 'best deal' rather than necessarily on what is best for us in the long term. As rationally obvious as it may seem to retailers who introduce 'everyday low-price' strategies, customers still want a deal, even if it is a false economy (see case study at the end of this chapter).

DIGITAL MARKETING THEORY

Digital marketing has undoubtedly changed the process of marketing communications in the past few years, but has it changed the underlying theory behind marketing and marketing communications? Some would undoubtedly argue that this is the case, although cynics would suggest these are the same marketers who are simply repeating the mistakes of the past (albeit digitally). Digital technology has allowed us to communicate faster and more effectively. Unfortunately, the competition has access to it as well. According to Kevin Roberts, CEO of Saatchi and Saatchi: 'the Web is functionally fantastic, but it's a tool. A terrific place to present information but not, at this stage, a tenably emotional location.' The marketer's job, therefore, is still to get over the message in a targeted and creative way, understanding those concepts we have learnt though a century and more of the study of marketing in general and marketing communications in particular.

summary

This chapter reviewed those concepts and theories associated with marketing communications research and practice. It introduced the 'simple communications model' and described the important elements of it. It reviewed the characteristics of the 'source' and the 'message' that are associated with message clarity and those that restrict effective communication. The 'two-step model' introduced the concepts of 'opinion leaders' and 'opinion formers' and their influence on message management. The associated concepts of 'diffusion of innovation' and the 'product life cycle' were explained and their connection with marketing communications strategies explored. Returning again to the 'hierarchy of effects' models, various versions were analysed and alternatives suggested.

review questions

1. How would you illustrate the basic process of communication?

2. What would you consider to be the problems associated with ethnocentrism?

3. Explain the differences between semiotics, syntactics and semantics.

4. What do you consider are the key determinants of ineffective communication?

5. Why might the source of a piece of communication be important?

6. Define 'noise'.

7. What is the principle of 'wear-out'?

8. To what extent can hierarchical effects models incorporate the impact of post-purchase behaviour?

9. What do you consider to be the main advantages of using hierarchy of effects modelling?

10. Would you consider David Beckham to be an opinion former or an opinion leader and why?

discussion questions

1. Viral marketing is a phenomenon of internet advertising. What do you think the dangers might be for companies adopting this medium and under what circumstances do you feel this form of advertising might be inappropriate?

2. Repetition is an important aspect of message receipt and acceptance. To what extent do you feel this works and what would you need to consider if you were building this into a communications plan?

3. How valuable are hierarchy of effects models and to what extent can you use them in your communications planning?

4. How should digital marketing be viewed in terms of marketing communications?

case study 2.1: *J.C. Penney's* mistake? Assuming the consumer is rational

By Tom Denari, *Advertising Age,* 23 May 2012

In this article, the author remembers his childhood and how his mother would frequently buy goods because they were 'on sale' or she had a coupon. He examines this behaviour in the light of J.C. Penney's decision to follow an everyday low-price strategy.

Some of my fondest memories as a kid were the days when my mom would arrive home from an all-afternoon grocery-shopping trip. The blue Country Squire station wagon with the fake wood on the sides would pull into the driveway, full of produce, staples and snacks from the three or four different grocery stores she'd visited. Feeding a family of seven, my mom was an expert at determining which stores had sale prices, which had in-store coupons and which had specials on the eight-packs of Coke or Pepsi. (We went through a ton of those.) Sometimes she'd arrive with a rare carton of Dr Pepper. It was hardly ever on sale – those were special days.

I couldn't wait to dig through each of the brown paper sacks. Every once in a while I'd find a new product, or something she wouldn't typically buy. When I found one of these surprises, like a jar of dry-roasted peanuts, I'd ask, 'Wow. Peanuts. Cool. Why'd you get these?'

'It was on sale – and I had a coupon for it', she'd proudly proclaim. 'I saved seventy-five cents.'

My mom got great pleasure in buying products that were on sale, and in finding ways to get more for our money. But, over time, as I got older I realised that maybe she got too much pleasure from it. She enjoyed saving money so much that she would purchase things because they were on sale, not because we needed them. 'The deal was just too good to pass up', she'd say. In the end, my mom probably bought more, and ultimately spent more than if many of those same items had simply been marked at an 'everyday low price'.

But my mom's not unique. Most people are wired this way.

Last week, when I read about *JC Penney*'s struggles to get consumers to understand the company's new pricing strategy that eliminates 'sales', I chuckled and thought of my mom. CEO Ron Johnson's notion that they 'need to better explain our pricing system' misses the point. *JC Penney* isn't wrong for trying to change the nature of retail. I'm rooting for them. But the company overestimated consumers' rationality to think that they would change their behaviour so quickly.

JC Penney's desire to give more integrity to pricing – eliminating the traditional retail game of inflating suggested retail prices so that they can be quickly discounted – is admirable. And it makes logical, rational sense. For instance, a rational person would rather buy a $7 T-shirt for $7 than that very same T-shirt, typically listed at $12.99, marked down to $7.99 (almost a dollar more than the new price). But Penney's customers aren't buying more T-shirts, or the new pricing strategy. Johnson reported that his customers are making fewer visits and fewer purchases.

Why? The mistake *JC Penney* made was expecting consumers to behave rationally. As much as we prefer to think of ourselves as rational beings, loads of neuroscience studies over the past four decades have demonstrated that most decision making actually occurs through a very fast, imperceptible wrestling match between: (1) the parts of our brains that control rational thinking, which centre around slower, conscious, computational reasoning, and (2) the parts that control the non-rational aspects, which are fast, subconscious, intuitive and emotional.

This faster, intuitive, non-analytical functioning of the brain was introduced by Amos Tversky and Daniel Kahneman in the 1970s. Their compelling research, since built on by many others, revealed that this non-rational part of our brain is what allows us to make some judgements and behaviours effortlessly, like driving to work without having to analyse every turn or recognising whether the person walking toward you is your neighbour or a stranger. But environmental factors, memory and other stimuli can easily influence this intuitive processing into creating flawed judgements or distorted perceptions, which are referred to as cognitive biases. These distorted perceptions can also lead to phenomenona like stereotyping, or the halo effect, where we trust attractive people more than unattractive.

The cognitive bias at play in the *Penney* pricing initiative is an 'anchoring effect', meaning that consumers are typically heavily influenced by a specific piece of information, which all other information is evaluated against. Suggested retail prices are the most common anchors. Even when seemingly inflated, a suggested retail price serves as an anchor for which all other pricing information is compared. For instance, while the $12.99 original price tag for the T-shirt might have been an inflated price, it still creates a subconscious anchor. While the consumer's rational side may know that it's a bogus price, the irrational side is excited that it can get the T-shirt for a bargain at $7.99. The discount creates the yearning to make the purchase. For some, it even gives them a slight feeling of euphoria, or a mini rush.

The reason *JC Penney* is selling fewer items is because the anchor is gone. A $7 T-shirt is just a $7 T-shirt. If you buy it, you're paying full price. And what our irrational brains have learned over time – they do learn – is that paying full price, no matter what the cost, is no fun. This doesn't make us crazy, just human – and not nearly as rational as marketers think we are.

Case study questions

1. Why has the author criticised *Penney*'s strategy change?
2. What is the significance of the 'anchoring effect'?

further reading

Berglind, M. and Nakata, C. (2005) 'Cause-related marketing: more buck than bang?', *Business Horizons*, 48 (5): 443–53.

Kuster, F. and Eisend, M. (2012) 'Immediate and delayed effects of message sidedness', *Advances in Advertising Research*, 3: 55–65.

(Continued)

(Continued)

Lindgreen, A. and Swaen, V. (2010) 'Corporate social responsibility', *International Journal of Management Reviews*, 12: 1–7.

Menord, V.I. and Menord, M. (2006) 'No longer lost in translation', *Quality Progress*, 39 (8): 27–32.

Rucker, D.D. and Petty, R. (2006) 'Increasing the effectiveness of communications to consumers: recommendations based on elaboration likelihood and attitude certainty perspectives', *Journal of Public Policy & Marketing*, 25 (1): 39–52.

Shapiro, S.J. (2005) 'Looking backward – and ahead', *Journal of Public Policy & Marketing*, 24 (1): 117–20.

Wang, S. (Alex) and Nelson, R.A. (2006) 'The effects of identical versus varied advertising and publicity messages on consumer response', *Journal of Marketing Communications*, 12 (2): 109–23.

REFERENCES

Abrantes, R. (2006) The silent language: the human nonverbal communication. Etologisk Institute, at www.etologi.dk and Abrantes R&D International, at www.abrantes.org

Barry, T. and Howard, D.J. (1990) 'A review and critique of the hierarchy of effects in advertising', *International Journal of Advertising*, 9: 121–35.

Bovée, C.L., Thill, J.V., Dovel, G.P. and Wood, M.B. (1995) *Advertising Excellence*. Englewood Cliffs, NJ: McGraw-Hill.

Carl, W.J. (2006) 'What's all the buzz about? Everyday communication and the relational basis of word-of-mouth and buzz marketing practices', *Management Communication Quarterly*, 19 (4): 601–34.

Colley, R.H. (1961) *Defining Advertising Goals*. New York: Association of National Advertisers.

De Pelsmacker, P., Geuens, M. and Van den Bergh, J. (2007) *Marketing Communications: A European Perspective*, 3rd edn. London: Prentice Hall.

Fill, C. (2001) 'Essentially a matter of consistency: integrated marketing communications', *The Marketing Review*, 1 (4): 409–25.

Harper-Collins (2011) *English Dictionary*. Glasgow: Harper-Collins.

Kelman, H. (1961) 'Processes of opinion change', *Public Opinion Quarterly*, 25 (Spring): 57–78.

Klapper, J.T. (1960) *The Effects of Mass Communication*. New York: Free Press.

Lavidge, R. and Steiner, G. (1961) 'A model for predictive measurements of advertising effectiveness', *Journal of Marketing*, Oct.: 61.

Mano, H. (1996) 'Assessing emotional reactions to TV ads: a replication and extension with a brief adjective checklist', *Advances in Consumer Research*, 23: 63–9.

Mistry, B. (2006) 'Star spotting', *Marketing*, 7 June: 33–4.

Nielsen, A.C. (2003) 'Alternative marketing vehicles: future of markets', *Consumer Insight Magazine*, June, at www.marketingpower.com [accessed 31 October 2005].

Nielsen, A.C. (2009) *Global Faces and Networked Places: Nielsen Report on Social Networking's New Global Footprint*. London: Nielsen.

OED (2014) Oxford Concise English Dictionary. Oxford: Oxford University Press.

Petty, R.E. and Cacioppo, J.T. (1979) 'Effects of message repetition and position on cognitive responses, recall and persuasion', *Journal of Personality and Social Psychology*, 37 (Jan.): 97–109.

Pickton, D. and Broderick, A. (2001) *Integrated Marketing Communications*. Harlow: Prentice Hall.

Rogers, E.M. (1983) *Diffusion of Innovations*, 3rd edn. New York: Free Press.

Schramm, W. (1955) *How Communication Works in the Process and Effects of Mass Communications*. Urbana, IL: University of Illinois Press.

Smith, P.R. and Taylor, J. (2004) *Marketing Communications: An Integrated Approach*, 2nd edn. London: Kogan Page.

Strong, E.K. (1925) *The Psychology of Selling*. New York: McGraw-Hill.

Wells, W., Burnett, J. and Moriarty, S. (1997) *Advertising Principles and Practice*, 4th edn. Upper Saddle River, NJ: Prentice Hall.

USEFUL WEBSITES

Examples of 'slice-of-life' advertising can be found at:

www.youtube.com/watch?v=OQPLia_eu2Q and www.youtube.com/watch?v=ZXDvzPx8zTc
For examples of music used in advertising, see www.tvadmusic.co.uk/

For additional materials that support this chapter and your learning, please visit:
study.sagepub.com/egan

BUYING BEHAVIOUR   3

CHAPTER CONTENTS

LEARNING OBJECTIVES

Having completed this chapter, readers would be expected to:

- understand the different schools of thought on consumer decision making

- recognise the factors that affect decision making and the ways researchers classify them

- understand the importance of attitudes, perception, learning and motivation on buying behaviour

- understand how marketing communications strategies utilise buyer behaviour theory.

INTRODUCTION

What makes buyers buy? This question has troubled marketing scholars for well over a century. What is certain is that the answer is not straightforward. Every consumer is different as a result of their own unique characteristics and the effect society has on them. These all-powerful drivers are frequently referred to as **nature** (i.e. those characteristics we inherited) and **nurture** (i.e. the effect of society on those characteristics). Marketing communicators, while recognising this complexity, need to be aware of what stimulates audiences and what does not. This is very far from being an exact science.

Theories of decision making generally fall into two schools of thought: **the cognitive paradigm** and **the behavioural paradigm**. (A paradigm is a 'world view' underlying the theories and methodologies of a particular subject – in this case marketing.)

COGNITIVE PARADIGM

The cognitive paradigm is so-called because it focuses on an individual's thought processes and sees consumer choice as a problem-solving and decision-making series of activities, the outcome of which is determined principally by the buyer's intellectual functioning and rational goal-orientated processing of information (Pickton & Broderick 2005). This makes the rather rash judgement that consumers are highly rational, willing to put themselves out of their way, problem solvers. It also makes the assumption that most product choices are **routinised problem solving** (see Chapter 2) characterised by habitual behaviour with little thought going into the purchase and largely based on previous buying experience. The simple buying model (Figure 3.1) is an example of this perceived rational process.

FIGURE 3.1   Simple buying model

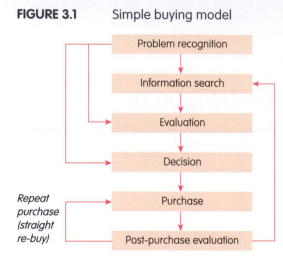

Most cognitive models, however complex, are generally based on a model similar to Figure 3.1. Such models involve a **problem recognition** (or **problem definition**) stage which acts as the trigger for the process. This *may* lead to an **information search** where the potential customer collects information on a range of products or services, and which aids their subsequent **evaluation**. A **decision** is made which *may* lead to a **purchase**. **Post-purchase evaluation** *may* mean that the next time it will be a **straight re-buy** if everything has been to the customer's satisfaction. Alternatively, it might end up in a further search for information if the experience was not a satisfactory one. The continual use of the word *may* emphasises that the model is not a straightforward linear model, that some stages are bypassed and that iteration can and does occur.

There are limitations to this process that have been identified by a number of authors:

- Consumers do not have perfect knowledge of all alternative products (the **total set**).
- Consumers are only aware of a percentage of the products (the **awareness set**).
- Consumers reduce this to a smaller, more manageable group (the **evoked set**) from which a decision is made.

The major management implication of this is that achieving awareness, although an important prerequisite, is not in itself enough. A key objective of any brand owner should be to get their brand into the evoked set (see Chapter 4 on **brand salience**). The term **front of mind** (or **top of mind**) is frequently used by marketers to emphasise that it is a principle objective of brand owners and their communications teams to aim for a prominent place in an evoked set (see Chapter 2).

Closely associated with the simple buying model is the concept of a **problem-solving** hierarchy. As discussed in Chapter 2, this suggests that there are various levels of problem solving and that the level affects how much care, attention and involvement we are prepared to undertake when making buying decisions. These levels are labelled **extensive problem solving, limited problem solving** and **routinised problem solving** and are described as follows:

- extensive problem solving: important decisions warrant greater deliberation (high involvement); usually high expenditure
- limited problem solving: known and familiar (modified or straight rebuys) (medium involvement); usually moderate pricing
- routinised problem solving: repeat behaviour, often with limited external knowledge (low involvement); usually low pricing.

BEHAVIOURAL PARADIGM

The behavioural paradigm is derived from operant behaviouralism research by Skinner, discussed in more detail on page 65. Proponents of this paradigm believe it is not possible to study what goes on in the consumer's mind because it is so complex. Instead, it is proposed, output is measured following a given stimulus. In effect, it is a 'black box' into which stimuli (or environmental cues) flow and out of which behaviour occurs. The consequence of this behaviour may in turn reinforce future behaviour and increase its occurrence (Pickton & Broderick 2005). An illustration of the process as conceived by behaviouralists is shown in Figure 3.2.

FIGURE 3.2   The behavioural paradigm

Behavioural theorists believe that marketing communications activity should be based on creating the correct environmental cues for the individual and monitoring the responses to these cues as a guide to future activity. According to Foxall (1993), the behavioural paradigm makes two assumptions. These are:

- The frequency with which the behaviour is performed is a function of the consequences of such behaviour in the past – that is, the success of previous outcomes are likely to determine the number of times that the stimulus is repeated.
- The determinants of behaviour must, therefore, be found in the environment rather than in the individual. The triggers to that behaviour can, therefore, be applied by the marketer.

ALTERNATIVE MODELS OF PROBLEM SOLVING

Although eminently logical, most decision-making models relate to **high-involvement purchases** and are **extensive problem-solving** types; most product or service choices involve, however, **routine problem solving** characterised by habit with little thought given to the range of alternatives (including, at times, price). Ehrenberg and Goodhardt (1979) suggest that the greater part of the buying experience is rooted in past experience, as indicated in the **ATR model** (see Figure 3.3).

Post-purchase evaluation
Evaluation of a product or service after consumption which may lead to re-purchase.

Straight re-buy
A business-to-business (B2B) term for re-buying a product without changing the supplier or the specifications.

Total set
All of the products available in a particular product or service category.

Awareness set
Those products in a category that the consumer is actually aware of.

Evoked set
Those products in a category that the consumer has 'front of mind' and will make the purchase choice from.

Brand salience
The importance and prominence of a brand.

Problem-solving model
An extensive, limited and routinised problem-solving model.

Extensive problem solving
A model that reflects important purchase decisions (e.g. high expenditure), which warrant great deliberation and high involvement; also known as the high-involvement model.

Limited problem solving
Known and familiar purchases (modified or straight re-buys) with medium involvement in the purchase.

Routinised problem solving
Repeat behaviour with low involvement, usually low cost and often limited external knowledge.

FIGURE 3.3   The ATR model

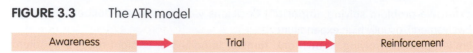

ATR model
Awareness, Trial and Reinforcement. Ehrenberg and Goodhardt (1979) suggest that the greater part of the buying judgement is rooted in past experience.

Trial packs
A new product, frequently in smaller than normal quantity and at a special price to encourage trial.

Giveaways
Products distributed (in-store or elsewhere) without cost as a means of encouraging trial.

Cognitive dissonance
The mental discomfort that an individual feels if they hold two conflicting cognitions (or views). Individuals will seek to reduce or eliminate this dissonance by either changing one or the other viewpoint or by introducing a third view that will account for and reduce the dissonance.

Post-purchase dissonance
The mental discomfort felt after a purchase is made regarding whether or not the buyer has made the right decision (e.g. is it value for money?).

The important thing here is to gain trial as there is a natural reluctance to try something new. This reluctance explains why so many new consumer products are introduced through **trial packs** and **giveaways**. The trial is a considerable barrier which, once overcome, can lead to repeat purchases in the future.

It is also quite common behaviour for normally brand loyal customers to shop around occasionally – a practice which may or may not lead eventually back to their original favoured brand.

COGNITIVE DISSONANCE THEORY

This theory was developed by Festinger (1957) and remains somewhat controversial. It is based on the presumption that if an individual holds two conflicting cognitions (or views) he or she will experience mental discomfort (**cognitive dissonance**). In this event, individuals will seek to reduce or eliminate this dissonance by either changing one or the other viewpoint or by introducing a third view that will account for and reduce the dissonance. In marketing terms, this cognitive dissonance is most likely to occur after a purchase (**post-purchase dissonance**) because any purchase involves some form of self-justification, particularly if high costs (monetary or emotional) are involved in the purchase. Blythe (2000) suggests that there are four general approaches to reducing dissonance and these are:

- Ignore the dissonant information (e.g. accept a car's poor performance as one of those things).
- Distort the dissonant information (e.g. pretend the car works well in certain circumstances such as in the rain).
- Play down the importance of the issue (e.g. look for the positive features and benefits such as comfort).
- Change the behaviour or situation (e.g. get rid of the car).

It is frequently proposed that brand-building communications (e.g. advertising) help reduce cognitive dissonance by emphasising to existing consumers the positive attributes of the purchase, reinforcing the view that they have made the right decision. In automobile advertising, for example, it is suggested that many of the viewers who pay attention to the message(s) are existing customers looking for such reassurance.

FACTORS AFFECTING BUYING BEHAVIOUR

It is probable that the best approach to understanding buying decision behaviour is through a combination of cognitive and behavioural decision making augmented by other factors including internal and external influences mediated through individual and unique personalities. A wide range of different factors affects our reception of information, what we do with that information and, consequently, our buying behaviour.

Race, religion and culture set the tone for our particular values, as modified by our membership of primary (e.g. family) or secondary (e.g. work colleagues) groups. Cultural factors have a significant impact on consumer behaviour. Culture is at the root of a person's personality, wants and behaviours. As they grow up, children learn basic values, perceptions and wants from their family, friends and other culturally specific groups. Marketers are always trying to spot 'cultural shifts' which might point to new products wanted by customers or to increased demand. Internally, our **attitudes**, **perceptions**, **learning** and capacity for memory, and **motivations** have a considerable influence. Our individual characteristics, such as age, gender, income, personality and family situation (see Figure 3.4), are seen as further determinants of what we choose to pay attention to and ultimately purchase. External factors such as our personal situation (e.g. health), the prevailing fashion, the availability of disposable funds, the legal position, time-associated factors (e.g. time to search), the power of the media and communication messages, the weather or even the current stock position act as further moderators to our behaviour. These diverse influences are shown graphically in Figure 3.4.

Attitude
A strongly felt, not easily changed view. Attitude forms an important part of consumer theory because it is believed to be the link between what consumers think and what they buy in the marketplace.

Perception
Perception is the result of how we interpret and make sense of the world. The way an individual perceives a situation may be different from how others perceive the same situation.

Learning
The human capacity to know about and act on a situation based on prior experience.

Motivation
An inner drive which causes human beings to strive for some level of satisfaction.

FIGURE 3.4   Factors affecting buyer behaviour

Basic demographic factors (age, sex, income, etc.) are traditional discriminators as they are seen to have an effect on purchase decisions. Other aspects (employment, motivation, etc.) are used as the traditional basis for creating 'groupings' of consumers. Perhaps the oldest such classification in the UK is the National Readership Survey's (NRS) socioeconomic groupings, much beloved of newspaper and magazine circulation managers. The NRS social grade definitions are shown in Table 3.1.

TABLE 3.1   Socioeconomic groupings

Social grade	Social status	Occupation
A	Upper middle class	Higher managerial, administrative or professional
B	Middle class	Intermediate managerial, administrative or professional
C¹	Lower middle class	Supervisory or clerical, junior managerial, admin/professioinal
C²	Skilled working class	Skilled manual workers
D	Working class	Semi or unskilled manual workers
E	Lowest level of subsistence	Pensioners or widows/ers, casual or lowest grade workers

The NRS socioeconomic groupings have considerable failings. They were developed at a time when the class structure was more pronounced than it is today. It was also based on the occupation of the head of the household with no consideration for the partner/spouse or other influencers. In 2001, a new classification was introduced based on the way people work. The classifications distinguish between employers, the self-employed and employees, who are further segmented by the nature of their job conditions including career prospects, the length of notice required, whether paid a salary or a wage and the standard of pension and insurance provision. The seven new classifications are shown in Table 3.2.

TABLE 3.2   Seven classifications of social class

Class	% *	Description
One	8.5%	Large employers and higher managerial and professional occupations
Two	19%	Lower managerial and professional occupations
Three	9.4%	Intermediate occupations (e.g. medical/legal secretaries)
Four	7%	Small employers and 'own account' workers (e.g. hotel manager)
Five	7.2%	Lower supervisory and technical occupations (e.g. traffic wardens)
Six	12%	Semi routine occupations (e.g. sales assistants, taxi drivers)
Seven	9.1%	Routine occupations (e.g. waiters, packers, couriers)
	29%	Unclassified are those who have never worked, the long-term unemployed, full-time students and others not covered.

Note: * because of rounding up the total exceeds 100.

VALs
Value, activity and lifestyle analysis.

It remains to be seen if this new classification (or others that might follow it) will eventually take over from the old. Given the traditional nature of the magazine and newspaper industries, it is unlikely to happen overnight.

Lifestyle is also seen as an important discriminator. Researchers investigate consumer **VALs** (values, activities and lifestyles) and will frequently give distinct groupings a name that describes these broad characterisations. The NRS, for example, uses a table of descriptors, each representing a particular lifestyle (see Table 3.3).

TABLE 3.3   NRS profiles

Class	Descriptor	Class	Descriptor
A	Affluent achievers	G	Senior citizens
B	Thriving greys	H	Producers
C	Settled suburbs	I	Hard-pressed families
D	Nest builders	J	Have-nots
E	Urban ventures	K	Unclassifiable
F	Country life		

An individual's life stage is seen as a particularly important discriminator. The key variables are age, marital/commitment status, career progress, disposable income and the presence or absence of children. Table 3.4 is a list of descriptors showing the changing circumstances experienced during a typical lifetime. At each stage, consumers have different needs and (given the cost of rearing children) different levels of disposable income with which to satisfy them.

TABLE 3.4   Family life cycles

Life stage	Description
Single	Living alone; no dependents
Single Parent	Alone with dependent child/children
DINKS	Double Income No Kids
Full Nest 1	Youngest child under 6
Full Nest 2	Youngest child over 6
Full Nest 3	Dependent children
Empty Nest 1	Children moved out but still working
Empty Nest 2	Retired couple
Solitary Survivor 1	Still working widow/er
Solitary Survivor 2	Retired widow/er

Even more detailed profiles are available in developed markets around the globe. For example, *CACI Ltd* produces **Acorn profiles** (Acorn is an acronym of 'a classification of residential neighbourhoods'). These describe residential areas and are based on the approximately 1.7 million postcodes in the UK. The full Acorn profile currently comprises of 5 categories, 17 groups and 56 types. It is **geodemographic** (i.e. combining both geographical and demographic features) and has been used by marketers to target consumers with particular characteristics. The current Acorn classifications are shown in Table 3.5.

A number of factors similar to those above are used to create composites of a brand's target audience. Known as **trait theory**, it suggests that individual personalities are composed of broad characteristics. For example, consider how you would describe the personality of a friend or colleague. A trait may be relatively stable which causes individuals to behave in certain ways. These traits are of particular interest to marketing communicators who study the relationship between broad personality traits and general types of behaviour. There are very many examples of this consumer typology, indeed some major brands develop their own typologies describing in some detail the types of consumer of their product or service. A typical example of a typology was that introduced by Young and Rubicam in the 1980s called the 4Cs (consumers). This is shown in Table 3.6.

Acorn profiles
Describe residential neighbourhoods and are based on the approximately 1.7 million postcodes in the UK. The full Acorn profile comprises of 17 distinct categories containing 54 Acorn neighbourhood types.

Geodemographic profiles
Combining both geographical and demographic features to provide a profile.

Trait theory
A theory that suggests individuals can be viewed as a composite of several behaviour traits or characteristics.

TABLE 3.5   CACI Acorn Profile of Great Britain

Category	Group	Type
1. Wealthy Achievers	1.A Wealthy Executives	01 – Wealthy mature professionals, large houses
		02 – Wealthy working families with mortgages
		03 – Villages with wealthy commuters
		04 – Well-off managers, larger houses
	1.B Affluent Greys	05 – Older affluent professionals
		06 – Farming communities
		07 – Old people, detached houses
		08 – Mature couples, smaller detached houses
	1.C Flourishing Families	09 – Larger families, prosperous suburbs
		10 – Well-off working families with mortgages
		11 – Well-off managers, detached houses
		12 – Large families and houses in rural areas
2. Urban Prosperity	2.D Prosperous Professionals	13 – Well-off professionals, larger houses and converted flats
		14 – Older professionals in detached houses and apartments
	2.E Educated Urbanites	15 – Affluent urban professionals, flats
		16 – Prosperous young professionals, flats
		17 – Young educated workers, flats
		18 – Multi-ethnic young, converted flats
		19 – Suburban privately renting professionals
	2.F Aspiring Singles	20 – Student flats and cosmopolitan sharers
		21 – Singles and sharers, multi-ethnic areas
		22 – Low-income singles, small rented flats
		23 – Students, terraces
3. Comfortably Off	3.G Starting Out	24 – Young couples, flats and terraces
		25 – White collar singles/sharers, terraces

Category	Group	Type
	3.H Secure Families	26 – Younger white-collar couples with mortgages
		27 – Middle-income, home-owning areas
		28 – Working families with mortgages
		29 – Mature families in suburban semis
		30 – Established home-owning workers
		31 – Home-owning Asian family areas
	3.I Settled Suburbia	32 – Retired home owners
		33 – Middle-income, older couples
		34 – Lower-income people, semis
	3.J Prudent Pensioners	35 – Elderly singles, purpose-built flats
		36 – Older people, flats
4. Modest Means	4.K Asian Communities	37 – Crowded Asian terraces
		38 – Low-income Asian families
		39 – Skilled, older family, terraces
	4.L Post Industrial Families	40 – Young family workers
		41 – Skilled workers, semis and terraces
	4.M Blue Collar Roots	42 – Home owning, terraces
		43 – Older people, rented terraces
5. Hard Pressed	5.N Struggling Families	44 – Low income larger families, semis
		45 – Older people, low income, smaller semis
		46 – Low income, routine jobs, terraces and flats
		47 – Low income, terraced estates
		48 – Families and single parents, semis and terraces
		49 – Large families and single parents, many children
	5.O Burdened Singles	50 – Single elderly people, council flats
		51 – Single parents and pensioners, council terraces
		52 – Families and single parents, council flats
	5.P High Rise Hardship	53 – Older people, many high-rise flats
		54 – Singles and single parents, high-rise estates
	5.Q Inner City Adversity	55 – Multi-ethnic, purpose-built estates
		56 – Multi-ethnic, flats

Source: CACI (as at July 2012)

TABLE 3.6   Young and Rubicam 4 Consumers Typology

Name	Description	Tendency to purchase
Aspirers	Seeking status and self-esteem	Symbols of achievement
Succeeders	Successful but need to control their lives	Quality (actual or perceived)
Mainstreamers	Basic need for security and belonging	Established products/brands
Performers	Self-fulfilment rather than status	Own brands, natural products

insight: Trait theories

The dangers of subjective profiles are outlined by the former marketing director of a major UK FMCG manufacturer interviewed as part of a research project. He stated that 'most of our brands had more off-strategy eating than on-strategy eating going on'. He went on to explain that they 'would very carefully target a brand at an archetypal consumer with a particular need ... the classic cube of who, why, when and frankly, when you analyse the numbers an awful lot more was getting eaten by the wrong people, at the wrong time, for the wrong reasons, than you would care to admit'. Although perhaps not a ringing endorsement, the same executive went on to say that it could be helpful: 'It can help you at least to have clarity, to have a clear view, of which customer you have in mind.'

Using these traits as guides, marketers establish target groups of customers who hold most promise for the brand. As the Insight above suggests, this does not always work.

ATTITUDE

Personal attitude plays a central part in consumer behaviour. Attitudes are what drive a human being to act in a certain way. Attitude forms an important part of consumer theory because it is believed to be 'the crucial link between what consumers think and what they buy in the marketplace' (Foxall et al. 1998: 102). The experiential combination of perception and learning processes can help influence the creation of predisposed attitudes, for example to imagery, situations or circumstances, which might influence the way in which consumers react, creating a bridge between the way they think and the way they behave. Attitude is a learned tendency to respond and react to something in a consistent (favourable or unfavourable) way (Onkvisit and Shaw 1994); put more simply, it is a predisposition to respond in a consistent manner to a stimulus; a tendency to act or behave in some predictable way. Attitudes are difficult to change. Even when change is affected, this is usually over a long period of time.

Attitudes (and in particular cultural attitudes) may be characterised as stereotypes which are very useful to marketers targeting particular groups (see Chapter 6). The influence of individual cultures (or sub-cultures) is very strong. Culture is not those features we are born with (nature) but those we derive from the society around us (nurture). Culture is everything a person learns and shares with members of a society, including ideas, norms, morals, values, knowledge, skills, technology, tools, material objects and behaviours (Sheth et al. 1999). These unique characteristics define acceptable patterns of behaviour within a given society and are usually visualised through:

- a society's values
- a society's norms or rules of behaviour
- a society's rituals and symbols
- a society's myths (stories describing key societal values). (Sheth et al. 1999)

Despite the importance of attitude to buying behaviour, a positive attitude is not necessarily a good predictor of purchase behaviour. For example, an individual may have an excellent attitude to the brand *Ferrari* but other factors (e.g. finance) may inhibit purchase. From the perspective of repeat business, it is also incorrect to assume that satisfaction with a product or service at any point in time will necessarily ensure re-purchase or longer-term loyalty. Research by Reichheld (1993) and Mittal and Lassar (1998) suggests that satisfaction is not necessarily a precursor to customer retention or loyalty. The researchers note that high levels of customers who defected to other brands had declared themselves satisfied or very satisfied immediately before the defection. What becomes more relevant, therefore, is the relationship between a change in attitude and that individual's intent to act in a particular way.

PERCEPTION

Effective marketing management rests on two fundamentals (Foxall et al. 1998):

- Consumers act on their perceptions and these come from the information they receive.
- Managers need to understand the nature of the perceptions their customers and potential customers have.

Perception is how we interpret and make sense of the world. A fundamental part of the function of marketing communications, therefore, is to ensure that the product or service finds the right place in the consumer's **field of perception'** or real world/'**world view**' (see Chapter 2). Not everyone perceives the same thing, thus two opposing football fans can see a referee award a penalty. One may (genuinely) see it as a definite penalty award while the other (genuinely) will see it as unjust.

We each create our own 'cognitive map', therefore, which is essentially an imaginative construct that will be influenced by:

- subjectivity: determined by each individual's own world view
- categorisation: how each individual develops information
- selectivity: how much the brain selects from the environment (see, later, selective attention)
- expectation: what leads individuals to interpret later information in a specific way (e.g. seeing only part of a familiar label enables the brain to complete the picture; see Figure 4.3)
- past experience: what leads us to interpret current experiences (e.g. sometimes sights, sounds or smells trigger appropriate responses).

The human brain is good at assembling evidence from less than complete information. The presentation of only part of a label or image, in the knowledge that the viewer's brain will complete the picture, is a common advertising ploy (see Figure 4.3). In the **gestalt approach** to perception, this is known as **closure**. In effect, the mind acts as the communication medium as it is only within the

World view
An individual's view or understanding of the world (see field of perception).

Gestalt approach
Gestalt (German for 'whole' or 'entirely') and gestalt psychology stress the fact that perception of a stimulus takes place within a known context and that the individual's reaction is crucially affected by his or her 'world view'.

Closure
The mind's ability (based on past experience) to complete something that is incomplete (e.g. part of a name, recognition based on shape, etc.).

mind that the image becomes visible. Gestalt (German for 'whole' or 'entirely') and gestalt psychology stress the fact that perception of a stimulus takes place within a known context and that the individual's reaction is crucially affected by his 'world view' (Foxall et al. 1998). A similar recognition takes place when a familiar script (e.g. *Coca-Cola*) is used in unfamiliar ways (for example, to spell out messages). The mind associates the script with the brand even if the brand name is not mentioned (see Insight).

insight: Coca-Cola font

The *Coca-Cola* font is the one used in the *Coca-Cola* drink logo. The Coca-Cola logo was created in 1885 by Frank Mason Robinson and the font is known as Spencerian script. It is sometimes used without mention of the brand but such is its fame it is still recognisable. As Spencerian script pre-dated the logo, the script itself is not under copyright. However, '*Coca-Cola*' written in Spencerian script is protected by trademarks.

Selective attention
The process of screening out information that does not interest us and selectively processing the information that does. Messages that successfully bypass 'selective attention' are likely to be perceived positively.

Selective exposure
Where consumers selectively expose themselves to certain messages as opposed to other messages.

Selective distortion
The tendency to hear what we want to hear. Distortion may occur because of attitudes, prejudice or stereotyping.

Before perception can even occur, **attention** has to be gained. Indeed, the greater the attention paid, the greater the likelihood that the receiver will perceive the right message. There are a number of concepts that are directly associated with perception. These include:

- **selective attention:** all consumers are each day exposed to hundreds of competing messages. Selective attention is the process of screening out information that does not interest us and selectively processing the information that does. Messages that successfully by-pass 'selective attention' are likely to be perceived positively
- **selective exposure:** where consumers selectively expose themselves to certain messages as opposed to other messages (e.g. by ordering a catalogue)
- **selective distortion:** the tendency to hear what we want to hear. Distortion may occur because of prejudice or stereotyping.

The basic principle, according to Foxall et al. (1998), is that consumers pay attention to stimuli they deem relevant to their needs, wants, beliefs and attitudes. Once attention is gained, the information is interpreted and stored in the memory so as to enforce and enhance existing attitudes and behaviour.

Distortion frequently takes place because of attitude and prejudice. For example, if an individual is a supporter of a particular political party s/he is unlikely to be persuaded by the positive messages of an opposing party, at least in the short term. Another distortion is the **halo effect**. This is when the attributes of one factor are transferred to another in such a way that it affects our judgement. This is the effect sought through **brand extension** (the halo effect of the original brand), **cause-related marketing** (the halo effect of the cause or charity) and **sponsorship** (the halo effect of the event).

LEARNING

According to Foxall et al. (1998: 75), learning is conceptually related to perception. Both involve the individual customer's response to environmental and psycho-social stimuli; both can be explained theoretically in terms of either a stimulus response or a cognitive paradigm; both processes are intrinsically connected with and shaped by an individual's attitude, personality and motivation; both are important in explaining several aspects of consumer behaviour and hence are of practical concern to the marketer.

Most of what consumers know about products or services is gathered though learning. Researchers suggest that there are two main types of learning: **behavioural** (or **experiential**) **learning** and **cognitive learning**, where the former sees learning as largely unconscious and the latter as a conscious mental activity.

BEHAVIOURAL LEARNING

Three factors are important to behavioural learning: association, reinforcement and motivation. Behavioural learning suggests an individual develops a pattern of behavioural responses due to the rewards and punishments offered by his/her environment (Sheth et al. 1999). For learning to occur, therefore, it is generally accepted that what is required is a '**time–space proximity**' between the stimulus and the response. Learning (or **conditioning**) takes place through the establishment of a connection between this stimulus and response. There are two forms of conditioning:

- **classical** (or respondent) **conditioning** originally identified by Ivan Pavlov; it describes a largely unconscious process through which we acquire both information and feelings about stimuli (see Table 3.7)
- **operant** (or instrumental) **conditioning** largely based on the work of B.F. Skinner with pigeons and rats (see page 65).

CLASSICAL CONDITIONING

Ivan Pavlov was a Russian psychologist who experimented on dogs. He began by presenting food to the animals who, on sight of the food, began to salivate. He then noticed that, over time, they began to salivate before the food was presented to them. The reaction was triggered on hearing the footsteps of his assistants who brought the food to them. He began to experiment with a bell being rung as food was presented. After some time, the dogs began to salivate just on hearing the bell. The salivating response to the food itself did not have to be learned as it existed as an instinctive response. The food, therefore, was the **unconditioned stimulus**. In effect, the bell became the **conditioned stimulus** and the salivating the **conditioned response**. This can be described diagrammatically, as in Table 3.7.

The psychology of conditioned response was popular in the early twentieth century and then fell out of favour but it may be coming back into favour, once again creating interest. The basic process, according to Foxall et al. (1998: 90), is as follows:

> A stimulus either well understood or viewed favourably produces a response in the consumer: for example, feelings of pride are elicited on seeing a nation's flag or feelings of warmth and love on seeing a baby. In these examples,

---

Halo effect
Those aspects of the brand that are portrayed to the outside world through marketing communications. The effect involves image management and the building up of benefits, brand personality and associations. It is the halo characteristics that consumers use to distinguish one brand from another.

Brand extension
Using an existing brand name to develop a product/service in a different product/service category.

Cause-related marketing
An activity in which commercial organisations join with charities or other good causes to market a product, service or the image of the organisation, for mutual benefit.

Sponsorship
A commercial activity whereby one party permits another an opportunity to exploit a situation with a target audience in return for funds, services or resources.

Behavioural learning
Suggests that an individual develops a pattern of behavioural responses because of the rewards and punishments offered by his/her environment (also referred to as experiential learning).

Cognitive learning
Cognitive learning theory suggests that humans store information for different periods of time (see, later, sensory storage, short-term memory and long-term memory).

Time–space proximity
The time between a stimulus and a response.

Classical conditioning
Originally identified by Ivan Pavlov, it describes a largely unconscious process through which we acquire both information and feelings about stimuli (also referred to as **respondent conditioning**).

Operant conditioning
Where reinforcement follows a specific action – for example, do this (e.g. push a button) and you will receive a reward (e.g. food); also referred to as **instrumental conditioning**.

Unconditioned stimulus
Something that is naturally stimulating (e.g. the smell of food).

Conditioned stimulus
Something that is associated with something else that is naturally stimulating (e.g. the ringing of a bell means food is coming).

TABLE 3.7   Classical conditioning

Pavlov's research

Unconditioned stimulus	→→→→	Unconditioned response
Food	→→→→	Salivation
Conditioned stimulus	→→→→	Conditioned response
Bell	→→→→	Salivation

In marketing communications, such associations are built up over time. For example:

Unconditioned stimulus	→→→→	Unconditioned response
Advertising commercial	→→→→	Positive attitude feeling
Conditioned stimulus	→→→→	Conditioned response
Brand	→→→→	Positive attitude feeling

the flag or baby are termed the **unconditioned stimulus**, and the feelings they evoke are the **unconditioned response**. Pairing or associating some other neutral stimulus, called the **conditioned stimulus**, such as a brand name, with the unconditioned stimulus will over time cause the consumer to feel the same feeling when only the brand name is encountered.

For advertisers, the ability to associate their product/services with specific elements, such as images, emotions or perceptions that have a positive response in consumers, can have obvious benefits. An example from a 2012 campaign is shown in Figure 3.5. This suggests that a popular piece of music (Only a Woman to Me) that produces a nostalgic feeling when played, which is then associated with a brand (*John Lewis*) during a campaign, will itself attract a positive response (nostalgia) after the campaign ends.

FIGURE 3.5   CONDITIONING

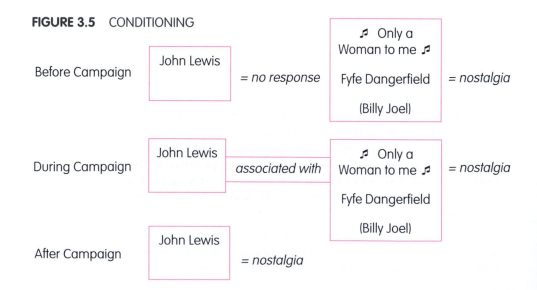

Marketers are not averse to using popular music (e.g. EDF Energy/Together in Electric Dreams, in April 2012) or film pastiches (e.g. *Thelma and Louise, Psycho, The Italian Job*) as stimulants to these feelings of happiness, nostalgia, suspense, etc. However,

- For learning to occur, it is necessary to create an association between the unconditioned and the conditioned stimuli and for this to be over a relatively short time frame, ideally occurring simultaneously or in close proximity.
- In order for conditioning to take place, there needs to be a relatively high repetition of the association. The more this happens the stronger the association will be.

Conditioned response
The outcome of a conditioned stimulus. For example, the ringing of a bell (conditioned stimulus) means food (unconditioned stimulus) is coming which may cause salivation (conditioned response).

insight: Classical conditioning

Batra, Myers and Aaker (1996) describe an experiment used to try to establish whether classical conditioning works. The research was carried out among 200 students who heard music being played while looking at an illustration of an inexpensive pen. Half the group heard familiar and popular music while the other half listened to music that was both unfamiliar and had previously been established as unpopular with this audience. Half of each of the two groups was exposed to a beige pen and the other half a blue pen. A total of 79% picked the colour associated with the popular music. When asked why, 62% said they had no reason for their particular choice.

Source: Batra et al. (1996)

OPERANT CONDITIONING

B.F. Skinner worked with rats that had learned to press levers in order to receive food and who later learnt only to press the lever when a light was switched on (**discriminative stimulus**). This aspect of reinforcement following a specific response is an essential feature of **operant** (or **instrumental**) **conditioning**. The response of the individual is likely to be affected by **positive reinforcement** (reward) or **negative reinforcement** (punishment), although the affect is likely to cease when the reinforcements are taken away.

At its simplest, operant conditioning is represented by A:B:C (Blythe 2000) where A is the antecedent (or prior) stimuli, B is the behaviour and C are the consequences or outcomes. (Note: the colons indicate that A does not automatically lead to B but is, however, likely to do so.) In commercial terms, organisational reinforcement is created by stressing the benefits and/or rewards that the customer will receive on buying this product or service.

Discriminative stimulus
A particular stimulus (e.g. a light being switched on) that suggests if you do something (e.g. push a button) you will receive a reward (e.g. food).

Positive reinforcement
A reward which reinforces the behaviour that led to the reward.

Negative reinforcement
Punishment which reinforces the avoidance of behaviour that led to the punishment.

FIGURE 3.6   Operant conditioning

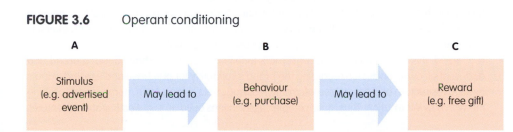

Marketers use this learning mechanism most effectively when they make the product its own intrinsic reward. However, when a product or service is a **parity brand** (i.e. with little or no intrinsically superior rewards compared with the competition), marketers offer extrinsic rewards (e.g. coupons, gifts, etc.) to attract patronage (Sheth et al. 1999).

COGNITIVE LEARNING

Cognitive learning theory suggests that humans store information for different periods of time in order to manage their memory to greatest effect and that they have three basic levels of access:

- **sensory storage**: information that is sensed for a split-second; if an impression is made this will be transferred to the short-term memory
- **short-term memory**: the maximum number of items stored (perhaps four or five) for short periods of time (perhaps 8 seconds)
- **long-term memory**: information stored for extensive periods of time, although constant reorganisation and re-categorisation take place as new information is received.

Four functions of memory increase the likelihood that information will be transferred from the short-term to the long-term memory (Foxall et al. 1998):

- **rehearsal**: by mentally repeating the information the individual increases the chance that it will be linked to other stored information (i.e. learning by rote/repetition)
- **encoding**: the process by which information is symbolically or verbally represented so that it can easily be stored and retrieved (e.g. jingles, taglines)
- **storage**: the way the memory is organised
- **retrieval**: the process where information is returned from the long-term to the short-term memory so it can be used to make evaluations and decisions.

Evidently, every consumer has differing learning capabilities so there are no hard and fast rules. A marketer can, however, assist this transfer through unique presentation, repetition, jingles, etc.

Cognitive learning is about processing information. In general, information processing is a 'generic term used to describe the series of stages or steps by which information is encountered in the external world, attended to by the consumer, interpreted, understood and stored in memory for future use' (Foxall et al. 1998: 79). The learning takes place though three main processes:

- **iconic learning:** developing an association between two or three concepts when there is an absence of stimuli. For example, advertisers of certain products that are low-value but frequently purchased will try and remind their target audience, repeatedly, of the brand name in an attempt to help consumers learn; this is again, effectively, learning by rote
- the **modelling approach** (also called **observational learning** or **vicarious learning**): this involves the consumer in the observation and imitation of others and the application of this to their own lives. An attractive model using a particular brand of aftershave (for example, 1 Million parfum by Paco Rabanne, featuring male model Matt Gordon) generates a need to pattern future behaviour. In other words, the same effect (the rapt attention of onlookers) is promised to those who do the same (i.e. purchase and use 1 Million)
- **reasoning**: this takes place where consumers take information they have about a brand and deduce their own conclusion regarding the brand's suitability for purchase and use. Individuals need to restructure and reorganise information already held in long-term memory and combine this with new information. Thus, quite complex associations build up (e.g. *Red Bull* and adventure).

With such activity going on, one might expect a degree of mental overload. Overload is, however, avoided because our mind has only the capability to process certain levels of information. To help limit and prioritise the input, consumers expose themselves to a limited number of messages (see selective attention and selective exposure).

MODELS OF ATTENTION

In terms of models describing attention, the majority fall into two broad categories: 'bottleneck' theories and capacity theories. Bottleneck theories, such as the Deutsch–Norman (Deutsch & Deutsch 1963; Norman 1968) Model of Selective Attention, describe why it is that of all the information that bombards us every day, only a small portion of it actually gets through. These theories suggest an apparent bottleneck effect or the narrowing down of the information that reaches our conscious awareness. Bottleneck theories are inherently theories of selective attention because they describe how some information is selected for processing while the rest gets discarded. Capacity theories also suggest limited processing capacity and how this attention is distributed among informational sources. Capacity models are really models that describe the division, rather than the selection, of attention. For example, the limited-capacity model of attention, developed by Kahneman (1973), explains this selectivity on the basis that:

- attention is a limited resource
- arousal levels determine capacity
- attention is determined by enduring dispositions and momentary intentions.

MOTIVATION THEORY

Motivation is what moves people to act. It is the driving force for all human behaviour or, more formally, 'the state of drive or arousal that impels behaviour toward a goal objective' (Sheth et al. 1999). Motivational research attempts to discover the underlying motives behind consumer activity. Maslow (1954) developed a model that suggested that different needs drive each of us and that when a particular level of need is satisfied, a higher, more aspiring need or want becomes dominant. Thus, at the most basic level it is our physiological needs (hunger, thirst, etc.) that require satisfying. Once these are attended to, safety needs (security, protection, etc.) dominate. Having satisfied both physiological and safety needs, social needs (love, belonging, etc.) and then esteem needs (recognition, status, etc.) come to the fore. Ultimately, the self-actualisation (or self-development) stage is reached where the drive for self-fulfilment is most obvious. The direction is not just upward. If disaster strikes (e.g. natural disaster or war) and the lower-order needs become once more apparent, then motivation will return to that level. The motivational process begins when a stimulus engenders arousal or a drive which is 'autonomic' (i.e. felt physiologically and involuntarily) when faced with danger; emotive when, for example, you feel lonely; or cognitive when, for example, you are negotiating a particular situation (Sheth et al. 1999).

Modelling approach
Where the consumer, through observation and imitation of others (for example, in an advertisement), associates something with their lifestyle; also called observational learning and vicarious learning.

Reasoning
Where consumers take the information they have about a brand and deduce their own conclusion regarding the brand's suitability for purchase and use. Individuals need to restructure and reorganise information already held in long-term memory and combine this with new information. Thus, quite complex associations build up (e.g. *Silk Cut* cigarettes and silk ribbon, *Red Bull* with flying).

Bottleneck theories
Theories that suggest an apparent bottleneck/ blockage of information that reaches our conscious awareness. Bottleneck theories are inherently theories of selective attention because they describe how some information is selected for processing while the rest gets discarded.

Capacity theories
Theories that suggest limited processing capacity and how this attention is distributed among informational sources. Capacity models are really models that describe the division, rather than the selection, of attention.

Physiological needs
Fundamental life-surviving needs, such as those that stave off hunger, thirst, etc. (Maslow's hierarchy of needs).

FIGURE 3.7   Maslow's (1954) Hierarchy of needs

Safety needs
Those needs which enhance our security, protection, etc. and that of those close to us (Maslow's hierarchy of needs).

Social needs
Those needs that are associated with love, belonging, etc. (Maslow's hierarchy of needs).

Esteem needs
Those needs which are associated with social recognition, status, etc. (Maslow's hierarchy of needs).

Self-actualisation
Described by Maslow (1943) as 'the desire for self-fulfilment, namely the tendency for him (the individual) to become actualised in what he is potentially. This tendency might be phrased as the desire to become more and more what one is, to become everything that one is capable of becoming' (Maslow's hierarchy of needs).

Autonomic motivation
Relating to the autonomic nervous system. A motivation or drive felt physiologically and involuntarily.

Emotive motivation
Strong mental or instinctive feeling (e.g. love, fear, etc.) that drives actions.

ERG theory
ERG (Existence, Relatedness and Growth) is Alderfer's (1972) theory of motivation. Unlike Maslow's hierarchy, it allows for different levels of needs to be pursued at the same time, differential personal ordering and regression.

Frustration–regression principle
Acknowledges that if higher needs remain unfulfilled, an individual may regress to lower-level motivations (ERG theory).

Later research suggested limitations in Maslow's theory. This included Clayton Alderfer's (1972) **ERG theory** which, like Maslow, describes motivational needs but they are not 'stepped' in any way. They are:

- existence: physiological and safety needs (approximating Maslow levels 1 and 2)
- relatedness: social and external esteem (approximating Maslow levels 3 and 4)
- growth: self-actualisation and internal esteem needs (approximating Maslow levels 4 and 5).

In addition to reducing the number of factors, the ERG theory differs from Maslow in three ways:

1. It allows for different levels of need to be pursued simultaneously.
2. It allows the order of needs to be different for different people.
3. It acknowledges that if higher needs remain unfulfilled, the person may regress to lower levels (known as the **frustration–regression principle**).

An alternative model of persuasion is based on **MAO factors** (Petty & Cacioppo 1986). This model suggests that it is not only motivation but the ability to process information and the opportunity to make it happen that have a role to play in successful communications. The MAO factors are:

- **M**otivation: a willingness to engage in behaviour, make decisions, pay attention and process information
- **A**bility: the resources needed to achieve a particular goal
- **O**pportunity: the extent to which the situation enables a person to obtain his/her goal.

If MAO factors are high, consumers are willing to elaborate on the information they have been given to evaluate the argument and what is on offer. If MAO factors are low, central information processing is very unlikely to occur and consumers are likely to process the communication peripherally. Decisions are made instead on the basis of certain characteristics known as **heuristic evaluation**. Heuristic evaluations range from a perception that the higher the price is, the higher the quality will be (e.g. Stella Artois' 1982–2007 UK advertising slogan 'reassuringly expensive') to the use of celebrities to reflect a brand (e.g. Usain Bolt and VISA). Examples of heuristic evaluations are shown in Table 3.8.

Marketing scholars have also identified some specific needs that are especially influential in marketing. These are (Sheth et al. 1999: 351):

- **arousal seeking:** the motive underlying **hedonic consumption** is the need to seek arousal; hedonic consumption refers to the use of products or services for sheer enjoyment rather than to solve a problem or need.

TABLE 3.8   Heuristic evaluation

Feature	Example of heuristic evaluation
Country of origin	Signifies certain characteristics (e.g. French quality, German precision)
Price	The higher the price, the higher the quality; the lower the price, the lower the quality
Celebrity	The more famous the celebrity that endorses it, the better the quality
Design	The more attractive the product, the better the quality
Status	The higher the perceived status (e.g. Cartier, Rolls Royce), the better the quality

- the **need for cognition:** a need to understand the world such that it develops a curiosity for further information
- the **need for attribution:** attributions are the inferences that people draw about events, other people and their own behaviour and include such factors as consistency, consensus and distinctiveness.

ORGANISATIONAL DECISION MAKING

The buying behaviour of organisations has traditionally been seen as entirely different from that of consumers. Whether or not this is wholly true (after all, it is still determined by human beings with complex individual needs), certain characteristics are seen to influence buying in this sector. Often, these are associated with expected practice, market structure and legal considerations which differ from consumer markets. What organisational buying is not is wholly rational. The individuals involved are equally subject to perceptions (and misconceptions), emotions, cultural influences and peer pressure as are consumers.

In B2B markets, fewer buyers account for higher percentages of the overall market, compared with the millions of individual consumers purchasing relatively small amounts. Emotion is seen as having less influence than, for example, price and utility and there is usually more complexity because of contractual arrangements, long lead times, high value or any number of other variables. One big difference is the network of relationships which develop and which are stronger and longer-lasting generally than in consumer markets.

Like consumers, organisational buyers are influenced by factors. Externally, market size and geographical spread, customer/supplier power balance and the prevailing economy are important. Within the organisation, variables include the nature of the firm's business, the buying structure and systems and purchasing policy. In most organisations, it is rare for decisions to be made by an individual. The array of contributors is often called the decision-making unit (DMU). In a DMU model (see Figure 3.8), purchases are requested by **initiators**; meanwhile,

MAO factors
Petty and Cacioppo's (1986) model suggests that it is not only motivation but the ability to process information and the opportunity to make it happen that have a role to play in successful communications. The MAO factors are Motivation (a willingness to engage in behaviour, make decisions, pay attention and process information), Ability (the resources needed to achieve a particular goal) and Opportunity (the extent to which the situation enables a person to obtain his/her goal).

Heuristic evaluation
Where evaluation is intuitive and made based on extraneous factors such as price, status, etc.

Arousal seeking
The motive underlying hedonic consumption is the need to seek arousal rather than satisfy more basic needs.

Hedonic consumption
The use of products or services for sheer enjoyment rather than to solve a problem or need.

Need for cognition
A need to understand the world such that it develops a curiosity for further information (see cognition).

FIGURE 3.8   Organisational decision-making unit (DMU)

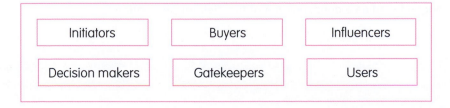

Initiators	Buyers	Influencers
Decision makers	Gatekeepers	Users

buyers have the formal responsibility to purchase under the guidance of **influencers** and the authority of **decision makers**. **Gatekeepers** manage the flow of information within the DMU and **users** will ultimately utilise the purchase. Evidently, one or more individuals can share these roles.

summary

This chapter reviewed those concepts and theories associated with consumer decision making. It reviewed the cognitive and behavioural theories associated with buying decisions and reviewed alternative suggestions. It looked at the geodemographic and lifestyle characteristics that affect consumers and the ways that these are used to build up consumer typologies (or buyer types). It illustrated the importance of attitudes, perceptions, learning and motivation and their affect on the buying process.

? review questions

1. Define the term 'front of mind'.

2. How would you differentiate between the cognitive and the behavioural paradigms?

3. What alternative models have been proposed?

4. How might brand-building behaviour reduce cognitive dissonance?

5. Identify two external factors that may influence or have an effect on purchase decisions.

6. What character traits might be associated with a person's age?

7. Explain 'VALs'.

8. In commercial terms, how is organisational reinforcement created?

9. Describe the concept of heuristic evaluation.

10. What is the 'ATR' model?

discussion questions

1. What influences an individual's buying behaviour and do you believe it is possible to categorise the factors in any way?

2. How might 'trait theory' influence the way in which you approached market segmentation?

3. What are the challenges faced as a consequence of the 'field of perception'?

case study 3.1: Save the planet marketing 'won't change consumer behaviour'

by Gemma Charles, *Marketing*, 3 May 2012

Brands rolling out catch-all 'save the planet' initiatives, such as Procter & Gamble's 'Future Friendly' drive, will fall foul of consumer complacency, according to new research.

Procter & Gamble's 'Future Friendly' campaign has been labelled dated and unfocused in a study by social enterprise Behaviour Change that looked at the current state of green consumer behaviour in the UK, covering everything from loft insulation to flying, using a nationally representative sample of 1,000-plus qualitative fieldwork.

It found that while easy behaviours such as recycling were now mainstream, sustainable living as a whole remained low on consumers' priorities.

On transport, for example, only a quarter of respondents said it was very important to be greener, while 61% of those surveyed admitted they 'can't ever imagine' changing holiday plans to avoid flying.

The report found numerous instances of over-claiming on green behaviour, suggesting that in many cases, consumers wrongly believe they are doing as much as they can.

It also found that communications and using the word 'green' increasingly elicited responses such as, 'I've had enough of green'.

The research was conducted in partnership with The Energy Saving Trust and Guardian Sustainable Business.

It concluded that while the conventional wisdom was that economic concerns had made it harder to attract consumers to the green movement, a 'more worrying green saturation' was taking place.

The research recommends companies 'take on each sustainability challenge on its own terms'.

David Hall, executive director, Behaviour Change, highlighted *Marks and Spencer*'s 'Shwopping' drive as a good example of this, as it 'is focused, super easy, highly relevant and it creates a feel-good factor without going anywhere near the word "green"'.

However, he criticised *Procter & Gamble*'s 'Future Friendly' campaign as 'dated and unfocused'.

Hall said: 'Conceived five years ago, in the days before green saturation, it is essentially a clumsy product sell, disguised as a sustainability initiative. It assumes people are more motivated by green than is really the case.'

In response to the criticism, a spokesman for *P&G* said: 'It's a shame that efforts in this direction still face such negativity, at a time when our whole industry is doing more than ever towards our responsibility to inform and shape consumer behaviour on this agenda.

'Future Friendly is an educational programme and it's all about "everyday little steps the consumers can make at home", and involves rewarding local community work that supports sustainability at the grassroots level.

(Continued)

(Continued)

'We see great numbers of communities wanting to get involved in Future Friendly. The website had more than 55,000 hits for the last campaign and in 2011, we saw a record number (more than 11,000) of votes received for the FF award entries.'

Source: Reproduced from *Marketing Magazine* with the permission of the copyright owner, Haymarket Media Group Limited

Case study questions

1. Are the critics being fair to *Procter & Gamble*?
2. What might *Procter & Gamble* expect to achieve through this type of promotion?
3. In what other ways might *P&G* become involved in cause-related marketing?

 ## further reading

Abendroth, L. and Heyman, J.E. (2013) 'Honesty is the best policy: the effects of disclosure in word-of-mouth marketing', *Journal of Marketing Communications*, 19 (4) 245–57.

Andersen, P.H. and Kumar, R. (2006) 'Emotions, trust and relationship development in business relationships: a conceptual model for buyer–seller dyads', *Industrial Marketing Management*, 35 (4): 522–35.

Bruce, M. and Daly, L. (2006) 'Buyer behaviour for fast fashion', *Journal of Fashion Marketing & Management*, 10 (3): 329–44.

Lancastre, A. and Lages, L.F. (2006) 'The relationship between buyer and a B2B e-marketplace: cooperation determinants in an electronic market context', *Industrial Marketing Management*, 35 (6): 774–89.

Lybeck, A., Holmlund-Rytkönen, M. and Sääksjärvi, M. (2006) 'Store brands vs. manufacturer brands: consumer perceptions and buying of chocolate bars in Finland', *International Review of Retail, Distribution & Consumer Research*, 16 (4): 471–92.

McFarland, R.G., Challagalla, G.N. and Shervani, T.A. (2006) 'Influence tactics for effective adaptive selling', *Journal of Marketing*, 70 (4): 103–17.

REFERENCES

Alderfer, C.P. (1972) *Existence, Relatedness and Growth: Human Needs in Organizational Settings*. New York: Free Press.

Batra, R., Myers, J.G. and Aaker, D.A. (1996) *Advertising Management*. Upper Saddle River, NJ: Prentice Hall.

Blythe, J. (2000) *Marketing Communications*. Harlow: Pearson Education.

De Pelsmacker, P., Geuens, M. and Van den Bergh, J. (2007) *Marketing Communications: A European Perspective*, 3rd edn. London: Prentice Hall.

Deutsch, J. and Deutsch, D. (1963) 'Attention: some theoretical considerations', *Psychological Review*, 70: 80–90.

Ehrenberg, A.S.C. and Goodhardt, G.J. (1979) *Essays on Understanding Buyer Behavior*. London: Thompson.

Festinger, M.J. (1957) *A Theory of Cognitive Dissonance*. Stanford, CA: Stanford University Press.

Foxall, G.R. (1993) 'Consumer behaviour as an evolutionary process', *European Journal of Marketing*, 27: 46–57.

Foxall, G.R., Goldsmith, R.E. and Brown, S. (1998) *Consumer Psychology for Marketing*, 2nd edn. London: Cengage Learning.

Kahneman, D. (1973) *Attention and Effect*. Englewood Cliffs, NJ: Prentice Hall.

Maslow, A.H. (1943) 'A theory of human motivation', *Psychological Review*, 50.pp 370-96

Maslow, A.H. (1954) *Motivation and Personality*. New York: Harper & Row.

Mittal, B. and Lassar, W.M. (1998) 'Why do customers switch? The dynamics of satisfaction versus loyalty', *The Journal of Services Marketing*, 12 (3): 177–94.

Norman, D.A. (1968) 'Toward a theory of memory and attention', *Psychological Review*, 75 (6): 522–36.

Onkvisit, S. and Shaw, J.J. (1994) *Consumer Behaviour, Strategy and Analysis*. New York: Macmillan.

Petty, R. and Cacioppo, J. (1986) *Communication and Persuasion: Central and Peripheral Routes to Attitude Change*. New York: Springer-Verlag.

Pickton, D. and Broderick, A. (2005) *Integrated Marketing Communications*, 2nd edn. Harlow: Financial Times/Prentice Hall.

Reichheld, F.F. (1993) 'Loyalty-based management', *Harvard Business Review*, 71 (2): 64–73.

Sheth, J.N., Mittal, B. and Newman, B.I. (1999) *Customer Behavior: Consumer Behavior and Beyond*. Cincinnati, OH: Thomson Learning.

USEFUL WEBSITES

Test to find your VALS type at: www.strategicbusinessinsights.com/vals/presurvey.shtml

Explore Acorn classifications at: www.caci.co.uk/integrated-marketing/data-products/acorn

Learn more about cognitive experiments at: http://psychclassics.yorku.ca/Tolman/Maps/maps.htm

For additional materials that support this chapter and your learning, please visit: **study.sagepub.com/egan**

IMAGE AND BRAND MANAGEMENT

4

LEARNING OBJECTIVES

Having completed this chapter readers would be expected to:

- recognise the importance of brands in the marketing communications process

- understand the factors and characteristics that contribute to the development of brands

- recognise the importance of branding to both the supplier and the consumer

- understand the theory behind brand naming, brand extension and multi-brand strategies and comprehend the importance of brand equity in the management of brands

- understand the importance of brand associations to the building of brand image and recognise the part played by positioning in successful brand management.

INTRODUCTION

Branding is essential to marketing communications, and the successes of individual brands owe much to effective brand communication with the public. Essentially, brands are the product of an organisational intent to distinguish themselves from their competition by augmenting their products and services with values and associations that will be recognised by and have a positive meaning for customers.

There are many definitions of branding although invariably each author selects those aspects that they see as important rather than an all-encompassing definition. Some prominent definitions of brand and branding are given in Table 4.1.

TABLE 4.1   Definitions of branding

Wells et al. (1997)	Branding: the process of creating an identity for a product using a distinctive name or symbol.
De Chernatony & McDonald (1998)	A successful brand is an identifiable product, service, person or place augmented in such a way that a buyer or user perceives relevant, unique added value which matches their needs quite closely.
Kotler (2000)	(A brand is) a name, term, sign, symbol or design or a combination of these intended to identify the goods and services of one seller or group of sellers to differentiate them from their competitors.
Pickton & Broderick (2005)	Branding is not just a case of placing a symbol or name onto products to identify the manufacturer – a brand is a set of attributes that have a meaning/an image and produce associations with the product when a person is considering that brand of product.
Dahlen et al. (2010)	What user imagery the brand has in terms of people's cognitive and affective disposition to the brand.

As can be seen from the above definitions, there is little overlap in the definitions of branding other than as an identifier. By way of clarity, the following is offered as a short but comprehensive working definition of branding:

> Branding is a collection of actual and emotional characteristics associated with a particular identified product or service that differentiates that product or service from the rest of the marketplace.

This definition recognises both the tangible and intangible nature of brands and the important part that branding plays in product and service differentiation.

BRAND CHARACTERISTICS

Although very much a simplification, it is useful to visualise a 'brand' as a **halo** around a product or service offering. Beneath the halo is the **core** (also called 'intrinsic') and **augmented** (also called 'extrinsic') aspects associated with a product or service, as represented in Figure 4.1. Core aspects of the brand include functional characteristics such as basic product/service, shape/texture, performance and physical capacity. Any changes in the core aspects will directly alter the generic product or service. Augmented aspects include packaging/presentation, price/terms, guarantees, extras (for example, built-in software) and after-sales support. Any change in the augmented characteristics does not alter the basic function or performance but may affect competitive advantage, trust and other subjective measures of the brand's value. The 'halo' is that aspect of the brand that is portrayed to the outside world through marketing communications. It involves image management and the promotion of the benefits, brand personality and brand associations. It is the halo characteristics that consumers use to distinguish one brand from another.

In communicating the brand halo characteristics, marketers choose those elements of the brand that will be most attractive to the target audience and which satisfy the current marketing communications objectives (awareness, trial, etc.).

FIGURE 4.1   Brand characteristics

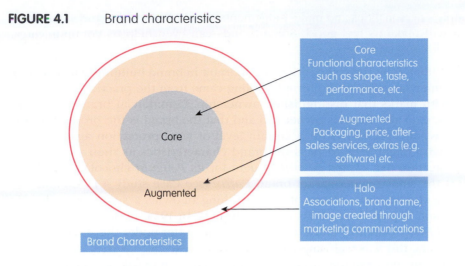

These factors may include (Biel 1997):

- brand skills/benefits – what the brand will do for you (e.g. *Anadin* relieves headaches, *Baby Bio* makes plants grow faster)
- brand personality – the perceived lifestyle associations and values (e.g. status – *Rolls Royce*, adventurous – *Red Bull*)
- brand interaction – the brand's relationship with the customer (e.g. loyalty, closeness, habit)
- brand experience – providing other brand-related experiences (e.g. *Barclays* Premiership, *Pepsi* NFL/Super Bowl, *Guinness* The Guinness Experience).

BENEFITS OF BRANDING

Customers and organisations both benefit from branding. From the customer perspective, recognition is an important feature. With experience a customer learns to recognise preferred (as well as non-preferred) brands. For the consumer, once they have experienced the brand (which may be through consumption or 'virtually' through communication) they are likely to be comfortable with that brand and this tends to lower perceived risk. If, for example, an individual is travelling for the first time in the Far East, they might chose to stay at a branded chain of hotels such as *Holiday Inn* or *Hilton*. This is not necessarily because these hotels offer better value or additional comfort but because the traveller has a good indication of what to expect from any of their hotels worldwide. This reduces the risk of any unpleasant surprises during the trip. In effect, the **brand promise** of these hotel groups is that they will deliver a level of service that consumers would recognise worldwide.

Brand names and symbols, therefore, provide information about quality, taste, performance and other attributes without the consumer having to undertake risk-reducing comparisons every time they enter the market. For the consumer, there is also a psychological reassurance or reward from association with certain brands. At one extreme are brands such as *Rolex* and *Rolls Royce* which undoubtedly give their owners pleasure as well as saying something about their owner's status in the world. Even on a lesser level, brands can be very effective communication devices. As Varey (2002: 156) notes:

We say something about ourselves by the brands we select, discard and consume. We enact rituals through selected brands. We can also read other

Brand promise
The promise(s) (e.g. to provide comfort, security, etc.) associated with a particular brand. Broken brand promises may lead to a reassessment of the brand.

people's personalities and make judgements about relationships and situations that will make us feel good. Some brands can even help us communicate something to ourselves.

Differentiation from the competition is important in brand building. The origin of the commercial usage of the term branding came from the practice of branding cattle with marks that distinguished ownership. Commercial branding (name, symbols, etc.) also denotes ownership and that the brand is the property of the brand owner. This allows for a certain level of legal protection against **brand pirates** who might seek to pass off brand characteristics as their own. It was this protection that *United Biscuits* sought for its *Penguin* chocolate snack bar against the similar supermarket brand *Puffin* (see Case study 4.1). Commercial branding also became a means of distinguishing an owner's 'superior product' in comparison to generic products or other brands. In 1924, for example, the *New Zealand Dairy Company* started to pre-package butter under the *Anchor* brand. For retailers, this was welcomed as a time-saving exercise (as they did not have to cut, weigh and wrap the product) but, importantly, it developed a relationship between the customer and the brand (Brierley 2002).

Where risk reduction is a factor in choice, successful brand owners are often able to obtain premier pricing over and above the competition from other branded and non-branded competitors. In the days when *IBM* was the world's leading computer brand, for example, there was a common saying in the computer purchasing industry that 'you would never get sacked if you bought *IBM*'. In other words, buying *IBM* was the safe option. You knew the standard to expect and that the purchase was relatively risk-free. You could buy cheaper brands, but would you take the risk of it all going wrong?

Branding also offers other benefits to the brand owner. As will be discussed later, it also offers opportunities for cross-product development (see **brand extension**) and encourages thematic consistency supporting **integrated marketing communications**, as well as strengthening corporate identity.

A summary of the perceived consumer and organisational benefits of branding are shown in Table 4.2.

TABLE 4.2   Brand benefits

Customer benefits of branding	Organisational benefits of branding
• Assists in the identification of those preferred products and services	• Helps differentiate the product or service from the competition
• Reduces level of perceived risk	• Enables premium pricing (e.g. in situations of perceived reduced risk)
• Makes it easier to assess product or service quality	• Enhances cross-product promotion and assists the development and use of integrated marketing communications
• Reduces the time taken in making product or service selection	• Provides for greater thematic consistency and uniform communications
• Can provide psychological reassurance and/or reward	• Encourages customer loyalty/retention and/or repeat-purchase behaviour
• Gives clues about the source and any associated values	• Contributes to corporate identity and provides some legal protection

BRAND IDENTITY

Brand identity is a composite of those features of a brand that make it recognisable. It essentially forms the trigger for recognition. These identity features include brand names, which can be vocalised or written, and symbols, colours, shapes, etc. that are recognised through sight, touch or smell. Key aspects in a brand identity programme (Pickton & Broderick 2005) are the:

- design element
- statements
- application.

Design elements include the **logo**, **graphic features**, **typeface**, symbols and colours that stimulate the recognition and remembrance of a brand. Examples of strong, immediately recognisable (to most), design characteristics include the *McDonald's* 'golden arches', the *Coca-Cola* traditional logo and bottle design, the *Facebook* logo, the *Starbucks* symbol and the *Nike* 'swoosh'. Many famous logos have not so much changed but evolved over the years.

Statements refer to how the brand is promoted and to copy style and **slogans** (or taglines). Slogans can become as distinctive as the brand itself. Thus, *Carlsberg* 'is probably the best lager in the world' despite Australians not giving 'XXXX for anything else' other than *Castlemaine*. *Audi* has a head start through technology (better known as Vorsprung durch Technik) while elsewhere 'it's a *Skoda* – honest'. *Stella Artois'* tagline, 'reassuringly expensive' (created by the agency Lowe Howard-Spink in 1981), helped a relatively obscure Belgian beer become the UK's best-selling brand by clever use of human psychology. It did not claim that it was any better than any rival, rather it let the customer make the connection with quality. 'Reassuringly expensive' flatters the *Stella Artois* drinker prepared to pay for this quality. In 2010, the brand has sought to reposition itself as 'a thing of beauty' and mimicking 1960s sophistication. Further examples of iconic advertising slogans are shown in Table 4.3.

Design elements (of a brand)
Include the logo, graphic features, typeface, symbols and colours that stimulate the recognition and remembrance of a brand.

Logo
An emblem or device used to distinguish an organisation or brand.

Graphic features
Those design features that are unique and which distinguish a brand (e.g. *McDonald's* 'golden arches') from its competition.

Statements
What is said about the brand and how it is promoted through copy style and slogans/taglines.

Slogans
Memorable phrases that sum up an important characteristic and/ or positioning of the brand (also referred to as a tagline).

TABLE 4.3 Selected slogans from advertising's Hall of Fame

Slogan	Advertiser	Advertising agency	Year
Impossible is nothing	*Adidas*	TBWA/180 Amsterdam	2004
Don't leave home without it.	*American Express*	Ogilvy & Mather	1975
We try harder.	*Avis Rent A Car*	Doyle Dane Bernbach	1962
Ah! Bisto.	*Bisto*		c.1919
The ultimate driving machine.	*BMW*	Ammirati & Puris	1975
The world's favourite airline.	*British Airways*	Saatchi & Saatchi	1983
It's good to talk.	*British Telecom/BT*	Abbott Mead Vickers/BBDO	1994
Are you a Cadbury's Fruit & Nut case?	*Cadbury's Fruit & Nut*	Young & Rubicam	1978
And all because the lady loves Milk Tray.	*Cadbury's Milk Tray*	Leo Burnett	1968

(Continued)

TABLE 4.3   (Continued)

Slogan	Advertiser	Advertising agency	Year
I bet he drinks Carling Black Label.	Carling Black Label	WCRS	1986
Does she or doesn't she?	Clairol	Foote Cone & Belding	1964
It's the real thing.	Coca-Cola	McCann-Erickson	1969
Simples.	Comparethemarket.com	VCCP	2009
A diamond is forever.	De Beers Consolidated	N W Ayer	1948
Go to work on an egg.	Egg Marketing Board	Mather & Crowther	1957
Put a tiger in your tank.	Esso	McCann-Erickson	1964
When it absolutely, positively has to be there overnight.	Federal Express	Ally & Gargano	1982
No FT, no comment.	Financial Times		1982
The best a man can get.	Gillette	BBDO	1989
Guinness is good for you.	Guinness	S H Benson	1929
Don't be vague. Ask for Haig.	Haig Scotch Whisky	Lord & Thomas	1934
Happiness is a cigar called Hamlet.	Hamlet	Collett Dickenson Pearce & Partners	1960
If you want to get ahead, get a hat.	Hat Council		1934
Heineken refreshes the parts other beers cannot reach.	Heineken	Collett Dickenson Pearce & Partners	1974
Beanz meanz Heinz.	Heinz Baked Beans	Young & Rubicam	1967
Snap! Crackle! Pop!	Kellogg's Rice Krispies	J Walter Thompson	1932
Finger lickin' good.	KFC	Ogilvy & Mather	1952
Have a break. Have a Kit-Kat.	Kit Kat	J Walter Thompson	1957
Because I'm worth it.	L'Oreal	McCann-Erickson, New York	1973
A Mars a day helps you work, rest and play.	Mars	D'Arcy Masius Benton & Bowles	1965
There are some things money can't buy. For everything else, there's MasterCard.	Mastercard	McCann Erickson	1997
Maybe she's born with it. Maybe it's Maybelline.	Maybelline	Lintas	1991
Just do it.	Nike	Wieden & Kennedy	1987
The future's bright. The future's Orange.	Orange	WCRS	1994
It's a bit of an animal.	Peperami	Lowe Lintas	1993

Slogan	Advertiser	Advertising agency	Year
Lipsmackin' thirstquenchin' acetastin' motivatin' goodbuzzin' cooltalkin' highwalkin' fastlivin' evergivin' coolfizzin' Pepsi.	Pepsi Cola	Dave Trott, BMP	1974
It's a lot less bovver than a hover.	Qualcast Concord	WCRS	1985
Does exactly what it says on the tin	Ronseal	HHCL	1994
No child born to die.	Save The Children	Adam & Eve	2011
Schhh…You-Know-Who.	Schweppes		1962
For mash, get Smash.	Smash	Boase Massimi Pollitt Univas	1978
Every little helps	Tesco	Lowe Howard-Spink	1993
All the news that's fit to print.	The New York Times	Adolph Ochs	1896
Hello Tosh, gotta Toshiba?	Toshiba	Gold Greenlees Trott	1984
The car in front is a Toyota.	Toyota		1996
Think Small.	Volkswagen	Doyle Dane Bernbach	1962
Hello Boys.	Wonderbra	TBWA	1995
Let your fingers do the walking.	Yellow Pages	Geers Gross	1964
The appliance of science.	Zanussi	Geers Gross	1981

Source: Basic Talk Ltd trading as AdSlogans © 2012

Application refers to **corporate advertising**, stationery, **signage**, **livery**, etc. and is not so much a separate category of design as a reminder that all organisational messages affect the image of the company/brand (see Insight), not just the planned communications associated with advertising, public relations, etc.

Application
Attention to other aspects of branding such as corporate advertising, stationery, signage, livery, etc., which maintains the organisation's positioning.

Corporate advertising
Advertising designed to promote and enhance the image of the company among its target publics.

Signage
The identity applied to buildings, vehicles, etc., denoting the organisation or its brand(s).

Livery
See Signage. Particularly relates to vehicles or uniforms.

insight: Social media brands

In a survey by *Headstrean*, it is claimed that 'social brands' have successfully become part of the 'people's media'. In this 2012 study, the brand *Innocent* topped the social media poll followed by *Starbucks* and internet provider *GiffGaff*. However, in a *Chartered Institute of Marketing* survey in the same year, senior managers were accused of not really understanding why companies would use social media at all. One in five companies polled admitted they were leaving it to under-skilled (but social media savvy) staff such as interns. Less than one in ten recognised the significant reputational risks in mishandling social media and half felt there were no risks at all. In addition, many are failing to take advantage of the data available to measure performance, still relying on unsatisfactory measures such as click-through rates. On the positive side, some good results are beginning to appear. In research carried out by *Marketing Sciences* for the *Internet Advertising Bureau*, three major brands – *Heinz*, *Kettle Chips* and *Twinings* – all saw an uplift in sentiment (by 22%, 17% and 19% respectively) following social media campaigns.

Source: Marketing, June and July 2012; **www.harpers.co.uk**

BRAND TRUSTWORTHINESS

Hand in hand with risk reduction goes trust in a brand. As trust grows, perceived risk is shown to diminish. Trust in a brand (whether it is a supplier's, distributor's or retailer's brand) is important in everyday retail situations but is particularly important when buying through direct response, mail order or over the internet. Indeed, it is doubtful whether online retailing would have reached a level, according to *Kelkoo,* where it represented (in 2011) 12% of total spend in the UK, 9% in Germany, 8.7% in Switzerland, without retail brands or producer brands being trusted. If you know the brand (even though you may not know the retailer) and you are confident enough to purchase from this unknown source (particularly if there is an internet trust mark or credit card guarantee against internet fraud), the risk may appear limited. In the reverse case, an online consumer may trust an unknown brand from a reputed (bricks and clicks[1]) retailer.

Research by Hoddleston and Cassil (1990) suggests that consumers use a brand name as a cue to assess quality and that this is used, where appropriate, to justify high prices. Ideally, both retail and supplier brands would be trusted (e.g. *Rolex* at *Goldsmiths, Sony* at *Harrods*) and you would have what is referred to as a **double-header**.

Double-header
Distinctive brands sold in distinctive retail (online or off-line) outlets.

Nationally some brands are trusted more than others. There is a strong correlation between trusted brands and those in a consumer's evoked set (see Chapter 3). As *Marketing* noted:

> Trust is a cornerstone of any successful brand. It reassures the customer that the product or service they are buying will live up to expectations. It's a basic deal: if the brand delivers, it's rewarded; if it falls short, the customer will almost certainly take their business elsewhere. (Curtis 2004)

BRAND SALIENCE

A desired outcome of brand marketing communications is to make a brand salient (i.e. important, prominent and noticeable) in its **consideration set** (Ehrenberg et al. 1997) or **evoked set** (see Chapter 3). A consideration set might be visualised as a basket of brands in a particular category from which the consumer's selection(s) are made. Consistency of quality and satisfaction over time may lead buyers to trust a brand, which in turn may raise it in the consumer's mind to a position of priority in their product choice set. In turn, this may positively influence their repeat purchase activity. Research indicates that few consumers stick loyally to one brand, however, and over time they will purchase from a number of brands in the consideration (or evoked) set. Even if a consumer is largely loyal to one particular brand, they may consider substituting this for another brand for a short or extended period when:

- the favoured brand is out of stock
- competitive factors tip the balance towards a competitive brand (e.g. a promotional price offer)
- a new offer (new or updated product) promises more than the existing offer
- the customer wants variety or acts spontaneously (i.e. impulse buying).

---

[1]   The term 'bricks and clicks' was originally used to distinguish established retailers who had gone online. Such is the ubiquitous nature of online retailing that the distinction has become less relevant.

Brand salience is more than just brand recall (i.e. the ability to recall from memory brands in a particular category) and may indeed be largely subconscious on the part of the buyer. Brand salience requires, on the part of the consumer (Varey 2002: 159):

Brand recall
The measure of brands in a particular category recalled from memory.

- awareness (of the product or service)
- interest (to a larger or lesser degree)
- assurances (as to quality, service, price, etc.)
- familiarity and acceptance
- consistency (of product or service attributes)
- habitual choosing (building up over time).

It is the responsibility of the marketer to convey these salient points to potential consumers.

DETERMINANTS OF SUCCESSFUL BRANDS

A successful brand is one that develops and sustains over time a strong, positive image in the minds of consumers. Dibb et al. (2012) suggested that there are certain determinants of brands that are regarded as successful. These are:

- They are invariably good quality – it is easier to build distinctiveness through quality than price.
- They frequently offer additional, superior services that are less easy to replicate.
- Pioneers (or first-movers) often become leading brands.
- Good brands have unique benefits that differentiate them from the competition.
- Successful brands adopt consistent and integrated marketing communications strategies.
- Good brands are not built overnight.

Shimp (2010) sees a successful brand as having several facets, represented by the mnemonic VIEW. These are:

- **V**isibility (implying exposure to the target audience)
- **I**nformative (concerning brand benefits)
- **E**motional appeal (building up the personality of the brand)
- **W**orkability (how the brand package functions).

Undoubtedly, successful brands appear to have these characteristics but will still require constant monitoring. No brand is totally safe and the fall from top-brand status may be the first step in a downward spiral unless action can be taken to halt the decline. What causes brands to become unpopular is often to do with more fickle factors such as fashion trends, although quality again seems to be an important determinant. A highly popular brand with many may be highly unpopular with some of the population. For example, both *Manchester United* and *British Airways* have appeared on both most popular and least popular brand lists[2] (in each case higher in the latter than the former). An unpopular brand can resurrect itself. Eastern European vehicle manufacturer *Skoda* was in the 1990s derided for the poor quality of its cars and the fact that they were extremely difficult to resell (even though they were relatively cheap). The purchase of the company by *Volkswagen* has led to a renaissance in design and quality. The legacy of the 1990s, however, is still there as the company in its advertising (introduced in 2000) asked consumers to believe that the car really is a *Skoda!*

---

[2]   *Marketing*, 13 May 2008.

NEW PRODUCT/SERVICE STRATEGIES

New product/service introductions pose particular communication problems. It starts with a decision as to whether or not to put an existing brand name on the item and if so what sort (see box 4.5). According to *Forbes Magazine*, 250,000 new products were introduced to the world in 2010 alone. The success rates for new product introductions, however, are not good, with some commentators putting failure at between 60% and 85%. A *Boston Consulting Group* study in the USA showed that in 19 of 22 consumer goods categories, the brand leader in 1925 was still the brand leader in 1985 (Varey 2002). However, if a new brand is introduced there are a number of brand-naming strategies designed to fulfil different brand objectives. These are shown in Table 4.4 (see also brand associations).

TABLE 4.4   Brand naming strategies

Stand-alone brands	Brands which are not directly associated with a particular manufacturer or retailer for the purpose of communication (*e.g. Persil*)
Corporate brands	Brands which rely heavily on the corporate name, whether or not a sub-brand is used (*e.g. Mercedes 320, Renault Clio*)
Own label	Carries the name of the retailer (e.g. Sainsbury's coffee) or the retailer's exclusive brand name (*e.g. Dunne's Stores – St Bernard*)
Super own label	Exclusive brands created for emphasis or thematic purposes (*e.g. Per Una at Marks & Spencer, George at ASDA*)
Generic brands	Basic own label range with limited packaging (*e.g. Tesco's value range*)
Exclusive brands	Brands that, although theoretically independent, trade on an exclusive basis with a single retailer (*e.g. Nautica at Debenhams as at March 2012*)
Component brand	Where a brand is incorporated into another product (*e.g. Intel, Nutrasweet*)
Complementary branding	Where two brands combine to strengthen an offer (*e.g. Braun and Oral B electric toothbrush*)
Co-operative branding	Joint venture schemes (*e.g. Apple with Nike to develop Sports Kit*)

New brands, if they are to be successful, require considerable investment. New brands need awareness if they are to be ultimately purchased and this can be expensive. According to *Harvard Business Review* (April 2011), consultant Jack Trout found that American families, on average, repeatedly buy the same 150 items, which constitute as much as 85% of their household needs. In this situation, it is difficult to get a new brand off the ground. At *Procter & Gamble*, less than 3% of new consumer packaged goods exceed first-year sales of $50 million – considered the benchmark of a highly successful launch. One brand that bucked this trend is *Febreze*. Launched in 1996 with considerable promotional support, by 2008 it had become *Procter & Gamble*'s 25th billion-dollar brand. By 2012 it had 67.9% of the worldwide fabric freshener market.

If the investment is considered too high to launch an entirely new brand, a company may decide to use an existing brand name in one of two ways:

- **line extension**: using an existing brand within a category for new lines within that category (e.g. *Apple* ipod > *Apple* Nano)
- **brand extension**: using an existing brand name in a different category (e.g. *Yamaha*, originally a Japanese manufacturer of motorbikes, into branded hi-fi equipment, pianos and sports equipment).

Line extension
Extending the products or services in an existing category using an existing brand name from that category.

Brand extension
Using an existing brand name to develop a product/service in a different product/service category.

Normally, brand extension is in complementary categories, for example the move by confectionery brand owners *Mars*, *Cadbury* and *Nestlé* into the ice-cream market. In some instances, the brand extension is much more dramatic. One of the best examples of this latter type of brand extension is *Virgin* whose brand name has adorned, at various times, everything from trains to transatlantic passenger planes and financial services to banking. Other examples of successful brand extensions include *Starbucks* coffee liqueur and the *Tide* stain removal pen. Among the more dubious is the *Harley-Davidson* cake-decorating kit.

In normal circumstances, brand extension requires some sort of fit with the existing brand although not necessarily in an associated category (*Virgin* is again an obvious exception to this maxim). Therefore, most consumers would question the company's strategy if a cereal company such as *Kellogg* were to enter the dog-food market, while snack bars are quite an acceptable and rational extension. In the same way, *Guinness* producing a clothing range does not raise too many eyebrows. *Bic*'s entry into the perfume market made sense to them because they perceived a gap in that market for inexpensive fragrances. They failed to realise that it was not just the scent that the consumer was buying but a lifestyle choice and not one associated with *Bic*'s brand image.

The advantages of line and brand extension to the communication process are manifold. Communication costs are lower if a consumer already holds a positive image of a brand. Retailers are more prone to using limited shelf space for an existing brand rather than an unknown one. To the consumer, the brand name contains a promise of quality that reduces the purchase risk associated with new, untried products or services. An obvious downside lays in the possibility that the brand or line extension may damage the brand's image. The problems associated with the introduction of the *Mercedes* A-series was nothing short of highly embarrassing for the company and without doubt affected the brand's formerly unblemished reputation for reliability. Some brand extensions have failed despite their association with big-name brands. These have included *Harley Davidson* perfume, *Bic* underwear and *Virgin* cola.

Multi-branding is in many ways the opposite of line and brand extensions and is where different names are used by an organisation in the same product category. An example of a producer who uses a multi-branding strategy is *Procter & Gamble* who manufactures and distributes more than 300 brands in 180 countries around the world. Many of these brands are particular to certain markets, such as *Duplex* (Latin America), *Era* (North America), *Dash* (Europe) and *Bonus* in Asia. *Axe* is familiar around Europe and North America but is called *Lynx* in the UK. In some markets, this proliferation of brand names is historical. As noted in Chapter 1, as markets became more saturated, segments were 'sliced' even thinner with brand variations created for each ever smaller segment. In other situations, suppliers introduced competition to its own brand. Known as **flanker brands** (Clow & Baack 2007), they took advantage of a supplier's market strength to compete against competitor brands for shelf space.

Given the production and communication costs involved, multi-brand owners have looked to rationalise the number of brands in their portfolios, particularly where the same product was being sold under different brand names in different markets. Thus, in the UK *Marathon* became *Snickers*, *Opal Fruits* became *Starburst* and *Jiff* became *Ciff*. In other instances, takeovers have led to brand changes, for example when *One-2-One* became *T-Mobile* and *Rowntree* became *Nestlé*. In these situations, investment in the original brand names (considerable in the case of *One-2-One* and historic in the case of *Rowntree*) is effectively lost and the brand owner must invest further resources in communicating the name change and the personality and associations allied to it. In some instances, the brand (or sub-brand) name(s) are the target of the takeover (e.g. *Nestlé*'s takeover of *Rowntree* and *Knorr*'s takeover of *Cadbury*). In *NCL*'s agreed takeover of *Virgin*

Multi-branding
Where different brand names owned by one company are used in the same product category (e.g. *Procter & Gamble* soap powders Dreft, Daz and Bold).

Flanker brands
Where a supplier takes advantage of its market strength to introduce additional brands to compete against the competition brands for shelf space.

Mobile, it was the latter's brand name that was retained as it was seen to be more in tune with the joint company's target audience. It is perhaps most difficult to change names when the 'old' and the 'new' brand personalities seem to be in conflict. This situation demands a degree of creativity if it is to be pulled off. Thus, when *Freeserve*, whose advertising was based on free-spirited, tree-hugging hippies, became *Wannadoo*, whose brand aspirations were those of a solid-citizen, mainstream brand, a creative approach was called for. In the advertising that announced the brand change, the *Freeserve* hippies were seen shaving off their beards and abandoning their 1960s lifestyle to re-join the mainstream. *Wanadoo* became *Orange* in 2006, necessitating yet another makeover.

Another reason for brand rationalisation in the fast-moving consumer goods (FMCG) category is the growing strength of grocery retailers. While in the period 1950–1970, it would be commonplace to see as many as four or five brands from one category on a retailer's shelves, today it is more commonplace to see, alongside the retailer's own brand or brands, the **brand leader**, and perhaps the second brand in the category. **Brand followers** are those who did not get to market first or who do not hold the dominant market share. It is extremely difficult for a follower to take market share from a brand leader but they are not wholly without competitive strength. The *Avis* 'we try harder' campaign is a good example of a follower establishing a competitive advantage that directly relates to the supposed weakness of the leader.

In the last decade of the twentieth century, there was a noticeable trend towards corporate branding particularly (but not exclusively) in the high technology categories where product turnover is high. This trend also reflects the high cost of launching new brands, often without a guarantee of long-term success. One estimate, for example, for the cost at that time of launching a brand in Europe or North America and supporting it in its early years would leave little change out of £1 billion /€1.25 billion (Mottram 1998). In recent years, corporate giants such as *Procter & Gamble* and *Unilever* have come out from behind their established (but in communications terms largely anonymous) brands. *Unilever*, for example, regularly includes a discreet corporate logo in its advertising. *P&G* has been much more visible, declaring itself 'the proud sponsor of mums' in its 2012 multi-brand campaign.

GLOBAL BRANDS

Many of the top brands in established markets are global brands. That is, the brands are recognisably the same (with a few local adaptations) in whatever market they are available in. They are often long established and supported by central, regional or local marketing teams. The influence and management of global brands will be discussed in more detail in Chapter 20.

BRAND LIFE CYCLE

The brand life cycle is an adaptation of the product life cycle discussed in Chapter 2. Just as product life cycles predict that a product or service has a natural (but immeasurable) life span, so brands are supposed to go through a process as indicated in Figure 4.2.

The **brand life cycle** suggests that brands have different life stages through which they pass. The introduction of a brand involves investment and starting from scratch in a market can be a slow process. It can take time for a brand to build up the level of confidence (and, therefore, reduce the level of risk) that

---

Brand leader
The leading brand in a particular product or service category.

Brand followers
Brands who did not get to market first or who do not hold the dominant market share.

FIGURE 4.2 Brand life cycle

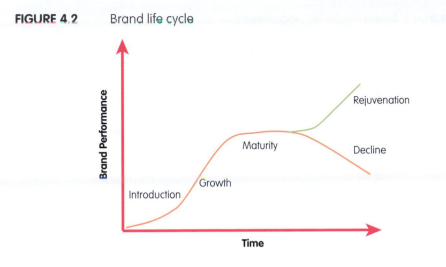

is a prerequisite to purchase. The growth stage represents a period of growing popularity and acceptance and, perhaps, greater competition. There then comes a point where growth levels off. When this occurs, brand loyalty can suffer and brand awareness decline At some point, however, a decision has to be made whether to let a brand naturally decline or to invest in its revival. To recover from a decline can take exceptional levels of creativity and effort. With brands such as *Harley-Davidson* and *Brylcreem*, investment (driven by changes in fashion) has reversed what appeared to be the terminal decline of these brands. Other old abandoned brands have also been brought back to life. In May 2011, *Procter & Gamble*'s iconic male toiletry *Old Spice* was resurrected with a new look, a new variant and a five-month marketing campaign in a bid to increase its appeal to a younger audience. According to *Vogue*,[3] former couture house *Mainbocher* and footwear brand *Herbert Levine* are set to be revived, after French entrepreneur Arnaud de Lummen acquired the trademark rights and intellectual property to both labels. In these and other cases, nostalgia is often the driver, however it may also be because it is less expensive to generate interest in a brand that has been retained in the collective memory than launch one from scratch.

Coopers and Simons (1997: 42) have taken the concept of brand equity one stage further with the brand equity lifestyle model, as shown in Figure 4.3. As with brand and product life cycles, the equity model proposes that a brand's value goes through life stages. These stages are indicated in the model and are represented as follows:

- P1: the rapidly rising brand equity of a relatively new brand. This does not apply to all new brands but for those with flair; often associated with entrepreneurial brands. Examples of P1 companies currently might be *Virgin Money, MoreThan*
- P2: mature brands. Major concerns here are brand maintenance and defence against competition. Examples might include *British Airways, Microsoft* and *Barclays*
- P3: perceived to be waning brands (e.g. *HMV, Habitat, Thorntons*) or those which seem to have disappeared completely (e.g. *Smedleys, PanAm*)
- S1: a formerly declining brand that is experiencing or has managed its own resurgence (e.g. *BHS, RAC, Brylcreem* and *Harley Davidson*)
- S2: a brand whose equity continues to fall without or despite efforts to turn it around (e.g. *Borders*).

---

[3] *Vogue*, 2 May 2012.

FIGURE 4.3   Brand equity life stage model

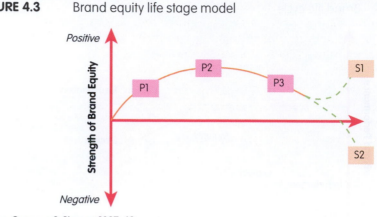

Source: Coopers & Simons 1997: 42

As noted in Chapter 2, brands, at differing points in the brand life cycle, will have differing marketing and marketing communications needs. The problem with product or brand/brand equity life cycles is that they are disconnected from time. One brand may last less than a year while there are many examples of brands over a century old that, un-rejuvenated, show little sign of decline.

BRAND EQUITY

An alternate way of expressing the strength and duration of a brand is through the concept of brand equity. Accountants have argued for years about the value of brands (i.e. the value of owning a particular brand name compared to a generic brand) with all its history, associations and personality. The equity is an important indication to the marketer of the return on investment of marketing and in particular marketing communications. It is this 'added value' that accumulates through investment over time. This 'added value' used to be termed '**good will**' and was the disparity between the firm's basic asset value and the true worth of the business (with its brands). Thus, when an organisation was sold it was valued as the sum of its assets, plus a figure for 'good will' that represented that business's appeal in the marketplace over and above a company starting in that marketplace from scratch. This 'added value' was most dramatically illustrated by *Nestlé*'s takeover of *Rowntree*. The value of the assets of the company (estimated to be £2.5 billion) paled into insignificance compared with the valuations put on brand names such as *Kit-Kat* and *After Eight*. *Nestlé* reportedly paid around six times the asset worth to secure ownership of these brands.

This good will value is now more often called **brand equity**. In economic terms, this brand equity might be regarded as the sum of future profits associated with the brand discounted over time.[4] The valuation is not fixed. A purchasing company may think that it can increase the brand equity by managing the brand in a different way. Thus, when *Ford Motor Company* acquired *Jaguar* the consensus at the time was that the purchase cost would never be recouped. *Ford*, however, believed that they could lever additional value under their ownership. The 2008 sale of *Jaguar* to *Tata* may indicate the sceptics were right.

Brand valuations are produced for various reasons including budget allocation, brand portfolio review, performance benchmarking, balance sheet calculations

Good will
The disparity in value between the firm's asset value and the estimated worth of the business.

Brand equity
The value associated with owning a particular brand compared to a generic brand of the same type in the same product or service category.

---

[4]   Other types of valuation such as cost-based valuation, market-based valuation and income-based valuation are used to value brands but the intricacies of these methodologies are beyond the remit of this text.

and other company valuations. Different methodologies will produce different valuations. Rather than using a simple discounted rate of return, *Interbrand*, the brand development agency which annually produces valuations of the world's biggest brands, uses four criteria for valuation:

1 **Financial analysis:** a review of the business earnings
2 **Market analysis:** the percentage of earnings attributed to the brand (branding index)
3 **Brand analysis:** the strength of the brand as perceived by consumers (brand strength score)
4 **Legal analysis:** how well the brand is legally protected.

A change in any of the financial, market, brand or legal factors can dramatically affect brand equity and, if a brand is owned by a quoted public company, that company's share price.

In Table 4.5 is *Interbrand*'s valuation of the world's top 20 brands for 2006 and 2012. Although many of these leading brands have maintained similar positions in the tables, there have been some winners and losers. While the estimated brand value of *Google, McDonald's* and *Apple* (up 129% over 2011) have shown substantial increases, the brand value of *Nokia, American Express* (24th in 2011), *Citi* (50th) and *Marlboro* (no longer in the top 100) have been significantly reduced.

TABLE 4.5   World's most valuable brands 2006 vs. 2012

Rank	Brand 2006	Value $ billion	Rank	Brand 2012	Value $ billion
1	Coca-Cola	67.00	1	Coca-Cola	77.84
2	Microsoft	56.93	2	Apple	76.57
3	IBM	56.20	3	IBM	75.53
4	GE	48.91	4	Google	69.73
5	Intel	32.32	5	Microsoft	57.85
6	Nokia	30.13	6	GE	43.68
7	Toyota	27.94	7	McDonald's	40.06
8	Disney	27.85	8	Intel	39.39
9	McDonald's	27.50	9	Samsung	35.89
10	Mercedes	21.80	10	Toyota	30.28
11	Citi (Citigroup)	21.46	11	Mercedes-Benz	30.10
12	Marlboro	21.35	12	BMW	29.05
13	Hewlett-Packard	20.46	13	Disney	27.44
14	American Express	19.64	14	Cisco	27.20
15	BMW	19.62	15	Hewlett-Packard	26.09
16	Gillette	19.58	16	Gillette	24.90
17	Louis Vuitton	17.61	17	Louis Vuitton	23.58
18	Cisco	17.53	18	Oracle	22.13
19	Honda	17.05	19	Nokia	21.01
20	Samsung	16.17	20	Amazon	18.63

Source: Interbrand's 100 Best Global Brands 2006 and 2012

BRAND ASSOCIATIONS

The building of brand associations is critical to developing the image and personality of a brand. As will be discussed in Chapter 8, this is normally through the development of a creative platform for the brand. The creative platform is a crucial part of campaign planning. This will be discussed in greater detail in later chapters but should be influenced by:

- the problem the campaign seeks to resolve
- the objective (e.g. building awareness or interest, creating desire, changing attitudes or moving to action)
- a full description of the product/service
- the key customer benefit
- evidence substantiating benefit
- a profile of the primary target audience
- a competitive analysis
- a conversational style and advertising appeal (soft vs. hard sell, rational vs. emotional, romance, fast action, excitement, relaxation, etc.)
- a sales strategy.

There are strategies that can be used to further develop positive brand associations:

- sponsorship
- co-branding
- geographical identifiers
- ingredient brands
- support services
- award symbols.

Sponsorship is one of the major ways that companies build brand associations. Beer companies (e.g. *Guinness, Heineken, Tetleys, Carling* and *Ansell)*, for example, frequently sponsor sporting events. They see their target customers as those audiences most closely linked with each particular sport and the sponsorship is a means of building that association in the consumer's mind. Sponsorship will be covered in more detail in Chapter 12.

Co-branding takes two distinct forms. The first involves joint marketing of products or services such that both (or more) brands benefit in terms of exposure (e.g. *Hotpoint* and *Persil, Aer Lingus* and *Hertz*). The second, more commonly known as **cause-related marketing**, involves a charitable partner (e.g. *NSPCC* with *Microsoft*). Research (e.g. Webb & Mohr 1998) suggests that, given the choice between purchasing a product or service from a company that supports a charity and one that does not, unsurprisingly most consumers would choose the one that was charity associated. It may also help those brands that wish to be associated with caring and/or community.

Geographical identifiers can help (and at times hinder) the building of positive associations with a place. *Caffries* beer exploits its Irishness, while *Walker's* shortbread, in its distinctive tartan packaging, leaves the consumer in no doubt about its Scottish origins. Welsh lamb, English beef and Jersey potatoes are also such identifiers. *Audi* and *Alpecin* (caffeine shampoo) trade on their German origins, while *Chanel* is quintessentially French. On the other hand, *McDonald's* North American heritage can make it a target for anti-globalisation demonstrations. A brand's heritage can be powerful and should be protected if it provides a distinct advantage. *British Airways* sought to distance itself from its British origins by re-designing its livery to reflect cultures from around the world. The decision was reversed when it became apparent that British passengers saw it as a form

---

Creative platform
The creative idea on which a campaign is built and which is guided by the problem the campaign seeks to resolve, the key benefit and other factors associated with the brand.

Co-branding
This appears in two forms: (1) involves joint marketing of products or services such that both brands benefit in terms of exposure; and (2) involves a commercial and charitable partner.

Geographical identifiers
Signs and symbols, associated with a particular brand, that suggest a geographical location.

of betrayal while overseas passengers saw the airline's 'Britishness' as part of the brand's personality.

Ingredient brands capitalise on the use of quality ingredients or components to enhance the value of another brand. *Intel* processors, for example, are regarded almost as a requirement in any brand of personal computer as is *Dolby* sound to any quality sound system.

Support services are frequently used to develop a distinct brand image. Indeed, in many product categories it is often the only thing that differentiates one brand from another. In the highly competitive carrier market, for example, *UPS* offers customers an internet-accessible tracking system that most of the competition cannot match, and that positions them as an efficient and trusted organisation.

Award symbols give credibility to a brand and set quality benchmarks. This may prove to be particularly important in situations where some form of guarantee is required to reduce purchase risk (e.g. internet purchases). In the highly intangible field of education, where status is an important asset, award symbols represent an important differentiator. In Europe, many business schools and other institutions offer a Masters in Business Administration (MBA) programme. Of these, only a limited number are accredited by the *Association of MBAs* (*AMBA*) who maintain standards through formal validations and inspections. This *AMBA* accreditation is seen as the quality benchmark for potential MBA students.

BRAND IMAGE POSITIONING

Positioning may be described as 'the act of designing the company's offering and image so that they occupy a meaningful and distinct competitive position in the target customers' minds' (Kotler 1967).

Positioning may be considered in various different ways:

- benefit positioning
- user positioning
- competitive positioning.

Benefit positioning takes account of the positive outcomes of using the brand. These can be functional/rational (e.g. *Headex Extra* cures headaches) or emotional (e.g. *Peugeot 407* is 'the drive of your life'). User benefits relate to the specific profile of the target audience. **User positioning** is commonly exercised through the use of demographic and psychographic variables which denote specific lifestyle characteristics (e.g. *The Working Women* clothing brand).

Competitive positioning focuses on the advantages of the brand relative to its competition. For example, *Hertz* may be 'number one' in car rentals but *Avis* 'try harder' in direct response to this claim. This type of positioning is often used to establish the profile of a new brand (e.g. *Plusnet* – good, honest broadband from Yorkshire) or to distinguish an existing brand in a highly competitive marketplace (e.g. *Tesco, ASDA and Sainsbury's* price comparison advertising).

Any attempt to reinforce or change what consumers think about a brand is normally achieved through marketing communications. Often, consumer perceptions are visualised in the form of a **multi-dimensional skills map** (or **perception map**), as illustrated in Figure 4.4. The particular example used in the illustration shows how *Lucozade*, a mature, perhaps even matronly brand, was successfully repositioned as a trendy, energy-enhancing drink. The messages associated with the brand from its introduction in 1927 until the 1980s was of a product designed to provide energy for the sick and sick children in particular. Those of a certain age in the UK will remember that *Lucozade* was a favourite gift for people

---

Ingredient brands
Where a branded ingredient or component is incorporated in another brand.

Award symbols
Symbols that represent a certain level of status that has been gained by the brand (e.g. through accreditation, awards, etc.).

Positioning
The process of creating a perception in the consumer's mind regarding the nature of the company and its products relative to the competition.

Benefit positioning
Positioning on the basis of brand benefits. These can be functional and/or emotional.

User positioning
Relates to the specific profile of the target audience and is commonly accomplished with the aid of demographic and psychographic variables which denote specific lifestyle characteristics.

Competitive positioning
Focuses on the advantages of the brand relative to its competition. This type of positioning is often used to establish the profile of a new brand or to distinguish an existing brand in a highly competitive marketplace.

Multi-dimensional skills map
A matrix used to establish a customer's view of the organisation relative to its competitors (also referred to as a perception map).

FIGURE 4.4   Multi-dimensional skills map

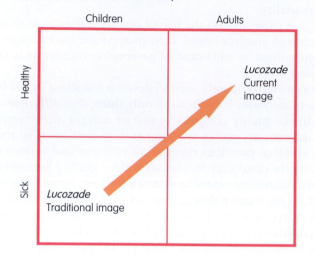

convalescing at home or in hospital. Advertising frequently showed a sick child being nursed back to health with the help of the drink and even the packaging (yellow plastic wrapping around a severely shaped bottle) exuded institutional care. In more recent years, *Lucozade* has re-positioned the product as a healthy, energy-inducing drink for sporty adults. This is backed up not only through their advertising, but with product placement at major sporting fixtures around the world. It is common to see footballers and athletes leaving the field of competition clutching a *Lucozade* container.

In addition to the matrix, other designs of multi-dimensional maps exist which can be used to compare the brand as it currently exists or where it is proposed to position (for a new brand) or reposition it (see the spider map in Figure 4.5 and the brand map in Figure 4.6). Repositioning of brands, even by a small amount, is fraught with dangers, notably whether your existing customer base will respond well or badly to it. *Abercrombie and Fitch*, who cater for the 18–25 market and use sexually explicit advertising, decided to target a younger age group with a

FIGURE 4.5   Spider map

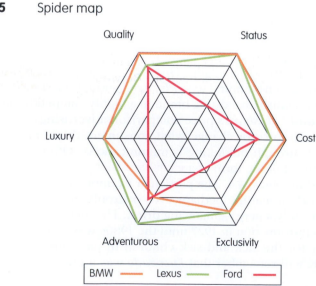

FIGURE 4.6   Brand map

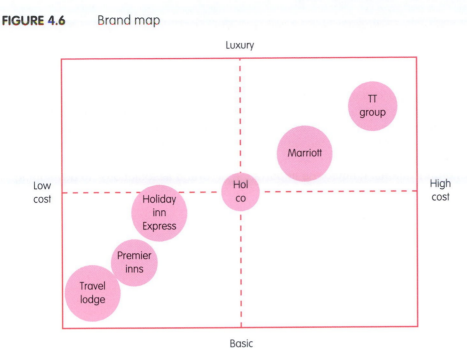

padded bra for pre-teen girls. Given the image of the company, it was heavily criticised for inappropriateness. Tropicana is another example of how playing with the image of a brand can go wrong (see box 4.7).

insight: Tropicana

In 2009, Tropicana decided to update its packaging by removing the iconic orange with a straw. According to the Tropicana press release, the re-launch promised 'a historic integrated marketing campaign designed to reinforce the brand and product attributes'. Neil Campbell, President of Tropicana, said, 'The straw and orange have been there for a long time, but people have not necessarily had a huge connection with it'. However, the company was dramatically mistaken regarding customer connection. Between 1 January and 22 February 2009, sales of products in the new packaging dropped by an estimated 20%, costing the company around $35 million. At the same time, competitors' sales grew. After two months, the company reversed the decision and re-adopted the old design. The reasons for the re-branding disaster have been long debated. Some

commentators point out that the critical blogging activity that followed the launch may have had a detrimental effect. Others suggest that shoppers simply didn't recognise their favourite brand when they searched in-store. Either way, the parent company, PepsiCo, will be more careful with any re-branding in the future.

Source: various

summary

This chapter emphasised the importance of branding to marketing communications. It reviewed the characteristics of product and service brands and the concept of the 'brand halo'. The chapter clarified that branding was not only important to the brand owner but that it reduced search time and risk for the consumer. It reviewed the determinants associated with successful brands and the differing strategies adopted to build or maintain them. The chapter reviewed the 'brand life cycle' and the relevance of 'brand equity' to modern organisations. It noted the importance of 'brand associations' to developing the image and personality of a brand and of 'brand positioning' as a way of expressing it.

review questions

1. How would you define 'branding'?

2. What are the 'augmented' aspects of a product or service?

3. What is a 'brand pirate'?

4. Suggest some potential brand extensions for well-known brands such as *Evian* or *OXO*.

5. Salience is an important aspect of brand communications. Why?

6. What factors determine the success of a brand?

7. Explain the mnemonic 'VIEW'.

discussion questions

1. The costs of both launching and supporting a new brand in Europe and North America towards the end of the twentieth century were very high. How do you think this cost will have changed since 2000 and what might be the main factors influencing this change?

2. Consider a well-known brand. Has its personality changed over the years? Why is this?

3. Using current market examples, under what circumstances would you consider developing new products using an existing brand name through either brand extension or line extension?

case study 4.1: Home is where the brand is

Almost all companies have an identifiable nationality and the same can be said of many (though not all) brands. However, the world is now much more interconnected and the relevance of the nationality of brands and their actual ownership is open to debate. What are the marketing consequences of foreign ownership of nationally associated brands?

Take, for example, four iconic British motor brands: the *Mini*, *Land Rover*, *Jaguar* and *Rolls Royce*. BMW (Germany) own *Mini* and *Rolls Royce*, while *Land Rover* and *Jaguar* belong to *Tata* (India). These are not the only motor brands with foreign ownership. *Fiat*, in addition to its Italian marks, own American brands *Chrysler, Dodge* and *Jeep*. *General Motors* has a controlling interest in *Opel* (Germany), *Vauxhall* (UK) and *Holden* (Australia). *Volkswagen's* non-German brands include *Bentley* (UK), *Bugatti* (France), *Lamborghini* (Italy), *SEAT* (Spain) and *Skoda* (Czech Republic), while *Volvo* (Sweden) is owned by Chinese automaker *Geely*. With most of these brands, manufacturing has largely (but not always exclusively) stayed in the country of origin but this may not always be the case in the future.

How British is the Mini really?

The question might be asked, does foreign ownership affect the identity of brands associated closely with their particular country of origin? *Kraft's* **£12 billion capture of** *Cadbury*, **the UK's best-known chocolate brand, reignited the debate on overseas ownership of UK brands.** This takeover in 2010 unleashed a wave of emotion by Cadbury brand loyalists similar to the furore, 22 years previously, when *Nestlé* bought *Rowntree*, the maker of Kit-Kat and other well-known names. **However, in a global economy, does it really matter that national brands end up in foreign hands?** *Cadbury's* ownership (technically) changed again when the US group went ahead with a surprise de-merger in 2012 that saw more than 100 of *Kraft's* internationally diverse snack brands, including Cadbury, Milka, Toblerone and Oreo, spun off under the newly created banner of *Mondelez International*, which, despite the foreign-sounding name, is based in Deerborn in the USA, the home of *Kraft*.

In a similar vein, does it really matter where something is made? Despite the worldwide manufacture and distribution of their products, *Coca-Cola* is very distinctly American and *Müller* (full name Unternehmensgruppe Theo Müller) undoubtedly German. Many foreign beer brands (e.g. *Carlsberg, Heineken* and *Fosters*) are actually brewed in the country of consumption rather than imported. Is the consumer being cheated? Is it not a truism that nationality is reflected not just in the location of the company's head office or actual place of manufacture but also in the culture and reputation of the business and that this is often associated with where (and when) it was established?

There are, in addition, brand names that sound as if they come from locations where they are unknown. *London Fog* may sound British but it's a decidedly US brand. *British Bulldog* is a chain of chip shops in Pakistan. *Munich Polo* and *Da Milano* are not of German or Italian origin but Indian brands of clothing and accessories respectively. Is this adoption of foreign-sounding brands the means by which consumers are misled or does it really matter?

Problems can arise when brands are too closely associated with a particular country. At the time of the Iraq war, there was an Indian government-inspired boycott of American goods, particularly ubiquitous American brands like *Coca-Cola, Pepsi* and *McDonald's*, as well as British-owned *Lever* soap. Following the publication of cartoons that offended many Muslims, Danish brands, including *Havarti* cheese and *Lego* toys, were taken off the shelves of stores in Saudi Arabia, Kuwait and other countries around the Middle East.

Case study questions

1. Does the nationality of brands matter and what messages do they send to the consumer?
2. What are the downsides of being closely associated with a particular country? Give examples.
3. Take three countries and list the features associated with them.

further reading

Caruana, A., Cohen, C. and Krenter, K.A. (2006) 'Corporate reputation and shareholders' intentions: an attitudinal perspective', *Journal of Brand Management*, 13 (6): 429–40.

Cataluña, F.R., García, A. and Phau, I. (2006) 'The influence of price and brand loyalty on store brands versus national brands', *International Review of Retail, Distribution & Consumer Research*, 16 (4): 433–52.

Chu, S. and Keh, H. (2006) 'Brand value creation: analysis of the Interbrand-Business Week brand value rankings', *Marketing Letters*, 17 (4): 323–31.

Ha, H.-Y. (2006) 'An exploratory study and consumers' perceptions of e-reverse bundling price in online retailing', *Journal of Strategic Marketing*, 14 (3): 211–28.

Herstein, R. and Gamliel, E. (2006) 'Striking a balance with private branding', *Business Strategy Review*, 17 (3): 39–43.

Rekom, J., Jacobs, G. and Verlegh, P. (2006) 'Measuring and managing the essence of a brand personality', *Marketing Letters*, 17 (3): 181–91.

Zarantonello, L. and Schmitt, B.H. (2010) 'Using the brand experience scale to profile consumers and predict consumer behaviour', *Journal of Brand Management*, 17: 532–40.

REFERENCES

Biel, A. (1997) 'Discovering brand magic: the hardness of the softer side of branding', *International Journal of Advertising*, 16: 199–210.

Brierley, S. (2002) *The Advertising Handbook*, 2nd edn. London: Routledge.

Clow, K.E. and Baack, D. (2007) *Integrated Advertising, Promotion and Marketing Communications*, 3rd edn. Upper Saddle River, NJ: Pearson/Prentice Hall.

Coopers, A. and Simons, P. (1997) *Brand Equity Lifestage: An Entrepreneurial Revolution*. London: TBWA Simons Palmer.

Curtis, J. (2004) 'Brands we trust', *Marketing*, 28 April: 28–30.

Dahlen, M., Lange, F. and Smith, T. (2010) *Marketing Communications: A Brand Narrative Approach*. Chichester: John Wiley.

De Chernatony, L. and McDonald, M. (1998) *Creating Powerful Brands in Consumer Service and Industrial Markets*. Oxford: Butterworth Heinemann/CIM Association.

Dibb, S., Simkin, L., Pride, R. and Fernell, B.R. (2012) *Marketing Concepts and Strategies*, 6th edn. London: Cengage Learning.

Ehrenberg, A., Barnard, N. and Scriven, J. (1997) 'Differentiation or salience', *Journal of Advertising Research*, 37 (6): 7–14.

Hoddleston, P. and Cassil, N.L. (1990) 'Female consumers' brand orientation: the influence of quality and demographics', *Home Economics Research Journal*, 18 (3): 255–62.

Kotler, P. (1967) *Marketing Management: Analysis, Planning, Implementation and Control*. Englewood Cliffs, NJ: Prentice Hall.

Kotler, P. (2000) *Marketing Management, Analysis, Planning, Implementation and Control*. Englewood Cliffs, NJ: Prentice Hall.

Mottram, S. (1998) 'Branding the corporation', in S. Hart and J. Murphy (eds), *'Brands': The New Wealth Creators*. London: Macmillan Press, pp. 1–12.

Pickton, D. and Broderick, A. (2005) *Integrated Marketing Communications*, 2nd edn. Harlow: Financial Times/Prentice Hall.

Shimp, T.A. (2010) *Advertising, Promotion and Supplemental Aspects of Integrated Marketing Communication*, 8th edn. Cincinnati, OH: Thomson Learning.

Varey, R.J. (2002) *Marketing Communication: Principles and Practice*. London: Routledge.

Webb, D.J. and Mohr, L.A. (1998) 'A Typology of consumer responses to cause-related marketing from skeptics to socially concerned', *Journal of Public Policy & Marketing*, 17 (2): 226–38.

Wells, W., Burnett, J. and Moriaty, S. (1997) *Advertising Principles and Practice*, 4th edn. Upper Saddle River, NJ: Prentice Hall.

USEFUL WEBSITE

For examples of the evolution of automobile brands, see: www.auch.cl/automoviles/curiosidades/evolucion-de-los-logos-de-las-marcas-automovilisticas

For additional materials that support this chapter and your learning, please visit:
study.sagepub.com/egan

MARKETING COMMUNICATIONS PLANNING

5

LEARNING OBJECTIVES

Having completed this chapter readers would be expected to:

- understand the importance of developing a marketing communications plan

- recognise the value of the situational audit

- be able to describe the relationship between objectives, strategies and tactics

- understand the concept of positioning

- be familiar with the way budgets are created and allocated

- recognise the importance of control mechanisms

- understand the various levels of customer knowledge and suggest strategies for improvement.

Marketing communications plan
A systematic plan to achieve organisational and marketing objectives relative to marketing communications.

INTRODUCTION

This chapter introduces the concept of marketing communications planning. In this chapter, the **marketing communications plan** itself is introduced and objective and strategy setting discussed. In addition, budgeting and control and evaluation measures are reviewed at an early stage in recognition of their importance in the overall plan. In subsequent chapters, marketing research and target marketing are discussed before returning to the tactical and operational aspects of the plan in the chapter on campaign planning (Chapter 8).

MARKETING COMMUNICATIONS PLAN

The purpose of a marketing communications plan is to systematically set out an organisation's communications objectives and devise strategies and tactics regarding how these might be achieved. Most marketing and marketing communications plans follow a pattern which involves elements of analysis, design, implementation and control (see Figure 5.1). Various formats exist and no particular form is proposed as necessarily greatly superior to any other. The plan presented in Figure 5.1, for example, is represented by the acronym SOSTCE (Situation, Objectives, Strategies, Tactics, Control and Evaluation) and, approximately, follows this well tried and tested format. One difference from many linear plans is that the model recognises that marketing plans are not 'one-off' but need to be continually revisited. Rather than a linear model, Figure 5.1 is seen as a continuous circle of activities.

FIGURE 5.1 Marketing communications plan

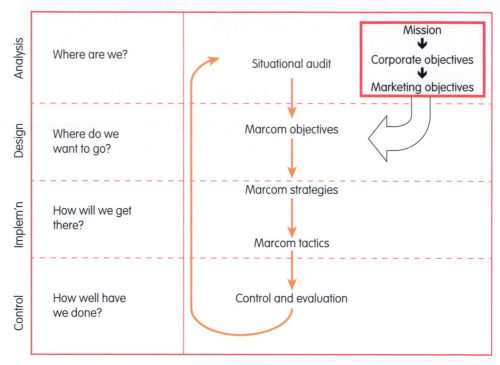

SITUATION (SITUATIONAL AUDIT)

The old adage rings true: how can you possibly decide on the direction to go in if you do not know where you are coming from? Many organisations begin (or resume) the planning process by establishing (or reiterating or adapting) their **mission** and **scope** (or **reach**). The mission and scope relate to the 'attitudes and expectations within the organisation with regard to the business that the organisation is in, how the organisation rates against competition and how it fits into its environment' (O'Malley et al. 1999: 37). These attitudes and expectations are often framed in the form of a **mission statement**. Some companies (e.g. *Pret a Manger*) are proud to proclaim their mission statement (in *Pret*'s case, 'Creates handmade, natural food, avoiding the obscure chemicals, additives and preservatives common to so much of the "prepared" and "fast" food on the market today') or a variation of it as visibly as possible.

The **situational audit**, on which decisions will be based, is a comprehensive assessment of the organisation and its competitive and macro environment. Analysts have commonly used versions (both simple and complex) of PEST(L), SWOT and competitive market models to develop such analyses.[1] Although we

Mission
The core business of an organisation and its ambitions usually set out in the company's mission statement.

Scope (or reach)
The boundaries of an organisation's operations (and perhaps aspirations).

Mission statement
A statement that asserts the core business of an organisation and its ambitions.

Situational audit
An audit of the current state of the organisation, often using SWOT and PEST(L) analysis.

---

[1]   PEST (or STEP) represents elements of the macro environment: political, economic, sociological and technological, to which legal is frequently added; SWOT relates to a company's strengths, weaknesses, opportunities and threats.

concentrate here on the marketing communications plan, this organisational analysis is likely to be reflected in the organisational and marketing objectives which should cascade down through the company. Elements of the PEST(L) model, however, may be a practical tool in a number of specific marcom situations, for example:

- political, e.g. the threat of restrictive communications legislation (see Chapter 18)
- economic, e.g. major job redundancies in a proposed campaign area
- sociological, e.g. public concern regarding advertising to children
- technological, e.g. new technologies (e.g. texting) revising media utilisation
- legal, e.g. legislation restricting the promotion of types of products or services (e.g. cigarette advertising) or rules and agreements that define it (e.g. sponsorship deals).

The identification and profiling of target markets is an important prerequisite to any plan (see Chapter 8). For 'customer acquisition' purposes, this may still require the use of socio-demographic, geodemographic and/or lifestyle (including propensity to buy) data, whether exercised through rented 'lists' or communications media audience classifications. From the customer retention and development perspective, the company's customer database is of paramount importance as it is a means of indicating customers' preferences and profitability, which can be analysed in a number of different ways. Direct and digital marketers, for example, use recency, frequency and monetary value (RFV) models that incorporate data on a customer's most recent purchases, the frequency of sales and the value of previous purchases to target potential '**cross-selling**' and '**up-selling**' (see Chapter 13) opportunities.

Cross-selling
Selling other items (sometimes from different categories) to an existing customer base.

Up-selling
Selling higher quality (and, therefore, higher priced) items to an existing customer base.

Another way to assess the organisation's current situation is to visualise it in the form of a **multi-dimensional skills map** (or **perception map**), as illustrated in Figure 5.2 (see also Chapter 4). Generally known as **positioning**, such analysis seeks to establish the brand's place in the competitive marketplace comparative to its main rivals. This positioning (or any necessary re-positioning) will be highly significant in establishing the **brand proposition** and is central in any campaign. In the simple example illustrated, 'OurCo' sees its position as a supplier of largely basic, modern furniture in an existing competitive market. It is, however, considering re-positioning itself to achieve its corporate expansion objectives. The multi-dimensional skills map suggests three 'gaps' in the market where the company might be more profitably trading. However, just because there is a gap in a particular sector does not mean that a profitable marketplace exists. The sector may not be big enough to sustain and/or the potential customers may be difficult (and therefore expensive) to reach. In this situation, the absence of competitors may be an indicator that such re-positioning may fail. On the other hand, changes in fashion and/or technological advances can rapidly change a sector's profile and re-positioning may lead to renewal of vigour and present **first-mover advantages**. Examples of this include the *HSBC*'s move into telephone-only banking through its specially created subsidiary *First Direct*, *Bank of Scotland's* entry into telephone-based insurance through *Direct Line*, and *Amazon's* passage into internet book retailing and, more recently, digital editions for its *Kindle* reader.

Brand proposition
The brand's central proposition; the focus of the brand campaign.

First-mover advantage
Advantage associated with being the first organisation in the marketplace and which may include experience, distribution channels, etc.

FIGURE 5.2   Multi-dimensional skills map

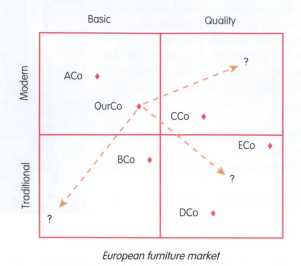

European furniture market

The organisation's 'position' in the market may be visualised based on a number of attributes and benefits (determined by the sector) including, but not restricted to:

- quality (e.g. *Stella Artois*)
- style (e.g. *Cartier*)
- status (e.g. *Rolls Royce*)
- cost (e.g. *Ryan Air*)
- originality (e.g. *Apple*).

Alternatively, organisations can be positioned by users or usage, breadth of offering, differentiation or indeed any descriptive variable relevant to the company and the marketplace.

OBJECTIVES

Objectives are what drive an organisation. They are the 'where we want to be' of any business. Objectives should be SMART (strategic, measurable, actionable, realistic and timely), communicable and aspirational. Corporate and/or business objectives play an important role in the activities of individuals, groups and organisations within the organisation because, according to Fill (2009), they:

- provide direction and an 'action focus'
- provide a means by which decisions, relating to an activity, can be made in a consistent way
- determine the time period within which the activity should be completed
- communicate the 'values' and scope of the activity
- provide a means by which the success of an activity can be evaluated.

Traditionally, marketing objectives are derived (or cascade down) from the organisational corporate/business objectives (see Figure 5.3) and the marketing objectives and these, in turn, inform the communications objectives. Top-level (corporate/business) objectives are usually financial and marketing objectives frequently (but not always) relate to sales. Certain marketing communications tools, including sales promotion, personal selling and point of sale, are of a direct action nature (i.e. they call on the customer to make an immediate response). In such cases, sales objectives may be appropriate. Other tools, such as advertising and public relations, are not directly measurable in the short term by sales and may rely on proxy measures for evaluation purposes such as **recall** (see Chapter 9). It may, however, also be the case that in certain mature markets companies have accumulated knowledge over the time of investment in marketing communications and can model the current effect of past investment and predict the future effects of current campaigns.

FIGURE 5.3   Cascading objectives

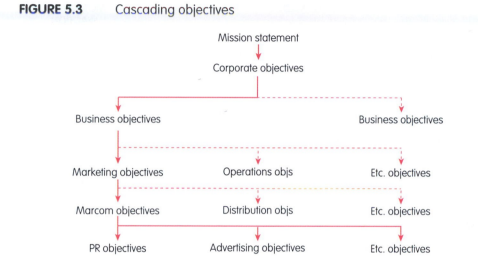

Although communications objectives cascade down through the company, two models can help sharpen the focus of marketing communications objectives, albeit they should not be regarded as having scientific validity. These are the **hierarchy of effects** and **life cycle** models.

Hierarchy of effects models were discussed extensively in Chapter 2. Among the models discussed was **DAGMAR**, introduced by Russell Colley in 1961 in a report to the American *Association of National Advertisers* entitled 'Defining Advertising Goals for Measured Advertising Results' (whose initials gave the incorporated model its name). DAGMAR was specifically designed to help with the setting of objectives and was built on the premise that consumers pass through various stages on their way to purchasing.[2] The DAGMAR model suggested that these were *awareness, comprehension, conviction and action* (other similar hierarchy models highlight similar terms), and that these were the primary goals of advertising.

In terms of DAGMAR, AIDA and other models (see Chapter 2), these objectives fell into three broad fields – knowledge-based (e.g. awareness, comprehension, etc.), feeling-based (e.g. interest, desire, liking, etc.) and action-based (e.g. sales):

- Knowledge-based communications objectives look to stimulate awareness and gain interest and may require creative attention-seeking strategies, involve demonstrations, scientific evidence and/or celebrity or technical endorsement to achieve the desired outcomes.

---

[2]   As noted in Chapter 2, the traditional hierarchy of effects models makes the assumption that consumers always go along the rational path of [learning] →[feeling] →[doing]. Although this might be considered logical, our knowledge of human beings suggests rationality is not always the observed response.

- Feeling-based objectives involve developing the 'aura' and 'personality' of the brand through growing reputation and prestige, developing associations and strengthening brand preference, and may involve seeking a change in attitudes to and opinions of the brand.
- Action-based objectives may be sales oriented but also include the building of competences in areas such as database management.

FIGURE 5.4   Hierarchy of effects models

	KNOWLEDGE		FEELING	MOTIVATION →ACTION
AIDA Strong 1925	Attention	Interest	Desire	Action
DAGMAR Colley 1961	Awareness	Comprehension	Conviction	Purchase
Lavidge and Steiner 1961	Awareness	Knowledge Liking	Preference	Conviction Purchase
Wells et al 1965	Awareness Perception	Understanding		Persuasion
	COGNITIVE		**AFFECTIVE**	**CONATIVE**

Marketing communications objectives may also be conceived in relation to a product's or service's perceived position in its **life cycle**. Notwithstanding the danger of investing too much in such models (not least because of the difficulty in establishing an organisation's position in the life cycle), they are a useful aid to developing broad marketing and communication objectives.

A newly launched product or service is looking initially for awareness and to inform potential customers that there is another alternative in an existing marketplace and/or that the newcomer offers something competitors do not (traditionally referred to as its **USP – unique selling proposition**). There are, however, very few introductions that are truly innovative and most are 'me too', copycat products and services or incremental improvements. Significantly new and unique products or services (for example, the iPhone) require considerably greater investment in marketing communications (including public relations publicity), not only to gain awareness but to provide understanding in the marketplace. When, for example, *Microsoft* launched *Windows 95*, $200 million was spent to raise awareness and develop interest in this innovative product. Such was the success of this campaign that customers queued to get into stores to buy it and it quickly gained an 85% market share. *Samsung* reportedly spent $142 million in US media for the *Galaxy* in 2011, up from $79 million in 2010 and a further $64 million just on the *Galaxy S II*, the new phone's predecessor, in 2011.

During the growth phase of the life cycle, brand building may be the major objective, particularly as and when other competitors enter into direct competition or develop new features attractive in the marketplace. **Channel development** (through distributor-targeted campaigns) may also be a priority (see 'push strategies') at this stage as the brand seeks extra sales outlets. Brand owners may seek a wide distribution or be more selective. When the iPhone was launched, *Apple* chose to give exclusivity in selected markets (e.g. *AT&T* in the USA and O_2 in the UK), while the *Samsung Galaxy* was made available through a wide range of providers.

Unique selling proposition (USP)
The proposition which sets the brand apart from any other brand.

Channel development
The development of distribution channels for the sale of products and services based on an organisation's distribution strategy.

In the maturity phase, there is little or no growth in the total market and, therefore, increased (or at least maintained) **market share** may be the principal objective. It is interesting to note that the cigarette industry, faced with a complete promotional ban, argued that, in a stagnant and/or declining cigarette market, their communications objective was not to attract new smokers to their brand but to improve market share at each other's expense. At the maturity stage, it may be beneficial to promote other uses (e.g. *Kelloggs Cornflakes* as an evening snack) or expand the scope of the brand (e.g. *Tesco* clothing, *Thomas Cook* sports travel). Brand extension and/or category extension are also potential considerations in a mature market.

In the decline stage, the level of communication expenditure supporting the brand may be minimal (e.g. concentrating on point-of-sale materials) or sufficient to keep it going as a niche or secondary brand or may herald its eventual withdrawal.

As noted previously, marketing communications objectives are frequently more troublesome to evaluate than higher level objectives as they often relate to highly subjective consumer behaviour measures (awareness, interest, desire, etc.). While targets can be set for aspects of the communications mix such as sales promotions and personal selling, the measurable effect of advertising (whether online or offline) or public relations may not be known for some time (if at all). Known as the **'lagged'** (or **'carryover') effect**, the immediate objective may to establish the brand at the **'front of mind'** of the consumer, ready for when the purchase decision will be made, rather than immediate purchase. A review of econometric studies which examined the duration of cumulative advertising effects found that, for mature, frequently purchased, low-priced products, the marketing communications effect lasted up to nine months (Belch & Belch 2011). At the other end of the price scale, motor manufacturers do not expect all potential customers to rush out to buy a new car on the basis of one campaign. Rather, they are hoping that, when the customer is ready to buy, their brand will be 'front of mind' and will be a strong contender for purchase. Where there is a 'lagged effect', **proxy measures** are used such as **'advertising recall'**; in public relations, **'media evaluation'** (see Chapters 9 and 11) is a favoured measurement. These, however, measure 'awareness' of a campaign rather than interest or commitment. An example of the use of recall

Market share
The brand's share of a market sector usually shown as a percentage of the whole sector.

Lagged effect
The time between when a consumer sees an advertisement and when they are ready to act on it (e.g. purchase.)

Proxy measures
Measures used when the marketing communications effect on sales cannot be directly measured.

Advertising recall
Unprompted awareness of recent advertising.

Media evaluation
Evaluation of a brand's media coverage over a specific time period.

FIGURE 5.5   Objectives and the product life cycle

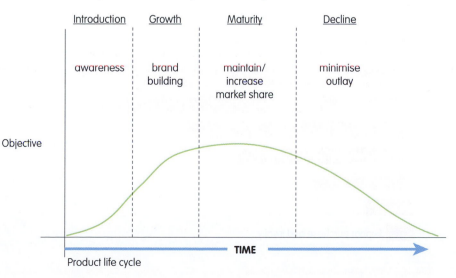

FIGURE 5.6   Adwatch analysis (*Marketing*, 4 February 2014)

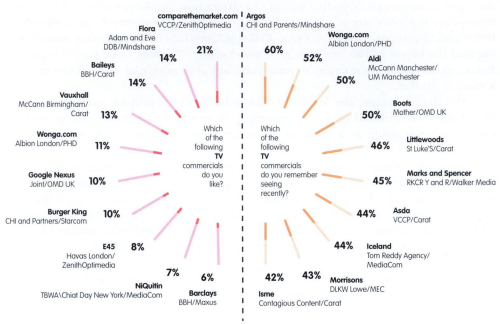

ADWATCH

comparethemarket.com VCCP/ZenithOptimedia — 21%

Argos CHI and Parents/Mindshare — 60%

Flora Adam and Eve DDB/Mindshare — 14%

Wonga.com Albion London/PHD — 52%

Baileys BBH/Carat — 14%

Aldi McCann Manchester/ UM Manchester — 50%

Vauxhall McCann Birmingham/ Carat — 13%

Boots Mother/OMD UK — 50%

Wonga.com Albion London/PHD — 11%

Littlewoods St Luke'S/Carat — 46%

Google Nexus Joint/OMD UK — 10%

Marks and Spencer RKCR Y and R/Walker Media — 45%

Burger King CHI and Partners/Starcom — 10%

Asda VCCP/Carat — 44%

E45 Havas London/ ZenithOptimedia — 8%

Iceland Tom Reddy Agency/ MediaCom — 44%

NiQuitin TBWA\Chiat Day New York/MediaCom — 7%

Morrisons DLKW Lowe/MEC — 43%

Barclays BBH/Maxus — 6%

Isme Contagious Content/Carat — 42%

Which of the following **TV** commercials do you like?

Which of the following **TV** commercials do you remember seeing recently?

measurements appears regularly in the pages of *Marketing* magazine (see Figure 5.6). This ranks the television commercials in the UK in a given week, based on an audience recall survey conducted by *NOP Research Group.* However, simply being aware of the advertisement does not necessarily imply an intention to purchase. On the other hand, unless you are aware of a product or service you are highly unlikely to buy it spontaneously! This relationship between awareness and ultimate purchase is an interesting and observable one, involving perceived stages of involvement with the brand, as illustrated in Figure 5.7.

FIGURE 5.7   Awareness to loyalty scale

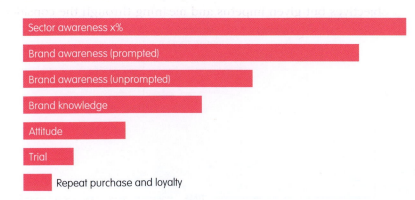

Sector awareness x%

Brand awareness (prompted)

Brand awareness (unprompted)

Brand knowledge

Attitude

Trial

Repeat purchase and loyalty

The model proposes[3] that, for a particular existing brand in a particular market-place, and when prompted by a researcher, sector awareness is highest (and may be close to or at 100%). If sector awareness is not high, it may benefit all competitors banding together to produce generic communications which may benefit the sector as a whole. Prompted brand awareness (or recognition – see Chapter 9) is measured in relation to sector awareness. Unaided brand awareness (or recall – see Chapter 9) is lower, as is relevant brand knowledge (e.g. benefits, features, positioning, etc.) about the product or service. Rather less people are perceived to have a positive attitude to the brand and fewer still might trial it. Ultimately, the brand owner is looking for loyalty, as indicated by repeat purchases and/or a high positive attitude, but this is likely to be a fraction of those measures that went before. For a new, re-launched or existing brand, therefore, there may well be multiple communication objectives for a campaign. For example:

1. Within four months, 75% of the target market is aware of the brand unprompted.
2. Within six months, 10% of the target market has trialled the product or service.
3. Within 12 months, 5% of the target market is repeat purchasing.

In a later campaign, the objectives may be set higher. There is also an expectation that increasing the numbers at one level leads to greater repeat purchases in the longer term, as illustrated in Figure 5.8. If consumers are aware of a number (or portfolio) of brands, brand attitude may be the deciding factor and the priority may be to improve this in the target market.

FIGURE 5.8 Effect of increased awareness

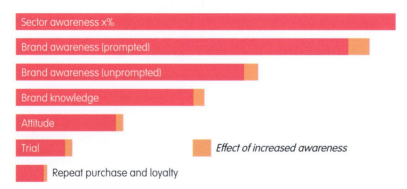

The setting of communication objectives may, therefore, be derived from the marketing objectives but given impetus and meaning through the consideration of hierarchy, life cycle and awareness models.

BUDGETING

Budgeting is introduced at this point, although the form of budget setting used by an organisation determines where in the process itself it is considered in the planning exercise. Too often, marketing communications are regarded as costs

---

[3] The model is not drawn to any form of fixed scale. It is the relative reduction between each level and not the exact scale that is useful.

Sector awareness
Consumer awareness that a sector (e.g. tablet computers) exists.

Generic communications
Communications designed to expand the sector rather than any individual brand within it.

Brand awareness
How aware a consumer is of a particular brand (also referred to as brand recognition) or a brand's promotion.

Brand knowledge
Knowledge of the benefits, features, positioning, etc. associated with the brand.
Trial
Buying a product or service for the first time.

Brand loyalty
Loyalty in behavioural terms is the repeated selection of the brand over time. Loyalty in attitudinal terms incorporates consumer preference and disposition towards the brand.

Portfolio of brands
A consumer's basket of brands from which final buying decisions are made.

Objective and task (for budgeting)
Establishing what needs to be achieved and setting the budget on the basis of achieving these objectives.

Budget modelling
Various econometric and simulation techniques which seek to model investment and subsequent performance.

Pay-back period (for budgeting)
Where budget decisions are made based on the time taken to repay the investment.

(rather than investments) and are often the first to be cut when times are hard. This is despite such investment in communications playing a major part in determining the brand's value in the future.

Budgeting 'processes' include everything from the ubiquitous 'back-of-an-envelope' calculation to major planning proposal exercises (Smith & Taylor 2004):

- **objective and task** (or **task**) approach: establishing what needs to be achieved and setting the budget on the basis of achieving the objectives set by the organisation. Effectively, it is a 'build-up' approach to budgeting that relies on setting the objectives, determining the strategies to achieve them and estimating the costs associated with these tasks
- **budget modelling**: various econometric and simulation techniques which seek to model investment and subsequent performance. This is prevalent in the direct marketing industry where testing is an important indicator to future action (see Chapter 13)
- **pay-back period**: where decisions are made based on the time taken to repay the investment
- **profit optimisation**: suggests that investment continues as long as the marginal revenue (i.e. each additional unit generated) exceeds the marginal cost (i.e. each additional unit invested to achieve that extra unit generated)
- **percentage of sales**: where the communications budget is set at a certain percentage of projected sales. This is widely used as a benchmark in many industries
- **competitive parity**: spending determined relative to the spending of major competitor(s)
- **affordable budgeting**: where costs and profit margin are deducted from turnover and the balance invested in marketing and marketing communications
- **arbitrary budgeting**: another 'build-up' approach where senior management arbitrates between different organisational priorities.

Budgeting is more than just purely financial. Organisational resources (both physical and in human terms) determine how finance can be leveraged to achieve the marketing communications objectives. Does enough 'in-house' expertise exist to manage a campaign or does the organisation need to look outside to agencies for professional support? Time restrictions too may determine whether additional resources are employed.

insight: Predicting the future – those who got it wrong

Predicting the future can be very difficult but there is no shortage of people (some of whom should know better) willing to put their reputation on the line. Below is a selection of such attributable prophesies which turned out to be somewhat inaccurate.

'This "telephone" has too many shortcomings to be seriously considered as a means of communication. The device is inherently of no value to us.' (Western Union internal memo, 1876)

'The Americans have need of the telephone, but we do not. We have plenty of messenger boys.' (Sir William Preece, chief engineer of the British Post Office, 1876)

'Radio has no future. Heavier-than-air flying machines are impossible. X-rays will prove to be a hoax.' (William Thomson, Lord Kelvin, British scientist, 1899)

'Who the hell wants to hear actors talk?' (H.M. Warner, Warner Brothers, 1927)

'There is not the slightest indication that nuclear energy will ever be obtainable. It would mean that the atom would have to be shattered at will.' (Albert Einstein, 1932)

'I think there is a world market for maybe five computers.' (Thomas Watson, chairman of IBM, 1943)

'Computers in the future may weigh no more than 1.5 tons.' (*Popular Mechanics*, 1949)

'Man will never reach the moon regardless of all future scientific advances.' (Dr Lee De Forest, inventor of the vacuum tube and father of television, 1952)

'We don't like their sound, and guitar music is on the way out.' (Decca Recording Co. rejecting the Beatles, 1962)

'There is no reason anyone would want a computer in their home.' (Ken Olson, president, chairman and founder of Digital Equipment Corp., 1977)

Source: various

CONTROL AND EVALUATION

Although **control and evaluation** appear in the latter stages of the communications plan (see Figure 5.1), the means by which the success of the plan will be monitored, controlled and measured needs to be established at an early stage. The advent of digital media has revolutionised the tracking of online campaigns (for example, through tools such as *Google* Analytics) but more traditional media often require time to pass before results can be appreciated. The budget will be a critical control and costs, particularly those associated with external agencies, should be closely monitored. Action plans should be established to determine what takes place and when and the resources (human and financial) involved. Given the long lead times in some media (e.g. television), plans should be subjected to 'what if' interrogation, for example 'What if the product launch falls behind schedule?' Measurable objectives are the basic evaluation tools. Some measures may be on the basis of pre- and post-campaign research (for example, into brand awareness) or **rolling research** (see Chapter 6) to determine the effectiveness.

Control and evaluation
The means by which a plan is monitored, controlled and measured.

Rolling research
Research that takes place on a regular basis and asks the same questions each time so that response comparisons can be made.

STRATEGIES

If the objectives are 'where we want to be', then the **strategies** are 'how we are going to get there'. Communication strategies are the way an organisation chooses to communicate with its customers and other stakeholders. Although the tactical dimension of marketing communications planning will be discussed in more detail in Chapter 7, it is worth distinguishing between strategies and tactics at this point, albeit in practice they tend to overlap. **Tactics** are the operational element of the communications plan and, by definition, short term. The choice may be between different media (including the internet) or techniques (e.g. advertising). The potential danger here is confusing the tactical with the strategic. For example, despite its influence on business in general, the internet is a tactical tool (although it may support strategic intent). The internet is part (certainly not all) of a company's communications armoury. It may promote different approaches but is, in strict terms, yet another media channel.

Marketing communications strategies may include sub-strategies based on the marcom tools (e.g. advertising strategies, public relations strategies, etc.) or be

Strategies
The ways that objectives are to be achieved. Communication strategies are the ways an organisation chooses to communicate with its customers and other stakeholders.

Tactics
The operational element of the communications plan and, by definition, short term. The choice may be between different media or various marcoms techniques.

cross-discipline (e.g. media strategy, creative strategy). These should, in the final analysis, blend into one plan.

Communications strategy setting requires knowing or establishing the:

- target audience (and the ways of communicating with them)
- positioning of the brand (or where it might be re-positioned)
- distribution channels (and/or the quality level of re-sellers)
- competition (and their communication strengths and weaknesses).

Strategies relate directly to objectives and also cascade down through the organisation (see Figure 5.9). Thus, the marketing objectives and strategy relate directly to the marketing communications objectives and strategies so that, for example, the:

marketing objective, e.g. increase sales by 5% &

determines the

marketing strategy, e.g. increase awareness of the brand &

determines the

communications objective, e.g. increase awareness by 20% &

determines the

communications strategy, e.g. develop advertising campaign and leverage through public relations campaign.

By definition, marketing communications strategies should be customer orientated and not media orientated. In other words, the focus is on reaching particular target audiences rather that media selection per se. The media tactics (see Chapter 8) should evolve based on strategic decision making.

Where objectives are derived from hierarchy of effects or life cycle models, these may suggest relevant campaign strategies, as noted in Table 5.1. So, for example, in the growth phase of the product life cycle, strategies to aid brand building may include sponsorship and/or a cause-related promotion or other brand-building tools (e.g. advertising, public relations). If, however, the objective is to develop distribution channels, then '**push strategies**' (see below) would be appropriate.

FIGURE 5.9   Cascading objectives and strategies

TABLE 5.1   Objective and Strategy Development

		Objectives	Example of possible strategies
Hierarchy of effects	Knowledge-based	awareness, comprehension	advertising campaign
	Feelings-based	interest, desire, liking	increased sponsorship
	Action-based	purchase	direct marketing campaign
LIFE CYCLE	Introduction	awareness, trial	advertising and point of sale
	Growth	brand building, distribution	sponsorship, cause-related promotion, 'push strategies'
	Maturity	market share	sales promotion
	Decline	management of costs	point of sale

PUSH/PULL STRATEGIES

Another way of differentiating between marketing communications strategies, particularly in the fast-moving consumer goods (FMCG) sector, is by whether they are push strategies or pull strategies. Push strategies are those designed to influence re-sellers or trade channel intermediaries (e.g. wholesalers, dealers, agents, retailers, etc.) to carry and promote particular brands (i.e. they are 'pushed' into the distribution system). Push strategies include:

- trade promotions (competitions, demonstrations, etc.)
- buying allowances (cash discounts, increased margins, etc.)
- advertising or sales promotion allowances (including joint advertising)
- slotting allowances (i.e. a payment in consideration of 'slotting' a new product into the merchandise mix)
- point-of-sale materials training (to encourage information flow to the consumer and promote good practice at the point of sale).

Pull strategies are those which look to influence the end-user and attract these customers (through marketing communications) 'over the heads' of retailers direct to the individual brand (whomsoever is selling it). Customer expectations are raised such that they expect promoted items to be available for them at their local store. By driving customers to purchase, they are 'pulling' merchandise through the distribution network. Pull strategies include:

- brand building (e.g. through advertising)
- consumer promotions
- consumer competitions.

For much of the twentieth century, 'pull strategies', determined by the major FMCG brands such as those owned by *Procter & Gamble* and *Unilever*, dominated primarily through pull strategies including mass media advertising but also promotions and competitions. Towards the end of that century, this dominance began to wane as the power of major FMCG retailers grew in most developed

Push strategies
Strategies designed to influence re-sellers or trade channel intermediaries (e.g. wholesalers, dealers, agents, retailers) to carry and promote particular brands (i.e. they are 'pushed' into the distribution).

Pull strategies
Strategies which look to influence the end-user and attract these customers (through marketing communications) 'over the heads' of retailers direct to the individual brand.

Re-sellers
Wholesalers, dealers, agents, retailers, etc., online or off-line, who distribute goods from producers to consumers (also referred to as trade channel intermediaries).

Trade promotions
Promotions designed to develop the brand through the trade (e.g. staff competitions, in-store demonstrations).

Buying allowances
Cash discounts, increased margins, etc., against goods purchased by the retailer.

Advertising or sales promotion allowances
Contributions made to retailers for advertising or promotions.

Joint advertising
Where the cost of advertising is shared, not necessarily equally, between retailer and supplier.

Slotting allowances
Payment made to the retailer in consideration of 'slotting' a new product into that retailer's merchandise mix.

Point of sale
In-store materials displayed at the time and place where the customer is making buying decisions.

Own brand
A retail brand that carries the retailer's name and/ or logo rather than that of any other brand.

Cooperative strategy
Retailers and suppliers working together to develop business through distribution and other efficiencies.

markets. Brand communication budgets were cut as manufacturers vied for shelf space with their competitors and retailers' '**own brands**'. In recent years, in these FMCG markets another, less combative, relationship has begun to develop between suppliers and retailers. This **cooperative strategy** involves a close relationship between retailer and supplier, such that the latter knows almost instantly when a product has been sold, at what price, from which location in the store and with what promotional support. Communication plans relating to the brand, by both supplier and retailer, can, therefore, be 'dovetailed' to provide the most effective response. The change in the balance of power in the FMCG retail market has, however, seen a considerable shift away from brand-building advertising to 'below-the-line' tools.

FIGURE 5.10   Promotional strategies

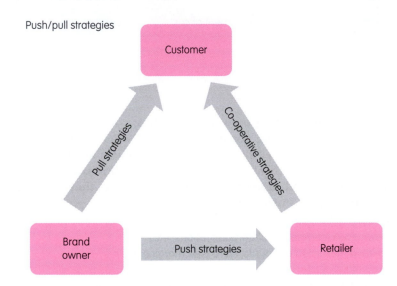

Push/pull strategies

This chapter introduced the concept of a marketing communications plan and proposed a model within which to frame it. A situation audit was proposed and the importance of target markets emphasised. Objectives and strategies were described as flowing down through the company in a cascade effect. Objectives should provide direction and focus and a means by which decisions can be made in a consistent way. They should be timely, communicate the scope of the activity and provide a means by which the activity can be evaluated. The hierarchy of effects and life cycle models were re-introduced as a guide to objective and strategy development. The importance of budget setting and the variety of different budget setting methods were discussed, as was the means by which control and evaluation are built into the communications plan. Other strategy models such as 'push' and 'pull' distinguished between campaigns designed for the distribution channel and those to be directed at the customer. The relationship between awareness and other levels of consumer knowledge was also proposed as an aid to strategy development.

summary

In subsequent chapters, **marketing research** and **target marketing** will be developed before returning to the communications plan to discuss **campaign planning**.

review questions

1. How would you describe the 'SOSTCE' circle of activities associated with a marketing communications plan?

2. What do you understand by the term 'first-mover advantage'?

3. Explain the terms 'pay-back period', 'competitive parity' and 'profit optimisation' in relation to budgeting.

4. What is the difference between strategies and tactics?

5. Define 'push' and 'pull' strategies.

6. What do you believe 'point-of-sale' materials will include?

7. What is the purpose of a marketing communications plan?

8. Objectives should be SMART. What does SMART stand for?

9. Who are the 'trade channel intermediaries'?

10. What is a 'slotting allowance'?

discussion questions

1. Marketing objectives are traditionally seen as cascading down from above. Using examples to illustrate the relationship between the various levels, how might corporate objectives evolve into communications objectives?

2. How do communications objectives relate to stages of the product life cycle?

3. Using examples, what techniques can be used for evaluating the effectiveness of advertising and how reliable do you think these might be?

case study 5.1: *Magners – 'Original vintage cider'*

The market

With beer the dominant player in the UK pub market, cider was until recently a mature market in decline. Cider was perceived to be a cheap drink attracting first-time drinkers, students and street alcoholics. It was considered mainly a man's drink or, at best, an occasional or summer drink, according to women. This negative image limited sales – which in 2005 amounted to £1.2 billion, compared with beer's £19 billion.

The world's largest cider maker is *Bulmers*, owned by Heineken International. *Bulmers*'s largest sub-brand, Strongbow, is the UK's market leader. Its largest competitor is *Magners*, owned by C&C Group. Once a small domestic Irish cider brand, *Magners* decided to challenge *Bulmers* by attacking the British market with an aggressive strategy to change the brand perception of cider.

(Continued)

(Continued)

Magners's marketing communications strategy

Magners's challenge was to change attitudes from negative to positive ones. Their aim was to create a new premium brand, 'original vintage cider', which would appeal to traditional drinkers and convert regular beer drinkers. *Magners* wished to re-position cider as a respectable, year-round alternative to beer. *Magners* targeted both males and females in the socio-economic ABC groups – a more sophisticated audience aged between 18 and 34 years.

Magners's campaign objectives were to persuade consumers that *Magners* is a credible alternative to beer and to achieve brand salience so that *Magners* would be top of people's minds for point-of-sale decisions. Using the observation that drinkers in pubs often ask for ice to be added to their *Magners* drink, 'serve over ice' became a central concept of the campaign. *Magners* bottled their cider and altered the packaging design, *Magners*-branded glasses were introduced and bar salespeople were encouraged to prepare *Magners* 'over ice'.

A TV campaign was initially tested in Scotland in 2003, followed by a regional roll-out, finally airing in London in 2005. TV was selected as the primary medium to allow the flexibility needed to use this roll-out strategy. Creative agency Young Euro RSCG chose the strapline 'Time – dedicated to you' in its 30-second advertisements.

The campaign's first commercial used various emotionally engaging elements to connect with the audience. Donovan's 1960's hit 'Sunshine Superman' played throughout. Rich colours like the green Irish countryside and ripe red apples were prominent, and the scene migrated from the *Magners* Clonmel Orchard to a warm and relaxing pub setting. A group of happy, relaxed young adults represent the target audience. They enjoy pints of *Magners* over ice: a clear 'user as endorser' strategy. *Magners* created a natural world their working target group could retire to at the end of their working day. Other ads adopted similar themes of 'time and heritage' with young adults, but adjusted the season of the natural setting to show the year-round appeal of the brand. Overall, the campaign gave the impression that *Magners* cider was a trendy yet natural, healthful drink.

Media agency MPG selected TV spots across major TV channels in diverse programmes including sport and upmarket dramas, films and documentaries to reach ABC males and females. The media mix also included premium magazine adverts, radio slots, posters in prominent locations like London Underground stations and a large outdoor billboard that showered passing traffic with apple blossom.

Magners additionally embarked on a large sports and arts sponsorship programme. They promoted stand-up comedy by sponsoring the Glasgow International Comedy Festival and Edinburgh and Brighton's Fringe Festivals. They also sponsored broadcast channel Paramount Comedy. To reach their new target group through sport, they paid for the naming rights to the *Magners* League, which featured the top rugby teams from Ireland, Wales and Scotland. They also sponsored the successful London Wasps rugby team. *Magners* partnered with the Scottish and Irish Golfing unions and the Scottish Club Golfers championship. The *Magners* website offered competitions to win tickets to sporting events. As a result of this campaign, several consumer blogs have appeared either endorsing or vilifying the product.

Results of the campaign

Cider sales increased by over 26% between 2005 and 2007, and this was largely attributed to the advertising and promotion efforts of *Magners*. The campaign rejuvenated the cider category, and *Magners* became the top-selling packaged, long, alcoholic drink sold in UK pubs and bars. The campaign also won the IPA Silver Effectiveness 2007 Award. However, for *Magners* itself this success was arguably somewhat short-lived. The competition copied the over-ice concept and *Magners* soon began to lose market share to *Bulmers*. It also struggled to persuade consumers to drink cider all year round as wet British summers depleted sales.

© Kim Roberts 2015

Case study questions

1. What was seen by the company as their biggest communications challenge and how did they go about addressing it?
2. Why was television chosen as the preferred medium?
3. What message was the television and other media advertising seeking to communicate?
4. For what reasons did *Magners* develop a sponsorship strategy?

 further reading

Anantachart, S. (2006) 'Integrated marketing communications and market planning', *Journal of Promotion Management*, 11 (1): 101–25.

Bauman, A., Smith, B.J., Maibach, E.W. and Reger-Nash, B. (2006) 'Evaluation of mass media campaigns for physical activity', *Evaluation & Program Planning*, 29 (3): 312–22.

Jenkinson, A., Sain, B. and Bishop, K. (2005) 'Optimising communications for charity brand management', *International Journal of Nonprofit & Voluntary Sector Marketing*, 10 (2): 79–92.

Keller, K.L. (2009) 'Building strong brands in a modern marketing communications environment', *Journal of Marketing Communications*, 15 (2/3): 139–155.

Piercy, N.F. (2006) 'Exploring the impact of sales upon the planning process: the strategic sales organization', *Marketing Review*, 6 (1): 3–28.

Reinold, T. and Tropp, J. (2012) 'Integrated marketing communications: how can we measure its effectiveness?', *Journal of Marketing Communications*, 18 (2): 113–32.

Schimmel, K. and Nicholls, J. (2005) 'Segmentation based on media consumption: a better way to plan integrated marketing communications media', *Journal of Applied Business Research*, 21 (2): 23–36.

Sinickas, A. (2006) 'Tailoring campaigns by audience', *Strategic Communication Management*, 10 (1): 12–13.

REFERENCES

Belch, G.E. and Belch, M.A. (2011) *Advertising and Promotion: An Integrated Marketing Communications Perspective*, 9th edn. New York: McGraw-Hill.

Colley, R.H. (1961) *Defining Advertising Goals for Measured Advertising Results*. New York: Association of National Advertisers.

Fill, C. (2009) *Marketing Communications: Interactivity, Communities and Content*, 5th edn. Harlow: Financial Times/Prentice Hall.

O'Malley, L., Patterson, M. and Evans, M. (1999) *Exploring Direct Marketing*. London: Thomson Learning.

Smith, P.R. and Taylor, J. (2004) *Marketing Communications: An Integrated Approach*, 2nd edn. London: Kogan Page.

Strong, E.K. (1925) *The Psychology of Selling*. New York: McGraw-Hill.

USEFUL WEBSITE

Marketing industry news can be found at:
www.marketingweek.co.uk and www.brandrepublic.com/magazines/marketing

For additional materials that support this chapter and your learning, please visit:
study.sagepub.com/egan

UNDERSTANDING MARKETING RESEARCH

6

LEARNING OBJECTIVES

Having completed this chapter readers would be expected to:

- understand the marketing communications research process and the factors which determine its importance

- distinguish between secondary and primary data collection, probability and non-probability sampling methods and quantitative and qualitative research techniques

- recognise the distinction between testing and research and the various testing methods in the communications industry.

INTRODUCTION

Marketing research
A collection of 'tools' of assessment, evaluation and measurement which seeks to reduce the knowledge 'distance' between the product or service provider and the consumer, primarily through the supply of pertinent information concerning that customer and the marketplace the customer operates within.

Samuel Johnson once observed that knowledge comes in two kinds. We either know about a subject ourselves or we know where we can find information about it. **Marketing research** is a means of developing the latter. It is, in basic terms, a collection of 'tools' of assessment, evaluation and measurement which seeks to reduce the knowledge 'distance' between the marketer and the consumer. Importantly, it should always be used as an aid to decision making, *not* as a decision-making method in itself. Regardless of the quality of the data collected, judgement will *always* play a part in the final analysis and will *always* determine the final decision.

Research has, since the development of modern marketing in the 1950s and 1960s, been seen as central to marketing and marketing communications. However, our traditional view of marketing research may have to alter given the enormous changes, many of them technological, that have taken place over the past few years. As Moran (2012: 414) speculates, marketing research is 'facing rapid social, technological, and economic change, (such that) the traditional marketing research industry will either adopt new tools and talent, repositioning itself in a more strategic, consultative space, or it will fall into decline'.

This chapter looks at existing research and new developments and speculates at future uses of research in the marketing communications industry.

MARKETING COMMUNICATIONS RESEARCH PROCESS

In terms of marketing communications research, the process is likely to be as illustrated by the diagram shown in Figure 6.1. As with most simplifications, however, this hides a number of variations in approach and complexity that have come to signify modern marketing research. The diagram also implies forward motion when there is as great a likelihood of iteration or abandonment at any stage in the process.

FIGURE 6.1

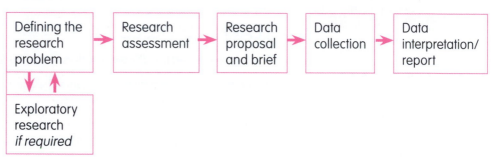

Research should not be a haphazard process. The objectives of the research should be clear and fulfil a defined need. Defining the **research problem** is a critical step as it specifies the areas of research and the types of data required to satisfy the research objectives. Whether the research is conducted using company staff or externally through a research agency, it is invariably the problem definition stage that is the most difficult as important issues might be masked by personal or organisational mindsets. In practice, much of the information required may be available in-house. Sometimes, however, and particularly where new markets and/or new media and/or new campaign techniques are considered, it may be necessary to carry out **exploratory research** to try and establish the issues and parameters of the research problem.

The importance of **research assessment** is growing within marketing communications as well as in marketing in general. This is in recognition of the costs associated with research and that these costs have to be justifiable in each particular case. The research assessment normally takes the form of a **cost–benefit analysis**: effectively the cost in monetary terms, in personnel and other resources and any other restrictions (e.g. time to market) against the expected benefits derived from the research. Not every company regards research as a viable option. It is the perceived wisdom that, as noted in a *Marketing* magazine article, 'while big companies use consumer research … smaller firms tend to go with gut instinct' (Dowdy 2004: 39). Brands launched without the benefit of research include *Amé*, the herbal drink, and *Clipper Teas*. Other companies have used less than conventional research methodologies. Market research detractors complain that it causes product launch dates to be delayed, makes managers indecisive and inspires the phrase 'analysis paralysis'. Other charges are that findings don't get translated into insight or insight into action and/or that research is often used as a comfort blanket to justify decisions that were going to be made anyway (Mitchell 2012).

Most major companies and agencies, however, will look for valid reasons for their research. Factors that determine the value of desired information include (Webb (2002: 17):

Research problem
What the research is designed to solve.

Exploratory research
Initial research designed to establish the parameters of the research problem.

Research assessment
Assessing the value and benefits of the research against the monetary costs and other limited resources (e.g. time).

Cost–benefit analysis
The ratio of cost to benefit used to establish whether a project (e.g. research, campaign) should proceed.

- the degree of 'newness' and, therefore, uncertainty in a particular environment
- the degree of complexity in the environment
- the strategic importance and cost of making the wrong decision(s)
- the degree of importance the company attaches to the decision(s) being made.

The more the uncertainty and complexity and the higher the costs associated with making the decision, the more important it is to consider in-depth research.

At the other end of the scale, too much data can confuse and hide clear meaning. This proliferation of data has become more of a problem as the cost of data storage has plummeted. In 1980, the cost of a gigabyte of storage was over $1 billion, by 2000 it was $10 and by 2009 it was calculated as less than $0.07 (www.nkomo.com). In August 2012, *Amazon* rolled out Glacier, a cloud service that charges as little as $0.01 per month per gigabyte for storage and it will not end there. Data sources continue to develop including social media and mobile phone data (including geo-location) to add to the rapidly developing 'point-of-sale' collection. According to Edwards (2012:1), many marketers see it as 'a badge of honour that data is piling up at a stunning rate while the ability to use and process this data is lagging farther and farther behind. There is a gleam in the eye of the data-miner, who believes there are more nuggets because there are more mines (and certainly more work for data miners!)'. As one research analyst notes, 'Not all data source is a good one' (Mitchell 2012:2).

In some sectors, 'time to market' has become an important factor as to how much (or indeed whether) marketing and marketing communications research is carried out at all. In highly volatile and fast-developing technological markets, research frequently takes place in the marketplace itself (to the annoyance of 'innovators' who feel they are being used as guinea pigs). Given the need for speed and message dissemination to particular consumer groups, marketing communicators frequently use '**word-of-mouth**' techniques such as **viral marketing** or **guerrilla marketing** (see Chapter 1) in such markets to communicate the benefits and obtain reaction and critical feedback.

If the need for the research is established and the estimated costs (monetary and other resources) justified, a research proposal should be drawn up. In constructing this, marketers should concentrate on the precise information needs of the organisation. This is set out in the form of a brief. This is particularly important when an external organisation is carrying out the research as not only does it aid accurate explanation, but it can also help management focus attention on the problem itself. In the course of a long and complicated research project, the brief can act as a guide and reference point.

Data collection methods can be sub-divided into two principal types: secondary data and primary data. Secondary data is data which is already available from one or more sources, while primary data is undertaken specifically for the project concerned. Secondary data may include internal company data or come from external agencies including research agencies, analysts, omnibus surveys, syndicated research or audit data,[1] trade association reports or departments of local, national and supranational government. This type of research can be very cost-effective as the costs are shared. Omnibus surveys, which involve the long-term tracking of consumer attitudes and opinions, are a good way of gathering longitudinal research data without the need to commission independent research. With a good knowledge of the market, a specialised research company, such as *Ipsos-MORI*, can bring together co-sponsors for the survey, thus saving costs for each participating organisation. In these surveys, forms, covering a wide range

Time to market
The amount of time it takes an organisation to get a product, service, idea or concept into the marketplace from its original inception.

Research proposal
A proposal detailing the resources required for a particular research project.

Brief
A presentation or report detailing the marketing problem and issues involved, directed at either an internal or external audience with a view to commissioning research.

Data collection
The collection of data that will inform a particular research project.

Secondary data
Data available from one or more existing sources.

Primary data
Data collected specifically for a particular research project.

Omnibus survey
Long-term tracking of consumer attitudes and opinions.

---

1 It should be noted that none of these terms is mutually exclusive and that there is considerable overlap in definitions.

Syndicated research or audit data
Carried out by specialist agencies who collect and analyse data on a regular (rolling research) or one-off basis. Clients normally pay a subscription for these services.

Outdoor advertising
Posters, billboards, transport and other signs that publicly display advertising in an outdoor location.

Questionnaire or survey research
Research which uses structured or semi-structured questions delivered personally, via mail, telephone, email or through online means.

In-depth interviews
A qualitative research technique that involves conducting intensive individual interviews with a small number of interviewees.

Focus groups
A research method that brings together a group of consumers to discuss a product/service or communication device (e.g. advertising), under the guidance of a trained interviewer.

Insights
The understanding, in a particular context, of a specific cause and effect.

Observation
Examining actual as opposed to predicted behaviour, such as an observation of consumers by a researcher interested in the effect on sales of an in-store promotion.

of interests including those of specific interest to the sponsoring company, are sent to a pre-selected panel of respondents. Syndicated research or audit data are carried out by specialist agencies, each collecting and analysing data on a regular (**rolling research**) or one-off basis. Clients normally pay a subscription for these services which are available for retail (e.g. AC Nielson) and specialist markets. In the UK, various organisations gather data on the effectiveness of media, for example. *The National Readership Survey* examines the readership of over 200 publications while the *Audit Bureau of Circulation (ABC)* validates circulation claims by national and local press. *Poster Audience Research (POSTAR)* uses statistical modelling to assess the effectiveness of outdoor advertising on billboards and other sites. The *Broadcasters Audience Research Board (BARB)* produces estimates of television viewing on the various available terrestrial, satellite and other digital stations, while *Radio Joint Audience Research (RAJAR)* does a similar job for audio-only transmissions. Specialist media, advertising and marketing communications research companies (e.g. Dipsticks Research) provide for more specialist data requirements.

In general, primary research data is required to answer specific marketing problems rather than for general information. Primary data may be collected in many different ways including (Webb 2002):

- **questionnaire** or **survey research**: through structured or semi'-structured personal, mail, telephone and (increasingly) email and online surveys. In this latter category, the advent of free online survey tools (for example, *Survey Monkey* and *Smart Survey*) has made such research much simpler and less expensive than in the past
- discussion: generally structured or unstructured in-depth interviews or group interviews (often called focus groups or panels). These techniques are used where direct questioning is unlikely to be informative and meaningful. Such interviews are used to generate ideas and insights or investigate feelings and attitudes
- observation: used as a means of examining actual as opposed to predicted behaviour. There may, for example, be observation of consumers by a researcher interested in the effects of an in-store promotion. EPoS (electronic point of sale) technology has, however, revolutionised in-store monitoring, particularly where the retailer shares information, in real time, with the brand supplier. There is also a growing trend towards electronic observation through set-top boxes (in the case of television audits) and the internet (through cookie technology).

While discussing data collection, it should be noted that some unscrupulous companies misrepresent themselves as researchers when their principal objectives are selling product/services or fundraising. These practices, specifically prohibited by research associations, are known as sugging (selling under the guise of research) and fugging (fundraising under the guise of research) respectively.

The selection of measurement techniques for data collection is largely but not exclusively associated with quantitative rather than qualitative research. Measurement is a means by which a property's characteristics may be quantified and should be appropriate to fulfil the research objective. The two main methods used in marketing are questionnaire analysis and attitude scales.

When analysing questionnaires, structured questions provide answers (e.g. yes, no, don't know) that can be tabulated to produce meaningful information on a wide range of marketing communications situations. *Marketing*'s Adwatch column (see Figure 5.6 in Chapter 5), for example, is based on research by *NOP Research Group* who interview around 500 adults per month. The advantage of such a methodology is that it produces precise, easily readable information. The downside is that accuracy may be lost in favour of simplicity and expediency (see Chapter 9 on advertising).

While structured, closed questions produce simplified information, unstructured questions produce 'messy' answers that may defy categorisation. This is, however, the 'rich data' that cannot be obtained through simplified questioning. In some qualitative research, **content analysis** is used to attempt to quantify the results of unstructured data. This is a technique for making inferences (or recognising patterns) from the data. Here, some counting can be done, and some researchers go on to use **factor analysis** on the data, although this does run the risk of substituting numbers for rich description (Goulding 2002).

As noted in Chapter 3, consumer attitudes are believed to be a crucial link between what consumers think and what they buy, despite the highly tenuous link between attitudes and behaviour. **Attitude scales** come in a variety of forms including (Webb 2002):

- **nominal scales**: where variables are categorised and used for classification, e.g. age, sex, place of birth
- **ordinal scales**: where objects are ranked in order
- **interval scales**: usually positive or negative values about an arbitrary zero point
- **ratio scales**: those with a predetermined zero point (e.g. the percentage of satisfied customers).

An example of an interval scale widely used in marketing and marketing communications research is the **Likert scale** (see Figure 6.2). The Likert scale was developed by Rensis Likert in 1932 and is sometimes referred to as a **summated scale** as scores for individual responses are frequently added together to produce an overall result. The advantages of the Likert scale are that it is widely used and generally understood worldwide and the responses are easily quantifiable and can be presented in a tabulated form. However, because the scale is one-dimensional and gives limited (and subjective) options, it fails to measure, in anything more than highly general terms, the true attitudes of respondents. Another example of an interval scale is the **image study**, which seeks to make image comparisons between an organisation and/or its brands and that of its competitors.

Electronic point of sale (EPoS)
Technology at the point of sale that enables transactions to be tracked on a merchandise and customer level.

Cookie
A small text file left on the user's computer that identifies their browser so that they are 'recognised' when they revisit a site.

Sugging
Selling under the guise of marketing research.

Fugging
Fundraising under the guise of marketing research.

Measurement techniques
Those techniques (largely quantitative) that are used to collect data. Examples include questionnaires and attitude scales.

FIGURE 6.2   Example of a Likert scale

	Strongly agree	Agree	Neither agree nor disagree	Disagree	Strongly disagree
XYZ is the brand I prefer most					
If XYZ was not available in my local store, I would go elsewhere					
XYZ is a quality brand					
XYZ reminds me of having fun					

Qualitative research
Looking to answer the 'why?' and the 'what?' questions, this type of research places greater emphasis on understanding consumer behaviour through insights and is often referred to as 'rich data'.

Attitude scale
A scale that measures a respondent's attitude to pre-defined statements. Examples include nominal, ordinal, interval and ratio scales.

Quantitative research
Seeking to answer the questions 'how many?' or 'who?', it is research that is looking to quantify something.

Image study
A study of the organisation's perceived image in relation to its competitors.

Sample selection
Determines the body of individuals to be targeted in a research project.

Population
In marketing research terms, population is the group (demographic, geodemographic, users, former customers, etc.) of interest to the marketer.

Target audience
A defined group of consumers (demographic, geodemographic, users, former customers, etc.) targeted by the marketer.

Probability techniques
Those techniques of selection that are independent of human judgement, producing a known and non-zero probability of any one particular case in the population of cases being included in the sample. They are representative of (but never an exact match with) the population as a whole and a determination is made of their statistical accuracy.

Sample selection determines the body of individuals involved in the research. To conduct a census of each member of a **population** would be extremely costly unless that population were small (e.g. local club membership). Population, in marketing research terms, means the group (demographic, geodemographic, users, former customers, etc.) of interest to the marketer. An alternative term, more often used in the marketing communications industry, is **target audience**. Normally, a sample group is used that reflects, as closely as possible, the population as a whole. This sample stands as a proxy for those situations or populations which share one or more characteristics with the target audience. Sampling can be described under two headings: **probability techniques** and **non-probability techniques**. Probability sampling includes those techniques that are independent of judgement, producing a known and non-zero probability of any one particular case in the population of cases being included in the sample. Non-probability techniques do not adhere to the law of probability and, therefore, the results cannot be generalised across the population. Rather, the sample is chosen at the convenience of the researcher or to fulfil the demands of some predetermined purpose. Some of the most popular of these techniques are shown in Table 6.1.

TABLE 6.1   Examples of sampling techniques

Probability techniques	Non-probability techniques
❑ Simple random sampling	❑ Convenience sampling
❑ Systematic random sampling	❑ Judgement sampling
❑ Stratified random sampling	❑ Quota sampling
❑ Cluster sampling	❑ Purposive sampling
❑ Multi-stage sampling	❑ Snowball sampling

Source: Webb (2002: 26)

QUALITATIVE VS. QUANTITATIVE RESEARCH

There are basically two approaches to research: (1) the one variously labelled as positivistic, natural science-based, hypothetico-deductive, **quantitative** or simply 'scientific'; and (2) that which is variously called interpretative, ethnographic, phenomenological or **qualitative** among other labels.[2] In simple terms, the positivist seeks to explain patterns of behaviour, while the interpretivist seeks to establish the motivations and actions that lead to these patterns of behaviour (Baker 2001). Simpler still would be to describe quantitative research as seeking to answer the questions 'how many?' or 'who?' and qualitative research as answering the 'why?' and the 'what?' type of questions. As previously noted, qualitative marketing research was in the past seen as of practical use only in the exploratory phase, before the 'real work' of quantitative measurement began. This viewpoint, although not completely eradicated, is changing. As Goulding (2002: 9) notes:

Even the realm of marketing research, once so heavily reliant on the survey instrument as the main source of data collection, is starting to place greater emphasis

2   This two-way division is not strictly accurate as it is possible to have positivist/qualitative and interpretivist/quantitative methodologies. The above, however, represents the more common approach.

on understanding consumer behaviour through qualitative insights, rather than rushing to measure and predict actions before such insights are established.

The different characteristics of qualitative and quantitative research are described in Table 6.2.

TABLE 6.2   Qualitative vs. quantitative research

Qualitative research	Quantitative research
❑ Open-ended, dynamic, flexible	❑ Statistical and numerical measurement
❑ Depth of understanding	❑ Subgroup sampling or comparisons
❑ Taps consumer creativity	❑ Survey can be repeated in the future and the results compared
❑ Database – broader and deeper	
❑ Penetrates rationalised or superficial responses	❑ Taps individual responses
❑ Richer source of ideas for marketing and creative teams	❑ Less dependent on research executives' skills or orientation

Source: Webb (2002)

The differences appear significant but then again the outcomes are designed to be different. While quantitative research techniques such as surveys emphasise theory testing and measuring, qualitative techniques are looking for meaning and understanding. Some techniques are less obviously one method or the other. There are numerous (perhaps, in theory, unlimited) research techniques on the continuum between highly quantitative and highly qualitative research, some of which are shown on the continuum in Figure 6.3.

FIGURE 6.3   Continuum of research techniques

<<<<<<< Quantitative/Positivist						Qualitative/Interpretivist >>>>>>		
research techniques					research techniques			
Surveys and other multivariate techniques	Causal modelling and structural equation modelling	Experiments	Instrumental case studies	In-depth interviews	Focus groups Consumer juries	Action research	Ethnographic studies

In the marketing communications industry, the most familiar qualitative techniques are in-depth interviews, **focus groups** and **consumer juries**. The objective of in-depth interviewing is to discover 'feelings, memories and interpretations that we cannot observe or discover in other ways' (Carson et al. 2001). They can range from an informal conversation to a highly structured interview. They might be used to seek an interviewee's perspective on a new campaign or to develop customer profiles covering a wide range of needs and preferences.

Focus groups have been used extensively in the marketing communications industry for many years. They normally consist of a small number (8–10) of target consumers led by a moderator, brought together to discuss elements of a campaign from the initial **concept stage** to post production. At the concept stage of

Non-probability techniques
Techniques which do not adhere to the law of probability and, therefore, the results cannot be generalised across the population. Rather, the sample is chosen at the convenience of the researcher or to fulfil the demands of some predetermined purpose.

Focus group
Normally consists of a small number (8–10) of target consumers brought together to discuss elements of a campaign from the initial concept stage to post production.

Consumer jury
A collection of target consumers who are asked to rank in order ideas or concepts put to them and explain their choices.

Concept stage
The period when campaign concepts, ideas, themes and content are being developed.

Storyboard
Artists' impressions of television, cinematic and online advertising campaigns prior to production.

FIGURE 6.4   Marketing communications testing

Elements to be tested	Example of research techniques
Attitudes and behaviour	Rolling or tracking studies
Perceptions, concepts, creative ideas	Focus groups
Awareness	Surveys, tracking studies
Brand building, persuasion	Focus groups
Recognition, recall	Surveys

Direct opinion measurement
Research that directly asks target consumers about aspects of a campaign such as message clarity, interest, feelings and attitudes.

Ethnography (ethnographic research)
Where researchers submerge themselves in consumer culture in order to view consumer dynamics. Photography and video diaries are used by market researchers to delve into consumers' minds.

Testing
Unlike marketing research, testing measures actual behaviour but does not answer the 'why' and 'how' questions.

an advertising campaign, for example, the target sample is presented with rough outlines or **storyboards** giving an idea of the campaign(s) under consideration. A professional moderator aims to understand the thoughts, feelings and attitudes of the group towards a product or service, media or message. Focus groups can last for one or two hours and the participants are usually paid. The downsides of such research are that it is statistically unrepresentative and that one or two contributors may dominate the discussion. They are, however, a mine of rich data and can supply insights not necessarily accessible through other forms of research.

Consumer juries also consist of a collection of target consumers who are asked to rank in order ideas or concepts put to them and to explain their choices. This type of research is also known as **direct opinion measurement** which, as it implies, asks jurors directly about aspects such as message clarity, interest, feelings and attitudes.

In addition to these common qualitative techniques, there is growing use of what some observers might consider more esoteric techniques. *Semiotic Analysis* is a company that studies signs and symbols and how they interact to create meaning. The company's research has formed the basis of many national and international television campaigns and brand repositioning for organisations such as *Unilever, P&G, Mercedes, CK, Diageo, PepsiCo, Levi Strauss, Vodafone, Pernod Ricard* and leading agencies such as Lowe, M&C Saatchi, McMannErickson, MCBD, EuroRSCG and AMV BBDO (see www.semiotic-analysis.com).

Ethnography is a current marketing research buzzword and might be described as situations where researchers submerge themselves in consumer culture in order to view consumer dynamics. Photography and video diaries are used by market researchers to delve into consumers' minds. Despite its current popularity, it is unlikely that many research agencies submerge themselves in consumer culture as deeply as might be expected by the term. According to David Iddiols, a partner at *HPI Research*: 'Nearly every agency out there claims to be doing it … but in reality, many are not getting close enough to view the consumer dynamics, which is where the value of ethnographic research resides' (cited in Barrand 2004: 48). Sanjay Nazerali, Managing Director of research agency *The Depot*, sees ethnographic techniques as a solution to 'the problem of artificial focus groups', but believes that to 'be of true value, ethnography needs to be about getting deeper, not closer' (cited in Barrand 2004: 49). The arguments against ethnographic research are less to do with its validity and more to do with the standard of its execution. The discipline's base in social anthropology gives a benchmark for future research which, currently, appears to fall well short of this standard.

TESTING

Strictly speaking, a distinction should be made between marketing research and testing (aspects of direct marketing testing will be covered in more depth in Chapter 13). Marketing research is used to reveal attitudes to a campaign, brand or some other aspect of the marketing process. Testing, by comparison, measures actual behaviour. Attitude, as discussed previously, is a poor predictor of behaviour. For example, a consumer may respond very positively to the launch of a new, top-of-the-range sports car. However, lack of funds or family circumstances may mean that this positive attitude will never result in a subsequent purchase. On the other hand, testing will tell you what an individual has done but not why a customer has made one choice over another.

Testing is also the term used for research into existing or modified factors associated with the marketing of a product or service. Marketing communicators will frequently use test markets to carry out controlled experiments before exposing the 'new feature' (product, service, campaign, distribution, etc.) to a full national or even international audience. Technology is such that national television, radio and newspapers have regional editions which may be supplemented by local media to create a test market inside which the new feature can be exposed. This geographical segmentation can also be applicable online. An Internet Protocol (IP) address is applied to every computer connected to the internet, making it relatively straightforward to establish where the owner or user resides.[3] Depending on the feature involved, another region or the rest of the market may act as the control sample against which results can be measured.

When an advertisement is developed, it may be subjected to a number of tests. In the print industries, dummy magazines may be prepared and distributed to the target audience. These magazines contain normal editorial material alongside test advertising. Current advertising is also included as a control against which the new advertising can be measured. Readers are asked questions relating to both the advertising and the editorial in an attempt to establish the impact of the planned campaign and/or the setting of the material. Online portals also offer the opportunity to compare different advertising formats and messages. For example, *Google* 'Comparison Ads' let users compare multiple offers (at various time periods) from advertisers quickly and easily.

Previews of finished advertising are common. In the case of television and/or online commercials, they are often given a test screening prior to final transmission. Following the screening, the views of the audience are sought. In certain instances, views are sought before and after the screening so that any persuasion shift (i.e. change in preferences) can be monitored. Although this adds to the perceived effectiveness of the advertising, persuasion shift is not, however, a good indicator of actual performance. For example, one of the key observations of a major evaluation of 400 individual advertising tests in the USA was that there was no clear relationship whatsoever between measures of persuasion shift and eventual sales performance (Lodish & Lubetkin 1992). Further research by Peter Field, Consultant to the *Institute of Practitioners in Advertising (IPA)*, used *IPA* Effectiveness Awards to argue that pre-tested advertising performed worse than those not tested (Mitchell 2012).

Post-testing of advertising is common with a number of techniques being used as proxy measures (i.e. not direct measures but subjective indicators) for advertising effectiveness. These include recall tests, or advertising awareness tests, which are

Test markets
Where geographically controlled testing takes place before fully exposing the 'new feature' (product, service, campaign, distribution, etc.) or new brand to a full national or even international audience.

Control sample
The sample which is unaffected by change against which altered variables can be tested.

Dummy
An uncirculated, trial edition of a magazine sent to target advertisers or target audiences.

Editorial
Although the term should strictly only be applied to copy written by a newspaper or magazine editor (or that publication's online equivalent), it is frequently used to describe all off-line and online newspaper or magazine copy.

Test screening
Screening of an advertisement to a sample audience prior to final transmission.

Persuasion shift
Changes in preferences which occur in people who have seen an advertisement or other communication.

Post-testing
Testing that takes place after a campaign and which may be compared with pre-campaign test results.

---

[3] This is not always the case. This is due to 'virtual hosting' where the domain of a company from one country or region is hosted in another usually because it is cheaper.

Awareness Index

Introduced by Millward Brown in the 1980s, the Awareness Index (AI) is a measure of brand-linked advertising recall.

designed to measure the impression that particular advertising has on the memory of the target audience using a nominal **Awareness Index** (AI), and recognition tests, which measure the level of attention paid to such advertising and its effect on the consumer (see Chapter 9). Neither test is perfect although supporters claim that 'ad awareness, or recall, is a metric that has stood the test of time and is viewed worldwide as the best means of assessing advertising effectiveness' (Miles 2004a). Its detractors point out that awareness and recall are not good indicators of ultimate purchase intentions. Robert Heath, founder of *The Value Creation Society*, cites the example of *Stella Artois* (in Miles 2004a: 57). Its initial UK press campaign, as measured by a competitor's tracking study, showed that it achieved a claimed ad awareness of just 4% in 1990, compared with 29% for the leading TV-advertised lager brand *Castlemaine XXXX*. Stella's rating for quality on the same survey was, however, 45% (compared to *Castlemaine*'s 19%). When all the other factors involved were studied, the advertising proved to have been given a star rating. This reinforced the view that *Stella Artois* had the ability to develop strong brand values without necessarily performing successfully on memory-based evaluative measures.

Access panel

Provides respondents for survey-style information and is made up of targets who have been invited by email to take part with a link to a web survey.

Proprietary panel

An online survey set up or commissioned by a client firm, usually made up of customers of that company.

ONLINE MARKET RESEARCH

With all the hype concerning the internet and electronic communications, it should be remembered that 'online' is, basically, just another medium and many of the techniques and concepts using lesser technology also apply here. There is no doubt, however, that online research has and will have an effect on marketing research in the future. **Access panels** provide samples for survey-style information and are made up of targets who have been invited by email to take part with a link to a web survey. **Proprietary panels** are set up or commissioned

FIGURE 6.5   Online panels

The pros of online research	The cons of online research
1 Clients and analysts can see results being compiled in real time	1 Online panels' demographic profile can differ from that of the general population
2 Online surveys save time and money compared with face-to-face interviews	2 If questionnaires take longer than 20 minutes to fill in, quality can suffer and they may go uncompleted
3 Consumers welcome surveys they can fill in when they want to and often need no incentive to do so	3 Poor recruitment and badly managed panels can damage data
4 A more relaxed environment leads to better quality, honest and reasoned responses	4 Technical problems, such as browser incompatibility, can mean panellists give up
5 Panellist background data allows immediate access to key target audiences unrestricted by geography	5 Programming costs are higher than for off-line questionnaires

Source: Miles (2004b: 40)

by a client firm and are usually made up of customers of that company. To encourage participation in these surveys, the researchers often use incentives such as the chance to win a substantial prize. According to Miles (2004b), there are both pros and cons involved with online research and these are shown in Figure 6.5.

THE FUTURE OF MARKETING RESEARCH

For some considerable time, researchers have been concerned about the public's increasing unwillingness to take part in marketing research (Nancarrow et al. 2004). One reason is most probably associated with the growing, some might say excessive, amount of research by mail, through newspapers or in response (usually by telephone, email and text messaging) to radio or television polling. Another reason may be the growing consumer-literate population who, in return for information, demand more and more incentives before parting with what they know is valuable information. A third cause may be the growth in the number of organisations supplying details to other organisations and the barrage of marketing material that results. Consumers are apparently becoming more selective about who should benefit from their valuable data. Undoubtedly, marketing research has changed and will change further. This might be summed up by Moran (2012: 414) who suggests that marketing research is accelerating to a position where:

> new entrants from the wider emerging marketing research insights industry (management consulting, customer relationship management [CRM], customer experience management [CEM], data mining, DIY desktop tools, predictive analytics, neuromarketing, social media analytics, prediction markets, and cocreative digital consultants) converge with and redefine the traditional marketing research space.

As with other innovations, no doubt some techniques and tools will carry on as new ones emerge (see Figure 6.6). The rise of 'do-it-yourself' tools that are easy and cheap to use may also have a significant effect on the industry. *Google* Analytics, for example, is the most used analytics tool online with an

FIGURE 6.6   Passing and future research tools

Passing tools	Timeless tools	Transitional tools	Emerging technologies
Telephone surveys	Marketing mix modelling Online surveys Focus groups	Social media Insight communities Text analytics	Mobile research Passive data (GPS, RFID) Web-use tracking
	Ethnography Econometric modelling	Virtual reality Neurobiometrics	

Source: Moran (2012: 416)

estimated 10 million users worldwide (McGee 2012). Other free or relatively inexpensive web analytics tools include *Piwik, Crazy Egg, Fire Stats, Woopra* and *AWStats*.

summary

This chapter considered the marketing research process. It noted the importance of setting research objectives and defining the research problem before constructing the research proposal. It reviewed data collection methods and sampling types and the differences between secondary and primary methods. It also discussed quantitative and qualitative techniques and the growth of more esoteric techniques such as ethnography. Testing was also defined and testing techniques were reviewed. The growth of online marketing research was also examined and the future of marketing research considered.

? review questions

1. Describe the marketing research process.

2. In deciding on what data to seek, what factors might determine the value of the information to be gathered when making an assessment of worth?

3. Why would you draw up a research proposal?

4. Explain 'sugging' and 'fugging'.

5. What is the difference between a nominal scale and an ordinal scale?

6. How would you classify 'judgement sampling'?

7. Explain the difference between qualitative and quantitative research approaches.

8. What do you understand by the term 'consumer jury'?

9. Why would you undertake a test before fully rolling out a market research exercise?

10. What are the pros and cons of online research?

discussion questions

1. If you were only able to gather research via the internet, what are the challenges this might pose both in terms of data gathering and the value of the data gathered?

2. What is the difference between exploratory research and conclusive research and how might your approach to these differ, if at all?

3. What difference do you think technological innovations will make to marketing research?

Case study 6.1: The launch of the *Amazon* Kindle Fire

Since its founding in the USA in 1994, Amazon. com has grown into the world's largest online retailer, a dominant player in just about all consumer goods markets. In September 2012, the company's UK subsidiary announced the launch of the Kindle Fire tablet range, a successor to the company's successful Kindle e-reader. Having been released in the USA the year before, the Kindle Fire was a major product launch for *Amazon* that targeted a market that research revealed to be lucrative and growing: tablets.

Market research revealed that, though young, the tablet market was already becoming competitive

just two years after *Apple* had launched the ground-breaking iPad. The Kindle Fire would be going up against products like the *Google* Nexus 7 and *Kobo* Arc, as well as the iPad and new iPad mini. Studies in 2012 projected iPad sales alone to increase by 56% that year to reach 127m units. IHS iSuppli, a market research firm, reported that 59% of tablet sales were for products with 9-inch screens. But the fastest growth in the tablet market was coming from smaller-format 7-inch screens, expected to take 32% of the market in 2012, up from 26% in 2011. *Amazon* chose to target this market with its Kindle Fire, going head to head with its main rivals – the Nexus 7 from *Google* and *Apple*'s iPad mini.

Consumer research

A survey, conducted by Wiggin, found that a third of Britons owned an ebook reader. According to a TGI survey, those aged between 35 and 44 were the most likely to have bought an e-reader (5.1%), followed by those aged between 25 and 34 (4.4%). Overall, penetration was much lower among respondents aged 55 and over, implying that the mature consumer may not be as interested in the digital alternatives of hardcopy books. Regionally, those situated in Greater London (6.4%) had the greatest penetration. It is known that consumers in high socio-economic grades are more likely to be avid readers, but with e-readers being expensive, the more affluent are even more likely to be the main purchasers. It was key for the Kindle Fire to appeal to a wide audience without losing its original e-reader audience.

The product

The Kindle Fire, as finally released, is a 7-inch touch-screen version of the Kindle. It offers a high-definition display, Dolby audio, 11 hours of battery life, a camera and an enhanced processor and graphics engine. It provides customers with access to over 10,000 apps, including those from *Facebook, Twitter, Pandora* and *Netflix*. The price ranges from £129 for an 8GB standard-definition Kindle Fire with adverts popping up on-screen up to £199 for a 32GB high-definition, advert-free version. The Kindle Fire HD undercut *Apple*'s new iPad mini, launched one day earlier in the UK, by the huge sum of £110. *Amazon* keeps its price so low that each Kindle Fire is in fact sold at a loss in the hope that sales of books and films through its store will make sufficient profits to justify the low price. In fact, *Amazon* founder and CEO Jeff Bezos said, 'We want to make money when people use our devices, not when they buy our devices. If somebody buys one of our devices and puts it in a desk drawer and never uses it, we don't deserve to make any money'.

(Continued)

(Continued)

The Kindle Fire's specifications and apps are designed to make it as easy as possible to purchase content from *Amazon*'s library of over 22 million movies, TV shows, songs and books; 40% of *Amazon*'s sales come from these products, all of which are being transformed by the digital revolution. Users also get one month's free subscription to its movie-rental service Love Film (in the hope they will sign up and pay for the service permanently).

Marketing communications

Amazon announced in September 2012 that it would launch its new products in the UK the following month. The product could be purchased from *Amazon*'s website and through all other major electronics retailers. The announcement caused a flurry of media reports about the future of the tablet market. For example, *The Telegraph*, using the headline, *iPad's grip on tablet market weakens,* speculated on a Pew research report which revealed that, while in 2011 81% of tablet owners were using an iPad, by 2012 this had dropped to 52% as competitors made up ground. On the day of the launch, many TV news channels reported the story and almost every tabloid and broadsheet, both online and off-line, mentioned it, affording *Amazon* some very positive publicity.

In addition to word-of-mouth support, *Amazon* pushed the new product prominently in advertising and on its website, with clear visuals proclaiming the Kindle Fire's power and portability, as well as its simplicity. Consumer reviews are enabled on *Amazon*'s website, and, though an unreliable gauge of the product's reception, they average a solid 4 out of 5 stars. *Amazon* is notoriously secretive about releasing sales figures so people outside the company have little idea of how many are actually sold, but it is clear from media interest and subsequently released iterations of the product that *Amazon* is highly committed to this market.

© Kim Roberts 2014

Case study questions

1. Why does *Amazon* sell its Kindle for near to cost price?
2. Who are the major competitors to Kindle and what, if any, are their unique selling points?
3. If you were asked to describe a typical Kindle Fire customer for an up-coming promotion, what features would they have?
4. How would you describe the type of advertising used prior to the UK launch?

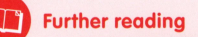 **Further reading**

Agafonoff, N. (2006) 'Adapting ethnographic research methods to ad hoc commercial market research', *Qualitative Market Research: An International Journal*, 9 (2): 115–25.

Agafonoff, N. (2006) 'Exploring the privacy implications of addressable advertising and viewer profiling', *Communications of the ACM*, 49 (5): 119–23.

McDougall, J. and Chantrey, D. (2004) 'The making of tomorrow's consumer', *Young Consumers*, 5 (4): 8–18.

Wyner, G.A. (2006) 'Coping with media fragmentation', *Marketing Research*, 18 (2): 6–7.

REFERENCES

Baker, M.J. (2001) *Critical Perspectives on Business and Management*. London: Routledge.

Barrand, D. (2004) 'Promoting change', Marketing, 6 October, pp. 43–5.

Carson, D., Gilmour, A., Perry, C. and Gronhaug, K. (2001) *Qualitative Marketing Research*. London: Sage.

Dowdy, C. (2004) 'Customer knows best', *Marketing*, 2 September, pp. 39–40.

Edwards, A. (2012) 'Too much data means too much data', at www.clickZ.com [accessed 20 July 2012].

Goulding, C. (2002) *Grounded Theory: A Practical Guide for Management, Business and Marketing Researchers*. London: Sage.

Lodish, L.M. and Lubetkin, B. (1992) 'General truths?', *Admap*, Feb.: 9–15.

McGee, M. (2012) 'Google Analytics is installed on more than 10 million websites', at www.marketingland.com [accessed 20 July 2012].

Miles, L. (2004a) 'Recall vs recognition', *Marketing*, 21 April, pp. 57–8.

Miles, L. (2004b) 'Online, on tap', *Marketing*, 16 June, pp. 39–40.

Mitchell, A. (2012) 'Make or break for market research', *Marketing*, 13 June, pp. 30–2.

Moran, R. (2012) 'The future of marketing research', in R.J. Kaden, L. Gerald and M. Prince (eds), *Leading Edge Marketing Research: 21st Century Tools and Practices*. Thousand Oaks, CA: Sage, pp. 414–39.

Nancarrow, C., Tinson, J. and Evans, M. (2004) 'Polls as marketing weapons: implications for the market research industry', *Journal of Marketing Management*, 20 (5/6): 639–55.

Webb, J.R. (2002) *Understanding and Designing Market Research*, 2nd edn. London: Thomson Learning.

USEFUL WEBSITES

For details on the activities of communications research agencies, see www.jigsaw-research.co.uk, www.spinter.lt and www.chime.plc.uk/

For details of the types of research carried out by *Dipstick Research*, go to: www.dipsticksresearch.com/

For details of a live research brief by *Smart Audiences* for *The Stables*, go to: http://culturehive.co.uk/resources/research-brief-samples

Free online survey tools can be found at: www.surveymonkey.com/ and www.smart-survey.co.uk/

For an example of how semiotics might be used in marketing communications, go to: www.semiotic-analysis.com/case-studies/semiotic-review-of-caffreys-ale/

For examples of commercial storyboards, go to: www.storyboards.com/

For examples of ethnographic research and photo clips, visit: www.everydaylives.com/

For further details on adwords, see: www.google.com/ads/innovations/

For details on how to use *Google* Analytics, see: www.google.com/analytics/

For additional materials that support this chapter and your learning, please visit:
study.sagepub.com/egan

CAMPAIGN TACTICS AND MANAGEMENT

7

LEARNING OBJECTIVES

Having completed this chapter readers would be expected to:

- understand the processes involved in campaign planning

- develop a campaign brief

- recognise the part played by creativity in developing a campaign.

INTRODUCTION

This chapter discusses those elements of the marketing communications plan (as discussed in Chapter 5) that form the tactical campaign. As Figure 7.1 illustrates, marketing communications strategies are informed by a company's marketing communications objectives (see Chapter 5). Given the perceived need for an integrated communications strategy, the campaign plan might be seen to represent the whole spectrum of communication tactics. Alternatively, it may represent one or more marcom tools (e.g. advertising). In some companies, it may be that elements of the communications mix (e.g. public relations and personal selling) are located in other parts of the organisation (e.g. corporate communications and sales management respectively). The chapter will assume a co-ordinated campaign but the model can be adapted to other organisational formats.

THE CREATIVE BRIEF

The objectives have been set and the strategies developed but this is meaningless unless ways are found to reach the target audience and fulfil whatever outcome is required. The creative **brief** outlines the way this will be achieved. It may be an internal document (if the bulk of the plan is to be operationalised in-house) or created

FIGURE 7.1   The campaign process

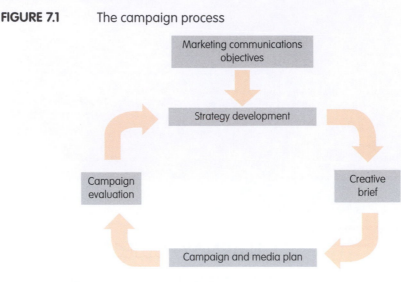

👁 insight: Bing and Jay-Z breaking new ground

For the release of Jay-Z's biography, *Decoded*, Manhattan-based agency *Droga5* broke new ground. Their 'big idea' was to release the pages of the memoir before the book was in retail stores. The *Decoded* campaign was actually a dual client brief – *Droga5* was also charged with creating an integrated campaign for *Microsoft*'s Bing. In the latter case, the brief was to connect their client to a new demographic that corresponded to the Jay-Z fan profile.

The campaign consisted of putting every page of Jay-Z's book in various locations, associated with incidents in the biography, one month before the official publication. This involved locating them in 13 major cities including New York, Chicago and London. Some appeared on huge billboards, others on bus shelters, but it was not only outdoor advertising that was used. Limited edition plates and tee shirts, pool table tops, a swimming pool and even a motor car became the canvasses upon which the pages were put.

As the campaign was rolled out, Bing launched an online game directing fans to each location. Clues were released daily through *Twitter* and *Facebook* and on the radio. Millions logged on to the search using Bing's Search and Maps facility. Fans were also able to assemble the book digitally before it was released. The campaign was extensively covered in newspapers and by broadcasters.

The results of the dual campaign were impressive. Average player engagement on the website was 11 minutes, Jay-Z's *Facebook* followers grew by 1 million and *Decoded* hit the bestseller list for 19 straight weeks. In one month, Bing saw an 11.7% increase in visits, entered the Global Top-10 for the first time and earned 1.1 billion global media impressions.

Source: various

by (or for) one or more agencies (advertising, public relations, etc.) if the bulk of this work is outsourced. In many organisations, it will be a mix of internal and external resources and, as such, no one model fits all or even a majority of situations.

The creative brief provides guidance to the creative team whose task is then to create a piece of communication that is designed to actively do something. It is not one document or the result of one internal or external meeting but a series of iterations and reconstructions. The term 'creative' does not only mean clever, original or funny (although it may be some or all of those things) but also refers to the creation of communications that will do the job they are supposed to do (create awareness, develop interest, sell products/services, etc.), despite the communications clutter from competitors (see Insight).

Whether it is an integrated campaign involving many or few of the elements of the communications mix, there are essentially two fundamental aspects to a creative brief:

- directional elements: clearly defining what the communication needs to achieve and/or the problem that needs to be solved
- inspirational elements: providing the creative team with context, purpose and focus in order to provide a robust starting point for the creative process to engage; this is often called the **creative platform**.

The process may begin or resume (particularly where agencies are involved) with a **brief** followed by one or more briefing sessions where ideas are explored. The brief should have consideration for current communications, even if the intention is to change direction. In some organisations, this assessment of current communications is built in to the planning process by way of a **communications audit.** In major companies, the tradition of one agency (usually advertising) has developed into multi-agencies each covering a particular communications specialism and is often directed by the organisation to co-ordinate campaigns using different tools in various media. Taking this to its logical conclusion, *Team Detroit* and *Blue Hive* (see box 7.2) are agencies formed from the *Ford* (USA) and *Ford of Europe* teams of specialist agencies including *Ogilvy*, *Wunderman* and *Mindshare*.

Creative platform
The 'big idea' on which a campaign can be built.

Brief
Details of the organisation, their brands and all other information pertinent to an agency making a 'pitch'.

Communications audit
A systematic assessment of an organisation's capacity and expertise in essential communications practices.

insight: Integrating agencies

Team Detroit was formed in 2006 by *WPP* to service its US client *Ford* by merging the client's teams from agencies *JWT*, *Y&R*, *Wunderman*, *Ogilvy* and *Mindshare*. In the UK, *WPP* have similarly established *Blue Hive* from the client's communications teams at *Ogilvy*, *Wunderman* and *Mindshare*, working together in one space to service *Ford of Europe* in what they call the 'post-digital consumer and media landscape'. *Blue Hive* describes itself as an integrated, ideas-led communications group. According to the company, whether the work is called 'integration', 'media-neutrality', 'multi-channel' or '360 marketing', the agency does it. *Blue Hive* has experts in a number of different fields so whatever the chosen media campaign, be it online or off-line, it can be covered. With over 100 employees, from 25 different countries, speaking 20 different languages, the group also brings different cultural experiences and views to bear across diverse European markets.

Source: thebluehive.com; *Marketing*, 15 August 2012

Tagline (or strapline or slogan)

A memorable phrase that sums up an important characteristic of the brand.

Certain themes, **taglines** (or **straplines** or **slogans**), music or visual features may represent continuity. Indeed, a change in agency or agencies often signals a change in the direction of that organisation's campaigns. At the extreme, past themes might be at the end of their shelf life and the aim may be to distance the brand (as far as is possible) from what went before. For example, Brylcreem, a product that kept men's hair under control in the 1950s, has been reinvented as a hair gel for the youth market in the new millennium and a new theme was obviously required. This re-positioning was best epitomised by the 'effortless' campaign featuring the music of indie band B. Rayond and the Voicettes (see Insight).

insight: Brylcreem

MEN IN THE PUBLIC EYE PREFER

BRYLCREEM FOR CLEAN GROOMING

BECAUSE the pure oils in BRYLCREEM are emulsified to prevent excessive oiliness

BECAUSE with massage BRYLCREEM ensures a clean scalp, free from dandruff

BECAUSE BRYLCREEM contains no gum, no soap, no spirit, no starch.

BRYLCREEM **YOUR HAIR!**

Since it was developed in Birmingham by County Chemicals in 1928, *Brylcreem* has been keeping men's hair in place, becoming an iconic product of men's hair styling. Clean, smart hairstyles were the dominant fashion of those times, and this trend continued right through the Second World War (when some RAF pilots were known as 'Brylcreem Boys' thanks to their slick hairstyles) and into the 1950s. At this time, popular sporting heroes were used to promote the brand, most notably cricket star Dennis Compton, who became the *Brylcreem* boy of his day. The popular TV series *Mad Men* shows that the 'teddy boy' image lasted into the early 1960s, but that was when men's hair fashions finally began to change.

With a more rebellious youth culture looking to new idols such as The Beatles, men began wearing their hair longer and without meticulous styling. This led to a fall in demand for *Brylcreem* and a corresponding drop in profits. Various attempts at reinvention through the following decades saw occasional revivals of the brand, but it really rebounded from the 1990s onwards. The company reclaimed its sporting pedigree by signing first David Beckham in 1997 and later cricketer Kevin Pietersen to front its campaigns. In another nod to the history of the brand, it is still available in the same packaging that has been used since the 1960s, but additional product lines including gels and waxes have been added. With cultural changes making male grooming a booming industry, the future for the brand looks strong. However, *Brylcreem* continues to think carefully about its branding plans, with one spokesman for the company recently saying, 'We have used sport in the past and it's not the case that we definitely won't use sports people again (but) we're reviewing the plans, and since *Mad Men*, we are looking at that kind of brand ambassador, too'.

Source: www.guardian.co.uk (accessed 2 April 2012) and various

Many agencies have some form of briefing document that aids the briefing discussion. This document usually includes questions such as:

(a) Why are we communicating?

(b) Who are we talking to?

(c)   What do they know about the brand?

(d)   What are we saying to them?

(e)   How are we saying it (the tone)?

(f)   What proof can we provide for any claim?

(g)   Are there executional guidelines and other requirements?

Tone

The 'personality' of your brand or company as expressed through the written or spoken word and/or imagery.

 insight: The importance of briefs

'Clients generally get the agencies they deserve! The best work flows from client/agency partnerships that are built on mutual respect, integrity and a joint humility of approach which allows the professional perspective of both parties to be recognised and respected.

In working together successfully, clients and agencies need to achieve the commercial equivalent of a 'Vulcan mind meld', which can only flow from clear, open and non-precious communications in both directions.

Establishing a clarity of purpose through the definition of objectives which are outcome focused and measurable is clearly at the heart of the briefing process. Clear briefs are not the only critical success factor in arriving at good advertising and marketing, but without this sound starting point you have little chance of success.'

Andrew Nebel, UK Director of Marketing and Communications, Barnardo's

Source: ISBA (2006)

The reason for the brief is to get everyone involved challenging the purpose of the communications. For example:

(A) WHY ARE WE COMMUNICATING?

The answer to this should be to fulfil the marketing communications objectives, however more detailed questions need to be asked. What are the communications intended to achieve? Is the strategy realistic? What do we want the target audience to do or think (e.g. build up an image, become aware, purchase)? As noted in Chapter 5, the objectives may be multi-level (awareness, interest, etc.) but the campaign should be as singular and targeted as possible. A brief resume of the 'problem' as specified by the brand owner would be appropriate.

Often, the principal reason for communicating (via any tool in any media) is to establish, maintain, enhance or, where necessary, adjust the brand (or company) **positioning**. According to Kotler (1997), 'positioning is the act of designing the company's offering and image so that they occupy a meaningful and distinctive competitive position in the target customer's mind'. Prior to the 1970s, market growth was the driving force for new products, particularly in the FMCG sector. With an expanding market, the safest new product launches were **me-too products**. Thus, every category had its market leader and several look-alike brands. The greater competition of the 1970s and later decades, coupled with the growing strength of large retailers (many of whom had own-label varieties of these brands), led to over-branding and a rethink about brand positioning in various markets.

Positioning

Creating a perception in the consumer's mind regarding the nature of the brand relative to competitive brands.

Me-too products

New products that are similar to existing products already available in the marketplace.

Most suppliers of both products and services tend now to believe that, in order to negate direct competition, organisations and brands should take up distinct positions in each marketplace. In order to do this, the organisation must know what its target customer wants, where its competitors are positioned, where it wishes to compete and then develop marketing and communication strategies to achieve this positioning of its brand (or organisation) in the minds of that target audience.

There are a number of ways to develop a positioning strategy, but it is generally accepted that they will incorporate the following:

- clearly identifying competitors
- undertaking an assessment of consumer perception of competitors
- determining the relative positions of competitors
- analysing consumer preferences
- establishing a positioning strategy
- implementing the positioning strategy
- monitoring the position over time.

First, the organisation must identify its major competitors, not just in the same product or service category but including competitors that satisfy the same needs in the eye of the consumer (e.g. air travel versus high-speed rail). Second, consumers' perception of competitive brands should be assessed. What attributes or benefits are important to this market and how do the competitors score on such an evaluation? The third and fourth stages are the determination of the positioning of competitors and analysis of customer preferences through in-depth interviews, focus groups or other qualitative research techniques. A major tool in this process is the **perceptual map** (or **multidimentional map**). This is a matrix consisting of two axes each with important attributes or features about the product or service. An example of a perceptual map is shown in Figure 7.2.

The perception map in Figure 7.2 shows the main competitors in a fictitious European furniture market where the most important attributes are seen to be style (traditional or contemporary) and quality (luxury or standard). Company A believed it had a reasonably good reputation but research shows that it is seen by its target market as 'stuck in the middle' of a highly competitive marketplace

Perceptual map (or multidimensional skills map) A matrix used to establish a brand's positioning against certain criteria.

FIGURE 7.2　　Perception map and competitive positioning

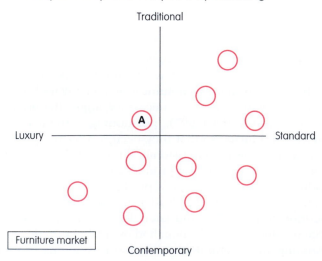

FIGURE 7.3   Re-positioning

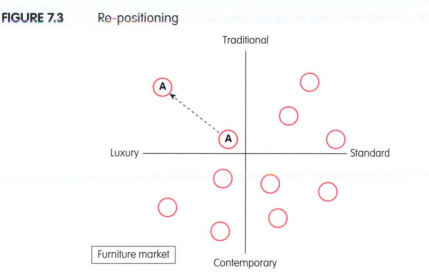

when it believed its target market would be more receptive to a traditional/luxury positioning. This may result in the adoption of a **re-positioning** (or **targeted differentiation**) strategy where the company identifies a specific market position and then redesigns its marketing programme to target it.

Implementing a new positioning would involve adapting the product, price and place (distribution) elements of the mix and communicating this re-positioned image (see Figure 7.3) to the target audience as a whole. The marketing imperative is to create a mix which reflects consumers' subjective, perceptive and cognitive processing of information, their personal lifestyles, values and motivations (Foxall et al. 1998).

There are, however, dangers associated with re-positioning. Although there may appear to be a gap in a market, this does not mean that it represents a good marketing opportunity. The *Mercedes Citan* was a brand extension designed to fill a 'gap' in the market for a top-branded small city van. The vehicle was based on the *Renault Kangoo* (the product of an alliance between the companies) and the same or similar to another van, the *Dokker*, available as *Renault's* discount brand *Dacia*. In addition, the van only scored three out of five stars in German autoclub ADAC's Euro-NCAP-Crashtest on a vehicle that was supposed to excel in safety. According to the *Truthabout cars.com* website, the rumour in the trade was that the launch of the Citan actually increased sales of the *Kangoo* and the *Dokker*. Why, they suggested, should customers pay more for something similar? The attempt to reposition the brand in a segment deemed profitable may have back-fired. Figure 7.4 details a perception map of brands in the European automobile industry which reflects *Mercedes's* perceived move to reposition itself in the market.

Depending on the industry, an organisation may have to reposition on a regular basis to keep up with the competitive landscape. Some well-known brands have had to reposition significantly based on changes in the competitive landscape. They include:

- *IBM*, formally the world's largest computer manufacturer, has been repositioned as a 'solutions provider'
- *Kodak* withdrew from film production in 2009 as the market switched to digital; in 2012 the company announced an end to digital camera production to concentrate on software and photo-booth technology

Repositioning or targeted differentiation
The process of recreating or changing the perception of a brand in the consumer's mind.

FIGURE 7.4   Repositioning in the European automobile market

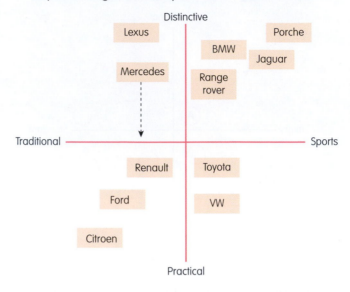

- *Lucozade* in the 1950s was a drink that you took to sick people in hospital; today it has been successfully repositioned as a drink for healthy sports men and women
- *Aer Lingus*, faced with competition from airlines such as Ryanair and EastJet, has reinvented itself as a no-frills, web-based, competitively priced airline that can compete in the short-haul market.

All of the above repositioning involved these companies in significant changes in their communications strategies, including rewriting brand messages, restyling brand images and redefining media channels.

(B) WHO ARE WE TALKING TO?

There are a number of ways of describing who you are targeting with your message (e.g. see box 7.5). Target marketing is where specific segments are selected and marketing plans developed to satisfy the needs of the potential buyers in that chosen segment. In order to ensure communications are coherent, consistent, uniform and successful, it follows that a clear understanding of the segmentation base is vital. For this reason, viable segments should meet a number of important criteria (represented by the mnemonic **ADMARS**). They should be:

ADMARS

A mnemonic which infers that segments are required to be accessible, differentiated, measurable, actionable, relevant and substantial.

- **A**ccessible: they can be reached through specific media
- **D**ifferentiated: different from other segments
- **M**easurable: they can be defined and measured to some degree of accuracy
- **A**ctionable: the company has the resources to reach this segment
- **R**elevant: the product/service is relevant to this segment
- **S**ubstantial: the segment is large enough (relatively) to warrant targeting.

There are various ways of segmenting the market, many of which were discussed previously in Chapter 3 and are summarised in Table 7.1.

Often, segmentation may take place on the basis of two or more variables. The example shown in Figure 7.5 assumes that vineyard holidays would be attractive to frequent leisure travellers but even more attractive to frequent travellers

TABLE 7.1   Segmentation types

Consumer market segmentation	Industrial market segmentation
❑ Demographics (including life stage, earnings, social class, learning, etc.)	❑ Company type (Standard Industrial Code)
❑ Geodemographics	❑ Company size
❑ Psychographics (personality and lifestyle based on analysis of interests and opinions (AIO))	❑ Company structure (e.g. central/ diversified)
❑ Benefits sought	❑ Location
	❑ Heavy/light users
	❑ Title/position of key decision makers
	❑ Benefits sought

FIGURE 7.5   Segmentation

Wine drinkers

Frequent travellers

Potential target market for vineyard holidays

Total market

who are also wine drinkers. The consumer information required to permit such segmentation may already be available within the organisation or be purchased (although strictly each list is rented[1]) as **lists** (see Chapter 13) available from **list brokers** or other commercial sources.

There are numerous ways with which to segment a market, indeed one of the biggest criticisms of segmentation is that marketers define segments to fit their own beliefs and prejudices rather than to reflect the market. Consultants are frequently criticised for developing customer typologies of dubious practical use. In their defence, such professionals argue that it is better to concentrate on one segment rather than no segment at all.

Not only might markets be segmented in many ways but frequently new segments appear as styles change, technology advances and society develops. More recent new segment introductions include tablet computers, apps and space travel.

List

A listing of potential customers with a specific characteristic (e.g. food-loving), available to rent for a specific direct mail, telemarketing or email campaign.

List broker

An intermediary between list owners and organisations wishing to rent lists.

---

[1]   Contracts vary but it is usual for organisations to be licensed to use a list for only one campaign.

At the same time, old market segments change. For example, it is estimated that the travel industry in India was worth $23 billion in 2012 and that 170m travellers will visit India by 2021, offering opportunities to many organisations.

Demographic segmentation remains an important classifier. Probably the most often used demographic is gender because large numbers of products and services are either gender-specific (e.g. lipstick) or dominated by a certain gender (e.g. children's clothing). Another obvious demographic is age. The financial services market is one that utilises age segmentation in a major way. In this industry, there is a recognition that different financial products are required at different life stages; as can be seen in Figure 7.6, the need for financial services changes as the average customer gets older. The skill of the financial services marketer is to reach these customers at the right time with the right product at the right price, and segmentation of this type contributes towards this.

FIGURE 7.6   Financial needs

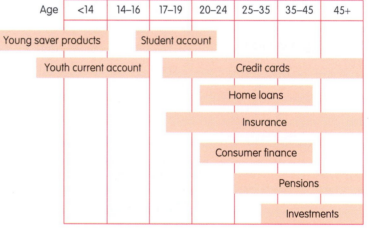

Demographic segmentation
Statistical data relating to the population and groups within it.

Geodemographics combine demographic and locational factors to provide an additional slant on the needs of customers. Among well-known commercial suppliers of such data are *Acorn* and *Mosaic*. *Acorn* is a classification of residential neighbourhoods which is based on the presumption of there being a relationship between the type of home people live in and their purchase behaviour (see Chapter 3).

It is arguable, however, that consumers, whatever their particular demographic profile, differ in personality and attitude and that a consumer lifestyle profile is a better indicator. **Lifestyle segmentation** (often referred to as **VALS** – values, attitudes and lifestyles) is, therefore, seen as an important segmentation tool. These lifestyle traits frequently form the basis of customer profiles or customer **stereotypes** (e.g. Essex Man) on which a campaign may be targeted. Stereotyping, despite its negative connotations, can be a useful communications tool. For example, in the run-up to the 2012 Olympic Games, French advertising agency *Leg* created a *Eurostar* campaign featuring Greek-style statues of what the French presumably saw as typical British athletic heroes playing darts and snooker.

Geodemographics
A method of segregating a market on the basis of social demographics and location.

Lifestyle segmentation
A method of segmentation based on lifestyle characteristics.

VALs
Values, attitudes and lifestyle analysis.

Stereotype
To categorise an individual as part of a group and inferring that s/he will have the qualities and personality possessed generally by that group.

(C) WHAT DO THEY KNOW ABOUT THE BRAND?

What are customers' attitudes to the brand? Are they those the company seeks? Do they require further information, assurance or perhaps more (correct) information? Does the image of the brand need a complete makeover? *Skoda* is an example of where consumer knowledge was out of line with the improvements made to products. In the 1980s and 1990s, the brand was regarded as a running joke, a symbol of shoddy eastern European manufacturing. Following the cold war, the company was purchased by *Volkswagen* who invested heavily in *Skoda* such that the car plant became one of the finest in Europe. However, it took substantial (and creative) promotion to convince a sceptical audience that the product had really changed.

(D) WHAT ARE WE SAYING TO THEM?

The **creative platform** is the foundation on which the campaign message is built. The creative platform must support the single **positioning statement** (or **single-minded proposition**). The positioning statement is designed to incorporate the essence of what the brand stands for in the minds of target audiences relative to their impression of competitor brands (its position). This can be based initially on two distinct approaches:

- **functional orientation**
- **symbolic/experiential orientation**.

Creative platform
The foundation (or big idea) on which a campaign message is built.

Positioning statement (or single-minded proposition)
A statement designed to incorporate the essence of what a brand stands for in the minds of target audiences relative to their impression of competitor brands.

Functional orientation
Where the positioning is based on that feature(s) or attribute(s) that is unique (or can be made to appear unique) to that brand.

⊙ insight: The Levis 501 campaign

The brief that originated the Levis 501 campaign is seen as a classic example of how to inspire the creative team. It asked: What must the advertising say?

501 from Levis are the right look and the only label.

Why should the consumer believe it?

Because they represent the way jeans should be worn today, and because they are the original jean, indelibly associated with the birth of teenage culture in the 1950s and its finest expression since.

Tone of voice: *Heroic, highly charged, American (but period).*

Source: Duckworth (1999)

Functional orientation suggests that the positioning is based on that feature or attribute that is unique (or can be made to appear unique) to that brand (the **unique selling proposition** or **USP**). This gives the consumer a distinctly differentiated reason for buying one brand over another. However, USPs can be fleeting as features can often be copied quickly by competitors. When it was suggested that *Gillette's* USP for a new razor was that it had three blades, their agency quite rightly asked what would happen to the campaign if a competitor came up with a four-blade razor! Examples of functional orientation, therefore, tend to be those where messages have become attached to the brand rather than necessarily to its uniqueness, such as:

Domestos – kills 99% of household germs

Orangina – shake it to release the taste.

Symbolic/experiential orientation
Where positioning is based on the emotional needs of consumers and is therefore concerned with psychosocial rather than physical differentiation (see also experiential orientation).

Unique selling proposition (USP)
The single feature that makes a brand stand out from other brands.

Sometimes these 'features' are strictly tongue in cheek, for example:

> *Peperami* – it's a bit of an animal
>
> *Heineken* – reaches the parts other beers cannot reach.

Pricing can also be a USP although again its advantages may be fleeting. The entry into the UK banking market of ING[2] with a high-interest, internet-based savings account supported by heavy advertising, which made savers aware of their superior rates, was quickly followed by other banks offering the same or a higher interest rate. The entry of low-priced competitors into the already crowded low-cost airline and supermarket businesses make it difficult to sustain an image of lower prices without constant promotion. However, this does not seem to have stopped organisations such as *Ryanair* and *ASDA* from continuing to keep cost a central theme in their communications campaigns.

Symbolic/experiential orientation is focused on the emotional needs of consumers and is concerned with psychosocial rather than physical differentiation. This is occasionally referred to as **'the soft sell'**. It involves using emotional appeals to produce positive feelings that may distinguish and enhance the brand image or, as it is increasingly described, the **brand personality**. This distinct identity or personality is particularly important in categories where there is little physical differentiation (beer, soft drinks, chocolate, cigarettes, fuel, air travel, etc.). Examples of campaigns that use this approach include:

> Land/Range Rover – rugged, unbeatable
>
> Volvic mineral water – using an ancient source of unpolluted, pure water.

Many male-orientated campaigns seek to be macho, if not seemingly misogynistic, such as:

> *Lynx/Axe* – the *Lynx/Axe* effect
>
> *Nestlé Yorkie* – it's not for girls
>
> *Fosters* – 'Good call'.

The choice between functional and symbolic orientation is not necessarily a straightforward one. It would be logical to assume that high-involvement decisions (see Chapter 3) are likely to require a more rational, informational emphasis (i.e. highlighting attributes and benefits), while low-involvement decision making may require the use of imagery. However, the investment of motor car manufacturers in developing brand status and personality would seem to go against this, as would the growing importance of delivering nutritional advice on what would normally be described as low-involvement groceries. As with many maxims associated with marketing communications, it is the exception that proves the rule!

Other creative strategies that may be employed include:

- resonance
- emotional
- generic
- pre-emptive.

Resonance (or **'slice-of-life'**) **strategies** attempt to match 'patterns' in the message with target audiences' shared experiences. This is frequently expressed in advertising through **indirect address**, where the potential consumer 'eavesdrops' on, for example, a family, a group of friends, an individual or other groups. Demonstrations may be used to get over important ideas such as ease of use,

Soft sell
Using emotional appeals to produce positive feelings for a brand.

Brand personality or branding
The character and essence of a brand, together with its perceived lifestyle associations and values (e.g. status, fashion, quality).

Resonance (or 'slice-of-life') strategies
These strategies match 'patterns' in the message with target audiences' shared experiences.

Indirect address
In advertising, where the potential consumer 'eavesdrops' on, for example, a family, a group of friends, other groups or individuals.

---

2   Since sold and renamed Bardays Direct.

insight: The Cadbury Gorilla

The Cadbury Gorilla advertisement premiered on 31 August 2007 and is still one of the most talked-about adverts of its generation. The commercial used a song and dance format and a simple but catchy song to humorous effect. From a branding perspective, it is associating the brand with this humour rather than any call to action. The camera angles used varied from mid shots to close-ups and slow motion was used in the build-up to a drum crescendo. The recognisable tune (Phil Collins's 'In the air tonight') and its lyrics suggested the gorilla had been waiting all his life for this opportunity. The only direct association with the *Cadbury* brand prior to the final shot was the purple backdrop and the reference to 'a glass and a half'. The final shot more specifically relates to *Cadbury*'s Dairy Milk. The campaign itself involved, in addition to television, appearances on posters, in newspapers and magazines, at the cinema and online, and event sponsorships. The campaign was handled by the advertising agency *Fallon London*. The advertisement scored high noticeability ratings whenever it was screened on television and this generated huge downloads from the web. Cadbury Schweppes reported that the Dairy Milk gorilla advert helped contribute to a 6% revenue growth in the UK, Ireland and the emerging markets.

Source: various

---

capability, flexibility or comparison with a named or unnamed competitor. On the other hand, the message may be spoken directly to the consumer. This **testimonial** may be delivered by a personality, an expert or a representative of the average consumer. Some communications use a mixture of indirect and direct deliveries, with the latter often summarising the benefits outlined in the previous discussions.

Emotional strategies appeal to emotions such as romantic feelings (*Gold Blend*), nostalgia (*Werther's Originals*), compassion (*Save the Children* and the *NSPCC*), excitement (*Nike*), joy (*BMW*), heroism (*Sony Play Station*), fear (all life insurance), guilt (anti-drink-driving campaigns), disgust (*Benetton*) and regret ('smoking leads to cancer' campaigns).

Generic strategies are associated with brands that are so dominant in a sector that there is (at that time) no need to differentiate the brand from its competitors. Effectively, these brands are looking to grow the total market in the knowledge that any increase will disproportionately benefit them. Examples of generic advertising[3] include *British Telecom's* 'It's good to talk' and, in the USA, *Campbell's* 'Soup is good for you'.

Pre-emptive strategies are those where the brand asserts its superiority in an undifferentiated market, making it difficult for competitors to match such assertions. Examples include:

'Carlsberg – probably the best lager in the world'

'Hertz – we're number one'

'Gillette – the best a man can get'

'Nothing is more effective than Anadin'.

(E) HOW ARE WE SAYING IT?

Humour, tension and other emotional triggers are used in varying degrees to create awareness and interest. The tone of the communication has, however, to

---

Testimonial
A testament to a brand delivered by a personality, an expert or a representative of an average consumer.

Emotional strategies
These strategies appeal to emotions, such as romantic feelings, nostalgia, compassion, excitement, joy, heroism, fear, guilt, disgust and regret.

Generic strategies
Where a brand is so dominant in a sector that there is (at that time) no need to differentiate the brand from its competitors. Effectively, these brands are looking to grow the total market in the knowledge that any increase will disproportionately benefit them.

Pre-emptive strategies
Where the brand asserts its superiority in an undifferentiated market, making it difficult for competitors to match such assertions (e.g. 'Carlsberg – probably the best lager in the world').

---

[3] This is not to be confused with generic advertising often undertaken by sector representatives such as the Wool Council.

Voice-over
Spoken commentary
over an advertisement.

be appropriate. It would be questionable for the inclusion of comedy in a campaign against road accidents. On the other hand, health warnings would be out of place (but perhaps appropriate) in a soft drinks commercial. **Voice-overs** can set the required tone, as in nostalgia-based advertising for *Hovis* and *Kerrygold*. Some voices resonate well and celebrity voices in particular. Hugh Laurie, for example, has been the voice of *Walker's, Johnson & Johnson, Bradford & Bingley* and *Marks and Spencer*, among others. As noted in Chapter 2, the accurate transfer and acceptance of messages is highly influenced by the characteristics of the source of the message, whether in the voice-over or acting role. Celebrities can instil confidence and enhance the personality of the brand. Some stars (e.g. David Beckham) no longer have to actively endorse a brand but only have to appear in an advertisement to create meaning. Animated characters are frequently used to convey information, often in a humorous way, and can become synonymous with the brand (e.g. Jolly *Green Giant*, the *Tetley* Tea Folk,[4] *Kellogg's* Tony the Tiger and Snap, Crackle and Pop).

Creative communicators will often use metaphors, analogies and stereotypes to create extra meaning. Mothers are frequently used as metaphors for homeliness and fast cars for success. The skill is to find an appropriate metaphor and ensure it means what it is intended to mean (Brierley 2002). Thus, *Tropicana* is associated with sunshine, *Bird's Eye* (frozen peas) with freshness, *Andrews'* toilet tissue with softness and *Häagen Dazs* with sexual expression! Analogies are sometimes used when a message cannot be realistically portrayed, for example a hammer striking a peach as a representation of a child in a road accident (2002) or a light bulb signifying a 'bright idea'.

Stereotypes abound and we use them in everyday conversation so it is unsurprising that they are used extensively by communicators as a short-cut towards meaning. For example, we all *know* men do not ask for travel directions or multi-task while women cannot read maps and are technophobic. Neither statement is true but there is enough truth (even if it is in our residual memory) that most people in society would recognise them. The communicator will choose those stereotypes that help create and fix meaning in the message. Absent-minded professors, inconsiderate white van drivers, protective mothers (usually in a *Volvo*) on school runs, talkative taxi drivers, unsympathetic traffic wardens, unscrupulous, grease-covered mechanics, over-bearing parents and angst-ridden teenagers all possess and portray meaning which enables us to share a joke at their expense. Stereotypes are frequently used to enhance meaning and instil values for products and services with geographical and cultural connections. *Foster's* beer advertising plays on the supposed tendencies of the Australian male to prefer his (cold) beer to his women, *Caffries* Irish beer evokes the fun-loving, congeniality of the 'old country', while *Rolex, Omega, Lindt, Swatch* and Longines *associate* themselves with the Swiss-made reputation for quality.

(F) WHAT PROOF CAN WE PROVIDE FOR ANY CLAIM?

Making a claim that is evidently unbelievable is unlikely to enhance the image and credibility of the brand, with the notable exception of those who do it tongue-in-cheek (e.g. *Red Bull* 'gives you wings'). Proof is sometimes made evident by demonstrations or comparisons. Claims to the effectiveness of particular constituents or the absence of perceived 'bad' ingredients have to be proved to be true. For example, television advertising for the *Sanex* bodycare brand, owned by

---

[4]   Introduced in 1973, phased out in 2001, resurrected in 2010 and currently central to *Tetley* campaigns.

Colgate-Palmolive, was banned in the UK after the Advertising Standards Authority (ASA) ruled that the advertising was misleading. The ASA considered that the overall impression was that the *Sanex* range contained only those ingredients essential for clean and healthy skin which they said was incorrect.

(G) ARE THERE EXECUTIONAL GUIDELINES AND OTHER REQUIREMENTS?

Having developed a creative strategy, there is a need to decide how it should be executed. The composition of the communication is crucial, whether it be advertising, sales promotion, personal selling or any other of the marketing communications tools. What legal requirements do I need to fulfil (see Chapter 18)? If advertising, sales promotion or direct marketing are involved in the campaign, which media will be used (see Chapter 8)? What public relations support does it require? Should there be colour, smell, movement or sound? Where should it be positioned (in a publication or broadcast)? What size should it be to create the required impact?

summary

This chapter continued the marketing planning process by considering campaign tactics and management. It began by discussing the creative brief and briefing sessions whose objective is to produce directional and inspirational elements for a campaign. Among the principal questions being asked by the creative team are: who are we talking to, what are we saying and how are we saying it? Conceptual terms such as the creative platform, positioning, functional orientation, symbolic/experiential orientation and the USP (unique selling proposition) were discussed, as was their contribution to brand image (or brand personality). The resource, emotional, generic and pre-emptive strategies were further defined. The importance of the message source was again reiterated and the contribution of metaphors, analogies and stereotypes highlighted as means to get across a message.

review questions

1. Give an example of a pre-emptive strategy.

2. What are the two main elements of a creative brief?

3. Explain the principle of functional orientation.

4. What is 'the soft sell'?

5. How would you define brand personality?

6. Why are testimonials seen to be effective?

7. Why is proof sometimes required when claims are made for a product or service?

8. What types of guidelines need to be followed when developing a campaign?

discussion questions

1. Why is the creative brief important, what do you think it should contain and what are the problems that could arise if it is not clear?

2. How would an emotional strategy take its form, and why might it work? Find examples of current advertising campaigns that use this approach and assess their potential impact on the implied target market.

3. Radio advertising has been popular in the past, but now only represents around 7% of UK advertising spend. Why might this be so and, as a potential advertiser, under what circumstances might you consider a radio campaign?

case study 7.1: The man who fell from space

Analysis of Felix Baumgartner's incredible jump from the edge of space on 14 October 2012 showed he reached a top speed of 843.6 mph. When he stepped out of his capsule above New Mexico at 127,852.4 feet, his heart was pumping at a rate of 185 beats per minute. In making the jump, he became the first person to break the sound barrier without help from a vehicle, reaching Mach 1.25. Baumgartner spent 5 (out of the 6) minutes in free fall, and had to use his years of training to recover from a terrifying spin which saw him at one point rotating faster than once every second. This event, under the campaign name *Red Bull Stratos*, was undoubtedly a great personal and, many would say, commercial achievement. Baumgartner and sponsor *Red Bull*'s records should remain intact for some time to come, having been submitted to the Federation Aeronautique Internationale (FAI) for official verification.

But why is Red Bull spending millions to send Baumgartner to the stratosphere and back? In fact, this event is merely the most spectacular manifestation of a long-running trend in the company's marketing. Red Bull attaches its name closely to sports, particularly extreme ones. Events ranging from cliff diving to the farcical Flugtag (Flying Day) carry the Red Bull name, as do two Formula One teams and several soccer teams. The company supports around 600 athletes worldwide in more than 150 sports, going as far as building snowboarding star Shaun White, a personal 'superpipe' in preparation for the 2010 Winter Olympics. Its corporate website is full of images of mountain bikers, racing drivers, surfers and skateboarders – with not a drink can in sight. According to Jim Andrews of sponsorship consultancy IEG, Baumgartner's jump 'is very in line with the Red Bull brand, which has established itself as a sponsor of extreme athletes and events, and has a heritage in flying, through its partnerships with aeronautic teams as well as its popular "Flugtag" events, featuring human-powered vehicles.'

Since the company was founded in 1987, it has built its promotional content creation just as rigorously as it has built its beverage distribution channels, or any product-related innovation. When Dietrich Mateschitz, founder of the company, was asked whether *Red Bull* was a drinks maker or a content producer (e.g. athletes and sports ventures), he said 'This is not either/or … It is both ways, the brand is supporting the sports and culture community, as well as the other way round.' Ben Sturner of the *Leverage Agency* commented: 'The value for *Red Bull* is in the tens of millions of dollars of global exposure, and *Red Bull Stratos* will continue to be talked about and passed along socially for a very long time.' For this sponsorship, the company cannot be displeased with the outcome as an unprecedented 8 million saw the jump live and millions more saw the replay on television and online.

Source: various

Case study questions

1. Why do *Red Bull* wish to be associated with the types of events noted in this case study?
2. What might have been the damage to the brand if things had gone wrong for Baumgartner?
3. What other types of sponsorship might *Red Bull* consider in the future?

further reading

Berglind, M. and Nakata, C. (2005) 'Cause-related marketing: more buck than bang?', *Business Horizons*, 48 (5): 443–53.
Holm, H. (2006) 'Integrated marketing communication: from tactics to strategy', *Corporate Communications: An International Journal*, 11 (1): 23–33.
Krieger, A.M. and Green, P.E. (2006) 'A tactical model for resource allocation and its application to advertising budgeting', *European Journal of Operational Research*, 170 (3): 935–49.
Percy, L. (2006) 'Are product placements effective?', *International Journal of Advertising*, 25 (1): 112–14.

REFERENCES

Brierley, S. (2002) *The Advertising Handbook*. London: Routledge.
Duckworth, G. (1999) 'Creative briefing', in L. Butterfield (ed.), *Excellence in Advertising*. Oxford: Butterworth-Heinemann/IPA, pp. 135–57.
Foxall, G.R., Goldsmith, R. and Brown, S. (1998) *Consumer Psychology for Marketing*, 2nd edn. London: Cengage Learning.
Incorporated Society of British Advertisers (ISBA) (2006) 'The client brief', Joint Industry Guidelines. London: ISBA.
Kotler, P. (1997) *Marketing Management: Analysis, Planning, Implementation and Control*. Englewood Cliffs, NJ: Prentice Hall.

USEFUL WEBSITES

Examples of creative briefs can be found at: www.adcracker.com/brief/Creative_Brief.htm
For examples of the *Leg* campaign for *Eurostar*, go to: www.creativereview.co.uk/cr-blog/2012/june/eurostar-olympic-ads
For examples of *Skoda* advertising, go to: www.pocket-lint.com/news/36582/new-skoda-made-meaner-stuff

For additional materials that support this chapter and your learning, please visit:
study.sagepub.com/egan

CAMPAIGN MEDIA AND MEDIA PLANNING

LEARNING OBJECTIVES

Having completed this chapter, readers would be expected to:

- be aware of the characteristics of the most important media for advertising and other communications

- understand the complexity of media planning

- recognise the importance of reach, frequency and gross rating points.

INTRODUCTION

This chapter discusses the media used principally in advertising and sales promotion (including what is termed direct and digital marketing) but whose characteristics also apply across all other communications tools (for example, sales promotion and public relations). The importance of targeted media cannot be over-emphasised and, as such, media planning becomes a critical part of the campaign process.

MEDIA CHARACTERISTICS

The overall goal of communications management is, within budget limitations, to design the best message for the most appropriate medium to reach the maximum number of people in the target audience. As such, the management of the media mix is crucial. Over the years, new mediums have developed which, despite dire predictions, have complemented rather than replaced what went before. Early hand-painted posters were replaced by larger signs which today may be digital and/or are three-dimensional. Meanwhile, printed 'bills' came to the fore with the arrival of the printing press which ultimately led to the development of newspapers and magazines. The print medium dominated until the 1920s and the advent of radio which gradually took over the former's prime position. This was also the golden age of the cinema and that too became a vehicle for commercial messaging. With the introduction of television, both radio and cinema dropped to lesser positions in the communications hierarchy but still continued to attract a definable and, therefore, targetable clientele. In the 1990s, direct marketing (both through mail and telephone) was heralded as the future of communication. The development of electronic media (internet, World Wide Web, emails, etc.) again brought predictions of the total dominance of this channel. In fact, rather than technical evolution making media decisions more straightforward, the plethora of choice makes it even more complex than in the past. Very few campaigns rely solely on one medium. The decision regarding which medium to use depends on campaign objectives, cost (always a limiting factor), the target audience to be reached and the characteristics of that medium.

As noted previously, the job of a media planner is, within the financial confines of the campaign, to reach the greatest number of target customers, more times. To achieve this, the characteristics of each medium, and the opportunities within that medium, need to be known. What follows is a review of the media currently available.

OUTDOOR MEDIA

Despite being perhaps the oldest commercial communication medium (outside of word of mouth), outdoor media has remained an important tool. Indeed, it has achieved something of a renaissance in the latter part of the twentieth century because of the potential formats available. The term **outdoor media** relates to posters (or billboards), hoardings, transport (including liveried balloons or blimps, airliners, trains, taxis and buses) and other non-traditional media. Examples of the latter include the *Ryanair*

jet painted with the *Hertz* livery and the *Eurostar* train decorated with images from the *Da Vinci Code* which, in 2006, took the stars of that film from London to the *Cannes Film Festival*.

Although still a major medium, the traditional poster (see Insight) has also been surpassed, particularly in high traffic locations, by rolling presentations or 3D designs (e.g. *Xerox* light bulbs). Giant posters, placed through companies such as *Blow-up Media* and *Mega Ltd*, now adorn large office buildings or factories in many major cities around the globe. As an example of the variety of poster/billboard opportunities, the Insight below details the services offered by one of the leading companies in this sector.

👁 insight: Outdoor billboards

Out of Home is an organisation specialising in outdoor advertising. Among the formats offered are:

48 Sheet: the most popular billboard size; also available in high definition; the dimensions are based on a traditional measure of 20 x 10 ft (609.6 x 304.8 cm)

96 Sheet: a larger format (40 x 10 ft) for higher impact; also available in high definition

Lenticular/prism/wave: a triple revolving poster that creates impact through movement

Scrolling 48: a backlit, boxed scrolling advertisement

Backlit 48 and 96: illuminated billboards

Mega 6: the largest portrait (as opposed to landscape) outdoor format; can also be illuminated

Golden squares: 20-ft square billboards

Landmark: unique premium formats targeting high traffic flow sites

3D builds: individually built for individual campaigns

Special builds: going beyond traditional posters to make a dramatic statement.

The term **ambient media** is often associated with outdoor advertising and is best described as anything that introduces a 'wow factor'. It is something not generally seen before that is capable of attracting attention and curiosity. In the past, this has included projections onto buildings (including the UK House of Commons), buses with white *Polo Mint* wheels and the 75 x 110 ft (approximately 23 x 33.5 m) *Maxim Magazine* cover in the Arizona desert that can be seen from space. Prior to and during the 2012 Olympics, *British Airways* painted an image of Jessica Ennis (who subsequently became a gold medallist) on Thornbury Playing Fields in Hounslow, about three miles from Heathrow Airport. This became the first image many passengers saw as they entered the UK during this period.

Ambient media
Advertising with a 'wow factor' placed in conspicuous but unusual places.

By definition, ambient media ceases to be ambient media once it has become popular (i.e. when it no longer has the same 'wow factor'), although the term is often used in a general sense for non-traditional outdoor media.

The advantages of poster and other outdoor media is that they are relatively inexpensive yet can offer high **frequency** and **reach** (see media buying). Much depends on location, with the areas of highest traffic having the densest advertising (e.g. New York's Times Square, London Piccadilly, etc.). There are few heavy traffic sites that do not have marketing messages dominating them. Indeed, it can sometimes appear that every conceivable vantage point has been taken by outdoor media in some central city locations.

Frequency
The number of times the target audience has an opportunity to see (OTS) or hear (OTH) the message.

On the downside, the poster is a largely untargeted medium although you could argue that the position of sites, for example at an airport, does offer some segmentation opportunities. By their very nature, outdoor media have a very short exposure time in which to get their message across to the passing public. The industry maxim is that it is unlikely to be an effective poster if there are more than eight words on it. Although 'eight words' is somewhat arbitrary, the message certainly must be easily conveyed in the short time the audience is exposed to it. Organisations that have used posters as a central vehicle in their campaigns include *The Economist* and *Benetton* where the messages (in words and/or pictures) are straightforward and to the point.

Reach
The percentage of the target audience exposed at least once to the message during a period (normally four weeks).

PRINT MEDIA

There are two major classifications of print media (other than leaflets, brochures, etc., which are covered in Chapter 13): newspapers and magazines. Newspapers have been a vehicle for advertising almost since their inception (see Chapter 1). For much of that time, they were limited to black on white and few type sizes and relied on repetition and blocks of print to create an effect (see Chapter 13).

In the late twentieth century, however, the introduction of colour and improvements in paper and printing quality went some way to improving their appeal. Advances in digital technology have taken this to new heights. Newspapers now have shorter lead times, enabling flexibility and rapid response where required. They can also be printed as local editions with appropriate editorial content (e.g. Irish *Sun* and the Scottish *Daily Mail*). Newspaper is a highly portable medium and individuals can choose when to 'consume' it, but it has a very short shelf life. The growth of free newspapers has had an effect on the industry. For example, when the *London Evening Standard* decided to distribute the newspaper free in 2010 volume rose by 60%. Readership surveys showed the free *Standard* was given away to 600,000 people a day, with a total readership of 1.4 million; while previously it had sold 1,600 copies a day at Oxford Circus, it could now distribute 20,000 for free (according to the *Observer*, 13 June 2010). The increased circulation naturally attracted advertisers, covering the revenue lost from sales.

Newspapers are good at explaining complex issues (in print and pictures), although practical demonstration is more difficult than in a televisual or cinematic medium. It is not a highly targeted medium (except for specialist publications such as the *Financial Times* or the *Racing Post*), although different national newspapers attract somewhat different demographic groups. Regional newspapers and local variations of 'nationals' allow for geographically based campaigns. From a public relations perspective, journalistic and editorial content has high credibility but this can also work against, as well as for, the organisation (see Chapter 11).

Blog
A website on which an individual author or group records their opinions or other information, often in the form of an article, on a regular basis.

Undoubtedly, in the past few years, newspapers have suffered from the challenge of online publication of relatively instantaneous news, while blogs have started to encroach on the domain of the feature writer. In the UK, the top 10 national newspapers' circulation fell 7.83% in the year to March 2012. Local newspapers have suffered even more. Circulation of the *Manchester Evening News* declined by 13.2% during 2011, while the *Leicester Mercury*, Teeside's *Evening Gazette* and the *Yorkshire Post* all showed falls. However, certain newspapers (in the UK, notably *The Guardian* and the *Daily Mail*) seem to have embraced the online medium while continuing (at present) to maintain a satisfactory paper circulation. In other parts of the world, newspapers continue to be a very important medium.

---

insight: World newspaper circulation

Printed newspaper circulation declined worldwide in 2011 but this was more than made up for by an increase in digital audiences, the World Association of Newspapers and News Publishers (WAN-IFRA) reported in its annual update of world press trends. The report focuses on the 69 countries that account for 90% of global industry value in terms of circulation and advertising revenue.

The survey suggested that media consumption patterns vary widely across the globe. Print circulation is increasing in Asia, but declining in mature markets in the West. The number of titles globally is consolidating. According to the Association, advertisers still see newspaper as more time efficient and effective than other media. Newspapers still reach more people than the internet. On a typical day, newspapers reach 20% more people worldwide than the internet. However, despite this digital advertising revenues are not compensating for the advertising revenues lost to print. The report suggests that social media are changing the concept and process of content gathering and dissemination. But the revenue model for news companies, in the social media arena, remains hard to find.

Source: World Association of Newspapers and News Publishers (www.wan-ifra.org)

Magazines have a number of similar advantages to newspapers (portability, ability to handle complexity, consumption choices, credibility, etc.) but generally have a much longer shelf life and an audience generally larger than the number of copies sold (i.e. multiple readership). The production qualities are generally considerably higher than with newspapers, consequently lead times are usually longer (although, again, digital presses have had a considerable impact). Dominant publications in the 1960–1980 period were often general interest, wide-circulation magazines such as the *Radio Times* and *Woman's Own*. Although general interest magazines still exist, many magazines today reflect particular interests and lifestyles, making them better vehicles for targeting (e.g. *Hallo, OK, Heat, Zoo, Nuts*, etc.). As with newspapers, magazines have been threatened by the internet. Indeed, many so-called magazines are now only available through the online medium. Even traditional children's comics are feeling the challenge of the internet (see Insight).

 insight: Desperate times for Desperate Dan

Desperate Dan was once the star of the world's best-selling comic book, the man who could 'chew iron and spit rust'. He even sunk U-boats with a peashooter and sailed off into the sunset with the Spice Girls. But this is the end of the line for Desperate Dan in traditional comic format. After 75 years of service to children, the *Dandy* ceased as a printed comic and went online on 4 December 2012. At its height in the 1950s, it sold 2 million copies a week but that was now down to around 8,000 so publishers *D.C. Thomson* bowed to the inevitable. The final issue features a cameo from Sir Paul McCartney, who said in 1963 it was his ambition to appear in the comic, and a pull-out of the first issue from 4 December 1937. The first online issue was free of charge, with following issues being priced at £1.49. A yearly subscription for the digital comic is, at the time of writing, £29.99, while access to the website is free.

OTHER MEDIA

RADIO

Radio was the driving force behind marketing in the USA in the 1930s and 1940s with sponsored programming and **spot advertising**. In Europe too, commercial stations grew in popularity pre and post the Second World War. In the UK, however, commercial radio stations were banned until 1973 when *LBC* became the first radio station (and *Bird's Eye* the first advertiser) to broadcast legally. However, many British listeners were exposed to radio advertising prior to that date. *Radio Normandy* and *Radio Luxembourg* broadcast from the continent in the 1940s and 1950s with adverts including the popular (*Ovaltine*-sponsored) 'Ovaltinees'. In the 1960s, so-called pirate radio stations, for example *Radio Caroline*, transmitted from off-shore vessels, also funded

Spot advertising
Advertising placed during or between broadcast programmes, typically lasting between 30 seconds and one minute.

by advertising. Although these stations were frequently closed down by the authorities, their popularity eventually created the pressure required to lift the ban on commercial radio.

In 2012/13, radio represented around 5.5% of advertising spend in the UK, a little below where it stood five years before that (5.9% in 2008). Among the advantages of radio are that it is relatively low cost, it is a portable medium and (because of the targeted audiences) can be usefully segmented.

In addition to geographical targeting (for example, through *Galaxy* in Yorkshire and *Real Radio* in Central Scotland), most radio stations limit their musical and/ or spoken output to attract specific audiences (for example, *FXM, Magic, Classic FM*, etc.). Production costs are a fraction of those for television and lead times are shorter.[1] In addition, radio (unlike visual media) enables the individual listener to create pictures in their own minds – a device used extensively by both radio programme producers and advertisers. On the other hand, radio lacks the impact of television as it is frequently no more than 'aural wallpaper' alongside other activities (driving, working, cooking, etc.). As such, it does not have the prestige of other media. However, commercial radio does still reach 64% of the UK population (see Table 8.1) and, despite any perceived failings, major companies such as *Unilever, News International, Volkswagen* and *Vodafone* still use radio extensively and find it a cost-effective medium for getting more out of their media budgets.

TELEVISION

It was the advent of television in the USA that rapidly expanded the platform for advertising in that country. The first television advertisement was broadcast there on 1 July 1941. In the UK, however, commercial television was late arriving, coming more than a decade after North America on 21 September

CPT/CPM
Cost per thousand – a calculation based on advertising costs x 1000, divided by circulation or target audience circulation.

TABLE 8.1   UK commercial radio statistics 2011

Total number of commercial radio stations	305
Total number of local stations	212
Total number of stations in England	239
Total number of stations in Scotland	39
Total number of stations in Wales	16
Total number of stations in Northern Ireland	11
Total number of ethnic minority stations	32
Total commercial radio reach (all adults)*	64%
Total number of commercial radio listeners*	33 million
Total number of hours listened to every week*	444 million

* *Source:* Rajar (www.rab.co.uk)

---

[1]   Particularly since the introduction of *J-ET*an electronic web-based advertising trading system that carries 90% of all UK radio advertising revenue.

1955.[2] The costs associated with television advertising are high but the **CPT**[3] (cost per thousand, in terms of audience exposure) is generally low because of the large audiences some stations and programmes attract. For example, the cost of a spot advert lasting 30 seconds during the televising of the 2012 US *Superbowl* was $3.5 million but it did reach an audience of perhaps 110 million viewers (according to ESPN). Advertising is normally carried on commercial stations (hence '**commercials**' are the alternate name for broadcast advertising). In Europe, however, many public-funded stations also carry a (sometimes restricted) amount of advertising while in the UK the BBC is still free from advertising (except for self-promotion).[4]

The main advantages associated with television are the visuals and sound that can be harnessed to produce a powerful and prestigious message. It can also be a good medium for demonstrations but not, given the time restraints, for complex explanations. A high amount of repetition is also necessary if the message is to become memorable.

Television was the dominant medium in the second half of the twentieth century and attracted around 26% of UK advertising spend in 2011/12. Although this is considerably down on the position a decade ago, advertisers continue to invest in TV campaigns, with UK '**adspend**' up 1.9% in 2011 to £4.16 billion. Total TV spend increases by a further £224 million once sponsorships, including branded content and product placements, are taken into account.

TV advertising may continue to be influential for some time yet, despite the problems associated with the traditional 'spot advertising' format. The introduction of the handset made changing channels during a commercial break (**zapping**) much easier, and evidence from the USA suggests that one-third of the potential advertising audience is lost to zapping activity (Shimp 2010). The introduction of pre-recordable videos and latterly satellite and free-to-air decoders (such as *Skybox* and *Freeview*) has led to an increase in **zipping** (the fast-forwarding of commercials during pre-recorded programmes), again enabling viewers to bypass spot advertising.

In an attempt to beat the zippers and zappers and in recognition of the growing power of the internet, the US television station *ABC* announced in April 2006 that it would make key programmes available on the internet the day after broadcast, paid for by advertisements from organisations such as *AT&T, Ford, Procter & Gamble* and *Unilever*. In the UK, *ITV Player* and *4 on Demand* similarly offer access to programmes that have already been broadcast, complete with advertising. While customers will be able to pause, rewind and fast-forward the episodes, they will not be able to skip the adverts which will be incorporated in custom-made interactive slots (Curtis 2006).

DIRECT MAIL AND TELEMARKETING

Direct mail (traditional 'snail mail' or electronic mail) and **telemarketing** are associated closely with direct marketing and are covered in more detail in Chapter 13, together with **direct response** media such as television (dedicated channels such as *QVC*, as well as 'spot' advertising) and **off-the-page**. Although direct mail can be a highly creative and flexible medium, it has been criticised for being **junk mail** (or

Commercial
A television or radio advertisement (also known as an advert or ad).

Adspend
The total advertising spend.

Zapping
Changing channel during a television commercial break.

Zipping
The fast-forwarding of pre-recorded programmes, enabling viewers to bypass the advertising.

Direct mail
Advertising, through the medium of the mail, to targeted, profiled customers.

Telemarketing
The use of telephony to maintain a relationship with your customers.

Direct response
Media where the customer can respond immediately to the offer.

Off the page
Newspaper or magazine offers with a direct-response mechanism (e.g. freephone, envelope, etc.).

Junk mail
Any mailing the customer decides is untargeted and obtrusive.

---

2   Although the British Broadcasting Corporation (BBC) began a regular, non-commercial service in 1936.
3   Also called CPM where 'M' is the Latin representation of 1000.
4   BBC Worldwide, transmitted outside of the UK, does carry advertising.

Spam
Unsolicited, untargeted emails usually sent out in bulk.

Door to door
The household delivery of leaflets, samples, etc.

with email **spam**) and having an image that the industry finds difficult to shake off. Telemarketing too is regarded as an effective but highly intrusive medium. Other direct marketing techniques (including **door-to-door** leafleting or inserts) can be effective in support of other media-led campaigns, particularly when the objective is the trial of a new brand or brand extension. In general terms, one of the most difficult issues is that of data protection. As a medium that relies on data, recent legislation has made data acquisition more difficult and data storage more restrictive.

INTERNET/WORLD WIDE WEB[5]

Nielsen UKOM data for 2012 shows that approximately 40 million people in the UK (out of a total of 62 million) used the internet every month and that some websites (for example, *Google, Facebook* and *MSN*) attracted audiences of over 25 million people each month, offering advertisers and other commercial messengers the ability to reach a huge proportion of the population through a single medium. It is not then a surprise that in 2009 the UK became the first major economy where advertisers spent more on internet advertising than on television advertising, with a record £1.75 billion online spend in the first six months of that year (versus £1.05 billion for television) (according to *The Guardian*, 30 September 2009). In 2012, the UK total online advertising spend was $8.64 billion and it was forecast to rise to $12.19 billion by 2016.

Banner ad
A vertical or horizontal website advertisement.

Pop-up
A message box that 'pops up' on websites, either to add additional information or as advertising.

Click-through rate
The number of times online users 'click through' or transfer to sponsored websites.

Early use of the internet as a commercial medium was not wholly successful. Initially, much of the advertising was on static **banner ads** or **pop-ups** and their value was questionable. Back in the days of the notorious '12k gif banner advert' there were lots of restrictions in available space, in the amount of animation and even in the number of colours that could be used. According to a study by *MSN*, recall of this type of advertising was even lower than that of mass-market television. According to *Nielsen/Net Ratings*, the **click-through rate** on banner advertising in 2001 was less than half of one per cent (Shimp 2010).

Cookie
A small text file left on the user's computer that identifies their browser so that they are 'recognised' when they revisit a site.

As the technology has developed, so have the commercial opportunities. More targeted advertising, driven by **cookie**-enabled technology, decidedly improved the effectiveness of online promotion. Internet advertising today enables targeting on many levels including:

Frequency-capped
Regulation of the number of times an advert is shown online in a particular period.

- demographic – by sex, age or location
- contextual – related to what a customer is looking at or looking for
- content – based around a specific piece of content such as video
- behavioural – based on previous interests or preferences.

The *Internet Advertising Bureau (IAB)* (2012) estimates that 13.5% of online advertising is now brand-based rather than direct response – an increase of 200% between 2008 and 2011. This may be associated with the introduction of online video content which has provided advertisers with opportunities for brand-based advertising normally associated with television. Online advertising can also be '**frequency capped**', such that users only see messages a certain number of times, increasing the efficiency of budgets, maximising campaign reach and reducing user frustration caused by seeing the same adverts again and again.

Social media
Online media primarily for social interaction, using highly accessible publishing techniques.

Social media or social networking sites are a relatively new phenomenon even in relation to the internet. *Facebook*, for example, only dates from 2004 although, by the end of that year, it had 1 million users. In 2012, it exceeded 1 billion active

---

[5]   See Chapter 20 for the distinction between these terms.

clients. Social networking sites include those sites that are defined as applications that enable users to connect with each other by creating personal information profiles. Users then invite friends and colleagues to have access to these profiles, thus enabling the sending of emails and instant messages between each other. These personal profiles can include any type of information, including photos, video, audio files and blogs. Other sites enable interaction through messaging sites (e.g. *Twitter*) or blogs.

Social media sites have long been seen as having a value in commercial terms but a number of issues have become evident. Notable is the objection of users of such sites to commercialisation. This has not stopped brands seemingly rushing to develop their presence on such sites. Paid-for advertising on social media sites has likewise been slow to become mainstream. Despite this, *Facebook*'s advertising revenue grew from $777 million in 2009 to $3.7 billion in 2011, and in the first quarter of 2012 was more than $1 billion. Social media marketing, it is said, provides organisations with a way to connect with their customers. However, organisations must protect their information, as well as closely watch comments and concerns on the social media they use. The dangers include employees sharing too much information in public forums, loss or exposure of confidential information, and increased exposure to litigation. It may also be interesting to note that according to research by *Associated Press/CNBC* in 2012, half of those polled believe *Facebook* is a passing fad (according to www.businessinsider.com).

Search engines are also becoming highly influential with companies looking for priority information retrieval based on specific keywords. So important have search engines such as *Google, Yahoo* and *Bing* become that **search engine optimisation** (SEO) has become a marketing specialisation in its own right. The earlier or higher ranked something is on a search results page and the more frequently a site appears, the more visitors it is likely to receive from the search engine's users. The importance of SEO is associated with the way that search engines work. **Crawling** is the name given to the process by *Google*. Search engines use computers to fetch (or 'crawl') billions of pages on the web. The program that does the fetching is called Googlebot (also known as a robot, bot or spider). Googlebot uses an algorithmic process and computer programmes determine which sites to crawl, how often and how many pages to fetch from each site. SEO may target different kinds of search, including image search, local search, video search, academic search, news search and industry-specific vertical search engines. In order to maximise your presence online, you will need to pay attention to:

- **content:** the keywords and key phrases that are most relevant to your site
- **link building:** the number of inbound links from other websites suggests the level of popularity which, in turn, is regarded as highly relevant by search engines
- **backlinking:** submission to directories and link pages, done in order to build the optimum number of backlinks to a site.

Search engine
A web-based information retrieval system.

Search engine optimisation (SEO)
The means by which the website owner can manipulate a site in such a way as to maximise the number of retrievals and page ranking of that site.

Crawling
The name given to the way the Google search engine builds profiles of web pages.

Content
The keywords or key phrases relevant to a site; also called key words.

Link building
The building of inbound links from other websites to increase relevance to search engines.

Backlinking
Submission to directories and link pages.

Paid placement
Where advertisers who pay receive priority placement from search engines.

Contextual advertising
A form of targeted advertising appearing on websites or other media, selected and displayed by automatic systems based on the content on display to the user.

Paid inclusion
Also known as sponsored listings, it is a service where the search engine company charges fees for the inclusion of websites in their search index.

In addition to offering search facilities, most search engines also offer **paid placements**, **contextual advertising** and **paid inclusions** (or sponsored listings) to further ensure that their clients' brands are visible to searchers.

MOBILE TECHNOLOGY

Mobile telephones are being extensively used as the medium of choice for participating in competitions or to obtain further product or service information. In May 2011, 21.3 million people in the UK used the mobile internet each month and 19.8 million used **apps** (software applications). The availability of a wide range of apps offers both brand-building and advertising opportunities. Many organisations offer the (usually free) download of their app to customers or clients. Free games and information-related apps are funded by advertising. According to the *IAB* (2012), 30% of all *Google* restaurant searches were made via internet-enabled mobile devices. Likewise, 17% of automobile searches and 16% of consumer electronics queries were made on mobiles. Importantly, not only are consumers surfing on their mobile, but they are also actually buying. *IAB* (2012) research shows that 51% of UK mobile phone owners have engaged with purchases online.

⊙ insight: The smartphone revolution

- The first smartphone was launched by IBM in 1993. It acted as a pager, e-mailer, calendar, address book, calculator and sketchpad. The retail price was $899.00.

- British 18–24-year-olds lead the world in accessing social networks by phone and tablet; 62% access them daily.

- Apple iPhone users are the biggest mobile gamers.

- Two-thirds of smartphone users sleep with their phone next to them and look at it first thing in the morning and last thing at night.

- The average UK consumer sends 50 texts per week.

Source: *Marketing*, May/June 2013

App
A software application, typically of a small, specialised programme available to download onto mobile devices such as mobile telephones, personal computers and tablets.

Gross rating points (GRPs)
An advertising media currency calculated by multiplying 'reach' and 'frequency'.

MEDIA MANAGEMENT

Selecting the right medium for the message depends on individual medium characteristics. Each has advantages and disadvantages and the skill in media management is to find the most effective way to fulfil the communications objective. Although simplistic, Figure 8.1 suggests that various media, given their particular strengths and weaknesses, are more effective than others, as determined by their contribution to fulfilling 'hierarchy of effects' objectives.

Media planners and buyers must also know not only which media might be effective but how many of the target audience they might reach, how many times and the costs associated with this. To do this they use a form of currency to describe the 'value' of each internet placement, radio or television slot or publication space. These are usually termed **gross rating points**[6] **(GRPs)** and are calculated by multiplying two measures – reach and frequency (see box 8.5):

---

[6]   In the UK television industry, GRPs are normally referred to as TVRs (television rating points).

FIGURE 8.1   Media influences

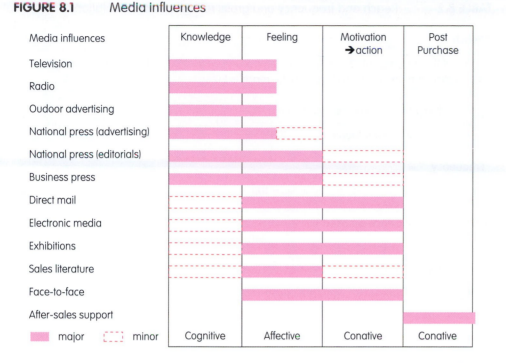

- reach: the percentage of the target audience exposed at least once to the message during a period (normally four weeks)
- frequency: the number of times (on average) the target audience has the **opportunity to see (OTS)** the message.

'Reach' is an important consideration because it reflects the ability to get through to the target audience. However, on its own it only gives us an insight into who might be exposed; it does not help us understand how frequently they need to see the communication for it to be effective. 'Frequency' takes us a step closer and is not just about getting the prospective customer to see one media type (e.g. a particular television advertisement), but also about reaching them through alternative channels or media. Media buyers, therefore, buy space or time in overlapping media to increase the frequency. But what is the ideal frequency? In the early 1970s, Herbert Krugman (1972) presented a paper in the *Journal of Advertising Research* that suggested only three exposures might be needed: the first initiating the response 'What is it?', the second 'What of it?' and the third, and those thereafter, were simply reminders of the first two exposures. An alternative approach to estimating effective frequency is the **Efficiency Index**. This assumes that with each exposure there is a greater chance of reaching and influencing an audience – up to a point. After this point is reached, an exposure no longer adds reach or improves effectiveness. The difficulty in quantifying when the point is reached still makes this an imperfect concept and it is effectively left to the experience of the media buyer as the final decision maker on the length of exposure.

Gross rating points (GRPs), although a product of reach and frequency, are the currency used by media buyers if frequency, distribution and reach figures are not available. For example, GRPs are assigned to a 'spot' by media researchers (e.g. *Nielsen Media Research*). **Target rating points (TRPs)** are a variation of GRPs whose points have been adjusted to reflect the chosen target audience. Media buyers make media purchases by deciding how many GRPs

Opportunities to see (OTS)
A calculation of the number of times the target audience has a chance to see (or hear) an advertisement.

Efficiency Index
An index which assumes that with each exposure of an advertisement there is a greater chance of reaching and influencing an audience – up to a point. After this point is reached, each exposure no longer adds 'reach' or improves effectiveness.

Target rating points (TRPs)
A variation of gross ratings points adjusted to reflect the chosen target audience.

TABLE 8.2   Reach and frequency and gross ratings points calculations

Reach

If 75% of the audience of 12 million *Coronation Street* viewers are C_2DE and the total C_2DE in this particular market is 10 million, then the reach is 80%

$$\text{Reach} - \frac{(\text{No. of target viewers}) \times 100}{(\text{Size of taget market})} = \frac{80 \times 100}{100} = 80$$

Frequency

10% of target audience exposed 10 times = 100
25% of target audience exposed 7 times = 175
65% of target audience exposed 1 time   = 65

$\qquad\qquad\qquad\qquad\qquad\qquad 340 \div 100 \quad = 3.4$

Gross ratings points

GRPs = Reach x Frequency = 80 x 3.4 = 272

or TRPs are required to fulfil objectives. In 2012, *Nielsen* launched a campaign ratings service for online advertisers using GRPs as its major metric.

The cost of space or time in particular media is determined by a number of factors, including the size and nature of the audience and what the rest of the market is prepared to pay (Brierley 2002). In the UK, the publication *British Rates and Data (BRAD)* is the media buyers' reference book as it lists circulation/audience figures, **Rate Card** costs,[7] deadlines and other mechanical data (column sizes, etc). Expenditure is expressed as a 'cost-per-thousand' (CPT or CPM) of consumers reached by a particular medium. Some CPT rates include weightings for such things as colour, quality of editorial, etc. There is also an important distinction to be made between the actual CPT and the CPT for reaching a particular target audience.

Choices also need to be made regarding **scheduling**. Is it to be a short, sharp campaign, relatively continuous or any of the myriad of combinations in between? Choices include the:

- **burst**: concentrating the 'spend' on a short period to raise awareness and increase reach
- **drip**: extending the campaign over time which increases potential frequency; this is often used for '**reminder campaigns**' or when an objective is to change long-term attitudes
- **continuous**: relatively even expenditure over the period
- **pulsing**: continuous campaigning which is higher at different times of the year and which may reflect seasonal considerations
- **flighting**: expenditure concentrated on some periods, leaving other periods with zero expenditure.

As noted previously, online advertising can be 'frequency capped', such that users only see messages a certain number of times, increasing the efficiency of budgets, maximising campaign reach and reducing user frustration.

One approach to scheduling proposed by Erwin Ephron, a New York media specialist, is the **recency principle** (or shelf-space model) (Shimp 2010). This principle

---

[7]   Although the costs shown on rate cards are published, these are usually highly flexible.

FIGURE 8.2   Scheduling

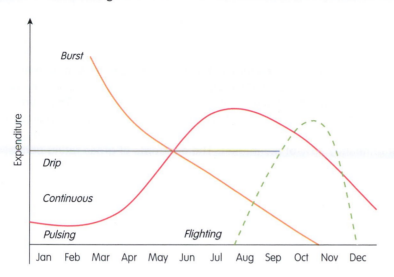

reflects what is known as the **'weak theory' of advertising**, discussed further in Chapter 9. The 'weak theory' questions the power of advertising to persuade (as suggested by the **strong theory**), proposing instead that it acts more as a reminder or gentle nudge toward a particular brand than a highly influential force. The recency principle supposes that:

- a consumer's first exposure to an advertisement is the most powerful
- an advertiser's primary role is to influence brand choice (when the customer is ready to buy)
- achieving a high level of weekly reach for a brand should be emphasised over acquiring heavy frequency.

Although the first exposure may be the most powerful, one exposure is probably not enough. However, short-term additional exposure is likely to be wasted on those consumers not in the market for the product or service. This suggests a continuous or near-continuous presence where advertising is used to remind, reinforce or evoke earlier messages rather than teach consumers about benefits or uses. The objective is to reach as high a percentage of the target market audience as possible for as long a period as is practical.

Another approach in media planning is that known as **media-neutral planning**. This is where market communicators see media planning from the consumer's perspective (see case study at the end of this chapter), rather than base media selection on traditional criteria. Media-neutral evaluation is not straightforward as it means using qualitative research to understand the target audience and to understand how they interact. In theory, agencies should be assessing all media but many are not designed to be neutral because of the structure of the industry, agency remuneration and long-term habitual behaviour. *Networked Insights* is an online research company, funded by Goldman Sachs, that enables networks and brands to more accurately understand how consumers are responding to advertising and media.

Despite the various theories available, decision making is frequently down to the media buyer's experience, industry case studies and, above all, an intuitive understanding of the marketplace.

Weak theory of advertising
Sees advertising power as much more benign than the 'strong theory of advertising'. It questions the power of advertising to persuade, suggesting instead that it acts more as a reminder or gentle nudge toward a particular brand than as a highly influential force.

Strong theory of advertising
Where advertising is presumed to have the power to inform, persuade and sell.

Media-neutral planning
A customer-focused review of media based on research, analysis and insight and not on habit and/or preference.

summary

This chapter looked at the media available to marketers and media management. Although the chapter largely concentrated on advertising, these media are available to the whole gamut of communications tools including public relations, sponsorship, sales promotions and personal selling. There are dangers of dismissing 'old media' (for example, print, radio and television) in favour of digital despite the growth in that area. Currently, UK internet advertising spend is around 25% of the total, leaving the more traditional outlets with a not unhealthy 75% of the market. The concepts of gross rating points, reach and frequency were covered and the merits of burst, drip, continuous, pulsing and flighting scheduling discussed, as was the recency principle and media-neutral planning.

review questions

1. What are the positive and negative characteristics of television, radio and online media?

2. What changes have affected the newspaper industry in the past few decades?

3. What is the Efficiency Index?

4. What scheduling opportunities are available to media planners?

5. What is the difference between 'frequency' and 'reach' in assessing media?

6. What are gross rating points (GRPs)?

7. What is the recency principle?

8. Explain the term 'media-neutral planning'.

discussion questions

1. Is social media a real revolution in marketing communications?

2. Is there a future for print media?

3. Is there any need to segment and target customers when search engine technology is available?

case study 8.1: Super Bowl advertising

The Super Bowl has always been an advertising phenomenon. In 2014, advertisers shelled out a record $4 million for a 30-second commercial during the contest. Afterwards, the media world held its breath to see how the commercials went over with TV audiences. The 2014 NFL season finale ended up being the biggest to date. An average 112.2 million viewers tuned in to see the Seattle Seahawks destroy the

Denver Broncos, making it the most watched Super Bowl and the most watched television programme in US history.

During the match, *Networked Insights Inc.* analysed more than 25 million consumer conversations that took place across the web. Sources included social network sites *Twitter* and *Facebook*, comment sections in *YouTube, Wordpress* and *Disqus*, along with millions of blogs and forums. Real-time analysis of consumer conversations indicated that *esurance, T-Mobile* and *H&M* were most talked about but only *esurance* made it into the top three in 'net sentiment' – the balance between favourable and less favourable comment. The top three were *Budweiser* (+26%), *esurance* (+25%) and *Maserati* (+23%).

Family differences were analysed. Fathers preferred *Bank of America* and *T-Mobile* while mothers, perhaps surprisingly, put *Budweiser, Jaguar* and *Axe* (*Lynx*) in the top three places. More predictably, 'Generation X' (those born from the 1960s to the early 1980s) preferred the *esurance* advertisement.

Celebrity endorsement played its part. *H&M* used David Beckham to front its offering while Quvenzhane Wallis headlined the *Maserarti* advert; 35% and 38% of viewers, respectively, said these adverts were their favourites. Other celebrities included Bruce Willis (*Honda*), Arnold Schwarzenegger (*Bud Light*), Bono (*Bank of America*) and Scarlett Johansson (*SodaStream*). The latter advert for the Israel-based in-home soda machine manufacturer was initially banned by Fox because it contained the line 'Sorry Coke and Pepsi', both of which are heavy sponsors of the Super Bowl. In the end, *SodaStream* removed the offending line and the edited version was shown. That was not the end of the story though as Johansson was subsequently attacked for severing her ties with the humanitarian group *Oxfam International*, who criticised her endorsement of *SodaStream*, which operates in an Israeli settlement in the West Bank, a territory captured by Israel in 1967 and claimed by the Palestinians.

Another Super Bowl controversy was associated with *Coca-Cola*. Toward the end of the first half, *Coca-Cola* premiered an advert called 'It's beautiful', featuring the hymn 'America the beautiful' sung in seven different languages. It immediately caused outrage on *Twitter*: hash tags like #SpeakAmerican were instantly trending, commenting on the 'unpatriotic' nature of the advert.

All in all, the 2014 Super Bowl was probably more exciting from a competitive advertising perspective than for the one-sided match on the field.

Case study questions

1. What does the above case study say about celebrity endorsement in advertising?
2. What, if any, is the value of 'net sentiment' over other measures?
3. 'All publicity is good publicity' is an old adage in the publicity sector. Do you believe that the adverse publicity will help or hurt *SodaStream* and *Coca-Cola*?

 **further reading**

Berglind, M. and Nakata, C. (2005) 'Cause-related marketing: more buck than bang?', *Business Horizons*, 48 (5): 443–53.

Hanna, R., Rohm, A. and Crittenden, V.L. (2011) 'We're all connected: the power of the social media ecosystem', *Business Horizons*, 54 (3): 265–73.

(Continued)

(Continued)

Holm, H. (2006) 'Integrated marketing communication: from tactics to strategy', *Corporate Communications: An International Journal*, 11 (1): 23–33.

Krieger, A.M. and Green, P.E. (2006) 'A tactical model for resource allocation and its application to advertising budgeting', *European Journal of Operational Research*, 170 (3): 935–49.

Percy, L. (2006) 'Are product placements effective?', *International Journal of Advertising*, 25 (1): 112–14.

Walker, L. (2014) 'Helping students understand the relevance of social media tools to marketing practitioners', *The Marketing Review*, 14(1).

REFERENCES

Brierley, S. (2002) *The Advertising Handbook*. London: Routledge.

Curtis, J. (2006) 'Revenue channels', *Marketing*, 20 April, p. 15.

Internet Advertising Bureau (IAB) (2012) IAB Internet Advertising Revenue Report. Available at: www.iab.net/insights_research/industry_data_and_landscape/adrevenuereport

Krugman, H.E. (1972) 'Why three exposures may be enough', *Journal of Advertising Research*, 12 (6): 11–14.

Shimp, T.A. (2010) *Advertising, Promotion and Supplemental Aspects of Integrated Marketing Communication*, 8th edn. Cincinnati, OH: Thomson Learning.

USEFUL WEBSITES

For examples of spectacular poster designs, go to: www.tutorialchip.com/inspiration/30-truly-dramatic-examples-of-advertising-poster-designs/

For further details on billboards, see: www.oohinternational.co.uk/billboard-advertising/billboards

For billboard poster sizes, see: www.vinyl-banners.co.uk/billboard_poster_sizes.htm

For the *British Airways* Jessica Ennis image, see: www.dailymail.co.uk/news/article-2159373/London-2012-Olympics-Jessica-Ennis-painted-field-near-Heathrow-airport.html

For more on radio advertising, see: www.rab.co.uk/radio-basics/seven-reasons-using-radio/

For additional materials that support this chapter and your learning, please visit: **study.sagepub.com/egan**

ADVERTISING 9

LEARNING OBJECTIVES

Having completed this chapter, readers would be expected to:

- understand how advertising developed and the part it played in creating modern consumer markets

- recognise and describe the strong and weak theories of advertising

- discuss the means by which the advertising industry measures effectiveness and the problems associated with such measurements

- describe those characteristics of good advertising

- understand how advertising standards are maintained

- discuss the factors currently affecting the advertising industry.

INTRODUCTION

Advertising, it has been suggested, is the world's second oldest profession. Certainly, as Chapter 1 illustrated, it can be traced back to the Babylonian, Greek and Roman civilisations. Up until the mid-nineteenth century, the term advertising was used to refer to any and all forms of promotional activity. However, by the twentieth century it came to be more narrowly defined by academics in such a way as to differentiate it from sales promotion. Thus, it may be described as a **paid-for, non-personal form of mass communication from an identified source, used to communicate information and influence consumer behaviour.**

This also differentiates advertising from public relations or general publicity as it implies paying to place your message, constructed wholly to promote your product or service, in the media (and the position in that media) of your choice. Advertising is also seen as non-personal (or untargeted) as it is directed through the mass media at groups of consumers rather than at individuals and from an identified source whose product or service is being selectively promoted.

THE GROWTH OF ADVERTISING

Advertising developed considerably in the three hundred years prior to the twentieth century. The late 1700s through to the twentieth century was an era when mechanisation and factory systems revolutionised industrial output. Mass production demanded mass consumption through mass distribution to mass markets. Prior to the Industrial Revolution, trade in other than basic commodities was largely the preserve of the rich. Most goods were produced locally in quantities suitable for local consumption. With the Industrial Revolution came enormous increases in supply. As we have seen in Chapter 1, advertising essentially emerged as a means of getting an over-production of goods to the wider market with money to spend. The underlying problem it was addressing, therefore, was that of under-consumption and so advertising was not acting as a mechanism for satisfying wants, as it is seen today. Instead it was concerned with creating that want.

One of the first manufacturers to try to expand his potential market through advertising was Josiah Wedgwood, the founder of the pottery *Wedgwood*, who in the late 1700s began to target the growing middle classes through newspaper advertisements, posters, handbills and shop signs. Other manufacturers of pioneering branded goods also began to recognise the value of advertising, seeing its potential in a number of areas, including:

- giving information to the consumer
- compensating for any weaknesses in wholesalers
- boosting sales efforts in the retail trade
- attacking competitive brands
- keeping aggressive rivals at bay.

The ability to mass-produce goods at a vastly reduced cost ensured that they were affordable to a great many more people and advertising was the means by which their availability would be made known to the public at large. Indeed, advertising has been credited as one of the main economic factors driving consumer spending and economic growth for the best part of two centuries. According to Franklin D. Roosevelt (1882–1945): 'The general raising of the standards of modern civilisation among all groups of people during the past half century would have been impossible without the spreading of the knowledge of higher standards by means of advertising.'

HOW ADVERTISING WORKS

There are countless models and theories which purport to suggest why advertising may work. There are, however, broadly two main perspectives. In the first, the **strong theory** of advertising, it is presumed to have the power to inform, persuade and sell. This is the traditional viewpoint taken by practitioners (and many academics) over the past hundred or more years. Under the 'strong' theory, advertising was seen as an almost irresistible force driving consumption. Such was the belief in the power of advertising that it often attracted hostile criticism. C.P. Snow, speaking in a debate broadcast by the BBC in 1936, claimed:

Strong theory (of advertising)
Suggests that advertising has the power to inform, persuade and sell products, services or ideas.

> I see modern advertising as an attempt to impel people to buy what, if it were not for the advertisement, they would never think of buying. Advertising begins by taking our money and ends by depriving us of our freedom. (cited in Nevett 1982)

The second theory sees advertising's power as being much more benign. The **weak theory** questions the power of advertising to persuade, suggesting instead that it acts more as a reminder or gentle nudge toward a particular brand.

Weak theory (of advertising)
Suggests that advertising can act as a reminder and/or nudge a consumer towards a brand or idea.

STRONG THEORY OF ADVERTISING

In Chapter 2, **hierarchy of effects** models were introduced. Hierarchy models are classically 'strong' theory models which suggest a rational, sequential approach to advertising. As noted previously, these models are some of the oldest of all marketing communications models with the first (AIDA) being published in 1898 and further developed by Strong in 1925. Their considerable influence on advertising lasted largely unchallenged at least until the 1980s, when opposition to the rigidity of the structure began to appear. It is arguable, however, that despite these challenges they are still not without influence today. The models purport to describe the outcomes of advertising. Take, for example, Colley's (1961) **DAGMAR** (standing for **D**efining **A**dvertising **G**oals for **M**easuring **A**dvertising **R**esults), a popular model developed in the 1960s, which was seen as a means of developing the objectives of an advertising campaign. Other models offered similar proposed insights (see Figure 9.1).

DAGMAR
A model promoted as a means of establishing the objectives of an advertising campaign (Colley 1961), standing for Defining Advertising Goals for Measuring Advertising Results.

FIGURE 9.1   Hierarchy of effects models

	KNOWLEDGE	FEELING	MOTIVATION →ACTION
AIDA Strong 1925	Attention Interest	Desire	Action
DAGMAR Colley 1961	Awareness Comprehension	Conviction	Purchase
Lavidge and Steiner 1961	Awareness Knowledge	Liking Preference	Conviction Purchase
Wells et al 1965	Awareness Perception Understanding		Persuasion
	COGNITIVE	AFFECTIVE	CONATIVE

Hierarchy of effects models imply that for advertising to be successful it must guide consumers usually from one stage (e.g. non-awareness) to another (e.g. awareness) and so on until the ultimate goal (the sale) is reached. These models, while using different terminology, were largely similar in construction, having cognitive (knowing), affective (feeling) and conative (motivational) dimensions (see Figure 9.1). The objective of any particular campaign (e.g. awareness) then determined the content and form of the advertisement.

Other 'strong' advertising models follow a similar linear development. One of the most widely used is the **cognitive response model**. This model (see Figure 9.2) maintains that exposure to advertising elicits different types of response and purports to suggest how these responses relate to attitudes and purchase intentions.

In the cognitive response model, the response to an advertising stimulus is one of three 'thought' processes. The first category (**product/message thoughts**) comprises those directed at the product/service and/or the claims made in the advertising.

Cognitive response model
A model that maintains that exposure to advertising elicits different types of response and purports to suggest how these responses relate to attitudes and purchase intentions (Belch & Belch 2011)

Product/message thoughts
Those thoughts directed at the product/service and/or the claims made in the advertising (see cognitive response model).

FIGURE 9.2   Cognitive response model

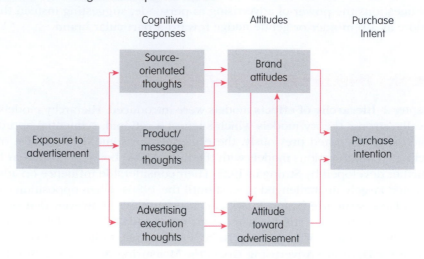

Second, **source-orientated thoughts** represent those associated (positively or negatively) with the origin of the message. **Advertising execution thoughts**, thirdly, relate to how favourably or unfavourably the messages are received. These in turn determine consumers' attitude toward the advertisement and the brand. Advertisers are particularly interested in consumers' attitudes to particular forms of advertising, as studies suggest (e.g. Ambler & Burne 1999) that people who show a positive response to an advert are more likely to purchase a product than those whose attitude is neutral. It is attitude which, this model suggests, affects purchase intentions.

These 'strong theory' models assume that advertising can ultimately persuade consumers to purchase a particular brand. It underwrites the view of many in the advertising industry that advertising is powerful and can have a substantial influence on the way consumers behave. As one prominent practitioner, John Bartle[1] (1999), suggests:

'I do not think it is too fanciful to talk of the best of advertising, with the greatest powers of transformation, as almost performing magic, turning the familiar and similar into the very special and unique.'

The problem with hierarchy of effects and other linear models is that there is very little evidence to show that they are in fact predictive. Indeed, they appear to be more descriptive of a few rare cases that are generalisable across all situations and have been heavily criticised as such.[2] One of the major realisations and a fundamental criticism is that there is no empirical evidence to actually support the argument that consumers pass through each stage in turn. The essence of a hierarchical model is this implied progression yet it is clear that influences can be cumulative and there will not only be intervention between stages but post-purchase experience will also be a factor. On this basis, one may have assumed that, as Crosier (1999) notes:

One might expect these theoretical shortcomings would inhibit practical application of the Hierarchy of Effects as a framework for decision making. On the contrary, case histories show that campaign objectives are repeatedly couched in (these) terms.

---

[1]   Founding partner of Bartle, Bogle, Hegarty, and President of the Institute of Practitioners in Advertising from 1995 to 1997.

[2]   See Crosier (1999) for a more detailed criticism of hierarchy of effects models.

Despite the evident shortcomings, there *are* some advantages in discussing the hierarchy of effects models and their alternatives (see Chapter 2). To begin with, it is possible to overlook issues of accuracy or predictive ability and draw out an acknowledgement of the importance of the brand. Such models may also help distinguish between the likely objectives (awareness, etc.) at each stage of a campaign. As Crosier (1999) notes, a 'deficient but codified basis for objective formulation is preferable to no common framework at all'. A third value of hierarchy models may be in exploring the relative importance of all the marketing communications tools (including advertising) at various times during the perceived process (see Figure 9.3). As noted in Chapter 2 (and illustrated in Figure 2.9), marketing communications tools are regarded as more or less effective depending on the objective(s) of the campaign. Advertising is seen to be most valuable in long-term brand building through the generation of awareness and interest but is seen to contribute less to the closing of a sale.

There is little doubt that advertising has contributed over time to the creation of very powerful brands such as *Nike, Coca-Cola, Microsoft, Sony* and *Vodafone,* nor that it has had a part to play in the development of the so-called consumer society. However, while it is clear that advertising can inform and contribute to a brand's image, its ability to persuade and/or to sell (particularly in the short term) is a more dubious claim. If there is any direct link between advertising and sales, it is typically delayed or lagged, particularly regarding goods or services that are infrequent purchases (e.g. insurance, vehicle sales, etc.).[3] Brierley (2002) suggests that, based on industry estimates, immediate response to an advertisement[4] is as little as 0.01%. If advertising is seen to be working in this situation, it must affect behaviour over time towards some future purchase. To illustrate this, consider an advert for any motor vehicle. It is highly unlikely that the advertising would generate an immediate, high level of response as the element of the market it can attract is restricted to those who are ready to buy. Other research into television advertising indicates the impact emerges typically within six months but this may be an over-simplification. Research by Schmit and Kaiser (2004) indicates

FIGURE 9.3   Perceived Influence of Advertising

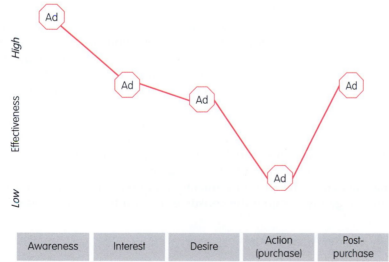

---

3   What we regard as **hard sell** (buy now while stocks last, etc.) type communications are not, arguably, advertising as such; rather, they have the features of sales promotion, where this is defined as the use of incentives to generate a specific (usually short-term) response.

4   This distinguishes between advertising as defined in this book and direct marketing which is sometimes called direct response advertising.

substantial elasticity between categories and brands. They propose that these elasticities indicate the response to advertising can be enhanced by targeting.

Although advertising may be inefficient in driving an immediate sale, it may become influential again after it. The suggestion is that in the post-purchase period there is a point when advertising can be used to bolster the customer's sense of satisfaction about the action or purchase (see also **cognitive dissonance**). The concept suggests that having made a decision to purchase a product or service (particularly where high cost and/or high salience are involved), the consumer looks for reasons to justify their buying decision (i.e. reassure them they have made the right decision), and that this may be found through advertising and some other communications tools (e.g. public relations).

In this 'limited benefits' model, advertising may be seen to be most effective when it is used to:

- stimulate interest and trial
- extol features and benefits (pre- and post-sale)
- create positive brand values and associations (pre- and post-sale)
- differentiate the brand from the competition (pre- and post-sale).

Cognitive dissonance
A situation involving conflicting attitudes, beliefs or behaviours that produces a feeling of discomfort, leading to an alteration in one of the attitudes, beliefs or behaviours to reduce the discomfort and restore cognitive balance.

WEAK THEORY OF ADVERTISING

Other authors see advertising as less powerful. One explanation for this may be because, although advertising allows for a high degree of control over the design and placement of a message, it is never either neutral or unbiased and, therefore, may suffer from a low degree of credibility unless accompanied by a high degree of (brand) trust. Most products and services are unlikely to be so highly trusted (although there are some notable exceptions). In addition it has been noted that, as the decades have gone by, consumers have become more sceptical and less trusting of advertising messages. In *Nielsen*'s Global Trust in Advertising and Brand Messages (April 2012), which is contributed to by more than 28,000 respondents in 56 countries, research showed that while nearly half of consumers around the world say they trust television (47%), magazine (47%) and newspaper advertising (46%), confidence declined by 24%, 20% and 25%, respectively, between 2009 and 2011. Advertising's potential for persuasion may, therefore, be continuing to wane.

With this in mind, researchers have proposed alternatives to hierarchy of effects models and other 'strong theories'. Ehrenberg and Goodhardt (1979), for example, suggest that the greater part of the buying experience is rooted in past experience, as indicated in their **ATR** (awareness, trial, reinforcement) **model** (see Figure 3.3 in Chapter 3). Having become aware of and eventually trialling a product or service, advertising acts to remind and reinforce the decision made. Ehrenberg (1997) was later to adapt this model further to suggest that the power of advertising was less in persuasion than gentle 'nudging' (see Figure 9.4). In this model, advertising stimulates trial and subsequently reinforces any positive associations with the brand, gently nudging the consumer toward that brand in the future.

ATR(N) model
A model that suggests that advertising may help awareness, trial and reinforcement, and may 'nudge' the consumer toward the brand.

FIGURE 9.4   The ATR(N) model

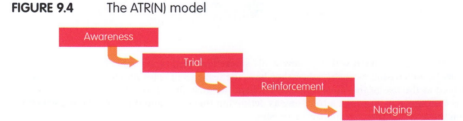

Ehrenberg also suggested that consumer purchasing behaviour can be described through statistical analysis in what he called 'negative binomial distribution' (more popularly known as '**double jeopardy**'). This theory suggests that advertising does not generally work to persuade as it fails to attract new buyers to a product or service, although it may help to keep existing purchasers 'loyal' by default. There is an appearance of brand loyalty because big brands are bought more often by more people and the number of consumers defecting to other brands is proportionately smaller for big brands than for small ones. The statistics suggest that the only way to increase brand loyalty is to create a bigger brand. This theory also extends to sales promotions as it suggests that short-term campaigns (such as 'buy one, get one free') have only a short-term impact and do not affect a brand's subsequent sales. The apparent new sales generated by the promotion are almost entirely to people who would have brought the product anyway.

Ehrenberg's (1997) ATR(N) theory appears to be a reasonable explanation for low-priced, fast-moving consumer goods (FMCG) brands, but what about products or services that consumers are unlikely to be able to trial (in the consuming sense), such as a new car or an expensive overseas holiday? In this respect, brand promises (claims associated with a particular brand) become important. These promises are communicated through advertising and may as such replace trial as the reason for including individual brands in the individual consumer's portfolio. This may also be particularly relevant when a new brand is introduced into a category or when a brand is re-launched (Jones 2004).

The 'weak' perspective also includes those who suggest that advertising helps maintain a brand within the consumer's repertoire of brands. This viewpoint is generally referred to as the '**portfolio**' or '**broad repertoire**' view. This perspective suggests that we each generate, through trial, a portfolio of brands from which we make our choice. Advertising keeps individual portfolio brands **front of mind** while the advertising (or promotion) of other brands may encourage us to try 'new' products which may or may not become part of our portfolio. Rossiter and Percy (1998) suggest that with new products that have been supported by heavy television advertising, such that 90% of the target audience have an **opportunity to see** the commercial, the advertiser might expect 60% to be attentive to the advertising, of which a third may be sufficiently impressed to consider sampling it, and the majority of which (70%) may trial purchase. From the original target audience, approximately 13% may reach the stage of trial purchasing. This supposition is illustrated in Figure 9.5. The similarity to the awareness loyalty scale in Figure 5.6 should also be noted.

Negative binomial distribution (or double jeopardy)
A theory that suggests that advertising does not generally work to persuade as it fails to attract new buyers to a product or service, although it may help to keep current purchasers 'loyal' by default.

Brand promises
The inherent promises associated with a brand regarding quality, reliability and other factors.

Portfolio or broad repertoire view
This perspective suggests that we each generate, through trial, a portfolio of brands from which we make our choice.

Front of mind
Where the brand is kept at the forefront of the consumer's mind through advertising and other marketing communications.

Opportunity to see (OTS)
The number of times a target consumer has to see (or hear) an advertisement.

FIGURE 9.5

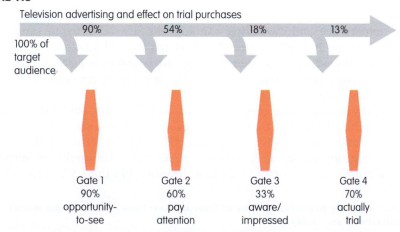

Television advertising and effect on trial purchases

100% of target audience

90%   54%   18%   13%

Gate 1   Gate 2   Gate 3   Gate 4
90%   60%   33%   70%
opportunity- pay   aware/   actually
to-see   attention   impressed   trial

Smith and Taylor (2004) take this portfolio theory a stage further by suggesting various levels of filtering out of brands before making the final purchasing decision, as illustrated in Figure 9.6.

FIGURE 9.6   Filtering brands

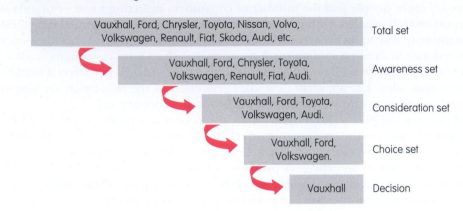

Vauxhall, Ford, Chrysler, Toyota, Nissan, Volvo, Volkswagen, Renault, Fiat, Skoda, Audi, etc.	Total set
Vauxhall, Ford, Chrysler, Toyota, Volkswagen, Renault, Fiat, Audi.	Awareness set
Vauxhall, Ford, Toyota, Volkswagen, Audi.	Consideration set
Vauxhall, Ford, Volkswagen.	Choice set
Vauxhall	Decision

Low-involvement theory
A theory that suggests that consumers scan the environment, largely subconsciously, to identify anything worth in-depth consideration.

Another concept associated with the portfolio or 'weak theory' viewpoint is **low-involvement theory**. Low-involvement processing is essentially the continual, regular and largely subconscious scanning of the environment in order to identify anything that might be worth considering in greater depth. For consumers, advertising serves to remind them of their preferred products, services and brands and to act as a post-purchase reassurance medium. Indeed, the majority of adverts actually reflect this view as they concentrate on talking points, either visual or verbal, and are designed to bring these to the fore with impact and in a creative way, rather than delivering strong selling propositions.

Weak theory, therefore, suggests that advertising works in the same way as strong theory in improving knowledge, but where it differs is that consumers are not only sceptical but thought to be selective in the way they decide which adverts they pay attention to and only acknowledge those which promote products that they either use or have some prior knowledge of. Consequently, advertising mainly supports existing buyers and helps to reinforce past sales and improve the pattern of repeat buying.

MEASURING ADVERTISING EFFECTIVENESS

Theories, experience and modelling can suggest how advertising should work but not always how it works in practice. Perhaps the old advertising adage[5] – 'I know that half my advertising doesn't work, the problem is I don't know which half' – sums up best the problem of accurately or even approximately measuring the effectiveness of advertising.

Day-after recall
(recall surveys)
Unprompted recall of the previous day's advertising, a methodology originally developed by Gallup in the 1930s.

The difficulty of measuring effectiveness has not, however, stopped the industry from developing the means by which to gauge advertising's contribution and using this as evidence of advertising effectiveness. In terms of the 'high-involvement' or strong model of advertising, recall has traditionally been the most popular measure. **Day-after recall** was first developed in the USA in the 1930s by

---

[5]   Attributed variously to Lord Leverhume of *Lever Brothers* (now *Unilever*), John Wannamaker, US retail tycoon, and Henry Ford.

George Gallup for *Procter & Gamble* but is still much in evidence today. With these **recall surveys**, respondents are asked what advertising they remember, as the understanding is that only advertising that has made a high impact will be recalled unprompted by the interviewee. Table 9.1 is an extract from recall research published weekly in the trade publication *Marketing*. In the 'adwatch' for this particular week in 2012, the Argos television advertisement was remembered (unprompted) by 62% of the respondents interviewed and as such has been judged to be very effective.

TABLE 9.1   *Adwatch:* The weekly analysis of advertisement recall (*Marketing,* 05/12/12)

	Account	Agency/TV buyer	%
Q: Which of the following TV commercials do you remember seeing?			
1	Argos	CHI & Partners/Mindshare	62
2	EE	Saatchi & Saatchi/MEC	60
3	Littlewoods	St Luke's/Carat	70
4	Apple iPad Mini	TBWA/Media Arts Lab	45
5=	Tesco	Wieden & Kennedy/Initiative	44
5=	Very.co.uk	St Luke's/Carat	44
7	DFS	Krow/MediaCom	43
8	eBay	TribalDDB/Carat	42
9	Febreze	Grey Dusseldorf/Starcom	41
10=	McDonald's	Leo Burnett/OMD UK	37
10=	Barnes & Nobel e-reader	Mullen/Initiative	37

In the 'low-involvement' model, advertising is believed to have made only a small impact and measurement may be sought through a **recognition survey** (i.e. a positive response to one or more of a selection of products presented to the interviewee). The thinking here is that as advertising only 'nudges' the consumer toward the brand, this may not be remembered unaided but will be remembered when the consumer is prompted.

Both recall and recognition testing are used to justify current and/or future campaign planning but are inherently flawed. The ability of a consumer to recall or recognise a brand does not mean that a respondent will ultimately buy that brand now or in the future. Brand awareness, recall or recognition, while being easy to measure precisely, is not directly associated with sales and might be said to be strictly an incorrect measure (it is, therefore, **precisely wrong**). On the other hand, actual sales directly related to advertising are almost impossible to gauge accurately (but if estimated based on past sales may be said to be **vaguely right**). Thus, we have allusions or indirect measures that serve mainly to remind both advertisers and their agencies that absolute dependence on recall of recognition can be misleading.

The contribution that advertising makes to sales can be approximated. This is normally achieved by calculating actual (advertising supported) sales against **simulated sales** (i.e. sales calculated on the basis of no advertising). The means used to establish the value of simulated sales are, however, largely subjective in that

Recognition survey
A survey which looks for a positive response to one or more of a selection of products presented to the interviewee.

Precisely wrong
Strictly a precise but incorrect measure. Proxy measures such as brand awareness, recall or recognition, while being easy to measure precisely are not directly associated with sales and might be said to be precisely wrong (see vaguely right).

Vaguely right
Actual sales directly related to advertising are almost impossible to gauge accurately but an estimation can be said to be vaguely right (see precisely wrong).

Simulated sales
Sales calculated on the basis of no advertising, which can then be used to measure the contribution of advertising.

Attitude scale
A scale that measures a respondent's attitude to pre-defined statements. Examples include nominal, ordinal, interval and ratio scales.

Rolling research (syndicated research or audit data)
Research carried out by specialist agencies who collect and analyse data on a regular (rolling research) or one-off basis. Clients normally pay a subscription for these services which are available for both retail (e.g. Nielsen) and specialist markets.

no established brand can truly be matched against an impartial control sample. With new introductions, however, the effect of advertising may be measured using different geographical regions and/or different media for the advertising against non-advertised control samples.

In the 1960s, new methods of measurement involving usage and attitude came to the fore. Rather than measuring the affect of advertising after a campaign has been launched, this suggested measuring consumer attitudes both before and after a campaign. One method is to use an **attitude scale**, as illustrated in the simplified example in Figure 9.7. A random selection of consumers are asked to rate each pair of statements to establish their attitude towards the brand. Following the campaign, the exercise is repeated, using the same or different random sample. The 'before' and 'after' scores show the change in attitude to the brand as a result of the campaign. Some companies (e.g. *Intel*) use **rolling research** of this type to monitor attitudes to their brand over time. Attitude research is, however, expensive and it is worth reiterating that a good attitude toward a brand, although desirable, does not necessarily lead to positive purchase behaviour.

FIGURE 9.7   Attitude scale

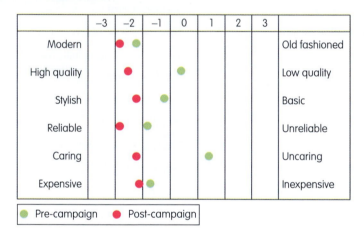

In summary, measuring the effectiveness of advertising continues to be a problem in the industry and, in a world of tighter budgets and the requirement to justify costs, this has contributed in no small part to the relative decline in the importance of advertising (see 'the advertising industry').

ADVERTISING CHARACTERISTICS

Whether working with the 'weak' or 'strong' theories of advertising, it is recognised that certain characteristics cause us to remember and empathise with some advertising messages over and above others. Any one advertisement has to compete with thousands of paid and other messages every day.[6] Unless your message catches sufficient of the target customers' (or other influencers') attention, and is relevant to them, it can be said to have been ineffective. Creating an advert with the power to do this requires creativity.

---

[6]   Yankelovich, a market research firm, estimates that a person living in a city 30 years ago saw up to 2,000 ad messages a day, compared with up to 5,000 by 2007.

Creativity in advertising is the ability to attract and hold the attention of the target audience through the manner and composition of the advertisement. It is an art and not a science (although the industry has built up a body of knowledge on what is likely to be successful) and can be affected by a myriad of factors, each of which can make or break the creative effect.

To begin with, however, the product or service has got to have merit and this has long been recognised. As Marcel Bleusteun-Blanchet, founder in 1926 of the *Publicis* agency, once observed: 'you can't have good advertising for a bad product'. If it is a poor product, according to William Bernbach, another veteran of creative advertising: 'a great ad campaign will make a bad product fail faster'.

Advertising may prompt you to investigate but close examination (sampling, test-drive, etc.) of a poor (relative to price and function) product or service will restrict sales, whatever the level of advertising investment. Similarly, advertising may encourage the consumer to trial a particular FMCG but only if that trial is satisfactory will the consumer consider purchasing it again in the future. Playing around with an existing product, whatever the advertising support, can also lead to dire consequences, as *Coca-Cola* discovered when it reformulated the drink (based on market research) in 1985 and caused uproar among traditional drinkers.

Establishing the **advertising problem** (the reason the company is resorting to advertising) is the next stage of the advertising creation process and is derived from the advertising objectives. Much good advertising is based on a creative concept (or **creative platform**), an idea on which the campaign is built. Effective advertising is not, however, creativity for creativity's sake. David Ogilvy, legendary advertising guru, attacks strongly 'pretentious and incomprehensible nonsense' advertising which he said was designed to win awards rather than promote products or services. As James R. Adams noted: 'great designers seldom make good advertisers because they get overcome by the beauty of the picture and forget that the merchandise must be sold.'

The answer lies in what might be called **effective creativity**: creativity that meets the commercial objectives of the campaign. The creative idea expresses the brand's positioning through the brand proposition. This 'proposition' (sometimes known as the '**single-minded proposition**'[7] to emphasise its importance in the advertising process) needs to capture the qualities of the brand and incorporate the right mix of functional properties and emotional characteristics.

The profile of the target audience is also key to establishing the creative platform, on which the campaign is based, and the **media strategy**, which defines the means of its distribution (see Chapter 8). It is interesting to note in this regard that product producers frequently use advertising to promote the intangible factors (prestige, reputation, etc.) associated with their brand while service providers often attempt to promote the physical, tangible outcomes (comfort, relaxation, etc.).

Although no strict formula exists, experience suggests that certain characteristics appeal to the consuming public. To this end, good advertising is said to generate **the Waterloo effect**. The Waterloo effect (based on the story below) is where good advertising is said to have one or more of the following features:

- uniqueness
- repetition or frequency
- relevance.

Creativity (in advertising)
The ability to attract and hold the attention of the target audience through the manner and composition of the advertisement.

Advertising problem
The reason(s) why an organisation is advertising.

Creative platform
The 'big idea' on which the campaign is built.

Effective creativity
Creativity that meets the commercial objectives of a campaign.

Single-minded proposition
A brand's unique selling proposition.

Media strategy
Decisions on which media to use for a given campaign.

Waterloo effect
An industry maxim which suggests that the features of good advertising campaigns are uniqueness, frequency and relevance.

---

[7]   The original view was that consumers could only sustain one idea at a time.

insight: The Waterloo effect – uniqueness, frequency and relevance

Long ago, an advertising practitioner used the following story to describe what he called the Waterloo effect. He explained that on his way home each night he would pass the time waiting for his train sitting in the bar at Waterloo Station, drinking a pint of beer and watching his fellow passengers go by. Occasionally, out of the thousands of people in the station, his gaze would fall on somebody different from the rest. It might be because of their behaviour or they might be dressed outrageously or be sporting a crazy hairstyle. Because they were different (or *unique*), they stood out from the crowd. At other times, he would become aware that the same person kept passing in front of the bar. He might not notice that person the first few times but invariably the more often they passed the more conspicuous they became. Repetition (or *frequency*), therefore, made them stand out from the crowd. On yet other occasions, he would be gazing into the crowd when he saw someone he recognised. Out of all those people in the station, this person was *relevant* to him personally and, therefore, attracted his attention. In the same way that these factors made people stand out from the crowd at Waterloo Station, good advertising should incorporate *uniqueness, frequency* and *relevance*.

Media chatter
Subject matter that is discussed by, and in, the media.

Impression
A single instance of an advertisement being displayed/broadcast.

Stopping power
Advertising that has the effect of gaining immediate attention.

Demonstration advertising
Advertising that demonstrates the effectiveness of the product or service and the way it may be used.

Typical-person endorsement
The use of everyday characters (usually played by actors) to endorse a product or service.

Expert endorsement
Advertising which uses known or supposed (from their description or appearance) experts to recommend a product or service.

Unique advertising undoubtedly stands out from the rest and gets talked about through 'word of mouth' and/or '**media chatter**'. Repetition meanwhile fixes a message in our memory. Popular and memorable taglines such as 'Beanz meanz Heinz' (*Heinz*), 'the world's favourite airline' (*British Airways*) and 'probably the finest lager in the world' (*Carlsberg*) rely on repetition to become memorable. More recently, *webuyanycar.com* and *gocompare.com* have shown that even online product/service providers need to establish recognition through repetition. Memorability is further enhanced by consistency (message, image, storyline, etc.) in message delivery.

Relevancy is, however, seen as the strongest influence of all. If advertising is relevant to the consumer's needs, at the time s/he wants to satisfy them (or in the foreseeable future), attention will be paid to the advertisement. For this reason, advertisers look to target those consumers (by age, by income, by lifestyle, etc.) who most clearly fit their existing customer profiles in the expectation that the advertising will be most relevant to them.

In the USA, research suggests that people are exposed to between 300 and 20,000 advertising **impressions** per day and that by the age of 18 the average American will have seen approximately 350,000 commercials.[8] Advertising, therefore, must aim for **stopping power**, whether through uniqueness, repetition or relevancy. To do this, advertisers use one or more proven formats, including:

- **demonstration advertising**: advertising which demonstrates the effectiveness of the product or service (e.g. *Shake-n-Vac*) and the way it may be used (e.g. 'have a break, have a *Kit-Kat*') or its use extended (*Lea & Perrin's* Worcester Sauce in spaghetti bolognaise, *Knorr* stock cubes in casseroles, etc.)
- **testimonials or typical-person endorsement**: where advertisers use everyday-type people (usually actors) to say how good the product or service is and any other messages the advertiser wishes to convey
- **expert endorsement**: advertising which uses known or supposed (from their description or appearance) experts to recommend a product or service, such as a former police

---

8   University of Washington Teen Futures Network (accessed 2 January 2013).

officer endorsing burglar-alarm equipment. Frequently, the 'expertness' is a creation of the advertiser. For example, the advertising of products said to include special formulations (haircare, headache relief, etc.) often appears to be based in a laboratory with people in white coats giving the scientific claims (to sometimes unpronounceable ingredients) more supposed validity

- **celebrity endorsement**: uses the credibility associated with a celebrity to carry the message. The greater the celebrity's influence on a particular target audience, the greater the wish to mimic that celebrity. The celebrity, therefore, should be appropriate for both the product/ service and target audience (David Beckham endorsing *Stannah* stair lifts or Thora Hird endorsing *Police* sunglasses is unlikely to be as effective as the original advertisements have been)

- **slice of life**: simulated 'real-life' situations have long been a vehicle for advertising messages. Here, the viewer is supposed to get involved with the action, either in an everyday setting (e.g. the various incarnations of Katie and the rest of the *OXO* family), a long-running romance (e.g. *Goldblend*) or a drama (*Ensure, AA, Mini*, etc.). These 'slice-of-life' adverts are in fact 'mini soaps'[9] or continuing dramas

- **comparative advertising**: the direct comparison of one brand with, usually, its main competitor. This may be to establish the brand's position in the marketplace (e.g. *Hertz:* 'Number one'; *Avis:* 'We try harder') or to claim price or functional superiority over an opponent. Limitations exist in some markets as to the level of direct comparison that can be made. In Europe, the EU permits comparative advertising, provided it:

  ○ is not misleading
  ○ does not create confusion
  ○ does not discredit or denigrate third-party trademarks
  ○ does not take unfair advantage of the reputation of a trademark
  ○ does not present goods or services as imitations or replicas of goods or services bearing a protected trademark or trade name.

Within these broad formats, advertisers use particular features to enhance the appeal of the advertising. These include:

- **logical appeals**: appeals to our sense of logic and reason, for example 'this product out-performs everything else on the market'. Many early advertisers used the **'reason-why'**, logical appeal, format as the basis for their advertising. This was developed further in the 1920s, by US advertising agency boss Rosser Reeves, into the **Unique Selling Proposition (USP)**. The USP concept assumes consumers can only comprehend one major factor about a brand and that the brand's total advertising message should concentrate on this

- **emotional appeals**: these develop atmosphere and appeal to an individual's ego, status or sense of worth. As early as 1916, *Coca-Cola* was running full-colour posters, with little **copy** and much white space, featuring two young and fashionable women drinking *Coke*. Far from a logical appeal (e.g. it satisfies your thirst), this advertising sought to establish the drink as youth-associated, fashionable and, perhaps, associated with meeting members of the opposite sex

- **stereotyping**: shorthand notions of what people and places are or are supposed to be in order to communicate messages quickly and effectively. Examples include the *OXO* mum (mother knows best), the *Marlboro* cowboy (manliness), *Audi*'s German heritage (well engineered) and *Foster's* Australian men (sexist drinkers who know a good beer) (see Chapter 8)

- **humour**: according to research, one-third of all global advertising contains humour (de Pelsmacker et al. 2007) and 26% of all positive responses to television advertising are because consumers are 'amused' (Lach 1999). Humour is, as such, a staple of the advertising industry.

---

[9]   An irony because the name **'soaps'** came originally from the sponsorship of radio programmes by soap companies in the USA.

Celebrity endorsement
Advertising which uses the credibility associated with a celebrity to endorse the message. The greater the celebrity's influence on a particular target audience, the greater the wish to mimic that celebrity.

Slice of life
Advertising that uses simulated 'real-life' situations and where the viewer is encouraged to get involved with the action.

Comparative advertising
Direct comparison of one brand with another, usually its main competitor. This may be to establish the brand's position in the marketplace or to claim price or some other superiority.

Logical appeal (or reason why) advertising
Advertising that appeals to our sense of logic and reason, for example 'this product out-performs everything else on the market'.

Emotional appeal advertising
Advertising that develops atmosphere and appeals to an individual's ego, status or sense of worth.

Copy
Relates to written material. Advertising copy is the text in an advertisement. Journalistic copy relates to published articles.

Stereotyping
Shorthand, generalised characteristics of people and places, used in order to communicate messages quickly and effectively.

Humorous advertising
Designed to attract, through humour, consumer attention. If it is good enough and is memorable, it may also generate 'word of mouth'.

Creatives
Individuals who work in
the creative industries
(e.g. designers).

The reason is that humour attracts our attention and, if it is good enough, is memorable and may generate '**word of mouth**' (as does other highly creative advertising). There is, however, a narrow line between success and failure. Some 'humorous' advertising can, with repetition, become annoying (e.g. Michael Winner in *Esure* advertisements), although some **creatives** would argue that mild annoyance is yet another way of keeping a brand at the front of mind of the consumer. Although much humour is 'culture-specific', many humorous commercials (especially those based on visual gags) do travel, as witnessed by the increasing number of television shows around the world based on this genre. There are a number of theories which suggest why humour in advertising attracts our attention. In incongruity resolution theory, a humorous advert evokes a situation that does not fully fit what the recipient of the message was expecting. Disparagement theory sees humour as a little evil as it often uses humiliation of some kind to ridicule other people or a group. If humour deals with disliked people, it is considered even funnier than humour dealing with nice people. Release theories maintain that laughter releases tensions and psychic energy, and/or that humour releases

◉ insight: Comparethemeerkat.com

Comparethemarket.com does what it says on the label. Like its numerous competitors, it compares rates and deals from a multitude of largely service suppliers and puts forward recommendations. It is a seemingly lucrative business, going by the intense activity in the area of comparison sites and herein lies the problem. All of *Comparethemarket.com's* competitors provide similar benefits and marketing messages with no real understanding of brand difference among consumers. That was before the introduction of Aleksandr Orlov who first aired in 2009 and is still going strong five years later.

In this industry, there was a compelling need to differentiate *comparethemarket.com* from its competitors. The brand needed to create and drive consumers to its website. Naturally, search engines were targeted but it was becoming expensive. Intense competition for the word 'market' on search engines drove the price up to £5 in paid search auctions.

The challenge was to create something consumers would relate to. It settled on a humorous theme, coupled with the functional and rational benefits offered by the company. The solution was the meerkat. The word 'meerkat' had a pay-per-click cost of just 5p – substantially lower than more common phrases. Aleksandr Orlov was introduced as a loveable but frustrated character, annoyed by the confusion caused between *comparethemarket.com* and *comparethemeerkat.com*. By encouraging his audience to 'pay attention', he and his assistant Sergei became popular for their various exploits on *Facebook*, *Twitter* and *YouTube*, as well as other microsites where fans can find out more about the errant meerkat.

The impact of Aleksandr Orlov has been considerable. Agencies report that clients come into their offices asking for campaigns just like the meerkat one. Orlov's 'Simples!' has become a catchphrase. But was the campaign effective? In the first nine weeks of the campaign, the cost of attracting visitors to its sites was 80% down while the volume of traffic was more than 100% up. So successful has been the campaign that the company has registered the trademarks 'comparethemeercat.com' and 'Aleksandr the Meerkat', as well as 'Orlov', 'Simples' and others.

👁 insight: Ryanair

Towards the end of the Iraq war, budget airline Ryanair ran an advertising campaign which put its main competitor Easyjet on the defensive. The advertisement featured Iraq's Information Minister Mohammed Saeed Sahaf, nicknamed 'Comical Ali', who became well known during the conflict for his highly unrealistic view of Iraq's fortunes during the war. Under the heading 'Easyjet's Head of Information', the Minister was portrayed as saying 'We are winning the war! We are beating the Americans! Easyjet have the lowest fares!' Easyjet failed to see the funny side, describing the advert as 'insensitive'. Samantha Day, spokesperson for Easyjet, said: 'We haven't lost our sense of humour, but this ad was released on the day the Information Minister was rumoured to have committed suicide and we thought it was distasteful to say the least.'

Source: various

us from inhibitions, norms and laws. Whatever the reasons behind it, humour has been seen to increase source liking of and decrease sceptical attitudes towards a product. Marketing studies also show that humorous adverts get higher scores in the categories of source liking and product preference

- **erotica**: 'Sex sells' is another old advertising maxim and there is little doubt that it can, at times, yield enormous stopping power.[10] The use of sexual imagery has, however, changed over the decades. Semi-clad models draped over motor cars are now seen as tacky and dated while the erotica associated with the sophisticated advertising of *Häagen-Dazs* ice cream or *Organix* shampoo has undoubtedly differentiated these brands in their particularly crowded marketplaces. *Levis 501* advertising has used both sexes in mildly erotic advertising. Adverts for the *Yves St Laurent* perfume *Opium*, featuring model Sophie Dahl, and the *Club 18–30* poster campaign[11] (both subsequently banned as potentially offensive) succeeded in generating considerable media comment (media chatter). The *Wonderbra* 'Hallo Boys' campaign, which cost around £500,000 to produce, was said to have generated additional publicity worth £50 million (Brierley 2002). There are, however, two ironies associated with much 'erotic advertising'. The first is that although mild erotica is powerful, overt erotica is seen as a turn-off by consumers. The second is that most, what is seen as erotic, advertising, that featuring naked or part-clad women, appears directed at female consumers (e.g. lingerie and perfume)!

  Erotica (in advertising)
  Where sexual imagery is used to attract attention and enhance stopping power.

- **shock tactics**: shock advertising techniques aim to make the consumer sit up and think about the message. *Benetton* has for many years used images such as newborn children, AIDS patients and death-row prisoners to 'promote' a message of international solidarity with their brand. Whatever the ethical issues surrounding the use of such images, they have rarely failed to cause comment. In the not-for-profit sector, charities such as *Barnardo's* and the *NSPCC* have used images of child abuse to shock potential contributors to take action. Health campaigns regularly use shock treatment (e.g. interviews with dying cancer patients) to try to change personal lifestyles, and road-safety campaigns use horrific images (e.g. a car crash without seat belts being on) to drive messages home. Shocking advertising invariably attracts the attention of the media and often prolongs **media chatter**; and **word of mouth** ensures the brand (or, in the case of health campaigns, the message) is kept forefront in the public mind

  Shock tactics (in advertising)
  Advertising that is shocking but attracts attention.

- **fear**: again, a staple of advertising. The fear can be around the physical well-being of the individual or his/her dependents (e.g. 'what will happen to your family if you die?'), social

  Fear (in advertising)
  Advertising that uses fear of something happening (e.g. a house fire) as the central theme.

---

[10]   The small number of minor road accidents reported around the *Wonderbra* 'Hallo Boys' poster sites in the UK and Ireland are perhaps evidence of this.

[11]   Including such slogans as 'Beaver Espania', 'The Summer of 69' and 'It's not all sex, sex, sex, sex, sex … there's a bit of sun and sea as well'.

status (e.g. 'will you be able to afford to retire?') or performance (e.g. 'can't sleep?'). The purpose of this advertising is to offer the consumer a remedy that will reduce the specific fear factor (e.g. insurance, pension funds or sleep aids, respectively)

- **sensory appeal**: yet another old advertising maxim is that you should be selling the sizzle not the sausage. For many years, *Marlboro*, the world's largest cigarette brand, used the image of the cowboy and the big country as the setting for all of its advertising. *Citroen's* fire-raising visuals, complemented by the 'Take my breath away' soundtrack, had enormous resonance with audiences. Fantasy, escape and nostalgia are also seen as attractive. For example, *Bounty* tastes of paradise, the *National Lottery* can make your dreams come true and *Hovis* is supposedly endowed with qualities associated with a bygone age. Until relatively recently, *British Airways* used a piece of music in its advertising first introduced in 1983. Although the *Flower Duet* from Delibes' opera *Lakmé* has been adapted and re-scored on several occasions, the basic melody is said to express everything the airline wants to say to its customers. Even though the advertisers are no longer using the theme, it is now so established that in the UK market the playing of the first few bars is instantly associated by most people with the airline. Indeed, music often becomes better known and more popular after it has been used in advertising (see Table 9.2)

Sensory appeal (in advertising)
Creating fantasy and/ or an aura to attract attention to a message.

TABLE 9.2　　Advertising theme tunes

Advertiser	Title	Artist
Vodafone	Bohemian Like You	The Dandy Warhols
Citroen Xantia	The Passenger	Iggy Pop
Adidas	Peaches	The Stranglers
Rolling Rock	Drinking In LA	Bran Van 3000
Levis Twisted	Before You Leave	Pepe Deluxé
Gap Denim	Digital Love	Daft Punk
Mercedes Benz	If Everybody Looked The Same	Groove Armada
Guinness	Phat Planet	Leftfield
The Times	Barber's Adagio For Strings	William Orbit
Lynx	Bentley's Gonna Sort You Out	Bentley Rhythm Ace
Miller Genuine Draft	Loco	Fun Lovin' Criminals
Nike	Mas Que Nada	Sergio Mendes
Peugeot 306	Can't Take My Eyes Off You	Andy Williams
Diet Coke	Lady Marmalade	LaBelle
Fiat Punto	Don't You Want Me	The Human League
Smile Internet Bank	Smile	The Supernaturals
Levis 501s	Inside	Stiltskin
Levis TV	Sarabande (Suite No.4 in D Minor)	Academy of St Martin-in-the-Fields
Kroenenberg 1664	Slip Into Something More Comfortable	Kinobe
Adidas	Beautiful Crazy	Space Raiders

Advertiser	Title	Artist
Levis	Before You Leave	Pepe Deluxe
Grolsch	I'm Bored	Iggy Pop
Levis	Itchy & Scratchy	Boss Hogg
Carling	Much Against Everyone's Advice	Soulwax
Baileys	One Way Or Another	Blondie
Levis	The Second Line	Clinic
American Express	Cars	Gary Numan
Mercedes Benz	If Everybody Looked The Same	Groove Armada
Sainsburys	Got Myself A Good Man	Pucho & His Latin Soul Brothers
XFM	Yellow Butterfly	Tahiti 80
Carling	6 Underground	Sneaker Pimps
Daewoo	Purple	Crustation
Tic Tac	27 Women	La Honda
Levis	Death in Vegas	Dirge
BUPA	Cry	Howie B
Citreon Xsara	Rise	Craig Armstrong
Vodafone	Smokebelch	Sabries of Paradise
Guinness	Original	Leftfield
Adidas	Right Here Right Now	Fatboy Slim
Renault Kangoo	Run On	Moby
Virgin Cola	With You	Alex Gopher
Caffreys	Clubbed To Death	Rob D
Levis	Novelty Waves	Biosphere
Compaq	Carrera Rapida	Apolla 440
Levis	Underwater Love	Smoke City
Guinness	Guaglione	Perez Prado & His Orchestra
Lynx	Chewy Chewy	Ohio Express
Dairylea	Gimme Dat Ding	The Pipkins
McDonalds	Hot Diggity Dog Ziggity Boom	Perry Como
Maxell Tapes	The Israelites	Desmonds Dekker
British Gas	Wipeout	The Safaris
Lynx	Miniskirt	Esquivel & His Orchestra
Alliance and Leicester	Baby Elephant Walk	Henry Mancini
Guinness	Babarabateri	Beny More/Perez Prado & Orchestra

(Continued)

TABLE 9.2   (Continued)

Advertiser	Title	Artist
PPP Healthcare	Boum!	Charles Trenet
Guinness	Incidentally Robert	Tot Taylor
Triumph Bras	Va Ba Boom	Edmundo Ros
Nike	Soul Bossa Nova	Quincy Jones
Go! Airlines	Theme From 'The Fox'	Hugo Montenegro & His Orchestra
The Guardian Newspaper	Dean Fraser	Dick Tracey
Powergen	Green Bossa	Tot Taylor
Halifax	Surfin	Ernest Ranglin
Ariston	Da Da Da	Trio
Maynard's Wine Gums	Hoots Mon	Lord Rockingham's XL
Fiat Bravo	Rubber Biscuit	The Chips
Kellogg's Fruit 'n' Fibre	The Banana Boat Song (Day-O)	Harry Belafonte
Wrangler	Follow The Yellow Brick Road	Victor Young & His Orchestra

- **shape and colour** play a part in aiding recognition: the *Coca-Cola* and *Heinz* ketchup bottles and the *McDonald's* golden arches are icons of design and instantly recognisable. Cigarette brands frequently use colour, in some cases to circumvent advertising restrictions. Examples include *Marlboro*'s red livery, *Silk Cut*'s purple silk and *Benson and Hedges*'s gold. *Cadbury* (purple), *Virgin* (red) and *McDonald's* (red, gold and more recently green) are other examples of brands with strong colour associations.

In summary, advertisers use a wide range of different characteristics individually or in combination to draw the attention of the consumer toward their branded product or service.

THE ADVERTISING INDUSTRY

Undoubtedly, advertising was the communications tool of choice for most of the twentieth century. It was endowed with the ability to create and maintain the profile of a wide range of national and international brands and was the backbone on which the communications industry was built. By the end of the century, however, the ratio of promotional expenditure to advertising was 3 to 1. This distribution of marketing communication funds would have been unthinkable to advertisers and agencies during the 1960s (Jones 2004).

Although advertising spending worldwide has doubled per person in real terms since the 1950s, the year-on-year growth rates in traditional media have declined substantially. According to the UK *Advertising Association*, advertising expenditure rose by 1.1% in the first quarter (Q1) of 2012, which is anticipated to grow to 2.2% by the end of that year. Online advertising distorts the overall total as it grew 11.1% in Q1 with a 10.1% growth for the year. In a report from the V12 Group (2006) on above- and below-the-line expenditure trends, it states:

> traditional, brand-oriented advertising is no longer the primary driver of customer behaviour. Whether it's reflected in dwindling print newspaper circulation or the stagnant market for network television commercials, significant evidence suggests that the marketing landscape has fundamentally shifted – from an 'above-the-line' focus on reaching a broad population with emotionally-oriented appeals, to a 'below-the-line' approach that stresses targeted, customer-centric communications, measurable results and concrete return-on-investment.

The reasons for the relative decline in advertising are manifold and include:

- **consumer markets in relative decline**: much of the success of advertising in the first half of the century was on the back of expanding populations and developing markets. By the 1960s, markets were becoming saturated and population growth was stagnant or in decline. When it was recognised that advertising could no longer stimulate growth in market demand, the emphasis switched to developing market share. Advertising agencies now claimed that the power of advertising lay in its ability to build long-term brand loyalty, a claim that is very difficult to quantify
- **a branding crisis**: many branded FMCGs came under pressure toward the end of the last century, particularly with the sectoral dominance of a few large supermarket retailers in each of the most developed markets and the growth of own-label brands produced for these stores. While, in earlier years, it had been the norm for medium to large retailers to stock the brand leader and up to three **follower brands** in any category, the reality today is that the brand leader vies for space on the shelves with other brands alongside the store's own-label produce. Individual retailers are less interested in brand advertising (because the brand can be purchased at any of that retailer's competition) and more interested in using promotion (frequently on the basis of price or multi-pack offers) to attract consumers to their store. To guarantee shelf space, brand owners have had to transfer much of the money that previously went into 'brand-building' advertising to sales promotion within stores
- **sector bans**: two sectors that had traditionally attracted high advertising expenditure are those of cigarettes and alcohol. In 1965, the UK government banned cigarette advertising on television. The cigarette industry responded by increasing its spending on poster, magazine and cinema advertising, in addition to 'point-of-sale' materials and sponsorship. Despite arguments from the industry that advertising did not encourage new smokers and only affected market share, a ban on all tobacco advertising and sponsorship was announced prior to the millennium. Alcohol too has had a number of restrictions put on what can be sold and when. For the advertising (and sponsorship) industry, this has meant a considerable drop in revenues. Other sectors such as medicines and children's toys, while not being wholly banned, are severely curtailed in many markets
- **media fragmentation**: in the nineteenth century, mass media advertising, largely through the press and magazines, was cheap and relatively focused. By 2000, the sheer number of different media had become a major problem for advertisers. While in the 1950s to 1980s *Independent Television (ITV)* companies accounted for between 90% and 100% of television advertising, today they represent (despite extra channels) around 40% and this is still falling. While for many of these years there was only one UK commercial television channel, today the *Broadcaster's Audience Research Board (BARB)* reports figures on over 100 stations and these exclude overseas channels available to many cable or satellite subscribers. Even in 1995 there were still 225 television programmes watched by over 15 million people. By 2004 this had fallen to 6 million. Commercial radio stations have also multiplied. New media (internet, email, etc.) is fast expanding and offers almost endless opportunities. While the press is one medium where the number of titles has decreased, there has been a huge explosion in magazine titles in the past 30 years. With more potential outlets for advertising and fewer consumers seeing individual media, the fragmentation of the media has increased substantially the cost-per-thousand (CPT) of individual campaigns

Follower brands
Brands that are not leaders in their particular category.

Media fragmentation
The dilution of TV or radio station audiences due to the proliferation of channels.

- **advertising effectiveness**: the 1990s and beyond saw the tightening of purse strings and a disillusionment with marketing expenditure in general and advertising in particular. For the brand leaders, ironically (given the above discussion concerning cost-effectiveness) the UK's high television advertising costs in the 1950s, 1960s and 1970s (due to the ITV monopoly) protected them against new entrants to the market challenging their status. In addition, established brands, looking to maintain awareness, do not need to do quite as much advertising as new brands fighting to establish their place. The fragmented media, while generally increasing the cost-per-thousand rates, have, however, produced a more level playing field, particularly for targeted products or services. Modern companies, run largely by accountants,[12] look for short-term reward rather than long-term brand building. They are looking for proof, which is not always readily forthcoming, that their advertising expenditure is justified. To the extent that advertising is notoriously difficult to measure, accountants have been more willing to invest in direct marketing and sales promotion where success or failure can be easily and quickly measured.

summary

This chapter examined the growth of advertising in the twentieth and into the twenty-first century and suggested two theories (weak and strong) as to why advertising may work. The strong theory of advertising, which suggests it is highly persuasive, has been the dominant viewpoint in the industry for the majority of the twentieth century. The weak theory, however, is probably more realistic in suggesting that the most advertisers can do is 'nudge' consumers towards their products or services. The chapter looked at the means by which advertising effectiveness is measured while recognising the flaws in such measurements as recall and recognition. It continued by examining those characteristics of good advertising such as uniqueness, repetition and relevance and other factors that give advertising stopping power. The chapter concluded by examining the problems faced by the advertising industry over the last five decades.

review questions

1. What is the difference between the strong and weak theories of advertising?

2. Describe the processes associated with the cognitive response model.

3. Explain the ATR(N) model.

4. What is low-involvement theory?

5. Explain the difference between 'recall' and 'recognition' in advertising research.

6. Describe the phenomenon known as the Waterloo effect.

7. It is recognised that advertisers need to achieve stopping power. How might they do this?

8. Give an example of a logical appeal in advertising.

9. What is the main assumption of the USP concept?

10. What is DAGMAR?

---

[12] According to *Accountancy Age* (24 April 2012), post-recession the majority of CEOs in the biggest UK companies (51%) have a financial background now compared to just 31% in 2008 – a massive 65% increase.

discussion questions

1. If it is true that the majority of consumers do not believe advertising claims, why does it continue to be used?

2. Shock tactics are often used by advertisers to gain attention. Under what circumstances would you consider these to be appropriate or inappropriate?

3. Media fragmentation and digital technology have had an impact on the advertising industry in recent years. How do you feel this will impact on advertising campaigns over the next 10 years?

case study 9.1: Paddy Power and Ryanair – two punk brands separated by marketing intent

By Noelle McElhatton, marketingmaga-zine.co.uk,
23 August 2012

Where do we stand on *Paddy Power*? The betting brand attracts a full gamut of views ranging from 'cheekily irreverent and fun marketer' to 'tasteless troublemaker'. If you fall into the latter bracket, it would be tempting to badge *Paddy Power* as the betting equivalent of *Ryanair* – two punk outfits with Irish provenance that delight in cocking a snook at the authorities.

Paddy Power is, like its compatriot brand, fulfilling a customer need that generates notable financial success. The betting group saw a 28% increase in revenues and a 40% increasing in online customers in the first half of 2012. And a la *Ryanair*, *Paddy Power*'s advertising is driven by stunts, some of them in poor taste. The 2010 TV ad featuring visually impaired footballers kicking a cat was that year's most complained about advert.

But that's where the comparisons end. For since then *Paddy Power* has shown serious marketing intent, as it attempts to realise its global ambitions with aggressive marketing that retains the *craic* at its heart. The first statement of that intent came last year with the hiring of agency Crispin Porter & Bogusky with its suitably disruptive creative track record. We're told the agency is being driven hard, turning around the brand's ads almost overnight, with ideas geared to what's going on in the world.

Perhaps the most significant expression that the bookmaker wants to inject discipline into its marketing was the appointment, also last year, of blue chip marketer Christian Woolfenden.

Now settled in his second year on the job, former *Procter & Gamble* marketer Woolfenden reflects on how he was persuaded by *Paddy Power* CEO, Patrick Kennedy, to join up. Former KPMG accountant Kennedy will doubtless approve of Woolfenden's efforts to make the brand's considerable marketing output more accountable, the marketer professing to be 'a big fan' of econometrics.

(Continued)

(Continued)

Woolfenden clearly takes no pleasure in seeing expensive ads such as 'Ladies Day', created by CP&B for this year's Cheltenham festival, being pulled off air. Despite *Paddy Power*'s all-powerful imperative to generate PR through controversy, my money's on Woolfenden not having his marketing instincts overridden.

But oh, to be a fly on the wall in meetings between the marketer and his PR equivalent, *Paddy Power*'s 'head of mischief' Ken Robertson.

Case study questions

1. Why is *Paddy Power*'s advertising seen as successful?
2. Will the need to be more accountable affect *Paddy Power*'s future marketing?
3. What direction might *Paddy Power*'s advertising take in the future?

further reading

Calder, B.J. and Malthouse, E.C. (2005) 'Managing media and advertising change with integrated marketing', *Journal of Advertising Research*, 45 (4): 356–61.

De Pelsmacker, P. and Neijens, P.C. (2012) 'New advertising formats: how persuasion knowledge affects consumer responses', *Journal of Marketing Communications*, 18 (1): 1–4.

Ehrenberg, A.S.C. (2000) 'Repetitive advertising and the consumer', *Journal of Advertising Research*, 40 (6): 39–48.

Horsky, S. (2006) 'The changing architecture of advertising agencies', *Marketing Science*, 25 (4): 367–83.

Lichtenthal, J.D., Yadav, V. and Donthu, N. (2006) 'Outdoor advertising for business markets', *Industrial Marketing Management*, 35 (2): 236–47.

Logan, K. (2013) 'And now a word from our sponsor: do consumers perceive advertising on traditional television and online streaming video differently?', *Journal of Marketing Communications*, 19 (4): 258–76.

REFERENCES

Ambler, T. and Burne, T. (1999) 'The impact of affect on ad memory', *Journal of Advertising Research*, Mar./Apr.: 25–34.

Bartle, J. (1999) 'The advertising contribution', in L. Butterfield (ed.), *Excellence in Advertising*. Oxford: Butterworth-Heinemann, pp. 25–44.

Belch, G.E. and Belch, M.A. (2011) *Advertising and Promotion: An Integrated Marketing Communications Perspective*, 9th edn. New York: McGraw-Hill.

Brierley, S. (2002) *The Advertising Handbook*, 2nd edn. London: Routledge.

Colley, R.H. (1961) *Defining Advertising Goals for Measured Advertising Results*. New York: Association of National Advertisers.

Crosier, K. (1999) 'Advertising', in C. Fill (ed.) *Marketing Communications: Principles and Practice*. London: Thompson.

De Pelsmacker, P., Geuens, M. and Van den Bergh, J. (2007) *Marketing Communications: A European Perspective*, 3rd edn. London: Prentice Hall.

Ehrenberg, A. (1997) 'How do consumers buy a new brand?', *ADMAP*, March.

Ehrenberg, A.S.C. and Goodhardt, G.J. (1979) *Essays on Understanding Buyer Behavior*. London: Thompson.

Jones, J.P. (2004) *Fables, Fashions and Facts about Advertising: A Study of 28 Enduring Myths*. Thousand Oaks, CA: Sage.

Lach, J. (1999) 'Commercial overload', *American Demographics*, 21 (9): 20.

Lavidge, R. and Steiner, G. (1961) 'A model for predictive measurements of advertising effectiveness', *Journal of Marketing*, Oct.: 61.

Nevett, T.R. (1982) *Advertising in Britain: A History*. London: Heinemann.

Rossiter, J.R. and Percy, L. (1998) *Advertising Communications and Promotion Management*, 2nd edn. Singapore: McGraw-Hill.

Schmit, T.M. and Kaiser, H.M. (2004) 'Decomposing the variation in generic advertising response over time', *American Journal of Agricultural Economics*, 86 (1): 139–53.

Smith, P.R. and Taylor, J. (2004) *Marketing Communications: An Integrated Approach*, 3rd edn. London: Kogan Page.

Strong, E.K. (1925) *The Psychology of Selling*. New York: McGraw-Hill.

V12 Group (2006) *Tracking the Trends: A Comparison of Above-the-Line and Below-the-Line Expenditure Trends*. New York: Winterberry Group.

Wells, W., Burnett, J. and Moriaty, S. (1997) *Advertising Principles and Practice*, 4th edn. Upper Saddle River, NJ: Prentice Hall.

Yeshin, T. (2006) *Advertising*. London: Thompson Learning.

USEFUL WEBSITES

For details of the Institute of Practitioners in Advertising (IPA) advertising effectiveness awards, see www.ipa.co.uk/Framework/ContentDisplay.aspx?id=3551

For debate on current advertising issues, see the Advertising Association website at: www. adassoc.org.uk/advertising-issues

For additional materials that support this chapter and your learning, please visit:
study.sagepub.com/egan

SALES PROMOTION

10

CHAPTER CONTENTS

LEARNING OBJECTIVES

Having completed this chapter readers would be expected to:

- distinguish between advertising and sales promotion and between consumer, retail and trade promotions

- explain the theories, concepts and generalisations associated with sales promotion

- understand the reasons behind the rise of sales promotion relative to advertising

- describe the tactics associated with sales promotions and the differences between price promotions and creative promotions (or incentives)

- analyse the outcomes of sales promotions and their effect on general communication strategies.

INTRODUCTION

Sales promotion has a very modern ring to it but it has actually been practised for a very long time. Free samples, money off and additional value (e.g. two for the price of one) have been used by traders for centuries to attract and stimulate new and existing customers. The arrival of newspapers not only saw an explosion in advertising but sales promotion as well. In the *Daily Telegraph* on 4 June 1900, there was a full page advertisement for *Eiffel Tower* lemonade ('the largest users of lemons in the world'). Incorporated in the text was an early example of the 'freepost' offers that are so prevalent today:

> 300 bottles are given away weekly. The firm has adopted the following novel method to induce everybody to try their lemonade. The first 50 letters opened every day not only have the lemonade sent by return post, but the stamps are also returned to the fortunate applicants.

SALES PROMOTION VS. ADVERTISING

Sales promotion
The offering of a short-term incentive, encouraging people to act.

There is often confusion between what is regarded as advertising and what is defined as sales promotion. Indeed, many choose not to distinguish between them at all. Those insertions placed in the *Daily Telegraph* above are, from an academic sense, part advertisement and part sales promotion. **Sales promotion is the offering of an incentive to make people act**. By its nature, it implies there is a built-in urgency to purchase (or otherwise act), either within a time period or until the offer is sold out. It has the function of accelerating purchases, being designed to increase the volume of sales by directly influencing the choice-making process and influencing the speed of the decision. In contrast to advertising, which, as has been discussed, is regarded as being more influential in the longer term and best suited to enhancing buyer attitudes and building brand equity, sales promotion is decidedly short term and capable of influencing behaviour rather than (in a primary objective sense) attitudes. While advertising creates value that is intangible (and largely immeasurable), sales promotion adds tangible value to the offering. In terms of the hierarchy of effects model discussed in Chapter 2, sales promotion comes into its own by motivating people to act. This relative effectiveness is illustrated in Figure 10.1.

FIGURE 10.1   Sales promotion relative to advertising

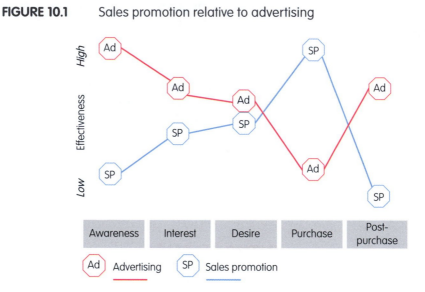

Sales promotion may be classified into four types:

- salesforce
- consumer
- trade
- retail.

Salesforce promotions are used in many industries to increase sales and generate leads and will be discussed in more detail in Chapter 14. **Consumer** and **trade promotions** are supplier initiated and frequently referred to as examples of **pull** and **push strategies** respectively (see Chapter 5). Pull strategies are those aimed at 'pulling' consumers to the brand (rather than any particular retailer). Instant-win promotions have become among the most heavily featured in this category. For example, in 2012 *PG Tips* ran an instant-win competition with a top prize of

£5,000 and *Dr Pepper* ran its instant-win 'Pants or Prizes' promotion through a competition website. Prize draws were also popular, as can be seen in Figure 10.2. The attraction for someone to purchase and enter a competition associated with a brand (or group of brands) is generally to the brand itself and not usually to a specific retailer.[1] **Retail promotions** are also pull strategies but in this case the attraction is to the retailer rather than the brand. These could include competitions, price or volume (e.g. buy one, get one free) promotions or in-store events.

FIGURE 10.2   Techniques

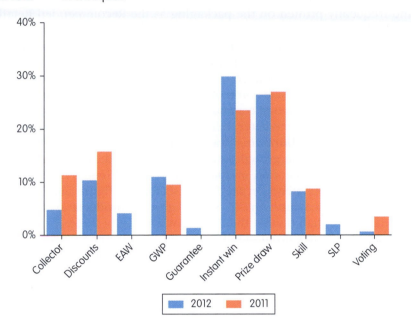

Push strategies are designed to attract product into the distribution network – that is, to encourage participating stores to purchase more product in return for promotional support of some kind. This might include **buying allowances**, **advertising** or **sales promotion allowances**, **slotting allowances** (slotting in new products) and other incentives such as product training, point-of-sale material, etc. Figure 10.3 shows the relationship between consumer, retail and trade promotions.

FIGURE 10.3   Push, pull and retail promotion strategies

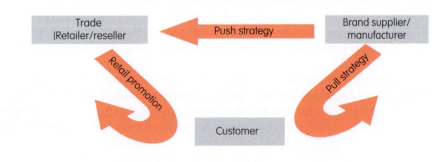

---

[1]   There are, however, a number of exclusive retailer/brand competitions that do take place.

THE GROWTH OF SALES PROMOTION

Over the past few years, sales promotion techniques have been introduced in areas such as financial services, media, IT, telecom, travel and leisure. Even national and local government are using sales promotion with various agencies handing out cigarette replacement therapies, free condoms and vouchers for fruit and vegetables to promote aspects of a healthier lifestyle. However, sales promotion in the consumer goods area had, for a considerable number of years, been restricted. At one time, in the not too distant past, UK prices on consumer goods were subject to Retail Price Maintenance (RPM) – effectively a price at which goods had to be sold and frequently printed on the packaging as the Recommended Retail Price (RRP). This legislation was withdrawn on most goods in 1964.[2] From this point on, manufacturers and retailers were free to promote their goods at any price.

There was also a change taking place in the world of advertising. Up until the 1980s, advertising was commonly 60% of the marketing communications budget. In the intervening period, sales promotion has, however, taken over from advertising as the principal marketing communications tool in most developed markets.[3] In the UK, in the years immediately before 2001, it was growing, according to the *Institute of Promotional Marketing* (formerly the *Institute of Sales Promotion*), at 20% per year although the growth rate has since slowed. According to research by Kim (2011), sales promotion in 2008 represented three-quarters of the total advertising/promotion spend. In the FMCG sector, the figure may be higher. In the UK, according to *SymphonyIRI*, 56% of grocery products are sold through promotions – more than double the European average of 25.6%.

The reasons why sales promotion has become so dominant in marketing communications are varied and frequently interconnected. They include:

- stagnating markets: a reduction in population growth in most developed markets, leading to a slow-down in market growth and subsequently increased competition
- increased costs and fragmentation in the advertising industry and decreased advertising effectiveness, which have encouraged spending on **below-the-line** activities in general and sales promotion in particular
- increased price sensitivity: it would appear that consumers are more knowledgeable and price sensitive than previously; indeed, consumers now expect bargains and may be prepared to search them out
- short-termism: the growing tendency of organisations to want to be seen to be successful (measured by turnover and market share) in the short term; sales promotions usually have an immediate positive impact on sales
- measurability: sales promotions generally have a specific beginning and end and it is, therefore, easy to measure results; this is in direct contrast to advertising where measurement of results is difficult, if not impossible, particularly in the short term
- a decline in brand loyalty as products and services have become more similar
- an increase in repertoire or portfolio buying: the repertoire or portfolio perspective (see Chapter 9) suggests that the majority of the population generate, through trial, a portfolio of brands from which they make their choice, rather than being loyal to one particular brand
- increased power and concentration of retailers: retailers are less interested in brand-building advertising per se because this is not of particular benefit to them alone. Rather, they see in-store support for price reductions and other 'extra value' offers as the vehicle for attracting customers and/or increasing customer spend. This is understandable as research suggests

Below the line
All marketing communications tools except advertising, which is referred to as above the line.

---

[2]   RPM on books stayed in force until 1997.
[3]   According to the American Marketing Association by 1986 sales promotion represented 66% and advertising 34% of total spend on these tools.

as much as 70% of buying decisions are made in-store. At the extreme is hostaging where the retailer/reseller is able to exert power over the brand owner and to insist on trade promotions on a more or less permanent basis (Fill 2009)

- the spread of own-label (or private-label) goods and a subsequent reduction in the shelf space allocated to brands
- improvements in technology: technology has enabled more variation in the types of promotion offered and further simplified the process. Scanning technology means that the operational software can recognise 'multi-offers' and 'price reductions' without human intervention. It also means improved planning for the retailer and the supplier. Many promotions are now internet-based and driven either though the brand website (e.g. *Coca-Cola*) or a social media site (e.g. *Budweiser* on *Facebook*).

Hostaging
Where the retailer/reseller is able to exert influence over the brand owner and to insist on trade promotions on a more or less permanent basis.

 ## insight: Promotions on Facebook

- Disney regularly launches games on *Facebook* and has over 100 million fans across its 200 brands, at one stage adding 5 million fans per week.

- Samsung launched the Galaxy SIII mobile phone on *Facebook*, and spends twice as much money maintaining its presence on the social network as it does on advertising.

- In 2010, Budweiser offered its *Facebook* following a free beer to people turning 22.

- VISA offered the first 20,000 small businesses to sign up on their *Facebook* page $100 in free advertising in that medium.

- In 2012 Starbucks launched its pumpkin spice flavouring with a contest on *Facebook*.

Source: **www.businessinsider.com**

SALES PROMOTION THEORY

Sales promotion is giving the customer something extra, rewarding them for their behaviour on this particular purchasing occasion. There are several theories which support the concept of reward as a motivator. In Chapter 3, classical and operant conditioning were discussed. While *classical conditioning* is largely associated with advertising, *operant conditioning* is seen as an explanation for consumer behaviour in relation to sales promotion.

Operant conditioning suggests the response of the individual is likely to be affected by positive reinforcement (reward) or negative reinforcement (punishment), although the effect is likely to cease when these reinforcements are taken away. In commercial terms, an organisation uses reinforcement by stressing the benefits and/or rewards a customer will receive on buying a product or service. The incentive is additional to the basic brand benefits and temporarily changes its perceived value (Shimp 2010). Similarly, Edward Thorndyke (1874–1949) suggested that the '**law of effect**', associated with the positive and negative consequences of actions, is also relevant to sales promotion. The law states that the consequences of behaviour *now* will govern the consequences of that behaviour in the *future*. In other words, once a buying pattern has been laid down it will continue. John Watson (1878–1958), US psychologist and founding father of American behaviouralism, introduced the concept of **shaping**. This suggests that a final response can

Shaping
Suggests that a final response can be explained as 'appearing after preceding acts which, taken together, constitute a chain of successive approximations' (John Watson).

be explained as 'appearing after proceeding acts which, taken together, constitute a chain of successive approximations' (Foxall et al. 1998). Shaping breaks the desired behaviour into a series of stages and the parts are learnt in sequence. This is particularly important with new products because trialling involves a complex set of behaviours which might be represented as:

inducement > trial > repeat purchase

Chaining is a concept that suggests behaviour emerges from sequences of actions in which the preceding action becomes the discriminative stimulus for the final response (inducement > purchase). **Priming** is yet another theory that suggests that a short exposure to a particular stimulus can evoke an increased drive to consume more of a product (de Pelsmacker et al. 2007). All of these different theories offer reasons why you can motivate people to buy more by offering incentives, although the longevity of this behaviour is open to doubt. Perhaps at its simplest, promotions rely on the human tendency to seek a bargain and/or other rewards.

In purely practical terms, Shimp (2010) suggested a number of intuitive generalisations that can be made about sales promotions:

- Temporary price reductions can substantially increase sales.
- The greater the frequency of deals, the lower the increased sales.
- The frequency of the deals changes the customer's reference point.
- Higher market-share brands are less 'deal' elastic.
- Advertised promotions increase store traffic.
- Higher quality brands tend to steal sales from lower quality brands.

To emphasise these and other observations about sales promotion, Figure 10.4 suggests four possible scenarios that may exist during and after a sales promotion.

Scenario 1: supports the proposition that price-related sales promotions merely bring forward sales. Ideally, sales promotion should generate extra sales

Chaining
Suggests behaviour emerges from sequences of actions in which the preceding action becomes the discriminative stimulus for the final response (inducement > purchase).

Priming
Suggests that short exposure to a particular stimulus can evoke an increased drive to consume more of a product.

FIGURE 10.4　　Effects of sales promotion

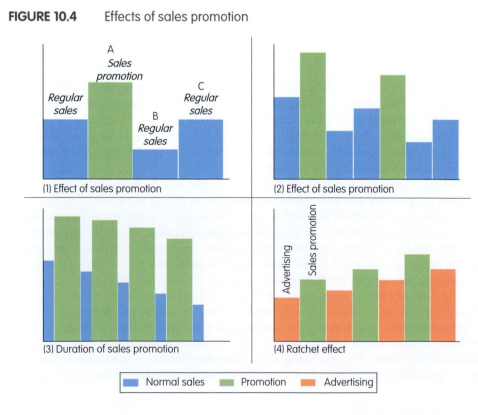

(1) Effect of sales promotion

(2) Effect of sales promotion

(3) Duration of sales promotion

(4) Ratchet effect

Normal sales　　Promotion　　Advertising

that cannot be guaranteed in any other way and should not lead to stocking up. However, Jones (1990) suggests there is overwhelming evidence that the sales effect is limited to the duration of the sale and that 'when the bribe stops the extra sales stop'. Another generalised observation is that sales, rather than returning to 'normal', often fall back for a period. This phenomenon, known as the **mortgaging effect**, suggests that with the promotion volumes rise (A) and fall back after the promotion to below normal sales levels (B), only eventually rising (C) back to normal over time. This implies that regular buyers simply bring forward their purchases. While sales (in volume terms) remain the same, profits fall.

> **Mortgaging effect**
> Where, after a promotion, rather than returning to 'normal', sales levels fall back for a period.

Scenario 2: here there is a similar effect to scenario 1 but over time there is a diminishing series of returns on the promotions themselves. Although the sales promotion increases sales, it is by an increasingly smaller amount, perhaps due to the frequency of the promotions. In addition, regular turnover is falling.

> **Marked down**
> Products or services where the normal retail price is reduced.

Scenario 3: similar to the above, this scenario predicts a situation where the frequency of sales changes the customer's reference point. Sales promotions are so frequent that sales outside those periods fall away. There have been many examples where it appeared that certain brands (or retailers) were constantly having sales. The internet has undoubtedly added to this feeling of continuous sales with the opportunities for online bargains continuously available.

Scenario 4: known as the '**ratchet effect**', this is the most optimistic of the scenarios as it predicts that with an integrated communications strategy credibility is built up through advertising and extra volume through inducements. In terms of an integrated campaign, this is an example of using two or more communications tools to create synergy.

> **Ratchet effect**
> Predicts the advantages of an integrated strategy that builds credibility through advertising and extra volume through promotional inducements.

Two principal schools of thought exist on the long-term effect of promotions. The first is that they discredit the brand (especially price-led promotions) over time. This is an ongoing debate and something that seems to have a degree of intuitive credibility, however there has been little by way of evidence provided to support it (see Srinivasan et al. 2002). Indeed, a major study in the UK, the USA, Germany and Japan, involving dozens of brands in 25 consumer goods categories, into the effects of price-related promotions suggested that promotions have no impact (positively or negatively) on a brand's long-term sales or on consumers' repeat-buying loyalty (Ehrenberg et al. 1994). What may occur with too frequent price reductions is a revaluation of the price/quality ratio such that the lower price becomes the expected norm.

Others, and in particular promotion practitioners, would suggest that sales promotion can actually add to brand value over time, particularly through 'creative promotions' that exclude discounting or **cause-related** events. In FMCG retailing, the strategy of **hi-lo** (or **high-low**) pricing is frequently used as the principal promotion strategy. Each week, a percentage of products is heavily discounted and promoted throughout the store. This is in direct contrast to an **everyday low-price** strategy which looks to spread savings across the whole store. Despite the obvious rational appeal of everyday low pricing, it is not always effective. In the USA, a significant feature in *K-mart*'s decline was its misjudged shift from 'hi-lo pricing' to 'everyday low pricing' in its attempt to compete with *Wal-Mart*. This was because *K-mart*'s core customers were 'deal-hunters' and the new value proposition did not satisfy their needs (McGovern et al. 2004).

> **Hi-lo (or high-low) pricing**
> A strategy, prevalent in FMCG retailing, where each week a percentage of products is heavily discounted and promoted throughout the store.

> **Everyday low prices**
> A strategy where the emphasis is on low prices across the store (in contrast to the hi-lo pricing strategy).

SALES PROMOTION OBJECTIVES

There are numerous organisational objectives for sales promotions. For consumer-focused promotions, these include:

- increased sales: looking to increase or defend market share or encourage repeat or multiple purchases
- stimulating trial: sales promotions can facilitate the introduction of new products, brands or brand extensions
- encouraging brand switching: encouraging consumers to break any bonds of loyalty to other brands
- highlighting novelty: bringing the consumer to a realisation of change (new, improved, etc.) or the re-positioning of a brand
- invigorating mature brands: brands that are no longer new and vibrant and/or where the similarity to other brands is high may benefit from sales promotion. For example, the tabloid newspaper industry is one where frequent promotions are used to set the brands apart
- rewarding loyal customers: one argument suggests that rewarding your customer for doing what they would do anyway is unprofitable. The counter-argument is that without these promotions your customers would go elsewhere for a bargain. There is also the suggestion that customers receive hedonic, non-functional benefits from such programmes, such as a sense of achievement at being a wise shopper, the positive effects of stimulation and variety through trying out new products and the entertainment value associated with certain promotions
- locking customers into loyalty programmes: to continue accumulating the rewards, the customer must remain largely loyal to the same supermarket, airline, petrol supplier, etc.
- targeting a specific segment: promotions may be aimed at particular customer types. For example, *Guinness* has for many years targeted young rugby fans during major events when many choose to watch the games in public houses or clubs. During major competitions, for example, in exchange for a set number of purchases of *Guinness*, drinkers can claim hats, tee-shirts and other merchandise. In 2011, for the Rugby World Cup Finals in New Zealand they offered a free *Guinness* alarm call mobile app to wake up fans with a direct alarm call from a famous rugby player to remind them that a game is about to start on the other side of the world

Spoiler campaign
A campaign designed to neutralise or disrupt the competition.

- neutralising or disrupting the competition: **spoiler campaigns** designed to thwart the competition. A good example of this was in October 2012 when *Vodafone* launched a £4.7 million campaign promoting the quality of its network ahead of *EE's* launch of its 4G services
- building databases: obtaining valuable data on customers. This is now frequently done through loyalty schemes. It is suggested, for example, that the *Tesco Clubcard* has saved over £500 million through the generation of data that was subsequently used by the company. Alternatively, companies may offer gifts or entry to competitions in exchange for information
- generating publicity: sometimes the magnitude of an offer is guaranteed to be newsworthy. For example, on 5 April 2013 the UK publishing industry handed out 1 million books as part of the inaugural World Book Night. This made news headlines and guaranteed coverage of the promotion's aims

Cause-related marketing
Where a commercial organisation is involved with a charity or other good cause to the benefit of both.

- **cause-related promotions** commercial organisations involved in promotions where a charity or other good cause is seen to benefit: these are seen as a way of creating a positive image for brands. For example, in the Computers for Schools initiative, Tesco boosted customer loyalty and attracted new shoppers to its store by rewarding customers with vouchers that could be redeemed to help local schools obtain free computers and computer equipment.

The objectives of trade promotions (i.e. push promotions) mirror those directed at the consumer. They are designed to encourage the retailer to facilitate particular goals. These may include:

- helping to introduce new products: new products/brands represent a risk to retailers which may require incentivisation to overcome. In FMCG retailers in particular, shelf space is at a premium and making room for a new product/brand may mean losing currently performing products/brands

- encouraging distribution penetration: increased sales through extended shelf space or improved positioning
- encouraging special displays (on- or off-shelf)
- thwarting the opposition: providing incentives more attractive than those of the competition
- stimulating salesforce motivation: for example, certain airlines have, in the past, offered above normal commission to agents, encouraging them to divert business that may have gone elsewhere
- helping overcome stock imbalances: incentives can help move excess stock and/or smooth out seasonal variations.

It is generally recognised that what sales promotion cannot do is compensate for the poor quality of products or permanently halt the decline of a brand.

SALES PROMOTION TACTICS

In essence, sales promotion tools can be divided into two types: price promotions and creative promotions (or incentives).

Sales promotion is not, therefore, simply a discount strategy but a wide range of tactical marketing techniques that include:

- money off (online, delivered or point-of-sale coupons)
- bonus pack offers (e.g. 50% extra free)
- bonus offers (e.g. buy one, get one free)
- refunds
- combined offers (e.g. buy product A and get product B free of charge)
- sampling
- premiums and self-liquidating premiums
- loyalty schemes (including money off or rewards)
- competitions.

Money-off, **bonus pack**, **bonus offers** and **combined offers** are self-explanatory and are in widespread use in retailing. **Coupons** are still the most popular means of offering targeted customers discounts on selected items. Technology is now such that supermarkets can issue coupons at the **point of purchase** or direct to the home (as part of a loyalty scheme) based on the shopper's buying pattern. So, for example, soft-drink buyers may be enticed to try new brands or flavours or products from an associate category such as snacks. In addition, there are now specialised online websites, such as *Groupon* and *Vouchercodes.com*, offering discount coupons or codes on a range of branded goods and services. Combined offers are frequently used to introduce a new product or flavours and to create **trial** of a new product. **Refunds** (by way of cash or coupons) may involve one or more purchases and may mean submitting proof of purchase by mail but more recently via the internet (e.g. *Kellogg's* book offer). **Sampling** may take place in-store or at any other location (e.g. train stations) or, if appropriate, may be delivered through a **door-to-door** distribution. **Direct response** television and other media campaigns are also used to encourage sampling. Sampling can be expensive but is often used when advertising alone is unable to communicate the brand's benefits, when the brand has benefits that are superior to the competitor or where the objective is to encourage product switching. **Premiums** are gifts given to consumers either with the product or, if terms (e.g. collect five wrappers or wrapper codes) have to be fulfilled, at some later date. *Ovaltine* was reputedly the first company to offer a premium when, in 1930, they distributed a 'de-coder ring' that required the participant to get information from the *Little Orphan Annie* radio show. In the 1950s, *Procter & Gamble* began offering plastic daffodils in the UK

Incentive
An extra inducement to purchase.

Combined offer
A joint brand promotion (e.g. free hair gel with shampoo).

Coupon
A voucher printed in-store or from packs, magazines, etc. which offer a money-off or other incentive to buy a product(s).

Refund
Given by way of cash or coupons, this may involve one or more purchases and submitting proof of purchase by mail or through claims managed via the internet.

Sampling
Free-of-charge trialling of products in-store or at other locations.

Direct response
Media where the customer can respond immediately to the offer.

Premium
A gift given to consumers either with purchase or, if terms (e.g. collect five wrappers) have to be fulfilled, by other means (e.g. through an online site).

with packets of *Daz*. Historically, the *Daz* flower is regarded as one of the most celebrated promotions ever; its success seems to be due to the gift being seen as bringing brightness into customers' lives in those days of post-war austerity. Some products are offered at a much reduced price rather than free of charge. If the income received covers the outgoings of the promotion, this is known as a **self-liquidating premium**.

Loyalty schemes may seem a relatively new innovation but they go back over a century. Although **loyalty cards**[4] were introduced relatively recently (becoming popular in the 1980s), a collection of coupons and **saving stamps** (in the UK, *Green Shield* was the largest of the saving stamp companies) have always been used to give the customer an extra incentive to shop at the retailers (including at one time *Tesco*) who distributed them. Even earlier, the *Co-operative* movement, founded in Rochdale in the nineteenth century, distributed its profits (or dividends) to loyal customers who shopped with them. Many, of a certain age, remember being sent to the *Co-op* and quoting the 'divi-number' whereby their sale would be entered in a divi-book, which in time would be tallied up and a 'dividend' (cash bonus) distributed. In time, this 'divi' book was replaced by saving stamps and ultimately loyalty cards (although in essence they all served the same function).

There can be little doubt that we live in the age of the loyalty card. In 2012, 86% of all UK adults owned at least one card and 29% had five or more. A survey by *Plastic Card Services* suggests that card holders save an average of £100.32 a year by using their loyalty points, however, while £4.39 billion is cashed in, £351 million annually is unredeemed. According to Uncles (1994), the popularity of loyalty schemes is based on the fact that customers actively seek an involving relationship with their brand and this, in turn, offers psychological reassurances to the buyer and creates a sense of belonging. The goal of these schemes is to establish a higher level of customer retention in profitable segments by providing increased satisfaction and value to certain customers. The reality is that although there is some evidence of 'first-mover advantage' (e.g. *American Airlines'* Frequent Flyer programme and *Tesco*'s Clubcard) when loyalty schemes become the industry norm, potential benefits can turn into the unavoidable costs of doing business. From the customer perspective, many of these schemes offer 'me-too' benefits which it would be nice to have (because people like getting something for nothing), but they are no guarantee to their continued loyalty and are often marginal to their brand choice (Uncles 1994).

With competitive promotions, the extra value is in the potential to win the prize. From the organisational perspective, the brand can be promoted without tampering with the price/quality/value equation, rather adding value by enabling entry to a competition. Competitive promotions add excitement and are also a popular way of collecting customer data.

SALES PROMOTION OUTCOMES

The simplest way to promote your product or service is to cut the price. The best way to promote your product, however, is to add value. It follows, therefore, that to add value, sales promotion becomes a strategic tool when it is not utilised for that 'quick-fix', immediate response solution. It needs to become part of a planned set of marketing communications activities over time, with each building on the other.

---

4   In Canada, it's called a rewards card or a points card, and in the USA a discount card, a club card or a rewards card.

Self-liquidating premium
A premium (or gift) where the income received covers the outgoings of the promotion.

Loyalty scheme
A scheme that rewards customers for purchases over time.

Loyalty card
A card issued to consumers by loyalty scheme organisers to facilitate the management and control of the scheme.

Saving stamps
Now largely defunct, saving stamps were a method of managing a loyalty scheme where stamps were issued with purchases, collected and ultimately exchanged for gifts of cash. Another form is still used in connection with savings clubs by some retailers.

insight: Costa Coffee

Three main companies dominate the British coffee scene: *Starbucks*, *Caffé Nero* and *Costa Coffee*. Every day, 70 million cups of coffee are consumed and the total UK turnover in 2012 was £5.8 billion, up 7.5% on the previous year. *Costa Coffee*, which in 2012 became the market leader with over 1 billion in sales, has an interesting history. The business was founded in 1971 by two Italian brothers, Sergio and Bruno Costa. By 1995 they had built up a chain of stores across the UK and the business was sold to *Whitbread*. At the time of writing, they currently have 1578 outlets in the UK (more than *McDonald's*) and a further 900 overseas.

In 2010 the company felt it had a potential problem. Brand research showed that regular customers were likely to visit the competition in addition to their own shops. They needed to find a reason for customers to choose *Costa Coffee* over its rivals. This prompted the development of a points-based loyalty scheme, The Coffee Club. Around 3 million customers used the card in a six-month period, according to the company. The scheme has also created a large database of customers who are emailed twice a month with further details about rewards. The database has also enabled *Costa* to set up customer panels to research ideas and product development.

Source: Bolger (2013)

The effect on profitability, particularly in the short term, must be regarded as a downside of sales promotion. The calculation in Table 10.1 shows the effect of a 3-for-2 offer based on a gross margin of 15%. This 'loss' may be taken by the manufacturer or retailer[5] and it may be used as a **loss leader** to stimulate **footfall**, thus generating increased sales in other products. The calculation should also be viewed with care because retailers frequently make use of our poor knowledge of prices beyond the basics (bread, milk, etc.). The actual saving on any promotion is determined by the original retail price which can vary significantly between retailers. A sales promotion 'trap' develops when the competition start to imitate each other's activities, often based on price reductions.

There is a need for careful planning, particularly in relation to competitions, and insurance against mishap is now commonplace. When such promotions go well, they can be very successful. One of the best-remembered and most successful was the *Shell* 'make money' competition where drivers collected half a note on each visit to the petrol station. Such was its success that the competition has been repeated three times since its original introduction in 1966 and has

Loss leader
A product sold at or below cost to attract customers into a store. Any 'loss' is made up by the purchase of other products.

Footfall
Retail jargon for the number of customers who visit a store during a specific time period.

---

[5]   This is a simple example and could relate to either retailers or brand owners.

TABLE 10.1   Sales promotion calculation

Non-promotion	Period 1	Period 2	Period 3	Period 4	Totals
Sales (units)	2000	2000	2000	2000	8000
Price	£1.00	£1.00	£1.00	£1.00	
Margin (15%)	£0.15	£0.15	£0.15	£0.15	
Gross profit	£300.00	£300.00	£300.00	£300.00	£12000.00
Promotion (period 2)	Period 1	Period 2	Period 3	Period 4	Totals
Sales (units)	2000	4000	1000	2000	8000
Price	£1.00	£0.66	£1.00	£1.00	
Margin (15%)	£0.15	(£0.19)	£0.15	£0.15	
Gross profit	£300.00	(£760.00)	£150.00	£300.00	(£10.00)

also appeared in other formats (e.g. matching cars). The dangers are, however, apparent as revealed by examples of three famous sales promotion disasters in the Insight below.

insight: Promotional disasters

Three well-publicised promotional disasters serve as warnings about the potential dangers of planning promotions and insuring against things going wrong.

In the UK, *Hoover* offered free flights to the USA in return for purchasing any product over £100. The company wildly underestimated the response because, in the planning stage, they had looked at response rates for a 2-for-the-price-of-1 offer rather than a comparable (if there was one) promotion. The response was huge (100,000 within the first month) with people buying two *Hoovers* at a time just to qualify for the flights. It was exacerbated by the fact that some retailers increased the price of some lines, bringing them into the promotion. The agency through which the competition was organised quickly went into liquidation and *Hoover*, who was not insured, became liable. Disgruntled customers complained and at least one blockaded a *Hoover* van and refused to release it until the travel tickets were produced. The promotion cost *Hoover* £48 million, numerous careers and was a public image disaster.

KFC in the USA decided to promote their new grilled chicken by giving it away for free. Wanting to be relatively discreet, they decided to announce it on the *Oprah Winfrey* show. Unfortunately for them, approximately 16 million people printed off coupons. *KFC* were so unprepared for this onslaught that most stores ran out of product before lunchtime. In New York, respondents that complained were dismissed by the company and responded with mini riots and sit-ins.

Pepsi in the Philippines offered one million pesos (£26,000) to anyone finding a bottle top with the number 349 printed on it. *Pepsi* paid out £8 million before they realised that thousands of winning tops were appearing everywhere. They immediately stopped the payments. In all, 500,000 bottle tops were printed with that number which would have cost *Pepsi* $18 billion. Instead, *Pepsi* reduced the prize money to $19.00 which still cost them $10 million. Following riots and attacks on *Pepsi* bottling plants, lorries burnt out and three people killed, many *Pepsi* executives left the country and were later the subject of thousands of lawsuits.

Source: various

LEGAL CONSIDERATIONS

There are laws and voluntary codes that govern most sales promotions and these vary by jurisdiction and can change at any time. Organisations should, therefore, always take legal advice before holding any sales promotion. Failure to comply with the regulations could result in an organisation being fined, attracting adverse publicity and possible prosecution. Across the world, sales promotion is regulated to a greater and lesser degree. What is permissible in one jurisdiction is not necessarily allowable in the next. In the European Union, the UK and Spain were among the most liberal in attitude to sales promotions while France, Belgium and the Netherlands were the most restrictive. However, in 2010, three cases went before the European Court of Justice whose outcome has rendered most former restrictions on promotional marketing in the European Union invalid, a development which has made it considerably easier to run promotions in the EU than prior to these verdicts.

Competitive promotions are basically of two types: skill-based **competitions** or **prize draws** where the winning is randomised (e.g. scratch cards, instant-win packs, etc.). In UK competitions, the winning of prizes must depend to a substantial degree on skill and participation can be made dependent on the payment of a contribution. A prize draw, however (if not deemed to be a lottery which is strictly licensed in the UK and in many other countries), must be free to enter. This means that the price of the product cannot be inflated nor any other cost demanded. The competition may require the entrant to pay transmission (e.g. telephone or postal) charges associated with entry but these cannot be inflated. An organisation may restrict participation to individuals who accept certain conditions (for example, those who provide personal data) but the chances of success must be the same, however the contest is entered. Successful participants in an 'instant win' competition should receive their prize immediately or be able to claim it without delay, costs or other barriers. Creating an impression that a consumer has already won a prize when none exists or the claimant having to incur cost to claim, may lead to a criminal conviction.

Price and value (e.g. extra volume) promotions must, by law, be genuine and applied for a specified amount of time (or while stocks last). Quality must be maintained, it must be clear what the comparison is with the regular price and unambiguous in describing the value offered (e.g. 10% more volume or 10% less cost). If the comparison is with the organisation's usual price, then it must be the most recent price and that offered for a minimum of 28 days previously. Businesses should not suggest that a sale is for a shorter time than intended and any extension must be clearly announced as such. Notices such as, for example, 'up to 60% off' can only be used if this applies to at least 10% of the products or services on offer. Introductory offers must be time restricted and the goods or services still available after the promotion, albeit at the higher price. Offers including free products (e.g. 'buy one, get one free') cannot involve increased pricing nor other charges being added.

The above relates to the UK excluding Northern Ireland and will differ from other markets around the world. As legislation is also prone to change, it is imperative that an organisation keep itself up to date. Other statutory legislation and voluntary codes apply to the area. For example, any claims made that are under the remit of the Advertising Standards Authority must be 'legal, decent, honest and truthful' and products truthfully described under a raft of consumer legislation.

Competition
In sales promotion terms, where the challenge is skill-based.

Prize draw
Where the winning of a competition is randomised.

summary

This chapter opened with a brief reflection on sales promotions of the past and distinguished sales promotion, as an incentive to people to act, from the brand-building qualities of advertising. It further distinguished between consumer, trade and retail promotions and how they interact with general organisational strategy. The growth of sales promotion was highlighted and it was noted that, since 1980, it had replaced advertising as the main medium in the consumer goods field. The reasons behind this were discussed. They included increased advertising costs; corporate short-termism; the measurability of promotions; stagnating markets; the decline of brand loyalty; the spread of own-label; increased repertoire buying; the increased power and concentration of retailers; increased price sensitivity; and the implications of new technologies. Sales promotion theories were discussed in the light of classical and operant conditioning theories, the law of effects, shaping, chaining and priming. Intuitive generalisations and potential scenarios were further discussed and analysed. Sales promotion consumer and trade objectives, including increased sales, trial stimulation, brand switching and rewarding of loyalty were analysed and the difference between price and creative promotions was highlighted. Outcomes, including the potential downsides to promotions, were discussed and the legal issues considered.

review questions

1. What are the four types of sales promotion?

2. What is the difference between positive and negative reinforcement in relation to sales promotion? Give examples of each.

3. Explain 'chaining'.

4. Describe the phenomenon known as the 'mortgaging effect'.

5. What do you understand by the term 'self-liquidating promotion'?

6. Explain the benefits behind undertaking a cause-related promotion.

7. How might a trade promotion differ from a consumer-based promotion?

8. List a range of sales promotion tactics that an organisation could use.

9. How might sales promotion activities assist in building or maintaining loyalty?

10. Why are loyalty programmes supposed to be effective?

discussion questions

1. What are the similarities and difference between advertising and sales promotion?

2. A number of intuitive generalisations can be made about sales promotion. What are they and what might their impact be on campaign planning?

3. For consumer-focused promotions, there can be many sales promotion objectives. List these and discuss how they might be achieved.

case study 10.1: Strategically building the brand – the case of iPhone

The introduction, in 2007, of the *Apple* iPhone was set to revolutionise the mobile phone market around the world. *Apple*'s marketing strategy from the start was to differentiate the iPhone from other smartphones on the market. Their principal target customers were middle–upper-income professionals that needed a PDA (personal digital assistant) device to co-ordinate their busy schedules and communicate with colleagues, friends and family. Their secondary consumer targets were high school, college and university students who also wanted a multifunction device. With this group there was a certain amount of cannibalisation as they expected the iPhone to replace the iPod in younger people's affections.

Credit: Canadapanda/Shutterstock.com

Apple set itself challenging objectives. In year one, the aim was to get a 2% market share of sales in the USA and the UK, rising to 10% in year two. They planned to do this by partnering with large mobile phone service suppliers and aggressive marketing. Advertising for the iPhone was created by TBWA/Media Arts Lab, a multidisciplinary advertising division of TBWA Worldwide that works exclusively with *Apple*. TBWA Worldwide itself is a unit of Omnicom Group Inc., one of the largest advertising, marketing and corporate communications parent companies in the world.

When the iPhone was originally launched in 2007, most contemporary mobile phones were very clunky, with limited, if any, online functionality. *Apple*'s aim was to change that and this was evident both in the product's features and in the way it was publicised. Advertising for the iPhone in 2007 trumpeted the integration of the iPod, video playback, full Web browser, glass multi-touch screen and its aluminium body. It was not, in itself, a wholly revolutionary product but the iPhone's overall design elegance and standout features made it attractive and, as a result, sales grew rapidly.

Apple sought to build on the initial momentum. In 2008, it announced cheaper iPhones, along with more professional versions with greater memory, battery time, video conferencing and professional application support, at appropriate price levels. To support this, the company released another new advertising campaign emphasising the new features. This was promoted heavily during the Beijing Olympics to further internationalise the presence of *Apple* and the iPhone.

In 2008, *Apple* released the iPhone 3G, with its 'game-changing' support for third-party applications (apps). While the 3G body changed to a curved, plastic exterior, the really exciting innovation concerned the software and an array of applications that meant that consumers could get far more from their mobile phones. By now the iPhone was a major force in the marketplace with 17.4 million purchased by the end of 2008. More innovation followed. In *Apple*'s 2009 iPhone campaign, the company promoted the new model's video and improved camera functions as a way of luring consumers looking for a reason to upgrade. The exterior of the phone did not change much, but the hardware was significantly improved.

In 2010 the iPhone 4 arrived with a new front and back glass design and a metal antenna along the sides. This time the advertising campaign concentrated on its high-resolution display, the App Store and Facetime, the phone's video-calling feature. iPhone users in the adverts were also shown using 'Siri', the new virtual personal

(Continued)

(Continued)

assistant. By March 2011, *Apple* had sold approximately 108 million iPhones worldwide and it appeared that the technological innovations, supported by aggressive marketing, were paying off.

The iPhone 5 arrived in 2012, with a thinner body and longer screen and with it came a change in the focus of the advertising message. The campaign now reinforced the idea that a person's life was less meaningful without an iPhone. The company illustrated how deeply embedded the iPhone already was in their owner's lives, and in the lives of people across the globe. As the advertising said, 'If you don't have an iPhone, well, you don't have an iPhone'. This emphasis continued with the iPhone 5c, launched in 2013, and the iPhone 5s. Indeed, *Apple*'s first iPhone 5s television commercial clearly positioned the main iPhone line as an expensive, decadent product. It was no coincidence that the company also made available a gold-coloured case.

In six years, *Apple* has gone from telling consumers how much they need an iPhone to showing them how much they love having one and how important it is in their lives. The advertising has won numerous awards over the years including, in 2009, Adweek's 'Brand of the Decade' for 'relentlessly improving its products' and its 'emotional connection to consumers'. The campaigns owed their success to a combination of ground-breaking technology and marketing. The obvious question now is, where will *Apple* go next?

Case study questions

1. What creative messages did *Apple* use to attract its target markets?
2. Why was the emphasis in the advertising message changed?
3. Where will *Apple* go next?

 ## further reading

Alvarez, B.A. and Casielles, R.V. (2005) 'Consumer evaluations of sales promotion: the effect on brand choice', *European Journal of Marketing*, 39 (1–2).

Bigne-Alcaniz, E., Curras-Perez, R., Ruiz-Mafe, C and Sanz-Blas, S. (2012) 'Cause-related marketing influence on consumer responses: the moderating effect of cause–brand fit', *Journal of Marketing Communications*, 18 (4): 265–83.

Borges, A., Cliquet, G. and Fady, A. (2005) 'Buying association and its impact on promotional utility', *International Journal of Retail & Distribution Management*, 33 (5): 343–52.

DelVecchio, D., Henard, D.H. and Freling, T.H. (2006) 'The effect of sales promotion on post-promotion brand preference: a meta-analysis', *Journal of Retailing*, 82 (3): 203–13.

Laroche, M., Pons, F., Zgolli, N., Cervellon, M. and Kim, C. (2003) 'A model of consumer response to two retail sales promotion techniques', *Journal of Business Research*, 56 (7): 513–22.

Peattie, K. and Peattie, S. (1995) 'Sales promotion: a missed opportunity for services marketers?', *International Journal of Service Industry Management*, 6 (1): 22–39.

REFERENCES

Bolger, M. (2013) 'Caffè culture', *The Marketer*, pp. 20–3.

De Pelsmacker, P., Geuens, M. and Van den Bergh, J. (2007) *Marketing Communications: A European Perspective*, 3rd edn. London: Prentice Hall.

Ehrenberg, A., Hammond, K. and Goodhardt, G.J. (1994) 'The after-effects of price-related consumer promotions', *Journal of Advertising Research*, Jul./Aug.: 11–21.

Fill, C. (2009) *Marketing Communications: Interactivity, Communities and Content*, 5th edn. Harlow: Financial Times/Prentice Hall.

Foxall, G.R., Goldsmith, R. and Brown, S. (1998) *Consumer Psychology for Marketing*, 2nd edn. London: Cengage Learning.

Jones, J.P. (1990) 'The double-jeopardy of sales promotion', *Harvard Business Review*, 68 (5): 145–52.

Kim, C. (2011) 'An exploratory analysis of marketing budget allocation: advertising vs. sales promotion', *The Ritsumeikan Business Review*, 1 (2–3): 91–111.

McGovern, G.J., Court, D. Quelch, J.A. and Crawford, B. (2004) 'Bringing custom to the boardroom', *Harvard Business Review*, Nov.: 70–80.

Shimp, T.A. (2010) *Advertising, Promotion and Supplemental Aspects of Integrated Marketing Communications*, 8th edn. London: Thomson Learning.

Srinivasan, S., Pauwels, K., Hanssens, D.M. and Dekimpe, M. (2002) 'Who benefits from price promotions?', *Harvard Business Review*, Sept.: 22–3.

Uncles, M. (1994) 'Do you need a loyalty scheme?', *Journal of Targeting, Measurement and Analysis for Marketing*, 2 (4): 335–50.

USEFUL WEBSITES

Visit the Institute of Promotion Marketing's website at: www.theipm.org.uk

For details on the top promotions on *Facebook*, see: www.businessinsider.com/the-30-biggest-advertisers-on-facebook-2012-9?op=1

For additional materials that support this chapter and your learning, please visit:
study.sagepub.com/egan

PUBLIC RELATIONS

11

CHAPTER CONTENTS

LEARNING OBJECTIVES

Having completed this chapter, readers would be expected to:

- understand the importance of public relations in the modern organisation

- describe the purpose of publicity and the importance of media management

- recognise the significance of corporate image and the importance of research and counselling as a function of PR

- understand the part played by internal marketing and how organisations manage it

- appreciate the importance of specialist areas of PR such as financial relations, lobbying and crisis management.

INTRODUCTION

Public relations (PR), although considered by some to be a relatively young profession, can (like other marcom tools) be traced back to the earliest times. Edward Bernays (regarded as one of the fathers of modern PR) has argued (1945) that the rulers of ancient Egypt, Sumeria, Babylonia, Assyria and Persia all used techniques that would today be described as public relations (although the term had not yet been identified). Indeed, a clay tablet found in Iraq from around 2000 BC, showing farmers how to sow crops, is considered by some to be the earliest known example of PR. In ancient Greece and Rome, PR tactics were used in these highly politicised states. Greek philosophers like Socrates and Plato promoted the value of honest communications. Aristotle studied persuasion as a method of manipulating public opinion to support particular political causes. The earliest formal PR activities were undertaken largely to promote something or to 'spread the faith' – the original definition of propaganda (Gruning and Hunt 1984). Machiavelli, for example, was not only a consummate politician but a PR practitioner of the highest order. After all, throughout history politicians have always needed to communicate with different **publics** (see Insight below). For example, British politician Lloyd George, as Chancellor of the Exchequer, used PR to promote the old-age pension in 1912, and Sir Steven Tallents (the first President of the Institute of Public Relations) used PR to promote the *Empire Marketing Board* between 1926 and 1933 (Baines et al. 2004). Harry S. Truman saw his job as US President as akin to PR when he wrote: 'all the president is, is a glorified public relations man who spends his time flattering, kissing, and kicking people to get them to do what they are supposed to do anyway' (CIPR at: www.cipr.org.uk). PR's rise to prominence in the commercial sector also began earlier than is often realised. Industrial growth during the nineteenth century meant that by 1900 powerful business interests in the USA were employing public relations professionals to 'defend their special interests against muckraking journalism and government regulation' (Cutlip et al. 2006).

PR has seen enormous growth, particularly in the latter part of the twentieth century. PR expenditure in the UK increased 150-fold from an estimated £50 million in the early 1960s to approximately £7.5 billion in 2011. The numbers of people employed in the business over the same period grew from 4,000 to 61,600. In parallel with its growth has come its increased importance. According to one of the world's richest men, Bill Gates: 'If I was down to my last dollar I would spend it on PR' (Moloney 2006).

Others see PR's importance continuing to rise: 'as members of the public become increasingly marketing savvy, anecdotal evidence suggests that a more subtle approach to engaging emotions has become the key to successful campaigns' (Siegle 2005: 41).

By the end of the twentieth century, the term 'PR' had entered everyday language as had certain PR jargon such as campaign, **press release**, **image**, **spin doctor**, **soundbite, on-message, prebuttle** and **relaunch** (Moloney 2006). The Institute of Public Relations (IPR) became the CIPR as it gained 'chartered status', signalling both its increased prominence and managerial acceptance. Indeed, CIPR membership figures have more than doubled in the last 10 years. Approximately 55% of its members are female (from 20% in 1987), 45% of its members work in PR consultancy and 55% work in-house (www.cipr.org.uk). In 1998, the *Spectator* magazine declared PR the 'profession of the decade'. Public relations in the new millennium is, it would seem, the new advertising!

PR DEFINITIONS

The Chartered Institute of Public Relations (www.cipr.org.uk) defines PR as:

> the discipline which looks after reputation, with the aim of earning understanding and support and influencing opinion and behaviour. It is the planned and sustained effort to establish and maintain good will and mutual understanding between an organisation and its publics.

The Public Relations Consultants Association (PRCA) offers the following simple statement which gets to the core of PR:

> Public relations is all about reputation. It's the result of what you do, what you say, and what others say about you. It is used to gain trust and understanding between an organisation and its various publics.

These definitions place PR at the very top of the organisation hierarchy. Indeed, the increasingly popular term **corporate communications** is strongly associated with these definitions. It is not uncommon in many organisations for advertising and sales promotion managers, as well as **public relations officers (PROs)** and press officers, to report to the director of corporate communications rather than the marketing director. In this type of organisation, marketing communications is seen as part of public relations. According to IPR/DTI research, 20% of organisations have PR decision makers at board level and a further 47% as a top-line management responsibility.

The alternative argument to this is that PR is part of the marketing communications mix. While suggesting that the evolution of corporate communications and 'marketing PR' were different, Kotler and Mindak (1978) argued that they consisted of overlapping activities and encouraged their integration. This view is not without controversy. One American academic, Martha Lauzen, has argued that by aligning PR with marketing the latter is attempting to subsume the former through what she calls 'marketing imperialism' (Briggs and Tuscon 1993). Certainly, by volume of production there is more **marketing PR** than any other type of public relations (Moloney 2006). PR as a subset of marketing is often associated with the term publicity. With 'publicity', the 'good will and mutual understanding' of the earlier definition relates more to building the image of the brand and creating associations between that brand and its publics (see Insight below). In effect, PR style and function is heavily determined by the organisational type and PR's recognised role within the individual organisation.

Corporate communications
An organisational function that controls all aspects of communication with an organisation's publics outside of marketing.

Marketing public relations
Those aspects of public relations directly associated with communication with customers or prospective customers (i.e. publicity).

Publicity
Building the image of the brand and creating positive associations between that brand and its publics.

◉ insight: PR publics

Public relations departments are not concerned with the general public per se but with a range of different communities. These are known in PR jargon as '**publics**'. The word 'publics' has a very particular meaning and one peculiar to PR. 'Publics' are those people, internal and external to the organisation, with whom the organisation communicates. These may include (but are not necessarily limited to):

- customers
- shareholders
- the community
- financial markets
- existing and potential employees
- media and other opinion formers
- suppliers of goods and services
- government and other legislators
- distributors
- other stakeholders.

Around the world, people work in PR departments (or associated agencies) although many such departments have names such as Public Affairs or more contemporary titles such as Corporate Affairs or Corporate Communications (Dolphin & Fan 2000). Despite the difficulties in accurately describing public relations, PROs' managers or directors (by whatever title) are usually involved with one, some or all of the following activities:

- publicity: positive messages about the organisation, its employees or other newsworthy stories designed to improve the image of the brand
- media management: sustaining and utilising long-term relationships with the media
- corporate image: publicising the positive aspects of the organisation
- research and counselling: monitoring public and other (e.g. government) opinion
- internal marketing: managing the organisation's relationships with its employees (see Chapter 16)

- shareholder and other financial relations: informing and maintaining good relationships with shareholders and other stakeholders
- lobbying: making the organisation's views and arguments known to law makers
- crisis management: limiting damaging publicity and managing the organisation's response
- community relations: managing the relationship between the organisation and the local community.

This breadth of coverage suggests a wider role than that suggested by the earlier CIPR definition, particularly in relation to research and monitoring. This aspect was discussed at an international public relations conference held in Mexico City in 1978 and the following definition (which became known as the **Mexico Statement**) was issued (cited in Baines et al. 2004):

Public relations practice is the art and social science of analysing trends, predicting their consequences, counselling organisational leaders, and implementing planned programmes of action that will serve both the organisation's and the public interest.

This statement spells out the full role of PR and highlights five important responsibilities associated with the broad function of research and monitoring. These are:

- analysing trends: to investigate the current situation inside and outside of the organisation
- predicting the consequences: making determinations of likely outcomes
- counselling leaders: giving advice on future strategy and tactics
- implementing planned programmes of action: defining the needs and managing the functional aspects of PR including press relations, internal marketing, etc.
- serving the public interest: social responsibility and ethical commercialism.

Public relations, therefore, has the potential to be a powerful and complex tool within the organisational armoury. There are, however, no set models applicable to all organisations, rather the organisation develops the format it requires determined by its individual needs.

PUBLICITY

One of the major functions associated with PR is that of publicity. Publicity is normally described as a series of positive messages about an organisation, its brand(s) or its employees designed to improve the image of the organisation or brand. Positive brand associations, it is suggested, develop sales over time but, as with advertising, it is almost impossible to measure the effect of publicity in anything but the broadest of terms. Proxy measures are used to gauge the success of an ongoing publicity campaign. The most extensively used measure is **media evaluation** (according to research by *Metrica*, 90% of organisations use media evaluation – Siegle 2005). Media evaluation is, according to the Association of Media Evaluation Companies, 'the systematic appraisal of a company's reputation, products or services, or those of its competitors, as measured by their presence in the media' (cited in Theaker 2011: 255). This evaluation is carried out either in-house or by media evaluation specialists and, by way of estimating the value of publicity, an approximate **Advertising Cost Equivalent (ACE)** is established. Media evaluation of this type has long had its critics but at the very least it shows how frequently and in what context the organisation has appeared on the media agenda (see Insight).

Directly ascribing PR investment to increased output, however, remains contentious. According to David McLaren of leading PR agency *Hill & Knowlton*, 'the industry's Achilles heel is its inability to show the relationship between PR output and marketplace effect, affordably'. Indeed, according to research at *Henley*

Management College over half of PROs cited 'gut feel' as their primary way of evaluating the success of their campaigns (Siegle 2004).

Although positive publicity is a major PR objective, there is evidence to suggest that even negative publicity can generate potentially valuable awareness. Sacha Baron Cohen's satirical film *Borat: Cultural Learnings of America for Make Benefit Glorious Nation of Kazakstan* was banned in Kazakhstan because it appeared to make fun of the country. However, the foreign minister there now credits the film for an increase in tourism. Other examples of companies for whom negative publicity appears regularly are *Ryanair* and *Benetton*. Again, adverse comment does not seem to have harmed these companies' profits, and may well have contributed (through wider exposure) to increased turnover. However, the danger for companies that provoke anger among the public has risen considerably with the advent of anti-company websites (or **gripe sites**) which may have an effect in the longer term.

PR publicity contributes to a brand in ways similar to those discussed in the chapter on advertising. There are, however, some significant differences. Unlike

Gripe site
A website created to carry negative messages concerning an organisation(s) and/or brand(s).

insight: Media evaluation

Effective media evaluation combines both qualitative and quantitative analysis. Media evaluation company *Paperclip Partnership* lists those aspects it considers make up a good evaluation:

Qualitative media evaluation

Tonal bias: does the article have a positive, neutral or negative slant?

Tone of the media: reflecting the mood of the press

Target publications: is there coverage in target publications?

Core message: tracking what publications are picking up your core message

Press release: tracking how much of your release has been published verbatim

Sector analysis: measuring the industry sector's media coverage as a whole

Competitor analysis: what are your competitors up to?

Quantitative media evaluation

ACE value: measuring the success of campaigns in advertising terms

PR value: measuring the success of campaigns in PR terms

Impressions/impacts: viewing opportunities x number who see it

Column centimetre data: how many column centimetres does your editorial cover?

Demographics: what sort of people see your coverage?

Keyword tracking: the number of times keywords appear

Media breakdown: the publications your message appears in.

Source: www.paperclippartnership.co.uk/media-evaluation.html

FIGURE 11.1   Public relations in context

advertising, the organisation does not pay to place its message in the media of its choice. In effect, the publicised messages (in the form of press releases, speeches, etc.) must compete for attention with other newsworthy stories. Even if the story is taken up by one or more media outlets, there is no guarantee that the message will be published in the form and with the positive content favoured by the company because journalists will interpret the message in whichever way they wish. Publicity is not, therefore, 'free advertising' (particularly because it involves costs in terms of management and other resources) and there is no guarantee (unlike advertising) of message placement or prominence. Another distinction is that while the cost of advertising is dictated by the media into which it is placed, the costs involved in PR are measured largely in terms of the expenditure of personnel resources. Figure 11.1 shows the relationships between PR publicity and other major marcom tools in terms of their brand- and image-building contribution and the major source of costs.

Another difference between the PR practitioner and other marketing communications specialists is that their interest goes well beyond that of the consumer. Other 'publics' (see Insight page 215) have to be targeted and the objective may be other than increased sales. In the case of bad publicity, other 'publics' of importance to the company (e.g. financiers, shareholders, government regulators) may receive messages that would both affect the confidence of shareholders and the company's ability to raise, at competitive rates, funding from financial markets. Here the PR responsibility would be that of **crisis management** (see page 224). This might include in some circumstances distancing the company from ex-directors and reassuring shareholders and markets of the organisation's current financial probity.

Publicity, like other marcom tools, is frequently more effective in combination with other tools than alone (see Chapter 15 on integrated marketing communications). *Wonderbra* advertising, costing £50,000, was said to have generated publicity in excess of £50 million.[1] *Camelot's* sponsorship of the British Olympic rowing team generated publicity far in excess of the company's investment. When *Apple* launched its latest version of the iPad (in September 2012), the publicity generated crowds of expectant buyers who, in turn, were publicised on broadcast and print media around the world.

Crisis management
Management of a crisis situation that has the capacity to severely damage an organisation.

---

[1]   This type of estimate is based on media monitoring and a calculation of the cost of any coverage in paid-for advertising terms.

In addition to companies wishing to publicise themselves, the rise of the 'cult of celebrity' has led to a sub-genre of PR professionals known as **'publicists'**. Most famous among these is Max Clifford who, until his recent personal notoriety, had represented the famous and the infamous over his 40-year career. Publicists, in essence, differ little from the traditional PRO in keeping their clients in (or out) of the public eye, thus enhancing their celebrity and/or earnings potential.

Publicist
A professional who seeks to promote or protect their clients in or from the media.

MEDIA MANAGEMENT

In terms of PR activities, media relations is the largest volume activity (Maloney 2006). According to Center and Jackson (2003), the PR practitioner serves two masters: the employer and the public interest, and the media, they suggest, stand between the two. Although this has an element of hyperbole, it stresses the importance to good public relations of a thorough knowledge of and close relationship with the media. The terms **'press office'** and **'press officer'** (PRO) are still the terms most widely used to describe the unit and personnel responsible for communications with the media despite the extension of their role to cover other news mediums (e.g. television, radio, internet, etc.). Although there is some evidence of a move to **'media office'** and **'media officer'** (MRO), the old titles have largely remained despite the broadening of the role. The press officer is there to act positively on behalf of the organisation, which means not only reacting to media requests for information but proactively working with the media in creating newsworthy stories.

Press office or media office
An office which handles press and other media enquiries and issues press releases.

Press officer (PRO) or media officer (MRO)
A representative of the company who handles press and other media enquiries and issues press/media releases.

The ability to produce and transmit properly written and targeted news releases and the kind of temperament to get on with journalists is crucial in the PRO/MRO role. The press officer's objective is not sending out **press releases** (or **media releases**) per se but getting them published. When this works, it can be very effective. It has been suggested that 80% of what appears in the business pages of newspapers and 40–50% of general news is produced or influenced by PR practitioners. It has been estimated, however, that in the UK, of the 130 million press releases sent each year 126 million go straight into editors' waste baskets (Smith and Taylor 2004).

Although the mass media has its place, it is vital to recognise the importance of targeting 'special interest' mediums. In some quarters, it is believed that the media are the 'publics' for an organisation, or indeed, by achieving media coverage that, in itself, achieves the goal. The reality is that the media is simply a conduit for accessing the true publics and that coverage in no way ensures that the message will be seen. It is important, therefore, to acknowledge that there are other conduits, such as face-to-face communication, and these too will need to be utilised as appropriate.

In order to develop a newsworthy story, the press officer needs to have good lines of internal and external communication so as to encourage the flow of news and develop the knowledge of where to place it. Mass-distributed press releases on subjects unlikely to interest anyone outside of a confined readership (and perhaps not even then) are, quite literally, not worth the paper they are written on. Targeted releases are both much more likely to be published and more cost-effective for the organisation.

CORPORATE IMAGE AND CORPORATE IDENTITY

The corporate image of an organisation is seen as a role managed by the PR practitioner. Corporate image and corporate identity are terms that are often confused. Although the latter should contribute positively and help define the former, they

FIGURE 11.2   The public relations transfer process

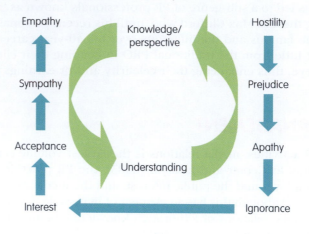

Public relations transfer process
A theory of public relations that suggests incremental stages between hostility and acceptance.

Mirror image
How internal management think outsiders see the organisation.

Current image
The image held by outsiders based on a consensus of perceptions modelled by their knowledge and experience.

Multiple image
Where different people see different images, dependent on their particular relationship with the organisation.

Wish image
The image that an organisation aspires to achieve.

Optimum image
The image a company aspires to (wish image) may not be possible and so a rather less than perfect image may be sought.

are different concepts. Corporate identity concerns the aims, values and ethos of an organisation and a key aspect of this is its visual cohesion and representation in terms of aspects such as company name, logo and livery. Corporate identity is physical and is how an organisation portrays itself to the outside world. Corporate image is, in contrast, highly subjective. It is what 'publics' see and feel when confronted by an organisation and is based on their knowledge and prior experience. Poor image problems can be two-fold. Either the company deserves its image or it has in some way been misunderstood. Misunderstanding can be resolved through communication and it is the responsibility of the PRO to implement this. This has been called the **public relations transfer process** (Baines et al. 2004). Whatever level of opinion is current, the PRO is looking to move that further in favour of the organisation through knowledge and greater understanding. This is illustrated in Figure 11.2.

An image that is deservedly poor can only be corrected by the organisation itself. Frequently, attempts to improve an organisation's image without dealing with the root cause lead to further negative publicity. The exposure of *Nike*'s use of overseas 'sweatshops' affected its corporate image significantly and no amount of public relations justification could resolve this until they changed their manufacturing policy.

An organisation's image can, of course, mean different things to different publics, as well as internally within the organisation. Baines et al. (2004) describe the different forms of image and their relationship with one another as follows:

- **mirror image**: how internal management think outsiders see the organisation. In the mirror held up to the company, the image looks rosier than from the outside
- **current image**: the image held by outsiders based on a consensus of perceptions modelled on their knowledge and experience
- **multiple image**: where different people see different images dependent on their particular relationship with the organisation. For example, a customer's view of a low-cost supermarket may be excellent whereas its suppliers may be highly critical of it
- **wish image**: the image that the organisation aspires to
- **optimum image**: what the company might aspire to may not be possible and so a rather less than perfect image may be sought. For example, petroleum companies are unlikely to be admired by the general public and, as such, might seek a more benign and responsive persona rather than being high profile.

An organisation wishing to sustain or adapt its corporate image should do this as part of its integrated communications strategy (see Chapter 15). This would include conducting regular **communications audits** (also called **reputation audits**).

FIGURE 11.3 Image management

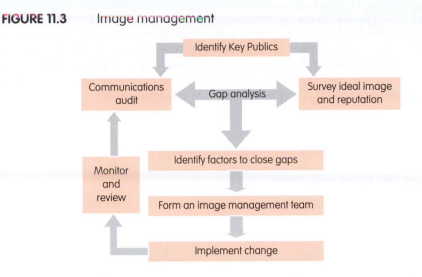

A communications audit examines a number of aspects, from the functional elements to the specific. Functional aspects include factors such as communication need, channels, technologies, patterns, etc. Specific aspects include content and content clarity of the message, its effectiveness, the effective fulfilment and inclusion of the needs of the various parties involved in its construction, the reflection of corporate culture and the wider impact of the communication in terms of organisational motivation and performance. Figure 11.3 outlines the process that might be followed when a firm needs to bring about an effective change in its image. The diagram suggests the disparity between how a company would like to see itself (wish image) and how management might regard it (mirror image), and contrasts this with how its publics see it (current image) through a communications audit. The factors contributing to the gap are analysed and the means of closing that gap in perceptions is sought.

Communications (or reputation) audit
Looks at communications' needs, patterns, flow, channels and technologies, examines content clarity and effectiveness, information needs of individuals, work groups, departments and divisions, non-verbal communications and corporate culture issues and communication impacts on motivation and performance.

RESEARCH AND COUNSELLING

Although outlined in the Mexico Statement (see page 216), this element of PR is often under-represented, particularly in relation to marketing communications. However, as early as 1922 Edward Bernays, in a book entitled *Crystallizing Public Opinion*, talked about the 'new profession of public relations counsel'. In this he explained that PR counsellors were different from press agents and publicists of the day and that they were using:

> the knowledge generated by social science to understand public opinion, public motivation, public relations techniques, and methods for modifying group points of view. The objective of the public relations counsel was to interpret the organisation to the public and the public to the organisation. (cited in Gruning and Hunt 1984: 3)

This act of mediation between the organisation and its public is an important one. The responsibilities are to evaluate public attitudes and ensure that the policies and procedures of an organisation are in line with it. Public attitude may be measured through survey methods or more qualitative methodologies such as focus groups. Public attitude may be informed and/or hardened by 'influencers' such as the media. In recent years, various media have been responsible for creating reaction to everything from the European Union to national football team management and much more in between. Public opinion changes and the PRO should understand its implications for the organisation. For example, in December 2012 global coffee chain Starbucks was one of several well-known firms criticised over the level of tax they paid in the UK. This was highly publicised by the media and there was a public backlash to the news. In response, the company held talks with the UK Revenue and Customs and the Treasury over how much UK tax it pays and admitted that it 'needed to do more' in the UK on tax.

SHAREHOLDER AND OTHER FINANCIAL RELATIONSHIPS

According to the *Public Relations Society of America*, financial PR is:

> that area of Public Relations which relates to the dissemination of information that affects the understanding of stockholders (shareholders) and investors generally concerning the financial position and prospects of a company and includes among its objectives the improvement of relations between corporations and their stockholders. (PRSA 1995: 22)

This is probably an over-simplification as it is not only existing shareholders that are important as financial intermediaries can also have a considerable influence on existing or future shareholders. The main financial publics are, therefore:

- current shareholders
- prospective shareholders
- financial intermediaries (banks, credit rating agencies, stock markets, etc.)
- financial media (specialist financial press such as the *Financial Times* and the *Wall Street Journal*, as well as the financial sections of national and international newspapers).

Financial publics are highly active and interested in a company's financial status and react to information accordingly. With 'good news' (frequently transmitted through press releases to the financial media), existing shareholders may decide to retain or extend their investment while new shareholders help stabilise or increase the share price. Organisational stability and profitability may attract a favourable **credit rating** from **ratings agencies** such as *Moody's* and *Standard and Poor's*, which will affect the organisation's ability to borrow and the rate on which that loan is based. Since the financial crisis, the importance of credit ratings has become important at national and international level as the 'bad news' emanating from some Eurozone countries was reflected in poorer ratings and higher interest on national debt. In addition, as confidence in major financial institutions has fallen, and stakeholders and regulators have demanded greater corporate accountability and transparency, the more important the role of financial PRO has become.

Shareholders, in public limited companies, are its financial backbone. In essence, the primary objective of such organisations should be the creation of maximum shareholder value although short-term management-driven objectives are often seen to be in opposition to this. Shareholders generally come in two forms. First is the institutional investor who buys and retains shares as a fundraising device on behalf of pension funds, unit trusts and other investment mediums. In this instance, loyalty to a particular company is small as the institutional investor looks for the best return on behalf of his/her fund or investment trust. At the other end of the scale is the private investor, who is also looking for a return on their investment, however, rather than invest in general cross-market funds (e.g. investment trusts), they buy shares from one or more specific organisations. If a publicly quoted company has a large number of private shareholders, they can prove to be a very powerful constituency. It is widely believed that Philip Green's failure to take over *Marks and Spencer* in 2005 was due in large part to the loyalty of private shareholders to the existing management.

Credit rating
Ratings based on the perceived financial integrity of the organisation; ratings are set by ratings agencies.

Ratings agency
An organisation such as *Dun and Bradstreet* or *Standard and Poor's* who monitors companies and establishes credit ratings based on perceived commercial risk. These ratings affect the company's ability to lend and the rate on which the loan is based.

Responsibilities under the heading of financial PR are varied and diverse. They include:

- the preparation and distribution of financial news releases
- media placement of newsworthy, positive stories about the organisation, ensuring company spokesperson involvement where pertinent
- production and circulation of annual reports and the conduct of shareholder meetings
- the production and distribution of shareholder newsletters and/or the maintenance of shareholder websites
- in the event of financial activity (e.g. takeover, share issue, buy-back) the transfer of news and information to relevant stakeholders.

An in-house public relations officer's (PRO) responsibility for financial PR may not extend beyond existing shareholder relations and day-to-day contact with the financial media. Other financial PR functions may be associated directly with the organisation's financial director. Often, specialised agencies (see Insight) are used on a contract basis, particularly in relation to complex financial activity.

insight: Selecting a public relations agency

The Public Relations Consultants Association (PRCA), an industry body representing many PR agencies, offers the following advice on selecting the right sort of PR agency.

Generalised benefits	Specialised benefits
• Agencies who provide the potential to translate key learning/successes from one market to another. • Agencies who generally have a bigger market and geographical spread and who can reach those audiences required by the organisation. • Agencies who have a bigger base of staff and in-house resources to call on. • Agencies that have access to more or higher supplier discounts. • Generalised agencies who have specialised departments.	• Agencies who have specialist expertise of markets, audiences and/or communication streams. • Agencies that understand niche markets/audiences and how to communicate with them effectively. • Agencies who are closely networked with key opinion formers within niche markets. • Agencies who provide smaller working teams and, therefore, the potential for the development of client–consultancy relationships. • Agencies reputed to have lower overheads.

Source: www.prca.org.uk

LOBBYING[2]

As with financial PR, lobbying is seen as a specialist area of public relations. In many organisations, this is often called **public affairs** to emphasise that it largely

Public affairs
A specialist area of practice within public relations concerned with public policy making, legislation and regulation that may affect the interests of the organisation.

---

[2] There is some dispute over the origin of the term. The name derives either from the practice of UK Members of Parliament meeting constituents and others in the lobby of the House of Commons or from the habit of US politicians meeting petitioners in the lobby of the Willard Hotel in Washington.

involves relationships with governmental organisations and, perhaps, to distance it from the somewhat tarnished reputation of some lobbyists. Public affairs has been defined as a specialist area of public relations concerned with those relationships involved in public policy making, legislation and regulation (see Insight). Lobbying, meanwhile, has been described as a specialist part of public relations that builds and also maintains relationships with government largely for the purpose of influencing legislation and regulation (Cutlip et al. 2006). The differences appear to be more semantic than substantial.

Lobbying is all about knowledge and relationships. The knowledge of how the various levels of government work and how they can be best influenced is coupled with access to those people (not necessarily the final decision makers) who can best affect it. These may be politicians, civil servants or other influencers. Some lobbyists successfully use the media to put their case and build up public opinion for and against an issue. Such is the specialist nature of lobbying that in all but the largest corporations lobbying is usually undertaken either by trade or management associations (e.g. the *Confederation of British Industry (CBI)*) or specialist lobbying agencies.

insight: What is public affairs?

According to *PubAffairs*, the public affairs, government relations, policy and communications network, public affairs:

is a term used to describe an organisation's relationship with stakeholders. These are individuals or groups with an interest in the organisation's affairs, such as MPs, civil servants, shareholders, customers, clients, trade associations, think tanks, business groups, unions and the media. Public affairs practitioners engage stakeholders in order to explain the organisation's policies, to provide statistical and factual information and to lobby on issues which could impact on the organisation's ability to operate successfully. Their work combines government relations, media communications, issue management, corporate and social responsibility, information dissemination and strategic communications advice. They aim to influence public policy, build and maintain a strong reputation and find a common ground with these stakeholders. (www.publicaffairsnetworking.com)

CRISIS MANAGEMENT

Response to crisis situations has become an important function of PR. According to Hayes (2001), the best way to destroy one's reputation is to be ill-prepared for all types of crises and to fail to take a stand on appropriate issues. A crisis is not a day-to-day problem but one that has the capacity to severely damage the organisation. The crisis may be caused for all manner of reasons but is likely to have one or more of the following characteristics (White and Mazur 1995):

- a high degree of threat to life, to safety or to the continuing existence of the organisation
- time pressure (ensuring that decision makers have to work quickly)
- stress placed on those responsible for managing the situation.

Examples of possible crises include industrial accidents, environmental problems, hostile takeovers, strikes, kidnapping, product tampering, product recall, security leaks, unethical behaviour, workplace violence, employee fraud and government action (Baines et al. 2004). Managing the response to the situation is of paramount importance as it may not be the incident per se that causes the critical episode but the company's response to it (see Insight).

insight: Tesco crisis management

On 15 January 2013, it was reported that horse DNA had been discovered in processed foods sold in several Irish and British supermarkets. Foods, such as beef burgers and lasagne, advertised as containing beef, were found to contain undeclared horse meat, as much as 100% of the meat content in some cases. While horse meat is not harmful to health and is eaten around the world, it is considered a taboo in many countries, including the UK and Ireland. Of all the supermarket chains, Tesco were seen to react among the quickest to the crisis. In addition to withdrawing 26 lines, the head of Tesco, Philip Clarke, pledged to bring meat production 'closer to home' and work more closely with British farmers. Tesco were seen to employ an open stance by activating crisis communications strategies during the scandal. In particular, Tesco informed their publics that all the suspect products were withdrawn and emphasised there was no potential risk to health. In the meantime, they apologised, showed sympathy and promised to investigate the whole event and take steps to prevent the situation happening again. The crisis team managed to take control of the first 48 hours of the situation and communicate early with customers, the news media and other stakeholders by various communications tools.

Source: various

Although crisis management is not a day-to-day activity, preparedness should regularly be on the agenda. Active preparedness is described as 'a systematic approach that engages the whole organisation in efforts to avert crises that may affect the firm and manage those that do' (Baines et al. 2004). Crisis management is dealing with the sporadic, the unlikely and the unpredictable, so how can a crisis be foreseen? Although a specific crisis is unlikely to be predictable, it is, however, possible to imagine exceptional situations in advance. On a university campus, for example, the possibility of fire, flooding, etc. may cause those responsible for drawing up contingency measures to develop emergency procedures. Similarly, the PRO may wish to ensure that they have important contact details internally and externally to be able to respond to a crisis effectively and responsibly. More unlikely scenarios such as attack or occupation may not be considered in detail but the general response to a crisis situation (e.g. the formation of a crisis team) can and should be planned for.

Although the media have no right to information, they may often demand it and it is part of crisis decision making to ascertain what information should be released at what time. Attempts to deny responsibility or conceal information in crisis situations (e.g. *Jarvis PLC* during the Potters Bar rail crash or *Ford*'s attempt to blame *Firestone* for a series of accidents in the early 1990s) can often backfire, while openness (e.g. New York Mayor, Rudolf Giuliani's handling of the aftermath of the World Trade Centre attacks on 11 September 2001 or *Transport for London*'s response to the 7 July 2005 bombings) is, generally, seen as a positive move in most situations.

COMMUNITY RELATIONS

This aspect of public relations acknowledges the importance of an organisation maintaining good, or at least respectable, relationships with local, national and wider communities. In addition to wishing to generally avoid 'bad press', there is the likelihood, with consumer goods and services companies in particular, that these communities will, or can, influence your customers. Thus, some organisational policies can have considerably wide-ranging effects, such as *Nestlé*'s marketing of baby milk formula in poorer countries or *Reebok*'s purchasing strategy, which both led to consumer boycotts of these companies. On a more localised note, it is likely that current and future employees are going to come from communities influenced by the activities of the organisation.

CONCLUSION

The heading 'public relations' covers a wide and diverse set of responsibilities that can affect the organisation (and its brands) in widely different ways. From encouraging well-being and association through publicity to lobbying for legislation which will benefit the company, and from maintaining or enhancing financial standing to research and counselling, the PR process is at the heart of an organisation's marketing communications.

summary

This chapter examined the part public relations plays in the modern organisation. In particular, it looked at publicity and media management and how this can be managed to the benefit of the organisation. It examined the growing importance of the research and counselling function within PR and analysed the part played by corporate image and how this might be managed. Internal marketing and internal communications were considered and their importance noted. More specialist areas such as financial relations, lobbying and crisis management were examined and the importance of community relations was noted.

review questions

1. How would you define public relations and why?

2. List a selection of public relations' publics.

3. What are the main responsibilities of public relations in relation to research and monitoring?

4. Who are the main financial publics?

5. What is 'lobbying' and what does it entail?

6. Why might public relations be used for community relations?

7. What was the 'Mexico Statement'?

8. Why might a 'clippings service' be of value?

9. Would you consider publicity to be free advertising?

10. What do you associate with the term 'optimum image'?

discussion questions

1. Public relations is often concerned with managing a company's image. However, this means different things to different people. What are the different ways that image could be interpreted?

2. What might be the responsibilities under the heading of financial public relations and under what circumstances might organisations undertake financial public relations activities?

3. How might you select a public relations agency and what might the problems of selection be?

case study: 1.1 Media management of the 7 July London bombings

On 7 July 2005, at 0850, three simultaneous explosions on the London Underground were followed by a further explosion just under an hour later on the Number 30 London bus in Tavistock Square. A total of 52 people were killed in what transpired to be one of the most devastating terrorist attacks the capital city had witnessed. Within 10 minutes of the first explosions, it was clear that this was an incident of international importance and one that would lead the news headlines around the world during the days that followed. By 1100 that day, over 250 requests for media interviews had been received by the *TfL (Transport for London)* press office, who, by the end of the day, had received around 2000 phone calls.

Hits on the press centre website rose from the daily average of 402 to a staggering 56,562 on the following day.

The TfL press team was in charge of crisis communications. Having undertaken crisis exercises in London, elsewhere in the UK and overseas, the team was well trained for such an eventuality. However, prior to the bomb attacks the press team had been heavily involved in Live8 and the 2012 Olympic bid, which London won the day before the bombings. In the space of 24 hours, the team had had to switch from managing a celebratory national story to managing an unprecedented crisis. Five crisis communications objectives were established on the day of the incident:

- to inform the public to allow them to make travel decisions
- to support operational staff by reducing the impact of media activity
- to show that *TfL*, the emergency services, the GLA (Greater London Authority) and the government were co-ordinated in their response
- to reinforce *Transport for London*'s key message that passenger and staff safety is the top priority
- to minimise the long-term impact on passenger confidence.

In order to achieve these objectives, the press team had to ensure that fast, accurate information was provided to the media, and that the media demand for access was balanced with operational requirements. It was also imperative that co-ordination was maintained with Mayoral, emergency service and government teams, as well

(Continued)

(Continued)

as across TfL itself. The press team also had to ensure that it would be in a position to sustain a professional operation over an unspecified period of time, in demanding circumstances.

After a quick risk assessment, and within 20 minutes of the initial explosions, six press officers were sent, in pairs, to Liverpool Street, Russell Square and Edgware Road tube stations to tackle questions from the media. In order to shorten lines of communication, a press officer joined the NCC (Network Control Centre) to act as an information bridge. At 1030, the first London Resilience communications conference call took place.

The initial messages placed the emphasis on operational information and practical advice for travellers. The fast pace of events involved the evacuation of the entire tube network followed by the withdrawal of the London bus fleet and the suspension of the congestion charge. Buses were subsequently re-introduced within a matter of hours and the following day communication focused on the restoration of a full bus service and around 85% of the tube network by the morning 'rush hour'.

Over the days that followed, the press office assisted in the management of three police press conferences, two Mayoral press conferences, two Mayoral visits to stations and two royal visits. It also organised a multi-language briefing for the Foreign Press association and managed over 270 media broadcast and print interviews. Furthermore, it assisted operational staff by assigning press or British Transport Police officers to stations with large numbers of media, and maintained round-the-clock staffing during this period. Communication aimed to cover three key aspects:

- security: this included urgent reminders not to leave bags
- recovery: it was important for the organisation, their passengers and London as a whole that normal services resumed as quickly as possible
- professionalism: close liaison with staff, senior management and counsellors ensured that the demand from the media was managed without exposing staff to further trauma.

As a result of the prompt actions taken and the well-considered strategy underlying those actions, recovery was relatively quick and passenger levels were soon back to normal. The crisis management strategy had not only dealt immediately with the priorities on the day itself, it had looked ahead to the challenges TfL would face in the days and weeks that followed.

The handling of media communications during the crisis earned the in-house team at *TfL* a high level of critical acclaim from within the PR industry. It was one of the two top media relations case studies presented at the 2006 PR Week 'PR and the Media Conference' and won the award for 'Crisis Communications' at the CIPR Excellence Awards 2006.

Source: www.ipr.org.uk

📖 further reading

Brody, E.W. and Brody, E.W. (2005) 'The brave new world of public relations: a look back', *Public Relations Quarterly*, 50 (4): 31–4.

Edelman, D.J. (2006) 'The golden age of public relations', *Public Relations Quarterly*, 51 (1): 20–1.

Robinson, D. (2006) 'Public relations comes of age', *Business Horizons*, 49 (3).

Ruck, K. and Welch, M. (2012) 'Valuing internal communication: management and employee perspectives', *Public Relations Review*, 38 (2): 294–302.

Scammell, A. (2006) 'Business writing for strategic communications: the marketing and communications mix', *Business Information Review*, 23 (1): 43–9.

Waters, R.D., Burnett, E., Lamm, A. and Lucas, J. (2009) 'Engaging stakeholders through social networking: how nonprofit organizations are using Facebook', *Public Relations Review*, 35 (2): 102–6.

REFERENCES

Baines, P., Egan, J. and Jefkins, F. (2004) *Public Relations: Contemporary Issues and Techniques*. Oxford: Elsevier Butterworth-Heinemann.

Bernays, E.L. (1945) *Public Relations*. Norman, OK: University of Oklahoma Press.

Briggs, W. and Tuscon, M. (1993) 'Public relations versus marketing', *Communications World*, March.

Center, A.H. and Jackson, P. (2003) *Public Relations Practice*, 6th edn. Englewood Cliffs, NJ: Prentice Hall.

Cutlip, S.M., Allen, H.C. and Broom, G.M. (2006) *Effective Public Relations*, 9th edn. Upper Saddle River, NJ: Prentice Hall.

Dolphin, R.R. and Fan, Y. (2000) 'Is corporate communications a strategic function?', *Management Decision*, 38 (2): 99–106.

Gruning, J.E. and Hunt, T.T. (1984) *Managing Public Relations*. New York: Holt, Rinehart & Winston.

Hayes, R. (2001) 'The importance of crises management', *Intermedia*, 29 (4): 36.

Kotler, P. and Mindak, W. (1978) 'Marketing and public relations: should they be partners or rivals?', *Journal of Marketing*, 42 (Oct.): 13–20.

Moloney, K. (2006) *Rethinking Public Relations*, 2nd edn. London: Routledge.

Public Relations Society of America (PRSA) (1995) 'Code of conduct', *Public Relations*, June, pp. 22–5.

Siegle, S. (2004) 'PR league's top 100', *Marketing*, 19 May, pp. 41–9.

Siegle, S. (2005) 'PR league's top 100', *Marketing*, 25 May, pp. 41–50.

Smith, P.R. and Taylor, J. (2004) *Marketing Communications: An Integrated Approach*, 2nd edn. London: Kogan Page.

Theaker, A. (2011) *The Public Relations Handbook*, 4th edn. London: Routledge.

White, J.B. and Mazur, L. (1995) *Strategic Communications Management: Making Public Relations Work*. London: Addison-Wesley/Economist Intelligence Unit.

For additional materials that support this chapter and your learning, please visit:
study.sagepub.com/egan

SPONSORSHIP AND PRODUCT PLACEMENT

12

CHAPTER CONTENTS

LEARNING OBJECTIVES

Having completed this chapter readers would be expected to:

- understand the place of sponsorship in the marketing communications mix

- recognise the reasons behind the growth of sponsorship in recent decades

- discuss the theory underpinning sponsorship

- determine the various sponsorship types and the factors which make them viable

- discuss the advantages and disadvantages of sponsorship.

INTRODUCTION

Sponsorship has never been as prominent in the marketing communications mix as it is today. As one industry commentator notes (Duffy 2004: 19):

> some marketers have long held the belief that, with relevantly matched and effectively leveraged sponsorship, brand loyalty can be built between consumers and sponsors; that sponsorship has the power to build strong brands and drive the bottom line better than any other single form of communication.

In spite of its apparent power as a marketing activity, there does seem to be ambiguity about its role (Dolphin 2003). The area of research that incorporates sponsorship is closely associated with both public relations, within whose management remit sponsorship often falls, and advertising, which is frequently an integral part of any sponsorship arrangement. There is a reasonable argument for placing sponsorship within the field of advertising as the most frequent objective of sponsorship activities is that of creating awareness. This, however,

FIGURE 12.1   Total global sponsorship spending

excludes the element of philanthropy (which is still sometimes evident) and/or the risk that is associated with some forms of sponsorship. Writing at a time of great expansion of sponsorship, Nevett (1982: 194) perhaps reflects yet another viewpoint when he suggested that 'the future of sponsorship seems to lie not so much in its effectiveness as an advertising medium as in providing a means for companies to parade their social consciences in public'.

Modern sponsorship, however, while maintaining in some quarters an element of philanthropy and social consciousness, is primarily viewed as a commercial arrangement. For big-name brands targeting mass consumers, sponsorship today is as carefully thought through as any other marketing tool. According to IEG,[1] sponsorship has been elevated to the level of corporate planning and is much more likely now to be discussed in the context of an integrated marketing communications campaign.

WHAT IS SPONSORSHIP?

Sponsorship is about involvement outside of an individual or company's normal range of activities. A sponsor is 'the provider of funds, resources or services to an individual event or organisation in return for some rights and associations usually to be used for commercial advantage' (Copley 2004: 289).

This definition does not necessarily exclude philanthropic support as there is frequently an association between social recognition and commercial advantage, albeit a tenuous one. Some sponsors do see sponsorship as 'enlightened self-interest' (Smith and Taylor 2004). However, as Warner Canto of *American Express* notes, 'if your primary goal is to donate to a cause, the experts say it's a lot less complicated simply to write a check [cheque]' (cited in Bovée et al. 1995: 510). A cynic might suggest that no sponsorship is undertaken without at least the hope of some commercial (or personal) pay-back.

Notwithstanding the complex and sometimes personal objectives of some sponsorship, within a marketing communications strategy it is essentially a

---

[1]   IEG is a leading North American sponsorship consultancy; see www.sponsorship.com

commercial-based activity wherein access to the target audience of one party is made accessible to another in return for finance, services or resources.

The growth of sponsorship in the last two decades of the twentieth century and into the twenty-first owed much to difficulties associated with advertising. Not only were the costs increasing but some sectors, notably the cigarette industry, were banned from advertising on television, radio and, ultimately, all other media. Brands such as *Marlborough, John Player, Benson & Hedges* and *Silk Cut* moved heavily into sponsorship which was not (at that time) subject to such restrictions. *Formula 1* and other motor racing events and most snooker championships were soon heavily under the patronage of one of the cigarette brands. This coincided, in the UK, with a relaxation in the rules concerning the broadcasting of sponsored sports events. The expansion in the number of such events, partly driven by an increase in available leisure time, provided further sponsorship opportunities.

In the world of communications, sponsorship was coming to be seen as a cost-effective alternative to traditional advertising. For the majority of sponsors, however, this was not the only or even the main promotional activity undertaken by them. Indeed, sponsorship is one marcom tool that should never be used in isolation. Rather, it is supported by other marketing communications tools including advertising, sales promotion and public relations. The role played by sponsorship in the promotional mix is shown in Figure 12.2. It is an informing and image-building tool that requires support from the mix.

In the 2000 Olympics, for example, while approximately 20% of communications expenditure was on sponsorship, over 50% was on advertising. In general terms, it is suggested that whatever the initial cost of a sponsorship deal, the sponsor will spend about 150% on other marcom tools, again notably advertising (Barrand 2004).

WHY SPONSORSHIP WORKS

While sponsorship clearly creates awareness and may be the basis of a trial, there is no direct evidence to suggest that increased awareness leads directly to increased sales although there is a perceived relationship (see Chapter 5). The

FIGURE 12.2   The role of sponsorship in the promotional mix

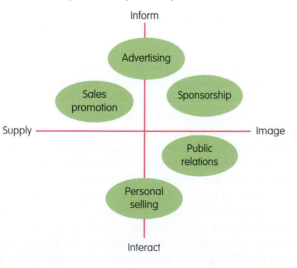

Adapted from Eriksson & Hralmsson (2001)

insight: Why sponsorship?

Marketing magazine (29 June 2012) asked sponsors of the Olympic Games, 'how did you make the case for Olympic sponsorship to your boards?'

Sally Hancock, Director, Olympic Marketing and Group Sponsorship, *Lloyds Banking Group:* It stemmed from our 'For the Journey' repositioning. 2012 seemed a great representation of that. We wrote a detailed case with lots of numbers, which we don't look at now. It has been a leap of faith in LOCOG (London Organising Committee Olympic Games) and a marker that we believed in ourselves as the first sponsor.

Norman Brodie, General Manager, London 2012, *Cadbury*: The original sign-up was around taking *Cadbury* to a global status. However, *Kraft* could have pulled the plug in that it might not have activated the sponsorship, but that hasn't been the case.

Lionel Benbassat, Director of Marketing, *Eurostar*: We knew that we would have a role. Whether (the Games were held) in Paris or London, we were winners. We took a classic business case to the board based on economics, but also how it would position the brand. We are known in Paris, London and Brussels, but not more widely.

Suzi Williams, Group Marketing and Brand Director, *BT*: I wasn't emotionally pro-Olympics, so we ran a meaty piece of research looking at propensity to purchase, and, to my surprise, it showed how Olympic association would build consideration, favourability and purchase. It took a year to get the process signed off. It's a notoriously complicated thing to get involved in, particularly in telecoms.

Ian Symes, Marketing Director, UK, Ireland and London 2012, *Cisco*: There were two drivers: the effect on staff, and to counter a perception that, in the UK, *Cisco* was the sales company for a Californian IT business. For us, the Games is a starting point, not a finish.

Jat Sahota, Head of Sponsorship, *Sainsbury*'s: Respecting the rights of existing food and beverage retailers was important, and we found that it was going to be quite complex for any supermarket. Then the question was posed: 'What about the Paralympics only?' The values were a good fit, and we built the business case from there.

James Eadie, Olympic Portfolio Director, *Coca-Cola*, North West Europe: *Coke* signed up in 1928. As a worldwide partner, you have to understand the host country. (For every Games) we look at what the Olympics can help us transform and address. For London it's worked well because it's a cool city that young people admire.

Source: Stuart Derrick, **www.marketingmagazine.co.uk,** 29 June 2012

building of longer-term associations must also play a part. There are a number of theories as to why sponsorship may work, including those associated with the behavioural and cognitive paradigms discussed in Chapter 3. In behavioural terms, enjoyment of a sponsored event may act as a reinforcement of previous experiences with the brand. The evidence certainly seems to suggest that consumers do feel some gratitude towards sponsorship of events but whether this is affective linking, however, is harder to confirm (Blythe 2000). From a cognitive perspective, it is believed that sponsorship, as with advertising, works through associations that consumers make with the brand and the event or otherwise being sponsored. Positive brand associations may even be more achievable through sponsorship than advertising as the former may be perceived to be less commercial. Consumers may make a judgement based on the fit between the event and the sponsorship in that the greater the degree of compatibility the more readily acceptable the sponsorship is likely to be (Fill 2009). Association between the

FIGURE 12.3 Sponsorship perspective, consumer perspective

$$PI = SL \times DL \times (GL + PL)$$

| Persuasion impact | Strength of link | Duration of the link | Feeling of gratitude | Change in perception |

sponsor and sponsored event is, therefore, important but emotional involvement (attitude strength, actual purchases and word of mouth) is also crucial in terms of recall because of the way attitudes to brands are formed (Copley 2004).

Crimmins and Horn (1996) argue that the persuasive impact of sponsorship is determined in terms of the strength of the links generated between the brand and the sponsorship and the effect on the target audience. They suggest (see Figure 12.3) that the persuasion impact (PI) is a combination of the strength and duration of the sponsorship link and the gratitude and perceptual change associated with it, and they proposed the equation PI = SL x DL x (GL + PL). In this model, 'strength of link' (SL) refers to how integrated the marketing communications is with the event. For example, sponsors who fail to advertise at such events are being less than fully effective at building links with the attending and viewing public. Duration of the link (DL) refers to how long the exposure can be maintained. For example, main sponsors at the Olympic Games may have up to four years' association with the event. A feeling of gratitude (GL) may seem far-fetched, however in a survey 60% of US adults said they try to buy products that support the Olympics and felt they were contributing by buying a sponsor's products (Fill 2009). Finally, the change in perception (PL) due to the sponsorship is introduced into the equation. While not suggesting that such a calculative model can truly represent sponsorship, it highlights those aspects that are seen as important for a successful sponsorship campaign.

Hoek (1999: 366) offers an alternative model (see Figure 12.4) which emphasises the advantages of sponsorship from the consumer perspective. While not putting this forward as a workable equation, it does suggest that it will be the consumer's attitude to the event, to the commercialisation surrounding the event and their ultimate behavioural outcome (e.g. awareness) that determine the success or otherwise of sponsorship. Again, it throws some light on the perceived processes going on.

Abrahamsson, Forsgren and Lungren (2003) suggest that the main objectives of sponsorship include awareness, meeting competitive threat, reaching target markets, building relationships with clients, image building and increasing sales, but that it is important that there is high relevance, uniqueness and compatibility. In addition, they suggest that there are advantages in a long-term agreement and the ability to create 'spin-off' promotions to maximise impact.

SPONSORSHIP TYPES

Sponsorship may be divided into several, not exclusively mutual, types. These are:

- arts sponsorship
- events sponsorship
- sports sponsorship
- broadcast sponsorship (and product placement)
- cause-related sponsorship.

FIGURE 12.4   Sponsorship perspective, consumer perspective

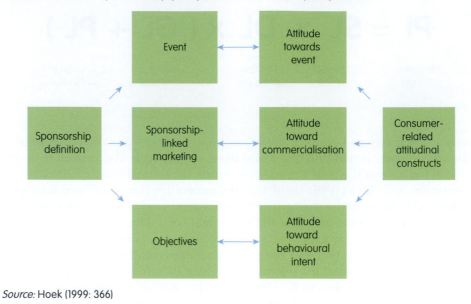

Source: Hoek (1999: 366)

Historically, sponsorship was largely directed towards the arts. Personal sponsorship of musicians and artists by ruling families, church dignitaries and the growing number of wealthy traders, could be said to have supported and nurtured fine art and music throughout the centuries. The de Medici family's sponsorship of Michelangelo and the support of Mozart by both church and state are but two examples of a system of patronage that enabled the arts to develop throughout the world. In 1976 in the UK, the *Association for Business Sponsorship of the Arts (ABSA)* was founded by a group of business leaders. This organisation has been particularly influential in promoting arts sponsorship and today many major corporations are seen to promote the arts. *ABSA* was also a co-founder of the *Comité Europeén pour le Rapprochement de L'Economie et de la Culture* (*CEREC* – The European Committee for Business Arts and Culture). In 2008, the *Prince of Wales Medal for Arts Philanthropy* was created to honour leading philanthropists who have made an outstanding contribution to cultural organisations in the UK. *Ernst and Young* is a good example of a corporate sponsor, following a wholly arts-based, hospitality-associated, sponsorship strategy. According to the company, 'art offers a personality – a different face to the firm' (Gillis 2004: 17). In 2012 the company sponsored the British Design Exhibition at the *Victoria & Albert Museum*. This was *Ernst & Young's* third collaboration with the V&A as the firm had sponsored the highly acclaimed exhibitions Maharaja in 2009 and Art Deco in 2003. Research would seem to back up the effectiveness of art sponsorship. In a report by *Performance Research*, over 50% of those with an interest in the arts indicated they would almost always buy from a company that sponsored cultural events (Dolphin 2003).

Events sponsorship might be seen to come in two forms: those events organised and supported wholly by the company (e.g. *Red Bull*'s cart races) and the more traditional financial sponsorship of existing or future events (e.g. *Virgin* 2013 London Marathon). Either way, there is a good argument that events are more memorable and motivating than a more passive brand message. In recent years, there has been a growth in an offshoot of events marketing known as **experiential marketing**. An early example of this was *Disney* whose theme parks integrated the

Experiential marketing
A strategy that encourages customers to engage and interact with brands, products and services in sensory ways.

brand into a consumer experience. More recent examples include the *Guinness* experience in Dublin and *Cadbury World* in Bournville, Birmingham. These are not just museums or showcases but interactive theatrical events. More extreme was *Red Bull*'s sponsorship of athlete Felix Baumgartner in 2012 to break the world record for the longest free-fall jump (128,000 feet/39,000 metres) in the world, in which he reached speeds of 833.9 miles (1342 kilometres) per hour. Over 8 million people watched the jump live and over 30 million people (and counting) have viewed the jump on *YouTube*. The jump was shown live by over 40 TV stations and 130 digital outlets and was a trending topic on *Twitter* worldwide. *Red Bull*'s *Facebook* photo of the jump generated 216,000 likes, 10,000 comments and over 29,000 shares.

Sports sponsorship has grown incrementally over the past few decades. Its popularity is derived from the ability of some sports at the top level to attract large audiences and extensive media coverage. Demand for top-level sponsorship is high and this is reflected in the ever-increasing costs. For example, it was reported in February 2013 that *Emirates Airlines* had agreed to sponsor *Formula 1* to the tune of $200 million over a period of five years. Such is the demand to sponsor some football events that as well as the teams, the ball, the stadiums (e.g. *Aviva* Stadium, Dublin; *Emirates* Stadium, London) and even the referees (by *Specsavers* in Scotland[2]) have been made available for sponsorship. In 2003, *Barclays* initially signed a three-year £57 million deal with the *Football Association* for the top English league to be known as the *Barclays Premiership* and associated rights. This agreement has been renewed on several occasions with the latest (2012) valued at £120 million. From 2007 to 2014, there were to be six top-tier event sponsors of football's governing body *FIFA* (including the 2010 and 2014 World Cups). They include *Sony, Hyundai and Adidas* who will pay a total of between £160 million and £180 million each (Gillis 2005).

---

[2]   The re-signing in 2012 of the substantial six-figure sponsorship deal will see the partnership between Specsavers and Scotland's referees entering its 10th year – one of the longest agreements of its kind in sport.

The largest sporting event in the world is the Olympic Games. In a survey by *Sponsorship Research*, 81% of participants associated the Olympic rings with success and high standards; the Games inevitably attract those companies who wish to be associated with these attributes. The first Olympics to be televised widely was the 1960 Games in Rome when it was broadcast live to 18 European countries, time-delayed to the USA, Canada and Japan and supported by 46 brands (Britcher 2004). At the Olympic Games in Sydney in 2000, over 3.7 billion people (over half the world's population) saw one or more of the events. Control of Olympic Games sponsorship rights lies at various levels: at Olympic organisation level, national Olympic association level and individual sports association level, which can lead to confusion (see ambush marketing). At the highest level are 'The Olympic Partners' (TOPs). Established in 1985, TOP sponsors contract with the Olympic Committee for a period of four years prior to the games. For the 2012 London Games, TOPs sponsors included *Coca-Cola, ATOS, Dow, General Electric, McDonald's, Omega, Panasonic, P&G, Samsung* and *Visa*, who each paid approximately $100 million for the privilege and raised 40% of the revenue for the Games. TOPs sponsorship from 2001 to 2004 was $603 million more than that spent on tickets for the Games. By 2012, TOPs revenue totalled $947 million. *Coca-Cola*, who has sponsored every Olympic Games since 1928 and was an original TOPs sponsor, uses the event as a centrepiece for their brand marketing. At the 2012 London Games, the company created a campaign that sought to fuse Olympic sport with music. Award-winning music producer Mark Ronson is said to have travelled the world, capturing the sounds of five different Olympic sports and blending them into one song (with vocals by Katy B) that sought to bring the spirit of London 2012 to life.

Sports sponsorship in general is particularly attractive to marketers as it enables the targeting of large numbers of consumers sharing similar characteristics. On the downside, it may have reached a point where costs have become so inflated that return on investment must be becoming questionable.

Broadcast sponsorship is when an individual or organisation, other than the makers or broadcasters of the programme, sponsor all or part of the production and/or transmission costs in return for the right to promote its brand or other interests. In the USA, broadcast sponsorship is an established communications medium. The first commercially targeted radio station KDKA ran programmes such as the *Wrigley* Party and the *Maxwell House* Hour in the 1920s. Television was introduced much later but sponsorship was still prevalent; indeed, the *Hallmark* House of Fame, first broadcast in 1951, is the longest-running primetime series in the history of television. In the UK, *Cadbury*'s 10-year sponsorship of long-running 'soap' *Coronation Street* began in 1996 and was said to cost the company £10 million each year when all promotional materials are taken into account.[3] Other companies, notably *HSBC* and *Stella Artois*, are also getting more involved in programme sponsorship. The market has a considerable way to grow before competing with television commercials but it is anticipated that this gap will narrow considerably in future years. The television market has altered dramatically, due in large part to the advent of digital television and the growth of the internet. With the plethora of television channels, some record such low audience figures as to be immeasurable (less than 1.0% of the UK population). Therefore, the massive reach advantage that advertising held over sponsorship no longer applies (BDS 2013). As such, media agencies are now forced by brand owners to consider 'properties' that deliver 'niche' rather than 'mass markets'. The sponsorship of programmes is controlled by the *Independent Television Commission*'s

---

[3]   The latest *Coronation Street* sponsor, Compare the Market, signed a three-year contract in 2012.

code of conduct. This code contains rules concerning advertiser involvement in programmes and the coverage of events (e.g. major sporting events) which may themselves be sponsored or include advertising at the venue. The code also gives effect to a number of requirements relating to television sponsorship in the European Union Directive on Television Broadcasting and the Council of Europe Convention on Transfrontier Television.

⦿ insight: Soap operas

The history of the 'soap opera' in the USA is inexorably tied to sponsorship. In the 1920s, daytime radio attracted few advertisers because it was thought that housewives did not have time to listen to the radio. In 1932 the *Blackett-Sample-Hummert* agency in Chicago began producing long-running, sentimental, human interest stories with continuing characters in daily instalments. One of the most enduring was '*Oxydol's* Own Ma Parker' which ran for over 27 years. The association of *Oxydol* and other detergent manufacturers with these shows led to them being labelled 'soap operas'.

Source: Sivulka (1998)

Although not strictly sponsorship per se, **product placement** is an area of substantial growth and should be discussed alongside broadcast sponsorship. Product placement is defined by the US *Association of National Advertisers* (*ANA* – see www.ana.net) as 'the convergence of advertising and entertainment industries where a brand message is integrated within the appropriate context as part of the interaction', which covers a broad range of potential uses. It is not, however, a new phenomenon with its origins in the 1890s motion picture industry when French film directors the Lumiére brothers produced the film *Défilé du 8eme Bataillon*, which included the logo of *Sunlight Soap* on the side of a wheelbarrow in exchange for assistance with publishing and distributing the film. In the 1930s, *Warner Brothers* and *Buick* entered into a 10-film product placement arrangement and in this and subsequent decades US tobacco companies regularly paid movie stars to use their brand on-screen (Hudson & Hudson 2006). Since 1982 (when *ET* followed a trail of *Reese's Pieces* chocolate which led to a reported 65% rise in sales), the number of placements has grown to majestic proportions. The use of *Ray-Ban* sunglasses in the 1986 film *Top Gun* is credited with turning around the company's performance. In the 1997 film *Tomorrow Never Dies*, the automobile company *BMW* supplied 17 model 750L vehicles worth an estimated £75,000 each, thus replacing the *Aston Martin* as the traditional mode of transport for James Bond. In addition, the film included product placements from *Visa, Avis, Smirnoff, Heineken, Omega* and *Ericsson*. In the 2002 film *Minority Report*, there were appearances by *Lexus, Guinness, American Express, USA Today, Pepsi* and *Gap*. In 2013, the Superman film *Man of Steel* featured 94 brands and earned $160 million through product placement. *Mercedes-Benz* is the most frequently placed brand, appearing in 29.4% of all top box office films. For the communications industry, product placement is designed to lead to increased awareness and a more positive attitude toward that brand. According to research by *Mediaedge:cia*, 61% of filmgoers said they noticed brands promoted this way and 30% said that they could be persuaded to buy a brand having seen it in a film (Jones 2004).

In the US television industry, product placement has been a major revenue earner since its inception. In addition to straightforward endorsement, brand-owners are looking at ways of incorporating the brand into the fabric of programming. In 2004, for example, *Procter & Gamble* provided $50,000 budgets for *each* team on the reality television programme *The Apprentice*, whose task it was to launch *Crest*'s latest flavoured toothpaste (Hudson & Hudson 2006). **Advertising funded programming (AFP)** is a particular growth area. AFP is where a sponsor part funds the programme in return for product placement. *Coca-Cola, BMW* and *Ford Motor Company* have all adopted roles in programme production.

Since 2011, television programmes made for UK audiences have been allowed to contain product placement as long as they comply with the rules of the regulator *Ofcom*. Soon afterwards, *Nationwide* cash machines began appearing on *Coronation Street* and the characters on teen soap *Hollyoaks* began to prominently display *Nokia* mobile phones. In Italy, 'surreptitious advertising' is frowned on and in France it is currently illegal (Hudson & Hudson 2006). Given that many satellite, cable and other digital television channels are largely outside the control of European television regulators, however, the likelihood is that the remaining restrictions will ultimately be withdrawn. Indeed, the European public have for some time been viewing product placements in US television programmes such as *Sex in the City* (*Apple* laptops), *24* (*Ford*), *Friends* (US store *Home Depot*) and *Desperate Housewives* (*Buick*).

Product placement has also invaded the video-games industry. It is estimated that the video-games business reached $11 billion in 2006 and, as has happened for decades, advertisers have followed audiences. As each game can cost up to $25 million to develop, game producers are anxious to attract revenue from as many sources as possible. The exposure of the brand is in two forms: traditional advertising as the game downloads and the placement of brands within the game itself. It was estimated (Financial Post 2005) that by 2009 one-third of product placements in video games would be in the form of **advergaming** where practitioners create a game around the brand rather than place their brand within a well-known title. Specially designed story-led commercials for brands such as those for *Volvo* are in the ascendancy on the internet. Consumers are also entreated to visit brand websites for 'extra-value' information and rewards.

Cause-related sponsorship is another growth area. Perhaps closest to the original philanthropic origins of sponsorship, contemporary cause-related marketing is, however, largely based on consumers' positive attitude to organisations that support good causes. According to *Business in the Community*'s Brand Benefits Report:[4]

> Cause Related Marketing is not philanthropy or altruism. It is based on a recognition by businesses that linking with charities or good causes can be mutually beneficial. It is a way of addressing current social issues by providing resources and funding, while addressing business marketing objectives.

The report included research which suggested that:

- 86% of consumers agreed that when price and quality are equal they are more likely to buy a product associated with a cause
- 61% of consumers said they would change retail outlets for the same reason
- 86% of consumers agreed that they have a more positive image of a company if they see that it is doing something to make the world a better place.

Sue Atkins, Director of *Business in the Community*, believes that cause-related marketing will grow substantially in the future. She says 'people are cash-rich and time-poor so cause-related marketing fits beautifully into the way they go

---

[4]   Available to download from www.bitc.org.uk/our-resources/report/brand-benefits-cause-related-marketing (accessed 23 August 2013).

about their daily lives – they're going to the shops anyway and by making a selection for a cause-related marketing product or service, they can also make a contribution' (Murray 2002).

SPONSORSHIP OBJECTIVES

Sponsorship is usually seen as more than patronage, altruism or benefaction although it can indeed help others while simultaneously achieving specific communication objectives (Smith and Taylor 2004). Commercial sponsorship objectives may, for example, include:

- awareness: making a target audience aware of the organisation
- image building: associating the organisation with a cause or an event
- citizenship: developing bonds with a community
- alteration of perceptions: changing people's attitude about a brand
- building trade relationships: extending hospitality (an estimated £750 million market) to clients at sponsored events
- motivating employees: building the reputation of the company and, in the case of charity sponsorship, actively encouraging the participation of staff
- media attention: leveraging the news value of the sponsorship
- shareholder reassurance: associating the organisation with success and/or corporate altruism and/or corporate responsibility.

The advantages of sponsorship are that it can be more cost-effective than advertising and can enable organisations to target consumers (usually when they are relaxed and possibly more susceptible) on two levels: those of the immediate audience and those wider audiences to whom it may be transmitted or who come to hear about the sponsorship through other sources. It is difficult to watch or listen to any sports broadcast or read any sports section of a newspaper without mention of the *Barclays Premier League,* the *Capital One Cup*, the *Sky Bet Championship*, the *Emirates* and *Aviva* stadiums and many more. In the arts section, companies such as *Bank of Scotland* and *Ernst and Young* sponsor classical concerts. In the case of *Ernst and Young*, it is selective targeting. The company claims it has entertained every *FTSE 100*[5] chief executive during a single season. Musical events targeted at a younger audience are sponsored by *Pepsi, Visa, Tennants* and *T-Mobile* (who have sponsored concert tours by the Rolling Stones and Kylie Minogue). Such is the perceived value of sponsorship that you can now sponsor the *possibility* of having an event. For example, *Granada* sponsored Manchester's bid for the 2000 Olympics and *BT, British Airways, Virgin Atlantic* and *EDF Energy* each paid £1 million to be premier partners in London's (ultimately successful) 2012 Olympics bid.

Companies also use sponsorship as a differentiator. According to Nicki Major, Head of Sponsorship at *Ernst and Young*, 'the majority of the public don't need to know who we are, so we aren't using it to generate mass profile but we are in a relationship-based business in a market where we all offer relatively similar products' (cited in Gillis 2004: 17). Sponsorship has one further advantage over most other forms of communication. It can overcome the barriers of language and culture. For international brands, sponsorship of events that will be broadcast around the world ensures a powerful and consistent brand message.

The disadvantages of sponsorship are that many of the variables (weather, attendance, media coverage, etc.) are uncontrollable. It can also be seen, particularly in

---

[5]   *Financial Times'* listing of the top 100 shares on the London Stock Exchange.

the arts, as undermining artistic integrity and/or as an act of excessive corporate indulgence. Over-commercialisation is a constant charge in the arts world. It is, however, unlikely that many arts venues could continue with their current output without some level of commercial sponsorship. Ethical concerns are also a consideration. In the USA, the decision to link *Tylenol* with arthritis, through the *Arthritis Foundation*, ran into trouble when the media questioned whether it was appropriate for an arthritis charity to be in partnership with one brand of painkiller (Murray 2002). Sponsorship of individuals and events can also become a focus for discontent. In the 1998 World Cup, *Adidas*'s sponsorship of England football star David Beckham (and the associated advertising that accompanied it) was halted following Beckham's dismissal in the game against Argentina. In 2012, a group of former professional cyclists and fans picketed *Nike* offices over their continuing support of Lance Armstrong. It is argued that there are further threats associated with sponsorship, including **negative association, sponsorship clutter**, over-commercialisation and evaluation problems (Pickton & Broderick 2005). Negative associations can occur through the sponsorship of a controversial event or group that attracts both highly positive and negative associations. In the latter category, the sponsorship of particular football teams can generate negative associations with rival fans. This is particularly true when arch-rivals are involved (e.g. *Manchester United* and *Manchester City*, *Arsenal* and *Tottenham Hotspur*, *A.C. Milan* and *Inter Milan*). Such is the partisanship among supporters of Glasgow's *Rangers* and *Celtic* teams that from 1999 until 2013 the only way to resolve this was to have one main sponsor for both clubs. 'Sponsorship clutter' acknowledges the preponderance of sponsors, particularly in high-profile events such as the Olympic Games, the World Cup, the Super Bowl and Formula 1. In all these cases, the events and teams seem over-burdened with sponsors' logos and advertising hoardings to the possible detriment of the individual sponsor. Evaluation problems, seen as a particular problem with sponsorship, will be discussed later in this chapter.

Another threat is so-called **ambush marketing**. The phrase was first coined in the mid-1980s in response to competitive clashes between *Kodak* and *Fuji* during the 1984 Los Angeles Olympic Games (Hoek 1999). Meenaghan (1994) defines ambush marketing as 'the practice whereby another company, often a competitor, attempts to deflect some of the audience to itself and away from the sponsor'. Examples of ambush marketing are given in the Insight.

SPONSORSHIP EVALUATION

As with public relations, the most common methods of evaluation of sponsorship are media audits. These calculate sponsorship exposure in terms of advertising costs and awareness, image or behaviour surveys. According to one leading practitioner, 'the usual method for sponsorship value measurement is to analyse brand exposure, compare it with (an) advertising rate card, and apply a discount' (cited in Rines 2003: 25). Surveys have similar problems. As Hoek (1999: 371) notes: 'the difficulties, either logical, practical or both, in using awareness, image and behaviour as an indication of sponsorship effectiveness inevitably raises the question of whether sponsorship can be evaluated (and may explain why so few managers appear to undertake any formal research)'. A notable exception to this is *Coca-Cola* who is reported to spend 8% of its total sponsorship budget (which in an Olympic year can be $400–$500 million, including support costs) on research (BDS 2013).

Nationwide, who is heavily involved in sports sponsorship, tracks the exposure generated in the major media and judges the return on investment using

⊙ insight: Ambush marketing

Ambush marketing is the sponsorship equivalent of a 'spoiler campaign'. The 1996 Olympics in Atlanta, as well as being dubbed the most over-commercialised, had numerous examples of ambush marketing. In the figure-skating event, while *McDonald's* was the main sponsor, *Wendy's*, a fast-food competitor, sponsored US star Kristi Yamaguchi who attracted most attention from the US audience. In subsequent research, *Wendy's* was seen to have generated greater awareness. In the same year, the US basketball 'dream team' was officially sponsored by *Reebok* and the team's tracksuits carried the *Reebok* logo. Several members of the team, however, endorsed *Nike* products and at the medal ceremony these players carried US flags to obscure the *Reebok* logo. Two days before the men's 100 metres, Linford Christie appeared at a press conference wearing contact lenses with the *Puma* logo on them and pictures of this went around the world. This was a coup for *Puma*, particularly as *Reebok* had sponsored the event. Ambush marketing did not stop in Atlanta. In 1998, *Adidas* paid approximately £20 million to sponsor the football World Cup. *Nike,* however, sponsored nine of the 16 teams, including the favourites Brazil, and, it was rumoured, were willing to spend an equivalent £20 million to highjack the coverage. The *Euro 2004* (the European nations' football championship) tournament was sponsored by *Coca-Cola*. *Pepsi*, however, had a £5 million sponsorship deal with David Beckham and a £20 million deal with the England team. Beckham also had a £3 million personal deal with *Adidas* while he turned out in kit sponsored by *Umbro*. Wayne Rooney also had deals with *Nike* and *Coca-Cola*. Michael Owen meanwhile had a deal with supermarket *ASDA* when the official England partner was *Sainsbury.* During the Athens 2004 Olympics, the authorities either took down or covered with sheets 'illegal' posters around Olympic venues. However, they could not catch everyone. Anyone watching the Games in Brazil would have seen spectators wearing clothing bearing the *Banco do Brazil* logo, even though the bank was not a sponsor. In the 2006 World Cup, hundreds of Dutch fans had to watch the Netherlands–Ivory Coast match in their underwear after stewards at the stadium rumbled an ambush marketing ploy. The fans all turned up in bright orange lederhosen displaying the name of Dutch brewery *Bavaria*. *Anheuser Busch's Budweiser* was the official beer of the tournament and world football's governing body *FIFA* fiercely protects its sponsors so ordered that the Dutch could not enter the stadium with the lederhosen. According to *FIFA*, they were alert to the kind of ambush marketing *Bavaria* had attempted. A *Bavaria* spokesman said it was 'going too far'. At the World Cup in 2010, *Bavaria* were again accused of ambushing the South African tournament. This time 36 women who attended a match dressed in sponsored 'Dutchy dresses' were detained by police in Johannesburg.

Source: various

advertising rates. It then blends this with traditional consumer awareness research to give an overall gauge of the sponsorship effect. According to research by strategic sponsorship consultancy *Redmandarin*, 12% of organisations who spend money on sponsorship fail to set clear objectives (Collett 2004), making measurement of success or failure even more difficult.

It is also difficult to separate sponsorship from advertising, promotion, public relations and other marcom tools. Where does one element begin and another end? According to Richard Berry, Managing Director of sponsorship research specialists *S:Com*, 'in many respects sponsorship is beginning to be seen as a media buying exercise' (Rines 2003: 24). There are also some signs that investments in sponsorship are not producing the returns of earlier times when perhaps their significance was under-valued. In the sporting field in particular, inflated figures have made the true value of sponsorship hard to gauge (Rines 2003). The good news for sponsors comes from research done into sponsorship of the Rugby

World Cup (BDS 2013). The vast majority of attendees agreed that sponsorship benefits rugby (92%) and was appropriate at the World Cup (84%). The majority of fans also felt more positive towards sponsors (63%), believed they were more innovative than non-sponsoring companies (62%) and appreciated them more because of their involvement (62%).

Despite the problems with evaluation and notwithstanding the element of risk involved, sponsorship is seen as a medium with considerable brand-building potential. Dolphin (2003: 184) sums this up when he notes:

> sponsorship – ambiguous or otherwise – has proved itself to practitioners and scholars alike as a cutting edge marcoms activity; one with the potential to reach specific audiences and to reach them with sharply focused messages and themes – ones capable of achieving and sustaining real competitive advantage. Thus sponsorship has become a global tool in an age when the global village has become a reality.

summary

This chapter has discussed the importance of sponsorship to the marketing communications mix. The different types of sponsorship were discussed, including arts sponsorship, events sponsorship, sports sponsorship, broadcast sponsorship and cause-related sponsorship and the features of each reviewed. It analysed the reasons why sponsorship might work with reference to behavioural and cognitive paradigms, the persuasive impact of the sponsorship model and the consumer attitude model. The chapter went on to discuss the objectives behind sponsorship campaigns, including awareness, image building, citizenship, changing of perceptions, external and internal relationship building and gaining of media attention. The potential disadvantages were also analysed, including negative association, sponsorship clutter, over-commercialisation and ambush marketing, and the risks evaluated. Finally, the problems surrounding evaluation were highlighted.

? review questions

1. List the various types of sponsorship.
2. Define sponsorship.
3. What is 'advergaming'?
4. What is experiential marketing?
5. What is the point of product placement?
6. What is the meaning of the phrase 'sponsorship clutter'?
7. Why is 'ambush marketing' a concern for sponsored events?
8. How might sponsorship be monitored in financial terms?

discussion questions

1. Are sponsorship and product placement the future for funding television services?

2. How likely will it be that experiential marketing will increase and in what ways might it develop?

3. Why do sponsors sponsor?

case study 12.1: 007 and product placement

The association between product placement and James Bond is not new. After all, author Ian Fleming himself dropped a few brand names such as *Cartier* and *Bentley* into his stories. Bond's breakfast when in London, according to the author, included coffee from *De Bry* in New Oxford Street, brewed in an American *Chemex*, drunk from *Minton* china and toast with Norwegian heather honey from *Fortnum and Mason*. Knowing that Fleming himself used real products in his books, it seems natural that product placement should also find its way into the Bond films. The difference is that, unlike the current

Piotr Zajac/Shutterstock.com

franchise owners, Fleming (almost certainly) did not receive a penny from the featured brands. In Bond movies, however, since the very first instalment in 1962, brands such as *British Airways, PanAm, Perrier, Finlandia Vodka, Smirnoff, Ford, Omega, Mattel, Calvin Klein, Virgin Atlantic, Revlon, Samsonite, Sony Ericcson, Kodak* and many more have paid millions to associate themselves with the franchise.

In the early Bond films, the placement was incidental rather than part of the process. Films, especially fast-action thrillers, required props. If James Bond needed to drive a car, they had brands offering to supply them. In *Dr. No* (1962), it was a Sunbeam Alpine but it could have been any car. The franchise, however, pioneered auto placements in movies, starting with *The Man with the Golden Gun* (1974). In this film, American Motors made a historic $5 million deal to have Bond drive its cars, exclusively. This included the shots taken in Thailand, where the brand was not even on sale and which would require steering wheels to be on the opposite side of the car. Today, it is more likely that you obtain the car sponsorship first and then write a scene afterwards. In *Golden Eye* (1995), Bond's iconic Aston Martin was swapped for a BMW. In *Die Another Day* (2002), Ford Motor was said to have paid $35 million to replace BMW as the official Bond car, with Bond speeding away in a hand-built, $230,000 Aston. In *Casino Royale*, it was reported that *Ford* paid $14m to have James Bond drive the new *Ford* Mondeo in the movie. In *Skyfall* (2012), Landrover Defender and Audi were to be seen in a car chase: Eve drove a Landrover, while the bad guys tried to escape in another Audi. During the chase, a

(Continued)

(Continued)

few VW Beetles fell from a train, a Range Rover was used to transport Bond to MI6's new location and M and Bond used a Jaguar XJ.

Another interest that developed first in Fleming's novels and has translated to the big screen is the importance of alcohol in defining Bond's personality and lifestyle. The phrase 'Vodka Martini – shaken, not stirred' is perhaps one of the best-known lines in film history. Indeed, it was seen to perfectly encapsulate the nature of James Bond and became synonymous with the suave British spy. That did not stop the redefining of Bond's drinking habits courteousy of the sponsors. In the very first Bond movie *Dr. No* (1962), Bond perched at a bar beside a Red Stripe beer. He has also drunk various brands of vodka, soda and other prominently labelled beverages. The Heineken tie-in for *Skyfall* (2012) was one of the largest product placement packages in history. The $45 million deal covered almost one third of the film's budget and, according to the *New York Times*, the deal required Bond to drink Heineken in at least one scene in the movie. However, it was the whisky brand Macallan that was probably the most visible placement in this film. It occurred during the first meeting between Bond and Silva (the main villain), where the latter offers Bond a drink of a 50-year-old Macallan, because he knew it was his favourite drink.

Air travel plays a significant part in the Bond films. Pan Am, at one time among the world's largest intercontinental airlines, was visible throughout the Bond franchise. In *From Russia With Love* (1963), Bond nonsensically flew from London to Istanbul on the US-based airline. In *Moonraker* (1979), Bond crashes through a *British Airways* billboard and the airline pops up again in *Golden Eye* (1995) and *Die Another Day* (2002). For the latter film, *British Airways* also ran a multimillion-pound campaign for its 'Save your moneypennies' sweepstakes, including magazine and internet advertising. In *Casino Royale* (2006), *Virgin*'s Richard Branson made a cameo appearance. Such is the supposed power of brand placement that *British Airways* cut the Branson scene from its in-flight version and blurred the tailfins of *Virgin* planes that also appeared in the film.

Film tie-ins have also been prevalent. In *Quantum of Solace* (2008), *Coca-Cola, Omega, Sony, Avon, Heineken* and *Virgin Atlantic* pulled out all the stops. *Avon* released a Bond Girl 007 fragrance, *Sony* held a competition that gave consumers the chance to win $1 million and a trip to a top-secret location, *Virgin Atlantic* launched a 'you only live once' campaign and both *Coca-Cola* and *Heineken* released Bond-themed commercials.

There has been some backlash from James Bond purists, particularly when a scene has obviously been altered to allow for product placement. *Casino Royale* (2006) was ridiculed for a string of clumsy lines that appeared to have been included solely to refer to a product. An example is when Bond is asked if he wears a Rolex and he quickly replies, 'Omega'. Though 2012's *Skyfall* was a box-office smash, there was plenty of response on *Twitter* expressing cynicism, and even calls of 'sacrilege'. Never mind that Bond has drunk other booze in the past, and that he has on at least one occasion had his martini stirred, not shaken. The onslaught of brands prompted many fans to complain. Comments such as 'Wow, sickening number of Bond product placement ads', 'Am sick of 007 and Skyfall hasn't even started yet!' and 'My Skyfall highlight was the obscene amount of product placement and Bond themed ads' were among the more polite.

In an industry dominated by mega-budget blockbusters, product placement might be regarded as a necessary evil for film makers attempting to recoup the huge costs of making a blockbuster film. On the positive side, it is doubtful whether without this funding *Skyfall* would ever have been made. After all, we are talking here about a true icon: 'Bond – James Bond'.

Case study questions

1. Why are brands prepared to spend so much on product placement in James Bond films?
2. How is the sponsorship leveraged to extend it beyond the film itself?
3. Are consumers fed up of being bombarded by brands while they are being entertained?

📖 further reading

Farrelly, F., Quester, P. and Greyser, S.A. (2005) 'Defending the co-branding benefits of sponsorship B2B partnerships: the case of ambush marketing', *Journal of Advertising Research*, 45 (3): 339–48.

Meenaghan, T. (1998) 'Current developments and future directions in sponsorship', *International Journal of Advertising*, 17 (1): 3–28.

Pringle, H. and Binet, L. (2005) 'How marketers can use celebrities to sell more effectively', *Journal of Consumer Behaviour*, 4 (3): 201–14.

Wang, R.T. and Kaplanidou (2013) 'Exploring the relationship between team (as brand) personality and geographic personality: linking consumer perceptions of sports teams and cities', *International Journal of Sports Marketing and Sponsorship*, 15(1).

Wiles, W.A. and Danielova, A. (2009) 'The worth of product placement in successful films: an event study analysis', *Journal of Marketing*, 73 (4): 44–63.

REFERENCES

Abrahamsson, J.-T., Forsgren, T. and Lungren, H. (2003) Sports Sponsorship as a Marketing Communications Tool. Lulea University, Lulea, Sweden.

Barrand, D. (2004) 'Promoting change', *Marketing*, 6 October, pp. 43–5.

BDS (2013) Measuring Successful Sponsorship. Available at: www.sponsorship.co.uk (accessed 18 March 2013).

Blythe, J. (2000) *Marketing Communications*. Harlow: Pearson Education.

Bovée, C.L., Thill, J.V., Dovel, G.P. and Wood, M.B. (1995) *Advertising Excellence*. Englewood Cliffs, NJ: McGraw-Hill.

Britcher, C. (2004) 'Lessons from Athens', *Marketing*, 2 September, p. 15.

Collett, P. (2004) 'Sponsorship can prove worth', *Marketing*, 16 February, p. 33.

Copley, P. (2004) *Marketing Communications Management*. Oxford: Butterworth-Heinemann.

Crimmins, J. and Horn, M. (1996) 'Sponsorship: from management ego trip to marketing success', *Journal of Advertising Research*, Jul./Aug.: 11–21.

Dolphin, R.R. (2003) 'Sponsorship perceptions on its strategic role', *Corporate Communications*, 8 (3): 173–86.

Duffy, N. (2004) 'Doing it for the fans', *The Marketer*, 6 October, pp. 18–19.

Fill, C. (2009) *Marketing Communications: Interactivity, Communities and Content*, 5th edn. Harlow: Financial Times/Prentice Hall.

Gillis, R. (2004) 'FIFA turns the screw', *Marketing*, 20 April, p. 17.

Gillis, R. (2005) 'Alternative invitation', *Marketing*, 4 August, p. 27.

Hoek, J. (1999) 'Sponsorship', in P.J. Kitchen (ed.), *Marketing Communications*. London: Thompson, pp. 361–80.

Hudson, S. and Hudson, D. (2006) 'Branded entertainment: a new advertising technique or product placement in disguise', *Journal of Marketing Management*, 22 (5–6): 489–504.

Jones, H. (2004) 'The silent screen idols', *The Marketer*, 6 October, pp. 16–17.

Meenaghan, T. (1994) 'Point of view: ambush marketing – immoral or imaginative?', *Journal of Marketing Research*, 34 (3): 77–88.

Murray, S. (2002) 'Cost effective philanthropy', *Financial Times*, 4 December.

Nevett, T.R. (1982) *Advertising in Britain: A History*. London: Heinemann.

Pickton, D. and Broderick, A. (2005) *Integrated Marketing Communications*, 2nd edn. Harlow: Financial Times/Prentice Hall.

Rines, S. (2003) 'Headline deals and half truths', *Marketing*, 27 November, pp. 24–5.

Sivulka, J. (1998) *Soap, Sex and Cigarettes: A Cultural History of American Advertising*. Belmont, CA: Thomson Learning.

Smith, P.R. and Taylor, J. (2004) *Marketing Communications: An Integrated Approach*, 2nd edn. London: Kogan Page.

For additional materials that support this chapter and your learning, please visit:
study.sagepub.com/egan

DIRECT AND DIGITAL MARKETING

13

CHAPTER CONTENTS

LEARNING OBJECTIVES

Having completed this chapter, readers would be expected to:

- describe the characteristics of direct and digital marketing

- explain why direct and, more recently, digital marketing has grown in prominence

- recognise the importance of customer retention and customer acquisition

- describe the various direct and digital marketing media and their characteristics

- analyse the various components of the direct and digital marketing offering

- recognise the importance of testing and digital analytics to direct and digital marketing.

INTRODUCTION

Interactive marketing techniques (which include those traditionally known as direct marketing) have always used mediums which target specific customers and, where possible, develop a relationship with them. It differs from mass marketing in that it is the means by which dialogue can be established with potential or actual customers rather than simply being the medium for messages. The enormous growth of digital marketing mediums has not majorly affected the original prime objectives of direct marketing to attract and maintain customers. Rather, the creative opportunities available have increased, the speed of response has substantially reduced and the speed of analysis has been substantially improved. It was recognition of the growing importance of digital which led, in May 2011, to the *Institute of Direct Marketing* rebranding itself as the *Institute of Direct & Digital Marketing*. In the same year, the *Direct Marketing Association* announced it was repositioning itself as 'a modern, digitally attuned trade body'. Both organisations recognised the influence on the market of the digital revolution.

Direct and digital marketing is often characterised as the most recent addition to the marketing communications mix because of its association with database technology and, more latterly, the power of the internet. However, the fundamentals of direct marketing have been around for centuries. The **catalogue** business, a staple of direct and digital marketing activity over the centuries, grew out of the invention of the printing press by Johannes Gutenberg around 1450. In the seventeenth century, the first seed and nursery catalogues appeared, with the earliest of these by Emmanuel Sweerts, a Dutch merchant, in 1612. In the UK, William Lucas (1667) and Leonard Meager (1668) both produced gardening catalogues to tempt their customers in London. In 1862, Barr & Sugden and James Veitch of Chelsea, London launched catalogues that included both plant descriptions and wood engravings. The first US example of a catalogue is attributed to Ben Franklin who produced his book catalogue in 1774. In 1872, Chicago-based *Montgomery-Ward* issued their first **flyer** (i.e. distributed pamphlet) and went on from there to become a US catalogue institution. In 1891, *Avon Cosmetics* introduced the concept of direct marketing of beauty products. The first UK consumer catalogue (*Freemans*) began life in 1905. Notable entrepreneurs such as Josiah Wedgewood, Chippendale and Thomas Edison also used recognisable direct and digital marketing mediums such as flyers to generate sales of their wares.

In the 1930s and 1940s, as marketing concepts began to take shape, direct marketing became a laudable aim and a logical extension of the ideas surrounding segmentation and targeting. At this time, researchers began asking groups of consumers about their likes and preferences but were without powerful analysing tools to help them. The term 'direct marketing' itself was probably first used in a speech by Lester Wunderman in 1967. He was responsible for developing direct marketing techniques with brands such as *American Express* and *Columbia Records*. It was not until later in the century that technology developers came up with tools that could rapidly analyse data and enhance interactivity.

In our digital world, it is easy to forget how recent (in terms of commercial history) are many significant developments in digital technology. It was in 1989 that Sir Tim Berners-Lee first proposed the World Wide Web and in 1991 that the first web page was created and the first webcast made. Yahoo (formerly Jerry's Guide to the World Wide Web) was launched in 1994 and Netscape and Infoseek (an early search engine) followed a year later. *Google* was a relative latecomer, appearing in 1998, the same year as 3G telephony was launched. Second-generation web technology (Web 2.0) was introduced in 2004 and what have come to be called 'social media' sites began to appear in the early part of the century, with *Facebook* launched in 2005 and *Twitter* in 2006; 4G telephony was also launched in 2006 while the iPhone appeared in 2007.

With the most recent technological developments, therefore, come the tools to rapidly analyse data and the platforms on which to publicise messages. Content-driven websites allow for appropriate display on whatever devices are used (e.g. PCs, tablets, phones). Whether we are utilising these platforms well, however, is more of a moot point and we will probably need time to evaluate more recent developments (e.g. the online watch) to establish whether they will prove attractive for consumers and a medium for marketers. In the 'rush to digital', we should recognise that the underlying theory behind interactive marketing (whether direct or digital) remains fundamentally the same. This chapter begins, therefore, with the theory and development of direct marketing and tracks the adoption of digital mediums later in the twentieth century.

Catalogue
A list of things (e.g. books, gifts) usually arranged systematically.

Flyer
A pamphlet which promotes a brand(s) and which may be delivered or collected by consumers.

DIRECT AND DIGITAL MARKETING DEFINITION

The UK *Direct Marketing Association* (*DMA*) describes direct marketing as an interactive system of marketing which uses one or more advertising media to affect a measurable response and/or transaction in any location. The addition of the word 'digital' does not affect this definition. The use of the term 'advertising', however, may confuse (in part because of the way advertising was described and defined in Chapter 9). While advertising builds up the image and personality of a brand in the longer term, direct and digital marketing (in most cases) asks people to act and often incentivises them to do so. In this regard, it is closer to the earlier definition of sales promotion (Chapter 10). A major difference, however, between direct and digital marketing and either sales promotion or advertising is that, once an interest has been established (e.g. through an enquiry or sale), individual customers become the priority targets rather than market segments.

Direct and digital marketing not only exploits a consumer's wish to acquire goods and services but also to be involved. Relationships are developed over time. It can be argued that, in addition to fulfilling sales objectives, direct and digital marketing can maintain these relationships between sales (sometimes referred to as **affinity marketing** or **loyalty marketing**). The digital revolution has particularly benefited small and medium-sized organisations (SMEs). According to a 2013 *YouGov* poll,[1] almost one-third of SMEs handle their own online marketing.

Direct and digital marketing is also, because of the interactive element, frequently described as the nearest thing to face-to-face **personal selling** (see Figure 13.1). Given the expense of personal selling and the relatively low cost of direct and digital marketing, it is seen as particularly useful in developing a dialogue prior to personal contact. Indeed, personalisation is a defining issue in much direct and digital marketing (although not in all). According to research by *Drayton Bird*, a direct marketing specialist, putting someone's name in a message increases responses by 50% (Bewick 2005).

Affinity marketing or loyalty marketing
Developing customer relationships over time.

Personal selling
An interpersonal tool where individuals, often representing an organisation, interact in order to inform, persuade or remind an individual or group to take appropriate action, as required by the sponsors.

FIGURE 13.1   Relative personalisation and interactivity

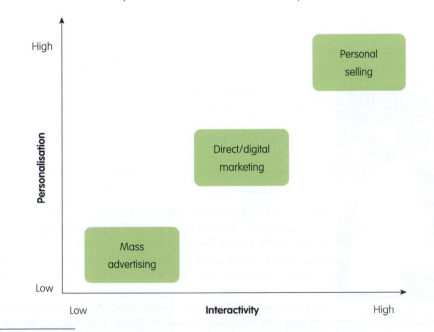

---

[1]   The survey, commissioned by HTML5 web-publishing platform wix.com, looked at over 500 small business owners.

DIRECT AND DIGITAL MARKETING DEVELOPMENT

The growth of direct marketing in the 1980s and 1990s and subsequent developments in digital marketing in the twenty-first century can be traced back to a number of different drivers. In addition to the search for better targeting and closer customer relationships, the increased cost of advertising and the fragmentation of advertising media were undoubtedly an influence on its development. Importantly, however, it is the introduction of tools and the technological sophistication to handle the complexity involved with personalised marketing which is seen as the greatest promoter of direct and digital marketing growth. Among these technological advances are:

- increased processing power
- analytical systems development
- development of telephone technology (e.g. freephone access, voice recognition, smartphones)
- electronic point-of-sale (EPOS) technology
- smartcard touch and touchless card technology
- interactive/internet-enabled television
- internet and World Wide Web technology.

Each played their part in enabling direct and digital marketing (DDM) to become a powerful proactive tool in the hands of the marketer. In the USA, the US Direct Marketing Association reported in 2010 that $153.3 billion was spent on direct and digital marketing, generating approximately $1.798 trillion in sales (DMA 2010). In the UK, DDM expenditure rose to £14.2 billion in 2011, with sales worth around £700 billion representing over a quarter of total UK sales (DMA UK 2012). The power of direct and digital marketing has even crossed into the field of political marketing, as the Insight below shows.

insight: Team Obama's tech genius says 2012 campaign 'redefined brand communications'

Brand marketers must follow in the footsteps of Barack Obama's 2012 re-election campaign to succeed in producing personalised communications with customers, claims Harper Reed, the technology and data guru behind Obama's campaign. Reed made the comments at the announcement of his first live UK speaking engagement in April, at the Direct Marketing Association's Technology Summit.

Obama's campaign manager Jim Messina appointed Reed to spearhead the pioneering project to crunch huge chunks of Democrat voting data and produce sophisticated profiling techniques that brought the president closer to his actual and potential supporters than ever before. Reed assembled a team of developers from *Google, Facebook, Amazon* and *Twitter* to produce a data platform codenamed 'Narwhal' to give the president the edge over his rival, Mitt Romney. In total, the campaign raised $1 billion in donations from 4.4 million donors, including $690 million online. Narwhal helped create a social network for supporters who organised 358,000 events, made 125,646,575 campaigning phone calls and mobilised 600,000 *Facebook* fans to recruit five million more active users to support the campaign. Sophisticated TV audience modelling helped to buy 20,000 more TV ads than Romney's campaign for $100 million less.

Reed fast made a name for himself in November last year, being photographed hugging Obama on election night after he won the presidency for a second term. Commenting on the implications for brand communications, Reed said:

> The Obama campaign was the product of the smartest people in the room producing tools to put together a detailed picture of every one of Obama's millions of supporters. From there we were able to understand what interested them, what was important to them and what would motivate them to donate, vote and persuade others to vote for Obama. We worked out how to get Obama to speak one-to-one with tens of millions of voters in ways that have never been achieved before. This has redefined how campaigns should be run and redefined how all brands should communicate with their customers.

Source: Tristan Garrick, DMA (UK), 20 March 2013

DIRECT AND DIGITAL MARKETING CHARACTERISTICS

Direct and digital marketing relies on a number of characteristics which make it a valuable tool whatever the medium or media used. In particular, DDM is highly measurable and there is the ability to test the significant variables regularly or even instantly through tools such as *Google* Analytics. It is targeted, cost-efficient (especially in relation to personal selling), flexible, fast and interactive. These are all characteristics which distinguish it from traditional mass marketing. In addition, while traditional marketing relies on reaching large audiences through mass media, DDM aims to communicate with individual customers through personalised messages. Budgets in DDM are determined through testing the various components of the offering and generating decision-making data to establish the optimum return, rather than being defined by the availability of budget and incomplete segment-based and/or surrogate measures (e.g. recall). The speed with which this testing can be done in the digital environment allows for changes to be made as appropriate. DDM also requires specific action(s) to be taken which is then measurable against expected outcomes, while the objectives of traditional marketing can be unclear and/or long term in nature, making measurement difficult if not impossible. Additionally, while traditional marketing campaigns are

TABLE 13.1   Comparisons between general marketing communications and direct and digital marketing

General marketing communications	Direct and digital marketing
• Mass audiences through mass media	• Direct communication with customer
• Impersonal communication	• Personalised
• Controlled by size of budget	• Budget determined through testing
• Desired action unclear or delayed	• Specific action requested
• Incomplete data for decision making	• Data drives promotion
• Analysis at segmentation level	• Analysis at individual level
• Uses surrogate measures (e.g. recall)	• Measurable (and, therefore, controllable)
• Promotions highly visible	• Promotions largely invisible

highly visible and, therefore, vulnerable to competitive spoiler campaigns, DDM campaigns, through mediums such as email and personal messaging, are largely invisible (because they are personalised), even after the campaign launch. These various advantages are summarised in Table 13.1.

It is interesting to note that sponsored ads or suggested posts on social media sites such as *Facebook* or *LinkedIn* are closer in definition to mass advertising than DDM, albeit they may be driven by profiling.

Data warehousing and **data mining** are two terms associated with direct and digital marketing. Data warehousing, as the term implies, is the taking and storing of data from a variety of sources. The data is stored because it may not be seen as currently usable, either because its value is not immediately appreciated or because it requires further qualification. According to *ikeydata.com*, a data warehouse should be:

- **subject-oriented**: data is used to analyse a particular subject area (e.g. sales)
- **integrated**: data from multiple sources is integrated
- **time-variant**: historical data is kept in a data warehouse and can be retrieved as required
- **non-volatile**: once data is in the data warehouse, it will not change, so historical data in a data warehouse can never be altered.

Data mining (sometimes called data or knowledge discovery) is the extraction and analysis of this data from the data depositories in a form useful to marketers.

Both data warehousing and data mining imply that data gathered may not necessarily be used immediately but held until such time as it can usefully generate information useful to the marketer. The term **big data** has come to be used to describe data sets that are so large and complex that they are difficult to capture, manage and process within a tolerable time period. This is driving further development of more complex tools to help solve the big data conundrum.

According to Miller (2012), supermarket company *Tesco* use data from their Clubcard operation to improve promotions, ensure 30% fewer gaps on shelves, predict customer behaviour in relation to the weather to deliver £6 million less food wastage in the summer and £50 million less stock in warehouses, and to optimise store operations to give £30 million less wastage. For example, a 10-degree increase in temperature can mean that 300% more barbeque meat, 45% more lettuce, 50% more coleslaw and 25% fewer sprouts are sold in their stores.

The value of a database and associated software, therefore, is that it allows direct marketers to identify:

- the most profitable customers, for **up-selling** and **cross-selling** activities
- the most profitable potential customers, for new sales
- past customers who are still valid prospects, for reactivation
- the most profitable products and services in the portfolio, to drive merchandising activities and predict trends
- the most appropriate pricing policies, both that the market will stand and that are competitive
- the most appropriate and effective promotions and media, to assist with the planning and implementation of communications campaigns
- new market opportunities for development
- channel efficiency evaluation, to help maximise opportunities
- opportunities to increase profitability through identifying and reducing waste and inefficiency.

There are, however, potential downsides that should be considered. Sometimes data is incomplete or out of date, rendering it potentially damaging. Some data may be inaccurate through human error or where the source deliberately enters false data (as has been particularly the experience online). Duplication is also

---

Data warehousing
The storing of data from a variety of sources. The data is stored because it may not be currently usable, either because its value is not immediately appreciated or because it requires further qualification.

Data mining
The extraction of data from a data depository in a form useful to marketers.

Big data
Data sets that are so large and complex that they are difficult to capture, manage and process within a tolerable time period.

Up-selling
Selling higher quality (and, therefore, higher priced) items to an existing customer base.

Cross-selling
Selling other items (sometimes from different categories) to an existing customer base.

a continuous problem, particularly where data is stored using various styles of address (e.g. J. Smith, John J. Smith, J.J. Smith). Despite this, the same name at the same address is no guarantee of duplication as it may be two members of the same family. Advanced software is used to search for potential duplication so that '**de-duping**' can take place, although this is far from infallible (see Insight below). Another problem directly associated with emails is that it is widely reported that one-third of people change their emails every year. With such a turnover, it is a major problem keeping updated.

De-duping
The removal of duplicate names from mailing and other lists.

insight: Updating databases

Dun and Bradstreet report that 7% of businesses move location annually and *Experian* that 5% of businesses have name, address or contact changes every month. In research undertaken by *Wegener DM* in 2004 of 51 business-to-business databases and a total of 1.53 million records, they reported:

- 13% of records had no name present

- 21% had no postcode

- 19% had incorrect or incomplete postcodes

- 19% of records were duplicates

- 3% related to companies that had ceased trading.

There are, however, several sources of updated information including directories such as *Yell* or *Thomson* or data-gathering companies such as *Dun and Bradstreet*. In addition to these 'business universe' lists, there are others which concentrate on contact details for the UK's largest companies or those in specialist sectors.

Source: Murphy (2005)

DIRECT AND DIGITAL MARKETING OBJECTIVES

There are two principal objectives of direct and digital marketing:

- **customer acquisition**
- **customer retention.**

There are also two subsidiary objectives associated with the above which are:

- **lead qualification** (adding to the information known about the customer/prospect)
- **customer relationship maintenance** (maintaining contact with customers).

The importance of customer acquisition and retention is illustrated by the 'leaky bucket' metaphor (see Figure 13.2). This suggests that for a company to maintain or increase customer numbers they must either increase the flow (acquire new customers) or stem the leakage (retain more customers). All companies lose customers for competitive (e.g. attracted by a competitor's promotion) or non-competitive (e.g. customer changes location) reasons. In a booming, fast-expanding market, the loss of existing customers is less than crucial as there are usually plenty of others

Customer acquisition
The process of acquiring new customers.

Customer retention
The process of retaining existing customers.

Lead qualification
Improving the quality of the information known about a customer/prospect.

Customer relationship maintenance
The maintenance of regular contact with a customer.

to take their place. In slow-growth or highly competitive markets, the acquisition of new customers becomes considerably harder (and often more expensive) and retention of existing customers becomes the priority.

FIGURE 13.2 Leaky bucket metaphor

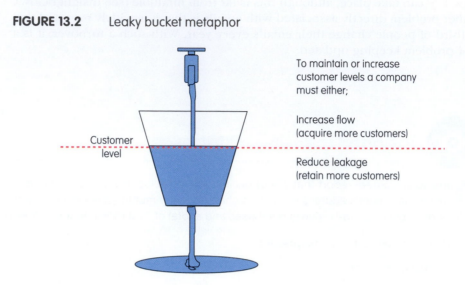

To maintain or increase customer levels a company must either;

Increase flow
(acquire more customers)

Reduce leakage
(retain more customers)

The significance of customer acquisition and retention to the direct and digital marketing concept can be seen in the '**wheel of prosperity**' in Figure 13.3 (Smith & Taylor 2004). This 'wheel' illustrates those aspects of direct and digital marketing that contribute to commercial prosperity.

FIGURE 13.3 Wheel of prosperity

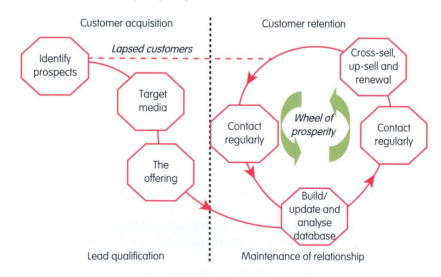

IDENTIFYING PROSPECTS

Prospect
A potential customer.

As the model suggests, **prospects** are first identified. Even if your initial objective is to lead these prospects to the organisation website, they will need to become aware (through advertising, search engines, etc.) that the website exists and/

or have a link to that website. Prospects (i.e. non-customers to whom a varying degree of sales potential can be attached) may be described on the basis of a **prospect hierarchy**.

FIGURE 13.4   Prospect hierarchy

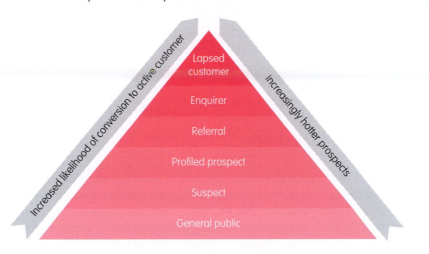

SUSPECTS

At the lowest level of this hierarchy (above the public at large) are the '**suspects**'. This category may be based on **geodemographic profiling**, **values, attitudes and lifestyle profiling (VALs)** or previous purchase behaviour which indicates they *may* have the same profile as current customers. These names may be obtained in the form of commercially available **lists**. Lists are collections of contact inform-ation (names, addresses, phone numbers, email addresses, etc.) under some form of segmentation. Lists may be divided into three types:

- **response lists**: individuals with **identified product interest (IPI)**
- **compiled lists**: individuals with identified characteristics (but not IPI)
- **house lists**: compiled from a company's own database.

Lists (unless in-house) are generally rented on a one-time-only basis and the **cost-per-thousand** (CPT) is determined by the quality of the list. Lists are obtained from **list compilers** (who use house lists, surveys and other available data), **list brokers** (who act as brokers between list owners and renters) or through **list exchanges** with other companies.[2] In addition to the traditional forms of data collection, the practice of using **cookie** technology to track customers' movements (and therefore their interests and desires) continues to rapidly expand in scope and depth of precision (see Insight below). In May 2012, a new EU e-Privacy Directive was introduced which required that users or subscribers consent to the use of cookies and that the user knowingly indicates their consent (albeit that there can be implied as well as explicit consent). The UK *Information Commissioner's Office*, at that time, issued definitions of the types of cookies covered by the legislation.[3] They were:

---

[2]   Subject to legal restrictions in many countries.
[3]   Guidance on the rules on use of cookies and similar technologies, May 2012.

Margin glossary

Prospect hierarchy
A hierarchy of potential customers ranging from lapsed customers at the top to 'suspects' at the bottom.

Suspects
Geodemographic profiling, values, attitudes and lifestyle profiling (VALs) or previous purchase behaviour indicate that these customers *may* have the profile of current customers.

Response list
A list of prospective customers with identified product interest (IPI).

Identified product interest (IPI)
An interest in a particular product or service category.

Compiled list
A list of individuals with identified characteristics but *not* identified product interest.

House list
A list compiled from a company's own database.

List broker
An intermediary between list owners and organisations wishing to rent lists.

List exchange
Exchange of customer data between companies (illegal in certain countries).

Hand raiser
A prospect who has indicated by their behaviour (e.g. ordering a catalogue) that they *may* want to become a customer.

Cookie
A small piece of information stored as a text file on a computer that a web server uses when browsing websites that have been visited before. Typically, a cookie records preferences when an individual visits a particular site.

- **session cookies** allow websites to link the actions of a user during a browser session
- **persistent cookies** are stored on a user's device in between browser sessions which allows the preferences or actions of the user across a site (or in some cases across different websites) to be remembered
- **first-party cookies** are those set by a website visited by the user – the website displayed in the URL window
- **third-party cookies** are those set by a domain other than the one being visited.

insight: The AdChoices icon

Many of the advertisements we see online are based on the content of the website we are visiting or on predictions based on interests suggested by visits to other websites. The AdChoices icon (shown) was created by online advertising trade associations to show that these 'interest-based' advertising practices may be being used to decide what adverts to show an individual. Operators do not have the names of those they are targeting nor any other personal details. They simply recognise a number stored on your browser via a cookie and show the adverts inferred by the democratic categories associated with it. By clicking on the icon, viewers are redirected to a website explaining interest-based advertising and offering the opportunity to opt out if required.

Profiled prospect
A prospect whose general profile suggests they *may* become a customer.

Referral
A prospect who has been encouraged by an existing customer to contact the company.

Enquirer
A prospect who has directly contacted the company for specific information.

Lapsed customer
A customer who has not purchased from the company for a particular length of time.

Win-back strategy
A marketing strategy designed to bring back lapsed customers.

Above the level of 'suspect', the details are likely to come from the company's own records, internet intelligence or cookies, or derived from compiled or response lists. '**Profiled prospects**' are those whose general profile suggests a likelihood of them becoming customers (for example, a wine lover buying wine). '**Referrals**' are those who have been influenced by existing customers to contact the company, while '**enquirers**' have directly contacted the company for specific information either through their website or another source (e.g. a search engine). In both the last two categories, potential customers may be influenced by customer testimonials and/or reviews which have become ubiquitous on the internet.

At the top of the prospect pyramid are former or **lapsed customers**. Customers who have already purchased the product/service, brand or category and who, by definition, are closest to your customer profile and always the most likely to come back to you again. For this reason, organisations may go further in incentivising these customers (often referred to as '**win-back strategies**') than any others. For example, organisations may offer substantially reduced prices to lapsed customers to get them back into the habit of ordering from them. In other instances, email messages may remind you that you have not visited the company website for a while or otherwise attract you back through promotional means (e.g. 'visit our website and win').

The management of such systems has changed substantially over the past few decades. More commonly today referred to as **customer relationship management** (CRM), it previously relied on paper-based formats including ledgers and 'Rolodex' systems. The principles behind modern computer-driven CRM systems revolve around enhancing detailed profiles of individual customers and tracking inter-actions. Depending on your source of reference, a number of different aspects are associated with CRM. These include sales, customer service systems, call centres, technical and other support. According to Kelly (2000), key analytical CRM applications include:

- *sales analysis*: offering the organisation an integrated perspective on sales and enabling the sales function to understand the underlying trends and patterns in the sales data
- *customer profile analysis*: allowing the organisation to distinguish, from the mass of customer data, individuals as well as micro-segments
- *campaign analysis*: providing the ability to measure the effectiveness of individual campaigns and different media
- *loyalty analysis*: measuring customer loyalty with reference to the duration of the customer relationship
- *customer contact analysis*: analysing the customer contact history of any individual
- *profitability analysis*: measuring and analysing the many different dimensions of profitability.

Customer relationship management (CRM)
A system for managing a company's interactions with customers.

TARGET MEDIA

FIGURE 13.5   Target media

The reference to 'target media' on the 'wheel of prosperity' model refers to the media most likely to generate a response from targeted prospects. In terms of direct and digital marketing, organisations may use **direct mail**, telemarketing, email, **SMS texts** or interactive media (including internet site-based and search engine advertising) to stimulate a response. Alternatively, they may use media normally associated with advertising (e.g. internet, television, radio, magazines, posters), as long as it includes a **response mechanism**. Basically a response mechanism is a means of communicating with the organisation by whatever means (via an internet site, email, SMS, freephone number, freepost, etc.) is convenient to the customer.

Direct mail, until relatively recently, was the most powerful of the direct marketing mediums. With the advent of the internet and email, physical mail-outs have become a more expensive option and mail volume has fallen accordingly. However, direct mail is still a flexible communications medium with considerable creative potential. It can still be affective as both a customer acquisition and/or customer retention tool. As such, while the volume of direct mail packs in the UK declined from 2.2 billion in 2006 to 1.5 billion in 2010, it appears to have stabilised and even rose slightly to 1.73 billion in 2011 (Benady 2012). For some brands, it is still bigger than other forms of advertising (including digital). An example is *Virgin Media*, who send out around 100 million mail packs per year. The reasons behind the continued use of direct mail may be physical. As John Townshend, creative partner at advertising agency *Now*, notes: 'The truth is, mail still works. As the culmination of a marketing campaign, a piece of material in the hand that allows you to digest information in your own time is still effective' (Benady 2012). Response rates also appear to be higher than

Direct mail
Promotion through the medium of mail.

SMS
Short message (or messaging) service that enables messages to be sent or received by mobile phone.

Response mechanism
The means by which a customer responds to an offer (e.g. internet site, email address, SMS text details, freephone number, freepost).

for digital mediums. According to the US DMA,[4] response rates for direct mail to existing customers average 3.4% against 0.12% for email (an approximate 30-fold difference), although the return on investment was higher on the latter (see Insight below).

On the downside, the mail order industry has a reputation for **junk mail**. In direct mail campaigns, responses between 3% and 5% *may* represent a successful campaign which implies 95–97% are disinterested or could not be bothered to respond. There are both ethical and ecological factors associated with this level of mass mailing. According to *www.ecofuture.org*, the direct mail industry uses 100 million trees annually and the majority of household waste now consists of unsolicited mail.

Junk mail
Any mailing the customer decides is untargeted and obtrusive.

TABLE 13.2   Average direct and digital marketing return on investment (ROI)

For every $1.00 invested in	Total ROI forecast 2012
Direct mail (catalogue)	$ 7.25
Direct mail (non-catalogue)	$15.40
Insert media	$11.34
Internet display	$22.38
Internet search	$19.71
Social media/networking	$12.90
Commercial email	$39.40
Telemarketing	$8.26
Mobile phone marketing	$11.37

Source: Direct Marketing Association (USA), The Power of Direct Marketing 2011/12

Catalogue retailing
A means by which products or services can be purchased from a selection of those on offer in a catalogue.

Mail order
The ability (through selection in a catalogue, internet site or flyer) to order products for delivery by mail.

Internet shopping
The process that enables consumers to buy directly any goods or services from a seller in real time, without visiting a retail intermediary.

Catalogue retailing (or **mail order**) has long been associated with direct mail. More recently, **internet shopping** has supplemented and, in some cases, replaced many of the formerly printed editions. However, print catalogues do retain some advantages. In addition to being a flexible and creative medium, catalogues have the advantage of an extended life as a reference document. On the downside, catalogue production and distribution costs can be high and this has prompted the switch of many catalogues wholly or partially online (see Insight). The catalogue has a long and distinguished history, as was noted at the beginning of this chapter. It did not necessarily grow in the same way in each market. In the USA, long distances between towns prompted the generally well-to-do to order catalogue merchandise not available locally. Similarly in Germany, travel difficulties, coupled with legal restrictions on retail opening hours, prompted affluent customers to turn to mail order. In the UK, however, it was the availability of credit and 'easy payment terms' that attracted customers largely from lower socio-economic groups.

Following a decline in the 1970s, catalogue sales saw a resurgence in the 1990s with the introduction of more specialist catalogues made possible by

---

[4]   The Direct Marketing Association's 2012 Response Rate Report.

lower publishing and design costs. More recently, there has been evidence that the printed catalogue may be acting as a driver of internet sales. According to *Royal Mail*,[5] 60% of recipients go online to make a purchase within a week of receiving a catalogue. The same research suggested that 70% of consumers keep catalogues for over a month and 34% for up to a year. It also revealed that people interact with catalogues for longer (up to half an hour) than an internet retail site (on average 11 minutes).

 insight: Argos catalogue

rgos introduced its catalogue in 1973 and at its peak 20 million copies of the bi-annual catalogue were produced. Customers could browse at home and come to an *Argos* store to collect their goods. Although the company eventually introduced online ordering and home delivery, they continued to rely on the catalogue and in-store collection. In September 2012, however, the company announced that it was cutting the circulation of the catalogue and scrapping the laminated versions used by customers in-store. The company will introduce web-based browsers and wifi so that customers can use their smartphones to order and pay for products instead of using the catalogue. Argos boss John Walden was quoted as saying it was unlikely the catalogue would be axed altogether, but admitted it may decline 'precipitously' as sales shift online. He said it would be 'foolish' to pull it now, as around 85% of customers still look at the catalogue before they buy.

Source: various

Despite the continued relevance of the printed catalogue, recent years have seen a continuing upward trend in online purchases with social media now playing a part. According to the *Centre for Retail Research* (www.retailresearch.org), 2011 online sales in the UK were £50.34 billion (€60.41 billion) or 12.0% of UK retail trade, up from 8.6% in 2008. For Europe (including the UK), the total market was worth £169.9 billion (€203.9 billion) in 2011, up from £143.7 billion (€172.4 billion) the previous year and £101.8 billion (€122.2 billion) in 2008. Online retailers in only three countries – the UK, Germany and France – accounted for 71% of European online sales in 2011. According to *Royal Mail* research (in September 2010), the top 10 online shopping categories are (% is of total UK sales):

1   Books (39%)
2   Homeware (36%)
3   Clothes – women's (33%)
4   DVDs (purchased) (30%)
5   CDs/video or audio tapes/records (27%)
6   Clothes – men's (23%)
7   Food or drink (21%)
8   Footwear (21%)
9   Phones/mobile phones/MP3 players (19%)
10   Electrical goods (17%)

---

[5]   *Royal Mail* MarketReach initiative, February 2013.

Multi-channel retailer
A retailer with a number of channels, such as online and retail space.

Shopping cart abandonment
Where an online transaction is halted before completion.

Search engine
A programme that searches sites on the World Wide Web for specified keywords and which returns a list of where the keywords can be found.

Search engine optimisation (SEO)
The process of improving the visibility of a website or web page in a search engine's 'natural' or unpaid search results.

Natural search
A search (using a search engine) where results are returned based on the natural indexing of the website, as opposed to those that are returned based on paid advertising and/or editorial changes made by the search engine itself.

Meta tags
A special HTML (or XHTML) tag that provides information about a web page which provides detail on what the page is about, and which keywords represent the page's content. Many search engines use this information.

Paid-for placement (PFP)
Where an advertiser pays to guarantee their listing appears on a search page when particular keywords are searched. The ranking of paid placement listings is usually determined by a competitive bidding process.

What drives consumers to particular websites are principally direct mail shots (including catalogues), word of mouth and search engines (see Insight below). One of the most troubling issues with online retailing is the number of sales abandoned before they are completed (so-called **shopping cart abandonment**), which is estimated to have cost **multi-channel retailers** an average of £1 billion each in 2010 (according to Royal Mail). The main reasons given were unhappiness with delivery charges (48%) and out of stock items (41%). Interruptions (40%) and website technical difficulties (39%) were also stated as reasons to abandon online purchasing.

TABLE 13.3   Prompts to purchase online

According to *Royal Mail,* the main influences on consumers going online to purchase are:

Direct mail/catalogues	25%
Word of mouth	24%
Search engine	19%
Email	12%
Seeing products in shops	12%
Auction sites	12%
Price comparison sites	12%
Television advertising	8%
Newspaper/magazine advertising	8%
Online marketplace(s)	8%

The search for products and services now often begins with a **search engine**, of which *Google* (who got around 4.7 billion searches per day in 2011) is the current market leader. This has spawned the new sub-discipline of **search engine optimisation (SEO)**, sometimes referred to as search engine marketing. SEO relates to the promotion of websites by increasing the site's visibility in a search engine's **natural search** (i.e. unpaid search). Search engines read through volumes of information on the Web with software programs called 'robots' or 'spiders' (because they navigate, or 'crawl', through the web). These create an index which contains all the pages they have found and the words associated with them. Identifying those keywords or key phrases that customers are likely to use is vital to SEO. Once established, they need to be incorporated into the pages of the organisation website in the form of **meta tags**. These are coding statements in the Hypertext Markup Language (HTML) that describe the content of the page. Other ways of improving visibility are associated with page set-ups and links to other websites. Some practices are seen as unfair as they manipulate artificially web page rankings (see Insight below). In addition, search engines accept **'paid-for placement' (PFP)** advertising which guarantees top ranking in such listings. As these PFPs are normally determined by a competitive bidding process, it can become a very expensive process for popular search words (e.g. MBA).

◉ insight: The dark side of SEO

According to Google, certain bad practices are used to try to artificially improve website rankings. These include:

- automated content: content that's been generated consisting of paragraphs of random text that make no sense to the reader but which may contain search keywords

- link schemes: any links that are part of a link scheme intended to manipulate PageRank or a site's ranking in search results

- cloaking: this refers to the practice of presenting different content or URLs to human users (where it is hidden or disguised) and search engines

- sneaky redirects: some redirects are designed to deceive search engines or to display different content to human users than to search engines

- hidden text: any text or links included solely for search engines and not visitors

- doorway pages: typically large sets of poor-quality pages where each page is optimised for a specific keyword or phrase. In many cases, doorway pages are written to rank a particular phrase which then funnels users to a single destination

- scraped content: content taken ('scraped') from other, more reputable sites on the assumption that increasing the volume of pages on their site is a good long-term strategy

- affinity websites: pages where product descriptions and reviews are copied directly from the original merchant without any original content or added value

- keyword stuffing: the practice of loading a web page with keywords or numbers in an attempt to manipulate a site's ranking in *Google* search results.

Adapted from *Google* at: https://support.google.com/webmasters/answer/35769 (accessed 5 October 2013)

Social media (or social networking) is having more of an influence with consumers using an online forum, review or chat room to inform purchases. In North America, 72% of adults are reported to use social media.[6] Although the young represent the highest number of users, those aged 65 and older tripled their presence (13% to 43%) between 2009 and 2013. In Europe, the Netherlands, the UK, Sweden and Luxembourg lead the way with 65%, 57%, 54% and 50% respectively.[7] In Europe too, there is substantial increased usage of social media among the over 65s.

Social media enables people to comment, interact and collaborate with a wide number of people; as such, it is blurring the traditional boundaries between media and the audience. It enables self-promotion on an individual (and commercial) basis but also provides a platform for those 'frenemies' who may want to criticise individuals, organisations or brands. Brands appear to be rushing to set up their own platforms on the likes of *Facebook* and *Twitter* and many promotions direct consumers to such sites. According to the US *Social Media Examiner* report[8] in 2012, 83% of marketers indicated social media is important to their business

Social media
Online virtual communities and networks that people use to interact with others and where they can create, share and exchange information and ideas.

---

[6] The Pew Research Centre & American Life Project, 5 August 2013.
[7] Office for National Statistics/Eurostat, published June 2013.
[8] See www.socialmediaexaminer.com/SocialMediaMarketingIndustryReport2012.pdf

with the top four sites (in descending order) being *Facebook, Twitter, LinkedIn* and *YouTube*. In the case of *YouTube*, interesting or amusing files, associated with particular brands, are being circulated to friends and relations in a form replicating the spread of a virus (viral marketing). What is particularly attractive to organisations is that it is the social media environment that is most attractive to younger consumers, a segment notoriously difficult to reach via traditional media. According to research by *PEW Research Center* in 2013, 83% of 18–29-year-olds use social media compared to 77% aged 30–49, 52% aged 50–64 and 32% aged 65+. In addition to signifying the dominance of the 18–29 age group, these figures also indicate the growing appeal among older age groups.

Even conservative estimates predict that advertising on social media will grow substantially with companies attracted by the high involvement users have with the sites. BIA/Kelsey predict that ad spend on social media will rise to $11 billion by 2017, a 130% increase on 2012 (Business Insider 2013), driven in part by increased use of mobiles to access sites.

Viral marketing
Any marketing technique that induces websites or users to pass on (virus-like) a marketing message to other sites or users.

insight: Viral marketing

Viral marketing is the art of encouraging individuals to pass on a marketing message in a variety of forms (e.g. videos) to others. The advantage of this is obvious as these people become your marketing team and do it for no payment at all. All good virals need to have a built-in incentive for the individual to pass it on to others. Normally, this is because it has some element of fascination based on humour, shock or some other emotion that the individual would like to share and thereby gain some kudos in the process. More basic rewards (such as free gifts) also play a part and the exact choice of the incentive depends on your goals, resources and audience.

Google has used virals extensively, including a video of Lady Gaga interacting with fans through the brand's Chrome web browser. This was viewed a staggering 78 million times. *Facebook* and *Twitter* are being used to allow followers to preview, share and 'like' the video. *Carphone Warehouse*, for example, regularly releases virals, including a series demonstrating new facilities on gadgets. Within two months of release, the retailer quadrupled its *Facebook* fan base to 350,000 which led to the videos being viewed nearly 300,000 times.

Source: various

In-bound telemarketing
The use of telephony to facilitate responses from customers, usually via a 'freephone' or local call rate number.

Out-bound telemarketing
Planned use of the telephone to make unstructured calls to a target audience in a measurable and accountable way.

Telemarketing can be classified either as in-bound telemarketing or out-bound telemarketing. Inbound telemarketing is the use of telephone services to facilitate responses from customers usually via a 'freephone' or local call rate number. These are frequently handled by call centre operations which may be out-sourced nationally or internationally. Outbound telemarketing is where the customer has given permission for the company to contact them, or where the company believes it is in the customer's interest to do so, and is distinguishable (although not always clearly) from telesales where no such permission is given or implied and which is, in effect, 'cold calling'. Another persistent complaint is about 'silent calls' generated by predictive dialling technology. Designed to speed up agent productivity, it frequently leaves customers with a disturbing silence when they answer their telephone. In the UK, you can restrict telephone calls by registering with the *Telephone Preference Service*. In the USA, the *Do-not-call Registry* provides a similar service. In addition, according to the US *Federal Trade Commission*'s telemarketing sales rules, a consumer can claim $500 from companies who, if they have been told not to call, continue to do so. Telesales calls from outside a country's jurisdiction are, however, difficult to regulate.

A growing area of communications interest associated with telephony is **mobile marketing**. Mobile marketing is marketing using a mobile device such as a mobile phone or tablet. In the UK, 94% of the population own a mobile phone and more than half of these are **smartphones** which offer more advanced computing ability and connectivity than basic mobile phones. Indeed, the UK has one of the highest penetrations of smartphones of all the researched markets with 58% of the population owning a smartphone in 2012 (*Ofcom* 2012). Social networking is driving much of the use of smartphones in the UK. Four in ten adults (40%) use their mobile phones to visit social networking sites, while among 18–24-year-olds almost two-thirds (62%) do so. The growth of 3G, 4G and accessible wifi means that social media sites, films, games, etc. can be accessed on the move. Mobile phone **apps** (applications) can guide you to your favourite food, clothing or any other retail commodity or place of interest. By way of covering the cost of these apps, advertising is often incorporated. Alternatively, commercial organisations encourage customers to download their particular app as a way of accessing the company's offerings and promotions. As the technology for mobile web browsers advances, new applications will undoubtedly develop.

Telesales
Cold calling (without prior contact or permission) with the objective of making a sale or starting the process towards a sale.

Cold calling
The process of approaching prospective customers or clients, typically via the telephone, who have not agreed to be approached.

insight: Waitrose on Twitter

Waitrose, the rather upmarket supermarket with a Royal Warrant, ran a competition on its *Twitter* social media site. It asked customers to finish the sentence 'I shop at Waitrose because…' Instead of strengthening relations with their loyal customers, the supermarket chain found itself the subject of ridicule for its largely middle-class, upmarket image. Derogatory tweets, accompanied by the hashtag #WaitroseReasons, included one from a user who said that she favoured the store because she 'didn't like being surrounded by poor people'. Others included 'I shop at Waitrose because Clarrisa's pony just WILL NOT eat ASDA value straw', 'I shop at Waitrose because it makes me feel important and I absolutely detest being surrounded by poor people' and 'I shop at Waitrose because the toilet paper is made from 24ct gold thread'. Perhaps the most surreal entry was 'I shop at Waitrose because I was once in the Holloway Rd branch and heard a dad say "Put the papaya down, Orlando!"'

Source: various

More general media (described in an earlier definition as advertising media) include magazines and newspapers (often referred to as **off the page**), television and radio, inserts and door-to-door communications. These are normally used as customer acquisition devices (used to generate leads) rather than as retention media and their particular characteristics are covered more generally in Chapter 8. One area of distinct growth of interactive activity, however, is **direct response television**. Direct response television advertising might be described as any campaign which persuades customers to contact the company (or their agents) via the internet, telephone or any other means. ITV and the DMA conducted a major study into how effective TV is when used in conjunction with other communication channels, which showed that response levels to DM increase by 143% when TV is included, by 52% for press and by 175% for online. Internet-enabled television will, undoubtedly, refresh interest in this medium.

Silent calls
Calls generated by predictive dialling technology designed to speed up agent productivity but which frequently leave customers with a disturbing silence when they answer their telephone.

Mobile marketing
The use of the mobile telephone medium as a means of marketing communications.

Table 13.4 describes the advantages and disadvantages of the various direct and digital marketing media discussed.

Smartphone
A mobile phone offering more advanced computing ability and connectivity than basic mobile phones.

App
A software application typically of a small, specialised programme available to download onto mobile devices such as mobile telephones, personal computers and tablets.

Off the page
Direct marketing advertising in newspapers or magazines.

Direct response television (DRTV)
DRTV refers to commercials or paid programming made for television in which viewers are encouraged to order either through a web page or by telephone.

TABLE 13.4   Direct and digital marketing media comparisons

	Advantages	Disadvantages
Interactive media		
Direct mail	• Can generate leads, improve image and sell, up-sell, cross-sell and help build/qualify databases • Cost-effective • Creative opportunities	• Cost-per-thousand (CPT) high compared to advertising • Clutter (junk mail) • Environmental issues
Telemarketing	• Inbound responsive to customer • Outbound relationship building	• Customer intolerance against cold calling
Mobile marketing	• Inexpensive • Interactive	• Potentially intrusive
Internet marketing	• Inexpensive • Interactive	• Passive medium • Millions of sites
Catalogues	• As Direct mail • Frequently kept as reference	• High production costs
Direct response television	• Interactivity and movement • Explanation of features • Immediate ordering facility	• Must wait for specific offerings to be made
Advertising media		
Magazines (off-the-page)	• Enables advertising alongside relevant articles • Enables complex explanation • Relatively long shelf-life	• Mass media and, therefore, not highly targeted
Posters	• Relatively inexpensive	• Only very simple messages
Newspapers	• Enables advertising alongside relevant articles • Enables complex explanation	• Mass media and, therefore, not highly targeted • Short shelf-life
Television	• Interactivity and movement • Explanation of basic features	• Difficulty in explaining complexities • Relies on consumer remembering and responding to particular email, web address or telephone number
Radio	• Relatively inexpensive • Atmospheric	
Cinema	• Interactivity and movement • Relatively inexpensive	
Inserts	• Relatively inexpensive	• Easily ignored
Door-to-door	• Relatively inexpensive	• Easily ignored

THE OFFERING

FIGURE 13.6   The offering

The **offering** on the 'wheel of prosperity' model (see Figure 13.6) refers not only to the product and/or service but to the complete package being offered to the prospective customer. How attractive the complete package is determines whether the sale will ultimately go through and is as important online as it is in direct mail or catalogue offerings. This package comprises of a number of elements which include:

- the offer
- the timing
- the creative element
- the response mechanism
- distribution costs.

The *offer* is comprised not only of the product/service but the pricing and incentivising elements as well. Regardless of how successful you have been in attracting target customers to your website or catalogue or how creatively the offer is presented, unless the main product/service, any incentive(s) and the price quoted interest the customer, the customer will not respond. A secondary incentive may be associated with a prompt reply within a given time period. This is offered in the knowledge that the longer a customer takes to consider an offer, the less likely they are to respond.

The *timing* of the offer is also crucial as many items are either seasonal or associated with a particular time of the year (e.g. Christmas, Valentine's Day). Where information is known about a particular anniversary (birthday, insurance renewal date, etc.), appropriate communication can be made with the prospect. It is also generally true that, at different times in our lives, we have different needs. This is particularly true of the financial services industry. Few teenagers are interested in pensions but may be interested in small loans. Couples may require substantial loans, particularly if they plan to purchase their own property, but are unlikely to have money to spare for investments. 'Empty-nesters' (couples whose children have left home), however, may have the funds to invest on their own or on their children's behalf.

The *creative element* of the offer in particular is seen as crucial to its success. Developing a creative strategy means:

- defining the primary marketing problem
- developing key selling concepts
- creating message strategies
- specifying the desired action and the means by which it can be accomplished
- including mandatory (i.e. legal) requirements.

The creative element is the 'icing on the cake' and can make the difference between being noticed and acted on and being ignored.

Just as important is the response mechanism. How easily can the prospect contact you? Initially, mail was the preferred media and then the telephone. The growth of digital makes them no less crucial. Systems have become much more sophisticated but it is frustrating (and a possible deal-breaker) if the email link does not work or website navigation is poor.

Offering
A number of factors (product, price, etc.) which together make up the direct marketing offering to the customer.

Distribution costs are another possible deal-breaker, particularly online. According to *Forrester Research* (2012), 42% of online shoppers do not complete because shipping and handling costs are too high. While some retailers view free shipping to be a competitive advantage that attracts shoppers, the majority of retailers interviewed by *Forrester* perceived free shipping offers to be a 'necessary evil' in the online world (2012).

CUSTOMER RETENTION

FIGURE 13.7   Customer retention

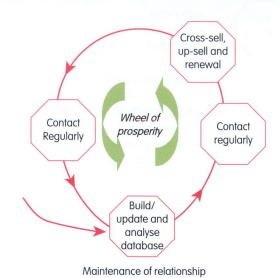

Maintenance of relationship

Once a prospect has become a customer, the work of retention begins. Direct and digital marketers build their database and continually qualify (i.e. update and improve) the data over time but, as Clive Humby of Dunn Humby[9] claimed it is not the detailed transaction data that is of interest per se but patterns in the transactions'. To enable patterns to emerge, direct marketers use software frequently based on three factors:

- **recency**: how long ago did this customer buy from us?
- **frequency**: how often does this customer buy from us?
- **monetary value**: how much does this customer spend with us?

As might be expected, it is likely that those customers who have most recently bought from the company and have most frequently spent relatively significant amounts with them are those most likely to be the most valuable in the future. Profiles can also be based more specifically on customer purchase and price preferences and other details. Online retailers such as *Amazon* use customer

---

[9]   Formerly an independent company that helped launch *Tesco* Clubcard, now a part of *Tesco*.

history (and that of customers who have purchased similar goods) to offer further suggestions at the time of the transaction and in regular updates. Once profiles have been established, the company *may* wish to contact the customer through newsletters, updates, etc. to maintain contact. Alternatively (or additionally), correspondence may be aimed at additional sales or targeted to **cross-sell** (sell an associated product) or **up-sell** (sell a higher quality product), increasing the value of that customer to the company. An example of this is *SportsDirect.com* whose regular newsletters promote special offers while encouraging regular sales. The retention of customers over time becomes the basis of the 'spiral of prosperity' for the organisation.

Customer retention is seen to be positive and organisations go out of their way to maintain relationships. Proactively, this may take two forms: sales communications and non-sales communications such as emails, e-newsletters, welcome packs (on- or off-line), out-bound telemarketing, etc. Sales communications have the advantage of both maintaining contact and generating profit but these may or may not be appropriate on every occasion. One undoubted problem with regular communication is deciding how often customers should be contacted. There is a fine line between 'acceptable' and 'too much'.

Another set of retention methods is associated with the **principle of negative option**. In effect, the principle takes advantage of our inclination to do nothing until something (often a negative perception) prompts us to take action. The principle of negative option is behind many club and other short-contract operations where, unless the consumer makes an effort to refuse that month's offer

Recency
How recently has a customer purchased from a company?

Frequency
How frequently does the customer purchase from the company?

Monetary value
What value does the customer spend with the company?

Cross-sell
Selling existing customers products or services outside of their existing purchase(s).

Up-sell
Selling existing customers products or services of a higher quality (and price) to their existing purchase(s).

👁 insight: Dynamic pricing

Dynamic pricing is a practice that has existed for many years. Prices differ on the basis of demand, date, geography and other variables. Initially, the internet was seen as a way of levelling prices because the internet is so seemingly transparent. However, as the internet became more sophisticated, new opportunities to leverage dynamic pricing presented themselves and the practice is widespread in some industries, notably transportation. However, when it comes to implementing these new profit opportunities, are retailers breaking any trust built up with them? Many consumers feel dynamic pricing is not fair. *Amazon* is well aware of this issue. The world-famous internet bookseller tried out a dynamic pricing strategy that varied the prices of products by determining the profiles of existing customers. Regular customers, it was hypothesised, would be more likely to pay more and, therefore, should be charged more for products! Discussions began on message boards and forums and stories began to spread about price differentials between whom *Amazon* perceived as new and existing customers. Confusion became outrage as customers found out what was going on. An *Amazon* spokesperson stated that the experiment 'was done to determine customer responses to different price levels'. Ultimately, the company admitted its mistake and promised its customers it would not happen again. *Coca-Cola* too tested dynamic pricing in vending machines where prices fluctuated based on the surrounding temperature. The theory was that a soft drink would be worth more when it is hot outside and that demand for soft drinks would decrease in cold weather. Adverse reaction caused the company to relent.

Source: various

(for example, the 'monthly choice'), you will be invoiced accordingly. Another example is also known as 'free-to-pay' conversion plans. Under this, a consumer receives goods or services for free (or for a reduced fee) for a trial period. After the trial period ends, the seller automatically begins to charge a fee (or a higher fee) unless the consumer cancels or returns the goods or services. Often, these 'free-to-pay' plans are placed in conjunction with another purchase. The reasoning is that anything that is 'free' (or substantially cheaper) is attractive to the consumer who, in many cases, fails to cancel at the end of the trial period. Certain financial devices also work on this principle. Insurance companies will automatically renew policies if the policy holder does not advise them to the contrary. Once a standing order or direct debit has been established, the customer must actively cancel the instruction before the relationship is ended. Research indicates that these devices substantially lengthen the **lifetime value** of the customer. Such is the value of such devices to organisations that they are frequently prepared to be exceptionally generous in the incentives offered for them to be set up. According to *MoneySupermarket.com* in 2012, nearly three million people in the UK are paying for services they no longer need because of forgotten direct debits. **Continuous credit** (offered by many mail-order and online companies) and leasing/rental agreements similarly keep relationships from terminating. Non-financial incentives to loyalty include clubs (where membership entitles members to certain privileges), **continuity series** (where a finite number of items are made available over time), subscriptions and loyalty programmes.

TESTING AND ANALYTICS

Testing is of central importance to the success of direct and digital marketing. Testing, as noted in Chapter 6, is different from market research. While research may tell you why something works and suggest a number of alternatives, testing establishes *whether* something works and *evaluates* alternatives. Testing (on- or off-line) can predict, therefore, the outcome of future marketing activities and is crucial to the integrity of direct and digital marketing. Effectively, all elements of the offering can be tested including:

- customer base: different lists, parts of lists, etc.
- the offer: variations in the offer (including price) or the incentives
- the timing: varying the timing of the offer, one-shot versus campaign, etc.
- the creative element: varying the creative element including the copy, physical format and media.

In simple terms, tests are made against a control sample, usually the existing best variable in the way shown in Table 13.5. **A/B tests**, as they are known, are usually performed to determine the better of two content variations. In this example, the response of each audience and each offer can be made.

   With the advent of online services, testing may take place in real time. According to the *Digital Analytics Association*,[10] **web analytics** is the measurement, collection, analysis and reporting of internet data for purposes of understanding and optimising web usage. In the online environment, **multivariate testing** is used so that one or more (sometimes many more) components of a website can be tested in a live environment. Where web analytics scores is

---

[10] See www.digitalanalyticsassociation.org

Margin glossary

Lifetime value
A calculation made (usually on the basis of likely future business discounted to present-day value) of the likely value to an organisation over a customer's lifetime.

Continuous credit
By paying in instalments, a line of continuous credit (to a maximum amount) is offered to the customer.

Continuity series
Where a finite number of items (usually in a series or set) is made available over time (e.g. monthly).

A/B tests
A testing method that uses randomised experiments with two variants.

Web analytics
The measurement, collection, analysis and reporting of internet data for the purposes of understanding and optimising web usage.

TABLE 13.5   A/B testing

Control	Test 1	Test 2
testing new offer ↓------------------------------------↓		
List A	List A	List B
Proven offer	New offer	Proven offer
↑--↑ *testing new list*		

Multivariate testing

A method of testing which uses different content for many elements across one or more web pages to identify the combination of changes that yields the highest conversion rate.

in the ability to provide data (including visitors, geodemographics, etc.) on a changing set of stimuli in real time. Different presentations can be made to different consumers and the 'offer' adjusted accordingly. It is essentially no different from the A/B tests referred to above except that, theoretically, the effectiveness of limitless combinations can be tested.

The reliability of any given test is determined by three statistical concepts relevant to direct and digital marketing.[11] These are:

- the sample: how representative it is of the population at large. Thus, the **sampling error** is the difference between the mean of the sample and the mean of the population as a whole. The greater the level of error you can tolerate, the smaller the sample can be
- the **significance**: analysing the differences between the observed and expected results and noting whether they are real and significantly different
- the **confidence interval**: how different the results must be before you can be confident of their significance.

Sampling error

The error caused by sampling only a small number of the total population. Using sample data presents the risk that results found will not represent the results that would be obtained from using data involving the entire population.

Significance

Analysis of differences between the observed and expected results, noting whether they are real and significant differences.

Testing is relatively low cost (especially online) and reliable if properly executed, and can save the organisation money and/or help realise future revenue. It can be analysed and refined over time and help secure competitive advantage. Indeed, testing provides information on the likely outcome of future marketing activity.

Confidence interval

In market research, how different the results must be before you can be confident of its significance.

summary

This chapter traced the development of direct and digital marketing which it described as an interactive system of marketing. It reviewed the reasons behind the growth of direct marketing and looked at how, more recently, the internet in particular has made it such a powerful marketing communications tool. The chapter reviewed those developments associated with the increase in processing power, analytical systems development and other technological advances. It described the characteristics of direct and

(Continued)

---

[11]   Although a brief description appears here, full statistical explanations are beyond the scope of this text.

(Continued)

digital marketing and compared them with traditional marketing and the outcomes achievable through effective database management. The chapter went on to describe the operation of direct and digital marketing in organisations where the principal objectives are to acquire and retain customers. Using the 'wheel of prosperity' as a model, it reviewed the identification of prospects through lists and other sources, the targeting of the media and the offering as an 'acquisition strategy'. Once this is achieved, building and updating, cross-selling, up-selling and win-back strategies are part of the maintenance and retention of relationships. In conclusion, the importance of testing to direct and digital marketing was highlighted.

 ## review questions

1. What do you understand by the term 'data mining'?

2. Explain the value of a database.

3. What factors have led to the growth of direct and digital marketing?

4. Give the principal objectives of direct and digital marketing.

5. Explain the differences between 'suspects' and 'profiled prospects'.

6. Explain the meaning of customer relationship management (CRM).

7. To what extent can telemarketing be used for CRM activities?

8. What are the benefits of online and off-line catalogues?

9. Testing is a feature of direct and digital marketing activities. What can be tested and why would you test at all?

10. Explain the leaky bucket metaphor.

discussion questions

1. Databases are crucial tools to the direct marketer. What are the problems associated with data capture and storage and how might this impact on a campaign?

2. Using an existing campaign, analyse it in terms of the wheel of prosperity. What is it trying to achieve and how does it integrate with other communications being undertaken by the same company?

3. Discuss the phenomena of junk mail and junk email. Why do companies send it out? Why is it considered junk and by whom?

case study 13.1: One Direction – Building the brand

Credit: Featureflash/Shutterstock.com

Despite only coming third in the 2010 *X Factor* final, behind Rebecca Ferguson and the series winner Matt Cardle, the manufactured group One Direction (1D) has built itself into one of the world's greatest music brands in a very short space of time. The official website, **www.onedirectionmusic. com,** boasts of the group's achievements so far:

- 61 album and single no. 1's worldwide
- the last album, 'Take Me Home', was no. 1 in 37 countries
- the debut album, 'Up All Night', was no. 1 in 17 countries
- the only UK band to have its first two albums debut at no. 1 in the USA
- the first UK band since The Beatles to have two no. 1 albums in the same year in the USA
- winners of two Brit Awards in 2012 for 'Best British Single' and 2013 for 'Global Success Award'
- awarded three MTV VMAs and three MTV EMAs
- received NRJ award for 'Best International Group'
- won three Billboard Music Awards for 'Top Duo/Group', 'Top New Artist' and 'Top Pop Artist'
- two *Sunday Times* bestselling books
- a sold-out 2013 UK arena tour
- over 18.5 million *Facebook* fans and 71 million combined followers on *Twitter*.

It is this last statistic that indicates what has helped rocket the group to worldwide fame so quickly. One Direction uses social media to interact with fans (known as Directioners) on a daily basis. Individual members of the band, Niall Horan, Zayn Malik, Liam Payne, Harry Styles and Louis Tomlinson average around 13 million *Twitter* followers each, with daily updates and fan interaction. *YouTube* is another medium used. The 'What Makes You Beautiful' track on the band's Vevo channel had an estimated 418 million views. 1D also has a comprehensive website to post information and sell products like T-shirts, hoodies, posters, bracelets and even dolls of each band member! The website is in several different languages and although the same worldwide, local news is personal to the country domain.

In early 2011, the band encouraged fans from outside the UK to get active on social media and help build a bigger fan base, with the 'super fans' who were the most successful winning an appearance from the 1D boys in their own country. This engagement strategy continues with fans being asked to help make decisions, such as what the boys should wear or where their next photo shoot should take place.

One Direction's 2013 North American tour was sold out nearly a year in advance. Tickets went on sale just months after the band's American breakthrough in March 2012 when 'Up All Night' debuted at no. 1. When the group hit the road on 13 June that year, a multinational brand partner was in tow in the form of Mondelez International's *Nabisco*, whose brands (Chips Ahoy, Oreo, Trident, Ritz, Stride, Cheese Nips, Dentyne and Honey Maid) were all sponsors of the One Direction North American tour. The sponsorship follows in a tradition that *Nabisco* brands have in aligning with major pop stars, with earlier examples being 'N Sync and Britney Spears.

The seeds of One Direction's US success were sown in the UK in 2012, when an online marketing campaign targeted at European fans quickly spread to both North and South America. Simon Cowell's

(Continued)

(Continued)

Sony-backed record label, Syco, teamed up with London advertising agency Archibald Ingall Stretton to create a 'transmedia adventure' that engaged fans in both online and real-world adventures. Over 50 days, the campaign increased two-fold the traffic to One Direction's website. It attracted 200,000 participants who completed 20 separate challenges, creating along the way 12 *Twitter* trends and more than 2.5 million *YouTube* views. The strategy was not to be overtly commercial but to engage fans and make them feel part of the campaign.

For 2014, a world stadium tour has been announced. The group is to launch their own fragrance, 'Our Moment', and a movie, *This is Us*, is set to be released in cinemas worldwide. According to the *Daily Mail*, 'One Direction aren't just a pop band. They're a hysteria-inducing, social media-fuelled, world-conquering phenomenon'.

Case study questions

1. How has One Direction used social media to build the group's international reputation?
2. Is the band's success 'hysteria-induced' or due to successful marketing?
3. What are the commercial benefits of *Nabisco* sponsoring the tour?

 further reading

Grosso, C., Shenkan, A., Guggenheim, S. and Hobart, P. (2006) 'A reality check for online advertising', *McKinsey Quarterly*, 3: 10–11.

Hoan Cho, C.-H., Kang, J. and Cheon, H.J. (2006) 'Online shopping hesitation', *CyberPsychology & Behavior*, 9 (3): 261–74.

Lagrosen, S. (2005) 'Effects of the internet on the marketing communication of service companies', *Journal of Services Marketing*, 19 (2): 63–9.

Pomirleanu, N., Schibrowsky, J.A., Peltier, J.W. and Nill, A. (2013) 'A review of internet marketing research over the past 20 years and future research direction', Journal of Research in Interactive Marketing, 7 (3): 166–81.

Pons, A.P. (2006) 'Biometric marketing: targeting the online consumer', *Communications of the ACM*, 49 (8): 61–5.

Sipior, J.C., Ward, B.T. and Bonner, P.G. (2004) 'Should spam be on the menu?', *Communications of the ACM*, 47 (6): 59–63.

REFERENCES

Benady, D. (2012) 'Special report: direct marketing', *Marketing Magazine*, 20 July.

Bewick, M. (2005) 'Charm school', *The Marketer*, 18 November, pp. 14–17.

Business Insider (2013) 'Why social media advertising is set to explode', 8 August. Available at: www.businessinsider.com/social-media-advertising-set-to-explode-2013-7 (accessed 6 October 2013).

DMA (2010) *The Power of Direct and Digital Marketing: ROI, Sales, Expenditures, and Employment in the US, 2009–2010 Edition*. New York: Direct and Digital Marketing Association.

DMA UK (2012) 'Putting a price on direct and digital marketing', 30 March. London: Direct and Digital Marketing Association.

Forrester Research (2012) *Smarter Strategies for Free Shipping: Understanding the Costs and Benefits to Retailers*. Cambridge, MA: Forrester Research, Inc.

Kelly, S. (2000) 'Analytical CRM: the fusion of data and intelligence', *Interactive Marketing*, 1: 262–7.

Miller, P. (2012) 'Tesco uses data for more than just loyalty cards', 1 October. Available at: www.cloudofdata.com (accessed 14 August 2013).

Murphy, D. (2005) 'A clean sweep', *The Marketer*, 18 November, pp. 11–13.

Ofcom (2012) *The Communications Market 2012*. London: *Ofcom*.

Reichheld, F.F. (1996) *The Loyalty Effect*. Cambridge, MA: Harvard Business School Press.

Smith, P.R. and Taylor, J. (2004) *Marketing Communications: An Integrated Approach*, 2nd edn. London: Kogan Page.

USEFUL WEBSITES

For information and news concerning direct and digital marketing, see the Institute of Direct and Digital Marketing at: www.theidm.com/ and the Direct Marketing Association at: www.dma.org.uk/

For direct mail campaign case studies, go to: www.marketreach.co.uk/

For additional materials that support this chapter and your learning, please visit:
study.sagepub.com/egan

PERSONAL SELLING, POINT OF SALE AND SUPPORTIVE COMMUNICATIONS

14

LEARNING OBJECTIVES

Having completed this chapter, readers would be expected to:

- describe the strengths and weaknesses associated with personal selling and its part in the integrated marketing communications mix

- comment on the value of field marketing and multi-level marketing

- recognise the importance of packaging in point-of-sale decision making

- assess the value of point-of-sale materials to marketing communications.

INTRODUCTION

Point of sale (point of purchase)
In-store materials displayed at the place where customers are making their buying decisions.

In the last chapter, it was suggested that direct and digital marketing was moving communications closer to the customer. This chapter gets closer still by looking at those elements of the marketing communications mix nearest the consumer and, by definition, closest to the point of purchase. We will examine, therefore, personal selling and those features which together are referred to as **point of sale (POS)** or **point of purchase (POP)**. In our brave new digital age, we sometimes forget how important these latter, seemingly boring, aspects of communication are. Approximately 80% of retailing is still off-line and of those customers who still shop 76% (and growing) of their decisions are made in-store.[1]

The logic behind presenting what at first might appear disparate tools in one chapter is that personal selling has such a wide spectrum of types from the complex negotiator to the supermarket shop-floor assistant. At the latter end of this continuum, point-of-sale features assume a more significant role in the purchasing process and should be included.

Figure 14.1 illustrates those influences closest to the (physical) point of sale. Advertising, public relations, sales promotion and sponsorship have a distant influence but may create the conditions

---

[1]   2012 Report, Point of Purchase Advertising International (POPAI).

FIGURE 14.1   Communications Tools Closest to the Customer

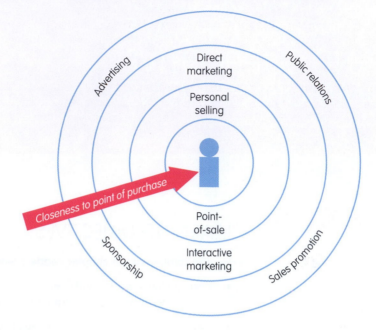

to prompt a sale. Direct and digital marketing is generally closer. Personal selling and point of sale are at the point of many purchases and have a direct influence on their outcome.

PERSONAL SELLING

Personal selling is as old as bartering and much older than any organised monetary system. It evolved from the time when humankind first found itself with a surplus of a commodity and sought to find others with whom to trade. Despite its traditional place within the 'marketing department', it is not universally accepted that personal selling should be regarded as part of the marketing communications mix. An argument sometimes used is that salespeople are there to sell what already exists (the antipathy of marketing) and/or that it's more to do with customer service than communications. The perspective taken in this text is that salespeople can be persuasive, acting as important communicators and contributing to a successful sale. Perhaps the term personal communications would describe it better than personal selling.

It is estimated that there are approximately 2.2 million professional salespeople in the UK.[2] Although the spectrum of personal selling types is wide, certain important characteristics set it aside from other communications tools. Most importantly, the communication is between two (or more) people who interact with each other in 'real time' and respond to each other's informational needs. This is important because it usually means much less **noise** (i.e. other distracting communications) and that the customer is involved and, therefore, plays a large part in the exchange process. It is frequently, but not always, face to face with exceptions being where part or all of the negotiation uses technology (e.g. online assistance, the telephone) as a medium between the salesperson and the

---

[2]   The *Hays* Market Overview 2011.

customer. Its fundamental aim is to inform, persuade or remind an individual or group to act, in the way desired by the initiator of the contact. The interactivity may, however, be part of a longer-term relationship between the salesperson and their customer. In this case, current negotiations may be heavily influenced by past experience.

Personal selling is seen as an action-driving tool which is most effective at or near the point of sale. As such, other longer-term, brand-building tools (e.g. advertising, public relations) are seen as complementary to personal selling. It is a tool that is heavily used in more complex, industrial or business-to-business (B2B) situations, whereas it is less intensely used in business-to-consumer (B2C) marketing. Personal sales are significant in the business-to-consumer sector in retailing and in the sale of products or services direct to the customer, frequently in their own homes (e.g. *Avon*) or through the personal technology (e.g. internet, telephony) medium.

In the marketing communications effectiveness model (see Figure 1.5 in Chapter 1), the influence of personal selling is seen to peak at the point of purchase. However, in many consumer services (e.g. financial services, personal care) and some retail operations, the importance of personal sales support continues after the transaction and the salesperson may well build up a long-term relationship with the customer. In the past, this level of relationship might have been with the local insurance salesman or woman (e.g. 'the man from the *Prudential*'[3]), the local shopkeeper or bank manager. Today, many of these interactions have been replaced by online technology although some conspicuous relationships may remain with a financial adviser, sales assistant (of your favourite store) or personal shopper. What they all have in common is relationships. The model of the effectiveness of personal selling (Figure 14.2) is amended to show that, in certain circumstances, the importance of personal salesmanship may extend into the post-purchase period.

Salespeople come in all types and utilise different approaches in their professional lives. There are those who fit the popular stereotype of the pushy,

FIGURE 14.2   Personal selling effectiveness

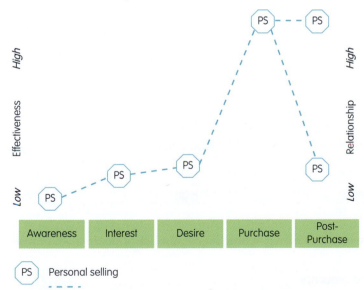

---

[3]   'Trust the man from the Pru' was a long-running tagline of the *Prudential Insurance Company*.

unrelenting, 'foot-in-the-door' individual whose particular skills appear to be a necessary feature of some industries (e.g. second-hand cars). Equally certain is that there are those who are honest, reliable and supportive – characteristics that are particularly important if any trusting relationship is to be built. Credibility also plays a large part. The best salespeople believe in the value of their product/service and are able to transmit this belief to the customer.

Personal selling is most effective when:

- new products are introduced
- new features are developed
- the product or service is complex and requires explanation and/or demonstration
- the product or service is recognised as a long-term expenditure/investment
- there is a need for negotiation and/or response to feedback
- relationship building is part of the marketing strategy.

Personal selling is important in situations where other communications tools are weak, particularly where instant response and complex explanations are needed and where relationship building and maintenance are major factors in the business. Where negotiation is the norm, salesmanship is also an important factor in finalising the sale. It is also logical to assume that the smaller the number of customers and, consequentially, the greater percentage contribution these customers make to turnover, the more likely the requirement for a relationship-based, personal sales operation.

The value and salience of a product or service also appears to be important. While many car purchases involve buyers searching for information on the internet, only 3% of actual UK sales take place using this medium versus one-third who use the traditional dealership, according to *Mintel*.[4] Many buyers still apparently want some form of human intervention (and the possibility of negotiation) that is not necessarily available through technological mediums. It may, however, be an age-related phenomenon that will spread out over time. Most internet automotive shoppers are in the 16–24 age bracket; beyond this age range, interest drops dramatically.

Table 14.1 compares the factors that influence the importance of personal selling with mass marketing tools.

TABLE 14.1   Comparisons of personal selling and mass communications

	Personal selling	Mass marketing
Information needs	High	Low
Complexity	High	Low
Number of customers	Low	High
Pricing	Negotiable	Set
Order size	High	Low
Value/Salience	High	Low

On the downside, personal selling has a number of distinct weaknesses, notably:

- cost
- reach and frequency
- control.

---

[4]   *Motoren*, 3 June 2011, at: http://motoren.wordpress.com

Cost has always been a major factor in the use of personal selling and how it is managed in organisations. There are effectively two types of salesperson – those located generally in one place and those who normally visit their customers. In B2B marketing, visiting salespeople spend between 5 and 10% of their time in negotiations with customers. Although a percentage of this time may be involved in relationship building, this still represents to many an inefficiency which organisations need to resolve. Organisations may be seen to reduce the impact of these inefficiencies through the management of their customer base and/or though the use of technology as a medium. **Pareto analysis** suggests that around 80% of orders are generated by 20% of the customer base, therefore the importance of individual customers may determine how this customer management strategy is implemented. Another tactic is to encourage customers to come to them at the organisation's showroom or at an appropriate exhibition. The importance of the customer to an organisation, therefore, acts as a measure of the importance of personal selling relative to other tools. Customers further down the chain may have considerably less personal contact, with most of their communications being through other tools (e.g. emails, catalogues). Even where customers travel to the salesperson (often at a fixed retail location), cost is a factor. There is, therefore, usually a direct correlation between the relative number of salespeople and profit margins in the sector.

From the salesperson's perspective, effectiveness is determined by the effort they put in (number of calls, emails, calling time, etc.) and their own personal effectiveness characteristics (e.g. experience, attitude, aptitude and education). Exogenous factors include the effect of sales management (type of supervision, experience, etc.), the marketing effort of the firm (e.g. advertising), the characteristics of the territory (potential, customer concentration, etc.) and the level of competitive activity they face.

In order to contain personal selling costs, back-office administrators will often contact prospects and create sales appointments and organise travel schedules to optimise the effect (and lower the costs) of sales personnel. This begins a process of what Smith and Taylor (2004) call the 7Ps of Selling and consists of:

- prospecting: looking for prospective customers
- preparation: customer research, objective setting, etc.
- presentation: demonstration and discussion
- possible problems: foreseeing and handling objections
- please give me the order: closing the sale and getting the order
- pen-to-paper: recording details accurately
- post-sales service: developing the relationship.

The problem of controlling organisational messages with a diverse salesforce is another important potential downside of personal selling (and one shared with public relations – see Figure 14.3). However well intentioned the salespeople, they may jeopardise the company's image by poor, inconsistent or inaccurate communications. **Over-selling** (i.e. claiming more for the product/service than can be achieved) is a particular problem. Customers do not usually complain if they get what they expect but not living up to expectations is a major cause of dissatisfaction. Salespeople often have a financial or other stake in a sale. This *may* encourage inaccurate information or highly speculative claims in an attempt to close the sale. The recent heavy fines by the UK financial regulator on organisations whose salesforce was involved in **mis-selling** financial products is an expensive case in point. Organisations may attempt to overcome this lack of control over salespeople by regular training and the updating of product/service information but there is always an unpredictability associated with human behaviour.

Pareto analysis
The general supposition that business relationships follow an 80:20 ratio (e.g. 80% of business comes from 20% of customers).

Over-selling
Promising more than is available through the sale.

Mis-selling
Selling something based on a falsehood.

Hard sell
Promoting heavily the tangible benefits available from a product or service.

Caveat emptor
Latin for 'Let the buyer beware'.

Soft sell
Using emotional appeals to produce positive feelings for a brand.

FIGURE 14.3   Personal selling control

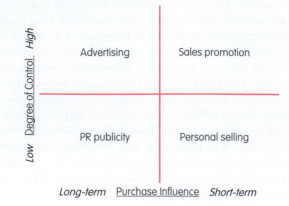

Another charge against a minority of sales personnel is that they may hustle and cajole customers into a sale. Commonly called the '**hard sell**', it was not so long ago that this was seen as evidence of good salesmanship and that it was up to the customer to beware (**caveat emptor**). Attitudes to this type of practice have changed and legislation introduced in most developed markets inserting 'cooling-off periods' during which the customer can withdraw from any commitment made through personal selling. Conversely, the term '**soft sell**' is often used to describe selling techniques where the salesperson's candour, perceived honesty and friendliness appear to disarm the customer's natural defences.

In business-to-business markets, salesforces are organised in a number of different ways depending on the industry, customer requirement and/or the history of sales in the organisation. Among the most common formats are those shown in Figure 14.4.

FIGURE 14.4   Salesforce organisation

Sales force type	Common titles
Geographically based	Area/regional sales manager
Product or brand-based	Product/brand manager
Market-based	Category manager
Account-based	Account manager

Geographically based sales personnel are the most common and straightforward means of organising a salesforce. It is usually highly responsive and represents the least duplication of calls on customers. It also concentrates the effort within the designated territory. The disadvantage in a multi-brand organisation is that this type of salesforce is unlikely to have specialist knowledge about all the products and/or services on offer. Product or brand-based sales teams will usually have a greater knowledge of the offering (which may increase credibility) but can involve duplicating visits of other members of the sales team. Account-based sales teams usually deal with one or a very few major accounts, while other customers (of lesser relative importance) are handled in more general ways (e.g. geographically, product-based). Account managers frequently build up close relationships with their customers and may even be based part or all of the time in the customer's workplace. The major danger associated with getting *too* close to the customer (particularly in B2B relationships) is that it may hamper or restrict negotiation and potentially add to overall costs.

IN-STORE SALES

In-store salespeople possess many of the same characteristics and personal skills associated with their B2B colleagues. As a generality, the greater the retail price and margin and the greater the salience, the more experienced sales staff are required to be. At this end of the scale, the salesperson at, for example, *Tiffany*, may only have to work with a few customers each day. At the other end of the retail spectrum, supermarkets have few (if any) dedicated sales staff.

Not all in-store sales are undertaken by employees of the company. The term **field marketing** is used to describe syndicated or shared teams who work, largely in the FMCG sector, and who carry out a number of selling and other 'sales' associated tasks on behalf of one or more suppliers. Field marketing originated in the 1960s when FMCG giants such as *Mars* sought to increase penetration in the independent stores sector (Benady 2002). The range of activities carried out by field marketing companies has become very wide, covering (and in many ways bridging) both personal sales and point-of-sale activities, including:

- sales calls (typically on smaller, independent retailers)
- sampling and other in-store promotions
- merchandising and in-store displays
- market research (including as a '**mystery shopper**')
- representing and promoting the brand at major events.

The advantage to the supplier of utilising field marketers is in the generally lower out-sourced costs of the syndicated teams and the avoidance of high fixed costs associated with employing a salesforce. On the downside, as field marketers are not employed directly by the organisation, the risks associated with controlling inconsistent or inaccurate communications are high.

Field marketing
Syndicated or shared teams working largely in the fast moving consumer goods sector, who carry out a number of selling and other 'sales' associated tasks on behalf of one or more suppliers.

Mystery shopper
A researcher who visits a store in the guise of a shopper for the purposes of research and observation.

insight: Field marketing activities

Field marketing is a form of personal selling that can involve a variety of different activities aimed at end consumers and/or trade outlets. *GfK NOP Field Marketing* is one company who carries out a wide range of activities, including auditing on-shelf availability, transport inspections, merchandising groceries and new technologies and point-of-sale (POS) legal compliance. As an example of the latter, the company carried out a POS refit for a UK supermarket chain following the introduction of legislation banning the open display of cigarettes. The team visited 1900 outlets within a five-day period to ensure that they were compliant with the legislation.

Another form of personal selling that has increased in the last few decades is '**multi-level marketing**', also known as '**network selling**' and (particularly when being disparaged) as '**pyramid selling**'. The terms broadly describe selling direct to the public, through a network of self-employed salespeople, often at house parties and other private gatherings. The multi-level marketing company initially recruits distributors who in turn recruit more distributors, and so on. Earnings come both from a distributor's own sales and the sales of those they recruit (and often even further down the line). The success of building and maintaining such a structure often relies on a form of corporate evangelism which infects and drives the participants not only to greater sales but (often more importantly) to recruit other distributors with the hope of significant future income as the 'pyramid' grows. Although some schemes may work well, many have

Multi-level marketing (network selling)
Selling direct to the public through a network of self-employed salespeople, often through house parties and other private gatherings. The multi-level marketing company initially recruits distributors who in turn recruit more distributors, and so on. Earnings come both from a distributor's own sales and the sales of those they recruit (and often even further down the line).

Pyramid selling
A form of multi-level marketing where the central purpose is to earn commission (or receive other payments) from those further down the line rather than make sales per se.

unscrupulously exploited distributors through high training fees and the high cost of sample packs, such that legal restrictions have been imposed in many developed markets, limiting the charges associated with this form of selling.

THE FUTURE OF PERSONAL SELLING

The future of personal selling as a major communications (and sales) medium will, as organisations look to curtail costs, be heavily determined by technological advances which are making physical location of diminishing importance. Where technology can effectively replace the salesperson (as, for example, in the case of travel agent services and insurance sales), it will inevitably lead to a decline. Electronic point-of-sale (EPOS) technology can calculate sales and order replacements more effectively than any travelling salesperson. Even in the business-to-business sector, where complex contract negotiation has to take place, personal meetings may be replaced by video-conferencing or *Skype*. Documentation can now be legally transmitted with electronic signatures, removing yet another reason for negotiators to meet face to face. In the business-to-consumer sector, traditional person-to-person contact between a customer and his/her bank manager or insurance salesperson are now largely handled by call centres using customer relationship management (CRM) technology.

Despite these advances, human beings crave personal contact as this is the basis of strong relationships. An attempt to use technology to wholly substitute interaction may prove destructive and there is ample evidence of the consuming public's annoyance at, and distrust of, call centres. A 2013 *YouGov* survey showed that 55% of people did not trust call centres in the UK to keep personal data safe, which rose to 83% for overseas call centres.

POINT OF SALE

Point of sale (POS) or (as favoured in North America) point of purchase (POP) has often been regarded as the least glamorous of the communication sectors, yet it is considerably important from a communications and sales perspective. POS is particularly important in FMCG retailing where POS materials play the part of the 'silent salesperson' (Kornblau 1961: 296), communicating the features, benefits and subtleties associated with the decision to buy. Research by the *Global Association for Marketing at Retail* suggests that, while in 1995 70% of decisions were made in-store, by 2012 this has risen to 76%. Of these, 55% of all purchases are made on impulse (POPAI 2012). Although impressive, these figures should be taken with a little scepticism as they ignore the (perhaps subconscious) influence of other marketing communications tools (i.e. advertising) on the ultimate purchase. However, this warning aside, POS marketing is significant and should not be underrated or ignored as a communications tool.

PACKAGING

The most basic (and often forgotten) communications tool is product packaging. It has been described as 'the least expensive form of advertising' and the 'five-second commercial'. Although it should not be forgotten that packaging serves to protect, contain and offer convenience to the purchaser, it is also a major communications device. Good packaging in this respect should:

- gain attention (through attractive, brash or familiar labelling)
- be distinctive (e.g. *Cillit Bang*)

- instruct and inform (e.g. legal requirements, serving suggestions, calorific and ingredient information)
- signify value for money (e.g. through size, promotion, etc.)
- help persuade (or 'nudge') the purchaser toward a purchase (e.g. money off, 50% extra free)
- reflect the personality of the brand (e.g. *Peperami*)
- motivate brand choice.

Shelf impact
The impact of product packaging in highlighting particular products.

Packaging (unlike other communications) offers instant gratification, is reasonably cost-effective and can be altered at relatively short notice. It helps 'brand loyalists' identify the product and more generally assists brand choice decisions. Packaging designers talk about the value of '**shelf impact**'. It is, however, not just the text and imagery that contribute to good packaging but shape (think of *Jiff Lemon, Bovril* and *Heinz Ketchup*) also adds to its impact. Brands such as *Orangina, Perrier* and *Coca-Cola* are instantly recognisable by the shape of their containers. It is interesting to note that this latter icon of the twentieth century, the *Coca-Cola* bottle, did not come about by accident. The original design brief from the company was (Smith & Taylor 2004):

> we need a new bottle – a distinctive package that will help us fight substitutes … we need a bottle which a person will recognise as a Coca-Cola bottle even when he feels it in the dark. The Coca-Cola bottle should be shaped [such] that, even if broken, a person could tell what it is.

Size and/or presentation can also be a feature. Normally, larger packs communicate better value but this is not always necessarily the case. Returning to *Coca-Cola* as an example in the UK consumer goods market, three main packages[5] are popular. These are the can, the traditional bottle (often now plastic rather than glass) and the 'family-sized' bottle. A quick calculation of prices (in whatever retail type) shows no real correlation between quantity and price. Even though all three sizes may be available at one outlet, they are aiming at different segments. The portability and throw-away nature of the can appears to be aimed at the young while the family-sized bottle is aimed (rather obviously) at the home market. The traditional bottle, however, remains associated with the product's history and reputation, and often sells at a distinct premium from other sizes. Aficionados might also suggest that the taste is somehow better from a bottle!

Colour has a particular part to play in conveying meaning and emotion to prospective buyers. The degree to which it can have an effect can be quite startling. A study by Tom et al. (1987) used three identical vanilla puddings with minor differences in their colour (induced by the addition of food colouring). Of the three shades of brown, the majority of interviewees described the dark brown pudding as the richest and with the best chocolate taste whereas the light brown pudding was the creamiest. Ernest Dichter's research (Smith & Taylor 2004) also suggests that colour affects perception. In this case, four containers were presented each with the same coffee but with different colour exteriors. When questioned about the flavour and aroma of the coffee:

- 73% believed the coffee in the dark-brown container was too strong.
- 84% believed the coffee in the red container was richer.
- 79% believed the coffee in the blue container was milder.
- 87% believed the coffee in the yellow container was too weak.

---

[5]   Although other sizes (e.g. miniatures) also exist.

TABLE 14.2   The influence of colour

Red	Red is a high-wavelength colour (as are yellow and orange) and generates excitement. It is described as active, stimulating, energetic and vital. It is the colour of prohibition and warning in Europe but it is also associated with love (e.g. *Hershey Hearts*). It is popular in China as it implies good luck and in India where it is a Hindu symbol of love and generally denotes life, action and gaiety. In Ireland (together with white and blue) and Paraguay (with green and blue), the colour has political connotations.
White	The colour for weddings in Europe and North America where it generally denotes purity and mildness (therefore, often used for toiletries and soaps, e.g. *Dove*). In China and South America, however, it denotes mourning and in India it is the most important priestly colour.
Blue	The colour associated with baby boys in the UK, baby girls in Belgium and Eastern France and females in Japan. It is seen as trustworthy in Europe and India. It is also associated with coolness and refreshment and is often used in skin products (e.g. *Nivea*) and spearmint products (e.g. *Wrigley*). Lighter shades of blue are associated with mildness (e.g. *Nescafé*).
Black	The European and North American colour for mourning and funerals. Combined with yellow in nature (e.g. wasps), it means warning and is similarly used in this combination on road signs. Also in this combination it is used for brash, over-the-top, signage associated with down-market retailers. However, combined with gold, it suggests elegance and superiority (e.g. *Johnny Walker Black Label*).
Yellow	A high-wavelength colour which is the colour of caution in Europe (usually combined with black in hazard warning signage). It is an Imperial Chinese colour which denotes grandeur and mystery. In India it is associated with merchants and second only to white in denoting sanctity. It is the colour of Sultans in Malaysia (and therefore never worn by the common people) and of despair in Brazil. It is the colour of lemons and frequently used where lemon is an important ingredient (e.g. *Jiff*).
Pink	The colour associated with baby girls in the UK, baby boys in Belgium and Eastern France and is a masculine colour in Japan.
Orange	A high-wavelength colour which is the national colour of the Netherlands. In Northern Ireland it is the colour of Loyalists and therefore unpopular with republicans north and south. It is often used, as yellow, for brash, over-the-top, signage associated with down-market retailers. Orange is the colour of *EasyJet*, perhaps reflecting its low pricing.
Green	The colour denoting the environment and environmental issues in Europe and brands to reflect their environmental concerns (e.g. *BP*). It is a significant colour for all Muslims and has religious significance in Malaysia. It is the colour most associated with Ireland and is often used to express Irish associations (e.g. *Kerrygold*). It is also associated with abundance, health, calmness and serenity and often used in packaging for beverages (e.g. *Heineken, Sprite, Seven-up, etc.*) and mint and mentholated products (e.g. *Wrigley*).
Purple	The colour of royalty in the UK and associated with quality and elegance and with superiority (e.g. *Cadbury*). It is also associated with mourning and sorrow in many countries.

It is understandable, given this information, why *Nescafé* uses colour to distinguish between various coffee strengths.

Of all colours, the colour red is among the most prominent and the chosen corporate colour for brands such as *Coca-Cola, The Economist, KFC, Virgin* and *Santander*. It is a colour that instantly attracts attention, energises and (according to Psychologist World[6]) increases the heart rate, raises blood pressure and improves the appetite.

Other colours give different messages but these may be culturally specific, as noted in Table 14.2.

POINT-OF-SALE MATERIALS

Point-of-sale materials are important because they communicate with consumers at the time and place that they are ready to make purchasing decisions. They are designed to inform, remind and encourage customers in regard to the promoted product. They act as in-store cues which capitalise on previous consumption experiences and/or media advertising. In-store displays (and packaging) carry themes through to the shop floor. They act as differentiators between these and other brands on the market.

Digital advances have further enabled effective POS displays. In November 2012, *Microsoft* relaunched its Windows phone. Using interactive digital touch screens in shopping centres throughout the UK, it sought to show consumers how they could personalise their phone. The strategy was to allow consumers to get 'hands-on' with the Windows phone in a mass-media environment, and to create immediate opportunities for personalisation and relevance.

Merchandising involves the logical placement of merchandise to fulfil the store's objectives. Increasing the shelf space given to a brand (manufacturer or own-label) and/or placing merchandise at the optimum height (eye level) both noticeably improve sales. The Insight below shows how placement can considerably affect sales. Merchandisers are also responsible for ensuring goods make it rapidly to the shelves. Failure to keep shelves stacked was seen as a major reason for *Sainsbury*'s poor sales in the early part of the millennium.

The way stores are designed can affect the sales of products within, and flow modelling (which takes into account that 90% of people who enter a store turn to the right) guides customers around each site (e.g. *IKEA*). Lighting and signage are used to emphasise and attract potential customers. In-store displays are designed to direct customers toward products and include:

- brand display units (normally supplied by the brand owner)
- dump bins
- show cards
- posters
- video
- sampling.

Technology is also being used to direct customers through in-store design technology (e.g. *B&Q*), interactive kiosks and coupon dispensers. According to *Retail Week* (5 April 2013), 'The explosion of in-store iPads has led to consumers increasingly expecting technology to bring education, entertainment and a bit of show business to a retail environment'. Proximity to the point of purchase is evidently an important influence on the consumer. The communications opportunities offered by managing point-of-sale materials should be managed as efficiently and effectively as any other marketing communications tools.

---

6   See www.psychologistworld.com/perception/color.php

insight: Point-of-sale research

To emphasise the effect POS displays can have on sales, Shimp (2010) presented research carried out in Canada in 80 stores selected from four major pharmaceutical (drugstore) chains involving the *Benylin* cough syrup and *Listerine* mouthwash brands. The stores were put into four groups (a control group plus three others), as seen in Table 14.3. The result of featuring these products in prime locations was certainly impressive. Even though the feature price evidently affected sales, it was the prominent positioning that showed the highest increase in turnover.

TABLE 14.3   Pricing vs. positioning in POS displays

	Pricing	Positioning	Benylin*	Listerine*
1	Regular price	Normal shelf position	control	control
2	Feature price	Normal shelf position	29% increase	11% increase
3	Feature price	End of aisle display	98% increase	141% increase
4	Feature price	Aisle/front aisle display	139% increase	162% increase

Source: Shimp (2010)

Note: *increase is over control sample results

summary

This chapter looked at those elements of the marketing communications mix that are nearest the point of purchase. It discussed the strengths and weaknesses of personal selling and the situations where it is deemed important and necessary. As a costly tool, it looked at the ways managers may handle a salesforce efficiently and effectively and the various ways a salesforce can be organised. It reviewed the selling process and emphasised the growing importance of retaining and developing existing customers. Field marketing, where syndicated teams carry out a number of sales and other associated tasks, was discussed, as was the sometimes dubious nature of multi-level marketing. Packaging was described as the 'silent salesman' as it was seen to gain attention through its distinctiveness, to instruct and inform and motivate brand choice. The importance of point-of-sale materials was described and the importance of prime display space discussed.

? review questions

1. Is there a difference between POP (point of purchase) and POS (point of sale)?

2. When is personal selling most effective?

3. What are the 7Ps of Selling?

4. Define 'field marketing'.

5. Explain the key weaknesses of personal selling.

6. What is 'pyramid' selling?

7. Explain the difference between a hard sell and a soft sell.

8. What is 'over-selling'?

9. Describe the key promotional roles of packaging.

10. List examples of in-store displays.

discussion questions

1. Explain the principal differences between personal selling and mass communications and discuss why these might be so. How might companies construct their personal-selling approach to reflect these differences?

2. Why might an organisation use mystery shoppers? How would you plan a mystery shopping campaign and what would it entail?

3. Is online retailing the future of shopping?

case study 14.1: Primark – budget fashion in upmarket stores

Primark Stores is a departmental clothing retailer, owned by Associated British Foods. The first *Primark* store opened in Dublin in 1969 and in the UK in 1973. It now has almost 300 stores, mainly in the UK and Ireland, though it is successfully expanding into other countries including Spain and Germany. *Primark* has emerged as one of the UK's most successful high-street chains. Now the country's second largest clothing retailer, after *Marks and Spencer*, it is the single largest value retailer.

All of the company's merchandise is made specifically for *Primark* under a variety of own brand names. Its main competitors in the value retail sector are *TK Maxx*, *Arcadia Group* and supermarkets such as *ASDA* and *Tesco*. *Primark*'s strategy is to provide quick turnaround of trends, offering consumers fast fashion, which sells at the budget end of the market. The company's success is based on sourcing supply cheaply, making clothes with simple designs and fabrics, and buying stock in huge bulk and varieties, all far more efficiently than its competitors. It maintains very low operating costs.

Although both *TK Maxx* and *Primark* have the same goal of providing high fashion at a low price, they approach their stores differently. While *TK Maxx* refers to itself as a 'no frills' retailer, with simple store layouts and no extravagant decoration, *Primark* operates in quite the reverse manner, investing in its stores. Large spaces

(Continued)

(Continued)

are purchased, completely gutted and virtually rebuilt. The mantra is a *Primark* store has to be big enough and be in the right place. This investment in property and shop fit is key to *Primark*'s strategy. The company aims to make its store interiors look expensive. They are spacious and bright with spot- and fluorescent-lighting combinations. Rich colour palettes are used to designate zones for easy navigation around stores. Each zone is fitted using high-quality materials such as baroque wallpaper and heavy timbering which add to the perception of sophistication. The colour co-ordination of products, shown as whole outfits on quality mannequins, is given a great deal of attention. Consumers often buy the whole look rather than single items, which is a concept more commonly associated with upmarket retailers.

These marks of quality have helped *Primark* to attract shoppers who are looking for more than just low prices. *Primark* transcends socio-demographics as it has taken a position that appeals to middle-class consumers, making them feel comfortable shopping 'down market'. Celebrities from Princess Beatrice to Arctic Monkeys' frontman Alex Turner have been reported wearing *Primark* fashions, lending legitimacy and a trendy vibe to the brand. While it was originally a haven for bargain-hunting women in their mid-30s, *Primark*'s emergence as the fashionista's choice has broadened its appeal, reflected in recent store openings in affluent areas.

These new store unveilings are carefully planned to create the right impression. *Primark* used to widely advertise store openings to generate excitement and publicity. However, online rumours (not of *Primark*'s making) of discounts at the opening of a new flagship Oxford Street branch in 2007 prompted riots among 3000 people and eventual police involvement. Subsequently, *Primark* decided on quieter store launches publicised by local door-to-door leaflet drops only. It simultaneously works with the local community to promote its shops as a good place to both work and shop. By building links with job centres, colleges and community groups, it recruits local staff who then undergo a three-week induction and training programme designed to communicate the company's culture and motivate employees to maximise sales.

Outside of new store launches, *Primark* does very little advertising. Nor does it pay for celebrity endorsements, hold end-of-season sales or run any promotions. It simply lowers prices of slow-moving products throughout the year. It focuses on providing an excellent shopping experience so that consumers tell their friends. Thus, it leverages its brand strengths to generate free publicity through word of mouth and media coverage, delivering its marketing communications goals for the minimum possible outlay.

© Kim Roberts 2014

Case study questions

1. What part does *Primark* stores' décor and point of sale play in their strategy?
2. How have *Primark* benefited from long-term changes in consumer trends?
3. *Primark*, according to the case study, 'transcends socio-demographics'. In what other ways might they segment the marketplace?
4. What are the major marketing communications tools used by *Primark* to publicise their offering?

 **further reading**

Doherty, N.F. and Ellis-Chadwick, F. (2010) 'Internet retailing: the past, the present and the future', *International Journal of Retail and Distribution Management*, 38 (11/12): 943–65.

Jaramillo, F., Mulki, J.P. and Solomon, P. (2006) 'The role of ethical climate on salesperson's role stress, job attitudes, turnover intention, and job performance', *Journal of Personal Selling & Sales Management*, 26 (3): 271–82.

Jones, E., Brown, S.P., Zoltners, A.A. and Weitz, B.A. (2005) 'The changing environment of selling and sales management', *Journal of Personal Selling & Sales Management*, 25 (2): 105–11.

Roper, S. and Parker, C. (2006) 'How (and where) the mighty have fallen: branded litter', *Journal of Marketing Management*, 22 (5/6): 473–87.

Sharma, A. (2006) 'Success factors in key accounts', *Journal of Business & Industrial Marketing*, 21 (2): 141–50.

Tom, G., Lopez, S. and Demir, K. (2006) 'A comparison of the effect of retail purchase and direct marketing on the endowment effect', *Psychology & Marketing*, 23 (1): 1–10.

REFERENCES

Benady, D. (2002) 'Fielding discussion', *Marketing*, 19 September, pp. 39–40.

Kornblau, C. (1961) 'Packaging and supermarkets: the package in the market place', in *Effective Marketing Coordination*. Chicago: American Marketing Association, pp. 296–306.

POPAI (2012) 2012 Shopper Engagement Study: Media Topline Report. Available at: www.popai.fr/textes/Shopper_Engagement_Study.pdf (accessed 5 May 2013).

Shimp, T.A. (2010) *Advertising, Promotion and Supplemental Aspects of Integrated Marketing Communications*, 8th edn. London: Thomson Learning.

Smith, P.R. and Taylor, J. (2004) *Marketing Communications: An Integrated Approach*, 2nd edn. London: Kogan Page.

Tom, G., Barnett, T., Lew, W. and Selmants, J. (1987) 'Cueing the customer: the role of salient cues in consumer perception', *The Journal of Consumer Marketing*, 4 (Spring): 23–7.

For additional materials that support this chapter and your learning, please visit:
study.sagepub.com/egan

INTEGRATED MARKETING COMMUNICATIONS

15

LEARNING OBJECTIVES

Having completed this chapter, readers would be expected to:

- describe the concepts behind integrated marketing communications (IMC)

- understand the market, industry and media drivers that have promoted IMC

- recognise the problems associated with IMC implementation

- assess the potential advantages and disadvantages of IMC.

INTRODUCTION

Integrated marketing communications (IMC) is a central tenet of this book. As noted in Chapter 1, IMC is a concept that has caused considerable debate since its theoretical inception in the late 1980s. Although most academics and practitioners regard IMC as a major communications development, it is neither fully accepted in academia nor fully adopted in the communications industry, largely because of its supposed difficulty to implement. While supporters of integrated marketing communications would argue that under current marketing thinking and in today's markets, effective implementation is critical to success, others would point to the belief that it is an old idea that has little evidence of ever being realised. It is indeed arguable whether IMC is a truly new innovation in communications or an old idea revived through the intercession of modern technology.

In the early days of commercial communication (see Chapter 1), little, if any, distinction was made between marketing communications tools. It was only as organisations expanded and the gap between customers and organisations grew that greater sophistication and specialisation were required, leading ultimately to the barriers built between the various marketing communications disciplines.

Like many concepts that continue to develop, it is subject to varying and sometimes colourful terminology. Thus, '360° branding', 'total branding', 'whole egg', 'seamless communication', 'new advertising', 'orchestration', 'relationship marketing', 'one-to-one marketing', 'integrated marketing' and 'integrated communications' (Kliatchko 2005; Pickton & Broderick 2005) have all been used to describe all or part of the IMC concept. This prompts the charge that IMC is yet another management fad. What most observers agree on is that IMC is a great idea in theory but hard to implement in practice. Indeed, even its most fervent supporters would be forced to admit that translating the theory into practice can present organisations with immense problems.

DEFINING IMC

The *Institute of Practitioners in Advertising (IPA)* in their criteria for integration use the phrase 'joined-up thinking' to describe the thread running through a co-ordinated campaign. The earliest definition of IMC came from the *American Association of Advertising Agencies (4As)* formulated in 1989. This stated that IMC was 'an approach to achieving the objectives of a marketing campaign through a well-coordinated use of different promotional methods that are intended to reinforce each other'. The American Marketing Association (AMA) calls it 'a planning process designed to ensure that all brand contacts received by a customer or prospect for a product, service, or organisation are relevant to that person and consistent over time'. These all see integrated marketing communications as the process of using promotional tools in a unified way to create synergy (Semenik 2002) and, by taking a holistic view, it is an approach that ensures the continual consideration of a brand's contribution to and inclusion in each and every communication. The emphasis is on using the various tools or disciplines and having one communications strategy or plan as the unifying theme, and is best summed up by the mantra 'one spirit, one voice, one look' (Kliatchko 2005). Consequently, integrated marketing communications is felt to be concerned with getting all of the various communications messages to work together in order to present a unified message, i.e. determining that 'above-the-line' and 'below-the-line' activities are mutually supportive, ensuring consistency in messages and presentation content, and duplicating key aspects such as colour, design, straplines and imagery.

Critics have pointed out, however, that there are inadequacies with this definition. If this is all that IMC delivers, then it is simply describing what many good marketers have been doing for decades. This definition fails to consider factors such as consumer orientation, creativity, measurability, cost-effectiveness and interactivity which are central to the argument for communications integration (Kitchen & Schultz 1999). From this more holistic viewpoint, IMC should include *everything* that the organisation and its people and brands communicate in their interaction with targets and publics, either deliberately or not (Copley 2004).

Another justification for IMC can be found in a theme that has run through this text. Notwithstanding earlier warnings regarding 'hierarchy of effects' models, the varying effectiveness of various marketing communications tools at different stages in the consumption process also supports the notion of synergy and communications impact through IMC (see Figure 15.1). Thus, advertising can keep the brand 'front of mind' and PR can maintain the brand's image while sponsorship helps build associations and sales promotion gives an added incentive to buy.

Novak and Phelps (1994) suggested that IMC, rather than just the co-ordination of marketing communications tools and messages, was based on three conceptualisations:

- one-voice marketing communications: integration which creates a clear consistent image, position, message and/or theme across all marketing communications disciplines or tools

FIGURE 15.1   Effectiveness of marketing communications tools

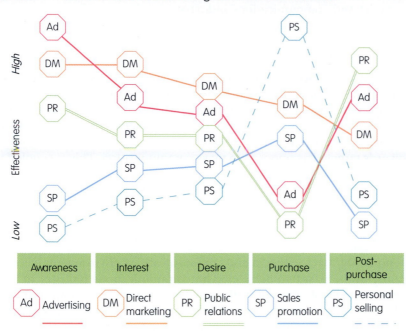

- integrated communications: the creation of both brand image and a behavioural response that emanates directly from marketing communications material (e.g. adverts)
- co-ordinating marketing communications: associating integration with the concepts of co-ordination of all marketing communications tools to produce a holistic campaign that both develops awareness and builds brand image, at the same time evoking a behavioural response from target audiences. This is what Smith and Taylor (2004) describe as wrapping communications around customers and helping them through the various stages of the buying process.

Schultz and Schultz (1998) offer a definition that expands the theme further. This includes the traditional view of marketing communications tools co-ordination but extends this, not only to all customer contact points but highlighting the importance of internal as well as external communications (Kliatchko 2005). This suggests that 'IMC is a strategic business practice used to plan, develop, execute and evaluate co-ordinated, measurable, persuasive brand communications pro-grammes over time with consumers, customers, prospects and other targeted, relevant external and internal audiences'.

This brings IMC in line with the more general concept of 'relationship market-ing' when it suggests that it should seek to address all of the organisation's relevant **publics** (or stakeholders) and not focus solely on the consumer (Kliatchko 2005). The rationale is that an organisation needs to establish relationships, internally and externally, 'in order to establish relationships with customers' (Berry 1995: 242). An organisation is looking, through IMC, to simultaneously consolidate its image, develop a dialogue and nurture its relationship with its customers at all points of contact.

DRIVERS TO IMC

Whether regarded as a new concept or a return to an earlier form of marketing communications, the current movement towards IMC has been hastened by dramatic changes in at least three main areas: the marketplace, the organisation, and the media and communications industry.

MARKET-BASED DRIVERS

The modern marketplace is highly competitive and with low levels of brand differentiation. The result is that organisations must work harder and harder to get their message noticed and appreciated by an audience that is both communications literate and sceptical of the accuracy of claimed benefits. In addition, media and audience fragmentation has led to a re-evaluation of mass media and a consequent move towards targeted as opposed to mass communication. This is coupled with a challenge to the traditional transactional marketing paradigm and the subsequent reappraisal of the importance of internal and external relationships.

MEDIA AND COMMUNICATIONS-BASED DRIVERS

There is no doubt that the media and communications environment has changed significantly in the past two decades. The communications industry in its many formats has been revolutionised by the advent of digital technology and the number of platforms that these can now be operated on. The increased sophistication has been responsible for increased commercial activity and a cluttered environment in which communication has to operate (Copley 2004). These advances have largely been driven by technology which is not only increasing the efficiency of the industry but also acting as the catalyst for greater targeting of consumers. On the downside, the same technology is creating information overload and clutter, devaluing the power of individual communications.

ORGANISATION-BASED DRIVERS

Organisations too have been evolving. They are paying more attention to brand development and the need to establish competitive advantage. In respect of the latter, some commentators suggest that in today's marketplace marketing communications is the only means of gaining competitive superiority. Organisations are looking to increase profits through improved efficiency, meanwhile utilising managerial time more effectively. On the downside, they are increasingly making decisions that produce short-term results. In another development, client organisations are looking to set the communications agenda rather than relying on formally powerful agencies to set it for them. International brands in particular have been looking to establish a clear image of themselves as the media by which it is carried crosses more borders than ever before. Recent technological advances, most dramatically the internet, have meant organisations have yet another reason to reconsider their marketing communications and re-evaluate their approach (Fill 2009).

Another organisational challenge is whether IMC is right for all types of company and there is some evidence that certain organisational types are more likely to implement IMC than others. They are:

- smaller firms (perhaps using less diverse marketing communications tools)
- firms involved with marketing services rather than products
- business-to-consumer (B2C) rather than business-to-business operations
- companies whose marketing communications budget is allocated primarily to advertising (as opposed to trade promotion)
- firms enjoying higher market share and realising greater profits
- organisations with experienced marketing communications managers.

Integrated marketing communications has emerged, therefore, for a number of reasons, some proactive and others reactive. Among the most powerful are in reaction to the structural inadequacies of the industry and the realisation by clients that their communications objectives could be achieved more effectively and efficiently. As IMC pioneer Don E. Schultz (Schultz and Schultz 1998) noted, 'integration just plain makes sense for those planning to succeed in the twenty-first century marketplace. Marketers, communicators and brand organisations simply have no choice'.

IMPLEMENTING IMC

Undoubtedly, the implementation of integrated marketing communications is an issue that has troubled even its most ardent supporters. Most commentators perceive change itself as a problem, as resistance to change is inherent in human beings who seek stability wherever possible. The development of integrated marketing communications requires change, and not simply change within the marketing function but stretching to 'part-time marketers'[1] and external suppliers (agencies) as well. Given the extent of such upheaval, an incremental approach to implementation is thought most likely to succeed. An example of an integrated marketing communications development model can be seen in Figure 15.2. Between initial co-ordination of promotional campaigns and functional co-ordination is where different parts of the organisation are introduced to a notion of internal marketing relationships. From here, a cultural shift is required if the organisation is to move towards stronger customer orientation. Such culture change is not a company-only activity. In research among clients and agencies (Eagle & Kitchen 2000), a crucial factor to success was seen to be the ability to match and harmonise client and agency cultures in order to build ongoing relationships.

FIGURE 15.2   An incremental approach to IMC

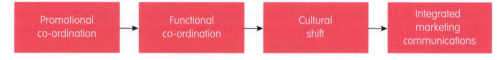

The perceived complexity in the planning and co-ordination of integrated marketing communications has also been a factor in resisting its introduction. Rather than concentrate on the scope and magnitude of integrated marketing communications implementation, an alternative approach would be to concentrate on the key aspects of what it entails:

- Customer focus: start with the customer or prospect and work backwards in determining the most appropriate messages (for example, customers do not differentiate between PR and advertising, the website and customer service so why does the organisation?).
- Contact: use any form of relevant contact (within reason and efficiency, the more points of contact the better) and be willing to use any communications outlets that are appropriate for meeting the target audience.

---

[1]   Gummesson (1990) uses the description 'part-time marketer' to describe non-marketers who have a significant influence on servicing the customer.

- Synergy: achieve synergy through use of the strengths of marketing communications tools in support and in co-ordination of a campaign.
- Relationships: build relationships between the brand and the customer.

Progress towards full implementation of IMC is regarded as a 'fairly steep learning curve' (Eagle & Kitchen 2000). As with any major change (particularly involving the reorganisation of organisational structures), training and staff development programmes are likely to be appropriate. Appointing a 'champion' or 'change agent' may also help direct the organisation toward a customer-focused approach. As one respondent in the Eagle and Kitchen (2000: 667) research noted, IMC implementation 'requires people whose professionalism is bigger than their ego … skilled and knowledgeable people who will consider all forms of communication'.

Many of these step changes are easier to describe than implement and the route to IMC is strewn with pitfalls and barriers. Among those barriers to IMC is the structure of the communications industry itself. The first agencies concentrated on advertising and these were well established by the time sales promotion and public relations began to become important. Personal sales too grew as a distinct function. This 'specialisation' was further entrenched by the development of trade associations, sometimes with more than one per industry. In the UK, organisations such as the *Institute of Practitioners in Advertising (IPA), Institute of Promotional Marketing (IPM) (*formerly the *Institute of Sales Promotion), Public Relations Consultants Association (PRCA), Chartered Institute of Public Relations (IPR), Direct Marketing Association (DMA)* and *Institute of Direct and Digital Marketing (IDM)* naturally defend their particular 'specialisation'. Research and education (including professional awards) are geared towards these specialisations and 'turf wars' have been known to break out. This structure has fuelled the functional divisions and expectations of marketing communications managers and industry employees since the Second World War and, once entrenched, has proven difficult to change. On the client side, it was (and in many instances still is) no less rigid with traditional hierarchical brand management structures that were slow to change, again focused on specialisation. For integrated marketing communications to work, it is clear that communications activities need to be cross-functional in the way they are operationalised.

Even though the concept has been debated for a decade, research suggests a strong commitment on both the client side and the agency side to integrated marketing communications research. On the one hand, clients perceive integrated marketing communications as a counter to the structural inadequacies of the communications industry as a whole and the means to rise above these and better meet their underlying objectives. As such, they essentially see integrated marketing communications as offering them a control they had previously lacked. Large agencies, on the other hand, argue that control and co-ordination should be left to them in their capacity as the 'dominant supplier'. Neither perspective though seems to wholly achieve the ambitions of integrated marketing communications. Total integrated marketing communications is clearly only achievable when all external agencies, outsourcing providers and partners work together with the organisation to deliver consistency to customers in terms of the promises given, the actions undertaken and in the overall customer experience. Sceptics, though, might question whether agencies can actually deliver these expectations. Inevitably, there will need to be some level of trade-off between the expertise an agency can provide and the degree of integration it can achieve, and no matter how agencies might develop or grow the need to compromise will not disappear.

insight: St John Ambulance – Lives Lost

Research by St John Ambulance revealed that 25% of us think we'd helplessly do nothing if a life were on the line. This shocking information prompted the first aid charity to launch a campaign to make people understand that just a little bit of knowledge could make the difference between a life lost and a life saved in an emergency.

'The campaign was a beautiful demonstration of strong integrated thinking', says Chris Beckles, Digital Creative Director at McCann Manchester. 'It's small and intimate in its channel mix but deep and engaging in its insight and appeal. What makes it so powerful is its delivery of the problem – and the solution.'

'Lives Lost' told five stories from beyond the grave; stories to which first aid could have made the difference. The posters and press ads first appeared in April 2010. Anyone who texted the dedicated number received a pocket-sized guide to first aid skills.

Beckles thinks that using the ads in such a hard-hitting way was 'bang on' and 'providing a text mechanism to receive more information is also seamless and psychologically empowering to the reader', he adds.

The creative team at BBH London wanted to make people see first aid as an essential skill, not something to put off learning about. 'People think first aid is complicated, hard to learn, and time-consuming', says former BBH creative director, Adrian Rossi. 'The reality is anything but.'

The creative team knew it had to handle the topic very carefully. 'Having an idea is the easy part', says creative director Alex Grieve. 'Bringing that idea to life is very, very hard.' Their solution was to build a great team.

The striking images in the press and poster ads are shot by photographer Nadav Kandar, and typographer Dave Wakefield created the unique and distinctive typefaces – both men world-renowned in their fields. Rossi and Grieve also give full credit to St John Ambulance for being such a brave client. 'Once you have a team like that, everything else is easy', says Rossi.

An iPhone app also formed part of the campaign, giving digestible first aid advice to people under pressure. It covered major and minor emergencies, with unique advice on infants. For Beckles, the app was the pièce de résistance. 'It's a branded utility that will be forever useful. Thus closing the "virtuous communication circle"', he says.

Source: Chris Beckles (2013), Digital Creative Director, McCann Manchester

ADVANTAGES AND DISADVANTAGES OF IMC

The potential advantages of integrated marketing communications are manifold. To begin with, the co-ordination of both creative application and production has obvious benefits in terms of cost and performance efficiencies. The increased control and co-ordination of brand-related messages increases the overall synergy of communications even further and, taken together, the impact should result in more effective communication. Integrated marketing communications also reduces dependence on mass-media advertising, encourages investigation of targeted mediums, heightens demand on agencies to multi-task and outsource and stimulates efforts to assess the return on investment (ROI) on organisational communications. This viewpoint has become known as being **media-neutral**. This involves a customer-focused review of media based on research, analysis and insight and not on habit and/or preference. Integration also offers the potential for reducing the ambiguity of messages coming from an organisation and reducing duplication of effort (Blythe 2000). Perhaps one of the strongest arguments of all is that through clear positioning and as a resultant power of synergy the drive for competitive advantage has more chance of success. As Hackley and Kitchen (1998: 233) note, 'creatively powerful promotional campaigns may be conceived as something which can slice through the cognitive debris of other half-remembered campaigns, memories of product trials and popular myths to create a new or more persuasive sense of meaning for consumers'.

Every concept has its dark side. Among the potential disadvantages of integrated marketing communications are that it encourages centralisation (which may or may not be a good thing) and bureaucracy. It also has the potential to dilute creative opportunities as a result. There is also danger in a strict uniformity of communication (although some authors support this) because this has the potential of boring the consumer. Researchers (Pechmann & Stewart 1990) found that irritation with a particular repeated message can lead to wear-out (see Chapter 2). Doubts have also been raised about the ethics of intrusive campaigns, some of which hide under the mantle of 'permission marketing', and about whether the resultant (physical and mental) clutter is socially justified. Another major criticism surrounds the ability to measure and evaluate IMC effectively (Eagle & Kitchen 2000), although this merely extends a deficiency that has long dogged the industry.

Summarising the literature to date in the field of integrated marketing communications and highlighting the problems with which it is associated, leads us towards a number of questions around whether it may or may not be:

- ethically sound
- an increasing form of social pollution
- increasingly integrative as an organisational function
- in need of radical theoretical and practical re-conceptualisation.

It would seem that integrated marketing communications is a concept designed for modern communications but which the communications world has yet to catch up with.

Media-neutral
A customer-focused review of media based on research, analysis and insight and not on habit and/or preference.

summary

This chapter reviewed the literature on integrated marketing communications (IMC), questioning whether its time had come or whether, however well supported in theory, its implementation posed considerable difficulties. The chapter reviewed the popular definitions of IMC and suggested it was more than just media and marketing communications tools co-ordination (one voice) and also included a dedication to customer focus, creativity, measurability, cost-effectiveness and interactivity. Further, it was seen to extend the organisation's marketing communications to all customer contact points and internally, as well as externally, to the firm. Dramatic changes in markets, in the marketing communications industry and in organisations were seen as drivers to IMC and the factors associated with these were discussed. The problems associated with implementation were reviewed and potential barriers assessed, including the 'specialist' nature of the industry itself. In conclusion, the potential advantages and disadvantages were reviewed.

review questions

1. What are the main drivers towards integrated marketing communications?

2. What is the 'mantra' used to sum up the concept of a single communications strategy or plan?

3. In the modern marketplace, what has led organisations to move towards targeted communication as opposed to mass communication?

4. Describe the driver responsible for the increase in commercial activity and a cluttered environment, in which communication has to operate.

5. What are organisations paying more attention to in order to establish a competitive advantage?

6. What recent technological advance(s) has most contributed towards organisations reconsidering their approach to marketing communications?

7. For integrated marketing communications to work within a company, what activity have clients and agents suggested must take place?

8. What might the appointment of a champion or change agent direct an organisation towards?

9. Describe two advantages that an organisation may experience as a result of implementing an integrated marketing communications strategy.

10. What are considered to be the potential disadvantages of integrated marketing communications?

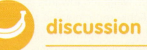

discussion questions

1. There is much debate around the realities of a company being able to fully implement an integrated marketing communications strategy. What do you feel are the challenges that might be faced and how might they be overcome?

2. All organisations have 'part-time marketers'. What would you need to do to ensure their support and contribution to customer-facing marketing communications activities?

3. When might it be appropriate for organisations not to adopt an integrated approach to their marketing communications activities?

case study 15.1: Boots No7 Protect & Perfect anti-ageing serum

Alliance Boots is one of only three retailers (including *Tesco* and *Marks and Spencer*) in the UK to break the £1 billion profit mark, with profits in the 2012–13 financial year reaching £1.27 billion. All three retailers notably have steady, strong marketing strategies. *Boots* is by far the largest specialist retailer of beauty and toiletries in the UK, with sales of £22 billion per year. It has strong brand elements: the logo with its rich blue colour is easily recognisable.

The British anti-ageing skincare industry is estimated to be worth over £6 billion and *Boots* is the largest player in this market. One of its biggest success stories has been the No7 Protect & Perfect serum, which competes very strongly with well-known branded anti-wrinkle products. It was clinically tested for 12 months before its launch in 2004 and claimed to contain renewing, protecting agents which scientists said repair photo-aged skin and improve fine wrinkles; 30ml of the serum is sold in attractive, cleanly designed packaging at a price [at the time of writing] of £16.75, a mere trifle compared with some other brand offerings priced in excess of £300.

Facial skincare marketing communications

Press and TV advertising accounted for the bulk of *Boots*'s above-the-line facial skincare media spending in 2008. A thoroughly integrated campaign for No7 Protect & Perfect continues to remind both male and female consumers of the benefits and value of the product. No7 was voted best skincare product on a BBC *Horizon* programme in April 2007 and, although *Boots* knew there would be an increase in sales following such positive publicity, it was not prepared for the frenzied demand for this 'miracle' cream. In the first 10 days after the programme aired, *Boots* sold 60,000 pots; previously it had averaged just 1000.

This created a shortage and *Boots* ran out of stock for several months. This only encouraged media hype and consumer demand. Over 100,000 women put their names on a waiting list for the product and it reputedly sold for as much as £100 on *eBay*.

Once it had restocked, *Boots* capitalised on its success through a concentrated £2 million advertising campaign and in-store promotions with suitably designed merchandise at point of purchase. A series of 30-second TV advertisements were aired with straplines such as 'my daily beauty must-have' and 'for younger-looking skin'. More recent campaigns in 2009 and 2010 featured a celebrity endorser, actress Keeley Hawes, or women 'just like you' who endorse the product. *Boots* claimed that 'when it comes to No7 Protect & Perfect, we let you do the talking' and '9 out of 10 women said their daily must have was Protect & Perfect – only at *Boots*'.

The ads used a combination of emotional and rational appeals, although very much weighted towards emotional elements, messages and cues which promised the 'magic cure' to ageing. Highly recognisable songs like Bananarama's 'Na Na Hey Hey Kiss Him Goodbye' were used in the background of the TV spots. To complement the commercials, *Boots* used radio and outdoor advertising as well as print adverts in glossy magazines. In 2010, ads featured a three-for-two product deal, with the same offer appearing on the product's official *Facebook* site.

Rave reviews on *Facebook* formed the heart of the product's first birthday campaign. 'We were so amazed by the sheer volume and passion, we created a campaign based on the fans' love for our product', said the No7 marketing manager. 'With fans' permission, we quoted them in-store, online, in press advertising and they had a starring role in our TV ad ("just like you" referred to above). It's clear that customers like engaging with the brand via digital channels'.

In fact, *Boots* features very heavily online, where a basic *Google* search for No7 Protect & Perfect produces six million hits. *YouTube* offers 49 ads featuring the product and it has a presence on many other sites. The buzz caused by the *Horizon* programme fuelled comments online by all the major newspapers and numerous magazines. *Stylist* magazine reported that an online survey of its readers resulted in 22,000 voting No7 the best anti-ageing product. Expert endorsers such as the Beauty Director of *Harrods* said that Protect & Perfect was 'an excellent product'.

It is not surprising then that with a consistently strong marketing strategy, an integrated campaign and products which feed consumers' desires, *Boots* has for four straight years now remained above the £1 billion profit ceiling.

© Kim Roberts 2014

Case study questions

1. What part did 'word of mouth' play in the success of *Boots*'s 'miracle cream'?
2. What marketing communications tools did *Boots* use in the campaign following the *Horizon* programme?
3. Why would *Boots* use an actress 'just like you' in their advertisements?
4. How are *Boots* using digital media to publicise their products?

 further reading

Bearden, W.O. and Madden, C.S. (1996) 'A brief history of the future of advertising: vision and lesson from integrated marketing communications', *Journal of Business Research*, 37 (3): 135–8.

Cornelissen, J.P. (2003) 'Change, continuity and progress: the concept of integrated marketing communications and marketing communications practice', *Journal of Strategic Marketing*, 11 (4): 217–34.

Fill, C. (2001) 'Essentially a matter of consistency: integrated marketing communications', *Marketing Review*, 1 (4): 409.

Hart, R. (2006) 'Measuring success: how to "sell" a communications audit to internal audiences', *Public Relations Tactics*, 13 (4): 9–19.

Kitchen, P.J. (2005) 'New paradigm – IMC – under fire', *Competitiveness Review*, 15 (1): 72–80.

Milart, C. (2012) 'Impact of integrated marketing communication on consumer behaviour: effects on consumer decision-making process', *International Journal of Marketing Studies*, 4 (2).

Olenski, S. (2012) 'Integrated marketing communications: then and now', *Forbes Magazine*, 31 May. Available at: www.forbes.com/sites/marketshare/2012/05/31/ integrated-marketing-communications-then-now/ (accessed 15 December 2013).

REFERENCES

Beckles, C. (2013) St John Ambulance: Lives Lost. Available at: www.dandad.org/inspiration/ features-and-opinion/st-john-ambulance-lives-lost (accessed 19 May 2013). London: D&AD.

Berry, L.L. (1995) 'Relationship marketing of services: growing interest, emerging perspectives', *Journal of the Academy of Marketing Science*, 23 (4): 236–45.

Blythe, J. (2000) *Marketing Communications*. Harlow: Pearson Education.

Copley, P. (2004) *Marketing Communications Management*. Oxford: Butterworth-Heinemann.

Eagle, L. and Kitchen, P.J. (2000) 'IMC, brand communications and corporate cultures: client/advertising agency coordination and cohesion', *European Journal of Marketing*, 34 (5/6): 667.

Fill, C. (2009) *Marketing Communications: Interactivity, Communities and Content*, 5th edn. Harlow: Financial Times/Prentice Hall.

Gummesson, E. (1990) *The Part-time Marketer*. Karlstad: CTF Service Research Centre.

Hackley, C.E. and Kitchen, P.J. (1998) 'IMC: a consumer psychological perspective', *Marketing, Intelligence and Planning*, 16 (3): 229–35.

Kitchen, P.J. and Schultz, D.E. (1999) 'A multi-country comparison of the drive for IMC', *Journal of Advertising Research*, 39 (1): 21–38.

Kliatchko, J. (2005) 'Towards a new definition of integrated marketing communications (IMC)', *International Journal of Advertising*, 24 (1): 7–34.

Novak, G. and Phelps, J. (1994) 'Conceptualising the integrated marketing communications phenomenon', *Journal of Current Issues and Research in Advertising*, 16 (1): 49–66.

Pechmann, C. and Stewart, D.W. (1990) 'Advertising repetition: a critical review of wear-in and wear-out', Working Paper, Cambridge Science Unit.

Pickton, D. and Broderick, A. (2005) *Integrated Marketing Communications*, 2nd edn. Harlow: Financial Times/Prentice Hall.

Schultz, D.P. and Schultz, S.E. (1998) *Psychology and Work Today*. Upper Saddle River, NJ: Prentice Hall.

Semenik, R.J. (2002) *Promotion and Integrated Marketing Communications*. London: Thomson Learning.

Smith, P.R. and Taylor, J. (2004) *Marketing Communications: An Integrated Approach*, 2nd edn. London: Kogan Page.

For additional materials that support this chapter and your learning, please visit:
study.sagepub.com/egan

INTERNAL COMMUNICATIONS

16

LEARNING OBJECTIVES

Having completed this chapter readers would be expected to:

- understand the reasons why organisations are putting more resources into internal communications

- describe the concepts that are involved with internal communications

- discuss ways in which internal communications can be implemented

- assess the potential benefits of an effective internal communications programme.

INTRODUCTION

Internal communications
The sharing of information within an organisation for business purposes that takes place via various communication channels.

Internal communications has, in recent years, received widespread attention in the academic and professional management literature. This has developed on the back of a general realisation that there is a basis of competitive advantage to be had through the improvement of organisational capability and delivery of customer services that actually matches customer needs and expectations. This development of interest in the internal workings of the organisation has not been restricted to the field of marketing. Human resource management and general management trends have also highlighted the need to communicate effectively internally. In the organisational context, internal communications may be seen to be a means of creating a more knowledgeable, democratic, training-oriented organisation, resulting in greater professionalism, greater empowerment and, ultimately, improved customer service.

In the marketing literature, internal communications (often referred to as internal marketing) is closely associated with developments in relationship marketing and with a recognition of the importance of the supplier–customer interface. While traditional marketing focuses wholly on the external customer, relationship marketing stresses the additional significance of the internal customer in successfully establishing relationships (Gummesson 1991). Modern marketing, therefore, calls not only for an external marketing orientation but also for an internal focus on employees. It is, according to one marketing consultant,[1] 'the application of marketing inside the organisation to instil customer focused values'. According to the CIPR,[2] having an internal communications strategy provides:

> a clear picture of the very business (or department or project) it is trying to support. It will be built on established values and principles and the ways it encourages discussion, conversation and feedback will highlight the organisation's very ambitions and aspirations. The importance of displaying clarity in terms of these issues links directly to the core of the communications strategy, what employees need to think, feel and do; to the priorities in terms of channel development and, ultimately, to the resources and budget that the internal communications function will require to deliver these objectives.

In business terms, internal communications seeks to supplement and rationalise the messages and communications which come from the company's employees at the customer interface that are normally difficult to control. It is seen as a means of moderation in what the employee says or does and what images and associations this creates in the mind of the customer. It is not, therefore, simply the managerial benefits that are associated with professionalism and empowerment but a conscious effort to align company communications with those of their staff.

The ideas associated with internal communications and internal marketing have had a chequered career. Perhaps the most prevalent view of employees is that they exchange their skills and labour, in relation to tasks performed, for remunerative reward. Not unsurprisingly, therefore, the historic and rather archaic role of internal communications was felt to be for the persuasion of staff to do as the management wished. It was not until the realisation that organisations have 'internal customers' within those internal markets that there was a change in mindset, a concept that arose from the idea of having to 'sell jobs' and make them more attractive to employees (Reynoso 1996): 'Marketing to employees of an organization to ensure that they are effectively carrying out desired programs and policies.' In more recent times, internal communications has become associated with a wide number of concepts, among them (Egan 2011):

- the orchestration of staff working together and attuned to the company's mission, strategy, goals and the wider operations of the company
- efforts to 'sell' the message of an organisation to its internal audience, using similar techniques to those used externally
- any activity which seeks to enhance the external marketplace performance
- activities that improve customer relationships with the organisation through its employees.

In practice, internal communications is concerned with developing responsiveness, responsibility and unity of purpose. The values transmitted externally to customers, suppliers and distributers through external communications, therefore, need to be both supported and reinforced by the values expressed by employees themselves, and especially those who interact with external stakeholders at whatever level. Successful internal communications requires:

- creativity and zeal
- consistency and alignment with the brand
- appropriate feedback mechanisms
- measurement.

---

[1]   Sybil Sterstic, cited in Duncan (2002).
[2]   Chartered Institute of Public Relations at: www.ciprinside.co.uk

Creativity and zeal suggests that communication should be across the most appropriate platforms (email, video, intranet, newsletter, etc.) and at the level of your external communication. Consistency and frequency and alignment with the brand get messages across successfully. There must always be a means of feedback and this should provide a basis for measurement.

CUSTOMER–EMPLOYEE INTERFACE

Recognition of the importance of the employee–customer interface has, in large part, promoted interest in internal marketing. Increased consumer sophistication and choice has meant that consumers are judging quality and value not just in terms of what they buy but also in terms of the 'exchange experiences' themselves. People are an essential part of those experiences and thus the total value package itself. As a consequence, employees' actions are important both in terms of the tangible aspects of service delivery and the intangible ones, such as presentation, attitude and the way in which the service is actually provided. Research suggests that the quality of relationships a company has with its customers is largely determined by how employees on the front line make customers feel (Barnes & Howlett 1998).

Reputation is based on quality service and quality service on employee know-how. Employees individually accumulate know-how (often referred to as **knowledge capital** because of its value to the organisation) over time. This in-company know-how is what turns knowledge into application and adds the extra value to the product or service offered. It is also suggested that while the customer–supplier interface is more immediate, the internal climate has a strong impact on employee satisfaction and customer retention (Payne 2000). In service organisations, internal communications can be seen to be of the utmost importance given the proximity of employees to customers. This does not, however, exclude manufacturing companies from consideration of internal communications. In all organisations, perception is influenced by the character and personality of the organisation as a whole and not just through its traditional paid or unpaid media. With advertising and sales promotion, the organisation can largely determine the message it wants to convey. Even public relations and sponsorship, although less controllable, are

Knowledge capital
The knowledge held within an organisation.

FIGURE 16.1   Organisational communication

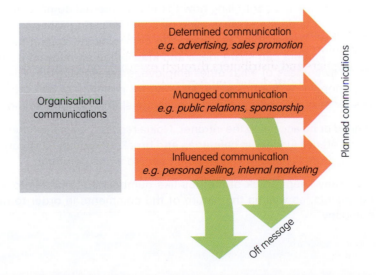

seen to be managed to produce, hopefully, a desirable outcome. With employees, however, the internal market consists of people with needs and wants which must constantly be assessed and, if practical, satisfied. It is this strategic intervention that can directly influence positive and/or negative communications from this source (see Figure 16.1).

Internal communications helps to dispense with the notion that it is only functional marketing staff who 'own the customer' and that they alone should be concerned with communications with them. Many companies have centralised marketing and sales staff, who might be called 'full-time marketers'. These employees do not, however, represent all the marketers and salespeople the firm has at its disposal (Grönroos 1996). The phrase 'part-time marketers' (PTM) is now widely used to describe these non-marketing specialists who, regardless of their position in the company, are crucial to the company's marketing effort. These part-time marketers include all of those employees who, in any way, influence customer relations, customer satisfaction and their perception of quality (Gummesson 1991). The impact on customer satisfaction and quality perception is more important to long-term success in the marketplace than is often realised. In building reputation, it is often the intangible aspects such as attitude and sincerity rather than the competence of the service provision, which has the most powerful influence.

⊙ insight: Nokia's social media communications team

With a tagline such as 'connecting people', you would expect *Nokia* to have implemented social media into their internal communications. Nokia uses a number of different vehicles for two-way communications and social media plays a big part in this strategy.

In 2008, *Nokia* established a social media communications team with the aim of improving inter-company communications and engaging employees. They were set the goal of encouraging the use of social media internally to bring out the company's unique authentic voice and to engage in social media externally on behalf of Nokia. With each of its social media tools, Nokia sought to foster knowledge sharing among its 125,000 employees worldwide.

The three most popular tools are BlogHub, VideoHub and Infopedia. According to a member of the team, 'The BlogHub lowers barriers for employees to find conversations relevant to them. Rather than the company dictating a corporate culture and controlling how the line of internal comms should flow, the BlogHub allows employees to better understand messaging by communicating with people whose opinions matter. Everyone has a voice'. This enables employees to communicate among themselves. By commenting on blogs, BlogHub members can share ideas and knowledge on relevant issues. It is also an effective tool to help raise awareness of what other employees are working on. The internal VideoHub has grown increasingly popular with employees, allowing for postings to be updated on a daily basis, and Infopedia allows for easy collaboration and knowledge sharing among employees.

To reach employees who have limited or no access to the intranet, Nokia regularly posts announcements on plasma screens around regional offices (usually in cafeterias and breakout rooms). This can include information pertaining to everything from flu jabs to what's being served in the cafeteria.

According to the team, 'The company keeps track of metrics like number of attendees to meeting, number of article views and comments, as well as the nature of the comments in order to measure success and progress at the company'.

Source: various

THE EMPLOYEE PERSPECTIVE

Obtaining and understanding the employee perspective is a critical tool in managing customer satisfaction as it enables managers to employ internal communications. Research suggests that employee commitment to the organisation requires that they have the opportunity to participate in company decision making and have a clear understanding of company values (Varey 2002). Internal communications, it is claimed, is a relationship development process in which staff autonomy and know-how combine to create and circulate new organisational knowledge (Ballantyne 1997: 354). It is built on the premise that employees want to give good service just as customers want to receive it, and managers who make it easier to achieve this will find that both customers and employees are likely to respond positively (Schneider 1980).

At a tactical level, internal communications may include ongoing training and encouragement of formal and informal communications (such as newsletters and social events). Patterns of working and expectations are transmitted through communication mechanisms such as training and socialisation programmes. These acquaint staff with the norms and expectations of the organisation. At the strategic level, internal communications extends to the adoption of supportive management styles and personnel policies, customer service training and planning procedures (Hogg et al. 1998). There is also a suggestion that implementing an internal customer approach involves a number of processes.

Internal communications are necessary in order that employees are motivated and involved with the brand in such a way that they are able to present a consistent and uniform message to anyone they come in contact with outside the company. The danger inherent in this is that internal communications may be limited in what it contributes to the wider issues of organisational culture as it all too often defaults to a one-way communications exercise (Meldrum 2000). What is required are proper mechanisms to ensure superior performance which requires support, flexibility and feedback.

Knowledge is a key driver to staff effectiveness (and indeed satisfaction). As Gummesson (1987) notes, all 'contact personnel' must be well attuned to the mission, goals, strategies and systems of the company, otherwise they would be unable to handle those crucial 'moments of truth' that occur during interaction with customers. This is particularly evident in service firms where interface with the customer is broad and intense but may also be generally true of all companies.

According to Kandampully and Duddy (1999), an internal communications programme should 'be considered the firm's life-blood – percolating through all ranks, departments, functions and assets of the firm – with the ultimate aim of simultaneously offering and gaining value at all levels'.

INTERNAL COMMUNICATIONS IN PRACTICE

In many organisations, internal communications has advanced a long way from the days of the corporate newsletter to well-organised systems of internal communications. Research by *Richmond Events* suggests that 75% of UK companies have a department responsible for internal communications but not all can be said to be implementing internal communications strategies. According to Jobber and Lancaster (2009), the implementation of internal communications is a process where:

- the organisation determines its must-have/would-like-to-have objectives
- the internal strategy is formulated

- the policy is implemented under the headings of (a) persuasion, (b) negotiation, (c) politics and (d) tactics
- the process is evaluated.

There are a number of reasons for this increased emphasis on including internal communications among the strategic processes of the organisation. These include (Baines et al. 2004):

- a greater requirement for companies to inform their employees about policy and financial affairs including annual reports and accounts
- the increasing democratisation of industry
- greater employee ownership of equity through privatisations, flotations, management buy-outs, share ownership schemes and performance-related pay schemes
- the availability of new communications technology, making it easier to organise and conduct internal communications
- the increasing significance of service industries and the consequent importance of the employee/customer interface.

Internally directed communications can be placed under the three headings of downward, sideways and upward communications (Baines et al. 2004), representing management–employee, employee–employee and employee–management relationships. Downward communication was traditionally through house journals or other printed material but much of this has been replaced with electronic versions (probably to the detriment of readership). Staff meetings are also used as they are more personal and enable instant feedback. A number of companies utilise internet technology to organise video-newsletters and video-conferencing. *Cisco Systems*'s employees, for example, are addressed regularly by their president via the internet. Research company *Melcrum* reported in 2011 that 93% of internal communications professionals now see video as an important tool (see www.melcrum.com).

Sideways communication (employee to employee) is encouraged in many businesses in the belief that it contributes to staff satisfaction. The organisation may, therefore, organise or facilitate employee events to promote collegiality, especially across departments. Upward communication has, traditionally, been difficult to encourage, even when management want to hear the opinion of staff. Some organisations hold regular staff surveys or focus groups to stimulate such debate. Others still rely on middle management to feed back from the front line – a notoriously ineffective strategy. It is generally supposed that the shorter the distance between the top and the bottom of the organisational pyramid, the better the communication. In effect, however, it is the systems in place to encourage this communication that determine whether interaction is successful or not.

INTERNAL COMMUNICATIONS BENEFITS

It is increasingly recognised that in order to sustain a competitive position, organisations must develop a customer service culture that both allows and encourages employees to give good service (Varey 2002). From a management and human resource perspective, internal communications focuses on the three core value-adding activities of innovation, effective processes and customer support, and builds networks which 'design in' quality (Doyle 1995). It involves retaining customer-conscious employees and the development of employee empowerment to better satisfy the needs of the customer. Internal communications reflects the belief that the company must be prepared to do a great deal for its employees if they want their employees to deliver an outstanding level of service to customers.

From a marketing communications viewpoint, this alignment between management and staff considerably improves the chances that the images and perceptions communicated by way of traditional marcom media will be reflected in the actions of staff. The calculation is that employees who believe that the organisation facilitates their performance, aids their career expectations and provides positive supervision will feel enabled to carry out the company's main work of serving customers (Varey 2002).

Effective internal communications, whether through personal contact or internal media, may have a positive effect on employees in a number of ways. It can:

- serve to clarify organisational roles by explaining the way the organisation works and the employees' part in it
- enable employees to make promises that can be delivered through knowledge of the strengths and limitations of the organisation
- demonstrate that the organisation is ethical and has values by informing employees of what the organisation has achieved in the local community, nationally and internationally
- improve employee loyalty because well-informed, empowered and satisfied employees are more likely to stay and be generally supportive of the organisation
- decrease employee turnover as a result of a satisfied and loyal workforce
- reduce training costs through reduced employee turnover.

Internal communications can also be seen to aid organisations going through crisis, in helping stabilise the confidence of employees.

It can, however, equally well have a negative effect if:

- claims are made by the company that employees know are unrealistic and/or undeliverable
- company messages are untrue and the workforce realises them as such
- the jobs of employees are unflatteringly portrayed.

summary

This chapter reviewed the concepts and themes surrounding internal communications. It suggested that the field of internal communications was receiving widespread attention because of the perceived need for improvement in organisational capability and in the delivery of customer service. It suggested that employee interaction is not only important in service delivery but also in intangible aspects such as attitude and the way a service is provided, and it contrasted this with more or less controllable tools such as advertising and public relations. The chapter discussed internal communications implementation and how this is delivered in practice. It also discussed the potential benefits which, in addition to better customer service, include the clarification of roles, capabilities and values and improved loyalty, decreased turnover and reduced training costs. These benefits were contrasted with the potential problems associated with unrealistic or untrue claims and employees being portrayed unflatteringly.

review questions

1. What is considered to be the focus of traditional marketing?

2. What concept has been recognised as being an important activity in developing a customer-focused organisation?

3. What term is used to describe the accumulation of know-how by employees?

4. What do the initials PTM stand for?

5. What is considered to be a critical tool in managing customer satisfaction?

6. Describe the process required when implementing an internal customer approach.

7. Why are internal communications a necessary part of internal management?

8. Give an example of downward communication.

9. What is considered to be the main factor in sustaining a competitive position?

10. How can internal marketing assist organisations that are going through crisis?

discussion questions

1. You are tasked with implementing a significant change within your organisation that will prove unpopular to some of the older staff. How would you go about minimising the resistance to change?

2. What means of communicating with staff are available to an organisation and how would you evaluate their effectiveness?

3. We now live in an age when text and email contact has become a normal way of communicating. What might the impact of this be in another 10 years on internal communications within companies?

case study 16.1: Nottingham City Homes and internal communications

Nottingham City Homes manages around 29,000 council homes across Nottingham. They see their mission as delivering excellent services. Their vision is to create homes where people want to live. Among the services they provide to tenants are repairs, allocations and lettings, advice and guidance on rent, advice on dealing with debt and tenant involvement. They also see fighting anti-social behaviour as a priority. Nottingham City Homes see themselves as a first-class housing organisation and a major player in transforming the quality of life in their neighbourhoods.

In achieving their vision, they recognised that success depends on well-informed, professional employees delivering excellent service. They believed that a strong internal marketing strategy could improve employee morale and motivation, increase productivity, lower absenteeism and staff turnover, develop a stronger commitment to organisational goals and improve job satisfaction.

At the heart of this is the organisation's internal communications. There is recognition in the company that internal communications is not just the responsibility of the communications and marketing team: all employees are seen to have a part to play. The strategy included ensuring that key messages from the executive management team reached everyone (top down), that stories about the successes of individual employees and teams were shared (sideways) and fostering a culture where all employees are able to voice their ideas and opinions (bottom up).

Most importantly, they wanted employees to have access to essential, up-to-date, accurate information so that they could do their jobs effectively and efficiently. They believe that when employees and colleagues are kept well informed and are listened to by the organisation, they are empowered to perform.

To achieve this ambition, they recognised that they needed strong internal communications messages and processes. They also wanted to stimulate cross-team working and encourage the development of ideas for improvement from other staff (internal customers) and external customers. Together with the performance team, they sought to establish a company-wide system for regularly communicating performance, with managers taking visible responsibility for and greater ownership of the information.

Case study questions

1. How might greater employee empowerment help the organisation fulfil its vision?
2. What processes may need to be put in place to achieve 'top-down', 'sideways' and 'bottom-up' communications?
3. Can you foresee any downsides to this strategy?

 ## further reading

Cockrill, M. (2006) 'Adapting to cultural diversity', *Strategic Communication Management*, 10 (5): 4.

Davis, S. (2013) 'Making the shift: transforming marketing through the eyes of change agents in the trenches', *Journal of Integrated Marketing Communications*, 8–14.

De Bussy, N.M., Ewing, M.T. and Pitt, L.F. (2003) 'Stakeholder theory and internal marketing communications: a framework for analysing the influence of new media', *Journal of Marketing Communications*, 9 (3): 147–61.

Goebel, D.J., Marshall, G.W. and Locander, W.B. (2004) 'An organizational communication-based model of individual customer orientation of non-marketing members of a firm', *Journal of Strategic Marketing*, 12 (1): 29–56.

Steyn, E., Steyn, T.F.J. and van Rooyen, M. (2011) 'Internal communication at DaimlerChrysler South Africa: a qualitative perspective on two-way symmetrical communication and internal marketing', *Journal of Marketing Development and Competitiveness*, 5 (4): 131–44.

REFERENCES

Baines, P., Egan, J. and Jefkins, F. (2004) Public Relations: Contemporary Issues and Techniques. Oxford: Elsevier Butterworth-Heinemann.

Ballantyne, D. (1997) 'Internal networks for internal marketing', *Journal of Marketing Management*, 3 (5): 343–66.

Barnes, J.G. and Howlett, D.M. (1998) 'Predictors of equity in relationships between service providers and retail customers', *International Journal of Bank Marketing*, 16 (1): 5–23.

Doyle, P. (1995) 'Marketing in the new millennium', *European Journal of Marketing*, 29 (12): 23–41.

Duncan, T. (2002) Using Advertising and Promotion to Build Brand. New York: McGraw-Hill.

Egan, J. (2011) *Relationship Marketing*, 4th edn. Harlow: Pearson Education.

Grönroos, C. (1990) 'Relationship approach to the marketing function in service contexts: the marketing and organization behaviour interface', *Journal of Business Research*, 20: 3–11.

Gummesson, E. (1987) 'In search of marketing equilibrium: relationship marketing versus hypercompetition', *Journal of Marketing Management*, 13 (5): 21–30.

Gummesson, E. (1991) 'Marketing orientation revisited: the crucial role of the part-time marketers', *European Journal of Marketing*, 25 (2): 60–7.

Hogg, G., Carter, S. and Dunne, A. (1998) 'Investing in people: internal marketing and corporate culture', *Journal of Marketing Management*, 14: 879–95.

Jobber, D. and Lancaster, G. (2009) Selling and Sales Management, 8th edn. Harlow: Pearson.

Kandampully, J. and Duddy, R. (1999) 'Relationship marketing: a concept beyond the primary relationship', *Marketing Intelligence & Planning*, 17 (7): 315–23.

Meldrum, M. (2000) 'A market orientation', in Cranfield School of Management, Marketing Management: A Relationship Marketing Perspective. Basingstoke: *Macmillan*, pp. 3–15.

Payne, A. (2000) 'Relationship marketing: managing multiple markets', in Cranfield School of Management, Marketing Management: A Relationship Marketing Perspective. Basingstoke: *Macmillan*, pp. 16–30.

Reynoso, J. (1996) 'Internal service operations: how well are they serving each other?', in B. Edvardsson, S.W. Brown, R. Johnston, E.E. Scheuing (eds), Advancing Service Quality: A Global Perspective. New York: ISQA, pp. 77–86.

Schneider, B. (1980) 'The service organisation: climate is crucial', *Organisational Dynamics*, Autumn: 52–65.

Varey, R.J. (2002) Marketing Communication: Principles and Practice. London: Routledge.

For additional materials that support this chapter and your learning, please visit:
study.sagepub.com/egan

MARKETING CHANNELS AND BUSINESS-TO-BUSINESS COMMUNICATIONS

17

CHAPTER CONTENTS

LEARNING OBJECTIVES

Having completed this chapter readers would be expected to:

- understand the characteristics of business-to-business (B2B) communications

- recognise the similarities and differences between B2B and consumer communications

- understand the reason(s) for supplier partnerships.

INTRODUCTION

The concept of 'channels' has been inherent in marketing since its inception. A channel suggests a flow. In this case, the flow is from the manufacturer or service provider to the consumer either direct or through intermediaries (wholesalers, retailers, catalogue operations, etc.). What also flows along the channel(s) are marketing communications, although this can and should be a two-way rather than unidirectional flow. Although Figure 17.1 is a simplification, particularly in our complex, multi-channel, digital and services dominant society, it remains a useful analogy in relation to business-to-business (B2B) markets.

The customer may be either another organisation or the general public. If the customer is another business, the original supply may be sold on unchanged (although frequently in less bulk), used in or combined with another product or service (which later re-enters the channel) or used to enable the company to carry out its main function (e.g. stationery, machinery). This inter-organisational trade is most commonly known as 'business-to-business'[1] (B2B) marketing and is distinguished from transactions with the public or 'business-to-consumer' (B2C) marketing. Where an organisation sells virtually the same products/services to both consumers and businesses (but not necessarily at the same price), this is commonly known as **direct channel marketing** (e.g. *Dell*).

---

[1]   In earlier times, it was more generally called industrial marketing.

FIGURE 17.1   Channel flows

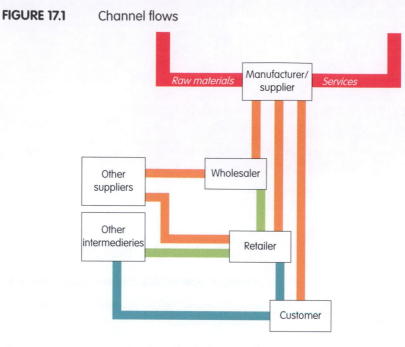

Business-to-business markets include the industrial and public sector, materials, components, consumables and services, and the total volume far exceeds that of consumer markets. One feature of the digital age, which initially forecast the demise of intermediaries, is the growing complexity of markets where consumers can be re-sellers (on *eBay*) and where companies encourage customers to participate in the product or service offering. The distinction between business-to-business and business-to-consumer may be becoming less important.

BUSINESS-TO-BUSINESS COMMUNICATIONS

The characteristics of the business-to-business sector are generally regarded as different from those of consumer marketing, although these are sometimes exaggerated to suggest that there is no commonality at all between business-to-business and business-to-consumer. In effect, there is little difference in the wants and desires of the two sectors, however the organisational dynamics and the implied rationality suggest that marketing communications should be formulated in different ways. Those business-to-business characteristics that most effect this application are:

- larger markets
- fewer customers
- higher spend
- wider geographical spread
- complex buyer–customer interaction.

The relative complexity and fewer (but higher spending) customers are reasons why personal selling is so important in business-to-business markets. A trained sales executive can demonstrate, answer technical questions and negotiate in real time. Although trade advertising, exhibitions, direct mail and public relations all play their part, these are frequently in support of personal sales, particularly in the customer acquisition phase. Once a relationship has been established, the communications dynamic changes. As noted in Chapter 14, most frequently the communication is between two (or more) people who interact with each other

FIGURE 17.2   Internal and external relationships

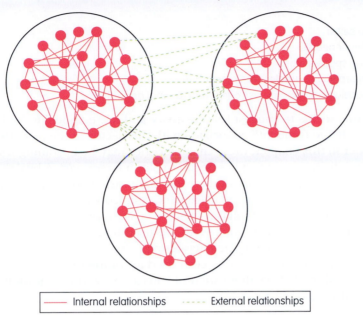

in 'real time' and respond to each other's informational needs. To facilitate these important relationships, supply organisations may appoint **key account managers** to work specifically with one or a limited number of accounts. These interactions frequently lead to long-term and sometimes close relationships between the individuals involved. It is generally accepted that organisations are networks in their own right but these relationships extend outside the organisation to other individuals in other organisations such that complex external networks develop (see Figure 17.2). It is along these lines of personal communication that a large volume of marketing messages pass.

   In overall communication terms, the relative importance of the various tools in business-to-business are almost inverse to that of business-to-consumer marketing. In business-to-business markets, personal selling replaces advertising and sales promotion as the main tool while others trail in relative significance (see Figure 17.3). However, personal selling is expensive and many business-to-business organisations use it as sparingly as possible, utilising other tools to create awareness, develop interest and ferment desire. Personal selling is then used where it is most effective in closing the sale and developing the relationship.

   Trade advertising, as the term suggests, utilises largely specialist publications including trade journals, newspapers and magazines aimed at particular industry buyers. The trade press is not the only media outlet. Business-to-business organisations do advertise in mass media publications for reasons associated with corporate image and brand awareness and development. It is also true that buyers and other decision makers are themselves consumers, which is important to recognise, particularly in re-sale industries.

Key account managers
Marketing and/or sales executives who work specifically with one or a limited number of accounts.

FIGURE 17.3   Perceived importance of marcom tools in B2B/B2C markets

According to de Pelsmacker et al. (2007), business-to-business advertising tends to:

- be more sexist
- depict fewer people
- give more space to copy
- mention product characteristics more often
- use psychological appeals less often than rational appeals.

All in all, this seems to suggest less creativity and more appeal to basic, rational instincts, a charge frequently associated with this sector in the past. However, as is noted later in this chapter, these characteristics may be becoming less distinct.

Direct and digital marketing has begun to play a larger part in business-to-business communications. Because of the continually rising costs of personal selling and the falling costs of database management, coupled with considerable advances in technology, direct and digital marketing is seen as the 'next best thing' to personal contact. Direct mail and email are used to create awareness, enhance image and establish credibility. Telemarketing helps establish and qualify leads, facilitate customer enquiries and is even used as a direct sales channel. As with consumer-based marketing, there are problems associated with **junk mail**, **spam** and **cold calling** (see Chapter 13).

TABLE 17.1   1 B2B content marketing usage 2012

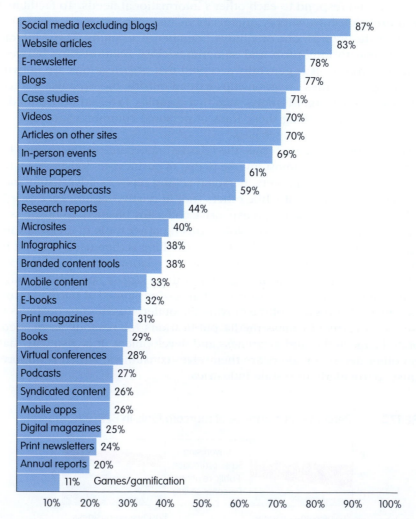

Adapted from the Content Marketing Institute www.contentmarketinginstitute.com

Web-based advertising and servicing is also growing in importance as business-to-business suppliers vie to create the best websites, with the most interactivity and effective customer care (e.g. order tracking). On the other side of the fence, customers looking to determine the best supply (in terms of quality and price) often use the internet to acquire this knowledge. This has led to the development of so-called **content marketing**. Content marketing is 'a marketing technique of creating and distributing relevant and valuable content to attract, acquire, and engage a clearly defined and understood target audience – with the objective of driving profitable customer action' (Content Marketing Institute at: www.content-marketinginstitute.com). It provides information attractive to customers, focusing on owning the media not renting it. The most used business-to-business content marketing mediums in the USA are social media and website articles.

Trade promotion at retail level includes buying allowances, advertising or sales promotion allowances, slotting allowances (slotting in new products, increasing shelf space) and others including gifts, training and other incentives (see Chapter 10). At all levels in the business-to-business sector, promotions include discounts or other offers to clear stock, increase sales during slow periods, introduce new products, increase distribution or counter competitive activity. Promotional offers may be targeted at specific buyers or made available through trade online and off-line publications. There is one major difference between business-to-business and business-to-consumer markets regarding sales promotion. While in business-to-consumer markets individual customers are incentivised (i.e. bribed) to change their buying behaviour, in business-to-business markets this may be considered as unethical (but goes on none the less).

Public relations (or corporate communications) is a tool used extensively in the business-to-business sector. PR style and function are heavily determined by the organisational type and by PR's recognised role within the organisation. However, suppliers of products or services and their customers are naturally keen to ensure that 'good will and mutual understanding' exist between them and so suppliers turn to PR techniques to deliver these messages.

THE BUSINESS-TO-BUSINESS MESSAGE

Business-to-business communications tactics are a series of activities designed to influence the target audience (usually, but not exclusively, the buyer) and persuade a percentage of these to ultimately purchase the product(s) and/or service(s). The characteristics of business-to-business have led observers to suggest that the content and targeting of messages is significantly different from business-to-business marketing. Suggestions concerning the differences are shown in Figure 17.4.

FIGURE 17.4   Business-to-business compared to consumer markets

	Consumer marketing	Business-to-business marketing
Decision making unit (DMU)	One or a few	Many
Priority communications methods	Sales promotion, advertising	Personal selling, direct and digital
Formality	Informal	Formal
Message orientation	Emotional	Rational
Decision period	Short	Long

In business-to-business, the decision-making unit (DMU) is assumed to involve many functions relative to consumer marketing where a purchase decision is made by a relative few. As a generality, this is indeed the case although some organisational buyers have considerable personal authority. According to Sheth et al. (1999), a business-to-business decision-making unit may consist of the buyer, decider, influencer, analyser, gatekeeper and (where appropriate) user, although some (or all) of these functions may reside in a few (or even one) individual(s). Who to target is, therefore, a major consideration and many companies compile or rent lists of such contacts to use for direct mailing, emailing or telemarketing purposes. The downside of this strategy is that individuals change jobs or leave organisations on a regular basis, making the upkeep of such lists a burden (see Chapter 13).

As noted above, personal selling (or personal contact) is a major conduit in many business-to-business organisations, although again it is the exceptions that make the rule. Organisations such as *Viking Direct* and *Niceday* deal with their largely organisational customers through catalogues (online and print), and some companies, for example *Intel*, use cooperative consumer advertising, in *Intel*'s case to maintain its influence on the computer processor market.

The assumed formality in procedure and rationality in decision making have long been seen as features of business-to-business, although IMP[2] research shows many inter-firm transactions are conducted within enduring business relationships where mutual trust and adaptation are commonplace, rather than the then prevailing rational view of inter-firm transactions conducted largely on a contractual basis (Brennan & Turnbull 2001). Buyers, influencers, etc. are all human and sometimes make decisions based not on rationality but on emotion. Nevertheless, much printed communication (flyers, catalogues, etc.) and the content of websites and business-to-business blogs concentrate more on features and specifications rather than on emotional appeals. A logical extension of this behaviour is the suggestion that brand image plays less of a part in business-to-business markets. The continued sale of premium brands at premium prices suggests otherwise. Indeed, contrary to what is sometimes suggested, many business decisions are based on psychological factors such as perceived performance, reputation, trust, flexibility and reliability, rather than on more basic reasons such as actual performance or cost.

The length of time between needs recognition and supply is likely to be longer than in business-to-business markets. While in the FMCG marketplace (i.e. supermarket retailers) this can be counted in minutes, most business have extended time cycles. The complexity and/or personalisation and/or bulk involved in some business-to-business ordering may extend waiting time into months (or even years in the case of the aircraft industry). If orders are going to tender (as is the case with most public sector spending), the ordering time requires extending to cope with shortlisting, obtaining tenders, evaluation and selection. In addition, strict delivery times may be crucial. For these as well as other reasons, continual, often personal contact over long periods is the norm.

SUPPLIER PARTNERSHIPS

In marketing communications terms, the format of any trade and cooperation and the inter-organisational relationships that may develop from this have a heavy influence on the nature and form of marketing communications activities. When it comes to business-to-business, no business is entirely independent of others, thus,

---

[2]   Industrial Marketing and Purchasing Group. The IMP Group was formed in the mid-1970s by researchers originating from the Universities of Uppsala, Bath, UMIST, ESC Lyon and Ludwig Maximilians (Munich).

by the very nature of the interdependency of most business-to-business markets, business relationships of one sort or another are inevitable. IMP research has noted that personal relationships between the employees and owners/directors of companies have for some time been explicitly recognised by both buyer and seller organisations and individuals within those organisations.

Relational 'bonding' between business-to-business traders is not even a twentieth-century phenomenon. The formation of trade guilds in the Middle Ages set standards and encouraged cooperation and many such trades, although competitors would gather in certain parts of towns or even dominate cities (e.g. Sheffield cutlery). In the pre-Industrial Revolution world, such associations were quite prevalent between traders, partly because of the need, in turbulent, minimally legislated and sometimes dangerous markets, to do business with others you could trust (Sheth & Parvatiyar 1995).

Communication within the supplier–customer channel is determined by three factors:

- channel structure
- channel climate and culture
- balance of power.

Channel structure may range from the traditional large industrial producer to the small, flexible supplier of creative services, and organisational climate and culture may be equally diverse. In organisational relationships, the 'balance of power' is rarely symmetrical with one party usually the stronger of the two (Gummesson 2002). During the so-called 'golden age of marketing' from the mid-1950s to the mid-1970s, it was the brand supplier who financed the development of individual brands, largely through mass advertising, and who dominated and manipulated the means of distribution. The observable tension in the distribution chain was evident in relationships between brand suppliers and their retail intermediaries. Only rarely did brand owners and retailers work together to achieve a result that would satisfy both parties. Most often, suppliers used 'pull strategies' (see Chapter 5) with the objective of attracting customers 'over the heads' of the retailer. Although 'push strategies' (effectively using trade incentives and promotions to 'push' product through the distribution chain) existed, they tended to be one-off tactics rather than strategic cooperative communication activity. The third quarter of the twentieth century saw a change in the balance of power between suppliers and retailers, particularly in the FMCG sector, but as yet little movement towards cooperation. As the power of large supermarket retailers grew, suppliers were often played off against each other. Information regarding production capacity on one side and sales on the other was regarded as commercially sensitive and distrust of one's supplier or customer was the norm. In the 1990s, however, retailers and suppliers began to recognise that in a relatively stagnant market one of the few opportunities to increase effectiveness was in channel distribution. To facilitate this **electronic point of sale (EPS)**, systems were introduced which enabled products to be replaced and sales to be monitored on a regular basis. From the marketing communications perspective, EPS allowed retailers and suppliers to monitor the effect of changing communications, ranging from the effect of moving a solus display to a major advertising campaign.

Another form of partnering involves generic campaigns organised by groups of suppliers. The trend to this type of cooperative behaviour began in the UK in the years between the world wars when the British public were asked to buy British cars, eat more fish and fruit, smoke imported Havana cigars, dress in Harris Tweed, protect woodwork with white lead and send their friends British Christmas cards (Nevett 1982). Cooperative campaigns today range from those for the meat, wool and other basic industries to those for the major airline groupings of *OneWorld*, *Sky Team* and the *Star Alliance*, and many in between.

Electronic point of sale (EPOS)
Technology at the point of sale that enables transactions to be tracked at the merchandise and/or customer level.

summary

This chapter reviewed the concept of marketing channels and business-to-business communications. It distinguished between business-to-business and business-to-consumer media and the messages they carry and the characteristics that affect this. The chapter reviewed the relative importance of various marketing communications tools and the importance of networks and relationships. It looked at the supposed rationality of B2B communications (epitomised by content marketing) in the recognition that emotion (and brand reputation) has a part to play too. The chapter also discussed supplier partnerships and the changes that have occurred in the past few years through the development of technologies.

review questions

1. Explain what is meant by direct channel marketing.

2. What do business-to-business markets include?

3. Describe the composition of a business-to-business decision-making unit.

4. What factors determine communication within the supplier–customer channel?

5. Explain the advantages of point-of-sale systems.

6. What is the difference, if any, between business-to-business and business-to-consumer markets?

7. For business-to-business markets, what is the major communications tool used?

8. What is 'trade advertising'?

9. How has technology changed business-to-business communications?

10. What do you understand to be the basis on which most business decisions are made?

discussion questions

1. Personal selling is important in business-to-business markets. Why might this be and what would companies need to do in order to be effective in this area?

2. Sales promotion activities in business-to-business markets risk being considered as unethical. Why is this so and in what circumstances would they be acceptable?

3. It is accepted that the decision-making unit within one organisation can be complex and bear no resemblance to that of a similar organisation. If you were tasked with trying to ensure your communications reached the right person, how would you plan this?

case study 17.1: *John Lewis* Partnership – Christmas advertising

John Lewis, historically, was very ambivalent when it came to advertising. The store's commitment to being 'never knowingly undersold' was introduced by founder John Spedan Lewis in 1925 and has retained its status in the group ever since. Such was the founder's apathy when it came to advertising that in June 1927 he wrote to all buyers and some key executives, asking their views regarding whether the group should give up advertising altogether in favour of an alternative strategy of plastering the group's stores, delivery vans, etc. with a notice that 'we do not advertise: we sell cheap instead'. The *John Lewis Partnership* also retained a preference for the earlier style of informative window displays, advertising the stock rather than the store. It was intended as a total trading philosophy. However, by the late 1990s 'never knowingly undersold' had been allowed to become just a price promise and one increasingly hard to defend against online retailers.

Given that *John Lewis*'s advertising (particularly its Christmas adverts) has since become an institution, it's hard to believe that the company's first Christmas commercial only aired in November 2007. Right from the start, the company was looking to distinguish itself from other retailers and the clever, elegant-looking film promised a more refined retailing experience. The following year, *John Lewis* introduced the first of its gentle cover versions ('From You to Me'). In the intervening period, *John Lewis* has consistently catapulted its cover versions into the Top 40.

Both of the first two campaigns were handled by the agency Lowe London but in 2009 newly-formed agency Adam+Eve won the *John Lewis* account. It used the Christmas advert as a means to ramp up sentimentality by making children the focus. The music was provided by a Guns N' Roses track ('Sweet Child of Mine'), although not in a form likely to appeal to the band's most loyal devotees. It was, however, a popular hit.

Elton John's 'Your Song' got the *John Lewis* treatment in 2010 as the focus shifted to the rituals associated with gift-giving at Christmas. Although most of the advert's emotional impact came from its soundtrack, there was some visual poignancy too, not least in the scene where a boy delivers a stocking to his dog's snow-bound kennel. Incidentally, although the advert was well received by the general public it attracted 145 complaints to the ASA, while a *Facebook* page, 'Stop the *John Lewis* Christmas Ad', received over 1500 'Likes'. Many people posted their outrage and concerns that the advert conveyed the wrong message about the conditions in which it is acceptable to keep a dog.

2011 was the year that *John Lewis* really hit the headlines. The twist in Dougal Wilson's film, showing a young boy's impatience for the big day, really caught the public's imagination and guaranteed that it wouldn't just be the advertising industry who were keen to know what *John Lewis* would be doing in 2012.

The following year, Dougal Wilson was again behind the Christmas commercial, and for the second year running it was a huge hit with the public. It showed a snowman going to great lengths to find the perfect present for someone very special. His journey was accompanied by a haunting version of Frankie Goes to Hollywood's 'The Power of Love', sung by 20-year-old Gabrielle Aplin. The instant verdict provided by *Twitter* was massively favourable when it was first broadcast during *The X Factor*.

By 2013, *John Lewis* had become one of the most talked-about and admired advertisers in the UK. The company planned to spend £7 million on its Christmas campaign (the advert itself cost £1 million). Once

(Continued)

(Continued)

again, expectation was going through the roof as the second Saturday of November approached, and this time it was directly fuelled by the agency as a short teaser campaign was broadcast during *Agatha Christie's Poirot*. The commercial itself was met with almost feverish anticipation by the media, an example of an advert being something of an event. Lily Allen sung Keane's 'Somewhere Only We Know'. Social media suggested it was another triumph. According to *Brand Republic*, 'Some 80% of the tweets praised the ad, describing it as "cute" and "sweet", while 5% of tweeters claimed the ad had reduced them to tears. One tweeter who admitted crying tweeted to say, "I well up at the *John Lewis* advert every time"'.

It is not only for Christmas that *John Lewis* has extended its iconic advertising. In 2010, its 'red dress' advert followed the life of one woman from birth to old age, going through all of life's stages wearing a red dress. The soundtrack was from Fyfe Dangerfield, of the band Guillemots, singing Billy Joel's 'Always a Woman'. This advert clearly had the intended effect, as *John Lewis* experienced a 39.7% leap in sales after its release. In an equally iconic 2012 advert, a split screen shows two parallel lives. It involves a young woman living out her romance in the 1920s while a young man lives out his in the same locations in 2012. It features a cover of an INXS song, 'Never Tear Us Apart', performed by Paloma Faith.

Was the investment made by *John Lewis* in advertising worth it? It would seem that the biggest reaction can be found in the period between 2009 and 2012, coinciding with the switch to sentimental advertising. In the period, total awareness of *John Lewis* TV advertising rose from 8% to 45%. In the same period, 10.5 million people have watched the adverts on *YouTube* alone. Coverage in the news media has an estimated 'advertising value equivalent' of £5 million. In this recession-hit period in retailing, *John Lewis* managed to increase sales from £2.8 billion to £3.6 billion (or just under 30%) while other retailers have foundered. *John Lewis*'s communications have propelled the brand into the nation's hearts, achieved a return on investment of over 500% and made every one of the 70,000 partners better off. For the three financial years to 2012, *John Lewis* bonuses have been generous at 15%, 18% and 14% of annual salary (equivalent to 7 to 10 weeks' pay).

case study questions

1. How important is emotion in the *John Lewis* advertising and what is it seeking to achieve?
2. What has *John Lewis* achieved since first introducing its Christmas adverts in 2007?
3. What part has celebrity played in the success of *John Lewis*'s advertising?

 **further reading**

Ahola, E.-K. (2012) 'Towards an understanding of the role of trade fairs as facilitators of consumer creativity', *Journal of Marketing Communications*, 18 (5): 321–33.

Berger, P.D., Lee, J. and Weinberg, B.D. (2006) 'Optimal cooperative integration strategy for organisations adding a direct online channel', *Journal of the Operational Research Society*, 57 (8): 920–7.

Blythe, J. and Zimmerman, A. (2004) *Business to Business Marketing Management*. London: Thomson Learning.

Ford, D. (2002) *Understanding Business Marketing and Purchasing*, 3rd edn. London: Thomson Learning.

Hutt, M. and Speh, T. (2006) *Business Marketing Management*, 9th edn. Cincinnati, OH: Thomson Learning.

Nink, M. (2013) 'B2Bs win by building relationships, not selling on price', *Gallup Business Journal*, 15 October.

Spencer-Matthews, S. and Lawley, M. (2006) 'Improving customer service: issues in customer contact management', *European Journal of Marketing*, 40 (1–2): 218–32.

REFERENCES

Brennan, R. and Turnbull, P.W. (2001) 'Sophistry, relevance and technology transfer in management research: an IMP perspective', *Journal of Business Research*, 55: 595–602.

De Pelsmacker, P., Geuens, M. and Van den Bergh, J. (2007) *Marketing Communications: A European Perspective*, 3rd edn. London: Prentice Hall.

Gummesson, E. (2002) *Total Relationship Marketing: Rethinking Marketing Management: From 4Ps to 30Rs*, 2nd edn. Oxford: Butterworth-Heinemann.

Nevett, T.R. (1982) *Advertising in Britain: A History*. London: Heinemann.

Sheth, J.N. and Parvatiyar, A. (1995) 'The evolution of relationship marketing', *International Business Review*, 4 (4): 397–418.

Sheth, J.N., Mittal, B. and Newman, B.I. (1999) *Customer Behavior: Consumer Behavior and Beyond*. Cincinnati, OH: Thomson Learning.

For additional materials that support this chapter and your learning, please visit:
study.sagepub.com/egan

ETHICAL MARKETING AND THE REGULATORY ENVIRONMENT

18

LEARNING OBJECTIVES

Having completed this chapter, readers would be expected to:

- understand the problems associated with ethical marketing

- detail those ethical breaches associated with the advertising industry and the arguments for and against them

- understand the relationship between self-regulation and legislation

- comprehend those advertising industry codes relating to misleading or offensive advertising

- be aware of ethical concerns in the sales promotion, public relations, personal selling and direct marketing industries.

INTRODUCTION

The purpose of this chapter is to review the much debated field of marketing ethics and the voluntary or legislative regulation that parallels much of this discussion. Whether justified or not, marketing is perceived in some sectors as 'an untrustworthy profession where duplicitous methods are used to sell customers products they do not particularly need or want' (CIM 2006: 11). Although much of the blame can (and should) be attributed to the management of such companies in general, it is the marketing communications specialists who invariably come in for most criticism.

ETHICAL MARKETING COMMUNICATIONS

Ethics, according to the *Oxford English Dictionary*, is 'a set of moral principles' (OED 2009). A concise definition of the term **ethical marketing** is as a set of moral principles that governs an individual's behaviour. Ethical marketing ethics is concerned with social well-being as related to marketing practice. Unethical conduct, it is suggested, has negative consequences for the contemporary organisation, ranging from adverse publicity and diminished corporate reputation to lower employee moral, customer boycotts and even legal sanctions

(Yeshin 2006). With such a potential downside, it might be logically assumed that marketers would avoid such controversy. In the marketing communications industry, however, ethical decision making is sometimes blinded by the need to attract attention to the brand or by crossing the line of 'good taste' in search of a humorous campaign (see Table 18.1). Simply being in bad taste, however, does not always equate to breaking (in the eyes of regulators) any ethical codes.

Ethical marketing
Concerned with social well-being as it relates to marketing practice.

TABLE 18.1   Britain's most complained about TV adverts in 2012

Advertiser/product	Advertisement	Complaints
Go Compare	Stuart Pearce	1008
Go Compare	Sue Barker	797
Channel 4	Big Fat Gypsy Wedding	373
Kerry Foods	Richmond Ham	371
Paddy Power	Transgendered Ladies	311

Source: The Guardian, 30 April 2013

Some 31,298 complaints were made about 18,990 advertisements in 2012, slightly down on 2011, according to the Advertising Standards Authority (ASA 2013). Complaints about financial services advertising, however, ballooned by 86%. Of the top five listed in Table 18.1, the two most complained about adverts, both for *Go Compare*,[1] were not upheld. Complaints regarding *Channel 4* and *Kerry Foods* were only partially upheld and the *Paddy Power* advertisement, because it aired on *YouTube* in Ireland, was seen to be outside of the ASA's jurisdiction. We shall return to discuss the ASA later in this chapter.

The problem with applying ethical consideration to marketing is that morals change with both time and place. What was unacceptable in parts of Europe 25 years ago may be quite acceptable today. An advertisement involving an unmarried, co-habiting couple (such as in a recent commercial for *BT*) would have been condemned in the 1950s or 1960s, indeed it would probably never have reached the production stage. It is also true that images of women regarded as inoffensive across Europe and North America would be regarded as highly offensive and would be banned in a state such as Dubai.

If morals are constantly shifting, is it marketers' responsibility to stand behind the moral white line or should they be challenging it? Given that creative communicators by definition push the frontiers of our experience, are they not bound to court controversy? Yet the dangers are evident and potentially costly. As eminent practitioner Francis Goodman (Director of the *Maiden Group*) has noted, 'we all have our own moral compasses and know right from wrong in what we are doing. It's up to the relative integrity of the person … (and) it's just as important for companies to engender an ethical way of operating' (Miles 2005).

As Malcolm McDonald notes, 'much of the criticism levelled against marketing is in fact directed against one aspect of it – advertising'[2] (CIM 2006: 11), and there are some who regard the whole advertising field as inherently unethical. Research suggests that advertising is seen to be one of the major factors as to whether a company is regarded as ethical (Snyder 2011). This is clearly not a new charge as the 1962 speech detailed in the Insight below clearly shows.

Advertising has been accused of a number of ethical breaches, most of which focus on its apparent lack of social responsibility (Yeshin 2006). These include accusations that advertising:

---

[1]   Both Stuart Pearce and Sue Barker attacked the iconic Go-compare opera tenor because he was perceived as annoying the public.

[2]   Malcolm McDonald is using a broad definition of advertising that almost certainly incorporates sales promotion, direct and digital marketing.

insight: Advertising to children

The fear of subjecting children to advertising is not new. Around 50 years ago at the 1962 Annual Conference of the National Association of Schoolmasters, Mr Terry Casey argued strongly in the following terms:

Perhaps the most pervasive anti-educational influence is that of modem advertising, for that exists to circumvent the reasoning faculty and weaken judgment. Some of it is puerile, but it can be subtle. Of the former kind are the many variants of the ex parte claim that 'Bloggs makes the best-whatever it is. This must be so because Bloggs says it is so'. Millions of young minds, which we seek to train to think, are constantly bombarded with this sort of nonsense. Not content with bad logic, resort is had to bad manners. Children themselves are recruited as advertising agents, and are urged to make importunate demands on their parents to buy this or that product. 'Don't forget my fruit gums, Mum!' is not even prefaced with the little word 'please'.

Under the rough treatment of the 'blurb' writers, adjectives have lost their vitality and almost their validity because of the excessive use of superlatives. In school we try to enrich vocabularies, but many children are reduced to the verbal poverty of using the prepositional prefix 'super' as an all-purpose adjective denoting approbation, thanks to the baleful influence of the 'Ads'. Psychology, the science which we thought was to be the handmaiden of education, has been prostituted to serve the ends of salesmanship, the panjandrum of the inflated economy. If advertising really is necessary to keep the wheels of industry and commerce turning, is it too much to ask that it be presented in ways which do not offend good taste nor affront good sense? (Nevett 1982)

- promotes materialism
- wastes resources
- creates unwanted needs
- perpetuates stereotyping
- causes people to use harmful products
- promotes unethical brands
- inhibits media coverage
- targets vulnerable groups
- delivers subliminal messages.

Advertising promotes materialism: There is a widespread argument that advertising bombards consumers with images associated with the 'good life'. Advocates of this viewpoint suggest that the acquisition of material possessions leads to contentment and happiness and adds to the general joy of living. Over 30 years ago, a Green Paper (government consultation document) on advertising castigated it for its 'tendency to over-encourage gross materialism and dissatisfaction and its tendency to irresponsibility' (Nevett 1982). Even earlier, George Orwell invoked this image when he described advertising as 'the rattling of a stick inside a swill bucket' (1936). The counter argument is that materialism promotes consumer spending and this is generally good for an economy. For all its faults, it is advertising that has driven prosperity to new heights, not only in so-called 'western' markets but also in emerging economies such as India and China.

Advertising wastes resources: Advertising, it is argued, adds costs to products and services, resulting in consumers having to pay more than they should. It may equally be argued, however, that advertising drives competition and acts as a downward pressure on prices.

Advertising creates unwanted needs: This suggests that advertising, because it exposes the public to products or services that they might not know existed, creates unnecessary wants and needs. While this is an evident truism, it seems to suggest that consumers would be satisfied in their ignorance and ignores their natural curiosity. A further argument against this manipulative affect of advertising can be found in the high rate of failure among new products for which advertisers are presumably looking to create such a need. Many new products are supported by huge advertising and marketing budgets, yet on average only one in ten succeed (Sheehan 2004). On the other hand, some products have become 'must-haves' without the support of any advertising. The global brand *Starbucks* markets itself with little or no advertising at all.

Advertising perpetuates stereotyping: The major charges here are against gender and ethnic stereotyping. For much of the twentieth century, women were portrayed either as home-makers or sex symbols. Advertising for domestic appliances promoted the benefits to the husband of his wife being relieved of the pressures of domestic toil. When it came to looking after the home, the *OXO* housewife always produced a delicious meal for her family,[3] *Flash* cleaned her floors, *Dettol* killed 99% of her household germs and *Fairy Liquid* helped her clean the dishes to the standard required. At the other extreme, women were used as sex symbols to sell everything from cars to cameras. Ethnic stereotyping has also long existed in advertising. In nineteenth and early twentieth century America, advertising for *Cream of Wheat* was accused of perpetuating the stereotype of African Americans as smiling chefs, minstrels, porters and servants, while *Rough-on-Rats* (rat poison) perpetuated the stereotype of Asians as long-haired, oddly attired people (Sivulka 1998). Stereotyping is indeed used extensively by advertisers as short-cuts to meaning (see Chapter 8). To counter the charge, advertisers would suggest that rather than perpetuating stereotypes they were holding a mirror up against the society of the day. That most stereotypes are recognisable at a particular time and in a particular place, and uncomfortable and outlandish in others, suggests some sympathy for this viewpoint.

Advertising causes people to use harmful products: The charge that advertising has promoted potentially harmful products is undoubtedly justified given that, for many decades, quack-medicinal cures, cigarettes and alcohol were the mainstays of the advertising world. The counter argument is that if a product or service can be sold legally then it should be allowed to be advertised. Cigarette manufacturers have frequently made this case. They have also argued that, in a declining market, they are using advertising not to attract new customers but to gain market share from their competitors! This latter argument has few sympathisers outside of that industry.

Advertising promotes unethical brands: The charge here is that advertising promotes brands whose owners have acted unethically in regards to such things as environmental breaches, 'sweatshop' labour, inhumane regimes, etc. While there is every right for individuals to object to or boycott such brands, it is difficult for an industry to take such a position, particularly when some of the world's most illustrious brands have fallen foul of such breaches over the years. The cost to the companies that are accused is not cheap. Boycotts have, for a time, cost *Shell* an estimated 20% of its sales, *Nestlé* $40 million and *Nike* a substantial loss of reputation. In August 2006, a number of UK universities began a boycott of *Coca-Cola* products on campus because of allegations regarding human rights abuses (*Marketing*, 23 August 2006). The ban was expected to severely dent the company's reputation.

Advertising inhibits media coverage: Another perennial charge is that advertisers use their strength to inhibit free speech or distort information flow. The term '**Chinese Wall**'[4] has been used to describe the relationship between the content

Chinese wall
A term relating to the separation between editorial and advertising.

---

[3] Times are changing. The OXO mum has recently been replaced by the OXO dad teaching his son to cook for his new girlfriend.

[4] The term 'Chinese Wall' was first used after the 1929 stock market crash to describe new regulations that provided a separation between brokerage and investment bankers, and only later to the separation between editorial and advertising functions (Sheehan 2004).

function (i.e. news, entertainment) and the advertising function (Sheehan 2004). The 'Chinese Wall' should guard against potential conflicts of interest between advertisers and the media but it is widely suggested that the concept fails to live up to its promise. In a 1972 Green Paper, the UK newspaper industry was accused of 'excessive reliance on advertising' (Nevett 1982), although it fell short of direct allegations of abuse. Evidence of actual and potential abuse comes largely from the USA. In one US study, it was suggested that magazines that relied on cigarette advertising were considerably less likely to publish articles about the health hazards associated with smoking (Belch & Belch 2001). In addition, magazines consider and often consult their advertisers when developing stories and selecting goods and services on which to report (Sheehan 2004). In another US study of 147 daily newspapers, 90% of editors said they had been pressured by advertisers and more than one-third said advertisers had succeeded in influencing news in their papers (Belch & Belch 2001). Benign censorship may also be evidenced. Large FMCG companies such as *Procter & Gamble*, who spend a huge percentage of their budget on television advertising, have been said to avoid airing commercials during any television programme that they regard as being controversial (Sheehan 2004). In 1993, *Chrysler* motor company instituted a pre-notification policy which said that any magazine wishing to run its advertising had to provide summaries of articles with sexual, political or social issue content against which such ads might appear (2004). **Advertorials** are a further problem that exists on both sides of the Atlantic. Advertorials can breach the 'Chinese Wall' between news/entertainment and advertising by blurring the distinction between them, creating potentially higher credibility in the confusion between advertising and editorial comment. While it is impossible to justify the charge of media manipulation, it is difficult to see how the advertising industry itself could stop such, often covert, acts. Even legislation against such practices would be very difficult, if not impossible, to enforce.

Advertising targets vulnerable groups: The targeting of vulnerable groups is a major issue. Advertising to children is a particularly contentious area and in a letter to *The Daily Telegraph* dated 16 June 2013, a group of academics, authors, MPs and charity leaders warned that aggressive advertising aimed at infants as young as 2 was leading to a rise in 'pester power', as children increasingly nag parents for the most expensive brands. The letter criticised the part the 'iniquitous' £12 billion-a-year advertising industry plays in undermining childhood, accusing companies of adopting techniques 'designed to manipulate adult emotions and desires onto children as young as two or three'. The Advertising Standards Authority (2013) insists that it already has strict rules in place to protect children, including ensuring that adverts do not contain inappropriate material and preventing children being exposed to age-restricted material.

Advertising delivers subliminal messages: That some advertising puts messages into our heads, below the level of our consciousness, has been a charge for many years. This idea was popular during the 1950s and 1960s and began to be taken seriously after experiments with cinema goers where messages such as 'drink *Coca-Cola*' and 'eat popcorn' were interspersed throughout the film (Sheehan 2004). Cinema owners reported that sales of soft drinks and popcorn increased because of the messages but this research was later discredited (Sutherland 1993, cited in Sheehan 2004). Claims continue to be made, however, that subliminal advertising works. Undoubtedly, whether you believe that advertising is a highly persuasive force or more a 'gentle nudge' toward a brand (the so-called 'strong' or 'weak' theories of advertising – see Chapter 9), it possibly has *some* effect on a potential consumer. Zapping (fast-forwarding through television commercials) may still trigger memory of the full advert seen at some point before. However, that it delivers messages that make consumers act significantly differently from their 'normal behaviour', as is suggested by the subliminal advertising charge, is highly debatable.

Advertorial
A magazine or newspaper advertisement that is written in the style of an editorial and which may be mistaken as such.

◉ insight: Selling the cigarette habit

The 1920s in the USA was a decade of delight, decadence, disaster, despair and an enormous rise in the number of smokers. According to Sivulka (1998), the 'selling of cigarettes proved advertising's ultimate triumph of the decade'. Many people before this time regarded smoking as an undesirable habit, and employers, such as Henry Ford, deemed smokers unemployable. Others stereotyped smokers as criminals, neurotics and possibly drug addicts.

The First World War and multi-million-dollar advertising campaigns, however, were to help cigarettes gain wider acceptance as both returning soldiers and civilians found smoking cigarettes to be 'more convenient, cheaper and more sanitary than chewing gum'. It was into this market that *R.J. Reynolds* directed its first nationally available brand, *Camel*, which quickly gained dominance as an 'upmarket' smoke. Within a short time, the *American Tobacco Company* had created *Lucky Strike*, described as a richer, sweeter product. *Camel, Lucky Strike* and a third national brand, *Chesterfield*, were to battle for market leadership from 1917 until after the Second World War.

The returning soldiers were, however, all men and *American Tobacco Company's* owner George Washington Hill, urged on by Albert J. Lasker of the *Lord & Thomas* advertising agency, wanted to reach an untapped audience – women – who could potentially double the market! Early on in the decade, women smoking was a controversial issue. Many colleges prohibited women from smoking and they were unable to smoke in railroad diners or in many smoking rooms in stations and on board ships. By the mid-1920s, many of these inequalities had been removed. To further fuel this cultural revolution, cigarette brands turned to advertising. In 1926, the *Newell-Emmett* agency daringly presented a poster showing a romantic, moonlit seaside scene with a man lighting his *Chesterfield* and a woman beside him saying 'Blow some my way'. The words shocked many people, yet the *Chesterfield* campaign continued on. Hill and Laskar quickly sensed an opportunity for the *Lucky Strike* brand and pitched it directly at the female audience. Hill used celebrities from the entertainment world, such as film stars, crooners and jazz musicians to promote *Lucky Strike*. For the first time, women endorsed the product and popularised the image of the fashionable lady who, while she indeed smoked, still appeared stylish and respectable. The company even promoted the brand as an aid to keeping a slender figure ('reach for a *Lucky* instead of a sweet'). *Lucky Strike* campaigns particularly favoured testimonials from operatic sopranos, actresses and society matrons who all attested to the brand's positive effect.

Source: Silvulka (1998) and various

Undoubtedly, ethics is such a pluralistic, complex and situational phenomenon that it is important for advertisers in particular and all marketing communicators in general to establish boundaries of latitude (Yeshin 2006). Charges of impropriety will not go away but attention to ethical principles, such as those set out in industry codes, may go some way to reducing them.

SELF-REGULATION AND LEGISLATION

Many of the charges levelled against advertising would be very difficult to legislate against and thus governments rely more on advertisers keeping to industry codes and norms than on legislation. For many years, it has been this self-regulation that has been the basis for controlling excesses in the marketing communications industry in the UK. The Advertising Standards Authority (ASA) was set up over 50 years ago to police the rules set down in advertising codes and works largely on the basis of voluntary restraint, although industry sanctions can be applied where necessary. Marketers, through their various trade organisations, have argued that self-regulation has advantages. In particular, it is much swifter to change a code than enact legislation. This is particularly important when technology is driving marketing and legislators into new areas of media (see Chapter 8) they have never been before. It is also true that legislation is nearly always 'black and white' when in the everyday practice of marketing it is sometimes the 'grey' areas that are potential cause for concern. The ASA acts as the regulator of choice in the industry. In 2010, online advertising became part of the ASA's remit and *Nike* became the first company to have a campaign banned from a social media site over endorsements made by Wayne Rooney on *Twitter*.

In the past few years, however, this self-regulatory framework has been challenged with formal legislation. Although much of this new law has a basis in European Union directives, according to Stephen Groom (2005: 10), a specialist in marketing and media law, 'it is a myth that UK marketers are constantly being assailed by wave after wave of changing Euro law'. Rather, public pressure, fuelled by well-publicised examples of dubious marketing practices, has encouraged legislators not only to harmonise legislation across boundaries but to strengthen it. In the UK alone, 21 new Acts of Parliament, regulations or amendments affecting marketers were passed in 2006 with a further 10 bills awaiting presentation to Parliament (CIM 2006) and more are added year on year. This is compounded by laws affecting marketing worldwide, particularly those related to data management. In the USA, a law was introduced forbidding companies inside or outside the USA from collecting data about minors (defined as children under 13) if that company is a commercial enterprise, whether or not the data is eventually used for commercial purposes (2006). Meanwhile, European Union legislation forbids personal data from inside the EU being transmitted to the USA because the same level of data protection is not available in that market. The law is also being used by companies globally in disputes among competitors. In the so-called 'razor-wars', *Wilkinson Sword/Schick* forced *Gillette* to withdraw an expensive advertising campaign for its *Turbo* and *Power* razors, featuring David Beckham, because a product claim was found to be false and unsubstantiated in a number of major jurisdictions such as Germany and the USA (2006).

Some legislation might be seen to benefit some (but not all) marketers. The 'Olympic' bill (introduced in the UK in preparation for the Games in 2012) was designed to combat ambush marketing (see Chapter 12), a phrase which was first coined in response to competitive clashes between *Kodak* and *Fuji* during the 1984 Los Angeles Olympic Games (Hoek 1999). This bill made it illegal to combine words such as 'games', medals', 'gold', '2012', 'sponsor' or 'summer' in any form of communication other than by an authorised sponsor. Despite the legislation, a number of companies got around the ban. *Paddy Power* claimed to be the 'official sponsor of the largest athletics event in London this year', with the rider that they were referring to London, France. Meanwhile, *Nike* (whose arch-rival *Adidas* was an official sponsor) launched a global campaign featuring sports people in places around the world called London.

On a more prosaic level, there are a number of areas of general concern to legislators. These fall into two sections – those relating to marketing practices and those product categories where potential abuse would be most damaging:

- marketing practices

  - comparative advertising
  - pricing claims
  - trademarks and passing off
  - product descriptions
  - promotions
  - international law
  - data protection
  - marketing to children and other vulnerable groups

- product categories

  - financial products and services
  - food and drink (including alcohol)
  - medicines
  - cigarettes
  - products associated with children.

Of all the above, it is comparative advertising and pricing claims that most frequently get organisations into trouble (CIM 2006). This is particularly prevalent in retail. Trademark infringement and 'passing off' are also commonplace and considerably difficult to enforce in some international jurisdictions (see Chapter 20). The need for international law is growing, as unscrupulous companies work from 'off-shore' locations and use the cross-border facility of the internet. Data protection is an issue that has grown exponentially alongside the greater use of data by marketers. Legislation has been tightened in past years concerning the collection and use of such data. UK data protection legislation demands consumers 'opt in' if they wish their data to be used rather than having to 'opt out' as in the past (see Chapter 10). Strict rules on what information can be held and what uses it may be put to are also included in the legislation. Marketing to children, as noted previously, is of uppermost concern and strictly policed because the industry, recognising the pressures, opposes any formal legislation in this area.

It is seen to be particularly important to monitor certain product categories. Customers of financial products or services rely heavily on trust and on the availability of accurate information. Food and drink must not be over-hyped and, in the case of alcohol, drinking should not be associated with attractive human characteristics. Medicines should not claim more than can be scientifically proven. Cigarette promotion, now largely constrained in European markets, continues to be monitored.

What is not considered either unethical or illegal (such as passing off) has been called **puffery**. Puffery is a claim made by advertisers, not capable of measurement, that the average consumer would not take seriously (Hoffman 2006). *Carlsberg* – 'probably the best lager in the world', first aired in 1973, falls into this category.[5] Another example is *Gillette* – 'the best a man can get'.

In the general field of advertising in the UK (including much of what has been described in this text as sales promotion and direct and digital marketing), the *Advertising Standards Authority* polices the rules laid down by the advertising code. Other bodies responsible for self-regulation include the *Direct Marketing Association (DMA)* who, through the *Direct Marketing Authority*, maintains the *DMA* Code of Practice and adjudicates on complaints against *DMA* members. Until recently, the *Financial Services Authority (FSA)* enforced a set of rules on the content of financial promotions and had the power to impose financial penalties and sanctions on organisations or individuals. In 2013, it was replaced by the *Financial Conduct Authority*. The *Medicines and Healthcare Regulatory Agency (MHRA)* monitors all medical claims. Complaints about an

Puffery
Claim(s) made by advertisers, not capable of measurement, that the average consumer would not take seriously.

---

[5]   The slogan was ditched by the company in 2011 after 38 years.

advertisement or any other communication concerning medicines can be made to the *MHRA* by a customer, a competitor or a patient. The UK watchdog for the collection and usage of data is the *Information Commissioner's Office* (see Chapter 10).

ADVERTISING STANDARDS

In most developed countries, advertising, whether on television, radio, the internet, newspapers and periodicals, posters or elsewhere, is regulated either by government legislation or by industry self-regulation or a combination of the two. In the UK, the *Advertising Association*, founded in 1924, very early on issued a set of ethical codes it encouraged its members to work to. This was encapsulated in the call to advertisers to seek truth and avoid exaggeration, misleading claims and unfair competitive criticism (Brierley 2002). These codes of practice have developed over the years and are still today administered by the industry in the form of the Advertising Standards Authority (ASA), whose role it is to 'make sure all advertising,[6] wherever it appears, is both honest and decent' (ASA 2013). A short history of the ASA is given in the Insight below.

👁 insight: The Advertising Standards Authority

When commercial TV started in the UK in 1955, advertisements were controlled by legislation. This was the first time that adverts and the claims they made were subject to any form of formal regulation. When commercial radio was launched in 1973, it too was subject to statutory control. In 1961, discussions between industry associations came to the conclusion that it was important that advertisements were welcomed and trusted by consumers in non-broadcast media as well. As a result, the industry (agencies, media and advertisers) came together to form the Committee of Advertising Practice (CAP) and produced the first edition of the British Code of Advertising Practice. As a direct result of the industry's actions, an official report on consumer protection by a parliamentary committee rejected the case for an American-style federal trade commission to regulate advertising by statute. The Molony Committee stated:

> We are satisfied that the wider problem of advertising ought to be, and can be, tackled by effectively applied voluntary controls ... and in particular on the continued quality and independence of the Authority at its pinnacle.

In 1962, CAP established the ASA as the independent adjudicator set up to supervise the working of the new self-regulatory system. In 1995, the ASA's remit was extended to cover adverts in 'non-broadcast electronic media', predominantly in 'paid-for space' such as banner and display ads and paid-for (sponsored) search. By 2007, the internet had become the second most-complained-about medium and the ASA was turning away nearly two-thirds of the complaints it received about online advertising, because they related to claims made on organisations' own websites, which were not subject to ASA regulation. In September 2010, CAP announced the extension of the ASA's online remit to cover advertisers' own marketing communications on their own websites and in other non-paid-for space under their control, such as social networking sites like *Facebook* and *Twitter*. Journalistic and editorial content and material related to causes and ideas – except those that are direct solicitations of donations for fundraising – are excluded from the remit.

Source: ASA (2013)

---

[6] One exception to this in the UK is political advertising. As this does not fall under the remit of the ASA, politicians are excused from the requirement to be honest and truthful.

The ASA Council is the body that adjudicates on formally investigated complaints in the UK. Although industry supported and funded, it has an independent chairman and the majority of its members are from outside the advertising industry. The key rules contained in the codes relate to:

- misleading advertising
- offensive advertising.

Misleading advertising: Advertisements are not allowed to mislead consumers. This means that advertisers must hold evidence for claims that they make about their products or services before the advert appears. As the *ASDA* example in Chapter 9 shows, there is a fine line between deliberately misleading consumers and competitive hyperbole or puffery.

Offensive advertising: Advertisements are 'not allowed to cause serious or widespread offence' (ASA 2013). Special care is taken regarding the portrayal of gender, race, religion, sexuality and disability, but the dividing line between what is offensive and what is not is an ever-shifting one, as what offends one person may be regarded as fair comment by another. The ASA considers various factors before deciding whether an advert is offensive, including the medium in which it appears, the target audience, the particular product or service and, most importantly, what is generally acceptable conduct at the time. This implies that a ban today need not necessarily mean a ban in the future. This has led some observers to suggest that the boundaries of what is acceptable are forever being tested and pushed forward by advertisers.

Other parts of the ASA codes contain specific rules about sales promotion and direct and digital marketing (see Chapters 10 and 13 respectively). There are rules that cover advertisements aimed at children and those for alcohol, health products, beauty products, financial services, employment and business opportunities and gambling. Rules also apply to the types of advertising that can be shown around certain programmes and at certain times (e.g. before the 'nine-o-clock watershed'[7]).

Although the ASA codes are not enshrined in legislation, the organisation can invoke sanctions against those who break the rules. If a complaint is upheld, the advertiser is requested not to use that advertisement again. The ruling is published on the ASA website and media owners will refuse to take this advertising. Misleading advertising or impermissible comparisons can also be referred to the UK *Office of Fair Trading* for legislative action where appropriate.

Just one complaint can trigger an ASA investigation and an advert being banned. At the other end of the scale, just because an advertisement attracts a large number of complaints does not necessarily mean it will be withdrawn. In 2005, *KFC's Zinger Crunch Salad* TV commercial became the most complained about UK advert of all time; not for reasons of sex or nudity, but because the call-centre staff portrayed were singing with their mouths full and complainants felt it encouraged bad table manners (Forbes 2005). As noted previously, no action was deemed necessary against the top two most complained about advertisements in 2012.

Advertising campaigns increasingly cross national boundaries and there is a growing movement to co-ordinate advertising standards, particularly across Europe. The *European Advertising Standards Alliance (EASA)* was formed in 1991, largely to try and circumvent *European Union* legislation by developing a Europe-wide code of practice for self-regulation of the industry. *EASA* currently consists of European (Austria, Belgium, the Czech Republic, Denmark, Finland, France, Germany, Luxembourg, the Netherlands, Portugal, Russia, the Slovak Republic, Slovenia, Spain, Sweden, Switzerland, Turkey and the UK) and four non-European (Canada, New Zealand, South Africa and the USA) self-regulating bodies. The organisation produces a publication with details on both statutory

---

[7]   The nine-o-clock watershed relates to the time that most young people will be in bed and denotes that this is adult viewing time.

and self-regulatory rules governing European advertising, known as the EASA Blue Book. This book also includes statistics on complaints across Europe and advice on the kinds of evidence needed to support advertising claims.

OTHER ISSUES

Although advertising has, to date, dominated ethical and legislative debate, other aspects of marketing communications have given cause for concern. In the promotional field, the use of incentives (discounts, allowances, etc.) to effectively buy shelf space and keep competitive products out has long been criticised but is a continuing practice. The use of high-cost telephone calls to enter promotions and/or the misuse of SMS/texting continue to cause concern (see chapter case study). Fraudulent competitions, particularly from off-shore locations, would also appear to be on the rise.

In the public relations (PR) field, the use of **advertorials** (promotions masquerading as editorials) is among the practices frowned on, but still prevalent, in the industry. There is also the dilemma posed in PR between protecting the company and freedom of information. The *Institute of Public Relations (IPR)* has a code of rules that they ask all members to apply which cover relationships with the media and the public. Fundamental to the code are high levels of integrity, competence, transparency and confidentiality (Baines et al. 2004).

Personal selling is an area of potential conflict. Salespeople are exposed to greater ethical pressures because they are largely unsupervised and evaluated and/or remunerated depending on what they sell. According to a *Sales and Management* magazine survey, 49% of managers say that their salespeople have lied on sales calls and 22% that they had sold customers products they did not need (Marchetti 1997).

In direct and digital marketing, the environmental and personal intrusion arguments against direct mail, email and telemarketing are heightened by discussion regarding the ethical collection and use of personal data. The commercial incentive to collect, merge, warehouse and sell customer information is enormous. This may include the provision of information or services (e.g. online news) in exchange for data. In the past few years, the emphasis of legislation has been on consumers proactively opting in (rather than having to opt out) and in May 2012 the EU e-privacy Directive extended this to the use of cookies (see Chapter 13). Some marketers have seen a benefit from this supposed restriction by promoting authorised data collection strategies under the heading of '**permission marketing**'. The logic is that consumers who proactively allow you access are going to be better prospects.

There is also some suggestion that customers react badly when they believe their personal details are being indiscriminately passed on, although the practice is difficult to control. On the other side of the coin, there is the irony that strictly regulating the collection of personal information could ultimately limit the quality and level of service that businesses can deliver to their customers.

THE ETHICS SOLUTION?

The legal and ethical minefields in the contemporary marketplace suggest that companies must be aware as never before. According to CIM (2006:3), 'companies need to take a more proactive role in order to assist and reinforce self-regulation, to avoid brand damage at best and costly legal proceedings at worst'. There is, therefore, a strong argument in medium-sized and large companies for the appointment of a **marketing compliance officer (MCO)** or, in small companies, an individual with part-time responsibility for this task. As noted earlier, marketers

Marketing compliance officer
An officer responsible for ensuring the organisation complies with laws and regulations.

are perceived as not having the best of reputations and the appointment of a MCO may show that the organisation is 'willing to identify and comply with their legal responsibilities, and communicate their actions to the wider business community, government … self-regulatory boards' (CIM 2006) and the general public.

summary

This chapter reviewed the ethical and regulatory environment in which marketing communications operates. Recognising the perception of marketers as untrustworthy, the chapter queries whether it is the place of marketers to submit to or push the boundaries of moral welfare and concluded that it was an individual marketer's responsibility to judge where to draw the line.

The chapter reviewed the accusations made against advertising of a number of ethical breaches, including that it promotes materialism, wastes resources, creates unwanted needs, perpetuates stereotyping, causes people to use harmful products, promotes unethical brands, inhibits media coverage, targets vulnerable groups and delivers subliminal messages, and the arguments for and against them. It also reviewed the relationship between self-regulation and legislation and considered whether the former, despite its advantages, was losing ground as more and more national and transnational legislation is introduced. It noted that advertising regulators were particularly concerned about certain marketing practices, including comparative advertising, pricing claims, trademarks and passing off, product descriptions, promotions, data protection, international law and marketing to children. They were also concerned with certain product categories, including financial products and services, food and drink, medicines, cigarettes, and products and services associated with children.

The chapter looked at the work of the Advertising Standards Agency and other UK agencies and noted that their focus was on misleading and/or offensive advertising. It also noted that as campaigns increasingly cross national borders so international advertising bodies are colluding in the hope of holding back legislation.

The chapter concluded by looking at ethical issues outside of advertising in the fields of sales promotion, public relations, personal selling and direct marketing.

review questions

1. What do you understand by the term 'ethical marketing'?

2. To what extent might advertising inhibit media coverage?

3. What do you understand by the term 'Chinese Wall'?

4. How would you use an advertorial?

5. To what extent might industry legislators be concerned with marketing practices?

6. What is the difference between 'opt in' and 'opt out' in direct response advertising?

7. Explain the role of the ASA.

8. What constitutes misleading advertising?

9. Define permission marketing.

10. Why might a company appoint a marketing compliance officer?

discussion questions

1. How do you decide if something is ethical or not?

2. Do you believe that advertising actually wastes resources? To what extent might this be true?

3. What are your views on stereotyping in advertising? Under what circumstances might it not be acceptable?

4. Does self-regulation work?

case study 18.1: Bacardi – Advertising ethics

Family-owned *Bacardi* was founded in Cuba in 1862 by Don Facundo *Bacardi* Massó, who produced the company's original 'light white' rum. The legendary *Bacardi* black bat set in a red circle logo was the idea of Don Facundo's wife, inspired by fruit bats living high in the rafters of her husband's first distillery. Bats were considered a symbol of good health, fortune and family unity in both Cuban and Spanish folklore. The bat symbol was a shrewd visual aid with which to recognise *Bacardi* rum. Don Facundo's signature also still features on every *Bacardi* bottle, signifying the timeless high quality of the products.

Bacardi continues to be a family-run business and is now the largest privately held spirits company in the world. Its portfolio includes more than 200 brands and labels, including *Grey Goose* vodka, *Bombay Sapphire* gin, ultra-premium *Eristoff* vodka and *Cazadores* tequila, in addition to its classic *Bacardi* Superior rum. The company also introduced ready-to-drink brand *Bacardi* Breezer, known commonly as an alcopop, in 1993. After huge initial success, it attracted controversy and lost sales when it became associated with under-age binge drinking.

Like other white spirits, the core of *Bacardi*'s market is among 18–34-year-olds, followed by the 35–44 age group (Keynotes 2012). Its advertising messages echo the activities, interests and personalities of young-at-heart drinkers. Its legendary spirit of Latin Quarter parties with music, dancing and fun have always been reflected in both its brand elements and advertising.

Binge-drinking culture

Binge drinking steadily increased in the UK and other countries at the end of the twentieth century and into the twenty-first, becoming a widely reported trend in the media. Binge drinking is referred to as 'a high consumption of alcohol during a single short drinking session' (Keynotes 2012). Figures show UK teenagers, who drank an average of six units of alcohol per week in 1994, were consuming 13 on average by 2007 (ITV 2012). However, binge drinking has been found to occur among most age groups. The 18–24 demographic drinks the most alcoholic units per session, but drink overall less frequently, while over-35s consume the highest total number of units, as they drink regularly at home (Mintel 2010). Binge drinking contributes to serious social problems, with almost 1 million alcohol-related violent crimes and 1.2 million alcohol-related hospital admissions recorded in 2010/2011. Alcohol is a factor in one in three sexual offences, one in three burglaries and one in two street crimes. The issue has become a real concern for the UK government, with various figures calling for a tightening of the regulation of alcohol marketing. The government has launched

(Continued)

(Continued)

its own 'drink aware' campaign to inform people that binge drinking can lead to anti-social, aggressive and violent behaviour.

Based on evidence that points to a link between alcohol advertising and people's awareness and attitude to drinking, the Advertising Standards Authority tightened rules around alcohol advertising in 2005 and again in 2009. The now stringent rules apply across all media, are mandatory and seek to protect young people. They stipulate that marketing communications must be socially responsible:

> Alcohol ads must not be directed at people under 18 years or contain anything that is likely to appeal to them by reflecting youth culture or by linking alcohol with irresponsible behaviour, social success or sexual attractiveness. The TV and radio advertising rules contain strict controls about the placement and content of alcohol advertising which are banned from appearing in and around programmes commissioned for or principally targeted at audiences below the age of 18, as well as programmes likely to appeal particularly to audiences below the age of 18.

Bacardi has continually committed to promoting responsible drinking since the early 1930s. The company pioneered programmes leading awareness against excess consumption and drink driving and its 1970s '*Bacardi* mixes with everything. Except driving' advertisement was widely acclaimed for its social responsibility. Successful versions of this campaign continue today under the 'Drink responsibly' slogan. The brand has recruited sports stars including Michael Schumacher and Rafael Nadal to front its *Champions Drink Responsibly* campaign. Former bad-boy spokesman Vinnie Jones was dropped in 2003 after being convicted of a drink-fuelled assault on a plane (Hastings 2003).

Age restrictions apply to *Bacardi*'s website, with those under 18 being redirected to a charity that works to prevent underage drinking and drink driving. The company's commitment to corporate social responsibility extends to other fields, including encouraging employee volunteering schemes, cutting its water usage by 50% and reducing its greenhouse gas emissions by 33% in six years. It is the only major spirits company to achieve certification in the top three international environmental and operating standards classifications.

Recent *Bacardi* advertisements continue to project an image that life is better shared with others. Its 'Island' advert shows friends coming together to build a '*Bacardi* Island' where they enjoy *Bacardi* drinks and embrace the rum's Latin spirit and dance all night. The party goers are all in their early to mid-20s, with no direct appeals targeting underage drinkers.

© Kim Roberts 2014

Case study questions

1. Why was Vinnie Jones used as the brand's ambassador?
2. For what reason were the Advertising Standards re-evaluated in 2009 and what effect might this have had on *Bacardi*'s advertising?
3. Why are *Bacardi* involved in a corporate social responsibility programme?
4. What message is *Bacardi*'s more current advertising seeking to communicate?

References

Advertising Standards Authority: www.asa.org.uk/

Bacardi: www.bacardilimited.com

European Association of Communications (2004) Bacardi-Martini, Welcome to the Latin Quarter, Agencies Finalist; World Advertising Research Centre.

Hastings C (2003) Vinnie Jones 'to forfeit *Bacardi* deal' over air rage. *The Telegraph* at: www.telegraph.co.uk/news/uknews/1449408/Vinnie-Jones-to-forfeit-Bacardi-deal-over-air-rage.html

ITV (2012) Teen drinking cases soar: 'binge-drinking gene found', ITV News at: www.itv.com/news/story/2012-12-04/gene-link-to-binge-drinking/

Keynotes (2012) Spirits & Liqueurs Market Report

Mintel (2012) White Spirits and RTDS Report, UK, March 2012

further reading

Beckett, R. (2003) 'Communication ethics: principle and practice', *Journal of Communication Management*, 8 (1): 41–52.

Capozzi, L. (2005) 'Corporate reputation: our role in sustaining and building a valuable asset', *Journal of Advertising Research*, 45 (3): 290–3.

Dawkins, J. (2004) 'Corporate responsibility: the communication challenge', *Journal of Communication Management*, 9 (2): 108–19.

Morsing, M. (2006) 'Corporate moral branding: limits to aligning employees', *Corporate Communications: An International Journal*, 11 (2): 97–108.

Payne, D. and Pressley, M. (2013) 'A transcendent code of ethics for marketing professionals', *International Journal of Law and Management*, 55 (1): 55–73.

Schroeder, J.E. and Borgerson, J.L. (2005) 'An ethics of representation for international marketing communication', *International Marketing Review*, 22 (5): 578–600.

REFERENCES

Advertising Standards Authority (ASA) (2013) 'Mission and performance', at: www.asa.org.uk/About-ASA/Our-mission.aspx (accessed 24 August 2013).

Baines, P., Egan, J. and Jefkins, F. (2004) *Public Relations: Contemporary Issues and Techniques*, 9th edn. Oxford: Elsevier Butterworth-Heinemann.

Belch, G. and Belch, M. (2001) *Advertising and Promotion: An Integrated Marketing Communications Perspective*. London: McGraw-Hill.

Brierley, S. (2002) *The Advertising Handbook*, 2nd edn. London: Routledge.

CIM (2006) *No Marketer is an Island: Marketing and the Law*, Hot Marketing Series, Issue 9, January. Cookham, Berkshire: Chartered Institute of Marketing.

Forbes, C. (2005) 'Be careful what you promise', *The Marketer*, 17 October.

Groom, S. (2005) 'You've never had it so good', *The Marketer*, 17 October, p. 10.

Hoek, J. (1999) 'Sponsorship', in P.J. Kitchen (ed.), *Marketing Communications: Principles and Practice*. London: Thomson, pp. 361–80.

Hoffman, D.A. (2006) 'The best puffery article ever', *Iowa Law Review*, 91 (5).

Marchetti, M. (1997) 'Whatever it takes', *Sales & Marketing Management*, 149 (13): 29–38.

Miles, L. (2005) 'Playing the game', *The Marketer*, 17 October.

Nevett, T.R. (1982) *Advertising in Britain: A History*. London: Heinemann.

Orwell, G. (1936) *Keep the Aspidistra Flying*. London: Harvest Books.

Oxford English Dictionary (OED) (2009) *The Concise Oxford Dictionary of Current English*. Oxford: Oxford University Press.

Sheehan, K. (2004) *Controversies in Contemporary Advertising*. Thousand Oaks, CA: Sage.

Sivulka, J. (1998) *Soap, Sex and Cigarettes: A Cultural History of American Advertising*. Belmont, CA: Thomson Learning.

Snyder, W. (2011) 'Making a case for enhanced advertising ethics: how a new way of thinking about advertising ethics may build consumer trust', *Journal of Advertising Research*, 51 (3). 477–83.

Sutherland, M. (1993) *Advertising and the Mind of the Consumer*. St Leonards, NSW, Australia: Allen & Unwin.

Yeshin, T. (2006) *Advertising*. London: Thomson.

USEFUL WEBSITE

For an up-to-date list of companies threatened with boycotts, go to: www.ethicalconsumer.org/boycotts

For additional materials that support this chapter and your learning, please visit:
study.sagepub.com/egan

THE COMMUNICATIONS INDUSTRY

19

LEARNING OBJECTIVES

Having completed this chapter readers would be expected to:

- understand the history and development of the modern communications industry

- comprehend the changes in structure and remuneration systems and what brought them about

- understand the basic functions associated with agencies and specialist independent and dependent agencies

- be aware of the factors involved in agency selection.

INTRODUCTION

The communications industry might be described as a simple network based on a tripartite relationship where the major players are the client, the agency and the media. Traditionally, the agency has been seen as an intermediary, first as the agent of the media and then on behalf of the client. The agency/client relationship is said to be 'a dynamic decision-making process in which the participants identify, evaluate and choose appropriate communication strategies and alternatives' (Yeshin 2006). This creative tension that develops is seen to drive the industry forward but not without its problems. The fact that (in modern times) agencies, while working for clients, were being paid by the media, has also complicated these relationships.

The communications industry today is a complex legacy of developments that continued throughout the eighteenth, nineteenth, twentieth and into the twenty-first centuries. In the beginning, it was the rapid expansion of both newspapers and magazines (seeking clients) and potential advertisers (seeking advertising space) that was the stimulus for this growth. As the numbers grew, relationships between both sides became complicated and a need developed in the industry to simplify arrangements. What clients required was someone who could advise on the suitability of a particular medium, write copy if required and simplify accounting (Nevett 1982). What newspaper and

FIGURE 19.1   The Tripartite Nature of the Marketing communications industry

magazine proprietors needed was a more efficient way of dealing with scores of individual advertisers. As such, these proprietors developed a preference for dealing with specialists who could both offer a professional approach to the placement of advertising and deal with the individual accounts. Advertising agencies, therefore, were the medium that developed to satisfy the needs of both sides of industry. It was the creation of this three-way relationship that first dominated and still influences the communications industry today.

HISTORICAL DEVELOPMENT

As noted in Chapter 1, the earliest agency for which records exist is that of William Taylor who described himself as agent to 'County Printers, Booksellers etc.' and first advertised his services in the *Maidstone Journal* of 1786. Early agents worked not on behalf of the client but for newspaper owners, both collecting news and selling advertising space on their behalf. By 1800, this was beginning to change and in that year James White founded an agency which was not just involved in placing advertisements but in writing copy too. In 1820, the *Edinburgh Review* reported that at the offices of *Newton & Co.* and *Barker & Co.*, two principal London agents, 'advertisements are received for all county papers without increased charge to the advertiser, the commission of the agent being paid by the newspaper proprietor'.

This system of remuneration, based on commissions from media owners, was eventually to become widespread and to dictate the structure of the industry well into the twentieth century.

By the 1830s and 1840s, agents were producing lists in the form of reference books which included information on newspapers such as the day and place of publication, political stance and, in some cases, average circulation. In addition to all the UK newspapers, some overseas media were included in these lists. These lists were a direct forerunner of modern industry publications such as *BRAD (British Rates and Data)*, which categorises and lists all UK media together with standard rates and technical data.

As the industry entered the twentieth century, competition became intense. While a few decades before it was not unusual to find rival chocolate or soap manufacturers using the same agent, clients were now complaining if there was any sign of conflicting interest. This caused some clients to leave an agency if they took on a rival competitor, while others forced agencies to resign if they had conflicting accounts (Brierley 2005). By 1906, there were 339 advertising agencies in London representing newspapers based in the capital – 22 who specialised in provincial publications and 79 who concentrated on overseas media. Although in the UK London was the main centre for advertising, regional centres in Manchester, Edinburgh and Bristol also began to grow at this time. Commission varied widely with up to 30% in the case of some 'weak and desperate publications' (Nevett 1982). Some **media brokers** who did not create copy for their clients undercut the main agencies by taking as little as 1% (Brierley 2005).

By the 1920s, mainstream advertising agencies were more clearly defined as intermediaries who managed, created and bought advertising space on behalf of their clients (Brierley 2005). 'Full service' agencies also offered sales support, creative input, research and sometimes product development in addition to purchasing media space. They were, however, continuing to be undercut by media brokers who did not carry the high overheads of the 'full service' agencies, and as such there was growing pressure from larger agencies to 'professionalise the industry' to the exclusion of the price-cutters. In 1907, the *Incorporated Society of Advertising Agents* was formed but it was short-lived, breaking up after continuous disagreements over rebating. In 1917, the *Association of British Advertising Agents*[1] *(ABAA)* was formed and in 1921 the London *Times* newspaper signed an agreement with the 60 members of the ABAA, restricting commission payments only to recognised agents affiliated to the Association. In 1932, the *National Publishers Association* produced an accord that formally banned rate cutting. The *NPA* agreement was effectively a cartel arrangement between the full service agencies and the media owners that squeezed out any other form of business such as media brokerage or consultancy. Although initially applying only to new agencies, it became the accepted norm and from then on dominated advertising remuneration for most of the rest of the twentieth century (Brierley 2005). Under the agreement, agencies also had to abide by the *IPA* (as successor to the *ABAA*) code of practice, reinforcing the *IPA*'s role as regulator and effectively as a 'closed shop' on industry knowledge (Ibid).

During and immediately after the Second World War, the main problem facing agencies related to the management of supply rather than to stimulating demand. Indeed, given the restrictions on European economies, advertising which encouraged consumption was something which was actively discouraged (Nevett 1982). By the mid-1950s, however, production and consumption were growing fast and advertisers had the new medium of television. Commission rates were also rising. Prior to the 1930s, many commission rates were in single figures but by the 1940s these had stabilised at 10% due to the *NPA* recognition system. On the introduction of commercial television to the UK, station owners offered a 15% commission to help cover the supposed additional costs of TV advertising (Ibid). Because of this, newspapers also raised their commission rates to 15%.

Changes were, however, in the air. American agencies had begun to establish offices in London during the 1950s and by 1960 there were 36 US agencies in London with 281 offices nationwide, bringing new techniques and a wider range of services to the market (Nevett 1982). When US advertisers wanted to use commercials (commercial advertisements) from their home or other markets and only wanted to buy 'space' and 'time' on the Independent Television (ITV) network, they started to use media independents who, although they received the full 15% commission, 'illegally' rebated 10–12% to the client supposedly for 'creative costs' (Brierley 2005). Many of these first media independents operated under 'flags of convenience' for small 'full service' agencies who in turn got a cut of the commission (2005).

By the 1970s, the recognition system was beginning to break down. The previous decade had shown a decline in business caused by economic uncertainty and unemployment and this subsequently increased competition between agencies. In 1976, the UK government introduced the Restrictive Practices Act and in 1978 the *Office for Fair Trading (OFT)*, set up under the act, ruled that fixed commission

Media broker
An intermediary who purchases media space (only) without the overheads of a full agency.

Full service agency
An agency that covers a full range of disciplines, including copy writing, design and media purchase.

Rebating
Giving the client part or all of the commission paid by media owners.

Commercial
A television or radio advertisement (also known as an advert or ad).

Media independent
An independent media broker.

---

[1]   This later became the *Institute of Incorporated Practitioners in Advertising* and is now the *Institute of Practitioners in Advertising (IPA)*.

was anti-competitive. In 1979, the *NPA* and the *Newspaper Society* dropped agency recognition. Agencies were forced to negotiate their commission rate individually with media owners and were under pressure from advertisers to rebate some part of this remuneration to them. Agencies that only handled the placement of advertising (media independents) began to openly appear again. Separate media buying was popular with many advertisers as it allowed them to dip in and out of different agencies and pick and choose the services they required. While in 1960 all media buying was controlled by 'full service' agencies, by 1980 there were 30 media independents. During the period 1986–1991, their share of revenue was to grow by 184%. By 2000, 90% of all media expenditure was handled by separate media agencies (Brierley 2005).

The response of the 'full service' agencies to the changing marketplace was to begin hiving off media departments into separate entities in order to compete. By the last decade of the twentieth century, it was established practice to have a creative advertising agency, a separate media planning and buying agency and another set of agencies to run direct marketing, sales promotion and public relations campaigns. Agency response to the growth of 'below-the-line' competition was two-fold. First, they tried to undermine client decision making by suggesting that compared with advertising other marcom tools were ineffective. Sales promotion was a particular target, with advertisers suggesting that it eroded brand values (Brierley 2005). Second, when it became obvious that this ploy was failing, large established agencies began to appropriate existing 'below-the-line' agencies or to create in-house such agencies of their own.

Media dependent
A media broker that is part of a larger agency group.

At the turn of the century, a number of substantial mergers took place and new '**media dependents**' (controlled by parent company agencies) were created such as *WPP's Mindshare*, launched in 1997 (Brierley 2005). By 1999, 70% of media buying companies were 'media dependents'. Reflecting the move toward integrated marketing communications (IMC), most advertising agencies were now subsidiaries of groups, usually operating on an international basis and also incorporating specialists in the fields of direct marketing, sales promotion, public relations, sponsorship, etc. (Yeshin 2006).

The history of the growth of the advertising industry today has, therefore, left a complex legacy. Many clients choose not to spend their money through full service agencies. Not only have functions been hived off but there is a growing number of independent agencies (or group dependents) who operate in narrow fields such as financial services, pharmaceuticals, tourism and business-to-business. Clients, as a result, may choose two or more agencies to obtain the skills and creativity they need to achieve their objectives.

It is also noticeable that client/agency relationships are not as longstanding as they once were. Long-term relationships (such as the 80+ year association between

insight: Agency merry-go-round

RHM Foods announced in January 2006 that it was reviewing *Mr Kipling* cakes' £3 million advertising account. The present incumbent *WCRS* won it from *Saatchi & Saatchi* and was responsible for handling the brand's £5 million re-launch in January 2005. *Saatchi & Saatchi* lost the account after it created a controversial TV advertisement depicting a woman giving birth during a nativity play. Following *RHM*'s purchase by *Premier Foods*, it was all change again. In 2012, the *Premier Foods* account was jointly held by *JWT* and *McCann*.

J. Walter Thompson (JWT) and *Kelloggs*) are now the exception rather than the norm, with fewer than 25% of major client accounts staying with agencies for 10 years or more (Brierley 2005).

AGENCY FEATURES

Given their history, agencies have grown up in a variety of types and structures that defy rigid definition. However, a 'typical' agency may have (or may have access to) the following functions:

- account management
- account planning
- creative design
- media management
- production.

The **account management** function is responsible for liaison with the client and ensuring that their needs are being fulfilled by the agency. Account managers are also charged with ensuring that timetables are kept and that all work is completed within budget.

Account planning is responsible for the changing requirements of the client and advising on the strategic direction of a campaign through pre- and post-campaign research. Account planners are expected to provide insight into and understanding of the consumer and their relationship with the brand and guide the strategic direction of communications, liaising closely with the creative team (Yeshin 2006).

To call the creative input of an agency a function may appear oxymoronic but as part of a process the creative team has to deliver. **Creatives** often work in teams and their role is to interpret the creative brief (see Chapter 8) and translate this into effective messages that suit the medium through which they will pass.

Media management involves getting the messages created into the appropriate media at a time and cost that fulfils the objective of the campaign and within the budget allocated. This 'function' has, more recently, been largely separated from agency management, with the creation of 'media independents' and 'media dependents'.

Production departments ensure that the creative elements are translated into the right format for the chosen media. In this area, **progress** (or **traffic**) **managers** ensure that the various stages of production are completed on time.

Although the above represents a typical structure, changes are happening very fast. As discussed in Chapter 15, client organisations are looking to set the communications agenda rather than relying on formally powerful agencies to set it for them. The move to more digitally driven advertising, social media and the merging of television, computing and mobile platforms has been significant in this regard. In 2011, internet advertising rose by 14.4% compared with a 2.7% rise in advertising overall (Internet Advertising Bureau UK) and advertising across all digital channels was forecast to reach one-third of all advertising spend in 2012 (Zenithoptimedia). This, coupled with the trend toward **integrated marketing communications**, has been the principal driver towards change in the industry. Current industry structures are reflected in these changed requirements. At one end of the scale, agency groupings (of dependents) are currently in vogue while at the other, small specialist service (digital media specialists, creative boutiques, etc.) agencies have developed in order to service the specialist needs of the industry.

Another dramatic change has been in the way agencies are remunerated. This has been a major cause of friction between agencies and clients for years, particularly as brand owners have sought to get the upper hand over the once-powerful agency cartels. As the power of advertising has declined relative to other marketing communications tools, so brand owners have demanded rebates and set standards to which agencies have been obliged to accede. As noted previously, commission was the backbone of agency power during most of the twentieth century. Today, a mixture of different methods has largely replaced the straightforward 10% or 15% commission payment. While in 1965 media commission accounted for 76% of agency income (the rest was mainly in additional **below-the-line** services), by 2000 the majority of the top 116 UK 'blue chip' companies were paying agencies on a fee basis or by results (PBR) (Brierley 2005). By 2010, fees of various types accounted for 90% of all creative agency agreements (IPA 2011). Contemporary reimbursement options reflect this diversity and now include:

- retainer fee
- project fee
- fee based on time spent
- scale fee and bonus
- consultancy and concept fee
- licensing fee
- output or 'off-the-shelf' rate fee
- commission fee
- performance-based fee or payment by results (PBR).

Retainer fee
A fixed amount of money that a client agrees to pay, in advance, to secure the services of an agency or specialist.

Negotiated commission maintains some connection to the original system and may involve rebating, sometimes on a sliding scale. Fee payment is currently the most popular form of remuneration and may be based on a quotation for individual projects or more complex arrangements. Occasionally, companies may pay an agency a **retainer fee** to enable them to maintain contact and ensure effective continuity. **Time-based fees** are an established form of recompense in public relations agencies but are also more generally used on special projects. **Cost-based fees** rely on an agreed mark-up on inputs such as media. **Performance-based compensation** or **payment by results (PBR)** is based on targets set against a particular campaign (see chapter case study). The majority of agency–client fee agreements have a minimum income guarantee and most retainer/resources fees also have a PBR element.

Time-based fee
A fee based on the amount of time spent on the project.

Cost-based fee
A fee that relies on an agreed mark-up on the campaign inputs (e.g. advertising).

Another major consequence of changes in industry structures and IMC is that organisations 'mix and match' agencies like never before. It is not unheard of for a company to employ separate creative advertising, media purchasing, promotion, public relations and sponsorship agencies. The key is co-ordination and this is often stipulated in the brief given to agencies.

Performance-based compensation or payment by results (PBR)
A fee based on measurable targets set for a particular campaign.

CHOOSING AN AGENCY

Apart from the specialisations noted above, agency structures are rarely that different from each other, with any significant innovations quickly being copied by competitors (Brierley 2005). Larger agencies, however, generally have extensive networks in the UK and abroad and will frequently incorporate more extensive research facilities than small or medium-sized agencies.

When initially choosing an agency or when a change of agency is considered, a starting point is whether potential organisations offer the services that the client requires. When selecting (or re-selecting) agencies to **pitch** for an organisation's communications business, many are automatically eliminated because of a requirement for:

Pitch
A presentation by an agency to the client organisation.

- sector experience and specialisation (e.g. pharmaceutical, financial)
- a particular agency type (e.g. advertising, promotions)
- particular facilities (e.g. European network, media buying)
- a lack of client conflict (i.e. no existing competitive clients).

Where an existing agency already has the company and/or brand brief, any consideration to change agency may be due to changed needs (e.g. technological media expertise required, full service agency preferred), although it may also be a result of a breakdown in the client/agency relationship. In this event, joint industry guidelines (ISBA 2006b) advise that the client should be clear that it would be in the best interests of the brand or business organisation, and enhance shareholder value, to change agency, and that efforts should have been made to re-establish a good working relationship. It is evidently not in the interests of industry bodies to encourage agency turnover.

The initial search may involve consulting trade bodies (e.g. *DMA, IPA, ISBA, MCCA* and *PRCA*), industry literature, agency websites and other sources (e.g. recommendation) and could include a pre-pitch **credentials presentation** from candidate agencies where they present to the client examples of past work. Some companies issue a questionnaire to agencies they are considering to assist in shortlisting and to try to ensure that the criteria they establish are met by potential contenders (Yeshin 2006). Even more influential than information from trade bodies or consultancies is reputation, which plays a big part in determining who appears on the **pitch list**.

The next step is the selection of the candidate shortlist and the issue of a **brief** which should include a clear indication of the brand and company marketing/communications budget (ISBA 2006b). The creation of a brief is seen as an important part in the selection process that potentially leads to better, more effective and measurable work, and a saving in time and money, making remuneration fairer (ISBA 2006a). Industry guidelines strongly suggest that in writing an agency brief companies should think not only 'Where am I now?' but 'Where do I need to get to?' (ISBA 2006a). Given the costs involved in preparing a pitch, some clients will pay agencies a fee for the expense, time and effort involved in making the presentation.

Agency responses to a brief may take many formats so it is important to bear in mind key pieces of information when preparing the brief. These fall into three main areas (ISBA 2006a):

- budgets: clearly stated and, where necessary, broken down into constituent parts in the brief or, alternatively, a suggested recommended budget to achieve a given set of objectives
- timings: what are the key delivery dates?
- other considerations: are there existing creative ideas to work with? Are there any legal constraints? Are there any brand or corporate guidelines which may affect an agency's work? Are other agencies involved in complementary promotions (for example, as part of an integrated marketing communications plan)?

Industry norms suggest that up to three agencies should be involved in the final pitch, or four if the existing agency is involved (ISBA 2006b). Organisations are encouraged to establish some form of objective assessment against which to measure a pitch presentation (Yeshin 2006). The client organisation should make clear in the brief the criteria on which the presentation will be judged, the length of time allowed for the presentation, the facilities available and the location (ISBA 2006b).

Following the decision to appoint a particular agency, joint industry guidelines give pointers to implementing an agreement and managing the relationship (ISBA 2006b):

Credentials presentation
Where an agency presents its reasons why it is a good fit with the organisation's campaign strategy.

Pitch list
Those agencies invited to pitch for the organisation's/brand's communications account(s).

Brief
A document produced by an organisation, detailing their needs, and used by professionals operating within the communications field to produce various deliverables.

- Give the losing agencies the courtesy of a full 'lost order' meeting.
- Ensure that losing agencies return all confidential material and information provided for the pitch and that the client returns details of the losing agencies' presentations.
- Honour the incumbent agency's contract in relation to the agreed notice period and payment of outstanding invoices.
- Ensure the incumbent agency fully cooperates in a hand-over to the new agency.
- Ensure that a new contract is signed with the successful agency covering all aspects of the agreement up to and including termination.
- Arrange for mutual induction meetings between client and agency personnel.
- Agree realistic objectives for brand and corporate communications, put measures of effectiveness in place and report key metrics at CEO/main board level.
- Carry out active management reviews and invest in the relationship through regular brainstorming sessions and 'away days'.

The client/agency relationship will always be complex, sometimes fraught and occasionally highly rewarding. Managing the relationship on both sides of the partnership is key to minimising the pain and maximising the gain from the experience.

 summary

This chapter looked at the modern communications industry from the perspective of its historical development and the changing needs of the twenty-first century. The industry today, it was suggested, is a complex legacy of developments that took place throughout the previous three centuries. Principal among these was the industry remuneration system that ultimately became standardised by agreement between the agencies and media owners and dominated the industry through to the 1970s. The demise of the commission system heralded change from 'full service' agencies to a more diverse system of independent and dependent agencies working within networks. Typical agency services were discussed, including account management, account planning, creative design, media management and the production function, and contemporary remuneration methodologies were highlighted. The chapter concluded by reviewing the way clients employ agencies with particular emphasis on the importance of the brief.

 **review questions**

1. What functions would you expect an agency to perform?

2. What is the role of media management?

3. Explain the function of account management.

4. What has been the principal driver to change in the traditional agency structure and why is this so?

5. How would you describe the function of a retainer fee?

6. How might companies shortlist an agency?

7. List the main agency reimbursement options.

8. Define 'PBR'.

9. What makes up the tripartite nature of the communications industry?

10. Explain what is meant by a full service agency.

discussion questions

1. If you needed to recruit a new advertising agency, how would you go about it and why? On what basis would you make your decision on who to use?

2. Where do you believe problems might occur between an agency and a company in the development of an advertising campaign?

3. You have a new product to launch. It needs to be kept secret from the competition but you are using an outside agency to do the above-the-line work. How much do you tell them and why? What might the consequences be of your decision?

case study 19.1: The changing face of the communications industry

In August 2013, *Ofcom* (the independent regulator and competition authority for the UK communications industries) produced a report looking at the possible evolution in the market for the advertising industry, given the likely developments in technology, consumer behaviour and service delivery by broadcasters and others.

The report, in line with many such reports over the last few years, suggested that technology will ensure dramatic change in the marketing communications market. The proliferation of broadband, smart mobile devices, cheap tablets, cloud-based services and social media will have a profound impact on consumer behaviour, business models and content services. As a result, there will be a chaotic but exciting period of innovation in technology and services which will have a disruptive impact on the marketing communications industry.

This presents a problem for *Ofcom* as well. How will it maintain its role while the communications world changes around it? The existing rules attempt to separate programme content from advertising. This is becoming more and more difficult as the brand message becomes part of the entertainment. Maintaining existing frameworks will be a struggle as the prolific innovation in advertising formats, together with the highly fragmented nature of their implementation, is bound to have a cumulative impact on consumers' attitudes. As a result, *Ofcom* will face increasingly difficult choices about the appropriate scope of regulation, how to implement regulatory change and how to balance consumer protection, innovation, investment in content and economic growth.

This disruption in the industry will particularly affect television spot advertising and its relative importance in the industry will diminish. Brands and agencies are already seeking new ways to engage consumers either directly or in association with producers and broadcasters. These new channels already include direct investment in television programmes, complementary advertising (on so-called 'second screens') and videos distributed via *YouTube*, *Google* Video, Daily Motion and others.

(Continued)

(Continued)

For the communications industry, it will require new capabilities that sometimes sit uneasily alongside agencies' core businesses. Traditional advertising agencies used to be the ones advising clients where the best mediums were to place advertising. Now, a host of technology firms, like *Adobe* and *Google*, offer online analytical services and software to help advertisers achieve success. Many online adverts are now bought and sold automatically with 'real-time bidding'. Advertisers can specify which sort of audience they want to reach and how much they want to pay, and use advertising 'exchanges' to buy space on websites that fit their requirements. *Procter & Gamble*, for example, now operate their own trading desks. All of this can be done in a fraction of a second.

How consumers utilise the various forms of technology available is what ultimately will affect the future of the industry. People seek immediate gratification and engagement, but also need to trust the brands they purchase. Marketers must learn to adapt to this and take into account the changing world of the target consumer.

Case study questions

1. What are the consequences of 'second-screen' behaviour to traditional television advertising?
2. Can the industry maintain its position of influence in the changing environment suggested?
3. What forms of advertising are most likely to be effective in the new media age?

 **further reading**

Daniels, C. (2006) 'Drawing the line', *Marketing Magazine*, 111 (25): 11–13.
De Gregorio, F., Cheong, Y. and Kim, K. (2012) 'Intraorganizational conflict within advertising agencies', *Journal of Advertising*, 41 (3): 19–34.
Hill, R.M. (2006) 'Advertiser satisfaction with advertising agency creative product', *European Journal of Marketing*, 40 (11–12): 1254–70.
Thompson, B. (2006) 'Do the right thing? Not with a rival's inside info', *Advertising Age*, 77 (29): 4.
Weiner, R. (2006) 'Mind your p's and q's', *Public Relations Tactics*, 13 (7): 7.

REFERENCES

Brierley, S. (2005) *The Advertising Handbook*, 2nd edn. London: Routledge.
Incorporated Society of British Advertisers (ISBA) (2006a) 'The client brief', Joint Industry Guidelines. London: ISBA.
Incorporated Society of British Advertisers (ISBA) (2006b) 'The guide', Joint Industry Guidelines. London: ISBA.
Institute of Practitioners in Advertising (IPA) (2011) *Agency Remuneration: A Best Practice Guide on How to Pay Agencies*, 2nd edn. London: IPA, ISBA, MAA, PRCA.
Nevett, T.R. (1982) *Advertising in Britain: A History*. London: Heinemann.
Simms, J. (2004) 'You're not paranoid, they do hate you', *Marketing*, 19 May: 32–4.

USEFUL WEBSITES

Visit the *BRAD* website at: www1.bradinsight.com/
For more on the history of advertising, go to: www.hatads.org.uk/

For additional materials that support this chapter and your learning, please visit:
study.sagepub.com/egan

GLOBAL MARKETING COMMUNICATIONS

20

LEARNING OBJECTIVES

Having completed this chapter readers would be expected to:

- understand the features and communications patterns of international, multinational, global and transnational companies

- be aware of the strategic arguments regarding standardisation and local adaptation

- comprehend the effect that international branding has had on the communications industry.

INTRODUCTION

There are many drivers to a company deciding to venture abroad. Although international trade has existed since the earliest times, it was the Industrial Revolution that created the surpluses that could then be exported to other sovereign countries and dependencies. Indeed, many British brands became famous and financially successful because they were shipped to all parts of the British Empire and beyond. *Guinness* is still promoted in Africa for its strength, a feature born out of its ability to be shipped long distances and still remain drinkable. It was not only one-way traffic. *Quaker Oats* arrived in Britain from the USA in 1894 and *Wrigley's* and *Palmolive* just after the First World War. Since the Second World War, there has been an increasing propensity towards the internationalisation of brands, frequently of North American and European origin, but with a growing number from countries in the Far East.

A common reason for developing overseas markets in the second half of the twentieth century was the saturation of domestic markets and the need to venture abroad or stagnate. A good example of this is *McDonald's* who (through subsidiaries and franchises) first moved into Western Europe and then, as that market too matured, to Asia and Eastern Europe.

In marketing communications terms, international markets provide a significant challenge to the company, ranging from the level of involvement to the development of meaningful brand messages. The skill of international communications management is defining what is optimal for the brand.

INTERNATIONAL AND GLOBAL COMPANIES

There are many ways of describing an organisation's level of international involvement from nil (the wholly domestic) to those organisations that are so globally orientated that their centres of control are no longer necessarily in their country of origin (e.g. *IBM*). Whatever typology is used, there are subtle differences in the way marketing communications operate, as determined by their level of international involvement, their degree of centralised control and their choice of whether to standardise brand messages or adapt them to individual markets. Fundamentally, there are four levels of international involvement (Keegan 1989; Bartlett and Ghoshal 1991). These are shown in Table 20.1 and they determine the key messages, management focus (standardisation or adaptation), control structure and agency involvement. As the chapter progresses, it may become apparent that such a straightforward typology is what we might call the global millennium. It is however a good starting point in recognising how an organisation's involvement with overseas markets leads to changes in its communications strategy.

International company
One whose home market dominates sales, but for whom the export market holds the promise of extra turnover.

An **international company** is one whose home market dominates its sales but for whom the export market holds the promise of extra turnover. It is unlikely that such a company has its own distribution system in overseas markets and may instead ship direct to trade customers, employ an agent or distributor or authorise a licensee to manufacture a product or supply a service on its behalf. As such, it is frequently a business-to-business (rather than direct to consumer) transaction where the key messages are based on the product/service features, although the company may sponsor consumer-directed, branded advertising or rely on the agent/distributor to do so on its behalf. Communication messages are likely to be the same as the domestic market although packaging may be adapted to the requirements of the overseas domain. Communication to and with potential customers (or agent/distributors) often takes place at international exhibitions or during overseas sales trips, although much international business-to-business now takes place online. The international company is unlikely to employ an overseas advertising or other communications agency although their collaborators may use

TABLE 20.1   International typology

	Home	International	Multinational	Global	Transnational
Communication stage	Domestic	Export	Multinational	Global	Transnational
Key message	Product features	Product/Brand	Corporate and brand	Corporate and brand	Corporate and/or brand
Standardisation/ Adaptation	Standardisation	Standardisation	Standardise/ adaptation	Regional adaptation	Global adaptation
Communications structure	Centralised	Centralised	Decentralised	Grouped centralisation	Network
Agency relationship	Domestic	Domestic	Domestic and foreign local	Global	Transnational network

Source: Fill (2009)

such services. Domestic agencies may, however, support an overseas campaign with resources such as point-of-sale material.

Multinational companies, as the terms suggests, operate in a number of overseas markets. Although they too may act through agents or distributors, they would normally secure more control over them. It may be the case that foreign-based partners are involved[1] and/or that the company has a wholly or partly owned subsidiary. From a communications perspective, multinational companies more readily perceive the differences between the markets they serve and often rely on an agent/partner/subsidiary to handle all marketing communications in that area (Yeshin 2006). Although there may be common themes, the company is not usually seeking a common transnational message, rather looking to the requirements of individual markets.

Global organisations are seen to strive towards commonality of products or services and communication themes, normally with some regional adaptations to respond to local pressures (Yeshin 2006). Indeed, Michael Perry's (former chairman of *Unilever*) definition of a global brand is a 'local brand reproduced many times' (cited in Lewis 2006). *Unilever* frequently works with this global-local (**glocal**) template with toiletry products such as *Lynx* (UK), *Ego* (South Africa) and *Axe* (rest of the world) and frozen food lines *Birds Eye* (UK), *Iglo* (Italy) and *Findus* (rest of Europe) carrying similar packaging and advertising and with comparable line extensions in each market. Another company with glocal strategies is *McDonald's* who offer different menus in different markets[2] accompanied by locally determined messages while still retaining a central product offering supported by globally recognised brand themes. Alternatively, some global organisations have pulled back from having too many local adaptations. Before 1998, *Johnny Walker*, the world's biggest-selling scotch whiskey had several different advertising campaigns around the world but since then it has effectively used the same theme around the globe. Today, the '*keep walking*' campaign uses celebrities to get across the global message and appears in 200 countries worldwide (Lewis 2006). The *Smirnoff* 'through the bottle campaign', developed by the agency *Lowe Howard Spink*, ran almost unchanged in 43 countries and *BBH's* advert for *Levis* was also virtually unchanged across the world (Yeshin 2006). Another example is *Royal Dutch/Shell* who has used a global theme since 1999. Since then it has worked to achieve consistency across its 45,000 outlets worldwide.

Transnational organisations make up a fourth category where the network structure is such that it is difficult to place their corporate centre (although not necessarily their original home). These types of organisation utilise the worldwide facilities for production and regard their markets as outlets in a global marketplace. Transnational companies may include motor manufacturers such as *Ford* or *General Motors*, financial organisations such as *American Express* and *HSBC*, and FMCG companies such as *Procter & Gamble, Unilever* and *Nestlé*. In 2012, *Lexus* moved its global nerve centre from Japan to California (see Insight below). The subtle difference between global and transnational is not easy to distinguish and may, from a marketing communications perspective, be a distinction too far, given the variety of differing strategies that appear to operate under the global and transnational heading. These transnational organisations frequently use a form of creative accounting to limit their tax liability in one country by transferring their profits (and headquarters in many cases) to one with a lower tax rate. This practice has become less acceptable to some governments such as the UK, France and Germany. In the UK, pressure has been brought to bear on companies such as *Starbucks* and *Google* to reform their procedures.

Multinational company
One that operates in a number of overseas markets, often through agents or distributors, but that would normally secure more (relative to international companies) control over them.

Glocal
Thinking global but acting local.

Transnational organisation
One whose network structure is such that it is difficult to place its corporate centre (although not its original home). These types of organisation utilise worldwide facilities for production and regard their markets as outlets in a global marketplace.

---

[1] This is particularly true where local legislation demands domestic involvement.
[2] For example, 'Croque McDo' (a variation of 'croque monsieur') and *Carte Noir* coffee in France and fruit salad in the UK.

insight: Lexus

U ndoubtedly, *Lexus* is a global brand associated with quality and a consistent message worldwide. Rather than leave the establishment of communications themes to local markets, decisions are made by representatives from key regions who meet in a forum known as the 'global communications council'. According to Paul van de Burgh, General Manager, Marketing for *Lexus Europe*, they work on the basis of 'global consensus'. If there is any opposition from any part of the group, then the suggested theme is immediately dropped and they search for another that will gain global support. The local markets do have a

contribution to make as each market can add 'local flavour' to the global message and translate advertising headlines. They also choose media schedules relevant to their marketplace. Currently, the *Lexus* global message is going out to 24 markets in 22 different languages. In 2012, 10 years after establishing the council, *Lexus* moved its nerve centre from Japan to California. According to General Manager Mark Templin: 'We want to create a global consistency ... We haven't had a hub for centralising our message. Now we can do that. We're at a point where we're ready to grow and enter more markets. So we want to create consistency before growing more.'

Source: various

STANDARDISATION VS. ADAPTATION

Whether to globally or regionally standardise or locally adapt is a dilemma that consistently arises with marketing in general and marketing communications in particular. Some international and global brands differentiate their product, others the message that is associated with the brand and still others both. This is often determined by the product or service characteristics involved. Figure 20.1, based on a model developed by Hankinson and Cowking (1996), illustrates how the fully global, product adaptive, proposition adaptive and fully adaptive strategies develop as determined by the needs of specific markets.

FIGURE 20.1 Strategic matrix of international brand options

While global brands are known to drive efficiencies and economies of scale, the practical role of global brand management consists of 'juggling global priorities with local nuances' and is as such 'fraught with complexity' (Lewis 2006: 7). In a seminal article over 30 years ago, Levitt (1983) argued that the world was moving inexorably toward homogenisation, globalisation and a 'converging commonality'. From a North American viewpoint, it may well have appeared that the advent of Galbrathian[3] corporate dominance and the drive for economies of scale made the move toward homogeneity inevitable. Despite the advantages of standardisation (discussed below), however, it has become evident that local markets can react poorly (or less than optimally) to both the composition and themes associated with global standardisation. Indeed, the very term 'globalisation' has come to be regarded pejoratively. Wholly adapting to the needs of each market, however, makes little use of potential economies of scale.

As is evident in most debates of this type, the answer lies somewhere in between and is rarely the same for any two organisations. The outcome is normally a mixture of strategies that look to make optimum savings from standardisation with the necessary local requirements in terms of product/service and messages – what Kenichi Ohmae (1990) summed up as 'think global – act local'. As Yeshin (2006) notes, 'international marketing in the twenty-first century is not about ignoring or over-riding cultural differences, but about understanding, accommodating and harnessing them in the service of global brand building'.

STANDARDISATION

The arguments for standardisation are rational and largely, but not exclusively, financial. They include:

- economies of scale
- increased homogeneity of markets.

Economies of scale relate to production, packaging and marketing communications. In the latter category, the cost of producing a television commercial can be around $500,000 and the development of individual creative themes can run into millions of pounds, euros, dollars or yen. The ability to use campaign themes, commercials or even point-of-sale materials across borders can considerably lower costs. For example, many vehicle advertisements use the same film material with various words and/or speech overlaid.

There is also the argument that the world is becoming more of a global village through technological developments and greater consumer mobility and that travelling customers expect more homogeneity. There is also a contention that in an increasingly cosmopolitan world there are more similarities between Londoners and New Yorkers than either have with the inhabitants of Burnley or Buffalo (although even this cosmopolitan/provincial distinction may also be rapidly disappearing). Certainly, luxury goods (*Rolex, Gucci, Burberry, Cartier,* etc.) and even more commonplace brands (*Johnny Walker, Toblerone, Walkers,* etc.) appear to be readily available at virtually every international airport, which would suggest that such international segments exist.

One global standardisation strategy increasingly used by multinational or global organisations is that of unifying brand names across markets. Despite considerable investment over time in the original brand name, the decision is taken that for it to be recognisable in the international market it requires brand name harmonisation. Significant UK brands that have been affected in this way include *Marathon* (to *Snickers*), *Opal Fruits* (to *Starburst*), *Jif* (to *Cif*), *Haze* (to *Airwick*),

---

3   From economist J.K. Galbraith (1908–2006).

Olivio (to *Bertolli*) and *One-2-one* (to *T-mobile*). Some brands have changed name several times as they sought greater international recognition (e.g. *Freeserve* to *Wannadoo* to *Orange* to *EE*).

Opportunities do exist for what at first sight would appear to be undifferentiated global brand messages in the form of international events. These global (or near global) attractions include the Olympics, the *FIFA* World Cup and the *Formula One* racing championships. Brands that can afford to appear on the world stage are, however, few and far between. For the 2014 FIFA World Cup, sponsors include *Budweiser, Castrol, Continental, Johnson & Johnson* and *McDonald's*. In addition to worldwide publicity, these sponsors look to tie in this coverage with local advertising and promotions. For example, prior to and during the 2012 Olympics, *UPS* advertised widely their participation as official couriers to the games. Local national teams were also heavily sponsored by organisations who wanted to make a statement both internationally and locally.

ADAPTATION

Despite the potential cost savings, there are several barriers to standardisation. These include:

- language
- culture
- management issues
- socio-economic conditions
- technological development levels
- brand status
- government regulation.

Language differences obviously produce difficulties in both packaging and in communicating brand messages. Even variations of the same language can throw up distinct anomalies (e.g. British, Australian and American English; French and Canadian French) and some markets have two (e.g. Canada, Belgium) or more (e.g. Switzerland, India, South Africa) languages to contend with. Many consumer goods companies cope with the multiplicity of languages by incorporating usage instructions in many regional languages in thick booklets (e.g. *Sony, Kodak*, etc.) and packaging with as few words as is practical. FMCG goods, particularly foodstuffs, which are obliged to carry ingredient and other information, are often so full of miniscule, almost unreadable print, that it makes a mockery of any packaging design. In advertising **copy** and other written communications (e.g. press releases), the most frequent mistakes are in understanding the meaning. Although the translation may be strictly correct, the interpretation may not. Most people have come across written communications (for example, furniture assembly instructions) that make no sense at all and there have been some notable examples of poor translation from prominent companies in the past (see Insight below). Another problem in translating copy, for example for newspaper or magazine advertising, is that some languages require more space to convey the same meaning. German requires 25% more space than English and some Arab languages require considerably more.

Some companies have made a virtue of using a one-language tagline in all (or nearly all) markets, for example 'the future's bright, the future's Orange'[4] was used by the company in almost all its world markets. It is, however, generally acknowledged that advertising and other communications work better in the

---

[4]   Prior to the company's merger with *T-mobile* and rebranding as *EE*.

◉ insight: Translation examples

Examples of reported mistakes in translation or interpretation:

Parker pens translated 'Won't leak in your pocket and embarrass you' as 'Won't leak in your pocket and make you pregnant'.

Coors' (beer) slogan 'Turn it loose' read in Spanish as 'Suffer from diarrhea'.

General Motors introduced the Nova model but it did not go down well in Spain: 'No va' means 'it doesn't go'.

Scandinavian firm *Electrolux* put the following in a US campaign: 'Nothing sucks like an Electrolux'.

Perdue's 'It takes a strong man to make a tender chicken' translated in Spanish as 'it takes an aroused man to make a chicken affectionate'.

Source: various

recipient's home tongue. Even the increasing international use of English is not always acceptable and sometimes wholeheartedly opposed. It is noticeable that one of the few exceptions to the use of *Orange*'s English tagline was in France, its corporate home.

In many ways, all marketing communications are culturally specific. **Culture** may be summed up as the values, beliefs, ideas, customs, actions and symbols that are learnt by members of particular societies (Fill 2009), or perhaps more simply as 'the way things are done at a given place at a given time … a shared understanding we have of the world that surrounds us' (Bewick 2006). Both definitions add something to the marketing communications debate. The first emphasises that it is a learning experience (nurture not nature) and specific to certain societal groups. The second emphasises that cultural understanding relates not only to place but to time. A simple commercial example of the latter is our taste in coffee. Traditionally, Latin American and Southern European countries prefer their coffee stronger than the rest of the world. The advent of coffee house chains (*Starbucks, Café Nero*, etc.) changed the drinking habits of many towards stronger blends and different preparations (e.g. latte, cappuccino, mocha). There is also the constantly changing meaning of language in various societies, particularly among the young. English words such as 'fit', 'buff', 'sick' and 'wicked' have decidedly different meanings in youth culture and in mainstream society and also have the capability of crossing borders.

Cultural differences may be affected by religious belief, moral codes, customs, history, education, work patterns and exposure to outside influences. This ensures that our interpretation of the colours, symbols and language around us are different in every culture. A historically difficult area to globalise is humour which can be highly culture-specific, particularly in writing or in speech. Humour that can travel is usually in the form of visual gags rather than metaphors or a play on words. However, even this is changing, with comedy from many nations' advertising in a variety of languages being posted on *YouTube* and spread through *Facebook* and other social media.

Consumers respond best to messages that are consistent with their own particular culture. Colours, habits and customs that are taken for granted in one culture can cause misunderstanding and even offence in another. It should, for example, have been easy for such global brands as *Unilever* and *Nestlé* to sell ice cream in Saudi Arabia. However, both companies withdrew from the market in 2001 – they had failed to realise that Saudi Arabians view ice cream as a dessert eaten at home and that female shoppers couldn't buy it at supermarkets because they had no driving licence and hence no way to get the ice cream home before it melted (Lewis 2006).

Country of origin can influence how a particular culture accepts products and services and once again stereotypical behaviour comes to the fore. The French have a decided bias for domestic products while the USA imports goods from beer to clothing and beyond. In the UK and other markets, German technology is admired as are Swiss watch-making and Japanese cars. Scotch whiskey, Cuban cigars, French Champagne, Italian pasta and Scandinavian furniture are accepted as segment brands in their own right around the world. Sometimes the country of origin can be problematical. Undoubtedly, many cultures around the world have been influenced by American cinema but many societies openly reject many of the nuances that these films and the culture that they represent contain. *Mecca* cola was launched for those who, for political reasons, did not want to associate themselves with American brands *Coca-Cola* and *Pepsi* (incidentally hurting sales of *Virgin Cola*[5] which had until then been the preferred alternative). *McDonald's* is a quintessential global brand that regularly has to put up with attack but not necessarily for the same reason in all markets. In France, there is pressure (and occasionally physical attack) from the farming lobby, in the UK it is from nutritionists and in Israel from the religious right. More recently, the printing of cartoons offensive to many Muslims has led to a backlash against products from Denmark across the Middle East and beyond.

Level of education and what might be grandly termed 'consumer knowledge' also differ significantly from market to market. There is a view that in 'unsophisticated markets' the emphasis is on the communication of information, while in more mature markets the concentration is on transformational communication. From a communications perspective, these are considerably different messages. In Western markets, for example, there is a high level of sophistication both in the use of advertising by organisations and, more specifically, in their interpretation by consumers. Advertising literacy is high, consumers have access to vast amounts of data on the world in which they live and can compare and evaluate wide ranges of brands, products and services with relative ease. The impact of this, however, is an equally high level of cynicism towards the motivations, techniques and activities of suppliers. In such markets, symbols (e.g. *Nike* ✓swoosh, *Adidas* stripes) replace words, celebrity associations replace product/service features and entertainment replaces the hard sell. In a similar vein, Goodyear (1996) distinguishes between **low consumerism** (unsophisticated markets) and **high consumerism** (sophisticated markets) – see Table 20.2 for these distinctly different markets and the messages they receive. In low consumerisation markets, the concentration is on rational, fact-based attributes in sales language and on featuring the product. In high consumerisation markets, the concentration is on emotionally charged benefits delivered in symbolic language and consumer-directed metaphors.

A further downside of centralised international communications is in the local management of campaigns. Although standardised communications may offer economies of scale, these might prove a false saving as locally placed marketers can often take advantage of opportunities in media placement, react rapidly to competitive activity and understand local nuances and the brand's response to them. Although local control may result in creative and production duplication, it

Low consumerism
In global marketing terms, undeveloped or unsophisticated markets.

High consumerism
In global marketing terms, developed or highly sophisticated markets.

---

[5]   *Virgin Cola* quietly died as a brand in 2009.

TABLE 20.2   Low/high consumerisation messages

Low consumerisation		High consumerisation
Product attributes	⇔	Product benefits
Focus on product	⇔	Focus on usage
Rational	⇔	Emotional
Realistic	⇔	Symbolic
Fact	⇔	Metaphor
Maker's language	⇔	Brand language
Sales person	⇔	Consumer
Pack shot	⇔	Consumption
Left brain	⇔	Right brain
Selling	⇔	Buying

Source: Goodyear (1996)

may reflect the best opportunities for the brand, particularly if the market is significantly different from home and if the brand holds a significantly different status in the overseas market than it does in the domestic market (see brand status).

The level of education is often, but not always, comparable with the level of socio-economic well-being in a particular culture (an exception to this is Cuba). Put in terms of Maslow's (1954) hierarchy of needs, some economies are fighting for basic survival needs (food, water, etc.), while other markets have high numbers for whom self-actualisation is the driving force (and every other level of need in between). This creates segmentation difficulties of huge proportions. Neither is it necessarily intuitive. India, for example, may have many for whom survival is the main priority but there are also more (US dollar) millionaires in that country than in any other. Although international and global brands are available in most markets, they may be well out of the price range of many. In some markets, a *McDonald's* hamburger[6] may represent a week's wages. This raises the question of whether mass advertising in such markets is socially and morally responsible.

Social nuances also affect the response to commercial messages. The cultural value associated with old age differs significantly from those societies where it is invested with knowledge and good sense to those where the 'grey market' is merely a target segment for investment products, health insurance and stairlifts. Decision-maker roles may also vary between men and women or a mixture of both depending on the position of women in the society and the importance and extent of family units. The level of class consciousness in particular societies may also affect how brand messages are composed. In such markets, aspiration may be a great motivator. Even regional segmentation can prove difficult. Hofstede (1980, 1991), in conducting a survey of *IBM* employees around the world, examined cultural differences based on such factors as individualism, authoritarianism (power distance) and risk (uncertainty avoidance). From this, he developed a series of national groupings but even they proved an uncertain fit. In terms of culture, each market (or subset of a market) has its own profile which frequently defies marketing communications standardisation.

---

[6]   The so-called 'hamburger index' (based on the price of a *McDonald's* burger) is a frequently used measure of economic prosperity (see case study).

The level of technological development in a market can have a great deal to do with the ability to communicate to different audiences. Access to media outlets is paramount and a lack of availability of newspapers, magazines, television and radio has always limited commercial communications. Global media stations (e.g. *CNN, MTV*), while perhaps being a vehicle for global brands, also need to adapt their messages to the local audience. Certain media may be unavailable, especially those driven by new technology (e.g. internet, broadband), or certain media may not be as important in a particular market as they are in others. The level of technological sophistication may also determine the available media, the level of agency expertise and the media specialisms available in the marketplace.

Other problems accompany brands when they enter a market. For example, although the product or service may be a major brand or even the market leader in its domestic market, this may not be the case overseas. In the new market, the brand's status may be different relative to the competition and the desired positioning (e.g. market leadership) may be occupied by someone else (Yeshin 2006). While in its own market the brand may have established an unassailable position with communications strategies which reflect this, in the new market it may have to fight for recognition, prove its credentials and/or encourage sampling, before getting off the ground. Brands such as *Hershey* and *Cadbury* may be market leaders in the USA and the UK respectively but they are minnows in each other's markets. The strategy may be to work off the back of existing brands rather than invest the amounts required to attain market leadership, were it even possible.

A final barrier to standardisation relates to government regulation. In Europe, there were, until recently, considerable restrictions in the area of sales promotion (for example, Sweden and Norway banned random-win promotions and France, Portugal and Greece insisted that promotions be registered). However, in 2010 three cases went before the European Court of Justice whose decisions effectively rendered most restrictions on promotional marketing in the EU invalid. There are, however, examples of differing legislative approaches, including tobacco advertising and sponsorship which is banned across Europe (but not North America) and comparative advertising (common in the USA) which is restricted in Germany and to a lesser extent in the UK. At the other end of the scale, some governments do not give enough protection to the integrity of brands in their markets. China has been the home of a great deal of intellectual property abuse in the past, although the government announced in December 2012 that it would change the law on 'malicious' trademark registrations after a series of legal cases in which well-known international brands had their copyright abused. Included in these legal battles were France's *Hermes International SCA* who had problems in China with its trademark, and *Apple* who agreed to pay $60 million to *Proview Technology* (*Shenzhen*) to end a protracted legal dispute over the iPad trademark in China.

GLOBAL AGENCIES

As noted in Chapter 19, agencies have played and are playing their own part in the globalisation of the communications industry but this is not a recent phenomenon. *Quaker Oats* was launched in Britain in 1894 by the London-based *Derrick* agency although many other US advertisers, such as *American Tobacco*, started a trend at the turn of that century of bringing their own agencies with them (Brierley 2002). These agencies brought new ideas and techniques to the

UK market and a new level of account supervision. *Lord & Thomas,* for example, who brought *Wrigley* and *Palmolive* to the UK, reviewed every poster position in London and developed a breakdown of class structure, whether the site was in a shopping, residential or industrial area and whether the sites were on major transport routes (Brierley 2002). As discussed previously, by 1960 there were 36 US agencies in London with 281 offices nationwide (Nevett 1982) and by 1972 US agencies held 86% of declared billings of the top-20 agencies (Brierley 2002). More recent mergers and takeovers have seen the further concentration of agencies, such that the top-10 agencies are estimated to control more than 80% of global markets and the same companies (or subsidiary companies) operating in Europe, America, Africa and Asia.

Overseas agency development is normally based on one of a number of growth strategies:

- organic growth (through the creation of overseas subsidiaries)
- acquisitive growth (through the purchase of an agency in the overseas market)
- cooperative growth (through networks and strategic alliances)
- co-ownership model (ownership shared with a local organisation).

Advantages of this development into overseas markets include the sharing of creative ideas (with the good ones being replicated – see Insight), standardised research methods and transnational coverage.

In the age of 'integrated marketing communications' (IMC), agencies should be playing a major part in global IMC (GIMC). Indeed, big global brands such as *eBay, HSBC, Samsung, Apple* and *UBS* are among those with clear guidelines that are consistent throughout the world. Global IMC has been described as 'a system of active promotional management which strategically co-ordinates global communication in all its component parts both horizontally in terms of countries and organisations and vertically in terms of promotional disciplines' (Grein & Gould 1996). In reality, however, the problems associated with domestic IMC (see Chapter 15) are often magnified in the international arena.

insight: Good ideas cross borders

In 2011, *Coca-Cola* Australia introduced the 'share a Coke' campaign: 150 of Australia's most often used forenames started to appear on bottles and consumers were encouraged to share the experience with friends. Messages were everywhere in both traditional and interactive media. In addition, *Coke* set up booths where individuals could get their own unique name on a can. So popular was the campaign that 50 new names were quickly added. In the three months of the campaign, young adult consumption (a key market) rose by 7%, it became the most talked about subject on *Facebook* and generated 242 articles which reached an estimated 14 million people (out of a total population of 23 million).

Good ideas cross borders. In 2013, the 'share a Coke' campaign was launched across Europe. Over one billion packs of Coca-Cola, Diet Coke and Coke Zero carried the most popular names in each country. For those who cannot find their own name, they can go online (in the UK, **www.shareacoke.co.uk**) where personalised virtual cans can be created and shared with friends.

Source: various

summary

This chapter reviewed the problems associated with global marketing communications. It discussed a typology that included international, multinational, global and transnational companies and the key messages, management focus, control structure and agency involvement seen to be associated with such companies. The chapter discussed the principal area of contention in international marketing communications, namely standardisation or adaptation, not only of the product/service but of the brand messages associated with it. The arguments for standardisation are based on potential economies of scale, supported by the proposal that markets are becoming more homogeneous. The arguments for adaptation are, however, powerful and largely relate to language differences, cultural nuances, management issues, socio-economic conditions, technological development, brand status and government regulation. Given the weight of evidence, the phrase 'think global – act local' is particularly relevant. The chapter concluded by looking at the internationalisation of communications agencies.

review questions

1. Describe what you understand by the term 'international company'.

2. What are global brands known to drive?

3. What strategy is used by multinational or global organisations to unify brand names across markets?

4. Name three barriers to standardisation.

5. What difficulties can language impose on standardisation?

6. Despite humour being highly culturally specific and a barrier to standardisation, there is one form of humour that can have international appeal. What is it?

7. In markets with high levels of consumerism, how are brand benefits delivered to the consumer?

8. What may happen to the status of a brand when it enters an international market?

9. What is the term used to describe a target segment associated with old age?

10. Describe the principal differences between high and low consumerisation.

discussion questions

1. There is evidence to suggest that the country of origin can impact on the appeal of goods in certain markets. To what extent do you believe this is true? Consider a selection of foreign products you are familiar with and consider to what extent their country of origin impacts on their promotion and presentation.

2. Redraw the strategic matrix of international brand options, adding your own examples. To what extent have the companies you have categorised as 'standardised' actually done so and why do you think this is?

3. As a product manager, how would you decide on the degree of standardisation or adaptation to be applied to your advertising activities? What data would you gather to help with this decision and why?

case study: 20.1 McDonald's global strategy

Of all the companies that have managed to endure the many challenges associated with global expansion, *McDonald's* stands out. It is, for example, the only brand powerful enough to be associated with world economics and world peace. *The Economist* publishes a global ranking of currencies' purchasing power, known as the *Big Mac Index*, based on the prices charged at the local *McDonald's*. Elsewhere, columnist Thomas Friedman has hypothesised that nations with *McDonald's* restaurants do not go to war with each other (the so-called Golden Arches Theory of Conflict Prevention).

Since its establishment in 1948, *McDonald's* has grown from a family burger stand to a global fast-food giant. By the end of the 1960s, it had more than 1000 outlets across the USA. British Columbia, Canada was the first international franchise, opened in 1967, and this was followed by Costa Rica in the same year. From there, the chain spread steadily. In a six-month period in 1971, *McDonald's* became established on three new continents, as stores opened in Japan, the Netherlands and Australia. A Brazilian *McDonald's* opened in 1979, bringing them to South America for the first time. After 14 years of discussions with the Kremlin, the Soviet Union's first *McDonald's* opened in Moscow in 1990. *McDonald's* reached its sixth continent in 1992, with the opening of a restaurant in Morocco. Four years later, the company heralded the expansion into its 100th nation, Belarus. By this time, the company had boasted it was opening a new restaurant every three hours somewhere in the world. By the end of 2008, *McDonald's* had grown to 31,967 locations in 118 countries. Of those, only about 14,000, or 45%, were in the USA; with 58 million daily customers worldwide, *McDonald's* was truly a global brand.

So why is *McDonald's* so successful? Largely in two ways: first, the company developed a franchise model that allows its franchisee, management and shareholders to share the risks and rewards of new business; second, by adaptation and innovation, coming up with new products and services to address the needs of consumer markets around the globe as shaped by the location's demographic, economic and local factors. For example, the biggest seller in France after the *Big Mac* is a mustard-topped burger called Le Royal Deluxe. Some Asian locations serve fried shrimp in a *Big Mac* roll, while *McDonald's* in India do not serve beef at all, relying instead on burgers made from vegetables, rice and beans. In Brazil, *McDonald's* offer baked banana pies for dessert. It has not always been plain sailing and knowing when to pull out of a location is sometimes as important as knowing when and where to expand. The company pulled out of Iceland, citing the collapse of the local economy and the high cost of imports. *McDonald's* has also pulled out of Bolivia, Jamaica and a handful of other countries due to poor sales.

Not everyone in the world is happy to welcome *McDonald's* when the fast-food giant moves into a country. Many see the corporate juggernaut as a symbol of globalisation. Some nations have viewed fast food as an insult to their own national cuisines. Bermuda banned all fast-food restaurants to stop *McDonald's* opening on the island. In 1999, a French farmer, Jose Bove, became a national hero when he and a band of activists destroyed a *McDonald's* that was under construction. As a result of these complaints in the 1990s and early 2000s, *McDonald's* made significant efforts to restore its corporate image with a radical overhaul of the company's product portfolio, including the introduction of healthier, more natural foods such as salads, fruit and carrot sticks.

Despite criticism from all sides (including anti-*McDonald's* websites such as McSpotlight), the company continues to offer the world what it evidently wants, regardless of the location.

Source: various

(Continued)

(Continued)

Case study questions

1. Explain why a model that allows its franchisee, management and shareholders to share the risks and rewards of new business should be so successful?
2. Do you believe the change in product portfolio will be enough to stem opposition to the brand?
3. If you were *McDonald's* global strategist, what would you propose to the company in the next 5 to 10 years?

 further reading

Aslam, M.M. (2006) 'Are you selling the right colour? A cross-cultural review of colour as a marketing cue', *Journal of Marketing Communications*, 12 (1): 15–30.

Bulmer, S. and Buchanan-Oliver, M. (2006a) 'Visual rhetoric and global advertising imagery', *Journal of Marketing Communications*, 12 (1): 49–61.

Bulmer, S. and Buchanan-Oliver, M. (2006b) 'Advertising across cultures: interpretations of visually complex advertising', *Journal of Current Issues & Research in Advertising*, 28 (1): 57–71.

Iyer, G.R., Sharma, A. and Evanschitzky, H. (2006) 'Global marketing of industrial products: are interpersonal relationships always critical?', *Industrial Marketing Management*, 35 (5): 611–20.

Kaynak, E., Kara, A. and Apil, A.R. (2011) 'An investigation of people's time orientation, attitudes, and behavior toward advertising in an international context', *Journal of Global Marketing*, 24 (5): 433–52.

Moon, T.W. and Park, S.I. (2011) 'The effect of cultural distance on international marketing strategy: a comparison of cultural distance and managerial perception measures', *Journal of Global Marketing*, 24 (1): 18–40.

Okazaki, S. (2005) 'Searching the web for global brands: how American brands standardise their web sites in Europe', *European Journal of Marketing*, 39 (1–2): 87–109.

REFERENCES

Bartlett, C. and Ghoshal, S. (1991) *Managing Across Borders: The Transnational Solution*. Cambridge, MA: Harvard Business School.

Bewick, M. (2006) 'Border crossing', *The Marketer*, 25 June, pp. 22–3.

Brierley, S. (2002) *The Advertising Handbook*, 2nd edn. London: Routledge.

Fill, C. (2009) *Marketing Communications: Interactivity, Communities and Content*, 5th edn. Harlow: Financial Times/Prentice Hall.

Goodyear, M. (1996) 'Divided by a common language', *Journal of the Market Research Society*.

Grein, A.F. and Gould, S.J. (1996) 'Globally integrated marketing communications', *Journal of Marketing Communications*, 17 (3): 141–58.

Hankinson, G. and Cowking, P. (1996) *The Reality of Global Brands: Cases and Strategies for the Successful Management of International Brands*. New York: McGraw-Hill.

Hofstede, G. (1980) *Cultures and Consequences: International Differences in Work Related Values*. Thousand Oaks, CA: Sage.

Hofstede, G. (1991) *Cultures and Organisations*. London: McGraw-Hill.

Keegan, W.J. (1989) *Global Marketing Management*. Englewood Cliffs, NJ: Prentice Hall.

Levitt, T. (1983) 'The globalization of markets', *Harvard Business Review*, May/June: 92–102.

Lewis, E. (2006) 'Global vs local', *The Marketer*, 25 June, pp. 7–9.

Maslow, A. (1954) *Motivation and Personality*. New York: Harper & Row.

Nevett, T.R. (1982) *Advertising in Britain: A History*. London: Heinemann.

Ohmae, K. (1990) *The Borderless World*. London: Collins.

Yeshin, T. (2006) *Advertising*. London: Thomson Learning.

For additional materials that support this chapter and your learning, please visit:
study.sagepub.com/egan

THE CHANGING FACE OF MARKETING COMMUNICATIONS

21

LEARNING OBJECTIVES

Having completed this chapter, readers would be expected to:

- recognise the potential areas of change in marketing communications

- be aware of potential technological developments and begin to question the outcome of such advancements

- understand the reasons behind potential changes in communications agency structures.

INTRODUCTION

As suggested by the title of this chapter, nothing stands still in marketing communications. Although marketers tend to operate on the basis of the here and now, they have to keep an eye on the future because change can happen fast. This year's success could be next year's failure. As eminent historian Peter Ackroyd (2011) has noted: 'The result of historical enquiry is the recognition of transience, the most fervent of beliefs will one day be discredited, and the most certain certainties will be abandoned.'

This applies as much to marketing as to life in general. It is, after all, barely a quarter of a century since the introduction of the internet, and who would have forecast then its enormous growth and the influence it would have not just on marketing communications but on all our lives? In the intervening period, we have seen the launch of *Google* (1998), *Facebook* (2005), *YouTube* (2005) and *Twitter* (2006). The effect of digital technology on marketing communications in general and on advertising in particular has been particularly significant. *PriceWaterhouseCoopers*[1] estimates that online spending in the UK increased by 14% and 11% in 2011 and 2012, respectively. Of the £607 million increase (to £5391 million) in 2012, over 50% of this increase was in mobile telephony (10% of the digital spend). Another significant sub-sector was video which increased by 46%

---

[1]   In research for the Interactive Advertising Bureau.

to £160 million. A rational prediction of the future, therefore, is that technology will play an increasingly more prominent part in marketing communications. We should, however, be careful not to ditch everything that went before to jump on the digital bandwagon. *Group M²* reported a significant worldwide digital advertising increase of 16.2% to $99 billion in 2012 but this only represented under one-fifth of the total spend on global advertising. So, as marketers, we should not throw the baby out with the bath water.

This text hopefully has indicated that there are lessons to be learnt from the past as well as from our expectations of the future. In addition to technological innovation, this chapter suggests that other potential changes (particularly in the socio-political area) may also have a great influence on marketing communications.

TECHNOLOGY

As noted, the increased sophistication of technology and its increased contribution to marketing communications is perhaps the easiest prediction to make, although its consequences are less immediately clear. For nearly a century, first newspapers, then radio and more recently television have at various times dominated mass advertising. Although 'direct response television' and more recently 'interactive television' have driven the dream of **one-to-one marketing** a little closer, generally this medium is proving difficult to adapt to the new communications age. Traditional advertising 'spots' are proving less effective (as viewers 'zip' and 'zap' their way past advertising on one of hundreds of different channels) and despite programme sponsorship becoming more commonplace, advertisers are questioning the medium's viability. Perhaps its salvation lies in the almost inevitable congress of television and the personal computer and/or further developments in hologram technology. Some advertisers are hoping that '**one-pipe convergence**' will remodel the landscape (Grose 2006). This is when a single broadband feed operates the television, PC, iPad, games console and stereo system. The advent of smart televisions is making this a reality in a short time.

Other traditional mediums may change through technological development. Outdoor poster sites have been replaced by digital screens and that is set to continue to expand. Some already deliver news and entertainment as well as advertising, particularly in travel termini. The survival of newspapers will depend on their capacity to either continue to raise revenue through advertising or find another revenue-raising model. Classified advertising (which Rupert Murdoch once described as the industry's 'rivers of gold') is fast disappearing. In the UK, the top-10 national newspapers' circulation fell 7.83% in the year to March 2012. Local newspapers have suffered even more. On the positive side, the website of the UK's Guardian newspaper now has half as many readers in the USA as it does in the UK (see Insight: Guardian USA, below). Formats too will change. Newspapers, magazines and catalogues, as well as podcasts, may be sent direct or downloaded onto mobiles, tablets or desk-top devices.

There are likely to be significant developments in point of sale. Point-of-sale technology will continue to become more efficient. This may result in an end to operator-assisted checkouts if 'smart trolley' scanning proves effective. Audio or video displays will alert shoppers to offers as they pass by and in-store terminals will enable the purchase of more complex services such as insurance. Face-recognition technology may recognise you when you enter a store and, based on your previous purchases, suggest specific products or services, as currently

One-pipe convergence
The movement in technology toward a single broadband feed which supplies all the televisions, PCs, iPads, games consoles and stereo systems in a house or other building.

---

²   A division of WPP. Report dated 2013.

happens with online retailers. The further extension of internet ordering and home delivery (or collection) is likely, although there will always be a place for physical retail therapy. Retailers may also use the information they hold about customers more efficiently. *Tesco* already utilises such customer knowledge to incentivise its Clubcard members. It is suggested, however, that *Tesco* currently only uses a fraction of the information collected (so-called **big data**). *IBM*[3] estimates that every day 2.5 quintillion (10^{18}) bytes[4] of data are produced and that 90% of the data held has been created over the last two years. More's law predicts that processing power will double each year and, were this to continue, even big data analysis would come within reach. Already, supermarkets can predict certain customer life changes from what they purchase. For example, folic acid supplement on a shopping transaction (online or off-line) is a good indicator that a baby is on the way, with all the lucrative trading opportunities that this entails. More effective management software and increased processing speeds may produce substantially more detailed information about individuals. This, of course, opens up the debate into privacy and all that that engenders. Although the possibilities associated with such targeting may excite some marketers, there are also considerable ethical considerations that come with such increased knowledge. For example, most supermarkets now offer life insurance. Would it be right for such companies to use the data from purchases (which may include cigarettes, alcohol, cholesterol-rich and fatty foods, etc.) as part of life-insurance risk assessment?

The growth in internet usage is a given. In 2013, there were 2 billion people online (compared with a total world population of 7 billion). The internet is still, however, a passive medium requiring constant direction (through advertising and/or promotion) to individual websites. How marketers will attract potential customers to their sites will be a continuing challenge. Cooperative networks of non-competitive suppliers are already cross-referencing (and earning commission) for each other's sites, particularly in the leisure and travel industries, and this strategy is likely to develop further into areas such as cross-purchasing and cooperative promotion as these networks stabilise. Social media is currently strong but those assuming that *Facebook* (and other currently heavily populated sites) will necessarily continue to be popular should look at how quickly *Second Life* (at the height of its power in 2008) virtually disappeared.

Once consumers reach a website, there is still the problem of keeping them interested and involved (sometimes referred to as **stickiness**) and stimulating them into action (e.g. purchase), and this will continue to challenge the creative abilities of marketers. Some innovative marketers are already using the medium of the internet to involve consumers themselves in the marketing of products and services. Interesting or amusing videos, associated with particular brands, are being uploaded onto sites such as *YouTube* where its location is spread in a form replicating the spread of a virus (viral marketing). On the downside, the democratic nature of the internet enables customers (and others) to post damaging messages. Some brands such as *McDonald's* have websites wholly dedicated to attacking them (e.g. currently McSpotlight and McCruelty*).*

The merging of technologies will almost certainly involve more services being available on mobile phones. Internet connection and email facilities are already available, and downloading, albeit currently restricted by size, on third-generation equipment, will improve dramatically as 4G technology is rolled out. According to David Black[5] of *Google*, currently 75% of mobile telephone users have smartphones and, on average, they look at their phones 150 times per day. So important has

Big data
Data sets so large that they are awkward or near impossible to work with.

Stickiness
Anything about a website that encourages its visitors to stay longer. A website is sticky if visitors stay for a long time and return frequently.

---

[3]   According to www.ibm.com (accessed 3 July 2013).
[4]   2,500,000,000,000,000,000 bytes.
[5]   Speaking at the *IDM* Employability conference on 21 June 2013.

our mobile become that there is a word (nomophobia) for fear of losing it and the disruption it would cause in our lives. The use of mobile phones for other than telephone calls continues to grow. According to *Forbes Magazine*,[6] in the year 2012:

- *texting* increased from 58% in 2007 to 80%
- *internet access* increased from 25% in 2008 to 56%
- *email* increased from 19% in 2007 to 50%
- *video recording* increased from 18% in 2007 to 44%
- *downloading of apps* increased from 22% in 2007 to 43%
- *accessing health/medical information* increased from 17% in 2010 to 31%
- *online banking* increased from 18% in 2011 to 29%.

As much as 80% of phone users use their phones to take photos (which they may instantly transfer to *Facebook* or another social media site). Other uses for mobile telephones already include charity donations and ticket confirmations by airlines and other travel companies, and these are forecast to grow. Apps (software applications) tell you the time of the next bus, train or plane, or how to get to your favourite store. Apps can guide you to where you want to visit, control your calorie consumption or deliver countless games (often with associated advertising). The use of mobiles for relatively small purchases (mobile phone companies are already charging small amounts to accounts) and as a door-opening (or key) device for entry to multiple locations is a small step away. At present, these facilities would prove a security risk and much will depend on how quickly such devices can be blocked if they are stolen.

One of the most popular uses (over 80%[7]) for mobile phones comes courtesy of the short messaging service (SMS), often called texting or text messaging. Organisations currently use SMS to invite further information and competition entry or to send brand messages. Transnational mobile phone networks (*Vodaphone, O₂*, etc.) send text messages to travellers and trade fair organisers use texting to remind visitors about particular events. Even universities are texting potential students with reminders about application procedures, and current students with details of their courses and important deadlines, as this method appears more effective than email. The trend will continue as advanced technology makes such communication easier and cheaper. The obvious danger is that as costs fall, spam email habits will cross over significantly to this medium.

We can, to some extent, forecast the technological changes that will affect the communications industry. What is more difficult to establish, with any accuracy, is how consumers will respond. A current example of innovation through available technology may serve as a warning. Call centres developed as a means of saving on customer communication costs but were presented (and continue to be presented) as enhanced customer service. Surveys consistently show general annoyance with call centres, in particular the menu options which can at times be completely baffling. Cost savings were extended by transferring many call centres off-shore to parts of the world where the cost of service personnel is low. It is interesting to note that a quiet backlash has caused a number of companies (including *NatWest* and *Direct Line*) to bring back domestic call centres and make this repatriation part of their brand message.

The main message for marketers in relation to technological innovation now and in the future is that just because technology makes things possible, it does not imply that marketers should always use it.

---

[6]   Issue dated 29 November 2012.
[7]   According to *Forbes Magazine*, issue dated 29 November 2012.

Insight: Guardian USA

The Guardian, a British newspaper founded in Manchester in 1821, had by 2011 15 million monthly readers in a country far away from its base: the United States of America. Seeking to capitalise on the opportunity presented by this international market and the ability to access it offered by online journalism, the company established a team of 30 journalists and staff in New York City to redefine its US presence.

US readers gained their own homepage, **www.guardiannews.com,** which gathered stories most relevant to that side of the Atlantic. The team of 30 New York-based staff, liberated from the need to produce a print newspaper, began creating content for the US web audience, beginning with a live blog of the Occupy Wall Street campaign. In July 2013, *The Guardian* went further, adding an Australian homepage and uniting its three presences under a new URL – **www.theguardian.com.**

Rather than competing with local rivals such as the *New York Times*, *The Guardian*'s international presence is focused on offering a different perspective for global readers – the chance to be part of an international audience, studying US or Australian events through the lens of a UK media outlet, while incorporating local voices. The plan seems to be working, with *The Guardian*'s US audience rising above the BBC's and it becoming the fourth highest-read newspaper in the world.

Source: **www.journalism.co.uk,** 26 March 2012; *New York Times*, 3 March 2013

MESSAGE

In technological terms, mediums have begun to merge and this integration is likely to continue. From the marketing communications perspective, decisions on how and through which medium to get a message across will become more crucial. The current 'innovation' of putting messages across prior to allowing access to downloaded material (on any device capable of downloading) may become the *quid pro quo* for covering the costs. If traditional mediums become more restrictive, can sponsorship (of programmes or films) or product placement (see Chapter 12) fully replace mass advertising? How can new brands gain attention or stimulate trial in the new communications era? Although it is now easier to connect with people than ever before, how do you attract their attention with the multiplicity of other messages bombarding the consumer? How do marketing communicators deal with message overload? Traditionally, they have used shock (e.g. sex, horror), emotion (human interest, love, etc.), fear (what will happen if...?) and humour (collectively, creativity) to get and maintain attention. Will communicators have to continue to push the boundaries of good taste and moral acceptance to maintain the status quo and can we trust the industry to control itself? It is doubtful whether industry bodies could keep control in an internet-dominated environment. Already, regulators are having difficulty monitoring activity within their own countries, let alone across borders. Increased cooperation between governments has potential but the track record so far has been poor, not only between the USA and Europe but among EU member states themselves. Many in the industry may welcome this continued indecision.

In addition, research shows that consumers are already highly sceptical of the messages they receive from organisations. Advertisers are widely vilified (see Chapter 9) for promoting consumerism and other societal evils. Personal sales assistants are frequently mistrusted (see Chapter 14), and direct and digital marketers are criticised for spam, junk mail, telesales (see Chapter 13) and, as noted previously, call centres, which are generally disliked. Even public relations

insight: Golf GTI

Alan Mitchell, in an article in *Marketing* (21 September 2012), argued that, in the information age, measuring the return on consumers' investment of time is becoming more important than the ROI of traditional campaigns. He points to the success of *Volkswagen* (VW) who, when launching its new Golf GTI in the USA in 2010, avoided the conventional paths of print ads, billboards and TV spots. What it did instead was launch an *iPhone* app: *Real Racing GTI*.

The app helped to promote the product in a number of ways. It encouraged social promotion by allowing users to post videos of their races on *YouTube*. It incorporated sales promotion by giving a customised GTI to a selected top performer. And it made it easy to book a test drive. The app itself proved a big hit and made it to the top of the apps chart in the USA and 35 other countries, generating huge public relations exposure and increasing sales leads, test drives and quote requests by 80%. Mitchell sums up the app's success by suggesting that Real Racing GTI was a great piece of brand communication, but it also did something else. It met the needs of its users and offered real value to them, just like any good product.

Source: Marketing, 21 September 2012

has not avoided controversy when, according to *PR Week*, 'the term PR is giving public relations a bad name' (Moloney 2006). The growing distrust may be here to stay. It probably took 30–40 years for western European and North American consumers to reach their current level of 'sophistication' (if this is the word to describe it), such that they have become antagonistic and less trusting of marketing. In developing markets such as India and China, this backlash has yet to begin in earnest but it is unlikely that it will take as long.

The creativity behind the message will become even more central to successful marketing communications strategies. Major brands are already replacing the product service 'message' or USP with much more intangible reputation and status 'messages' through association with wholesome activities such as sports or morally justifiable causes and charities, and involve themselves in (or responding to) social issues such as childhood obesity and the environment (often referred to as **social marketing**). Whether this will redeem the reputation of marketing communications remains to be seen.

THE COMMUNICATIONS INDUSTRY

As noted previously, the marketing communications industry prior to the twentieth century came holistically under the term advertising and it was only in that century that specialist functions and singular trade organisations developed (see Chapters 1 and 19). As that century ended, advertising had diminished in importance relative to sales promotion, public relations and sponsorship. In the same period, integrated marketing communications (IMC) (see Chapter 15) became the most talked about, although controversial, subject in the industry. Will IMC reunite

FIGURE 21.1   Marketing Communications over time

the disparate marcom tools and be a feature of marketing communications in the new millennium that is already a decade and a half old, as Figure 21.1 suggests?

As argued in Chapter 15, IMC has a powerful range of arguments to support it, although it is not such an easy thing to implement the strategy effectively. One must assume that technology (in the areas of project development, media planning, communications, design and research) will assist those companies and their agencies to develop the capability for integrated campaigns over time. Ironically, rather than create larger and larger 'full service' agencies to cope, more specialist agencies are likely to become parts of networks (contractually or less formally), albeit large groups may own several specialist agencies in the home market and overseas.

The issue of **marketing metrics** (or how to measure the success or otherwise of marketing tools) will continue to be an issue in the industry. Technology will continue to help estimate the success of parts of the communications mix but will the outcomes of advertising, public relations and sponsorship campaigns always be immeasurable? Certainly, online it is far easier to test and measure advertising response through tools such as *Google* Analytics. There is an old marketing fable that if everyone stopped advertising and promoting brands for a short time nothing much (in turnover terms) would change. Proving this is of course very difficult. A similar challenge faced scientists who were convinced that aeroplane exhaust fumes were contributing to a variation in the earth's temperature but could not prove it. Only after the major tragedy of 9/11, when all planes across the USA were grounded for a few days, were scientists able to prove their calculations to be correct. That any commercial companies (or sectors) would be willing to withdraw from advertising to test the market in this way is an intriguing if unlikely scenario. Legislation bans, such as advertising to children, may give more verifiable results of this claim.

In marketing's search for self-justification, there is perhaps as much danger in over-measuring or over-researching than in being under-informed. Reliance on focus groups or survey research can lead to safe, mundane and/or unadventurous results and the occasional result that is highly misleading. In a competitive communications market, is being 'safe' satisfactory or will the future inevitably require more risk taking? Some companies already launch products without the usual testing and research periods because of the need to get technological innovations quickly to market. Indeed, a number (e.g. *Microsoft*) have been accused of using customers to test-drive a new product. If 'messages' are going to appear fresh and meaningful in a rapidly changing, culturally diverse world, perhaps communicators too will see the need to use the market as the testing ground rather than following the path of traditional quantitative or qualitative research!

The industry has a difficult future to which it must adapt. Ignoring the criticism of customers and legislators is no longer a viable alternative, but neither are the mundane and safe strategies sometimes suggested by those promoting marketing metrics.

summary

This final chapter looked at the potential changes in the marketing communications industry. It noted that technical advancements will undoubtedly continue and that new media was already changing the face of the industry. A brief review of potential technological developments was undertaken and the convergence of mediums including television, personal computers and mobile telephones discussed. Communications at the point of sale is also likely to change both how we shop and how we receive information regarding brands. Although technological advances will be central to future changes in the industry, the way brand messages are constructed and conveyed is likely to be revolutionised. Traditional ways of attracting consumer attention may have to be set aside for the more creative and personal approach as the sophisticated consumer looks for attention, stimulation and entertainment. Consumer antagonism against marketers was discussed and the danger of over-measurement considered.

review questions

1. What developments have driven the 'dream' of one-to-one marketing?

2. What is 'one-pipe convergence'?

3. Why are traditional advertising spots on TV now proving less effective?

4. How does viral marketing work?

5. Explain the meaning of the term 'big data'.

6. What are 'marketing metrics'?

7. Why are consumers highly sceptical of marketing messages?

8. In terms of websites, what is 'stickiness'?

9. What is the future for texting?

10. When this book comes to be revised in a few years' time, where will the biggest changes be seen in marketing communications?

discussion questions

1. The development of technology has created choices now that did not exist a few years ago. One of these is the use of huge high definition screens to replace traditional poster sites. What advantages does this medium offer and to what extent do you think it will develop in the next five years?

2. Texting increased from 58% in 2007 to 80% in 2012. To what extent do you think that this change in behaviour has influenced the way in which people respond to and interact with traditional forms of marketing communications?

3. How might you cope with message overload?

case study 21.1: The Arab Spring and the future of communications

Nabil Sharif has had a distinguished political and media career. He was editor-in-chief of Jordan's Ad-Dustour newspaper, was Jordan's Ambassador to Morocco and has three times served as Jordan's Minister for Communication. According to Sharif, digital communications and the lightning speed of events surrounding the Arab Spring in the Middle East and North Africa took governments and experts by surprise. He noted that analysts had coined the term 'the Arab exception' to explain why the region had missed out on democratic reform. Governments in the area were confident that their control over the local communications media would suppress popular pressure for change. They were proved badly wrong.

Sharif explained that the strictness of these media curbs varied within the region. Some imposed almost total Soviet-style control over their media, simply repeating official government propaganda. Others, including Lebanon, Jordan, Kuwait and Morocco, permitted journalists to operate in relative freedom. However, in general, the Arab media were largely muzzled and acted mainly as mouthpieces for their governments.

It was the lack of belief and credibility in the official media which led the region's young to turn to the unrestricted and democratic world of digital media, according to Sharif. Here, they were free to speak their minds without fear while harnessing the power of solidarity and networking. Frustrations were shared, ideas discussed, slogans agreed and solutions hammered out. The result was the springboard for a democratic revolution.

Sharif explained that the digital media was the major tool of the new Arab spring. The internet became the medium of young activists to mobilise people against autocratic regimes. Mobile phones conveyed messages, captured photos and circulated them. Where correspondents were banned, young Arab activists were able to by-pass constraints by sending videos shot by mobile phones to widely viewed satellite stations such as *Al-Jazeera*.

Sharif observed that *Twitter* had become an alternative and powerful news agency as activists let the world know what was happening in Cairo's famous Tahrir Square. Meanwhile, *Facebook* gave young people encouragement and a sense of solidarity, *YouTube* gave them a video platform, and blogs and citizen journalism empowered them to challenge the status quo. It is not surprising, according to Sharif, that change came fastest in countries with a higher degree of internet penetration. Tunisia and Egypt have well-advanced networks. Countries like Mauritania, which are not well connected, have remained quiet by comparison.

Sharif asks: what does this revolution mean for the media in the region and for the way governments communicate with their citizens? He believes it has given a new understanding of the power of communication. Arab governments always knew it was important but now they have seen how it can topple regimes and change leaderships that had been in power for decades. Second, he believes, it has proved that censorship is obsolete. Satellite television had already broken the state's monopoly over the media scene but the way digital media was mobilised during the Arab Spring dealt it a fatal blow. Third, he is convinced that governments have realised that it was the failings of state-run media which gave the digital channels of communication such power. For example, at its most extreme, radio and TV broadcasters simply resorted to screaming and name-calling as they blamed foreign powers for their alleged roles in events.

(Continued)

(Continued)

Sharif believes that one of the most important outcomes of the Arab Spring has been the destruction of the old media regime and a move towards a new system based on international standards of professionalism and objectivity. He forecasts the birth of a new credible and independent media, as well as investment and effort going into making sure governments can communicate effectively through it with their citizens.

Source: Portland The Quarterly: The International Edition, May 2013, at: **www.portland-communications. com/publications/quarterly-issue-3/the-arab-spring-and-the-future-of-communications**

Case study questions

1. Why did the governments noted lose control of the media?
2. Does new technology promote democracy or could it become a means of control?
3. What effect might 'citizen journalism' have on news media?

 **further reading**

Bell, G.H., Ledolter, J. and Swersey, A.J. (2006) 'Experimental design on the front lines of marketing: testing new ideas to increase direct mail sales', *International Journal of Research in Marketing*, 23 (3): 309–19.

Clulow, V. (2005) 'Futures dilemmas for marketers: can stakeholder analysis add value?', *European Journal of Marketing*, 39 (9–10): 978–97.

Van Belleghem, S. (2013) 'Are you ready for marketing 2020?', Smart Insights, at www.smartinsights.com (accessed 15 December 2013).

REFERENCES

Ackroyd, P. (2011) *Foundation: History of England, Volume 1*. London: Macmillan.

Grose, T.K. (2006) 'Ad-ventures online', *Time* (European edition), 23 August, at www.time.com

Moloney, K. (2006) *Rethinking Public Relations*, 2nd edn. London: Routledge.

USEFUL WEBSITE

For a directory of anti-corporate websites, see: www.dmoz.org/Society/Activism/Anti-Corporation/

For additional materials that support this chapter and your learning, please visit: **study.sagepub.com/egan**

GLOSSARY

4Ps or the marketing mix   A model of marketing which incorporates product, place, price and promotion.

A/B tests   A testing method that uses randomised experiments with two variants.

Access panel   Provides respondents for survey-style information and is made up of targets who have been invited by email to take part with a link to a web survey.

Acorn profiles   Describe residential neighbourhoods and are based on the approximately 1.7 million postcodes in the UK. The full Acorn profile comprises of 17 distinct categories containing 54 Acorn neighbourhood types.

ADMARS   A mnemonic which infers that segments are required to be accessible, differentiated, measurable, actionable, relevant and substantial.

Adspend   The total advertising spend.

Advertising cost equivalent (ACE)   The value of publicity in terms of the equivalent cost of advertising for similar coverage.

Advertising execution thoughts   Those thoughts that relate to how favourably or unfavourably messages are received (see cognitive response model).

Advertising or sales promotion allowances   Contributions made to retailers for advertising or promotions.

Advertising problem   The reason(s) why an organisation is advertising.

Advertising recall   Unprompted awareness of recent advertising.

Advertising   A paid-for, non-personal form of mass communication from an identified source, used to communicate information and influence consumer behaviour with a high degree of control over design and placement but potentially a low degree of persuasion and credibility. It is never either neutral or unbiased.

Advertorial   A magazine or newspaper advertisement that is written in the style of an editorial and which may be mistaken as such.

Affective   Feeling processes relating to moods, feelings, attitudes and emotions.

Affinity marketing or loyalty marketing   Developing customer relationships over time.

Affordable budgeting   Where costs and profit margin are deducted from turnover and the balance is invested in marketing and marketing communications.

AIDA model   Generally attributed to Strong (1925), the model was designed to represent the stages through which a salesperson should take a prospect but was later adopted as a basic framework to explain how persuasive communication (mainly advertising) works. AIDA stands for attention, interest, desire and action.

Alternative or ambient media   Often associated with outdoor media and best described as anything that introduces a 'wow factor' capable of attracting attention and curiosity.

Ambient media   Advertising with a 'wow factor' placed in conspicuous but unusual places.

App   A software application typically of a small, specialised programme available to download onto mobile devices such as mobile telephones, personal computers and tablets.

Application   Attention to other aspects of branding such as corporate advertising, stationery, signage, livery, etc., which maintains the organisation's positioning.

Arbitrary budgeting   A build-up budget approach where senior management arbitrate between different organisational priorities.

Arousal seeking   The motive underlying hedonic consumption is the need to seek arousal rather than satisfy more basic needs.

ATR model   Awareness, Trial and Reinforcement. Ehrenberg and Goodhardt (1979) suggest that the greater part of the buying judgement is rooted in past experience.

ATR(N) model   A model that suggests that advertising may help awareness, trial and reinforcement, and may 'nudge' the consumer toward the brand.

Attention   Notice taken of something or someone; in communications theory, attention must be gained before a message can be delivered.

Attitude scale   A scale that measures a respondent's attitude to pre-defined statements. Examples include nominal, ordinal, interval and ratio scales.

Attitude   A strongly felt, not easily changed view. Attitude forms an important part of consumer theory because it is believed to be the link between what consumers think and what they buy in the marketplace.

Autonomic motivation   Relating to the autonomic nervous system. A motivation or drive felt physiologically and involuntarily.

Award symbols   Symbols that represent a certain level of status that has been gained by the brand (e.g. through accreditation, awards, etc.).

Awareness Index   Introduced by Millward Brown in the 1980s, the Awareness Index (AI) is a measure of brand-linked advertising recall.

Awareness set   Those products in a category that the consumer is actually aware of.

Backlinking   Submission to directories and link pages.

Banner ad   A vertical or horizontal website advertisement.

Behavioural learning   Suggests that an individual develops a pattern of behavioural responses because of the rewards and punishments offered by his/her environment (also referred to as experiential learning).

Behavioural paradigm   Proponents of this paradigm believe it is not possible to study what goes on in the consumer's mind because it is far too complex. Instead, output is measured following a given stimulus. In effect, it is a 'black box' into which stimuli flow and out of which behaviour occurs.

Below the line   All marketing communications tools, excluding advertising (e.g. sales promotion, public relations, etc.).

Benefit positioning   Positioning on the basis of brand benefits. These can be functional and/ or emotional.

Big data   Data sets that are so large and complex that they are difficult to capture, manage and process within a tolerable time period.

Blog   A website on which an individual author or group records their opinions or other information, often in the form of an article, on a regular basis.

Bottleneck theories   Theories that suggest an apparent bottleneck/blockage of information that reaches our conscious awareness. Bottleneck theories are inherently theories of selective attention because they describe how some information is selected for processing while the rest gets discarded.

Brand attitude   How the consumer feels about the brand.

Brand awareness   How aware a consumer is of a particular brand (also referred to as brand recognition) or a brand's promotion.

Brand confusion   Any misunderstanding concerning brand values and benefits – an outcome of indistinct communication.

Brand equity   The value associated with owning a particular brand compared to a generic brand of the same type in the same product or service category.

Brand extension   Using an existing brand name to develop a product/service in a different product/service category.

Brand followers   Brands who did not get to market first or who do not hold the dominant market share.

Brand knowledge   Knowledge of the benefits, features, positioning, etc. associated with the brand.

Brand leader   The leading brand in a particular product or service category.

Brand loyalty   Loyalty in behavioural terms is the repeated selection of the brand over time. Loyalty in attitudinal terms incorporates consumer preference and disposition towards the brand.

Brand personality or branding   The character and essence of a brand, together with its perceived lifestyle associations and values (e.g. status, fashion, quality).

Brand personality   The character and essence of a brand; the perceived lifestyle associations and values (e.g. status, fashion, quality, etc.).

Brand pirates   Those who seek to pass off characteristics of a recognised brand (e.g. package design) on their own product or service.

Brand promise   The promise(s) (e.g. to provide comfort, security, etc.) associated with a particular brand. Broken brand promises may lead to a reassessment of the brand.

Brand proposition   The brand's central proposition; the focus of the brand campaign.

Brand recall   The measure of brands in a particular category recalled from memory.

Brand salience   The importance and prominence of a brand.

Brand values   Those values associated with a brand (e.g. status, youth, etc.).

Brief   A document produced by an organisation, detailing their needs, and used by professionals operating within the communications field to produce various deliverables.

Budget modelling   Various econometric and simulation techniques which seek to model investment and subsequent performance.

Burst   Concentrating the campaign 'spend' on a short period to raise awareness and increase reach.

Buying allowances   Cash discounts, increased margins, etc., against goods purchased by the retailer.

Capacity theories   Theories that suggest limited processing capacity and how this attention is distributed among informational sources. Capacity models are really models that describe the division, rather than the selection, of attention.

Catalogue retailing   A means by which products or services can be purchased from a selection of those on offer in a catalogue.

Catalogue   A list of things (e.g. books, gifts) usually arranged systematically.

Causal research   Testing hypotheses about cause-and-effect relationships (e.g. advertising and sales).

Cause-related marketing   An activity in which commercial organisations join with charities or other good causes to market a product, service or the image of the organisation, for mutual benefit.

Caveat emptor   Latin for 'Let the buyer beware'.

Celebrity endorsement   Advertising which uses the credibility associated with a celebrity to endorse the message. The greater the celebrity's influence on a particular target audience, the greater the wish to mimic that celebrity.

Chaining   Suggests behaviour emerges from sequences of actions in which the preceding action becomes the discriminative stimulus for the final response (inducement > purchase).

Channel development   The development of distribution channels for the sale of products and services based on an organisation's distribution strategy.

Character-based trust   Trust in individuals (particularly important in personal selling).

Chinese wall   A term relating to the separation between editorial and advertising.

Classical conditioning   Originally identified by Ivan Pavlov, it describes a largely unconscious process through which we acquire both information and feelings about stimuli (also referred to as **respondent conditioning**).

Click-through rate   The number of times online users 'click through' or transfer to sponsored websites.

Closure   The mind's ability (based on past experience) to complete something that is incomplete (e.g. part of a name, recognition based on shape, etc.).

Co-branding   This appears in two forms: (1) involves joint marketing of products or services such that both brands benefit in terms of exposure; and (2) involves a commercial and charitable partner.

Cognitive dissonance   A situation involving conflicting attitudes, beliefs or behaviours that produces a feeling of discomfort, leading to an alteration in one of the attitudes, beliefs or behaviours to reduce the discomfort and restore cognitive balance.

Cognitive learning   Cognitive learning theory suggests that humans store information for different periods of time (see, later, sensory storage, short-term memory and long-term memory).

Cognitive paradigm   Focuses on an individual's thought processes and sees consumer choice as a problem-solving and decision-making series of activities, the outcome of which is determined principally by the buyer's intellectual functioning and rational goal-orientated processing of information.

Cognitive response model   A model that maintains that exposure to advertising elicits different types of response and purports to suggest how these responses relate to attitudes and purchase intentions (Belch & Belch 2011).

Cognitive   The process of thinking involving the mental processes of memory, perception, judgement and reasoning.

Cold calling   The process of approaching prospective customers or clients, typically via the telephone, who have not agreed to be approached.

Combined offer   A joint brand promotion (e.g. free hair gel with shampoo).

Commercial   A television or radio advertisement (also known as an advert or ad).

Communications (or reputation) audit   Looks at communications' needs, patterns, flow, channels and technologies, examines content clarity and effectiveness, information needs of individuals, work groups, departments and divisions, non-verbal communications and corporate culture issues and communication impacts on motivation and performance.

Comparative advertising   Direct comparison of one brand with another, usually its main competitor. This may be to establish the brand's position in the marketplace or to claim price or some other superiority.

Competition   In sales promotion terms, where the challenge is skill-based.

Competitive parity (for budgeting)   Spending determined relative to the spending of the organisation's major competitor(s).

Competitive positioning   Focuses on the advantages of the brand relative to its competition. This type of positioning is often used to establish the profile of a new brand or to distinguish an existing brand in a highly competitive marketplace.

Compiled list   A list of individuals with identified characteristics but not identified product interest.

Complaints   A statement that a particular situation (or series of situations) gives rise to dissatisfaction (also called **customer voice**).

Conative   Doing/action processes; behaviour directed towards positive action.

Concept stage   The period when campaign concepts, ideas, themes and content are being developed.

Conditioned response   The outcome of a conditioned stimulus. For example, the ringing of a bell (conditioned stimulus) means food (unconditioned stimulus) is coming which may cause salivation (conditioned response).

Conditioned stimulus   Something that is associated with something else that is naturally stimulating (e.g. the ringing of a bell means food is coming).

Confidence interval   In market research, how different the results must be before you can be confident of their significance.

Connectors   A collective name for opinion formers and opinion leaders and others (e.g. family) who help to carry the message to the consumer (also referred to as **influentials, carriers, trendsetters** and **evangelists**).

Connotative   Words having meaning unique to the individual.

Consumer jury   A collection of target consumers who are asked to rank in order ideas or concepts put to them and explain their choices.

Content analysis   Used to quantify the results of unstructured (qualitative) data. This is a technique for making inferences (or recognising patterns) from the data.

Content   The keywords or key phrases relevant to a site; also called key words.

Contextual advertising   A form of targeted advertising appearing on websites or other media, selected and displayed by automatic systems based on the content on display to the user.

Continuity series   Where a finite number of items (usually in a series or set) is made available over time (e.g. monthly).

Continuous (advertising)   Where there is relatively even advertising expenditure over the year.

Continuous credit   By paying in instalments, a line of continuous credit (to a maximum amount) is offered to the customer.

Control and evaluation   The means by which a plan is monitored, controlled and measured.

Control sample   The sample which is unaffected by change against which altered variables can be tested.

Cookie   A small piece of information stored as a text file on a computer that a web server uses when browsing websites that have been visited before. Typically, a cookie records preferences when an individual visits a particular site.

Cooperative strategy   Retailers and suppliers working together to develop business through distribution and other efficiencies.

Copy   Relates to written material. Advertising copy is the text in an advertisement. Journalistic copy relates to published articles.

Corporate advertising   Advertising designed to promote and enhance the image of the company among its target publics.

Corporate communications   An organisational function that controls all aspects of communication with an organisation's publics outside of marketing.

Cost-based fee   A fee that relies on an agreed mark-up on the campaign inputs (e.g. advertising).

Coupon   A voucher printed in-store or from packs, magazines, etc. which offers a money-off or other incentive to buy a product(s).

CPT/CPM   Cost per thousand – a calculation based on advertising costs x 1000, divided by circulation or target audience circulation.

Crawling   The name given to the way the Google search engine builds profiles of web pages.

Creative platform   The creative idea on which a campaign is built and which is guided by the problem the campaign seeks to resolve, the key benefit and other factors associated with the brand.

Creatives   Individuals who work in the creative industries (e.g. designers).

Creativity (in advertising)   The ability to attract and hold the attention of the target audience through the manner and composition of the advertisement.

Credentials presentation   Where an agency presents its reasons why it is a good fit with the organisation's campaign strategy.

Credit rating   Ratings based on the perceived financial integrity of the organisation; ratings are set by ratings agencies.

Crisis management   Management of a crisis situation that has the capacity to severely damage an organisation.

Cross-sell   Selling existing customers products or services outside of their existing purchase(s).

Current image   The image held by outsiders based on a consensus of perceptions modelled by their knowledge and experience.

Customer acquisition   The process of acquiring new customers.

Customer relationship maintenance   The maintenance of regular contact with a customer.

Customer relationship management (CRM)   A system for managing a company's interactions with customers.

Customer retention   The process of retaining existing customers.

DAGMAR   A model promoted as a means of establishing the objectives of an advertising campaign (Colley 1961), standing for **D**efining **A**dvertising **G**oals for **M**easuring **A**dvertising **R**esults.

Data collection   The collection of data that will inform a particular research project.

Data mining   The extraction of data from a data depository in a form useful to marketers.

Data warehousing   The storing of data from a variety of sources. The data is stored because it may not be currently usable, either because its value is not immediately appreciated or because it requires further qualification.

Day-after recall (recall surveys)   Unprompted recall of the previous day's advertising, a methodology originally developed by Gallup in the 1930s.

Decision (in terms of buyer behaviour)   The decision to act on information gathered to fulfil a previously recognised problem.

Decoding   Translating the message into understandable ideas/concepts.

De-duping   The removal of duplicate names from mailing and other lists.

Demographic segmentation   Statistical data relating to the population and groups within it.

Demonstration advertising   Advertising that demonstrates the effectiveness of the product or service and the way it may be used.

Denotative   Words having meaning for everybody.

Design elements (of a brand)   Include the logo, graphic features, typeface, symbols and colours that stimulate the recognition and remembrance of a brand.

Differentiation   The process of making the organisation's brand different from other brands through marketing.

Diffusion of innovation   The way that new product or service developments (e.g. mobile telephones) enter the market. Rogers' (1983) theory of diffusion suggests that various consumers adopt over different time periods. These he called innovators, early adopters, early majority, late majority and laggards.

Direct channel marketing   Where an organisation sells virtually the same products/services to both consumers and businesses.

Direct mail   Advertising, through the medium of the mail, to targeted, profiled customers.

Direct marketing   Seeks to target individual customers with the intention of delivering personalised messages and building a relationship with them based on their responses to direct communication.

Direct opinion measurement   Research that directly asks target consumers about aspects of a campaign such as message clarity, interest, feelings and attitudes.

Direct response television (DRTV)   DRTV refers to commercials or paid programming made for television in which viewers are encouraged to order either through a web page or by telephone.

Direct response   Media where the customer can respond immediately to the offfer.

Discriminative stimulus   A particular stimulus (e.g. a light being switched on) that suggests if you do something (e.g. push a button) you will receive a reward (e.g. food).

Door to door   The household delivery of leaflets, samples, etc.

Double-header   Distinctive brands sold in distinctive retail (online or off-line) outlets.

Drip   Extends the campaign over time which increases potential frequency. This is often used for 'reminder campaigns' or when an objective is to change long-term attitudes.

Dummy   An uncirculated, trial edition of a magazine sent to target advertisers or target audiences.

Early adopters   Frequently the opinion leaders. Their entry into the market is significant. They are generally younger with an above average education and/or income.

Early majority   Entry of the early majority of customers represents the first move towards general acceptance. The speed of adoption can be seen to have increased considerably by this stage.

Editorial   Although the term should strictly only be applied to copy written by a newspaper or magazine editor (or that publication's online equivalent), it is frequently used to describe all off-line and online newspaper or magazine copy.

Effective creativity   Creativity that meets the commercial objectives of a campaign.

Efficiency Index   An index which assumes that with each exposure of an advertisement there is a greater chance of reaching and influencing an audience – up to a point. After this point is reached, each exposure no longer adds 'reach' or improves effectiveness.

Electronic point of sale (EPOS)   Technology at the point of sale that enables transactions to be tracked on a merchandise and customer level.

Emotional appeal advertising   Advertising that develops atmosphere and appeals to an individual's ego, status or sense of worth.

Emotional strategies   These strategies appeal to emotions, such as romantic feelings, nostalgia, compassion, excitement, joy, heroism, fear, guilt, disgust and regret.

Emotive motivation   Strong mental or instinctive feeling (e.g. love, fear, etc.) that drives actions.

Encode, encoded (messages)   Putting the idea into a format (e.g. speech, print, etc.) using a combination of appropriate words, pictures and symbols so that it can be transmitted via a medium.

Encoding   The process by which information is symbolically or verbally represented so that it can easily be stored and retrieved (e.g. jingles, taglines, etc.).

Enquirer   A prospect who has directly contacted the company for specific information.

ERG theory   ERG (Existence, Relatedness and Growth) is Alderfer's (1972) theory of motivation. Unlike Maslow's hierarchy, it allows for different levels of needs to be pursued at the same time, differential personal ordering and regression.

Erotica (in advertising)   Where sexual imagery is used to attract attention and enhance stopping power.

Esteem needs   Those needs which are associated with social recognition, status, etc. (Maslow's hierarchy of needs).

Ethical marketing   Concerned with social well-being as it relates to marketing practice.

Ethnography (ethnographic research)   Where researchers submerge themselves in consumer culture in order to view consumer dynamics. Photography and video diaries are used by market researchers to delve into consumers' minds.

Evaluation   Consideration of information collected prior to purchase.

Everyday low prices   A strategy where the emphasis is on low prices across the store (in contrast to the hi-lo pricing strategy).

Evoked set   Those products in a category that the consumer has 'front of mind' and will make the purchase choice from.

Experience (in relation to purchasing)   The extent to which the consumer has accumulated prior knowledge of the product or service.

Experiential marketing   A strategy that encourages customers to engage and interact with brands, products and services in sensory ways.

Expert endorsement   Advertising which uses known or supposed (from their description or appearance) experts to recommend a product or service.

Expertise   Expertise includes aptitude, required training and experience and is domain specific.

Exploratory research   Initial research designed to establish the parameters of the research problem.

Extended problem solving   A model where purchase decisions are characterised by their importance (high involvement) and rational decision making.

Factor analysis   A systematic review of the correlation between research variables, which groups together those that are highly correlated to reduce a large number of variables to a smaller set of variables that are not correlated.

Fashion icons   Celebrity fashion leaders (e.g. David Beckham and Lady Gaga).

Fear (in advertising)   Advertising that uses fear of something happening (e.g. a house fire) as the central theme.

Feedback   Information regarding the receiver's reaction to a message used as a measure of understanding and, where appropriate, response to any call to action (e.g. a sale).

Field marketing   Syndicated or shared teams working largely in the fast moving consumer goods sector, who carry out a number of selling and other 'sales' associated tasks on behalf of one or more suppliers.

Field of perception   An individual's range of understanding. Overlapping fields of perception enable understanding (also referred to as realm of perception and realm of understanding).

First-mover advantage   Advantage associated with being the first organisation in the marketplace and which may include experience, distribution channels, etc.

Flanker brands   Where a supplier takes advantage of its market strength to introduce additional brands to compete against the competition brands for shelf space.

Flighting   Expenditure concentrated on some periods, leaving other periods with zero expenditure.

Flyer   A pamphlet which promotes a brand(s) and which may be delivered or collected by consumers.

Fly-posting   Posters randomly affixed to walls rather than licensed hoardings.

FMCG   Fast-moving consumer goods (such as those sold in supermarkets).

Focus group   Normally consists of a small number (8–10) of target consumers brought together to discuss elements of a campaign from the initial concept stage to post production.

Follower brands   Brands that are not leaders in their particular category.

Footfall   Retail jargon for the number of customers who visit a store during a specific time period.

Frequency   The number of times the target audience has an opportunity to see (OTS) or hear (OTH) the message.

Frequency-capped   Regulation of the number of times an advert is shown online in a particular period.

Front of mind   Where the brand is kept at the forefront of the consumer's mind through advertising and other marketing communications.

Front-of-mind awareness   Maintaining awareness of the brand in the consumer's mind.

Frustration–regression principle   Acknowledges that if higher needs remain unfulfilled, an individual may regress to lower-level motivations (ERG theory).

Fugging   Fundraising under the guise of marketing research.

Full service agency   An agency that covers a full range of disciplines, including copy writing, design and media purchase.

Functional orientation   Where the positioning is based on that feature(s) or attribute(s) that is unique (or can be made to appear unique) to that brand.

Generic communications   Communications designed to expand the sector rather than any individual brand within it.

Generic strategies   Where a brand is so dominant in a sector that there is (at that time) no need to differentiate the brand from its competitors. Effectively, these brands are looking to grow the total market in the knowledge that any increase will disproportionately benefit them.

Geodemographic profiles   Combining both geographical and demographic features to provide a profile.

Geodemographics   A method of segregating a market on the basis of social demographics and location.

Geographical identifiers   Signs and symbols, associated with a particular brand, that suggest a geographical location.

Gestalt approach   Gestalt (German for 'whole' or 'entirely') and gestalt psychology stress the fact that perception of a stimulus takes place within a known context and that the individual's reaction is crucially affected by his or her 'world view'.

Giveaways   Products distributed (in-store or elsewhere) without cost as a means of encouraging trial.

Glocal   Thinking global but acting local.

Goodwill   The disparity in value between the firm's asset value and the estimated worth of the business.

Graphic features   Those design features that are unique and which distinguish a brand (e.g. McDonald's 'golden arches') from its competition.

Gripe site   A website created to carry negative messages concerning an organisation(s) and/or brand(s).

Gross rating points (GRPs)   An advertising media currency calculated by multiplying 'reach' and 'frequency'.

Guerrilla marketing   A marketing tactic, originally described by Jay Conrad Levinson, which uses surprise and/or unconventional (and sometimes personal) interaction to promote products, services, ideas, etc. and which intends to get maximum results from minimum outlay.

Halo effect   Those aspects of the brand that are portrayed to the outside world through marketing communications. The effect involves image management and the building up of benefits, brand personality and associations. It is the halo characteristics that consumers use to distinguish one brand from another.

Hand raiser   A prospect who has indicated by their behaviour (e.g. ordering a catalogue) that they may want to become a customer.

Hard sell   Promoting heavily the tangible benefits available from a product or service.

Hedonic consumption   The use of products or services for sheer enjoyment rather than to solve a problem or need.

Heuristic evaluation   Where evaluation is intuitive and made based on extraneous factors such as price, status, etc.

Hierarchy of effects models   Models that purport to show how marketing communications can help the buying process. AIDA and DAGMAR (see Glossary) are among the best known.

High consumerism   In global marketing terms, developed or highly sophisticated markets.

Hi-lo (or high-low) pricing   A strategy, prevalent in FMCG retailing, where each week a percentage of products is heavily discounted and promoted throughout the store.

Hostaging   Where the retailer/reseller is able to exert influence over the brand owner and to insist on trade promotions on a more or less permanent basis.

House list   A list compiled from a company's own database.

Humorous advertising   Designed to attract, through humour, consumer attention. If it is good enough and is memorable, it may also generate 'word of mouth'.

Hypodermic effect   An early model of marketing communications that inferred communication was one way (also known as **magic bullet**).

Iconic learning   Developing an association between two or three concepts when there is an absence of stimuli.

Identified product interest (IPI)   An interest in a particular product or service category.

Image study   A study of the organisation's perceived image in relation to its competitors.

Image   A perception of an organisation or brand that exists in the minds of customers, stakeholders and publics.

Impression   A single instance of an advertisement being displayed/broadcast.

In-bound telemarketing   The use of telephony to facilitate responses from customers, usually via a 'freephone' or local call rate number.

Incentive   An extra inducement to purchase.

In-depth interviews   A qualitative research technique that involves conducting intensive individual interviews with a small number of interviewees.

Indirect address   In advertising, where the potential consumer 'eavesdrops' on, for example, a family, a group of friends, other groups or individuals.

Information search   Where the customer collects information on a range of products or services prior to purchase.

Ingredient brands   Where a branded ingredient or component is incorporated in another brand.

Innovators   Those customers who are at the forefront of trends, particularly in technical innovation. They are likely to have a high disposable income and are willing to pay a high price for being first in the market.

Insights   The understanding, in a particular context, of a specific cause and effect.

Institutional trust   Trust that is based on the rule of law (e.g. minimum standards legislation) or qualification (e.g. doctors, lecturers, etc.).

Integrated marketing communications   A concept of marketing communications planning that recognises the added value of a comprehensive plan that evaluates the strategic roles of a variety of communication disciplines and combines these disciplines to provide clarity, consistency and maximum communications impact.

Internal communications   The sharing of information within an organisation for business purposes that takes place via various communication channels.

International company   One whose home market dominates sales, but for whom the export market holds the promise of extra turnover.

Internet shopping   The process that enables consumers to buy directly any goods or services from a seller in real time, without visiting a retail intermediary.

Involvement   The degree of perceived relevance and personal importance attached to the purchase.

Joint advertising   Where the cost of advertising is shared, not necessarily equally, between retailer and supplier.

Junk mail   Any mailing the customer decides is untargeted and obtrusive.

Key account managers   Marketing and/or sales executives who work specifically with one or a limited number of accounts.

Knowledge capital   The knowledge held within an organisation.

Laggards   Sometimes technophobic, this is the last group to take up an innovation.

Lagged effect   The time between when a consumer sees an advertisement and when they are ready to act on it (e.g. purchase.)

Lapsed customer   A customer who has not purchased from the company for a particular length of time.

Late majority   Sceptical of new ideas, these customers eventually take up the innovation.

Lead qualification   Improving the quality of the information known about a customer/prospect.

Learning   The human capacity to know about and act on a situation based on prior experience.

Lifestyle segmentation   A method of segmentation based on lifestyle characteristics.

Lifetime value   A calculation made (usually on the basis of likely future business discounted to present-day value) of the likely value to an organisation over a customer's lifetime.

Limited problem solving   Known and familiar purchases (modified or straight re-buys) with medium involvement in the purchase.

Line extension   Extending the products or services in an existing category using an existing brand name from that category.

Link building   The building of inbound links from other websites to increase relevance to search engines.

List broker   An intermediary between list owners and organisations wishing to rent lists.

List exchange   Exchange of customer data between companies (illegal in certain countries).

List   A listing of potential customers with a specific characteristic (e.g. food-loving), available to rent for a specific direct mail, telemarketing or email campaign.

Livery   See Signage. Particularly relates to vehicles or uniforms.

Logical appeal or (reason why) advertising   Advertising that appeals to our sense of logic and reason, for example 'this product out-performs everything else on the market'.

Logo   An emblem or device used to distinguish an organisation or brand.

Long-term memory   Information stored for extensive periods of time, although constant reorganisation and re-categorisation take place as new information is received.

Loss leader   A product sold at or below cost to attract customers into a store. Any 'loss' is made up by the purchase of other products.

Low consumerism   In global marketing terms, undeveloped or unsophisticated markets.

Low-involvement theory   A theory that suggests that consumers scan the environment, largely subconsciously, to identify anything worth in-depth consideration.

Loyalty card   A card issued to consumers by loyalty scheme organisers to facilitate the management and control of the scheme.

Loyalty scheme   A scheme that rewards customers for purchases over time.

Mail order   The ability (through selection in a catalogue, internet site or flyer) to order products for delivery by mail.

MAO factors   Petty and Cacioppo's (1986) model suggests that it is not only motivation but the ability to process information and the opportunity to make it happen that have a role to play in successful communications. The MAO factors are Motivation (a willingness to engage in behaviour, make decisions, pay attention and process information), Ability (the resources needed to achieve a particular goal) and Opportunity (the extent to which the situation enables a person to obtain his/her goal).

Marcoms   A frequently used shorthand for 'marketing communications'.

Marked down   Products or services where the normal retail price is reduced.

Market share   The brand's share of a market sector usually shown as a percentage of the whole sector.

Marketing communications mix   The tools used in marketing communications such as advertising, sales promotion, public relations, personal selling, direct marketing, etc. (also referred to as the **promotional mix**).

Marketing communications plan   A systematic plan to achieve organisational and marketing objectives relative to marketing communications.

Marketing communications   The means by which a supplier of goods, services, values and/or ideas represents itself to its target audience with the goal of stimulating dialogue, leading to better commercial or other relationships.

Marketing compliance officer   An officer responsible for ensuring the organisation complies with laws and regulations.

Marketing public relations   Those aspects of public relations directly associated with communication with customers or prospective customers (i.e. publicity).

Marketing research   A collection of 'tools' of assessment, evaluation and measurement which seeks to reduce the knowledge 'distance' between the product or service provider and the consumer, primarily through the supply of pertinent information concerning that customer and the marketplace the customer operates within..

Mass media   Largely untargeted media, including newspapers, television, radio, etc.

Measurement techniques   Those techniques (largely quantitative) that are used to collect data. Examples include questionnaires and attitude scales.

Media broker   An intermediary who purchases media space (only) without the overheads of a full agency.

Media chatter   Subject matter that is discussed by, and in, the media.

Media dependent   A media broker that is part of a larger agency group.

Media evaluation   Evaluation of an organisation's media coverage over a specific time period.

Media fragmentation   The dilution of TV or radio station audiences due to the proliferation of channels.

Media independent   An independent media broker.

Media strategy   Decisions on which media to use for a given campaign.

Media-neutral planning   A customer-focused review of media based on research, analysis and insight and not on habit and/or preference.

Medium/Media   A means of carrying the message (also referred to as media channel), such as television, radio, newspapers, etc.

Message   The vehicle by which an idea is transmitted via a medium (e.g. television).

Meta tags   A special HTML (or XHTML) tag that provides information about a web page which provides information on what the page is about, and which keywords represent the page's content. Many search engines use this information.

Me-too products   New products that are similar to existing products already available in the marketplace.

Mexico Statement   A definition of public relations which originated at a public relations conference held in Mexico City in 1978.

Mirror image   How internal management think outsiders see the organisation.

Mis-selling   Selling something based on a falsehood.

Mission statement   A statement that asserts the core business of an organisation and its ambitions.

Mission   The core business of an organisation and its ambitions usually set out in the company's mission statement.

Mobile marketing   The use of the mobile telephone medium as a means of marketing communications.

Modelling approach   Where the consumer, through observation and imitation of others (for example, in an advertisement), associates something with their lifestyle; also called observational learning and vicarious learning.

Monetary value   What value does the customer spend with the company?

Mortgaging effect   Where, after a promotion, rather than returning to 'normal', sales levels fall back for a period.

Motivation   An inner drive which cause human beings to strive for some level of satisfaction.

Multi-branding   Where different brand names owned by one company are used in the same product category (e.g. *Procter & Gamble* soap powders *Dreft*, *Daz* and *Bold*).

Multi-channel retailer   A retailer with a number of channels, such as online and retail space.

Multi-dimensional skills map   A matrix used to establish a customer's view of the organisation relative to its competitors (also referred to as a perception map).

Multi-level marketing (network selling)   Selling direct to the public through a network of self-employed salespeople, often through house parties and other private gatherings. The multi-level marketing company initially recruits distributors who in turn recruit more distributors, and so on. Earnings come both from a distributor's own sales and the sales of those they recruit (and often even further down the line).

Multinational company   One that operates in a number of overseas markets, often through agents or distributors, but that would normally secure more (relative to international companies) control over them.

Multiple image   Where different people see different images, dependent on their particular relationship with the organisation.

Multivariate testing   A method of testing which uses different content for many elements across one or more web pages to identify the combination of changes that yields the highest conversion rate.

Mystery shopper   A researcher who visits a store in the guise of a shopper for the purposes of research and observation.

Natural search   A search (using a search engine) where results are returned based on the natural indexing of the website, as opposed to those that are returned based on paid advertising and/or editorial changes made by the search engine itself.

Nature   Those characteristics we inherit from our forebears.

Need for cognition   A need to understand the world such that it develops a curiosity for further information (see cognition).

Negative binomial distribution (or double jeopardy)   A theory that suggests that advertising does not generally work to persuade as it fails to attract new buyers to a product or service, although it may help to keep current purchasers 'loyal' by default.

Negative reinforcement   Punishment which reinforces the avoidance of behaviour that led to the punishment.

Noise   Anything that interferes with the proper delivery of the message (e.g. competing messages).

Non-probability techniques   Techniques which do not adhere to the law of probability and, therefore, the results cannot be generalised across the population. Rather, the sample is chosen at the convenience of the researcher or to fulfil the demands of some predetermined purpose.

Nurture   The effect of society on the characteristics and attitudes we are born with.

Objective and task (for budgeting)   Establishing what needs to be achieved and setting the budget on the basis of achieving these objectives.

Observation   Examining actual as opposed to predicted behaviour, such as an observation of consumers by a researcher interested in the effect on sales of an in-store promotion.

Off the page   Newspaper or magazine offers with a direct-response mechanism (e.g. freephone, envelope, etc.).

Offering   A number of factors (product, price, etc.) which together make up the direct marketing offering to the customer.

Oligopolies   A market situation in which there are few, dominant sellers in the market and where the marketing action of one firm will have a direct effect on the others.

Omnibus survey   Long-term tracking of consumer attitudes and opinions.

One-pipe convergence   The movement in technology toward a single broadband feed which supplies all the televisions, PCs, iPads, games consoles and stereo systems in a house or other building.

One-to-one marketing   A concept that proposes that customers can be individually targeted.

On-message   In political terms, the requirement for all prominent (therefore quotable) members of a political party to be delivering the same message.

Operant conditioning   Where reinforcement follows a specific action – for example, do this (e.g. push a button) and you will receive a reward (e.g. food); also referred to as **instrumental conditioning.**

Opinion formers   People with potential influence or authority over our lives, such as journalists, broadcasters, analysts, politicians, scientists or anyone with some real or imagined status who can be trusted (rightly or wrongly) to impart good advice.

Opinion leaders   May not be formal experts. They do not necessarily provide advice but consumers are prone to follow them. They are often, but not always, from a higher social status than their immediate contemporaries and frequently more gregarious.

Opportunities to see (OTS)   A calculation of the number of times the target audience has a chance to see (or hear) an advertisement.

Optimum image   The image a company aspires to (wish image) may not be possible and so a rather less than perfect image may be sought.

Out-bound telemarketing   Planned use of the telephone to make unstructured calls to a target audience in a measurable and accountable way.

Outdoor advertising   Posters, billboards, transport and other signs that publicly display advertising in an outdoor location.

Over-selling   Promising more than is available through the sale.

Own brand   A retail brand that carries the retailer's name and/or logo rather than that of any other brand.

Paid inclusion   Also known as sponsored listings, it is a service where the search engine company charges fees for the inclusion of websites in their search index.

Paid-for placement (PFP)   Where an advertiser pays to guarantee their listing appears on a search page when particular keywords are searched. The ranking of paid placement listings is usually determined by a competitive bidding process.

Pareto analysis   The general supposition that business relationships follow an 80:20 ratio (e.g. 80% of business comes from 20% of customers).

Parity brand   A product or service with little or no intrinsically superior rewards compared with the competition, typically leaving marketers to offer extrinsic rewards to attract patronage.

Pay-back period (for budgeting)   Where budget decisions are made based on the time taken to repay the investment.

Percentage of sales (for budgeting)   Where the communications budget is set at a certain percentage of projected sales.

Perception   Perception is the result of how we interpret and make sense of the world. The way an individual perceives a situation may be different from how others perceive the same situation.

Perceptual map (or multidimensional skills map)   A matrix used to establish a brand's positioning against certain criteria.

Performance-based compensation or payment by results (PBR)   A fee based on measurable targets set for a particular campaign.

Personal selling   An interpersonal tool where individuals, often representing an organisation, interact in order to inform, persuade or remind an individual or group to take appropriate action, as required by the sponsors.

Persuasion shift   Changes in preferences which occur in people who have seen an advertisement or other communication.

Physiological needs   Fundamental life-surviving needs, such as those that stave off hunger, thirst, etc. (Maslow's hierarchy of needs).

Pitch list   Those agencies invited to pitch for the organisation's/brand's communications account(s).

Pitch   A presentation by an agency to the client organisation.

Point of sale (point of purchase)   In-store materials displayed at the place where customers are making their buying decisions.

Population   In marketing research terms, population is the group (demographic, geodemographic, users, former customers, etc.) of interest to the marketer.

Pop-up   A message box that 'pops up' on websites, either to add additional information or as advertising.

Portfolio of brands   A consumer's basket of brands from which final buying decisions are made.

Portfolio or broad repertoire view   This perspective suggests that we each generate, through trial, a portfolio of brands from which we make our choice.

Positioning statement (or single-minded proposition)   A statement designed to incorporate the essence of what a brand stands for in the minds of target audiences relative to their impression of competitor brands.

Positioning   The process of creating a perception in the consumer's mind regarding the nature of the company and its products relative to the competition (see also benefit positioning, user positioning and competitive positioning).

Positive reinforcement   A reward which reinforces the behaviour that led to the reward.

Post-purchase dissonance   The mental discomfort felt after a purchase is made regarding whether or not the buyer has made the right decision (e.g. is it value for money?).

Post-purchase evaluation   Evaluation of a product or service after consumption which may lead to re-purchase.

Post-testing   Testing that takes place after a campaign and which may be compared with pre-campaign test results.

Prebuttle   The reply to a message (often an accusation) that has not yet been made.

Precisely wrong   Strictly a precise but incorrect measure. Proxy measures such as brand awareness, recall or recognition, while being easy to measure precisely are not directly associated with sales and might be said to be precisely wrong (see vaguely right).

Pre-emptive strategies   Where the brand asserts its superiority in an undifferentiated market, making it difficult for competitors to match such assertions (e.g. 'Carlsberg – probably the best lager in the world').

Premium   A gift given to consumers either with purchase or, if terms (e.g. collect five wrappers) have to be fulfilled, by other means (e.g. through an online site).

Press office or media office   An office which handles press and other media enquiries and issues press releases.

Press officer (PRO) or media officer (MRO)   A representative of the company who handles press and other media enquiries and issues press/media releases.

Press release   Newsworthy publicity distributed to selected media.

Primary data   Data collected specifically for a particular research project.

Priming   Suggests that short exposure to a particular stimulus can evoke an increased drive to consume more of a product.

Prize draw   Where the winning of a competition is randomised.

Probability techniques   Those techniques of selection that are independent of human judgement, producing a known and non-zero probability of any one particular case in the population of cases being included in the sample. They are representative of (but never an exact match with) the population as a whole and a determination is made of their statistical accuracy.

Problem recognition   Recognition that a purchase must be made to fulfil a need or want (also referred to as **problem definition**).

Problem-solving model   An extensive, limited and routinised problem-solving model.

Product/message thoughts   Those thoughts directed at the product/service and/or the claims made in the advertising (see cognitive response model).

Profiled prospect   A prospect whose general profile suggests they may become a customer.

Profit optimisation (for budgeting)   Suggests that investment continues as long as the marginal revenue exceeds the marginal cost.

Proprietary panel   An online survey set up or commissioned by a client firm, usually made up of customers of that company.

Prospect hierarchy   A hierarchy of potential customers ranging from lapsed customers at the top to 'suspects' at the bottom.

Prospect   A potential customer.

Proxy measures   Measures used when the marketing communications effect on sales cannot be directly measured.

Public affairs   A specialist area of practice within public relations concerned with public policy making, legislation and regulation that may affect the interests of the organisation.

Public relations transfer process   A theory of public relations that suggests incremental stages between hostility and acceptance.

Public relations   The planned and sustained effort to establish and maintain good will and mutual understanding between an organisation and its publics.

Publicist   A professional who seeks to promote or protect their clients in or from the media.

Publicity   Building the image of the brand and creating positive associations between that brand and its publics.

Publics   'Publics' are those people, internal and external to the organisation, with whom an organisation communicates.

Puffery   Claim(s) made by advertisers, not capable of measurement, that the average consumer would not take seriously.

Pull strategies   Strategies which look to influence the end-user and attract these customers (through marketing communications) 'over the heads' of retailers direct to the individual brand.

Pulsing A continuous advertising campaign which is stronger at different times of the year and which may reflect seasonal considerations.

Purchase The act of exchange of one commodity for another (usually money).

Push strategies Strategies designed to influence re-sellers or trade channel intermediaries (e.g. wholesalers, dealers, agents, retailers) to carry and promote particular brands (i.e. they are 'pushed' into the distribution chain).

Pyramid selling A form of multi-level marketing where the central purpose is to earn commission (or receive other payments) from those further down the line rather than make sales per se.

Quack medicine Derives from the arcaic Dutch word quacksalver (hawker of salve) – a derogatory term used to describe the promotion of unproven or fraudulent medicines.

Qualitative research Looking to answer the 'why?' and the 'how?' questions, this type of research places greater emphasis on understanding consumer behaviour through insights and is often referred to as 'rich data'.

Quantitative research Seeking to answer the questions 'how many?', 'what?' or 'who?', it is research that is looking to quantify something.

Questionnaire or survey research Research which uses structured or semi-structured questions delivered personally, via mail, telephone, email or through online means.

Ratchet effect Predicts the advantages of an integrated strategy that builds credibility through advertising and extra volume through promotional inducements.

Rate card The published cost of media advertising.

Ratings agency An organisation such as Dun and Bradstreet or Standard and Poor's who monitors companies and establishes credit ratings based on perceived commercial risk. These ratings affect the company's ability to lend and the rate on which the loan is based.

Reach The percentage of the target audience exposed at least once to the message during a period (normally four weeks).

Reasoning Where consumers take the information they have about a brand and deduce their own conclusion regarding the brand's suitability for purchase and use. Individuals need to restructure and reorganise information already held in long-term memory and combine this with new information. Thus, quite complex associations build up (e.g. Silk Cut cigarettes and silk ribbon, Red Bull with flying).

Rebating Giving the client part or all of the commission paid by media owners.

Recency principle A principle which supposes that a consumer's first exposure to an advertisement is the most powerful, that the advertiser's primary role is to influence brand choice (when the customer is ready to buy) and that achieving a high level of weekly reach for a brand should be emphasised over acquiring heavy frequency (also referred to as the shelf-space model).

Recency How recently has a customer purchased from a company?

Recognition survey A survey which looks for a positive response to one or more of a selection of products presented to the interviewee.

Reference groups Groups with whom consumers associate themselves, e.g. faith groups, social groups.

Referral A prospect who has been encouraged by an existing customer to contact the company.

Refund Given by way of cash or coupons, this may involve one or more purchases and submitting proof of purchase by mail or through claims managed via the internet.

Rehearsal   A process which aids memory. By mentally repeating the information, the individual increases the chance that it will be linked to other stored information (i.e. learning by rote).

Relationship marketing   To 'identify and establish, maintain and enhance and, when necessary, terminate relationships with customers and other stakeholders, at a profit so that the objectives of all parties involved are met; and this is done by mutual exchange and fulfilment of promises' (Grönroos 1994).

Relaunch   The reforming of an entity following a dramatic or negative occurrence.

Reminder campaign   Follows major campaigns and acts as a reminder and reinforcement of the message.

Repetition   Repeat exposure to the brand message (also referred to as frequency).

Repositioning or targeted differentiation   The process of recreating or changing the perception of a brand in the consumer's mind.

Reputation   Trust and confidence built up over time and based on past performance.

Research problem   What the research is designed to solve.

Research proposal   A proposal detailing the resources required for a particular research project.

Re-sellers   Wholesalers, dealers, agents, retailers, etc., online or off-line, who distribute goods from producers to consumers (also referred to as trade channel intermediaries).

Resonance (or 'slice-of-life') strategies   These strategies match 'patterns' in the message with target audiences' shared experiences.

Response list   A list of prospective customers with identified product interest (IPI).

Response mechanism   The means by which a customer responds to an offer (e.g. internet site, email address, SMS text details, freephone number, freepost).

Retainer fee   A fixed amount of money that a client agrees to pay, in advance, to secure the services of an agency or specialist.

Retrieval   The process whereby information is returned from the long-term to the short-term memory.

Rolling research (syndicated research or audit data)   Research carried out by specialist agencies who collect and analyse data on a regular (rolling research) or one-off basis. Clients normally pay a subscription for these services which are available for both retail (e.g. Nielsen) and specialist markets.

Rolling research   Research that takes place on a regular basis and asks the same questions each time so that response comparisons can be made.

Routinised problem solving   Repeat behaviour with low involvement, usually low cost and often limited external knowledge.

Safety needs   Those needs which enhance our security, protection, etc. and that of those close to us (Maslow's hierarchy of needs).

Sales promotion   The offering of a short-term incentive, encouraging people to act.

Sample selection   Determines the body of individuals to be targeted in a research project.

Sampling error   The error caused by sampling only a small number of the total population. Using sample data presents the risk that results found will not represent the results that would be obtained from using data involving the entire population.

Sampling   Free-of-charge trialling of products in-store or at other locations.

Saving stamps   Now largely defunct, saving stamps were a method of managing a loyalty scheme where stamps were issued with purchases, collected and ultimately exchanged for gifts of cash. Another form is still used in connection with savings clubs by some retailers.

Scheduling   The chosen media schedule format (see burst, drip, continuous, pulsing and flighting campaigns).

Scope (or reach)   The boundaries of an organisation's operations (and perhaps aspirations).

Search engine optimisation (SEO)   The process of improving the visibility of a website or web page in a search engine's 'natural' or unpaid search results.

Search engine   A programme that searches sites on the World Wide Web for specified keywords and which returns a list of where the keywords can be found.

Secondary data   Data available from one or more existing sources.

Sector awareness   Consumer awareness that a sector (e.g. tablet computers) exists.

Selective attention   The process of screening out information that does not interest us and selectively processing the information that does. Messages that successfully bypass 'selective attention' are likely to be perceived positively.

Selective distortion   The tendency to hear what we want to hear. Distortion may occur because of attitudes, prejudice or stereotyping.

Selective exposure   Where consumers selectively expose themselves to certain messages as opposed to other messages.

Self-actualisation   Described by Maslow (1943) as 'the desire for self-fulfilment, namely the tendency for him [the individual] to become actualised in what he is potentially. This tendency might be phrased as the desire to become more and more what one is, to become everything that one is capable of becoming' (Maslow's hierarchy of needs).

Self-liquidating premium   A premium (or gift) where the income received covers the outgoings of the promotion.

Semantics   The branch of linguistics concerned with meaning.

Semiotics   The study of signs and symbols in a language.

Sensory appeal (in advertising)   Creating fantasy and/or an aura to attract attention to a message.

Sensory storage   Information that is sensed in our mind for a split-second. If an impression is made, this will be transferred to the short-term memory.

Service-dominant logic   Traditional marketing had an exchange model based on goods. Service-dominant logic suggests a new approach in which service provision rather than goods or services is fundamental in any exchange.

Shaping   Suggests that a final response can be explained as 'appearing after preceding acts which, taken together, constitute a chain of successive approximations' (John Watson).

Shelf impact   The impact of product packaging in highlighting particular products.

Shock tactics (in advertising)   Advertising that is shocking but attracts attention.

Shopping cart abandonment   Where an online transaction is halted before completion.

Short-term memory   The maximum number of items stored (perhaps four or five) for short periods of time (perhaps 8 seconds).

Signage   The identity applied to buildings, vehicles, etc., denoting the organisation or its brand(s).

Significance   Analysis of differences between the observed and expected results, noting whether they are real and significant differences.

Silent calls   Calls generated by predictive dialling technology designed to speed up agent productivity but which frequently leave customers with a disturbing silence when they answer their telephone.

Silent communication   A non-verbal communication such as a shrug of the shoulders.

Simulated sales   Sales calculated on the basis of no advertising, which can then be used to measure the contribution of advertising.

Single-minded proposition   A brand's unique selling proposition.

Situational audit   An audit of the current state of the organisation, often using SWOT and PEST(L) analysis.

Slice-of-life advertising   Advertising that uses simulated 'real-life' situations and where the viewer is encouraged to get involved with the action.

Slogans   Memorable phrases that sum up an important characteristic and/or positioning of the brand (also referred to as a tagline).

Slotting allowances   Payment made to the retailer in consideration of 'slotting' a new product into that retailer's merchandise mix.

Smartphone   A mobile phone offering more advanced computing ability and connectivity than basic mobile phones.

SMS   Short message (or messaging) service that enables messages to be sent or received by mobile phone.

Social media   Online virtual communities and networks that people use to interact with others and where they can create, share and exchange information and ideas.

Social needs   Those needs that are associated with love, belonging, etc. (Maslow's hierarchy of needs).

Soft sell   Using emotional appeals to produce positive feelings for a brand.

Soundbite   The encapsulation of a message in very few words (for the purposes of television and radio journalism).

Source attractiveness   How attractive and persuasive the source is and how much the source identifies with the consumer.

Source credibility   How much confidence the receiver has that the source can provide an expert and/or objective opinion.

Source power   Where compliance with the request involves a real or perceived reward or actual or apparent avoidance of punishment.

Source   The originator of the message (also refers to the person delivering the message).

Source-orientated thoughts   Those thoughts that represent those associated (positively or negatively) with the origin of the message (see cognitive response model).

Spam   Unsolicited, untargeted emails usually sent out in bulk.

Spin doctor   Public relations jargon for a person who 'spins' or creates positive stories or deflects criticism. It is a term often used to ridicule political advisers.

Spoiler campaign   A campaign designed to neutralise or disrupt the competition.

Sponsorship   A commercial activity whereby one party permits another an opportunity to exploit a situation with a target audience in return for funds, services or resources.

Spot advertising   Advertising placed during or between broadcast programmes, typically lasting between 30 seconds and one minute.

Statements   What is said about the brand and how it is promoted through copy style and slogans/taglines.

Stereotype   To categorise an individual as part of a group and inferring that s/he will have the qualities and personality possessed generally by that group.

Stereotyping   Shorthand, generalised characteristics of people and places, used in order to communicate messages quickly and effectively.

Stickiness   Anything about a website that encourages its visitors to stay longer. A website is sticky if visitors stay for a long time and return frequently.

Stopping power   Advertising that has the effect of gaining immediate attention.

Storage   The way the memory is organised.

Storyboard   Artists' impressions of television, cinematic and online advertising campaigns prior to production.

Straight re-buy   A business-to-business (B2B) term for re-buying a product without changing the supplier or the specifications.

Strategies   The ways that objectives are to be achieved. Communication strategies are the ways an organisation chooses to communicate with its customers and other stakeholders.

Strong theory (of advertising)   Suggests that advertising has the power to inform, persuade and sell products, services or ideas.

Suggestions   Constructive feedback from staff, customers and others with a stake-holding in the organisation.

Sugging   Selling under the guise of marketing research.

Summated scale   Where scores are applied to individual responses that are then added together to produce an overall result (e.g. the Likert scale).

Suspects   Geodemographic profiling, values, attitudes and lifestyle profiling (VALs) or previous purchase behaviour indicate that these customers may have the profile of current customers.

Symbolic/experiential orientation   Where positioning is based on the emotional needs of consumers and is therefore concerned with psychosocial rather than physical differentiation (see also experiential orientation).

Syndicated research or audit data   Carried out by specialist agencies who collect and analyse data on a regular (rolling research) or one-off basis. Clients normally pay a subscription for these services.

Syntactics   The grammatical arrangement of words.

Tactics   The operational element of the communications plan and, by definition, short term. The choice may be between different media or various marcoms techniques.

Tagline (or strapline or slogan)   A memorable phrase that sums up an important characteristic of the brand.

Target audience   A defined group of consumers (demographic, geodemographic, users, former customers, etc.) targeted by the marketer.

Target rating points (TRPs)   A variation of gross ratings points adjusted to reflect the chosen target audience.

Telemarketing   The use of telephony to maintain a relationship with your customers.

Telesales   Cold calling (without prior contact or permission) with the objective of making a sale or starting the process towards a sale.

Test markets   Where geographically controlled testing takes place before fully exposing the 'new feature' (product, service, campaign, distribution, etc.) or new brand to a full national or even international audience.

Test screening   Screening of an advertisement to a sample audience prior to final transmission.

Testimonial   A testament to a brand delivered by a personality, an expert or a representative of an average consumer.

Testing   Unlike marketing research, testing measures actual behaviour but does not answer the 'why' and 'how' questions.

Time to market   The amount of time it takes an organisation to get a product, service, idea or concept into the marketplace from its original inception.

Time-based fee   A fee based on the amount of time spent on the project.

Time–space proximity   The time between a stimulus and a response.

Tone   The 'personality' of your brand or company as expressed through the written or spoken word and/or imagery.

Total set   All of the products available in a particular product or service category.

Trade promotions   Promotions designed to develop the brand through the trade (e.g. staff competitions, in-store demonstrations).

Trait theory   A theory that suggests individuals can be viewed as a composite of several behaviour traits or characteristics.

Transnational organisation   One whose network structure is such that it is difficult to place its corporate centre (although not its original home). These types of organisation utilise worldwide facilities for production and regard their markets as outlets in a global marketplace.

Trial packs   A new product, frequently in smaller than normal quantity and at a special price to encourage trial.

Trial   Trying a product or service for the first time.

Trust   A confidence in someone or something. There are three forms of trust: institutional trust, character-based trust and process-based trust.

Typical-person endorsement   The use of everyday characters (usually played by actors) to endorse a product or service.

Unconditioned stimulus   Something that is naturally stimulating (e.g. the smell of food).

Unique selling proposition (USP)   The proposition which sets the brand apart from any other brand.

Up-sell   Selling existing customers products or services of a higher quality (and price) to their existing purchase(s).

User positioning   Relates to the specific profile of the target audience and is commonly accomplished with the aid of demographic and psychographic variables which denote specific lifestyle characteristics.

Vaguely right   Actual sales directly related to advertising are almost impossible to gauge accurately but an estimation can be said to be vaguely right (see precisely wrong).

VALs   Value, activity and lifestyle analysis.

Vampire creativity   Occurs when the communication is too original, too entertaining or too involving, such that it distracts the consumer from the brand message. This leads to consumers remembering the advertising but not the brand it was associated with.

Viral marketing, buzz marketing or street marketing   Marketing spread by word of mouth; alternatively, marketing materials created by the brand owner that are passed on and spread 'virus-like' around the internet.

Voice-over   Spoken commentary over an advertisement.

Waterloo effect   An industry maxim which suggests that the features of good advertising campaigns are uniqueness, frequency and relevance.

Weak theory (of advertising)   Suggests that advertising can act as a reminder and/or nudge a consumer towards a brand or idea.

Web analytics   The measurement, collection, analysis and reporting of internet data for the purposes of understanding and optimising web usage.

Win-back strategy   A marketing strategy designed to bring back lapsed customers.

Wish image   The image that an organisation aspires to achieve.

Word of mouth (WoM)   Marketing messages that circulate around from person to person (or persons via electronic communications).

World view   An individual's view or understanding of the world (see field of perception).

Zapping   Changing channel during a television commercial break.

Zipping   The fast-forwarding of pre-recorded programmes, enabling viewers to bypass the advertising.

INDEX